*Major Problems in
American Military History*

MAJOR PROBLEMS IN AMERICAN HISTORY SERIES

GENERAL EDITOR

THOMAS G. PATERSON

Major Problems
in American Military History

DOCUMENTS AND ESSAYS
EDITED BY

JOHN WHITECLAY CHAMBERS II
RUTGERS UNIVERSITY

G. KURT PIEHLER
UNIVERSITY OF TENNESSEE

WADSWORTH
CENGAGE Learning™

Australia • Brazil • Japan • Korea • Mexico • Singapore • Spain • United Kingdom • United States

Major Problems in American Military History

John Whiteclay Chambers II,
G. Kurt Piehler

Editor-in-Chief: Jean L. Woy

Senior Associate Editor:
Frances Gay

Associate Project Editor:
Gabrielle S. Stone

Associate Production/Design
Coordinator: Jodi O'Rourke

Marketing Manager:
Sandra Mcguire

Manufacturing Coordinator:
Andrea Wagner

Cover Designer: Sarah Melhado

Cover Image: "Score Another
for the Subs," U.S. Navy
Combat Art Collection.

Photo Researcher:
Rose Corbett Gordon

Back Cover Photos: G. K. Pichler:
Scott Wynn J.W. Chambers:
Amy P. Chambers

For product information and technology assistance, contact us at
Cengage Learning Customer & Sales Support, 1-800-354-9706

For permission to use material from this text or product,
submit all requests online at **www.cengage.com/permissions**
Further permissions questions can be e-mailed to
permissionrequest@cengage.com

Library of Congress Catalog Card Number: 2003116168

ISBN 13: 978-0-669-33538-5
ISBN 10: 0-669-33538-X

Wadsworth
20 Channel Center Street
Boston, MA 02210
USA

Cengage Learning is a leading provider of customized learning solutions with office locations around the globe, including Singapore, the United Kingdom, Australia, Mexico, Brazil, and Japan. Locate your local office at: **international.cengage.com/region**

Cengage Learning products are represented in Canada by Nelson Education, Ltd.

For your course and learning solutions, visit **www.cengage.com**

Purchase any of our products at your local college store or at our preferred online store **www.ichapters.com**

Printed in the U.S.A.
13 14 15 12 11 10

To Four Special People
Who Served Their Country in World War II

John M. Chambers
U.S. Army
China-Burma-India Theater

Nichola P. Russo
U.S. Navy
Pacific Theater

Thomas A. Kindre
U.S. Army
European Theater

Ralph Schmidt
Essential War Worker
Home Front

Contents

CHAPTER 5
The Army, Professionalism, Jacksonian Democracy, and Manifest Destiny
Page 119

CHAPTER 6
Generals, Soldiers, and the Civil War
Page 152

CHAPTER 7
Indian Wars on the Great Plains
Page 187

C H A P T E R   1 2
World War II: Strategic Bombing in Europe and Asia
Page 339

C H A P T E R   1 3
The Korean War and MacArthur's Leadership
Page 374

CHAPTER 14

The Vietnam War: Political-Military Decisions and Combat Experiences

Page 409

C H A P T E R 1 5
The Persian Gulf War and Peacekeeping in the Post-Cold War World
Page 445

Preface

"The truth is that war is a dirty thing," General Henry H. Shelton, Chairman of the Joint Chiefs of Staff, told reporters in February 1998, as the administration of President Bill Clinton sought to prepare the nation for possible resumption of the use of military force against Iraq. "We will lose some people and that weighs heavily." Shelton was echoing the famous remark of Civil War General William Tecumseh Sherman: "War is hell." Nevertheless, war has remained a part of international relations and continues today to be a distinct possibility in trouble spots around the world. Despite the danger, however, millions of Americans have braved such risks to serve and defend the nation and its vital interests.

Today, even as the active-duty U.S. armed forces scaled back in the post–Cold War world from 2.1 million servicepeople in 1989 to 1.4 million in 1998, the restructured forces faced new missions—among them, containing regional aggressors, peacekeeping in areas of ethnic violence and civil war, and combating international terrorism in its many emerging forms. In May 1998, the U.S. Army alone had 34,000 soldiers in temporary duty in 81 countries, most of them on peacekeeping missions or training operations. At the same time, the role of the National Guard and other reserve forces has become more important in the military's new peacekeeping role; in the Total Force concept of military organization, they are fully integrated into deployment plans. New weapons technology and communications and control systems have partially reshaped the nature of warfare. The American military at the end of the twentieth century is also different from its predecessors in its social composition; in recent years, it has become sexually as well as racially integrated. Although there is a continuing debate about whether women should be sent into ground combat.

Military history too has changed dramatically in recent years. This volume, *Major Problems in American Military History,* reflects those changes: it includes not only the traditional study of battle and command but also the social and institutional focus of the "new" military history, including the combat experience of enlisted personnel, not just the generals. This book traces the evolution of American military institutions, strategic doctrines, and technology. It includes material on all of the major armed forces: army, navy, air force, and marines. It follows such historic themes as the nationalization of the militia, the professionalization of the officer corps, the question of civilian control of the military, the technological transformation of weaponry and munitions, and the evolution of what some have called an American view of war and an American way of waging war. Finally, *Major Problems in American Military History* explores the relationship between American military action and institutions and the unfolding role of the United States in the world.

Chapter 1 presents a diversity of approaches to the study of military history. After this general opening, each chapter addresses a major issue in the American experience with war and the military, which began in the early seventeenth century. Like other volumes in this series, *Major Problems in American Military History* includes primary documents in each chapter that introduce the problem, identify key issues, impart the flavor of the debate, and, particularly in the documents concerning the experience of ordinary servicepeople, convey the intensity of feelings as men and women risked their lives in the service of their country. In each chapter, the essays written by prominent scholars or military analysts reflect recent debate; they also disclose how different interpretations can derive from the study of the same actions and events, sometimes even from analysis of the same documents. An introduction to each chapter and the headnotes to the documents and to the essay sections help give historical and interpretive perspective to the readings. The aim is to enhance critical thinking and understanding of the subject by encouraging readers to evaluate the degree of credibility of the sources, assess the evidence, appraise the conflicting interpretations, and reach their own conclusions. To encourage further exploration of the subject, a list of relevant books and articles, emphasizing more recent historical works and some primary sources, is printed at the end of each chapter.

The contents of this volume derived in part from our experience since 1982 teaching a course on military history at Rutgers University in New Brunswick, New Jersey. We wish to thank the thousands of students who have taken this course at Rutgers and given it such high evaluations. We have benefited from their participation. We have also learned much from our discussions with other members of the Society for Military History and from syllabi for U.S. military history courses gathered from all over the country.

In the course of assembling the present volume, we have benefited from the kindness and invaluable support of a large number of persons. We gratefully acknowledge their generosity.

The present volume includes half a dozen essays written or updated especially for it. We would like to thank the following for doing so: Russell F. Weigley, Dennis E. Showalter, Gregory T. Knouff, Michael L. Grumelli, Robert Buzzanco, and H. R. McMaster. A number of persons provided us with their own original documents. Our thanks for this to Franklin J. Kneller, Mrs. Chester Szarawarski (for the diary of her late husband), William C. Boldenweck, and H. R. McMaster. Thanks also to David Culbert of Louisiana State University, who translated the selection from the diaries of Nazi Propaganda Minister Joseph Goebbels from a copy of the original manuscript version obtained by John Chambers in the Russian Archives in Moscow.

We also gathered previously unpublished manuscripts as documents from a number of depositories throughout the United States, and we wish to acknowledge the following institutions for their permission to use unpublished manuscript collections in this volume: the Library of Congress; the National Archives; U.S. Army Military History Institute, Carlisle Barracks, Carlisle, Pennsylvania; the Air University Library and Archives, Maxwell Air Force Base, Alabama; Special Collections, Joyner Library, East Carolina University, Greenville, North Carolina; and the Georgia Department of Archives and History, Atlanta, Georgia. David A. Keough and his fine staff at Carlisle Barracks helped us locate several crucial documents related to the Philippine-American War and the Vietnam War. Donald R.

Lennon, Coordinator of Special Collections, and his staff at the Joyner Library, East Carolina University, obtained original documents on the Mexican-American War and the Civil War. Margaret Luck of Greenville transcribed two of the handwritten documents found in the Joyner Library. Richard Peuser of the National Archives located General John Lejeune's February 1922 memorandum on the new amphibious mission of the U.S. Marine Corps; Michael Parrish of the Lyndon B. Johnson Presidential Library provided a declassified National Security Council document on the Vietnam War for us.

Some of our former and present students at Rutgers proved to be indefatigable research assistants. Tara J. Liston obtained copies of documents used in this collection at the Library of Congress, U.S. National Archives, and the Marine Corps Historical Center. Articles and documents were located and photocopied at Rutgers's Alexander Library by Melanie Cooper, Tara Kraenzlin, Elise Krotiuk, Linda Lasko, and Eve Snyder. We would also like to thank Scott Ceresnak and Carmen Godwin for their last minute assistance in reviewing page proofs. From the Rutgers Oral History Archives of World War II, Sandra Stewart Holyoak joined the editors in their search for relevant collections during a visit to the U.S. Military History Institute at Carlisle Barracks, Pennsylvania.

On the eve of completing this book, Kurt Piehler accepted a position at the Department of History at the University of Tennessee, Knoxville, as assistant professor of history and the new director of the Center for the Study of War and Society.

This volume would not be what it is without the guidance of a number of scholars who gave us invaluable advice, especially Richard H. Kohn, Allan R. Millett, and Charles Moskos. We are also grateful to the following reviewers who provided detailed and extremely helpful comments on the table of contents: Robert A. Doughty, United States Military Academy; Jeanne Heidler, United States Air Force Academy; James M. Johnson, United States Military Academy; Leslie A. Schwalm, University of Iowa; and Phyllis Zimmerman, Ball State University. Thomas G. Paterson, the editor-in-chief of the series *Major Problems in American History,* of which this volume is a part, kept faith in us and guided us through the entire project, even as the D.C. Heath series was acquired by Houghton Mifflin.

Never has there been a more insightful, helpful, and efficient editorial and production team as we have had at Houghton Mifflin. The senior editors, Jean Woy and Frances Gay, read every word and along with Tom Paterson gave us outstanding advice; this was particularly useful in reducing our original proposal to a manageable size. Production was ably moved along by Gabrielle Stone, the project editor; Margaret (Peggy) Roll, who obtained permissions; and Sandra McGuire, who handled marketing.

We dedicate this volume to four special people who served their country in World War II. John M. Chambers, father of one of the editors, served in 1944–1946 with the U.S. Army Medical Corps, first in India and then, after being flown over the Himalaya Mountains (the "Hump") in a C-47, in Kunming, China. Nichola P. Russo, John W. Chambers's father-in-law, served in 1943–1946 aboard the U.S. Navy battleship *South Dakota* in the Pacific theater of operations, including the battles of Tarawa, Philippine Sea, and Leyte Gulf. Thomas A. Kindre served in the U.S. Army, 1942–1945, in the Ordnance Company of the 34th Infantry Division, which advanced from North Africa through Italy. Ralph Schmidt, who tried to enlist in the army but wound up working on the "home front," 1942–1945, helped produce penicillin and other chemical substances that proved essential in maintaining the health of American servicepeople.

As alumni of Rutgers College, Class of 1942, Tom Kindre and Ralph Schmidt— along with Stephen E. Ambrose, Rudolph M. Bell, and John W. Chambers—were instrumental in 1993 in founding the Rutgers Oral History Archives of World War II. Frank Kneller, Rutgers Class of 1949, is the current chairman of the executive committee of that archive. The Rutgers Archives (and other oral history archives of World War II, such as those at the University of Tennessee, Knoxville, and the University of New Orleans) seek to make the U.S. wartime (and peacetime) military experience understandable to new generations of Americans. In a broader time frame, that is also one of the purposes of this volume.

J. W. C.
G. K. P.

Major Problems in
American Military History

Diverse Approaches to American Military History

What is military history and why study it? Military history has come a long way from its earliest origins in the histories of war and the military written by ancient Greek historians like Thucydides and his fifth-century B.C. political-military account of the Peloponnesian War. The idea of the practical applicability of studying past wars and battles, or learning from and avoiding similar mistakes of previous commanders, also has a long history, right up to its inclusion in the training of military officers today. Of course, many people read about past battles—Yorktown, New Orleans, Gettysburg, Little Big Horn, Meuse-Argonne, Normandy, Inchon— simply because such vicarious experience makes rattling good reading. But military history—like the broader discipline of historical writing itself—is now much more diverse than the traditional operational history of "drums and trumpets." The "new" military history has proliferated into institutional, sociological, and cultural studies of the armed forces, society, and war. It goes beyond the decisions of generals and admirals to the experiences of the rank and file, in combat and in peacetime, and includes the military experiences of women and minorities. It also seeks more widely to understand the connections between war and the military and other aspects of society: political, social, and economic systems, technology, and culture.

Fundamental questions about military history and the American military experiences are debated by military historians and other scholars today. What are the useful areas of war and the military for historians to study? How broad should the field become? What is the relationship of military history to the study of history in general and to American history in particular? What are the connections between American society, its military, and its warmaking? Is there an American way of viewing and waging war? How do the armed forces, war, and preparation for war achieve and protect U.S. national interests. How have they contributed to the development of the United States?

♠ E S S A Y S

The essays reprinted here illustrate the diversity in military history today. In 1973, Russell F. Weigley of Temple University wrote what many historians consider one of the most important interpretations of American military history. His thesis: There is a distinctive American way of war, and it emerged primarily as a result of American attitudes and resources. Here, in an essay written especially for this volume, Weigley revisits his seminal work. In an important milestone in the development of a social history of the military, reprinted here as the second essay, Richard H. Kohn of the University of North Carolina, Chapel Hill, and former Chief of Air Force History, called in 1981 for a history of American military service and its relationship to the larger society. The third essay, written by Alex Roland of Duke University in 1991, emphasizes the need for a broader approach to military technology, one that explores its relationship to American culture and strategic thought. Dennis F. Showalter of Colorado College has long challenged the direction of the "new" military history away from the study of battle; in the fourth essay, written specially for this volume, he revisits his provocative 1975 plea for "drums and trumpets." One of the most important new areas of historical scholarship in recent years has been women's history; in the fifth essay, D'Ann Campbell, dean of the College of Arts and Sciences at Austin Peay State University in Tennessee and a historian of women and war, examines the ways in which four countries in World War II dealt with the issue of women in combat, and emphasizes the need for scholars to include concepts of gender in the study of war and the society, particularly in regard to modern "total" war in the twentieth century.

How Americans Wage War: The Evolution
of National Strategy

RUSSELL F. WEIGLEY

In a university career of teaching United States military history, I have found again and again that there are two courses sure to draw a more than full enrollment: the American Civil War and the Second World War. Partly the popularity of studying those two wars lies in their being the military-history buffs' wars, the enthusiasts' wars. Gettysburg and the Ardennes, Vicksburg and Guadalcanal exert an endless emotional fascination. So do the technologies of the wars, from Minie balls to Flying Fortresses, and the resultant tactics. But 1861–1865 and 1941–1945 do more than simply tug at our national yearnings to find, in spite of war's horror, a measure of glory and of romance in war. Nearly every American senses also that the Civil War and the Second World War, of all the conflicts in our history, most embody the national image of what war inherently is and ought to be.

Americans fought both wars—in the Civil War, Americans on both sides fought—for causes large enough and vital enough to justify an all-out pursuit of victory, sparing no energies and resources. For most American participants, neither war presented blurred, difficult-to-define objectives, and therefore neither war brought with it only partial, limited commitments of military means to pursue the

---

"How Americans Wage War: The Evolution of National Strategy" written specially for this volume by Russell F. Weigley.

objectives, the kind of limited commitment that was to seem an incomprehensible anomaly to many Americans during the Korean and Vietnam Wars.

Long before the Civil War, the struggle against the North American Indians for possession of the continent had nurtured an American perception of war as implicitly a contest for total victory, because European-Americans early concluded that their way of life and that of the Native Americans could not coexist as neighbors, so that the Indians must depart, if not through extermination then to vastly distant places. The Civil War confirmed the American image of war drawn from the Indian wars by again posing total victory as the objective sought by each contestant: The South, the Confederacy, fought to defend its very society and culture, the same values that were at stake against the Indians; the North, the Union, fought for nothing less than the survival of the American experiment in democracy. The superior resources of the North, especially in manpower, then permitted the attainment of the total victory the North had pursued, the surrender of the Confederate armies, the practically complete military subjugation of the South, the consequently apparent malleability of the South to Northern political aims.

After the Civil War, the North's successful quest for nearly absolute military victory stood at the center of American military men's studies of how to wage war, and it shaped American conduct in the two World Wars. Lieutenant General Ulysses S. Grant's strategy of his 1864–1865 campaign aimed at the complete destruction of the fighting power of the enemy armies—preferably by forcing their surrender, as he had done to the Confederate Army of Vicksburg on July 4, 1863, but if not that then by their literal destruction—became the foundation of a confirmed American strategy of annihilation of the enemy armed forces. The supplementary strategy of Grant's favorite subordinate, Major General William Tecumseh Sherman, of undermining the enemy's armed forces by attacking the economy and the civilian morale that supported them, also became embedded in American military thought, to be translated in the twentieth century into the ideas of strategic air power. The United States entered the First World War too late, and its military might was only too partially mobilized at the end for this country to do much to shape Allied strategy in the conflict—although General John J. Pershing, commanding the American Expeditionary Forces, attempted to secure a march of the Allied and American armies across Germany to Berlin. In the Second World War, in contrast, the United States came to predominate in the strategic councils of the Western Allies, and the Americans won adoption of a strategy drawn from the experience of their Civil War.

Enjoying, as the North had done in 1861–1865, a preponderance of resources over the enemy, the United States favored against Germany a Grant-like strategy of direct confrontation with the enemy's main Western forces, by means of a cross-Channel invasion of northwestern France, to overwhelm those forces under superior strength and destroy them. The United States also employed a Sherman-like strategy of assault upon the German economy and civilian morale, by means of a strategic bomber offensive. In time, after British preference for peripheral rather than American direct strategy had helped delay the cross-Channel invasion until June 6, 1944, two and a half years after American entry into the war, the American strategic vision was realized, bringing about attainment of a characteristically American goal, Germany's unconditional surrender on May 7–8, 1945.

Against Japan, meanwhile, the United States Navy applied the Grant strategy of annihilation, filtered through the thought of Rear Admiral Alfred Thayer Mahan, seeking a battle of annihilation against the Imperial Japanese Navy and eventually achieving the virtual accomplishment of that destruction, albeit not in a single climactic battle as Mahan had seemed to suggest, but in a campaign of attrition closer to Grant's original methods. The American Army and Marine Corps similarly destroyed most of the Japanese ground forces they confronted. The Army Air Forces and the Naval Air Service applied a Sherman-style campaign against Japan's economy and people, with a hypertrophic climax in the atomic bombing of Hiroshima and Nagasaki on August 6 and 9, 1945. Unconditional surrender was again the outcome, arranged on August 14 and formalized on the deck of the battleship U.S.S. *Missouri* on September 2.

By the close of the Second World War, then, there had emerged out of an evolution from the Indian wars through the Civil War and reaching a climax in World War II, a preferred American way of war, which mobilized the material wealth and the plentiful manpower of the United States to overwhelm enemies, bring about the virtual annihilation of their armed forces and the destruction of their home front's economic and moral capacity to sustain war, and secure their unconditional surrender and almost complete malleability in the hands of American policymakers. The image of war and the preferred American form of warmaking drawn from the Indian wars, the Civil War, and the World Wars remains nearly unquestioned among a large public as the natural approach to the problem of war, as evidenced by the popular discontent generated by waging only limited war in Korea and Vietnam.

In the years since 1945, the classic American way of war identified with Grant, Sherman, and the American chieftains of World War II has served United States national interests much less well than it did against the Confederacy, Germany, and Japan. As long as the Soviet Union existed, through the Cold War, another major hot war would have found the superior resources, at least of manpower and military brute force, in the battalions of America's opponents rather than of the United States and its allies, which posed problems never satisfactorily resolved by American planners of a possible World War III who came out of the tradition of applying superior military power. Meanwhile the hot wars actually fought during the Cold War era were chiefly those controversial limited conflicts in Korea in 1950–1953 and Vietnam in 1965–1973 that grew highly unpopular largely because complex political and military constraints, notably the peril of nuclear war, prevented the United States government from pursuing the unconditional surrender of its adversaries through full-scale application of military might in the familiar style.

With the end of the Cold War and of the Soviet Union, moreover, the prospects for new conflicts on the model of World War II seem more remote than ever. Applications of United States military power are most likely to demand not overweening weight of resources but light, agile, maneuverable, politically sensitive and sophisticated armed forces for peacemaking and peacekeeping roles. Even a repetition of war on the scale of the Persian Gulf conflict of 1990–1991 is improbable, not least because without the stimulus of the Cold War it is not feasible, or sensible, to maintain American forces of the strength that overcame Iraq. Therefore a future

United States involvement even in a Middle East conflict otherwise resembling the Gulf War will also demand making the most of lighter forces.

To guide American military strategists into this uncertain new era in which the classic American way of war is unlikely to apply, however, United States history is not without models and precedents to study and ponder. The massive Union military power of the Civil War obscured from the vision of American military planners for many generations the preceding period when the United States lacked vast military resources and had to rely more on skill and guile, and on combining political with military strategies.

General George Washington may have been the master strategist of American history, particularly when judged by the magnitude of his accomplishments in relation to the poverty of his resources. Through most of the War of Independence, he avoided major battles while attempting through adroit maneuver to fall upon weak British detachments and win victories at small cost to himself but with accumulating moral weight. His objective was less the enemy than the enemy's psyche; he sought less a military triumph per se than political success drawn from limited military means.

The most successful American military commander between Washington and the Civil War was Winfield Scott. As major general commanding the United States Army, he led a relatively small force, just under 11,000 men at most, to the capture of the political objective of the enemy's seat of government, the City of Mexico. On the way, through skillful maneuver and for the most part the avoidance of large-scale battles, he was able to win the still larger political objective of favorable peace terms to end the Mexican War.

While they were not ultimately successful, several of the Confederate commanders of the Civil War also offer lessons in the effective use of relatively small forces by means of agility and maneuver, most notably Lieutenant General Thomas Jonathan "Stonewall" Jackson, but also General Robert E. Lee himself (albeit Lee's contradictory thirst for climactic, Napoleonic battle helped undermine him, especially by playing into U. S. Grant's hands).

Finally, though the Indian wars were fought for total objectives, the means of pursuing the objectives usually had to be small-scale forces, and probably the most able of the Indian-fighting leaders of the United States Army was a soldier who favored unconventional, guerrilla-style, low-intensity war: Major General George Crook. And at the very beginning of United States military history there stood alongside Washington a master of guerrilla warfare whose Southern Campaign has rarely been equalled for the achievements of a small conventional army interweaving its operations with those of guerrilla bands, Major General Nathanael Greene.

Thus, the American way of war as it came to be conceived of between 1864 and 1945 was by no means the only historic American approach to war. If American military history is studied and understood in all the diversity that has been its reality, then Americans should find therein rich guidance toward the solution of any military problems whatever, including the still not clearly defined difficulties ahead of us that will demand a deftness of maneuver and a subtlety in using military force as an instrument for securing political ends not demanded of our soldiers since before 1861.

The issue of blurred, difficult-to-define political objectives in war is another matter. All our post-1945 wars except the Persian Gulf conflict have posed that problem, and likely scenarios calling for American military intervention in the future will most probably offer it with at least as many puzzles to plague us as Vietnam. Policy, not military strategy, has to be the instrument for dealing with this issue. At least, however, if we disabuse ourselves of the notion that there has to be only one acceptable American way of war, if we devise military forces and tactics, operational methods, and strategies suited to conflicts of less than total means and objectives, if we learn to fight with measured applications of military strength and with adroit maneuver skills, then policies of intervention in complex circumstances need not be foredoomed by a military commitment to the unrelenting quest for unconditional surrender as our only way of war.

Exploring the Social History of the Military

RICHARD H. KOHN

Over the course of American history, few experiences have been more widely shared than military service. From the seventeenth century to the present, Americans by the millions have served in armed forces of one kind or another, in war and in peace, on frontiers and overseas, as career professionals and temporary militia conscripts. Universal military obligation is one of our oldest and most enduring traditions. Every generation has experienced military conflict of some kind, and through the twentieth century the military has increased dramatically in size and in its impact on national affairs. Between 1940 and 1973 the government through selective service touched the lives of nearly every American family directly, even if a male family member did not serve. In 1980 an estimated 37 percent of the male population over age seventeen were veterans, as many as 70 percent for those in the age bracket forty-five to sixty-four; and, in gross numbers, including women, some thirty million Americans were veterans in 1980. Nor are these figures likely to change significantly. Projections for manning the all volunteer army stress the need for fully one quarter of our eighteen-year-old males to enlist to maintain the armed forces at a strength of two million. And current projections estimate that 28 percent of the male population over seventeen, perhaps twenty-eight million men, will be veterans in the year 2000, even without conscription.

With rare exception, American historians, particularly social historians, have neglected this experience. In the last two decades scholars of the military have begun to abandon the old preoccupation with strategy and battle, but few practitioners of the "new" military history have chosen subjects that are frankly social. Of course, there has existed for generations a vast literature on American soldiers in the form of histories, memoirs, diaries, biographies, literary studies, popular hagiographies, government compilations of statistics, and sociological studies. But little of this material has been concerned with understanding soldiers per se, the

Abridged article "The Social History of the American Soldier: A Review and Prospectus for Research, " by Richard H. Kohn *American Historical Review* 86, no. 3 (June 1981): 553-567. Reprinted with permission of the author and the American Historical Association.

military experiences of Americans, or the impact of service on the nation. Most of the history has aimed at calling to memory the patriotism or loyalty of particular individuals and groups; the sociology, at advancing social science methodology or aiding the government in recruiting its armies and using manpower efficiently. What do we really know of this experience for Americans and, indeed, of the Americans who served through our history? Who were they? Why did they enlist or submit to coercion into service? Where did they come from? What did their leaving and their returning mean to their communities? What did they think? Why did they fight? How did they behave? What impact did service have on them and they on the nation? "Several scholarly studies of specific dimensions of the subject do exist and deserve . . . attention," one historian has written recently. "But such studies are . . . few in number" and focus primarily on the World War II and post-war eras. In point of fact, historians have neglected one of the most pervasive experiences in American life, one especially suited to the new social history. Because of the vast literary and statistical source material, examining service in the military ought to reveal much about the American population and society and, even further, begin to explain the significance of that service and fix it firmly in the mosaic of American history, where it has always belonged.

For most of our history, our vision of the American soldier—the prototypical enlisted man in the army, navy, or militia (marines have been by their own definition atypical)—has been expressed in various forms of symbol and myth. While historians, and a good proportion of the public, might no longer accept the old stereotypes, they still persist in patriotic rhetoric, in army thinking, and even in some forms of the old scholarship. The American soldier was a cross section of the American population; he enlisted and fought out of patriotism; his love of liberty, intelligence, and native individualism meant that the goals of war had to be explained to him. "[M]en must be thoroughly imbued with the spirit of their cause . . . , believe in it and want it with every atom of their being," a psychological handbook counselled prospective officers in 1943, echoing a theory first publicized by Freidrich von Steuben in 1779 and repeated as dogma ever since. In battle our soldiers were courageous; if captured, they remained loyal; once the battle ended, they reverted to the kind, adaptive, happy-go-lucky scroungers of Ernie Pyle's classic World War II reporting. Even as sophisticated an observer as General S. L. A. Marshall, who as an officer and writer studied Americans in four wars and often advised the army on training and leadership, perpetuated some of these generalizations. Marshall believed our soldiers had certain common characteristics, "true in times past from Lexington . . . to Pork Chop Hill": "resourceful and imaginative . . . , to a certain extent machine-bound . . . , optimistic . . . though their griping is incessant, . . . gregarious," impatient of "spit-and-polish," possessive of "an uncanny instinct for ferreting out the truth when anything goes wrong tactically, . . . wasteful of drinking water, food, munitions, and other vital supply," and hesitant to kill. But, if "led with courage and intelligence, an American will fight as willingly and as efficiently as any fighter in world history."

These myths have endured for a variety of reasons. Americans have long believed that how they have behaved in service and in battle reflected their character as a people and their virtue as a nation. Moral worth, and our special distinctiveness as a country, seemed somehow to hinge on the people's eagerness to serve, its bravery under fire, its loyalty in captivity, its virtue in bivouac, and its willingness to melt back silently into civilian life. The government down through our history has also contributed to stereotyping American soldiers. To mobilize the population and justify the cause, propaganda has consistently pictured the American in uniform in the best possible light. Veterans' organizations have also joined willingly in the celebration of the American soldier, lest they cheapen their own endeavors or call into question their sacrifice. And a good deal of the literature and rhetoric has emanated from ethnic groups who have wanted to prove their loyalty and patriotism by portraying their participation in laudatory terms.

Thus the American soldier has been a symbol, a political and cultural artifact for a nation diverse in culture, uncertain in unity, and concerned through much of its history with proving its superiority to the rest of the world. Of necessity has been anonymity, which has further muddied the truth and contributed to the making of myths. Artists from the Revolution to the present have depicted enlisted men in faceless terms: Winslow Homer's *Harper's Weekly* drawings in the Civil War, for example, or Harvey Dunn's "The Machine Gunner" of 1918. Even characters with as much realism as Bill Mauldin's World War II GI's, "Willie" and "Joe," were meant to represent an anonymous mass of citizen soldiers. And the government—for recruiting, in bond drives, in memorials—has insisted on typicality, an "unknown soldier." From such sources the nation produced symbols that from the outset bore no necessary relationship to reality, and, because of anonymity and repetition generation after generation, the myths have survived with remarkable durability.

While no scholar has yet put together a synthesis of what is known about American soldiers, enough good studies and source material have become available to put finally to rest the popular legends. First of all, our forces have never been homogeneous, but a bewildering mixture of ethnic and racial groups. Blacks served throughout American history, comprising, for example, as much as 20 percent of the Union Navy. Immigrants have also filled the ranks: over 20 percent of the Union Army, some 18 percent of the World War I draftees, and in peacetime in the nineteenth century even greater numbers—over 70 percent of army recruits in 1850 and 1851 and as late as 1894 one-quarter of enlisted ranks overall. In the navy, foreign-born sailors made up such a high percentage of enlisted ranks that officials wondered aloud whether the squadrons would be reliable in event of a crisis. Often the armed forces formed units from a single group: the four regiments of blacks in the post–Civil War army, the American Indian regiments in the Civil War, the Indian companies in the 1890s, the Philippine scouts in the twentieth century, the Japanese-American battalions in World War II, and the Eskimo battalions of the Alaska Territorial Guard and Alaska National Guard, formed in World War II and still in existence today.

Rarely have our forces constituted an economic or social profile of the general population. The Continental Army of the Revolution drew its soldiers from the poorest third of society and contained disproportionate numbers of drifters, servants, British deserters, captured loyalists, convicts, and drafted substitutes. Of the World War I draftees, three out of ten were illiterate or functionally so, five times the national illiteracy rate of 6 percent. In later conflicts men with college backgrounds or more education often became officers—in World War II, 40 percent of the men with some college background. (Of a sample of 231 select Harvard students and graduates, 80 percent held commissions.) The World War II ground armies could not have reflected the population, because so many of the skilled or technically apt were siphoned off into the air corps and navy. And our forces have rarely included another large group: the physically or mentally deficient. Selective Service rejected one quarter of those physically examined in World War II and nearly 50 percent of those eligible for the draft between 1950 and 1965.

Nor does the evidence support the belief that Americans enlist or fight purely out of patriotism. Often at the beginning of a war volunteers flocked to the colors in a surge of nationalistic fervor; invariably, however, the supply of willing recruits dried up as the realities of the sacrifice sank in. In the War of 1812 New England militia refused to turn out, and in 1814 the Madison administration considered introducing a national draft. In both the Revolution and Civil War, the states and the national government resorted to drafts. In both conflicts bounties were so pervasive and rose so high that they became a national scandal. Only in the Mexican and Spanish-American Wars has the nation manned its ranks without using large-scale bribery or coercion. And Americans have not submitted passively to coercion, except during World War II and the Cold War. When permitted in the Revolution and Civil War, thousands purchased substitutes. Others flouted the law. In World War I, 11 percent of those called evaded the draft, and nearly half of the evaders, some one hundred and seventy thousand men, were never apprehended. Long before Vietnam, Americans practiced medical chicanery. As one Civil War surgeon wrote in disgust, "They come fortified with elaborate certificates from sympathizing friends, kind-hearted family physicians, stupid quacks, and the learned homeopathist who has testified to the appalling infirmity of 'paralysis of the scrotum.'"

Our peacetime forces have never depended on patriotism. Augustus Myers, who joined the Army fife and drum corps at the age of twelve in 1854 and who served ten years on the frontier and with the Army of the Potomac, remembered his comrades as enlisting "for various reasons. Some had the 'Wanderlust'; others . . . a taste for adventure. . . . Some had joined from sheer necessity, or inability to find any other occupation to support themselves, . . . a very common cause." In the nineteenth and early twentieth centuries men joined the peacetime army, and deserted, in direct correlation to pay and treatment inside the army and the state of the civilian economy outside. In fact, pay and bonuses have influenced American soldiers for generations. During the Revolution soldiers mutinied over lack of pay, and their officers three times threatened Congress with resignation unless granted half-pay pensions for life. Until the Cold War, the military pension system primarily benefited our "patriotic" citizen armies, not the peacetime constabulary. The very first veterans' organization, the Society of the Cincinnati (for officers only), came into existence in 1783 in large part to press for promised pensions. By the end of the nineteenth century, veterans' lobbies had become such potent political forces that the government paid nearly five billion dollars in Civil War pensions alone. Not surprisingly, with over thirteen million men and women in uniform, the World War II Congress voted the most massive system of postwar benefits in history—before the fighting had even ended.

Like soldiers of other nations, Americans have on occasion deserted, run from combat, murdered enemy soldiers, assaulted superiors, and wounded themselves to avoid battle. Rather than being motivated by patriotism or political ideology, our soldiers have sustained themselves in the stress of battle by a variety of means, from the network of esteem and interdependence that creates the solidarity and cohesion of a unit to the will and the instinct for survival and, perhaps, even to the unspoken belief in the superiority of their nation and culture. Away from the constraints of family and community, they have sworn, drank, gambled, fought among themselves, and chased women with enough regularity and in sufficient numbers to dispel any claim to special virtue. (In World War I the army stubbornly determined to stamp out venereal disease by prohibiting all fraternization with French women—and failed utterly.) Soldiers often expressed hate and contempt for enemy and ally alike. A few, on occasion, have been actually attracted to war, to the spectacle and to the excitement, as the philosopher J. Glenn Gray, who in 1940 received his doctorate and draft notice in the same mail, noted. And Americans have not always melted peacefully back into civilian life: they have often demonstrated to hurry demobilization, to receive bonuses, or to settle economic grievances, and they have organized themselves into vocal lobbies that, even today, exercise political influence far beyond matters of specific concern to veterans.

Thus, as many historians have long known, the record casts grave doubt on some of our most cherished folklore. But to portray the American soldier as a self-interested, blue-collar scoundrel motivated solely by money and survival, interested primarily in drink and in the pleasures of the flesh, liable to desert or succumb to his captor at the first opportunity, and kept in check only by the threat of army punishment would be as gross a distortion as the myth of the virtuous patriot. In recent years some of these images have dominated the popular mind: Korean POW's demoralized, disloyal, and collaborating; Vietnam veterans as murderous drug addicts incapable of shedding their alienation and returning to normal civilian lives. The problem, in both scholarship and popular thinking, is our propensity to search for typicality, to think in terms of stereotypes, and to aim for universal generalizations that fit across all of American history. The truth of the matter is that the "American soldier" never existed; the most pernicious myth of all is that there has ever been a prototypical American in uniform. Common sense ought to remind us that the past was different: the pace of life, values and attitudes, occupations, the classes and social structure of the nation, technology and the conditions of battle, the character of discipline, the nature of war and military life. Our experience as scholars should warn us that few, if any, generalizations for something as varied as military service, experienced by so many diverse individuals under such disparate circumstances, can hold over as long a span of time as three centuries. We ought particularly to suspect broad surveys in the absence of very detailed research on specific periods of time. And what we as historians should seek is not some set of large generalizations, but history—change over time, evolution, development.

Certainly many aspects of military organization and experience are universal and timeless; scholars, soldiers, and other writers often emphasize the similarities across national borders and centuries. Battle and the reactions of men caught in combat provides an excellent example of the tendency to generalize—and its pitfalls. John Keegan, a historian on the faculty at the Royal Military Academy at Sandhurst, wrote recently that what "battles have in common is human: the behaviour of men struggling to reconcile their instinct for self-preservation, their sense of honour and the achievement of some aim over which other men are ready to kill them." Studying battle "is therefore always a study of fear and usually of courage; always of leadership, usually of obedience; always of compulsion, sometimes of insubordination; always of anxiety, sometimes of elation or catharsis; always of uncertainty and doubt, misinformation and misapprehension, usually also of faith and sometimes of vision; always of violence, sometimes also of cruelty, self-sacrifice, compassion; above all, it is always a study of solidarity and usually also of disintegration—for it is toward the disintegration of human groups that battle is directed." Yet Keegan also insisted that battle belonged "to finite moments in history" and that its character depended heavily on the nature of war, on the technology of the day, on the economies and societies of the opposing nations, on the armies, and even on the weather and the ground. In short, battle possesses a history of its own, an evolution over time that defines its dimensions and character.

Since battle has varied over hundreds of years, no single phenomenon could possibly explain the motives of soldiers, no matter how universal the emotions Keegan described. And yet many scholars have treated battle as a constant—have searched, with little regard for time and place, for the factors that explain why men fight. They have compared German soldiers in the latter stages of World War II with American soldiers in that war, and both of those with Americans in Korea and in Vietnam. Without doubt the phenomenon of primary group cohesion has, to some extent, been universal. Augustus Myers recalled that in the Civil War, "the fear of the contempt of his comrades" was "even more powerful a factor than discipline in keeping a timid or nerveless soldier in the ranks during a battle." In Vietnam, however, rotation loosened the ties of the unit by promising relief once the tour was over. One scholar has even argued that what sustained men in Southeast Asia was the understanding that only through collective action and cooperation could each individual hope to survive. The problem has been that the literature on primary group cohesion has never clearly shown whether solidarity with the group acted as a psychological prop to bolster men to endure the stress or as a motivation to carry out the mission and perform effectively in battle—or both. The same men in World War II who were supposedly welded together by the dynamics of the group were found by S. L. A. Marshall to have possessed an astonishingly poor frequency of firing their weapons at the enemy. . . .

It is time for historians to take a fresh look at the American soldier; for too long, political and policy concerns have dictated the very categories of inquiry. As we begin, we need to remind ourselves that the past in many respects did not resemble the present, that youth, battle, warfare, and enlisted life may have changed significantly since the seventeenth century. We ought also to cast a suspicious eye on old assumptions—for example, that military institutions reflect society. The army never reflected American society, unless a centralized, stratified, cohesive, authoritarian institution that has stressed obedience and sacrifice can reflect a decentralized, heterogeneous, individualistic, democratic, capitalist society. If our military forces at any given time have reflected American values and practices, it has only been in comparison to the forces of other nations or if measured against some sociological model of an ideal military organization. We should remember that there have been many different military forces in our history, most of which changed over the course of their existence, and rarely, if ever, comprised a representative cross-section of the American population. Peacetime constabularies and wartime armies have been organized for very different purposes and have been manned by very different types of individuals. Sometimes, the composition of forces differed radically; for a single Indian war in the early 1790s, the government raised three separate armies made up of mixtures of militia, militia substitutes, six-month volunteers, thirty-day volunteer cavalry, and regulars. Some services or units, like the navy and air corps, have purposely drawn on more educated and skilled groups. And through our history officers have almost always come from the wealthier or better educated segments of society, and at the other extreme large numbers of Americans have often been excluded by reason of race or for physical, mental, or moral deficiency. . . .

Until we, as historians, abandon both our stereotypes and our propensity to think in terms of stereotypes, the American enlisted man will remain as anonymous as the unknown soldier in the tomb at Arlington National Cemetery. For reasons of state, the tomb will continue to serve as a symbol of sacrifice and the gratitude of a nation. For the historical profession, however, the unknown soldier poses a special challenge: a sound, impartial rendering of the past.

Weapons and Technology Drive the American Military

ALEX ROLAND

. . . Technology has . . . shaped the United States, arguably the most technological of nations. The U.S. claim to immortality may be democratic government and free enterprise, but its world leadership and power rest on scientific, industrial, and technological prowess. The country was born rich in natural resources, but industry and mastery of the forces of nature propelled it to world prominence.

It was literally "born in an act of violence," as one historian has put it. And its "first major technological innovation," the American long rifle or Pennsylvania-Kentucky rifle, was a military as well as a civilian technology. Its Civil War was the first major conflict under the influence of the industrial revolution. The U.S. was the arsenal of victory in the two world wars, which were competitions in industrial production. Surely, then, technology must have been an influential variable in the evolution of American strategic thought, in ground warfare as well as air and naval warfare.

Upon further reflection, however, I found myself hard-pressed to move beyond the anecdotal. No significant generalizations occurred to me. I could think of no historical scholarship specifically addressed to the impact of technology on American strategic thought before World War II. I could identify no historical fig-

"Technology, Ground Warfare, and Strategy: The Paradox of American Experience," by Alex Roland *Journal of Military History* 55, no. 4 (October 1991): 447-48, 453-67. Reprinted by permission of the publisher.

ure who had written or acted influentially in this realm. In short I could find no pattern whatsoever, either in the historical record itself or in the subsequent historiography, that spoke persuasively to this topic. . . .

The paradox of the invisibility of technology in American strategic thought has at least four explanations. First, Americans are not alone. Hardly any major theorist of land warfare before World War II appreciated the full importance of technology. Sun Tzu, for example, barely mentions technology at all. Machiavelli and Clausewitz are regularly discounted for their insensitivity to changing technology. Jomini is now dismissed as a mere schematicist, who reduced Napoleon's magnificent campaigns to lines of operation and maneuver. Some strategists like Gustavus Adolphus, Napoleon, and the younger von Moltke were keenly aware of the importance of technology, but they are the exceptions that prove the rule. Most great captains before the nuclear age have been insensitive to the role of technology in war. The most important strategist of the nuclear age, Mao Tse-tung, understood the technology of warfare fully, but his insights were lost on Americans until Vietnam.

The second reason for the invisibility of technology in American strategic thought is that there has not been all that much American strategic thought. Americans are a pragmatic people. They have never been much given to theory of any kind, at least until recently. Throughout most of their history, Americans have been content to adopt European thought and adapt it to our particular needs. Furthermore, the United States has not faced continuing military threat in its history. Without a threat, there has been little incentive to develop a strategy. To invent a strategy in such a context would require inventing a threat. Different periods might have bred strategies for fighting Canada, Mexico, any number of European nations, half the banana republics, and a variety of Asian nations and Barbary pirates. None of these was a basis for sound strategy, let alone a strategy that made intelligent allowance for the role of technology. Instead, Americans invented a strategy each time they went to war. Until World War II, at least, this meant fighting with the technology at hand.

Finally, land warfare is simply less technologically based than naval warfare or air warfare. Without ships there is no naval warfare; without planes no air warfare. In those realms the vehicle is the sine qua non of combat itself, an integral part of how to fight. Choose battleships or submarines and you choose your strategy; choose bombers or fighters and you similarly define the game. But land warfare can go on without its vehicles, as in fact it has done throughout most of history. Regardless of their arms and armor, troops can still line up in a field and have at each other.

This last point really gets to the heart of the invisibility of technology in American strategic thought on land warfare. It is not so much that the technology was not there was that we did not see it. We took it for granted, accepted it as a given, in ways that naval theorists and air power theorists could not. Historians of American military thought and experience have simply reported what they found. Like the practitioners and thinkers who preceded them, they have viewed technology as part of the scenery, not as an actor in the play. The technology of ground warfare has been submerged all along in the other issues on which we have tended to focus.

When we look among those issues in search of technology, we find it everywhere, vitally linked to the main action, and determining in many ways the shape of our thought and behavior.

Take, for example, the half dozen most important themes in American military experience: personnel, civilian control of the military, suspicion of standing armies, preparedness, free security, and military conservatism. Participants and historians alike have been remarkably consistent in focusing on the same set of issues. Some historians would add or delete one issue or more, but most would agree that these six have been central to American military experience. I use this list for convenience, but I think any comparable list would do. All, I think, would have two identical characteristics. Technology would be invisible, and yet deeply embedded.

I would argue that personnel is the most important topic in American military experience. This view reflects more than just current fashion in the era of social history and the "new military history." It represents, rather, my considered judgment that the United States, especially in land warfare, has spent more time and energy on manning the army than on any other issue. Questions of personnel have come first in our military experience, from Washington's frustrations with enlistments through the drafts of the Civil War and the shortages of World War II right up to the all-volunteer army. Who is going to fight, under what terms, and with what consequences? This is the fundamental question of American military experience.

Consider the technological implications. First, the United States has been from colonial times resource rich and labor scarce. One reason for Americans' specialization in labor-saving devices is that they had so little labor. They were willing to use their abundant natural resources, profligately if necessary, to build and fuel the machines that would work the fields, run the mills, and lighten household chores. The same impetus gives you forts and minutemen, forts because they multiply the defensive power of people and minutemen because they can labor in their fields until needed for military service. Neither technique is entirely original to the United States, but both are well adapted to our natural and human resources.

The same scarcity of labor is manifest in national sentiment about casualties. Like citizens in all democracies, Americans deplore casualties because they value human life. But they also resent casualties because of our need for labor. Throughout much of American history the army was a place for misfits and ne'er-do-wells, the last refuge for the losers in our society who could not make it in a prosperous private sector. In spite of T. Harry Williams's assertion, in the context of the Mexican War, that Americans expected their generals to take heavy casualties, and in spite of a consistent pattern of violent death in American culture, Americans are still reluctant to see their youth cut down in military service. As a result, they have often sought the technological fix. Annihilation warfare in the Grant tradition breeds casualties; the American cure has been firepower. Overwhelm the enemy with profligate barrages of munitions so that American soldiers can take rubble with ease instead of bunkers with their lives. Thus began the growth of the huge support tail that now wags the army dog.

That tail has been further stretched by the American insistence that its soldiers have the best equipment. The quality of military technology compensates for the quantity of the enemy troops. Even before this predilection was manifest in government policy, it was evident in the behavior of the troops. In the American Revolution, colonials appeared on the battlefield armed with one of the greatest technological achievements of the era, the Kentucky or Pennsylvania long rifle. Europeans could not afford to arm their soldiers with such weapons, nor for that matter could the colonies. But individual soldiers provided their own arms, in part because they were the same arms that they used for hunting. In much the same way, many soldiers in the Civil War bought their own repeating rifles. By the twentieth century, Congress had taken up the cause, arming and equipping its soldiers second to none, if not in peacetime then at least in war. "Nothing is too good," so the saying goes, "for our boys overseas."

A second major theme that seems to run throughout American military experience is suspicion of standing armies. This is an English prejudice, dating to the Civil War of the seventeenth century and the interregnum of Cromwell and the New Model Army. It was reinforced by the colonial experience during the British wars of empire in the eighteenth century, when the colonists fought in wars peripheral to their interests and quartered British troops against their will. This same discontent fueled the flames of rebellion in 1776 and manifested itself once more when the new American nation got down to serious Constitution making in 1787.

The technology of ground warfare has been shaped by three provisions of the Constitution. First, the president is commander in chief of the armed forces, a law pregnant with consequences to be discussed presently. Second, Article I, Section 8, provides that Congress may fund the army for only two years at a time. This curious and now dated provision, which does not apply to the navy or the air force, has its roots in the English Mutiny Act of 1689. When the Glorious Revolution had wrested control from James II and placed William and Mary on the throne, Parliament sought legal protection against military rule. No tyrant must ever again be allowed to dismiss the legislature, as Cromwell had done in 1653, and rule indefinitely through armed force. The American Congress had similar concerns, and similarly made the army dependent on a sitting legislature.

So too did Congress worry about the defenselessness of the people if only the national military was armed. So it provided in Article II of the Bill of Rights that "a well regulated Militia, being necessary to the security of a free State, the right of the people to keep and bear Arms, shall not be infringed."

These last two provisions had enormous consequences for the development of the technology of land warfare in the United States. The two-year limitation on funding for the army made it all but impossible to support long-term development projects. All were subject to reconsideration by the Congress. Only innocuous and appealing technologies could survive this kind of biennial scrutiny. Similarly, the second amendment ensured that for many years, land warfare in the United States would be built around the technology of individual arms. In consequence, the United States has been preeminent in small arms development over the last two hundred years and retarded in artillery.

It also accounts in some measure for a third theme in American military experience, a consistent pattern of unpreparedness before wars and rapid demobilization afterwards. Development of artillery, tanks, transportation, and communication in these circumstances is almost impossible. Training troops adequately in the latest technology is out of the question.

Walter Millis and others have observed, however, that neither our unpreparedness nor our demobilizations were as dangerous and costly as has often been maintained. The reason is the fourth theme that runs throughout American military experience—free security. From the end of the War of 1812 until the launch of Sputnik in 1957, the United States faced no serious military threat from any nation. Even in the midst of the Civil War, during its period of greatest vulnerability, when England and other countries considered intervention on behalf of the Confederacy, no major power posed an offensive threat to the Union. During most of this period of free security, England guaranteed U.S. safety with her fleet, at first out of narrow self-interest and then out of truly common bonds and more enlightened self-interest. Diplomatic and even military disputes with Canada did not bar creation of the longest unarmed border in the world. After war with Mexico and another altercation during the Civil War, a similarly peaceful border emerged to the south. The Atlantic and Pacific Oceans were proof against all other threats—given the sympathies of the Royal Navy during the Pax Britannica—until the Soviet Union developed a missile that could reach New York.

Security like this breeds no incentive for arms development. While European nations rushed through generations of cannons and caissons, the United States muddled along in their trace. Some of the greatest developments in iron- and steel-making were taking place in the United States. We were becoming an international power in the production of locomotives, rails, ships, buildings, and engines. We even converted some of this technological prowess into armored warships and the big guns they came to carry by the end of the nineteenth century. But at no juncture did we seriously bend our prowess to the technology of land warfare. Like most other nations before World War II, we fought all our wars with the technology available at the outset. The problem in the United States was that, in the case of land warfare, this technology was painfully primitive, often imported.

A fifth theme running through American history grows out of the consequences of the previous two: civilian control of the military. Suspicious of standing armies and secure from foreign threat, Americans vested decisive power in civilian hands. The military was leashed to both a hierarchy of power in the Executive Branch and the power of the purse in Congress. One result has been a peculiarly American style of developing military technology. At least until World War II, civilian leaders of the military have been more receptive to new technology than uniformed officers.

This pattern is not peculiar to ground forces. The navy rejected or at least resisted such pivotal civilian inventors as David Bushnell, Robert Fulton, Samuel Colt, John Ericsson, and Simon Lake. And it suppressed, indeed at times persecuted, such internal reformers as John Dahlgren, William Sims, and Hyman Rickover. The air force, in its short history, has already resisted liquid fueled missiles, solid fuel missiles, and the cruise missile; an attachment to the manned bomber has been consistent and long-lived if nothing else.

The army, of course, has been guilty of more than its share of resistance to technological change. It drove off the Wright Brothers early on and then suppressed the apostle of their contribution, Billy Mitchell. It resisted mechanization in general, especially machines that threatened to displace its cherished horses. It suppressed in particular the repeating rifle, the revolver, the machine gun, and the tank, to say nothing of generations of improvement in artillery. General Joseph G. Totten, the longtime chief of the Corps of Engineers and an exemplar of army conservatism at its mindless worst, told Congress in 1844 that the army would adopt no new technology until it had proven itself in battle. Of course, failing adoption, it would never have a chance to prove itself in battle, leaving Totten and his fellow officers in the warm company of the weapons they knew as lieutenants.

There are good and cogent reasons why military officers are reluctant to trade existing technology for new. Those empowered to make such decisions have spent their whole careers in the embrace of the reigning paradigm; the old weapons had not only kept them alive but had gotten them to the top. Furthermore, all decisions about the battlefield demand caution, for lives are at stake. Better the tried and sure cannon of yesterday than a new and uncertain machine that had not yet earned its stripes. Finally, as Elting Morison has argued so persuasively, military officers are a community, and all communities resist change. To the extent that the society is autonomous and isolated from external influence, it will continue in the comfortable path it has known.

Thus it is that in the United States civilian leaders have been more receptive to new military technologies than the officers themselves. The most famous instance is Lincoln's receptivity to inventors and projectors during the Civil War. But there are countless other examples as well. Samuel Colt, for example, grew so frustrated with Joseph Totten and the army bureaucracy that he appealed directly to Congress for support. Congress was sympathetic to Colt's scheme for underwater mines but unable to judge the technical merits of the proposal. So he submitted it to the Patent Office, and then withdrew his application short of actually winning a patent, which would have revealed his secret. Instead he asked the director of the Patent Office simply to tell Congress that his device was patentable. Congress bought the project and Colt skirted the military bureaucracy.

Even insiders found themselves driven to similar tactics to sell their ideas. John Dahlgren, for example, played upon his political connections to bring his ideas for a new naval gun directly to the attention of Lincoln. William Sims similarly ran around the end of an obstructionist naval bureaucracy to bring his ideas on naval gunfire to Theodore Roosevelt. William Mitchell took his case to the public, in a failed attempt to influence Congress. Needless to say, this technique is not always successful, but that it ever works at all is a measure of the American commitment to civilian control of the military.

In ground warfare, especially, these traits combined to keep technology in the background. People were the main issue, not weapons. Civilian control of the military removed innovation, such as it was, from the hands of the user. Fear of standing armies put a focus on the minuteman, who chose his own weapon. Unpreparedness was as rampant in arms development as in other areas of military readiness. Free security meant arms could be produced ad hoc if the need arose. Military conservatism bred a satisfaction with the tools of the last war. The army, in short, was starved in peace and deluged in war. Beside these great issues, the question of technology appeared trivial and derivative.

World War II changed everything. It was the first war fought with weapons developed in the course of the conflict. Radar, jet propulsion, guided missiles, and the proximity fuse are only the more familiar of these. The atomic bomb is the most abiding symbol. If some of these weapons came late and short to the fray, they only reinforced the frightening discovery that Germany's laboratories were at work on devices that might have altered the outcome. The lesson for the military professional, including the army officer, was blindingly clear: the world wars may have been wars of industrial production; the next war would be won by technological development. Quality of arms replaced quantity as the desideratum of warfare in the second half of the twentieth century.

Adjustment to this new reality bred for the first time in American history a generation of theorists, if not of ground warfare, then at least of what came to be called strategic warfare, which included land war. Bernard Brodie, the dean of these, gathered the best early thought on the topic in *The Absolute Weapon*. He followed this with *Strategy in the Missile Age,* probably the most influential book ever written on the subject. The latter study joined a lively public debate being conducted in the late 1950s and early 1960s by scholars such as Robert Osgood, Henry Kissinger, Morton Halperin, Albert Wohlstetter, Herman Kahn, and Thomas Schelling. All these men sought strategies consonant with the new technologies, mindful always that the policies of brinkmanship and massive retaliation pursued by Secretary of State John Foster Dulles lent an urgency to their work that scholars seldom experience. Many of them advocated what was then called limited war, opening up a theoretical rationale for the tactical nuclear weapons that were rising from the laboratories in the late 1950s and early 1960s.

Since the climax of the Cold War in the Cuban missile crisis of 1962, nuclear strategy has continued to be a fruitful and prolific field of scholarship. If it has not quite matched the originality and insight of the early years, that is perhaps because most of the important issues were laid out then. The only original concept to emerge after 1965, nuclear winter, reflected the environmental movement and the politics of the late cold war; it was hardly a response to new military technology. The issue of tactical nuclear war, which attracted so much attention in the late 1950s and early 1960s, has moved from the realm of nuclear strategists to that of the strategists of ground warfare.

The revolution in the strategy of ground warfare experienced during the 1970s and 1980s resulted from external stimuli. First, the numerical superiority of Warsaw Pact conventional forces in Europe seemed capable of overwhelming America's reliance on firepower and qualitative superiority. Second, a military reform movement, originally centered on the technology of air force fighter aircraft, spread through the Pentagon and the halls of Congress. It prompted a searching examination of the focus on hardware that had dominated post–World War II military thought in the United States. Among the results was AirLand Battle, a strategy of ground warfare that emphasizes personnel and maneuver as components of strategy equal in importance to firepower. Technology is still at the heart of this strategy; its purpose in the new dispensation, however, is not simply to overwhelm the enemy materially but rather to achieve maximum combat effectiveness with the resources available.

Since World War II, technology has moved from the background to center stage. It is no longer invisible, as it was throughout most of American military experience. In fact, it has become a major focus of attention. Even the six traditional issues of greatest importance to participants and historians have now come to be couched in technological terms. The transformation is so great that it is easy to imagine, as some do, that these were technological issues all along. Instead, they are manifestations of the extent to which technology has penetrated every aspect of military activity in the last half century.

Personnel is still the most important issue in American military policy. Casualties in Vietnam proved the intolerable burden. Long after that war, Americans argued over who fought and who should have fought. An all-volunteer army capable of retaining its most highly trained technical specialists has been a national goal ever since. The national response to the continuing importance of people in a technological age is to protect the troops with firepower and armor. Americans spend money with profligate abandon to support their soldiers. The logistic tail now following our army abroad is the longest in the world, indeed the longest in the history of mankind. Behind every rifleman on the line are three soldiers in the rear providing intelligence, supplies, ammunition, medical support, entertainment, and letters from home. Every soldier in the trenches can call up an arsenal of artillery barrage, close air support, helicopter gunships, even naval gunfire from battleships and deep interdiction from strategic bombers. We dropped more munitions on tiny Vietnam than we did on our combined enemies in World War II. Where the Chinese spent their richest resource in human wave assaults in the Korean War, we spent our technological resources with equal abandon in an avalanche of firepower. The American style of war has come to be protection of its troops with material resources and technology.

Suspicion of standing armies has shifted to the military-industrial complex. Americans no longer fear a traditional military coup of the Cromwell variety, *Seven Days in May* notwithstanding; rather they fear an insidious coup by what Presidential Science Adviser James R. Killian called the delta of power. The Pentagon, the defense industry, and the Congress comprise the new, New Model Army. To this coalition has been added the defense research communities in universities and think tanks and the army of "Beltway Bandits" that orbit the nation's capital. From the fertile minds of these cold warriors have sprung countless projects that have posed a greater threat to our national solvency than to the evil designs of any potential enemy. Every solid contribution to national security, like the Polaris submarine, reconnaissance satellites, and helicopters, can be matched by a bum investment like the F-111, the Davy Crockett, and the Aegis. Since World War II, Americans have reconciled themselves to a standing army, but many perceive that it has not so much fought off our enemies or even marched on the White House as raided the Treasury.

To guard against further incursions, the old issue of civilian control has been focused with increasing precision on control of military procurement. Since the Eisenhower administration, if not before, there has been a continual series of efforts to rationalize and restrain the development of military technology. First came the National Defense Act of 1947 and its amendment in 1949, creating a Department of Defense with a potentially powerful civilian secretary. Then came civilian undersecretaries of the various services for research and development. In response to the missile mess of the 1950s, President Eisenhower appointed a missile czar. When Sputnik revealed the inadequacy of all these steps, President Eisenhower went still further, creating the Advanced Research Projects Agency, a Director of Defense Research and Engineering, and an elevated and invigorated Science Advisory Committee in the hierarchy of the White House. Robert McNamara went the Eisenhower administration one better, exploiting the statutory power available to the secretary of defense to take control of defense procurement. His record was mixed, but the pattern of civilian focus on this most essential element of control was clearly established.

The services appointed civilian advisers of their own, especially scientists and engineers. From the wartime Office of Scientific Research and Development during World War II, they learned to empanel advisory committees of civilian scientists, to contract with university professors and civilian experts in think tanks like the RAND Corporation, and to staff their own laboratories with civilians in key positions. One result has been, of course, a stalemate of experts, civilians in the services matched against colleagues in the White House and Congress. Officers have advanced degrees. Congressmen are reserve officers. All wear business suits in Washington. The Pentagon is politicized, and policy formulation is militarized. All in all, civilian control of the military seems more important and more elusive than ever.

The luxury of free security disappeared with the intercontinental ballistic missile. It may have succumbed when the Soviet Union first acquired nuclear weapons, even if they could not deliver them to the United States. The new security, such as it is, depends on deterrence, or mutually assured destruction. The Soviet Union is deterred from aggression by the sure threat that the United States can retaliate with unacceptable consequences. Traditional notions of air, sea, and land warfare lose their meaning in this strategic context. The weapons and their means of delivery are everything. It is a technological fix to the old problem of security, but with a strange new wrinkle. Stability comes not from security of the old sort, but from the mutual insecurity of the new terror. Vulnerability guarantees safety, a paradox unnatural and abhorrent to military minds on both sides of the Iron Curtain. So always there is a search for a new technological formula. The latest is Star Wars, or the Strategic Defense Initiative, which promises a return to island America. Where once the Atlantic and Pacific Oceans were proof against all potential enemies, now a great technological system will guarantee security. The issue is the same, but now the means are technological instead of geographic.

Until that return to guaranteed security, the United States must live for the first time in its history in a state of constant preparedness. Now troops must be trained and deployed at all times. Contingency plans must provide for immediate response. Supplies and equipment must be on hand, not on order. But most importantly, preparedness has come to mean research and development. The struggle for national security is being fought in the laboratories. The country lives in what William H. McNeill has called a command economy, one bent to the forced development and production of the technology of war. And that technology is being defined with ever broader sweep with every passing year. In 1989, when the Department of Defense was asked to identify the new technologies most important to national security, it selected twenty-two, including microelectronic circuitry, semiconductor manufacture, fiber optics, computer software, superconductivity, and biotechnology materials and processing. Even the civilian space program has become a component of national security, both because it generates prestige in the Cold War race for the minds and hearts of the world's people and because it produces technology that could have military applications. In the name of preparedness the federal government now promotes and protects a range of technologies that is spreading into virtually every corner of national life.

Finally, the traditional conservatism of the military mind, the force that gives us parade drill and dress swords, has virtually disappeared from defense technology. Previously a new weapon had to prove itself before it could be considered by the military hierarchy; now that same hierarchy force-feeds technological change, constantly reinventing the battlefield and racing its adversaries to the next generation of weapons. Instead of assuming that the old weapon will serve, officers now assume that the old weapon is obsolete, or at least obsolescent. Where inventors used to come to the military hat and plans in hand, the military now goes to the laboratory, specifications in hand for a faster plane, a quieter submarine, a more powerful tank. Instead of supply push, military technology now functions on demand pull. Some conservatism is still evident in the choice of technology—the air force's infatuation with the manned bomber, the navy's love affair with the battleship, the army's blindness to the vulnerability of the tank—but within each category the pressure is for more, better, and faster on demand. Once the military had been a desert where technological innovation withered for lack of nourishment. It is now a hothouse where exotic new breeds are created with scant attention to their survivability in the real world. The arms race has become the moral equivalent of war.

The curious, topsy-turvy world of Stingers and Star Wars helps make the past clearer in retrospect. Though technology now seems to shape strategy in general and ground warfare in particular, it is simply a focus of current concerns. The real issues in American military experience are the same: personnel, suspicion of standing armies, civilian control, free security, preparedness, and military conservatism. Once these issues masked the technology that lurked within all of them. Now the technology masks the issues. Only the focus has changed.

The paradox, then, turns out to be one of perception rather than reality. While this may be comforting at one level, it raises other concerns that historians may want to contemplate. It is hardly surprising that military thinkers before World War II failed to conceptualize American strategy in technological terms; "technology" was not then a conceptual category of much currency or power. Nor is it surprising that historians have tended to mirror their ways of ordering knowledge and discourse. But as technology becomes ever more important in our contemporary world view, we must beware that we do not allow it in turn to mask other issues of potentially greater import. The military reformers of the 1970s and 1980s have often made this point, but it bears repeating.

The Importance of Battle History

DENNIS E. SHOWALTER

The military historians of the 1970s were anything but a homogeneous group. They did, however, generally agree in their dislike for studying armies as military

"A Modest Plea for Drums and Trumpets -- Revisited," an 8 page typed essay, an updated version by Dennis E. Showalter specially written for this volume from his article "A Modest Plea for Drums and Trumphets," *Military Affairs 39* (April 1975): 71-74. Reprinted with permission of the author.

instruments. Operational history, the detailed analysis of who did what, where, and to whom, was even less highly regarded. At first glance, this is somewhat surprising. It is as though historians of science chose to ignore Newton's laws, or students of modern political history overlooked the conduct of elections. The apparent paradox of scholars disinterested in the essence of their subject had several causes. It involved a desire to make the study of military history respectable in an academic community that did not wish it well. It involved a commitment to distinguishing scholars from war-gamers and scale-modelers, buffs, amateurs, and popularizers, who as a rule are most strongly attracted to the nuts and bolts of military history. It involved a fear of romanticizing war, of satisfying unhealthy appetites for "colorful gore" or "the vicarious experience of crime and punishment." It incorporated a conviction that the study of war must move away from policy-oriented analyses that put evidence at the service of theory and drove evidence to the wall when the fit was imperfect. The common denominator of these imperatives was that military history must break from its traditional classroom format of a battle a day and its scholarly counterpart, the study of combat and preparation for combat. Instead a "new military history" sought less to understand specific aspects of war than to interpret the place of military institutions and military affairs in human development.

The result has been a growing body of research focusing on the cultural, social, and intellectual aspects of armed forces, on military-political relationships, and on the social impact of military systems. During the 1980s the new military historians began receiving significant reinforcements as scholars of gender and ethnicity turned to armed forces as reference points. It represents no denigration of these approaches, however, to argue that its contributions have come with a price tag. Class, race, and gender can be as restrictive as an earlier emphasis on battles, sieges, and dramatic tableaux. Armies and navies do not exist in a vacuum. They are not "things in themselves." Nor, at least ideally, are they foci of primary loyalties. They are subsidiary institutions, and like all such institutions they are justified by their principal intended function. Armed forces exist to fight, and they justify themselves on the grounds of their military effectiveness.

This does not mean stated functions and actual behaviors are always congruent. Institutions and attitudes can be generated and maintained for many reasons. But in armed forces they are justified in terms of actual or potential performance in war. Advocates of the citizen soldier in the United States between 1865 and 1940 may have been aware that the country would support neither a large professional army nor long-term peacetime conscription. Essentially, however, this case rested on the contention that citizen soldiers could be effective soldiers, that a citizen army could compare with its potential adversaries in both strength and efficiency. Similarly, contemporary supporters of expanding women's roles in the US armed forces have taken significant pains to deny that this will have any drastic or inevitable negative impact on warfighting capacities. Even the boldest pundits are reluctant to assert that social imperatives for such a change override considerations of winning the next war.

This is nothing new, nor is it confined to particular ideologies. Supporters of guard units in 19th century Europe, for example, had a vested interest in retaining socially select formations in an age of mass national armies. They also argued that such elite forces would perform significantly better than ordinary troops in battle.

Such arguments cannot be dismissed out of hand as special pleading. Evaluating them requires knowledge of armies as military instruments as well as sociological phenomena or political pressure groups. For example, analysis of the voluminous and often uninteresting literature on the failure of the Prussian Guard's attack at St. Privat during the Franco-Prussian War tends to refute suggestions that the guards were peacetime soldiers unintelligently committed to obsolete parade-ground formations. Their tactical shortcomings were common to the entire army, and a good case can be made that only its training, discipline, and high morale, based on a sense of being the best soldiers in Prussia, enabled the corps to advance as far as it did in a forlorn hope. The British Guards Division enjoyed a similarly high reputation throughout the BEF in World War I, even among hostilities-only soldiers like Robert Graves whose subsequent careers hardly qualify them as brass-bound militarists.

The neglect of operational history can have even more pernicious results. When the original version of this essay appeared it was distinctly unfashionable to suggest that historical watersheds can actually be crossed on the battlefield. General histories and specialized monographs alike argued that the Seven Weeks' War merely confirmed or reinforced Prussia's earlier success in achieving economic hegemony over Germany. But would Bismarck's Reich have come into being if the Austrians had won the Battle of Koeniggraetz? Four years later, had German armies reeled back across the Rhine under the blows of imperial France, would William of Prussia still have been crowned Kaiser? Such questions cannot be answered by interpreting wars' outcomes as entirely contingent on the strength and will of the sociopolitical structures involved. Reduced to its simplest terms, this thesis implies that the France of Napoleon III was incapable of developing a military system able to counter that of Prussia without changing essentially, becoming something different than it actually was or sought to be. The image of the computerized, mechanized, helicoptered American vainly lunging at his pajama-clad opponent armed only with a rifle and a cause became a popular cliché illustrating the same point long before the end of the Vietnam War.

The best that can be said for this approach is that it is incomplete. Close study of the battles of 1866 and 1870, for example, demonstrates that the overthrowing of the Austrian and French armies did not manifest some form of historical necessity. Their weaknesses have been highlighted by defeat, but miscalculated strategy, clumsy tactics, mismanaged mobilizations, and incompetent officers were deficiencies that could have been alleviated without making drastic changes in governments, societies, or, indeed, the armies themselves. The shock tactics of the Austrian infantry, which made the Prussians' task so much easier in 1866, reflected conclusions drawn from recent military experience and were justified, however mistakenly, in military terms. Nothing inherent in the Austrian army's structure or ethos directly prevented it from adopting tactics that would have taken advantage of the superior range and accuracy of its muzzle-loading rifles compared to the Prussian needle gun. Far from being a retrograde institution the French army of 1870 was as modern as its Prussian enemy, in the sense of directly reflecting in its structure and composition the country's perceived strategic requirements. Despite the shortcomings of the French staff system before 1871, the evidence suggests that the utilization of the railway network for military purposes could have been considerably improved by administrative reforms well within the capacity of the existing structure. To cite a more recent example, comparison of the plans, attitudes, and resources of the combatants in the Battle of France in 1940 shows that the allied defeat was anything but inevitable. The French collapse, in fact, can be explained in military terms without drawing on political or ideological factors.

Indirectly, of course, armed forces are products of their societies. Particularly in times of peace, but often during war as well, they respond to imperatives that are not directly focused on operational effectiveness. But since the beginning of history, fighting men have overcome handicaps imposed by defective organization, administration, and leadership. They have made good the failings of the systems that commit them to battle. The French and Austrians came closer to altering the destiny of 19th century Europe than is generally realized. Koeniggraetz, like Waterloo, was a near-run thing, with Prussian victory anything but predetermined. The fate of the Second Empire was ultimately decided not in arsenals, war ministers, or schoolrooms, but on the field, where good fortune was a consistently significant factor in the triumph of German conscripts over French professionals. . . .

This essay did not propose a headlong retreat to traditional military history. It suggested that social organization, military effectiveness, and victory in battle do not follow one another in anything resembling logical progression. This in turn implied that the study of armies both as military instruments and in the performance of their primary function continues to deserve an important place in military history and in history generally. It involves painstaking, frustrating labor. Only those who have attempted the process know the difficulties involved in even a marginally accurate reconstruction of a single phase of an uncomplicated action. But the labor is necessary, and its presentation is more than a footnote to studies of "war and society." . . .

When a Roman general was awarded a triumph, a slave rode in his chariot to remind the hero that for all the cheers, the praise, and the laurel wreaths, he was still nothing but a man. This modest plea for drums and trumpets had a similar purpose—to remind the military historian of the dangers of straying too far from the discipline's roots. Rediscovering the specific, unique function of armed forces, establishing the centrality of that function, has helped military history develop what it has never before possessed—a breadth, a stability, and a credibility that does not depend on external validation, whether by armed forces seeking precedents, government policy makers seeking advice or even academic search committees seeking job candidates.

The Evolving Relationship of Women and Combat

D'ANN CAMPBELL

Women are the invisible combatants of World War II. The concern here is with regular combat soldiers in uniform, not resistance fighters or guerrillas. "Combat" means an organized lethal attack on an organized enemy (and does not include

"Women in Combat: The World War II Experience in the United States, Great Britain, Germany, and the Soviet Union by D'Ann Campbell from *Journal of Military History* 57 (April 1993): 301-323. Reprinted by the permission of the publisher.

self-defense in emergency situations). Hundreds of thousands of women engaged in combat. They served on both sides and on every front. German women soldiers helped inflict casualties on American and British forces, and in turn they were killed, wounded, or captured. Likewise, Soviet and British women fought bravely.

American women were not sent into combat. The question is why not—and what does that tell us about gender roles in America? Historians in recent years have been exploring the changes in gender roles during World War II. The general consensus is that on the home front women temporarily assumed new roles ("Rosie the Riveter") but that no permanent or radical transformation took place. The question is more open regarding military roles: making women soldiers was the most dramatic government experiment in changing traditional sex roles ever attempted. Putting these women soldiers into combat constituted a radical inversion of the traditional roles of women as the passive sweetheart/wife/sex object whose ultimate mission was to wait for their virile menfolk to return from their masculine mission of fighting and dying for "apple pie and motherhood" (that is, for traditional social values). The Pentagon was well aware of the performance of European women soldiers, and Army Chief of Staff George C. Marshall conducted a full-scale experiment to see how well American women could perform. There was never a question of an all-female unit; the issue at stake was whether mixed gender units could perform combat roles effectively. The experiment stunned the General Staff: mixed gender units performed better than all-male units. As the draft scraped further and further down the barrel, the availability of large numbers of potentially excellent unutilized soldiers became more and more an anomaly. The demands of military efficiency called for assigning women to combat.

The Luftwaffe lost the Battle of Britain in 1940 but remained a powerful force. It had to be defeated, and the ground soldiers' preferred solution was strong anti-aircraft units (hereafter AA units). In 1941 the British began using their women Auxiliary Territorial Service (ATS) soldiers in "protected" AA units; protected because these soldiers were immune from capture and their living conditions could be closely monitored. To help emphasize the importance of women serving in AA units to free more men to fight on the European continent, Winston Churchill's daughter Mary served in one such brigade. Marshall asked General Dwight Eisenhower to investigate the effectiveness of these mixed-gender AA units. When Eisenhower gave a positive report, Marshall decided to conduct his own experiment. Security was tight—there were no leaks whatever until long after the war.

Marshall wanted to recruit for his experiment women who had already volunteered for military service. He turned to the only official American women's organization at that time, the Women's Auxiliary Army Corps (WAAC) which in July of 1943 would become the Women's Army Corps. Waacs from the 150th and 151st WAAC Technical Companies and the 62nd WAAC Operations Company, a total of 21 officers and 374 enrollees, were selected for this experiment. From 15 December 1942 to 15 April 1943, they were trained in the Military District of Washington on two composite antiaircraft gun batteries and the nearby searchlight units. The Waacs served with the 36th Coast Artillery Brigade AA. Colonel Edward W. Timberlake, the immediate commander of these experimental units had nothing but praise for them. "The experiences . . . indicate that all WAAC personnel exhibited an outstanding devotion to duty, willingness and ability to absorb and grasp technical information concerning the problems, maintenance and tactical disposition to all types of equipment." Indeed the Waacs learned their duties much more quickly than the men, most of whom had been classified as "limited-duty service." Colonel Timberlake recommended that in the future the training periods for women recruits could be shortened. When evaluating the searchlight units, he reported, "The same willingness to learn and devotion to duty has been manifested in these units as in the gun batteries."

In contradiction to generally existing stereotypes of women being physically too weak to perform combat jobs, Timberlake concluded that women met the physical, intellectual, and psychological standards for this mission. In an echo of a widespread belief at the time, he reported, "WAAC personnel were found to be superior in efficiency to men in all functions involving delicacy of manual dexterity." He specifically listed their operations at the director, height finder, radar, and searchlight stations, and concluded "their performance of repetitious routine duties is considered superior to that of men." Indeed he judged that WAAC personnel could be substituted for men in 60 percent of all AA positions. Because men and women were going to be working in close proximity, Timberlake was concerned about any possible scandals which might occur. Promiscuity, or even rumors of impropriety, could undermine the unit's combat effectiveness. He was relieved to find, "The relationship between the Army personnel and WAAC personnel, both enlisted and commissioned, has been highly satisfactory." No sexual harassment was noted; instead he found, "A mutual understanding and appreciation appears to exist." Timberlake asked his superior, Major General John T. Lewis of the Military District of Washington, to judge the experiment for himself. Soon Lewis was as enthusiastic as Timberlake. Lewis wrote that Waacs could "efficiently perform many duties in the antiaircraft artillery unit." Their high morale and a paucity of disciplinary problems "increases materially the relative value of WAAC personnel in antiaircraft artillery in fixed positions." Lewis was so proud of his Waacs that in May 1943, he asked Marshall for authority to continue the experiment, increase the number of Waacs to 103 commissioned and 2,315 enrollees, and replace half the 3,630 men in his AA Defense Command with these more efficient soldiers.

Marshall now had to make a choice. If he let Lewis have the women, the whole country would immediately hear that women were being sent into combat. What would that do to proposals to draft women? What would conservative Southern congressmen, who never liked the WAAC in the first place, do to Marshall's plans to expand the WAAC? Would the general public approve? Would women stop volunteering? Would the male soldiers react favorably or not? If Marshall approved, he could no longer keep this experiment secret. The Judge Advocate General's Office said that Congress would have to change the existing legislation and it provided the wording for a suitable amendment: the new Section 20 would read, "Nothing in this act shall prevent any member of the Women's Army Auxiliary Corps from service with any combatant organization with her own consent."

Marshall asked his staff for advice. They recommended that Marshall terminate the experiment immediately. General Miller White of the Personnel Division, General Staff, acknowledged that "The War Department believes the experiment . . . has demonstrated conclusively the practicability of using members of the Corps in this role." However, since the present strength of the WAAC was far

Isn't a woman's devotion more sincere and lasting than a man's?" The women developed bonds with fellow AA workers, male and female, which they did not share with former workers and friends. "After experiencing just a couple of months of communal life, I found that the girls (civilians) with whom I had worked before I enlisted were self-interested. . . . We no longer spoke the same language even and there seemed to be a barrier between us. It was even worse with the boys." Pile observed, "The girls lived like men, fought their lights like men, and alas, some of them died like men."

The first woman killed in action, Private J. Caveney (148th Regiment) was hit by a bomb splinter while working at the predictor—the device that predicted where the enemy plane would be when the shell finally arrived at the proper altitude. As had been practiced many times in the casualty drills, the woman spotter "stepped in so promptly that firing was not interrupted." In another attack, Privates Clements and Dunsmore stuck to their posts despite suffering injuries, caused "by being blown over by a stick of bombs dropped across the troop position." The total ATS battle casualties were 389 killed or wounded.

Morale was high in the mixed batteries; soon the women were allowed to wear the AA Command formation sign on the sleeves and to be called Bombardiers and Gunners (only on duty). As one recruit explained, "I don't know what it was about Ack girls but we always seemed to be smarter than the rest of the service" and they "acted accordingly." In 1944, morale in the mixed batteries soared when news came that some were to serve throughout England (not just around London) and even on the continent. . . .

The living conditions for both sexes were often primitive; the ATS women boasted how harsh it was out on the hilltops at night. Nervous uncles were appalled. Pressure soon mounted to provide better conditions for the women. Before such facilities could be built, one commander assembled the one thousand women of his brigade and offered to have any of them moved to another location within twenty-four hours. Only nine women asked for a change, and all of these were clerks who were not involved with the fire-control equipment. One male leader of a mixed battery unit confessed that he initially hated the idea of commanding a mixed battery, "But now that I have joined this battery, raised it, watched it grow up and shared in its sorrows and joys, I can say I have never been happier than I am now." After six months an AA corps commander told Pile that "It has been an unqualified success." . . .

It is possible to ask how women compared with men doing identical jobs. British AA leaders concluded that women were inferior as spotters, comparable as predictors and superior as height finders. The British experience was more complete than the American four-month experiment, but there were no major differences in the findings. The women excelled in several areas, were comparable in others, and were inferior in a few. But phrasing the question in terms of men versus women is highly misleading. The British were not interested in setting up all-female units in order to promote feminism. Rather they set up mixed units so they could shoot down more enemy planes and buzz bombs, while making the most efficient use of the limited human resources available. The effectiveness of a military unit depends on the team performance; team members who are better at lugging heavy shells can be assigned to that task, while those who are better at reading the dials should be doing that. The effectiveness of a team is not the average of each person measured as a Jack/Jill of all trades. Rather it is a composite of how well each specialized task is performed, plus the synergy that comes from leadership, morale, and unit cohesion. The mixed units did very well indeed.

Britain had to balance public doubts and ingrained gender norms against pressing needs. When Pile and Churchill first assigned women to AA jobs they encountered resistance from public opinion. It was not so much that the women were in danger—every woman in every British city was in danger of death from German bombs, and tens of thousands did die. The public would not support a proposal to allow women to fire the AA guns. But the British were a practical people, especially when bombs were falling. They soon decided, "A successful air defence was an even stronger political imperative than the possible moral and physical dangers to the daughters of the nation." The government did concede some details to public opinion by not formally classifying these AA jobs as combat and by symbolically prohibiting the women from pulling the lanyard. The mixed AA crews were as much combat teams as were the airplane crews they shot down.

One factor in whether nations employed women in combat roles was the urgency of the need for combat soldiers. The tail-to-teeth ratio was very high in the United States because Marshall felt only ninety combat divisions would be needed, and that the war would be largely won by the efficiency of the supply and support mechanism. Women were not needed in AA units (few men were actually needed), but they were urgently needed to handle clerical and administrative jobs. Marshall thought caution the better part of valor when he decided not to risk a confrontation with Congress and public opinion on the matter of gender roles. The British experience fits the next stage on this continuum. Men were urgently needed for front-line infantry units in North Africa at the same time the Luftwaffe threatened the homefront. British women were assigned to defensive missions to enable men to engage in offensive action. They were at risk of being killed, but there was little chance they could be captured. Living conditions, while difficult, protected them from unwanted sexual encounters. How did other European countries react to severe threats with their shrinking manpower assets? Did they employ maximum personpower?

Hitler had always insisted that women remain at home and be full-time wives and mothers; Nazi women were to guarantee the survival of the Aryan race in the labor room, not on the battlefield. Even single women were not recruited for jobs in industry at the beginning of the war. By 1941 women were holding jobs in industry and serving in Female Auxiliary Units doing administrative work for the military. After the invasion of Russia, German women in Female Auxiliary Units increasingly began replacing men who were sent to the Eastern front. Berlin did monitor its Finnish ally, which successfully used "Lottas" as auxiliaries to the army. But it was not until January 1943, when the war had clearly begun to turn sour and Albert Speer became the economic czar, that Germany began full mobilization of its human resources. Even so, measures to conscript women into industry were introduced "only with extreme reluctance, and were never efficiently implemented." Not surprisingly, then, measures to draft women into the military—including Goebbels's 1944 Second Order for the Implementation of Total War—were even less well-enforced.

German women, however, did serve in the military: in all, 450,000 joined the women's auxiliaries, in addition to the units of nurses. By 1945 women were holding approximately 85 percent of the once all-male billets as clericals, accountants, interpreters, laboratory workers, and administrative workers, together with half of the clerical and junior administrative posts in high-level field headquarters. These German women, in uniform and under military discipline, were not officially referred to as female soldiers. They were unofficially nicknamed "Blitzmädchen." While it may seem surprising that the Nazis ever allowed women to serve in the military in any capacity, to test our hypothesis we must examine the German model to see if women held more than combat support or combat service support positions.

Antiaircraft units became increasingly central to Germany's war effort, so on 17 July 1943, Hitler, at the urging of Speer, decided to train women for searchlight and AA positions. Basic training was to take four weeks. These AA auxiliaries were placed as follows: three to operate the instrument to measure distances, seven to operate the radio measuring instrument, three to operate the command instrument, and occasionally one woman served as a telephone platoon leader. By the end of the war, between sixty-five thousand and one hundred thousand women were serving in AA units with the Luftwaffe. Some searchlight units were eventually 90 percent female. Similar to the British experience, German women who joined AA units were soon "proud to be serving as AA-Auxiliaries," and were "Burning soon to be trained well enough to be able flawlessly to stand our ground at the equipment." In these units women developed the unit cohesion which had been evident in the British AA units. As one veteran recalled, "We have been raised with the same kind of spirit, we had the same ideals, and the most important was the good comradeship, the 'one for all.' " Here again these AA-Auxiliaries emphasized their continued femininity. As Lotte Vogt explained:

> In spite of all the soldier's duties we had to do, we did not forget that we are girls. We did not want to adopt uncouth manners. We certainly were no rough warriors—always simply women.

As in Britain, however, the German women serving with AA units learned all aspects of the guns, but were forbidden to fire them. Hitler and his advisers firmly believed that public opinion would never tolerate these auxiliaries firing weapons. Indeed, German propaganda warned all women in the auxiliaries not to become "gun women" (*Flintenweiber*). "Gun women" was the contemptuous German term for Soviet women who carried or fired weapons. Many Soviet women were without uniforms and thus considered de facto partisans. The Germans looked upon armed Soviet women as "unnatural" and consequently had no compunction about shooting such "vermin" as soon as they were captured. The verbal degradation of enemy females made it easier for German soldiers to overcome inhibitions about harming women.

In November 1944, Hitler issued an official order that no woman was to be trained in the use of weapons. The only exception was for women in the remote areas of the Reich which could be easily overrun by the Soviets. In one such area, a twenty-two-year-old Pomeranian woman, "Erna," was awarded the Iron Cross (second class) when she, together with a male sergeant and private destroyed three tanks with bazookas. Indeed, the German propaganda suggested that the bazooka was the most feminine of weapons. The Freikorps Adolf Hitler was formed in 1945 and trained in the use of bazookas, hand grenades, and automatic rifles. Lore Ley, daughter of a leading Nazi, once knocked out a Soviet armored scout car and took from its commander military documents and money. In all, thirty-nine German women received the Iron Cross (second class) for their duty near the front. The majority of these women, however, were nurses.

The true Nazis resisted weapons training for women auxiliaries serving with the Army or Luftwaffe until the final stages of the war. As Reichsleiter Martin Bormann sputtered to Reichsminister Dr. Josef Goebbels, as late as November 1944: "As long as there is still one single man employed at a work place in the Wehrmacht that could as well be occupied by a woman, the employment of armed women must be rejected." More and more desperate every day, in February 1945 Hitler capitulated and created an experimental women's infantry battalion. Ironically, this unit's mission was in part to shame cowardly men who were evading their natural gender role of dying for their country (thousands of men were deserting in 1945). The cowards ought to stay with their units and fight like real men. The war ended before the women's battalion could be raised and trained.

In contrast to the Germans, the Soviets mobilized their women early, bypassing the "auxiliary" stage entirely. About eight hundred thousand women served in the Red Army during World War II, and over half of these were in front-line duty units. Many were trained in all-female units. About a third of the total number of women serving were given additional instruction in mortars, light and heavy machine guns, or automatic rifles. Another three hundred thousand served in AA units and performed all functions in the batteries—including firing the guns. When asked why she had volunteered for such dangerous and "unwomanly" work, AA gunner K. S. Tikhonovich explained, "'We' and 'Motherland' meant the same thing for us." Sergeant Valentina Pavlovna Chuayeva from Siberia wanted to settle the score and avenge the death of her father: "I wanted to fight, to take revenge, to shoot." Her request was denied with the explanation that telephone operator was the most vital work she could do. She retorted that telephone receivers did not shoot; finally a colonel gave her the chance to train for the AA. "At first my nose and ears bled and my stomach was completely upset. . . . It wasn't so terrible at night, but in the daytime it was simply awful." She recalled the terror of battle: "The planes seemed to be heading straight for you, right for your gun. In a second they would make mincemeat of you. . . . It was not really a young girl's job." Eventually she became commander of an AA gun crew. Private Nonna Alexandrovna Smirnova, AA gunner from the Georgian village of Obcha, did not like the training program in which men with little education, often mispronouncing words, served as their instructors. The uniforms they received were designed for men. Smirnova, the smallest person in her company, usually wore a size 34 shoe but was issued an American-made boot size 42. "They were so heavy that I shuffled instead of marching." (In every nation the women's services had trouble with the quartermaster's notion of what a shoe should be.)

The noncombat-combat classification which preoccupied the Americans, British, and Germans proved an unaffordable luxury to the Soviets. In a nation totally controlled by the Kremlin, organized public opinion was hardly a factor. Implicit public opinion regarding the primacy of traditional gender roles was another matter, but the evidence available does not speak to that. (The Kremlin controlled the media and the historiography—and even the memories of World War II; perhaps someday *glasnost* will loosen some tongues.) Article 13 of the universal military duty law, ratified by the Fourth Session of the Supreme Soviet on 1 September 1939, enabled the military to accept women who had training in critical medical or technical areas. Women could also register as part of a training group and after they were trained they could be called up for active duty by the armed forces. Once war broke out, these Soviet women together with their fathers, brothers, and husbands went to the military commissariats, to party and Komsomol organizations to help fight. They served as partisans, snipers, and tank drivers. After one woman's tanker husband died, she enlisted herself, served in a tank she named "Front-Line Female Comrade" and perished in 1944. Women constituted three regiments of pilots, one of fighter pilots (the 586th Fighter Regiment), one of bombers (the 587th), and the most famous, the 588th Night Bombers who proved so effective at hitting their targets that they were nicknamed by the Germans the night witches. According to one veteran German pilot, "I would rather fly ten times over the skies of Tobruk [over all-male British ack-ack] than to pass once through [Russia where] the fire of Russian flak [was] sent up by female gunners." In all, Soviet women made up about 8 percent of all combatants. Between 100,000 and 150,000 of them were decorated during the war, including 91 women who received the Hero of the Soviet Union medal, the highest award for valor.

The Soviets boasted that their women were in combat units, and even sent some abroad on publicity tours. Combat roles were not publicized in Germany, Britain, or America, even as the generals realized that women soldiers in AA units had combat missions. They were shooting at the enemy, and he (or she) was shooting back. The British discovered that Luftwaffe gunners fired at everyone around the searchlights or the guns and not just the men there. As Shelford Bidwell, the distinguished historian of artillery and of the ATS, concluded, "There is not much essential difference between manning a G.L. set or a predictor and firing a gun: both are means of destroying an enemy aircraft." He noted that, "The situation became more absurd when the advance of automation was such that the guns were fired by remote control when on target, from the command post." After June 1944, most of the targets were V-1 robots, but the women still could not shoot. What stopped the British, Americans, and Germans from allowing the AA women to pull the trigger was their sense of gender roles—a sensibility that had not yet adjusted to necessity.

Understanding the reaction of the servicemen to women in combat involves study of the structure of gender roles in society at large and the military in particular, and calls out for a comparative framework. In the United States, most male soldiers were strongly opposed to the Women's Army Corps and urgently advised their sisters and friends not to join. Scurrilous rumors to the effect that Waacs were sexual extremists (either promiscuous or lesbian) chilled recruitment and froze the Corps far below its intended size. The rumors were generated almost entirely by word of mouth by servicemen. In point of fact, rumors were false because the servicewomen were much less sexually active than servicemen, and rather less active than comparable civilian women. The rumors therefore reflected a strong hostility, but to what? Senior officers had mostly been opposed to the WAC, but almost unanimously reversed their position when they realized how effective the women were and how many men they could free for combat. Most of the senior officers had been trained as engineers (especially at the military academies) and perhaps were more sensitive to efficiency than to human sensibilities. Most women themselves probably opposed going into combat. Some enlisted men with noncombat jobs were aghast at the idea (explicit in recruiting posters) that women who enlisted would send a man to the front. . . . Young men furthermore saw military service as a validation of their own virility and as a certificate of manhood. If women could do it, then it was not very manly. The exhilaration of combat could become an aphrodisiac, if not a sexual experience in its own right; perhaps like the "Tail-hookers" of recent days they felt this should be forbidden territory to females. The closure of territory to females was strongly enforced by every fifth word the men spoke—language deliberately offensive to women. At a deeper level, can society allow women to shoot at men? . . .

The question of women in combat has generated a vast literature that draws from law, biology, and psychology, but seldom from history. The restrictions against women in combat that persisted for decades in the United States were not based on experimental research (quite the reverse), or from a consideration of the effectiveness of women in combat in other armies. The restrictions were primarily political decisions made in response to the public opinion of the day, and the climate of opinion in Congress. Still horrified by Belleau Wood, Okinawa, and Ia Drang, many Americans to this day visualize "combat" as vicious hand-to-hand knife fighting. . . .

It was not feminism but fear of the lack of sufficient "manpower" to fight World War II, which served as the catalyst for Marshall's experiment, Pile's mixed batteries, and the Soviet Night Witches. Necessity, once it was dire enough, could overcome culture. "If the need for women's service be great enough they may go any place, live anywhere, under any conditions," concluded Major [Everett] Hughes. Success in combat was a matter of skill, intelligence, coordination, training, morale, and teamwork. The military is a product of history and is bound by the lessons it has "learned" from history. The problem is that the history everyone has learned about the greatest and best-known war of all times has airbrushed out the combat roles of women.

♠ F U R T H E R   R E A D I N G

George W. Baer, *One Hundred Years of Sea Power: The U.S. Navy, 1890–1990* (1994).
Edward L. Beach, *The United States Navy: Two Hundred Years* (1986).
Geoffrey Best, *Humanity in Warfare* (1980).
Walter J. Boyne, *Beyond the Wild Blue: A History of the United States Air Force, 1947–1997* (1997).
Bernard Brodie, *War and Politics* (1973).
John M. Carroll and Colin F. Baxter, eds., *The American Military Tradition: From Colonial Times to the Present* (1993).
Center of Military History, United States Army. *American Military History* (1988).
Joan R. Challinor and Robert L. Beisner, eds., *Arms at Rest: Peacemaking and Peacekeeping in American History* (1987).

John Whiteclay Chambers II, ed., *Oxford Companion to American Military History. (NY: Oxford University Press, 1999).*

———, *To Raise An Army: The Draft Comes to Modern America* (1987).

Calvin L. Christman, ed., *America at War* (1995).

Edward M. Coffman, "The Long Shadow of *The Soldier and the State*," *Journal of Military History* 55 (January 1991): 69–82.

Robert W. Coakley, *The Role of Federal Military Forces in Domestic Disorders, 1789–1878* (1988).

Eliot A. Cohen, *Citizens and Soldiers: The Dilemmas of Military Service* (1985).

Joseph G. Dawson, III, ed., *Commanders in Chief: Presidential Leadership in Modern Wars* (1993).

Charles DeBenedetti, *The Peace Reform in American History* (1980).

Robert A. Doughty and Ira D. Gruber, *Warfare in the Western World,* 2 vols. (1996).

Robert C. Doyle, *Voices from Captivity: Interpreting the American POW Narrative* (1994).

Dennis M. Drew and Donald M. Snow, *The Eagle's Talons: The American Experience at War* (1988).

Arthur A Ekirch, Jr., *The Civilian and the Military: A History of the American Antimilitarist Tradition* (1972).

John Ellis, *The Social History of the Machine Gun* (1975).

Louis Fisher, *Presidential War Power* (1995).

Kenneth J. Hagan, *This People's Navy: The Making of American Sea Power* (1991).

Charles E. Heller and William A. Stofft, eds., *America's First Battles, 1776–1965* (1986).

Robin Higham, *Air Power: A Concise History* (1972).

Margaret Randolph Higonnet, et al., *Behind the Lines: Gender and the Two World Wars* (1987).

Stephen Howarth, *To Shining Sea: A History of the United States Navy, 1775–1991* (1991).

Samuel P. Huntington, *The Soldier and the State: The Theory and Politics of Civil-Military Relations* (1957).

Morris Janowitz, *The Professional Soldier: A Social and Political Portrait* (1960).

Joan M. Jensen, *Army Surveillance in America, 1775–1980* (1991).

Robert Erwin Johnson, *Guardians of the Sea: History of the United States Coast Guard, 1915 to the Present* (1987).

Peter Karsten, *Soldiers and Society: The Effects of Military Service and War on American Life* (1978).

John Keegan, *The Face of the Battle (1976).*

———, *Fields of Battle: The Wars for North America* (1996).

Richard H. Kohn, "The Social History of the American Soldier: A Review and Prospectus for Research," *American Historical Review* 86 (June 1981): 553–567.

Paul A. C. Koistinen, *The Military-Industrial Complex: A Historical Perspective* (1980).

———, *Beating Plowshares into Swords: The Political Economy of American Warfare,* 3 vols. (1996–99).

Marvin A. Kreidberg and Merton G. Henry, *History of Military Mobilization in the United States Army, 1775–1945* (1955).

Edward Tabor Linenthal, *Sacred Ground: Americans and Their Battlefields* (1991).

Robert W. Love, Jr. *History of the U.S. Navy,* 2 vols. (1992).

John K. Mahon, *History of the Militia and the National Guard* (1983).

Allan R. Millett, *Semper Fidelis: The History of the United States Marine Corps* (1991).

Allan R. Millett and Peter Maslowski, *For the Common Defense: A Military History of the United States of America* (1994).

Walter Millis, *Arms and Men: A Study in American Military History* (1956).

Bernard C. Nalty, *Strength for the Fight: A History of Black Americans in the Military* (1986).

Peter Paret, ed., *Makers of Modern Strategy: From Machiavelli to the Nuclear Age* (1986).

Geoffrey Perret, *A Country Made By War: From the Revolution to Vietnam—the Story of America's Rise to Power* (1989).

G. Kurt Piehler, *Remembering War the American Way* (1995).

Alex Roland, "Technology, Ground Warfare, and Strategy: The Paradox of American Experience," *Journal of Military History* 55 (October 1991): 447–467.

Garry D. Ryan and Timothy K, Nenninger, eds., *Soldiers and Civilians: The U.S. Army and the American People* (1987).

Michael S. Sherry, *In the Shadow of War: The United States since the 1930s* (1995).

Dennis E. Showalter, "A Modest Plea for Drums and Trumpets," *Military Affairs* 39 (April 1975): 71–74.

Melvin Small, *Was War Necessary? National Security and U.S. Entry Into War* (1980).

Judith Hicks Stiehm, ed., *It's Our Military Too! Women and the U.S. Military* (1996).

James L. Stokesbury, *A Short History of Airpower* (1986).

Penny Summerfield, "Gender and War in the Twentieth Century," *International Historical Review* 19 (February 1997): 3–15.

Jerry K. Sweeney, ed., *A Handbook of American Military History: From the Revolutionary War to the Present* (1996).

Martin Van Creveld, *Technology and War: From 2000 B.C. to the Present* (1989).

Russell F. Weigley, *History of the United States Army* (1967).

———, *The American Way of War* (1973).

C H A P T E R
2

The Colonial Era: Native American Versus European State Warfare

Despite the fact that some colonists and Native Americans lived peaceably, war between Indians and Europeans came early to the English North American colonies. The Roanoke Island settlement off the Virginia coast was wiped out in the 1580s; Jamestown was almost destroyed by Powhatan Indians in 1622. In New England, Indians helped Plymouth colony survive, but within a decade after the founding of Puritan Massachusetts Bay colony in 1630 followed by the establishment of Connecticut and Rhode Island, New Englanders decimated an entire people in the Pequot War. Forty years later, when the colonists crushed an Indian uprising in King Philip's War of 1675–1676, some three thousand Native Americans (and six hundred colonists) were killed, and the independent power of the Indians in the region was broken.

For years, military history, like American historical writing in general, contrasted noble settlers with savage Indians. However, in the 1960s and 1970s the stereotypes were often reversed: The European-Americans became the savages, contrasted with the noble Indians. In recent years, the military history of Indian-European encounters has often been characterized by a more complex and sophisticated analysis, reflecting new attitudes and new directions in broader historical scholarship. In particular, the "new" military history looks at military institutions and war from a cultural as well as a strictly military perspective.

One of the continuing controversies about the colonial Indian wars concerns the Pequot War of 1636–1637, in which militia volunteers from the Massachusetts Bay Colony and Connecticut, aided by Narragansett Indian allies, destroyed the Pequots, an influential Indian nation that controlled much of the land and fur trade in the Connecticut River Valley and western Rhode Island. Traditional accounts, based on a history written by John Winthrop, the governor of Massachusetts Bay Colony at the time, ascribe the cause to the Pequots, who they alleged broke a treaty with Massachusetts and also murdered two traders, John Stone and John Oldham. However, revisionist accounts written in the 1960s and 1970s reversed

*this, blaming the war on the colonists' greed. Revisionists cite Pequot denials that
they had broken the treaty and note that no copy of the treaty has been found. In
regard to the murders cited by the Puritans as the reason for their punitive expedition, revisionists discovered that John Stone was no innocent trader; rather,
Massachusetts authorities had banished him for trying to hijack a vessel, and the
Pequots had captured and killed him after he had kidnapped some tribal members
and held them for ransom. Revisionists claim these incidents were merely pretexts
for an aggressive military action by the colonists to defeat the Pequots and acquire
their land.*

*The most controversial part of the conflict is the colonists' attack against a pal-
isaded Pequot village near the Mystic River not far from the present city of Stoning-
ton, Connecticut. The punitive expedition included 90 militiamen from Connecticut
led by Captain John Mason and 19 militia volunteers from the Massachusetts Bay
Colony under Captain John Underhill. They were accompanied by several hundred
Indian allies; traditional enemies of the Pequots, they included mostly Mohegans
but also some Narragansetts and eastern Niantics. On the night of May 25–26,
1637, the colonists, in a surprise attack, had first sought to shoot and stab the Indians and gain whatever loot they could find. Soon, however, they changed tactics
and decided to burn the entire village and all its inhabitants. Within minutes,
some seven hundred Pequots—men, women, and children—were slaughtered.
Seven were captured, and perhaps half a dozen escaped. Two colonists were killed,
one hit by a stray bullet from another colonist's musket. The Puritans' accounts
justified the slaughter primarily on religious grounds, as the destruction of heathen
savages.*

*The savagery of the colonists shocked their Indian allies, who, like the Pequots,
had traditionally fought a more ritualistic kind of intertribal warfare involving
comparatively few casualties. Subsequently, however, other Indians would adopt
this ruthless style of European warfare, reminiscent of the wars of religion and
conquest. Thus, did the nature of war change in North America. It was a change,
however, that ultimately included the total defeat and sometimes the annihilation
of Indian enemies. Some historians see in these early wars against the Indians,
the origin of an American view of war: Major threats to American security can
be eliminated through crusades by an aroused populace dedicated to complete
victory.*

♠ D O C U M E N T S

The first five documents reflect differing accounts of aspects of the Pequot War and of
Indian and European-American-style warfare. One of the declared causes of the war
was the killing of a trader, John Stone, by Pequot Indians. Governor John Winthrop of
the Massachusetts Bay Colony recounted in his journal, the first document, the death
of John Stone in 1634 and Winthrop's subsequent meeting with the Pequot ambassadors to prepare a treaty (the treaty provided for trade between Massachusetts and the
Pequots and also peace between the Pequots and Narragansetts; the latter never was
implemented.) As the second and third documents, taken from the subsequent and
somewhat defensive accounts by Captains Underhill and Mason, indicate, the two
commanders had decided to burn the village once the Indians had sounded the alarm;
the officers then extolled their men to put the Indians' quarters to the torch and destroy
every inhabitant. Two centuries later, one of the few surviving Pequot descendants,

William Apess, who had risen from extreme poverty, indentured servitude, and alcoholism, to serve in the War of 1812, and subsequently become a Christian convert and an itinerant Methodist preacher, defended the Indians in a number of sermons and writings. One of them was an essay from 1831, when at the age of 33, he decried the Puritan colonists' destruction of Mystic Village as being as immoral as the Pagan Gauls' sack of ancient Rome. Sympathizing with the Indians at the time of the Mystic attack, Roger Williams, the founder of Rhode Island colony, explains in his 1643 encyclopedia of Indian language and culture, excerpted in the fifth document, that the Indians' traditional style of warfare was originally much less bloody than that of the European Americans.

From their victories against the Indians, and later in the British colonial wars against the French, Americans took pride in their prowess as righteous warriors. In 1757, at the beginning of the French and Indian War, George Washington, then a colonel in command of a regiment of longer-term, volunteer provincial troops, writes to the royal governor of Virginia, in the sixth document, emphasizing the dedication and ability of his American soldiers and comparing them favorably with regulars in the British Army. Like Washington, historians differ over the relative effectiveness of the citizen-soldiers of the compulsory common militia and the volunteer, semi-professional soldiers in longer-term units, whether the Virginia Provincial Regiment or later the Continental Army.

1. Governor John Winthrop Recounts the Killing of John Stone and the Treaty with the Pequots, 1634

6.] There came to the deputy governor, about fourteen days since, a messenger from the Pekod [Pequot] sachem, to desire our friendship. He brought two bundles of sticks, whereby he signified how many beaver and otter skins he would give us for that end, and great store of wampompeage...[wampum: shell beads, Indian currency]. He brought a small present with him, which the deputy received, and returned a moose coat of as good value, and withal told him, that he must send persons of greater quality, and then our governor would treat with them. And now there came two men, who brought another present of wampompeage. The deputy brought them to Boston, where most of the assistants were assembled, by occasion of the lecture, who, calling to them some of the ministers, grew to this treaty with them: That we were willing to have friendship etc.; but because they had killed some Englishmen, viz. Capt. Stone, etc., they must first deliver up those who were guilty of his death, etc. They answered, that the sachem, who then lived, was slain by the Dutch, and all the men, who were guilty, etc., were dead of the pox, except two, and that if they were worthy of death, they would move their sachem to have them delivered, (for they had no commission to do it;) but they excused the fact, saying that Capt. Stone, coming into their river, took two of their men and bound them, and made them show him the way up the river, which when they had done, he with two others and the two Indians, (their hands still bound,) went on shore, and nine of their men watched them, and when they were on sleep in the night, they

From John Winthrop. Winthrop's Journal "History of New England," 1630–1639, Vol. 1, ed. James Kendall Hosmer (New York: Charles Scribner's Sons, 1908; Barnes and Noble, 1966), 138–140.

killed them; then going towards the pinnace to have taken that, it suddenly blew up into the air. This was related with such confidence and gravity, as, having no means to contradict it, we inclined to believe it. But, the governor not being present, we concluded nothing; but some of us went with them the next day to the governor.

The reason why they desired so much our friendship was, because they were now in war with the Naragansetts, whom, till this year, they had kept under, and likewise with the Dutch, who had killed their old sachem and some other of their men, for that the Pekods had killed some Indians, who came to trade with the Dutch at Connecticut; and, by these occasions, they could not trade safely any where. Therefore they desired us to send a pinnace with cloth, and we should have all their trade.

They offered us also all their right at Connecticut, and to further us what they could, if we would settle a plantation there.

When they came to the governor, they agreed, according to the former treaty, viz. to deliver us the two men, who were guilty of Capt. Stone's death, when we would send for them; to yield up Connecticut; to give us four hundred fathom of wampompeage, and forty beaver, and thirty otter skins; and that we should presently send a pinnace with cloth to trade with them, and so should be at peace with them, and as friends to trade with them, but not to defend them, etc.

The next morning news came, that two or three hundred of the Naragansetts were come to Cohann, viz. Neponsett, to kill the Pekod ambassadors, etc. Presently we met at Roxbury, and raised some few men in arms, and sent to the Naragansett men to come to us. When they came there were no more but two of their sachems, and about twenty more, who had been on hunting thereabouts, and came to lodge with the Indians at Cohann, as their manner is. So we treated with them about the Pekods, and, at our request, they promised they should go and come to and from us in peace, and they were also content to enter further treaty of peace with them; and in all things showed themselves very ready to gratify us. So the Pekods returned home, and the Naragansetts departed well satisfied; only they were told in private, that if they did make peace with the Pekods, we would give them part of that wampompeage, which they should give us; (for the Pekods held it dishonorable to offer them any thing as of themselves, yet were willing we should give it them, and indeed did offer us so much for that end).

The agreement they made with us was put in writing, and the two ambassadors set to their marks—one a bow with an arrow in it, and the other a hand.

2. Captain John Underhill Justifies the Attack on Mystic Village, in the Pequot War (1637), 1638

Having imbarqued our soldiers, wee weighed ankor at *Seabrooke* Fort, and set sayle for the *Narraganset Bay,* deluding the *Pequeats* thereby, for they expected us to fall into *Pequeat* River; but crossing their expectation, bred in them a securitie: wee landed our men in the *Narraganset Bay,* and marched over land above two dayes journey before wee came to *Pequeat;* quartering the last nights march within

---

From John Underhill. *News from America* (London: 1638; New York, 1971), 36–41, 42–43.

two miles of the place, wee set forth about one of the clocke in the morning, having sufficient intelligence that they knew nothing of our comming: Drawing neere to the Fort yeelded up our selves to God, and intreated his assistance in so waightie an enterprize. We set on our march to surround the Fort, Captaine *John Mason,* approching to the West end, where it had an entrance to passe into it, my selfe marching to the Southside, surrounding the Fort, placing the *Indians,* for wee had about three hundred of them without, side of our souldiers in a ring battalia, giving a volley of shotte upon the Fort, so remarkable it appeared to us, as wee could not but admire at the providence of God in it, that souldiers so unexpert in the use of their armes, should give so compleat a volley, as though the finger of God had touched both match and flint: which volley being given at breake of day, and themselves fast asleepe for the most part, bred in them such a terrour, that they brake forth into a most dolefull cry, so as if God had not fitted the hearts of men for the service, it would have bred in them a commiseration towards them: but every man being bereaved of pitty fell upon the worke without compassion, considering the bloud they had shed of our native Countrey-men, and how barbarously they had dealt with them, and slaine first and last about thirty persons. Having given fire, wee approached neere to the entrance which they had stopped full, with armes of trees, or brakes: my selfe approching to the entrance found the worke too heavie for mee, to draw out all those which were strongly forced in. We gave order to one Master *Hedge,* and some other souldiers to pull out those brakes, having this done, and laid them betweene me and the entrance, and without order themselves, proceeded first on the South end of the Fort: but remarkable it was to many of us; men that runne before they are sent, most commonly have an ill reward. Worthy Reader, let mee intreate you to have a more charitable opinion of me (though unworthy to be better thought of) then is reported in the other Booke [John Mason's account]; you may remember there is a passage unjustly laid upon mee, that when wee should come to the entrance, I should put forth this question: Shall wee enter: others should answer again; What came we hither for else? It is well knowne to many; it was never my practice in time of my command, when we are in garrison, much to consult with a private souldier, or to aske his advise in point of Warre, much lesse in a matter of so great a moment as that was, which experience had often taught mee, was not a time to put forth such a question, and therefore pardon him that hath given the wrong information: having our swords in our right hand, our Carbins or Muskets in our left hand, we approched the Fort. Master *Hedge* being shot thorow both armes, and more wounded; though it bee not commendable for a man to make mention of any thing that might tend to his owne honour; yet because I would have the providence of God observed, and his Name magnified, as well for my selfe as others, I dare not omit, but let the world know, that deliverance was given to us that command, as well as to private souldiers. Captaine *Mason* and my selfe entring into the Wigwams, hee was shot, and received many Arrows against his headpeece, God preserved him from any wounds; my selfe received a shotte in the left hippe, through a sufficient *Buffe* coate, that if I had not beene supplyed with such a garment, the Arrow would have pierced through me; another I received betweene necke and shoulders, hanging in the linnen of my Head-peece, others of our souldiers were shot some through the shoulders, some in the face, some in the head, some in the legs: Captaine *Mason* and my selfe losing each of us a man, and

had neere twentie wounded: most couragiously these *Pequeats* behaved themselves: but seeing the Fort was to hotte for us, wee devised a way how wee might
save our selves and prejudice them, Captaine *Mason* entring into a Wigwam,
brought out a fire-brand, after hee had wounded many in the house, then hee set
fire on the West-side where he entred, my selfe set fire on the South end with a
traine of Powder, the fires of both meeting in the center of the Fort blazed most terribly, and burnt all in the space of halfe an houre; many couragious fellowes were
unwilling to come out, and fought most desperately through the Palisadoes, so as
they were scorched and burnt with the very flame, and were deprived of their
armes, in regard the fire burnt their very bowstrings, and so perished valiantly:
mercy they did deserve for their valour, could we have had opportunitie to have bestowed it; many were burnt in the Fort, both men, women, and children, others
forced out, and came in troopes to the *Indians,* twentie, and thirtie at a time, which
our souldiers received and entertained with the point of the sword; downe fell men,
women, and children, those that scaped us, fell into the hands of the *Indians,* that
were in the reere of us; it is reported by themselves, that there were about foure
hundred soules in this Fort, and not above five of them escaped out of our hands.
Great and dolefull was the bloudy sight to the view of young souldiers that never
had beene in Warre, to see so many soules lie gasping on the ground so thicke in
some places, that you could hardly passe along. It may bee demanded, Why should
you be so furious (as some have said) should not Christians have more mercy and
compassion: But I would referre you to *Davids* warre, when a people is growne to
such a height of bloud, and sinne against God and man, and all confederates in the
action, there hee hath no respect to persons, but harrowes them, and sawes them,
and puts them to the sword, and the most terriblest death that may bee: sometimes
the Scripture declareth women and children must perish with their parents; sometime the case alters: but we will not dispute it now. We had sufficient light from the
word of God for our proceedings.

   Having ended this service, wee drew our forces together to battalia, being ordered, the *Pequeats* came upon us with their prime men, and let flye at us, my selfe
fell on scarce with twelve or fourteene men to encounter with them; but they finding our bullets to outreach their arrowes, forced themselves often to retreate: when
we saw wee could have no advantage against them in the open field, wee requested
our *Indians* for to entertaine fight with them, our end was that we might see the nature of the *Indian* warre: which they granted us and fell out; the *Pequeats, Narra-
gansets,* and *Mohigeners* changing a few arrows together after such a manner, as I
dare boldly affirme, they might fight seven yeares and not kill seven men: they
came not neere one another, but shot remote, and not point blanke, as wee often
doe with our bullets, but at rovers, and then they gaze up in the skie to see where
the Arrow falls, and not until it is fallen doe they shoot againe, this fight is more for
pastime, then to conquer and subdue enemies. . . .

   . . . Our *Indians* came to us, and much rejoyced at our victories, and greatly
admired the manner of *English* mens fight: but cried *mach it, mach it;* that is, it is
naught, it is naught, because it is too furious, and slaies too many men. Having received their desires, they freely promised, and gave up themselves to march along
with us, wherever we would goe.

3. Captain John Mason Explains the Decision to Burn the Village (1637), 1638

In the *Morning,* we awaking and seeing it very light, supposing it had been day, and so we might have lost our Opportunity, having purposed to make our Assault before Day; rowsed the Men with all expedition, and briefly commended ourselves and Design to GOD, thinking immediately to go to the Assault; the *Indians* shewing us a *Path,* told us that it led directly to the *Fort.* We held on our March about *two Miles,* wondering that we came not to the *Fort,* and fearing we might be deluded: But seeing Corn newly planted at the Foot of a *great Hill,* supposing the *Fort* was not far off, a Champion Country being round about us; then making a stand, gave the Word for some of the *Indians* to come up: At length ONKOS and one WEQUOSH appeared: We demanded of them, *Where was the Fort?* They answered, *On the Top of that Hill:* Then we demanded, *Where were the Rest of the Indians?* They answered, *Behind, exceedingly affraid:* We wished them to tell the rest of their Fellows, *That they should by no means Fly, but stand at what distance they pleased, and see whether* ENGLISH MEN *would now Fight or not.* Then Captain *Underhill* came up, who Marched in the Rear; and commending our selves to GOD divided our Men: There being *two Entrances* into the *Fort,* intending to enter both at once: Captain *Mason* leading up to that on the *North East Side;* who approaching within one Rod, heard a Dog bark and an *Indian* crying *Owanux! Owanux!* which is *Englishmen! Englishmen!* We called up our Forces with all expedition, gave Fire upon them through the Pallizado; the *Indians* being in a dead indeed their last Sleep: Then we wheeling off fell upon the *main Entrance,* which was blocked up with Bushes about Breast high, over which the *Captain* passed, intending to make good the Entrance, encouraging the rest to follow. Lieutenant *Seeley* endeavoured to enter; but being somewhat cumbred, stepped back and pulled out the Bushes and so entred, and with him about *sixteen Men:* We had formerly concluded to destroy them by the Sword and save the Plunder.

Whereupon Captain *Mason* seeing no *Indians,* entred a *Wigwam;* where he was beset with many *Indians,* waiting all opportunities to lay Hands on him, but could not prevail. At length *William Heydon* espying the Breach in the *Wigwam,* supposing some *English* might be there, entred but in his Entrance fell over a dead *Indian;* but speedily recovering himself, the *Indians* some fled, others crept under their Beds: The *Captain* going out of the *Wigwam* saw many *Indians* in the Lane or Street; he making towards them, they fled, were pursued to the End of the Lane, where they were met by *Edward Pattison, Thomas Barber,* with some others; where *seven* of them were Slain, as they said. The *Captain* facing about, Marched a slow Pace up the Lane he came down, perceiving himself very much out of Breath; and coming to the other End near the Place where he first entred, saw *two Soldiers* standing close to the Pallizado with their Swords pointed to the Ground: The *Captain* told them that *We should never kill them after that manner:* The *Captain* also

From John Mason, *A Brief History of the Pequot War* [c. 1656] (Boston: 1736 ed.), 7–10.

said, WE MUST BURN THEM; and immediately stepping into the *Wigwam* where he had been before, brought out a Fire Brand, and putting it into the Matts with which they were covered, set the *Wigwams* on Fire. Lieutenant *Thomas Bull* and *Nicholas Omsted* beholding, came up; and when it was throughly kindled, the *Indians* ran as Men most dreadfully Amazed.

And indeed such a dreadful Terror did the ALMIGHTY let fall upon their Spirits, that they would fly from us and run into the very Flames, where many of them perished. And when the *Fort* was throughly Fired, Command was given, that all should fall off and surround the *Fort;* which was readily attended by all; only one *Arthur Smith* being so wounded that he could not move out of the Place, who was happily espied by Lieutenant *Bull,* and by him rescued.

The Fire was kindled on the *North East Side* to windward; which did swiftly over run the *Fort,* to the extream Amazement of the Enemy, and great Rejoycing of our selves. Some of them climbing to the Top of the Palizado; others of them running into the very Flames; many of them gathering to windward, lay pelting at us with their Arrows; and We repayed them with our small Shot: Others of the Stoutest issued forth, as we did guess, to the Number of *Forty,* who perished by the Sword.

What I have formerly said, is according to my own Knowledge, there being sufficient living Testimony to every Particular.

But in reference to Captain *Underhill* and his Parties acting in this Assault, I can only intimate as we were informed by some of themselves immediately after the Fight, Thus *They* Marching up to the *Entrance* on the *South West Side,* there made some Pause; a valiant, resolute Gentleman, one Mr HEDGE, stepping towards the *Gate,* saying, *If we may not Enter, wherefore came we hear;* and immediately endeavoured to Enter; but was opposed by a sturdy *Indian* which did impede his Entrance; but the *Indian* being slain by himself and Serjeant *Davis,* Mr. *Hedge* Entred the *Fort* with some others; but the *Fort* being on Fire, the Smoak and Flames were so violent that they were constrained to desert the *Fort.*

Thus were they now at their Wits End, who not many Hours before exalted themselves in their great Pride, threatning and resolving the utter Ruin and Destruction of all the *English,* Exulting and Rejoycing with Songs and Dances: But GOD was above them, who laughed his Enemies and the Enemies of his People to Scorn, making them as a fiery Oven: Thus were the Stout Hearted spoiled, having slept their last Sleep, and none of their Men could find their Hands: Thus did the LORD judge among the Heathen, filling the Place with dead Bodies!

And here we may see the just Judgment of GOD, in sending even the very *Night before* this Assault, *One hundred and fifty Men* from their other *Fort,* to join with them of that Place, who were designed as some of themselves reported to go forth against the *English,* at that very Instant when this heavy Stroak came upon them, where they perished with their Fellows. So that the Mischief they intended to us, came upon their own Pate: They were taken in their own Snare, and we through Mercy escaped. And thus in *little more than one Hour's space* was their impregnable *Fort* with themselves utterly Destroyed, to the Number of *six* or *seven Hundred,* as some of themselves confessed. There were only *seven* taken Captive & about *seven* escaped.

Of the *English,* there were *two Slain* outright, and about *twenty Wounded.*

4. William Apess, a Pequot, Later Denounces the Mystic Massacre (1637), 1831

. . . In one of the homely narratives of the Indian wars in New England, there is a touching account of the desolation carried into the tribe of the Pequot Indians. Humanity shudders at the cold-blooded accounts given, of indiscriminate butchery on the part of the settlers. In one place we read of the surprisal of an Indian fort in the night, when the wigwams were wrapped in flames, and the miserable inhabitants were shot down and slain, in attempting to escape, "all being dispatched and ended in the course of an hour." After a series of similar transactions, "Our soldiers," as the historian piously observes, "being resolved by God's assistance to make a final destruction of them," the unhappy savages being hunted from their homes and fortresses, and pursued with fire and sword, a scanty but gallant band, the sad remnant of the Pequot warriors, with their wives and children, took refuge in a swamp.

Burning with indignation, and rendered sullen by despair—with hearts bursting with grief at the destruction of their tribe, and spirits galled and sore at the fancied ignominy of their defeat, they refused to ask their lives at the hands of an insulting foe, and preferred death to submission.

As the night drew on they were surrounded in their dismal retreat, in such manner as to render escape impracticable. Thus situated, their enemy "plied them with shot all the time, by which means many were killed and buried in the mire." In the darkness and fog that precedes the dawn of day, some few broke through the besiegers and escaped into the woods; "the rest were left to the conquerors, of which many were killed in the swamp, like sullen dogs who would rather, in their self-willedness and madness, sit still and be shot through, or cut to pieces," than implore for mercy. When the day broke upon this handful of forlorn, but dauntless spirits, the soldiers we are told, entered the swamp, "saw several heaps of them sitting close together, upon whom they discharged their pieces, laden with ten or twelve pistol bullets at a time; putting the muzzles of their pieces under the boughs, within a few yards of them; so as, besides those that were found dead, many more were killed and sunk into the mire, and never were minded more by friend or foe."

Can any one read this plain unvarnished tale, without admiring the stern resolution, the unbending pride, and loftiness of spirit, that seemed to nerve the hearts of these self-taught heroes, and raise them above the instinctive feelings of human nature? When the Gauls laid waste the city of Rome, they found the nobles clothed in their robes, and seated with stern tranquility in their curule chairs; in this manner they suffered death, without an attempt at supplication or resistance. Such conduct in them was applauded as noble and magnanimous; in the hapless Indian it was reviled as obstinate and sullen. How much are we the dupes of show and circumstance! How different is virtue arrayed in purple, and enthroned in state, from virtue destitute and naked, reduced to the last stage of wretchedness, and perishing obscurely in a wilderness.

Do these records of ancient excesses fill us with disgust and aversion? Let us take heed that we do not suffer ourselves to be hurried into the same iniquities. Posterity lifts up its hands with horror at past misdeeds; because the passions that urged to them, are not felt, and the arguments that persuaded to them are forgotten; but we are reconciled to the present perpetration of injustice by all the selfish motives with which interest chills the heart and silences the conscience. Even at the present advanced day, when we should suppose that enlightened philosophy had expanded our minds, and true religion had warmed our hearts into philanthropy—when we have been admonished by a sense of past transgressions, and instructed by the indignant censures of candid history—even now, we perceive a disposition breaking out to renew the persecutions of these hapless beings. Sober-thoughted men, far from the scenes of danger, in the security of cities and populous regions, can coolly talk of "exterminating measures," and discuss the *policy* of extirpating thousands. If such is the talk of the cities, what is the temper displayed on the borders? The sentence of desolation has gone forth—"the roar is up amidst the woods"; implacable wrath, goaded on by interest and prejudice, is ready to confound all rights, trample on all claims of justice and humanity, and to act over those scenes of sanguinary vengeance which have too often stained the pages of colonial history. These are not the idle suggestions of fancy; they are wrung forth by facts, which still haunt the public mind.

5. Roger Williams Ponders the Self-Imposed Limitations of Indian Warfare, 1643

Obs. Their Warres are farre lesse bloudy, and devouring then the cruell Warres of *Europe;* and seldome twenty slaine in a pitcht field: partly because when they fight in a wood every Tree is a Bucklar [shield].

When they fight in a plaine, they fight with leaping and dancing, that seldome an Arrow hits, and when a man is wounded, unlesse he that shot followes upon the wounded, they soone retire and save the wounded: and yet having no Swords, nor Guns, all that are slaine are commonly slain with great Valour and Courage: for the Conquerour ventures into the thickest, and brings away the Head of his Enemy.

6. Colonel George Washington Praises the Virginia Provincial Troops, 1757

Philadelphia March 10th 1757

Honble Sir

We may I think with great Propriety and Justice represent.

From Roger Williams. "A Key into the Language of America" (1643), *The Complete Writings of Roger Williams,* 7 vols., ed. by James Hammond Turnbull (New York: Russell and Russell, Inc., 1963), I, 264.

From George Washington to Governor Robert Dinwiddie, March 10, 1757, in W. W. Abbott, et al., eds., *Papers of George Washington: Colonial Series,* 10 vols. (Charlottesville: U.P. of Virginia, 1984–1995), IV, 112–115.

That—The Virginia Regiment was the first in arms of any Troops upon the Continent, in the prest War. That—The three Years which they have Servd has been one continued Scene of Action. That—whilst other Troops have an agreeable recess in Winter Quarters, the Nature of the Service in which we are engagd, and the smallness of Our Numbers so unequal to the Task, keep us constantly in Motion—That nevertheless, all these Services have hitherto been performed with great Spirit and cheerfulness but That continuing in a Service precarious and uncertain: hazarding Life Fortune & health to the chances of War, for the present, and a bare Subsistance, is matter for serious, and melancholy reflection: It tends to promote langour and Indifference: It sickens that laudable and generous Emulation so necessary among Troops: It is nipping in the bud our rising hopes. Hopes that we have been led to cherish: It is discouraging to Merit, and, I can't help repeating, that it is in the highest degree dispiriting to the Officers, more especially those, who, having thrown themselves out of other employments are now to look forward and see, that they are wasting the Prime of their Lives and Constitutions in a Service the most uncertain, and Precarious: In which they can expect to be continued no longer than hard blows, and continual Dangers require their Aid. and when those Causes Cease, are then dismissed, perhaps in a State of disability and Indigence from wounds, &ca. . . .

We cant conceive, that being Americans shoud deprive us of the benefits of British Subjects; nor lessen our claim to preferment: and we are very certain, that no Body of regular Troops ever before Servd 3 Bloody Campaigns without attracting Royal Notice. . . .

If it shou'd be said, the Troops of Virginia are Irregulars, and cannot expect more notice than other Provincials, I must beg leave to differ, and observe in turn, that we want nothing but Commissions from His Majesty to make us as regular a Corps as any upon the Continent—Because, we were regularly Enlisted attested and bound, during the King's or Colony's Pleasure—We have been regularly Regimented and trained, and have done as regular Duty for upwards of 3 Years as any regiment in His Majesty's Service—We are regularly and uniformly Cloathd; Officers & Soldiers—We have been at all the expence that regulars are in providing equipage for the Camp—and in few words I may say, we labour under every disadvantage, and enjoy not one benefit which regulars do.

How different from Us, the Establishment of all other Provincials is, may easily be discernd by considering, that they are raizd for a Season—assembl(ed) in the spring and are dismissed in the Fall. consequently are totally ignorant of regular Service—They know their Dependence, and had nothing to expect; therefore coud not be disappointed. They are never cloathd, and are at little expence, as they act as Irregulars and paid exorbitantly. There remains one reason more, which of itself, is fully sufficient to obviate scrupples: & that is—we have been in constant Pay, & on constant Duty since the commencement of these Broils, which none others have.

And we flatter ourselves, it will evidently appear, that the Advantages gaind by the Enemy, and the Ravages committed on our Frontiers are not owing to the Inactivity of the V. Regt In proof of which, we appeal to the many bloody Skirmishes with the Enemy last Campagn to our Beha[viou]r at Monogahela, & Services in the Campaign of 1754; To the number of Officers & Men killd in Battle, &ca &ca. . . .

I, in behalf of the Officers of the Virginia Regt beg, that your Honour will be pleas'd to take their Case into particular Consideration, and as they think themselves particularly entitled to your Honours Patronage, give them Reason by your earnest endeavours with His Lordship, to hope for a Soldiers reward, and redress their Grievances in whatever manner shall seem to your Honour most conducive to their Interest, and His Majesty's Service. . . .

Go: Washington

▲ *E S S A Y S*

Because of different evidence or perspectives, scholars sometimes offer differing interpretations of the same events; this is certainly true of the causes, nature, and meaning of the Pequot War and the attack on Mystic Village. In the first essay, Francis Jennings, a scholar of Indian culture, in a revisionist account published in 1975 blames the English colonists for the war and its savagery. Influenced by the new cultural history, as well as a perspective more sympathetic to the colonists as well as the Indians, Adam Hirsch, a student of New England history, drew a more complex picture a decade later in the second essay. In an exploration of the development of military institutions in the English North American colonies, Don Higginbotham of the University of North Carolina, Chapel Hill, asserts that contrary to tradition, American military institutions did not change suddenly from militia of the colonial period to the professional forces of the Continental Army during the Revolutionary War; the change had already begun in the mid-eighteenth century.

The Puritans Were the Savages

FRANCIS JENNINGS

. . . So many myths have circulated about savage warfare that the civilized European origin of war against noncombatants needs to be explicitly recognized. Armed conquest in New England was a special, though not unique, variant of seventeenth-century war, closely resembling the procedures followed by the English in Ireland in the sixteenth and seventeenth centuries. In these lands the English—Puritan and royalist alike—held the simple view that the natives were outside the law of moral obligation. On this assumption they fought by means that would have been thought dishonorable, even in that day, in war between civilized peoples. Four of their usages, transferred from Scotland and Ireland to America, profoundly affected the whole process of European-Indian acculturation: (1) a deliberate policy of inciting competition between natives in order, by division, to maintain control; (2) a disregard for pledges and promises to natives, no matter how solemnly made; (3) the introduction of total exterminatory war against some communities of natives in order to terrorize others; and (4) a highly developed propaganda of falsification to justify all acts and policies of the conquerors whatsoever. The net effect of all these policies in America has been the myth of the Indian Menace—the de-

From *The Invasion of America: Indians, Colonists, and the Cant of Conquest* by Francis Jennings. Published for the Institute of Early American History and Culture. Copyright © 1975 by the University of North Carolina Press. Used by permission of the publisher.

piction of the Indian as a ferocious wild creature, possessed of an alternately demonic and bestial nature, that had to be exterminated to make humanity safe. No Indian people has suffered more from this myth, either in its own time or in the historical records, than the Pequots. . . .

. . . Connecticut suddenly acquired a motive for accelerating the tempo of action against the Pequots. The settlers at Wethersfield had dispossessed sachem Sowheag (or Sequin) contrary to their agreement to let him live and make a living in his own lands, and Sowheag had gone to the Pequots for retribution. They accepted his cause and attacked Wethersfield. On April 23, 1637, they raided workers in the fields, killing six men and three women, destroying much property, and taking two girls prisoner. It is worth noting that the settlers had previously been so undisturbed and confident that they did not believe the first alarm given by a rider who had seen the Pequots approaching.

However the rank and file may have reacted, their leaders did not panic. A week went by before the General Court met at Hartford to act in a manner bearing the stamp of cool deliberation. There was no frenzied running about simply to ward off danger. Instead the General Court converted the situation to its own advantage by declaring "offensive warr" on the Pequots. Its undeclared reasons were sound and unemotional. Connecticut could gain nothing but security by staying within its prescribed limits of defense, but it could gain rights of conquest over the Pequot territory by beating the Indians in their homeland.

That the defiance of Massachusetts's sanction against offensive war was consciously done with foreknowledge of the Bay's displeasure is evidenced by a letter that Thomas Hooker felt constrained to write to John Winthrop, Sr. Without the background of interprovincial competition, the spectacle would be curious indeed. Here was Hooker excusing his people for attacking the enemies of Massachusetts, in spite of what seems like ample provocation. And the excuse was lame: Connecticut's Indian allies, said Hooker, had forced the action: "The Indians here our frends were so importunate with us to make warr presently that unlesse we had attempted some thing we had delivered our persons unto contempt of base feare and cowardise, and caused them to turne enemyes agaynst us: Agaynst our mynds, being constrayned by necessity, we have sent out a company. . . ." Winthrop, of course, knew how to interpret that, but he had to face the fact that Massachusetts's own blundering and delay had provided Connecticut's opportunity. The contest between the two colonies now turned into a race to see who could get at the Pequots first.

Connecticut mobilized a troop of ninety Englishmen under Captain Mason and about seventy Mohegans and "River Indians" under Uncas. These were instructed to attack sachem Sassacus at his main fortified village on the Pequot (Thames) River. They departed expeditiously, but encountered obstructions at Fort Saybrook, where neither Lieutenant Gardiner nor Captain Underhill showed any great enthusiasm for their mission. "They were not fitted for such a design," said Gardiner, and he raised questions about the competence of Mason's English soldiery as well as the trustworthiness of the Indian allies. Uncas satisfied him as to the latter by killing four Pequots of a company that had just passed by the fort. In the matter of English competence, the officer professionals made two decisions after "five or six days" of argument. They replaced twenty "insufficient" members of Mason's troop with twenty "of the lustiest" of the Saybrook garrison and assigned

Underhill to command the replacements. The second decision was to avoid a direct attack on Sassacus's strongly defended main village in order to attack instead from the rear with a large contingent of Narragansett auxiliaries. Following their new strategy, the troops embarked for Narragansett Bay.

Meantime John Winthrop, Sr., in Massachusetts had become disturbed by the news reaching him, but had been immobilized in his current position of deputy governor by the newly developed hostility of Governor Vane. This difficulty disappeared after the May 17 elections, in which Winthrop's faction elected him governor and routed Vane and the antinomians. Winthrop promptly sent forty soldiers by land to Narragansett Bay.

Connecticut's men got there first. A runner from Massachusetts's Captain Patrick brought his urgent request for them to wait for his arrival. If anything, it stimulated Connecticut's Mason to quicker action. After disembarking he sent his vessels back to the Pequot River to await his army's arrival by land. Then, with Narragansett guidance and an escort of about five hundred warriors, he marched westward to Mystic River, where the Pequot lesser village stood. Mason had chosen this strategy for reasons set forth in his narrative of the affair, "as also some other" that, he cryptically remarked, "I shall forebear to trouble you with." His forebearance becomes understandable as his other reasons emerged from their intended obscurity. Mason proposed to avoid attacking Pequot warriors, which would have overtaxed his unseasoned, unreliable troops. Battle, as such, was not his purpose. Battle is only one of the ways to destroy an enemy's will to fight. Massacre can accomplish the same end with less risk, and Mason had determined that massacre would be his objective. Gardiner and Underhill, hardened soldiers though they were, had opposed his plan and had concurred, Mason implied, only after the expedition's chaplain had spent a hard night "commending" their "condition" to the Lord and had brought forth clerical approval.

All the secondary accounts of the Pequot conquest squeamishly evade confessing the deliberateness of Mason's strategy, and some falsify to conceal it. Mason's own narrative is the best authority on this point. The Massachusetts Puritans' William Hubbard brazened out his own misquotation by telling his readers to "take it as it was delivered in writing by that valiant, faithful, and prudent Commander Capt. Mason." With this emphatic claim to authority he quoted Mason as saying, "We had resolved a while not to have burned it [the village], but being we could not come at them, I resolved to set it on fire." Despite Hubbard's assurance, these were not Mason's words. His manuscript said bluntly, "We had formerly concluded to destroy them by the Sword and save the Plunder."

Not only Mason's prior intent to massacre and plunder was suppressed by Hubbard. The rest of Mason's manuscript revealed what sort of inhabitants had been occupying the Mystic River village and proved conclusively that mere victory over them was not enough to satisfy Mason's purpose. After telling how the attack was launched at dawn of May 26, and how entrance to the village was forced, the account continued thus:

> . . . The Captain [Mason] facing about, Marched a slow Pace up the Lane he came down, perceiving himself very much out of Breath; and coming to the other End near the Place where he first entred, saw two Soldiers standing close to the Pallizado with their Swords pointed to the Ground: The Captain told them that We should never kill

them after that manner: The Captain also said, WE MUST BURN THEM: and immediately stepping into the Wigwam where he had been before, brought out a Fire Brand, and putting it into the Matts with which they were covered, set the Wigwams on Fire.

It is terribly clear from this description that the village, stockaded though it was, had few warriors at home when the attack took place. Mason claimed that 150 Pequots had "reinforced" the village only the day before his attack. Both the number and the suggestion that it supplemented a previous garrison find no confirmation in Mason's own account of the proceedings. There is enough testimony, even in Puritan accounts, of Pequot warriors' willingness to fight to the death, so that one may feel confident that the villagers overwhelmed by Mason were not warriors suddenly and uncharacteristically turned craven. Moreover, Increase Mather's version has revealed that the Pequot warriors had guns, a fact that is substantiated by Lieutenant Gardiner's earlier writing, and nowhere in Mason's account of the Mystic massacre is there mention of Indians with firearms. And if the supposed reinforcements had marched from the major fort at Pequot River to the lesser one at Mystic River, they would have been heading in exactly the opposite direction from the English settlements that Mason said they intended to attack. Such a march would have taken them eastward. Fort Saybrook was to the west, and the upper Connecticut settlements were to the northwest. There were no "reinforcements," and it was precisely for that reason that Mason struck where he did. Mason and Underhill had had advance intelligence from their Narragansett allies of the Pequots' dispositions, and Mason knew very well that the people at Mystic were the sort who could be destroyed easily "by the sword." The wretches crawling under beds and fleeing from Mason's dripping sword were women, children, and feeble old men.

The Narragansett allies had dissented sharply from Mason's procedures. After his intention became plain to attack Mystic instead of Sassacus's fort at the Pequot River, hundreds of the Indian allies withdrew. (Mason dissembled their motive by accusing them of cowardice.) Not trusting the remainder to be sufficiently ruthless, Mason and Underhill surrounded Mystic with two concentric rings, relegating the remaining Indian allies to the outer one. After firing the village the English closed up their interior ring, and as desperate Pequots tried to break through, the English intercepted and slew them before they could gain sanctuary among their formerly worst enemies. This episode was reported with some finesse by Captain Underhill in language equivocal enough to mislead the uninitiated but to be understood, with a wink, by his fellow participants. In the following passage from Underhill I have italicized key words: "Many were burnt in the fort, both men, women, and children. Others forced out, and came in troops *to the Indians,* twenty and thirty at a time, which *our soldiers* received and entertained with the point of the sword. Down fell men, women, and children; those that scaped *us,* fell into the hands of the Indians that were in the rear of us. It is reported by themselves, that there were about four hundred souls in this fort, and not above five of them escaped out of *our* hands."

Here were the Pequots coming in "troops" to the Narragansetts, but in order to "fall into the hands" of the Narragansetts they had to escape the English. The twists of phrase by which Underhill tried to implicate the Narragansetts in the killing were crude enough to reveal the real situation. In a following passage he was candid enough, or boastful enough, to tell of Indian protest against the killing in words that have been robbed of their full power, unfortunately, by semantic change over the centuries. He wrote that, after the slaughter, "Our Indians came to us, and much rejoiced at our victories, and greatly admired the manner of Englishmen's fight, but cried Mach it, mach it; that is, It is naught, it is naught, because it is too furious, and slays too many men."

In Underhill's day the word *admire* was used to express astonishment or wonder rather than respect, as in Milton's lines, "Let none admire / That riches grow in hell"; and the word *naught* meant bad or wicked. What Underhill smugly passed on as the Indians' comment was their incredulity at the ruthlessness of the English.

The toll of Pequot casualties ranges in estimate from three hundred to seven hundred. Of the English, two were killed and twenty were wounded, and some twenty of the allied Indians were also wounded. The allies complained that they had been shot by Englishmen, and one Englishman even seems to have been killed by his own cohorts in the hail of fire they let loose after igniting the village. They must have shot at everything that moved or seemed to move. Mason's men ran low on ammunition, and he had to beat a retreat to his ships to avoid a real battle with Sassacus's warriors, belatedly on their way to help their Mystic kinsfolk. The English retreated by themselves, abandoned by their shocked and guilt-smitten allies.

Now came great irony. Finding out somehow about the English attack, the warriors in Sassacus's fort about five miles away had rushed to Mystic. They arrived too late. At the sight of the smoldering ruins and corpses they gave way momentarily to disabling grief; then rage revived them, and they plunged after the perpetrators for revenge. They encountered the Narragansetts, who had just then drawn away from the English allies of whom they were so ashamed, and the Pequots' furious attack upon those wavering Narragansetts drove the latter back to the covering fire of the English. The allies were helped by the timely arrival of the English pinnaces with reserve ammunition and Massachusetts's company of forty men under Captain Patrick. Thereafter no alternatives but flight, death, or surrender could exist for the demoralized and despairing Pequots.

New expeditions were sent out from Massachusetts and Connecticut to harry and destroy the miserable refugees fleeing into the wilderness. A band of two hundred Pequots surrendered to the Narragansetts without fight. Only two were killed. The rest might have expected humane treatment in accordance with custom. In Roger Williams's words, "I understand it would be very gratefull to our neighbours [the Narragansetts] that such Pequts as fall to them be not enslaved, like those which are taken in warr: but (as they say is their generall Custome) be used kindly, have howses and goods and fields given them: because they voluntarily choose to come in to them and if not receaved will to the Enemie or turne wild Irish themselves." Such prospects faded when a company of Massachusetts's troops seized the captives from the Narragansetts. According to William Hubbard, "The Men among them to the Number of thirty were turned presently into Charons Ferryboat, under the Command of Skipper Gallop, who dispatched them a little without the Harbour; the Females and Children were disposed of according to the will of the Conquerors [i.e., the English], *some* being *given* to the Narhagansets and other Indians that *assisted* in the service."

The peculiar virtues of Hubbard's style show vividly in this passage. Not many writers could have so concisely insinuated that the English were really the conquerors of a group taken by the Narragansetts, at the same time suggesting that the Narragansetts bore some responsibility for an atrocity against which they protested. And his sprightly reference to "Charons Ferry-boat" speaks volumes about Puritan wit.

For present purposes we need not pursue every last band of Pequots to its capture and final disposition. There were more atrocities; the whole story of the Pequot "war" is one long atrocity. It is enough here to say that the Pequots scattered far and wide. Some found their way to Long Island. Others, including chief sachem Sassacus, took the tribal wampum treasury to the Mohawks and tried to purchase sanctuary, but the Mohawks killed Sassacus—perhaps because of their alliance with the Narragansetts, or because of fear of the English, or for other reasons. Most of the surviving Pequots hid themselves among Uncas's Mohegans and the Eastern Niantics. Uncas, who had been unable before the war to count more than fifty warriors in his following, suddenly emerged as the ruler of hundreds. Englishmen could not distinguish between a Pequot and a Mohegan—the difference indeed had been political rather than cultural—but the Narragansetts knew the names and pedigrees of individual persons, and they frequently complained to Roger Williams that Uncas had reaped the harvest of their own sweat and sacrifice. The old Narragansett-Pequot feud had not been ended, after all; it had simply become a Narragansett-Mohegan feud, and its rumblings momentarily threatened war once more.

However, it wore an important new aspect. Whereas formerly the Pequots had made a treaty with Massachusetts, now the Mohegans were clients of Connecticut. The Narragansetts continued to hold to their wartime treaty with Massachusetts. Uncas of the Mohegans and Miantonomo of the Narragansetts quarreled for reasons of their own, and their animosity was heightened by the continuing quarrel of Connecticut and Massachusetts. While the Indians struggled for larger shares of the Pequots' persons and former tributaries, the Englishmen strove for wampum and the Pequots' former lands.

The purported cause of the Pequot conquest was quite forgotten. In the wrangling over real issues nobody bothered to pursue "justice" for the killer of Captain Stone, who walked abroad flaunting his identity. In June 1639 the Dutchman David de Vries met him near the mouth of the Connecticut River and was struck by his scarlet mantle. "I inquired," wrote de Vries, "how he came by the mantle. He had some time ago killed one Captain Stone, with his people, in a bark, from whom he had obtained these clothes." That was as much attention as he got. He had served the Puritans' purpose, and they were now giving their energies to interests that had all along lain behind their voluble concern over Captain Stone.

The Pequot conquest did not bring interracial peace to New England. Rather it brought a new set of conflicting alliances in which Indians, as junior partners, fought with each other in ways that were permitted and encouraged for particular purposes of particular Puritan colonies. Pequots reconstituted as Mohegans fought Connecticut's covert war against the Narragansetts, which was, at second hand, a struggle with Massachusetts. Uncas understood his dependence and willingly played his role, but though he pulled the trigger, Connecticut provided the gun and prescribed its target.

To the English the experience seemed to prove that they could conquer Indians at will. They gloried in the terror that their conquests had inspired, and they labored as needed to keep it alive. The terror was very real among the Indians, but in time they came to meditate upon its foundations. They drew three lessons from the Pequot War: (1) that the Englishmen's most solemn pledge would be broken whenever obligation conflicted with advantage; (2) that the English way of war had no limit of scruple or mercy; and (3) that weapons of Indian making were almost useless against weapons of European manufacture. These lessons the Indians took to heart.

The Tragedy of Conflicting Military Cultures

ADAM J. HIRSCH

. . . To ensure their physical security in America, the New England colonists relied on experts. Miles Standish, John Underhill, and other professional soldiers accompanied the settlers to supervise the defense of their plantations. Those veterans carried with them a set of rules and customs governing every detail of the practice of war. To be sure, the Puritans insisted on a number of administrative reforms, over protests from the professionals who opposed any deviation from the orthodox "Schoole of warre." For the most part, however, the Puritans deferred to the experts and installed a military system rooted in European tradition.

Conceptions of the overall nature and purpose of war are fundamental to any military culture. In seventeenth-century European practice, armed conflict remained a ritualized activity, regulated by a code of honor and fought between armies, not entire populations. Yet, with the rise of the nation state, warfare had developed into a massive undertaking. Waged to settle economic and religious disputes of national significance, warfare came to entail substantial expense and bloodshed. Accordingly, the New England settlers did not rejoice at the prospect of war. But if events demanded it, the settlers were determined, in Underhill's words, to "conquer and subdue enemies."

To thwart enemies in time of war and provide security in time of peace, the colonists needed a fighting force, furnished with lethal weapons and versed in their use. For that service, military planners turned to a time-honored English tradition: the local militia or trainband. Every able-bodied male settler was obliged to serve in his town company, which mustered periodically for drill and mobilized at the call of the government or on alarum. To rouse the militia in the event of a surprise attack, every New England town instituted a nightly watch and designated signals to sound the call to arms.

Thus regimented, colonial militiamen received their equipment and a dose of martial training, as Standish, Underhill, and other officers labored to mold raw settlers into men-at-arms. Military apparatus and exercise in New England empha-

From Adam J. Hirsch. "The Collision of Military Cultures in Seventeenth Century New England," *Journal of American History* 74 (March 1988): 1188–1194, 1200, 1203–1204, 1209–1212. Reprinted by permission of the Organization of American Historians.

sized Old World conventions. Troopers wielded an assortment of muskets, swords, and wooden pikes. Bunched in tight formations on the open "champion field," militiamen marched about "in rank and file" to the beat of a drum, while company colors flapped overhead. Among all values, ritual discipline reigned supreme: On the training field, if not on the battlefield, a musket might require as many as forty-two preparatory motions before it could be fired. The settlers' evolutions, however impractical, must have made for a brilliant spectacle.

The Indians of New England, meanwhile, had different notions about the theory and practice of war. Though as steeped in ritual as its European analogue, Indian military culture had evolved to accommodate the separate needs of aboriginal society.

Central to Indian military culture was a distinctive conception of the purposes and objectives of armed conflict. Given ample land and a system of values by and large indifferent to material accumulation, the New England tribes rarely harbored the economic and political ambitions that fueled European warfare. Roger Williams, who knew the natives of New England better than most of his English contemporaries, traced Indian wars instead to "mocking between their great ones" or "the lusts of pride and passion." Other observers cited retaliation for isolated acts of violence as the most common *casus belli*. If waged in the name of retaliation, an Indian war ostensibly ceased when the aggrieved had inflicted retribution. Otherwise, native hostilities generally aimed at symbolic ascendancy, a status conveyed by small payments of tribute to the victors, rather than the dominion normally associated with European-style conquest.

The organization and execution of native warfare reflected its objectives. Often the demand to take up arms came from solitary tribesmen rather than their leaders. Hostilities frequently pitted kin group against kin group rather than tribe against tribe. Summoned to the call of battle, potential combatants "gather[ed] together without presse or pay" and agreed to fight only after weighing the instigators' "very copious and pathetical . . . Orations." On the march, an Indian war party might melt away as individual warriors had second thoughts and returned home. The contrast to colonial conscription speaks in part to the limits of tribal authority, but also to the characteristics of native warfare as such: voluntary participation in hostilities followed naturally from the Indians' individualistic motivations.

The most notable feature of Indian warfare was its relative innocuity. . . .

Indian battle array also contrasted sharply with European practice. Though Indians did occasionally assemble, as Williams noted, on a "pitcht field," native warfare more frequently consisted of guerrilla raids and ambushments conducted in forested regions by small companies. That style of combat took maximum advantage of the natives' renowned wilderness savvy, while also minimizing casualties.

In other respects, the Indians' martial temperance drew their military culture into line with that of the colonists, whose traditions included vestiges of medieval chivalry, ingrained when the aims of Old World warfare resembled those of native conflicts. Evidence indicates native adherence to a code of honor remarkably similar to the one governing European battlegrounds. Thus, native combatants ordinarily spared the women and children of their adversaries. Tribes typically opened hostilities with a formal declaration of war rather than an unannounced assault. And on at least one occasion, sources tell of a challenge to single combat between leading sachems to settle an intertribal quarrel.

Only in one particular was native warfare arguably more brutal than that of Europeans. Male prisoners of war frequently suffered ritual torture at the hands of their captors. Such isolated acts of cruelty did not add substantially to the death toll of native conflict and in fact may have served as emotional compensation for the participants' prescribed restraint in combat. But while torture remained an accepted element of European jurisprudence, martial tradition held it dishonorable in the nobler trial of arms.

Many of the contrasts between colonial and native military ordnance resulted from technological disparities rather than divergent social needs. Preparing for battle, the Indian brave donned war paint as his insignia, and he trooped off with his fellows to the sound of war cries rather than to the beat of a drum. For combat at a distance, he carried bow and arrows; for hand-to-hand fighting, a stone-headed knife or tomahawk. The mechanics of tribal security likewise coincided with more technically elaborate Puritan precautions: Round-the-clock sentries protected native villages from surprise assault, and networks of runners or other warning devices served to spread alarums. Had a fleet of menacing canoes appeared off the coast of Boston at any moment in the seventeenth century, a flurry of signal rockets and musket shots would have alerted the other settlements of impending attack. Similarly, when several shiploads of colonial militiamen cruised into Pequot Harbor on an August evening in 1636, the Indians greeted their arrival with the "most doleful and woful cries all the night (so that we could scarce rest) hallooing one to another, and giving the word from place to place, to gather their forces together."

What the Indians lacked in technology they made up for in the diligence with which they pursued the art of war. Like the colonists, northeastern Indians frequently relied on expert military commanders who were not necessarily the political leaders of their tribes. These native commanders, in turn, put Indian warriors through as much martial training as a colonial militiaman ever endured. In spite of such rehearsal, William Wood believed Indians to be wholly incapable of the military virtues of the Old World. But Roger Williams knew better. From his vantage point in Rhode Island, Williams testified to the "great Valour and Courage" evinced by his Narragansett Indian neighbors. . . .

That Indians might exhibit formidable martial prowess was a lesson skeptical colonists often learned the hard way. Lt. Lion Gardiner suffered such a painful initiation. When his scouting party spotted three Indians in the forest during the Pequot War, "they pursued till they were brought into an ambush of fifty, who came upon them, and slew four of their men, and had they not drawn their swords and retired, they had been all slain. The Indians were so hardy, as they came close up to them, notwithstanding their pieces." Gardiner eventually came to rate his tribal adversaries as better soldiers than the Spaniards.

Quite plainly, the natives of New England took their warfare every bit as seriously as the newcomers, however symbolic their objectives or bloodless the results. One student has characterized intertribal conflict as "a vigorous game," but that seems ethnocentric. From the standpoint of the participants, symbolic victories had significance, and bloodless battles were more than a diversion. Still, the overall patterns of native and European military cultures differed widely—and those cultures soon met head on in the New World. . . .

Why did the Pequots take up the gauntlet in 1636 despite their technological disadvantage? In part, the answer probably lies in the traditional character of native warfare. Custom compelled retribution for all offenses against a kin group or tribe, and here the offense had been substantial. What is more, the Pequots were a powerful tribe, "puffed up with many victories," and they doubtless placed great value on the maintenance of that stature. Had the Pequots submitted to the colonists, they would have lost face, both in their own eyes and in the eyes of their neighbors. Winthrop's ignorance of those cultural imperatives contributed to his indiscretion.

More fundamentally, however, the Pequots do not appear to have realized what they were risking by challenging the settlers in 1636. In all likelihood, they expected the struggle to resemble their previous conflicts with native enemies, in which a tribe lost little even when it faced defeat. Until colonial militiamen demonstrated that they marched to a different tune, that was a natural assumption for the Pequots to make—indeed, it was equivalent, *mutatis mutandis,* to Winthrop's assumption concerning the Indians' response. . . .

Cultural disparity between settlers and natives also speaks directly to the outcome of the Pequot War. Although traditional explanations of the settlers' victory stress the superiority of colonial weaponry, the foregoing analysis would suggest that more basic incongruities of strategy and decorum also helped decide the struggle. To Underhill, it seemed as if the Indians had prosecuted their warfare for "pasttime"—a description that, for all its ethnocentricity, cast the two cultures' differing levels of violence into sharp relief. Given their grimmer outlook on war, the Puritans would probably have prevailed over the Pequots whatever the quality of their respective arsenals. And by the time the Puritans made their intentions clear at Mystic village, it was too late for the Pequots to make the necessary strategic adjustments. Just as Indians reacted initially to colonial weaponry with panic, so now they panicked when confronted for the first time with colonial strategy; they fled in disarray. . . .

In some respects, the Puritans responded to native military culture by emulating it. Faced with an enemy who refused all invitations to the open field, colonial strategists presently realized that they had little choice but to match his stealth. When Mason prepared to set out against the Pequots in 1637, he therefore rejected the orthodox plan of attack mandated in his commission. Instead, Mason plotted a circuitous route to Pequot country, up the coast to Rhode Island and then back across Connecticut, so that his party "should come upon their Backs, and possibly might surprise them unawares." During King Philip's War in 1675, the colonists continued to adapt to native tactics, borrowing and honing the Indians' own guerrilla methods, without which they could never have engaged their adversaries.

Yet even as colonial military culture fell into step with its native analogue, it also struck out in new and ominous directions. Certainly the most startling characteristic of colonial operations during the Pequot War was their sheer wantonness. The slaughter of noncombatants at Mystic village, the ruthless pursuit of the vanquished tribe, the enslavement or execution of prisoners, all represented an approach to warfare more suggestive of the twentieth century than the seventeenth.

The battlefields of the Old World had been sanguinary, but honor-bound. In the New World, honor was tossed aside—and once the colonists set the precedent, the surrounding Indians followed suit. Out of the turmoil of New England's first Anglo-Indian conflict, an antecedent of total war had somehow emerged. . . .

The Pequot War is often dismissed as a minor episode in the military history of New England, a brief and limited skirmish eclipsed by the battles to come. Such appraisals miss the war's deeper cultural significance: From the standpoint of military acculturation, it was a watershed. The final period assayed in this study, 1637–1676, illustrates how initial cultural contact in the Pequot War left its imprint on the region's subsequent military affairs.

In one sense, the meeting of military cultures in the Pequot War was progressive in character: It facilitated the exchange of knowledge necessary for informed dealings between New England's native and colonial societies. Impolicies born of cultural ignorance—such as the settlers' decision to dispatch the Endicott expedition and the Pequots' decision to retaliate within traditional limits—therefore promised to be transient phenomena, irreversible in the event but incapable of repetition once cultural contact had disabused policy makers of their misperceptions.

Puritan settlers may have been a stubborn lot, but they would not close their eyes to stark reality. Having discovered in 1636 that precipitous military action against Indians could easily provoke hostilities, colonial leaders relied thereafter on other, safer vehicles of statecraft. Like most lessons learned through bitter experience, this was a dictum that John Winthrop took to heart. When the Connecticut Council in 1642 urged Winthrop, then governor of Massachusetts, to join in a preemptive strike against allegedly disloyal Indians, the suggestion opened an old wound. Winthrop responded that

> Our beginning with them could not secure us against them; we might destroy some part of their corn and wigwams, and force them to fly into the woods, etc., but the men would be still remaining to do us mischief, for they will never fight us in the open field.

That hard-earned wisdom prevailed.

Nor were the settlers alone in their appreciation of the Pequot War's harsh lessons. Native leaders proved quick studies, and their military policies after 1637 stood shorn of the naiveté so strikingly evident during the conflict. Even before the war erupted, Indians had shaken off their exaggerated fear of English firearms. And after the dust had settled in 1637, they understood all too well that conflict with the settlers meant war to the death. New England's native governments refrained from challenging their colonial neighbors for the next thirty-eight years, and although the Wampanoags' decision to launch King Philip's War in 1675 was certainly a reckless (or desperate) act, it was not an ignorant one. Philip fully comprehended that "he could expect no mercy" in the event of failure. His eventual defeat stemmed from the hopelessness of his cause, not from paucity of effort. That was one indiscretion the Wampanoags refused to repeat.

If military acculturation was thus a force for progress toward perceptive policy in New England, it also contained a distinctly retrogressive component. For even as contact built a foundation of mutual understanding and knowledge, it simultaneously demolished an old framework of practices that had regulated, and to some degree palliated, the carnage of armed conflict. Cultural contact reduced the danger of accidental war, but it also created the potential for *intentional* wars of unusually devastating character. The latter development embittered Anglo-Indian dealings in New England for the duration of its frontier history.

In 1660 Lion Gardiner ventured that "the Pequit war . . . was but a comedy in comparison of the tragedies which hath been here threatened since, and may yet come." When King Philip's War burst across New England some fifteen years later, Gardiner's forecast proved woefully accurate. From the outset, both settlers and Indians burned villages, destroyed food, slaughtered noncombatants, and abused their prisoners—all with scarcely a trace of moral unease. Before long, much of the region lay in a shambles, and contemporaries shook their heads in disbelief. Many Puritans were inclined to look skyward to account for their calamity. They should also have looked backward: Its seeds had been sown two generations before.

King Philip's War disclosed the final pattern of Anglo-Indian warfare in New England—a pattern that succeeding generations perpetuated as the frontier expanded beyond New England's bounds. With the eventual convergence and intermingling of regional societies in North America, New England's martial heritage contributed to the development of a national military culture that reflected traditions forged in an anguished, but unrelenting, past.

All told, military acculturation had a profound impact on the course of New England's military history—and thereby on the history of the country as a whole. That this impact proved as great as it did, in turn, seems related to several peculiar characteristics of military culture itself. Because military culture tended to express itself only in times of actual warfare (when theory ripened into practice), the acculturation process was not gradual, as in most other branches of culture, but "explosive," occurring at discrete intervals. This characteristic magnified the disorientation and misunderstanding that inevitably accompany the meeting of two disparate cultures. What is more, the bilateral nature of warfare intensified the pressures for customary adjustment that a meeting of cultures ordinarily entails: had the branch of culture under investigation governed a unilateral social activity, contact with a disparate analogue would have induced far less cultural stress. If an Indian, for example, saw the point of an English hoe, he remained free to integrate it into his unilateral scheme of agriculture thoughtfully and at his leisure. But when faced with a doctrine of organized violence to which he was directly subjected, that Indian enjoyed no such freedom. He was forced to react reflexively and on the spur of the moment. The need for rapid reaction enhanced the transformative impact of military acculturation and tended to harden hybrid patterns built on bilateral conceptions of retaliation.

An understanding of how military acculturation colored New England's military history may offer insights into the evolution of conflict along other frontiers. Scholars have noticed the emergence of wanton forms of warfare contemporaneously in such scattered hinterlands as Virginia, South America, and Ireland, as well as on the borders between Christendom and Islam. Whether cultural contact across the battlefield served to aggravate those conflicts merits further investigation.

Closer to home, an appreciation of the impact of military acculturation on events in New England helps us to understand why the parties to those events acted as they did. Throughout his monumental work, *The Invasion of America,* Francis Jennings insists that "human persons do have some power of choice over their own conduct," and he traces many of the grim episodes recounted therein to the willful decisions and ethical standards of the participants. This is undoubtedly part of the story. However, we must not forget that human persons also suffer from human failings. People aim, but they also err. In connection with cultural contact, such errors are the prolific offspring of a range of disabilities: ignorance, misunderstanding, and fear of the unfamiliar, to name a few.

The colonists and Indians of New England acted in accordance with their deliberate wishes, to be sure, but they also acted in response to the psychological shock of collision with what each perceived to be a strange and alien counterculture. It was as if a curtain rose and a pair of players converged confidently on center stage, each bearing a different script. The resulting dialogue rendered them both a bit confused, more than a bit angry—and prepared them for the darker roles that have left whole audiences of historians so shaken and moved.

A Different View of the Evolution of the Militia to the Continental Army

DON HIGGINBOTHAM

. . . The manner in which Americans moved from amateurism to professionalism in the conduct of warfare was not as dramatic and sudden as has usually been contended. It was not simply the replacing of the colonial militia system with a professional or standing army under George Washington in the Revolution. Rather, the change was evolutionary and subtle in nature, involving as it did the gradual appearance and development of semiprofessional military forces, which provided a transitional link between the seventeenth-century militia and the Revolutionary Continental Army. The point serves as a reminder that wars and their consequences provide us with maximum historical light when they are studied as part of an ongoing process rather than as episodic occurrences. But if the complexity of early American military history has only recently been recognized by scholars, and if it went unacknowledged by many eighteenth-century Americans as well, there is at least one very important reason—both then and later—for this omission. And that has to do with the power and persistence of myth.

It has scarcely been unique for peoples or nations to employ a distinctive and exaggerated rhetoric about their military prowess. Colonial Americans boasted of human tools of war—of minds and bodies: minds that acted out of disinterested patriotism and that were attached to bodies of upstanding citizens. As fighters they were infinitely superior to the riffraff thought to be the mainstay of European professional armies. American rhetoric almost wholly eschewed references to sophisticated weapons and other equipment of war and to formal training. All citizens

"The Military Institutions of Colonial America: The Rhetoric and the Reality," Don Higginbotham, ed., *War and Society in Revolutionary America: The Wider Dimensions of Conflict* (Columbia: University of South Carolina Press, 1988), 19-20, 22-24, 25-27, 38. Used by permission of University of South Carolina Press.

were capable of service in defense of their communities and often were called to do so, declared the Reverend Ebenezer Gay in 1738. There were "no Exemptions . . . for the High, nor the Low; for the Rich, nor the Poor; for the Strong, nor the Weak; for the Old, nor the Young; for the most buisy; the new-married, nor the faint-hearted." . . .

We must look more closely at the militia, to see what it was initially and to determine what it became later. Then we can endeavor to separate the myth from the history of that institution and to explain the development of semiprofessional military forces. Up to a point the seventeenth-century militia resembled what publicists always claimed. In most colonies, membership was nearly universal, consisting of able-bodied men between the ages of sixteen and sixty, who were required to possess their own firearms and other military paraphernalia and to assemble a certain number of times a year for drill and instruction. As a 1634 law in the Plymouth colony expressed it, all inhabitants were "subject to such military order for trayning and exercise of armes as shall be thought meet, agreed on, and prescribed by the Governor and Assistants." Everywhere the basic unit was the company—sometimes called the train band which was part of a county regiment. The statutes brim with rules and regulations for organizing, administering, supplying, and calling out men who were truly citizen soldiers.

There were, however, discrepancies between the theory and the practice of the seventeenth-century militia. Rarely did regular companies of militia take the field except in cases of emergency involving the protection of the immediate community. For service in the major Indian conflicts of the century such as the Pequot War and King Philip's War the militia served as the military body from which volunteers and draftees were secured for more extended duty in reconstituted militia companies and regiments. But draftees too were usually spared if they hired a substitute or paid a fine. What Harold E. Selesky observes for Connecticut came increasingly to apply throughout England's New World dependencies: namely, that "only in [the] early years of settlement and on the frontier were universal military obligation and universal military service the same thing.

As society became more stratified and as threats to the eastern, most densely populated regions receded in the late seventeenth century, we find that the militia eligible for combat were less a reflection of society than had been the case in the years of early settlement. Transients, paupers, and generally "loose, idle, dissolute persons"—along with blacks, Indians, and indentured servants—usually fell outside the militia system; and even some respectable elements of the population were excused from active participation. In Massachusetts, for example, magistrates, legislators, Harvard educators, school teachers, church leaders, physicians, ship captains, fishermen, and certain kinds of artisans fell into the exempted category.

All the same, if the militia no longer reflected society as it once did, its duty-eligible ranks still contained the vast majority of the freeholders, who were citizens with the vote. And their power of the ballot was never forgotten by the elites, whose domination of the provincial political scene rested more on responsible government than habits of deference on the part of the public. That explains why colonial assemblies were hesitant to call out the militia in behalf of unpopular or difficult and distant wars; and why, if they did assemble this home guard, they did so for short periods (normally three months), with service confined to their respective colonies—and, almost always, with the opportunity for the militiamen to buy their way out of actual participation by one means or another.

But the heterogeneity of society and the political clout of the freeholders were not the only reasons for the decline of the militia as the premier war-making institution in colonial America. The militia, both in the mother country and her trans-oceanic appendages, had always been primarily a defensive arm, infinitely more effective on its own turf than on distant offensive fields. Indeed, the home front aspects of its responsibilities cannot be too strongly emphasized. For one of its local functions had been and continued to be in the eighteenth century to serve as an instrument of social control, as one can see from examining its assignment as a slave patrol in the southern colonies, its hand in Bacon's Rebellion in Virginia in 1676, and its part in the War of the Regulation in North Carolina in 1771. This domestic dimension of militia activity gave that body new life throughout America in the Revolution as the local forces played a crucial role behind the lines in putting down the loyalists and giving sinews to the Revolutionary infrastructures at the colony-state levels. . . .

One must not be too critical of the Anglo-American militia, for changes in the nature of warfare and the onset of the imperial wars after 1688 provide us with additional reasons why this institutional importation from England could scarcely function any longer except as a defense force, as an institution for social control, and as a recruiting and drafting agency for semiprofessional colonial military forces.

Even before King Philip's War, in 1675–1677, the Indians of New England demonstrated that they had become increasingly dangerous opponents because they had learned to cope with the technological superiority of the colonists. First they turned from their rather limited, ritualistic style of intertribal combat to guerrilla tactics in order to counteract the settlers' superior weaponry. They also fairly quickly became proficient with firearms, a fact which serves as a reminder that technological advantage in military matters is rarely permanent and, in reality, is often short-lived. The tribesmen, notes Patrick M. Malone, "exercised careful judgment by choosing weapons with a firing mechanism suited for their environment and their methods of warfare. They rejected the inexpensive matchlocks carried by . . . most of the militiamen in the first New England military units," which were useless in bad weather and adopted instead the self-igniting flintlock.

The combining of firearms with their superior knowledge of the land made the Indians formidable adversaries in King Philip's War: the colonies suffered roughly a thousand deaths and saw many towns and farms of western New England reduced to rubble. The forces of Massachusetts Bay, Plymouth, and Connecticut—raised from the militia—often fought poorly, repeatedly falling prey to Indian ambushes, and eventually prevailed only because of their superiority in numbers and material resources and because of their effective use of Indian auxiliaries. One result of the war was the discrediting of the pike as a military weapon. Pikemen had often preferred their position in the Massachusetts Bay militia to that of the musketeers—they constituted a third of the membership of each company—because they received colorful attire and did not need to own firearms. Contrary to the militia myth, some not only failed to possess muskets but did not know how to use them. Young John Dunton was not alone in conceding that he "knew not how to shoot off a musket" and that his fellow militiamen "knew it well enough by my awkward handling" of one.

If King Philip's War brought the departure of the pike from the militia scene, and if, more important, that conflict forever ended the New England Indians' ability to launch a lengthy, unilateral offensive, the tribesmen continued to pose a sizable threat when allied with Britain's European adversaries. And increasingly that was the case, just as the colonists, especially in the northern and lower southern tiers of North American settlement, became participants in the mother country's imperial wars. Those conflicts involved the colonists in sending larger numbers of men than ever before into military service and in requiring them to serve great distances from their own communities—at one time or another between 1690 and 1760 in attacking French posts at Port Royal, Louisbourg, Ticonderoga, Duquesne, Quebec, and Montreal; and Spanish positions at St. Augustine, Cartagena, and elsewhere. Sometimes those provincial forces performed as intercolonial armies operating independently, while on other occasions American contingents served alongside or in conjunction with British military and naval commands.

As for the British government, it confronted imperial defense only on an ad hoc basis. It periodically asked the colonies to raise forces as best they could and without any plan of integrating them into a larger imperial military structure. Nothing better illustrates Britain's poor example than the London ministry's string of broken promises between 1706 and 1746 to contribute substantially to colonial military expeditions against Canada.

Left to their own devices, the colonies, because of the defects in the militia system and because of the lack of imperial direction, adopted semiprofessional forces that were actually a hybrid between the militia and a standing army. The term semiprofessional requires a definition, one that is employed strictly within an eighteenth-century context. We are usually speaking of fairly large numbers of men—several hundred to several thousand—who in return for a bounty enlisted for a year or more, who often reenlisted, who served if required outside the boundaries of their own colonies, who were subject to a stricter form of military law than applied to the militia, and who served under officers not infrequently possessed of a strong tinge of military professionalism (they read military literature and relished the opportunity to learn more about European methods from observing British forces in America). Generally, it was only in emergencies that these semiprofessional forces resorted to militia drafts and other kinds of compulsory service. . . .

Finally, what can we say about the usefulness of the colonial semiprofessional experience for Americans who won their independence between 1775 and 1783? Two points seem to stand out. First, Americans' sense of military accomplishment in the imperial wars may have given them a good deal of self-confidence for risking a violent break with Britain. For some Revolutionary military leaders, particularly Washington, that previous experience proved invaluable. . . . [T]he colonial semiprofessional experience enabled Americans to move by evolutionary stages to the creation of a Revolutionary army that became sufficiently professional by European measurements to acquit itself remarkably well against Britain; and to do so without arousing against it the deep-seated fears of standing armies that had been a part of their whiggish heritage. For Americans to have attained all that during the

War of Independence may seem amazing, but an examination of the semiprofessional military tradition helps to make their achievements explainable.

♠ F U R T H E R   R E A D I N G

Fred Anderson, *A People's Army: Massachusetts Soldiers and Society in the Seven Years' War* (1984).

James Axtell, *The Invasion Within: The Contest of Cultures in Colonial North America* (1985).

Russell Bourne, *The Red King's Rebellion: Racial Politics in New England, 1675–1678* (1990).

Alfred A. Cave, "Who Killed John Stone? A Note on the Origins of the Pequot War." *William and Mary Quarterly,* 3d series, 49 (1992) 509–521.

John Morgan Dederer, *War in America to 1775: Before Yankee Doodle* (1990).

John E. Ferling, *A Wilderness of Miseries: War and Warriors in Early America* (1980).

———, *Struggle for a Continent: The Wars of Early America* (1993).

Gerald S. Graham, *Empire of the North Atlantic: The Maritime Struggle for North America* (1950).

Laurence M. Hauptman and James D. Wherry, eds., *The Pequots in Southern New England: The Fall and Rise of an American Indian Nation* (1990).

Don Higginbotham, *War and Society in Revolutionary America: The Wider Dimensions of Conflict* (1988).

Adam J. Hirsch, "The Collision of Military Cultures in Seventeenth-Century New England," *Journal of American History* 74 (March 1988): 1187–1212.

Francis Jennings, *Empire of Fortune: Crowns, Colonies, and Tribes in the Seven Years' War in America* (1988).

———, *The Invasion of America: Indians, Colonialism, and the Cant of Conquest* (1975).

Paul E. Kopperman, *Braddock at the Monongahela* (1977).

Douglas Edward Leach, *Arms for Empire: A Military History of the British Colonies in North America, 1607–1763* (1973).

Jill Lepore, *The Name of War: King Philip's War and the Origins of American Identity* (1998).

Patrick M. Malone, *The Skulking Way of War: Technology and Tactics Among New England Indians* (1991).

Richard I. Melvoin, *New England Outpost: War and Society in Colonial Deerfield* (1989).

Barry O'Connell, ed., *On Our Own Ground: The Complete Writings of William Apess, A Pequot* (1992).

William Pencak, *War, Politics, & Revolution in Provincial Massachusetts* (1981).

Michael J. Puglisi, *Puritans Besieged: The Legacies of King Philip's War in the Massachusetts Bay Colony* (1991).

George A. Rawlyk, *Yankees at Louisburg* (1967).

Alan Rogers, *Empire and Liberty: American Resistance to British Authority, 1755–1763* (1974).

Peter E. Russell, "Redcoats in the Wilderness: British Officers and Irregular Warfare in Europe and America, 1740 to 1760," *William and Mary Quarterly* 35 (October 1978): 629–652.

Harold E. Selesky, *War and Society in Colonial Connecticut* (1990).

William L. Shea, *The Virginia Militia in the Seventeenth Century* (1983).

Ian K. Steele, *Betrayals: Fort William Henry and the "Massacre"* (1990).

James Titus, *The Old Dominion at War: Society, Politics, and Warfare in Late Colonial Virginia* (1991).

Allen W. Trelease, *Indian Affairs in Colonial New York: The Seventeenth Century* (1960).

John Underhill, *News from America* (1638; reprint ed. 1971).

Alden T. Vaughan, *New England Frontier: Puritans and Indians, 1620–1675* (1965).

Richard White, *The Middle Ground: Indians, Empires, and Republics in the Great Lakes Region, 1650–1815* (1991).

Roger Williams, *The Complete Writings of Roger Williams*, 7 vols. (1963).

John Winthrop, *Winthrop's Journal "History of New England, 1630–1639,"* ed., James Kendall Hosmer (1908; reprint 1966).

CHAPTER
3

The American Revolution: Who Fought and Why?

The United States was born in war: The American Revolution was a protracted conflict lasting nearly eight years and eventually ranging across most of the thirteen colonies. Unknown thousands fought on the side of the American revolutionaries as short-term, local militiamen, or longer-term Continental Army soldiers against the British Army and its allies—Hessians, Tories, and Indians. Among military historians, one of the most heated debates is: Who fought on the side of the American revolutionaries, and what was their motivation? Traditional nationalistic history celebrated the patriots as yeomen farmers fighting for liberty and self-government. A revisionist analysis beginning in the 1960s suggested that the rank and file, at least of the Continental Army, came from the lower classes, and suggested that their primary motivation was personal economic advancement. This belittling of ideology was quickly challenged, particularly by those who cited the perseverance of the revolutionary soldiers through the hardships of battle, prison camp, and shortages of food, clothing, and payment. A new historical emphasis on the eighteenth-century concept of republicanism has led to a renewed focus on ideology. But in reaction, some scholars are now stressing locally-based interests and identities and loyalties formed by a variety of factors: religion, ethnicity, race, and gender. The debate continues over who fought and why in the American Revolution.

DOCUMENTS

Like witnesses at a trial, historical primary sources should be examined and cross-examined to evaluate their credibility and veracity. In reconstructing past events, historians ask of a document: Who created it? Where? For what purpose? For what audience? How long after the event described was it created? (In other words: Who? Where? Why? When?) In the first document, Peter Oliver, a wealthy Bostonian loyal to the crown, in an account of the Revolution written in London shortly after he fled there in 1777, reports on a visit to an American prisoner of war, a Lieutenant Scott, who was captured at the Battle of Bunker Hill. In the second document, a March 1777 letter to one of his generals after the American successes at Trenton and Princeton that winter, General George Washington explains his overall strategy of concentrating the smaller Continental Army for hit and run raids upon detachments of the larger British and Hessian forces. Washington pursued that strategy the following year in his assault upon the rear guard of the British Army at Monmouth, New Jersey, in June 1778. In the third document, a diary entry, 20-year-old Jeremiah Greenman, who had risen from private to sergeant in the Rhode Island Regiment (and would end the war a lieutenant), jotted down the confusion of battle in the bloody encounter with British regulars, which included Charles Lee's order for retreat, later countered by George Washington's rallying of other units for the American victory. After Monmouth, the tale of "Molly Pitcher," the artilleryman's wife, who replaced her wounded husband at the cannon, soon became part of the American folklore, but did it happen that way? The only contemporary reference to a woman cannoneer at Monmouth is reprinted as the fourth document, a diary entry by Private Joseph Plumb Martin, of the New England Light Infantry, first published in 1830. Evidence of the localism, now emphasized by some historians, is evident in the fifth document, a 1781 petition from several freeholders (property owners) in the Westmoreland Militia Company from the Wyoming Valley in northern Pennsylvania (then also claimed by Connecticut) to the Connecticut government complaining that their service in the Continental Army had left their homes and families at the mercy of Tories and Indians. Some black slaves received their freedom for fighting in the Revolution; others did not, as the sixth document illustrates; it is a deposition taken around 1834 as part of an application for a federal pension for service in the Revolutionary War by Samuel Sutphin, then 87, who had been a slave from Somerset County, New Jersey, and who, in 1781, at the age of 35, had been sent into military service as a substitute for his owner. The final document, a pension application in 1837 by Sarah Osborn, then 81, recounts her experiences as the wife of a commissary sergeant with the Third New York Regiment; she accompanied her husband with the Continental Army as a cook and washerwoman from January 1780 through the British surrender at Yorktown, Virginia, in October 1781.

1. Loyalist Peter Oliver Tells How an American Prisoner of War Justified His Enlistment to His Captors (1775), c. 1777–1781

Among the Prisoners who were wounded, & confined in the Jail at *Boston,* was a Lieutenant, by the Name of *Scott,* a Person of a good natural Understanding. A Gentleman of Humanity went to the Jail to visit & converse with the wounded, & to offer the *Samaritan* Service, of pouring Oil & Wine into their Wounds. Among the rest, he found this *Scott* to be a sensible, conversible Man; he offered to send him some Refreshment, to alleviate his Distress. *Scott* seemed surprized at the humane Offer, & said to him, "are you in earnest Sir?" The Gentleman replied, "that he was; & if a Bottle or two of Wine, or any other Thing would be acceptable, that he'd send it to him." Such a kind Offer did *Scott's* Heart good equal to the

Peter Oliver. *Origin and Progress of the American Rebellion,* eds. Douglas Adair and John A. Schultz (San Marino, CA: Huntington Library, 1961), 129–130.

Medicine itself; & he accepted the Offer. The Gentleman then addressed him in this Manner: "*Scott!* I see you are a sensible Man; pray tell me how you came into this Rebellion?"

He returned this Answer: "the case was this Sir! I lived in a Country Town; I was a Shoemaker, & got my Living by my Labor. When this Rebellion came on, I saw some of my Neighbors get into Commission, who were no better than my self. I was very ambitious, & did not like to see those Men above me. I was asked to enlist, as a private Soldier. My Ambition was too great for so low a Rank; I offered to enlist upon having a Lieutenants Commission; which was granted. I imagined myself now in a Way of Promotion: if I was killed in Battle, there would be an end of me, but if my Captain was killed, I should rise in Rank, & should still have a Chance to rise higher. These Sir! were the only Motives of my entering into the Service; for as to the Dispute between *great Britain* & the *Colonies,* I know nothing of it; neither am I capable of judging whether it is right or wrong." This Instance will solve many Conjectures, relative to the Unanimity of the Colonists in this Rebellion; & seperate such Instances from the Numbers collected in carrying it on, the Justice of their Cause, when weighed in the Ballance, will be found wanting.

2. General George Washington Explains His Strategy, 1777

TO MAJOR GENERAL PHILIP SCHUYLER

Morris Town, March 12, 1777.

Sir: It is of the greatest importance to the safety of a Country involved in a defensive War, to endeavour to draw their Troops together at some post at the opening of a Campaign, so central to the theatre of War that they may be sent to the support of any part of the Country, the Enemy may direct their motions against. It is a military observation, strongly supported by experience, "that a superior Army may fall a sacrifice to an inferior, by an injudicious division." It is impossible, without knowing the Enemy's intentions, to guard against every sudden incursion, or give protection to all the Inhabitants; some principal object shou'd be had in view, in taking post to cover the most important part of the Country, instead of dividing our force, to give shelter to the whole, to attempt which, cannot fail to give the Enemy an Opportunity of beating us in Detachments, as we are under the necessity of guessing at the Enemy's intentions, and further operations; the great object of attention ought to be, where the most proper place is, to draw our force together, from the Eastward and Westward, to cover the Country, prevent the Enemy's penetration and annoy them in turn, shou'd our strength be equal to the attempt. There is not a State upon the Continent, but thinks itself in danger, and scarcely an Officer at any one post, but conceives a reinforcement necessary; to comply with the demands of the whole, is utterly impossible, and if attempted, would prove our inevitable ruin.

From John C. Fitzpatrick, ed. *The Writings of George Washington,* 39 vols. (Washington: GPO, 1931–1944), VII, 272–273.

3. Jeremiah Greenman, an Enlisted Man, Recounts the Bloody Battle of Monmouth, 1778

T. 25. this morn the Genl. beet / we peraded the Rijt. & slung our packs marcht as far as rockey hill ware made a small halt / then pushed on as far as kingstown ware we made a halt and sent out a large guard. very hot & sultry wether / we have Intiligence of the enemy being about fourteen milds off & the Militia clost [close] after them, we hear that a Number of hassans left the enemy. att Sun down marcht into a field ware we grounded our arms & order'd to stay by them ware we stayed about half a Nowr / then marcht 5 milds and halted in a flax field at a place cal'd long Bridge.

F 26. this morn started very early / pushed on 6 milds as far as a small town cal'd Crambury ware we made a halt ware we heard of the enemy being about 18 milds a head & the enemy a pushing on for Sandy hook. hear we stayed three owers & drawed sum provision / our Division was order'd forrid [forward] under the Command of Genl Lee / we went about 6 milds & made a halt / Sum very heavy Shower of wrain & Thundr.

S 27. this morn turn'd out from amung the wett grass. from [*illeg.*] pushed on 6 milds near Englishtown ware we draw'd 40 rounds of Cartireges / then marcht into the wood ware we heard a Number of Cannon fir'd toward the Surthurd of us / then we march'd about half a mild to the left of the army ware we stopt a Nower / then we ware order'd to sling our packs / we marcht half a mild into a Medow almost to the wright whare I took quarts. under a huckel bury buch. for it was very hot indeed / in the Night it wrain'd & cold.

S 28. Englishtown / this morn att two oClock we slung our packs / advanc'd towards the enemy about 3 milds from ware we lay / part of the militia & light hores that was on the wright engag'd the enemy / then our Division under the Command of Genl Lee advanced towards the enemy / thay form'd in a Sollid Collom then fir'd a voley att us / thay being so much Superier to our Number we retreated / thay begun a very heavy Cannading / kil'd a few of our Rijmt. then we form'd again under a fence ware the light horse advanced on us / we began a fire on them very heavy / then the footmen rushed on us / after firing a Number of rounds we was obliged to retreat. a Number of our men died with heat a retreating. a Number of troops form'd in the rear of us and sum artilira wich cover'd our retreat. they began a fire on the enemy, then they [the British] retreat'd / Left the Ground with about a thousand kil'd & wounded. on our Side about two hunderd kil'd & wounded & died with heat. after We retreated we went back to the ground ware we left in the morning att English town ware we buried sum of our officers. here rec'd a ball in my left thy.

M 29. Continuing in English town. this day we buried all the dead / the enemy gone off intirly / very hott indeed so that the men that wan [went] on a march

Jeremiah Greenman. *Diary of a Common Soldier in the American Revolution,* 1775-1783, eds. Robert C. Bray and Paul E. Bushnell, 1978. Reprinted by permission of Northern Illnois University Press.

retreating yesterday throy'd away thay packs & so forth and a Number dyed before ye enemy retreated back.

T 30. Continuing in a field near to English town / water very scarce indeed / Such a Number of Solders that water is almost as scares as Liquor & what is got is very bad indeed / we hear that the enemy is got to Statton Island. this afternoon we draw'd two days provision & fit for a march.

4. Private Joseph Martin Provides the Only Contemporary Account of "Molly Pitcher" (1778), 1830

[June 28, 1778]

One little incident happened during the heat of the cannonade, which I was eye-witness to, and which I think would be unpardonable not to mention. A woman whose husband belonged to the Artillery, and who was then attached to a piece in the engagement, attended with her husband at the piece the whole time. While in the act of reaching [for] a cartridge and having one of her feet as far before the other as she could step, a cannon shot from the enemy passed directly between her legs without doing any other damage than carrying away all the lower part of her petticoat. Looking at it with apparent unconcern, she observed that it was lucky it did not pass a little higher, for in that case it might have carried away something else, and continued her occupation.

5. A Militia Company Worries About Indians and Local Safety, 1781

To the Honourable the General Assembly of the State of Connecticut or in their Recess to his Excellency the Governor and Council of Safety for Said State.

Humbly Sheweth that your Humble Pititioners whose names are hereafter Subscribed Humbly Beg leave to Say before your Honours this our Present State & Situation. Your Pititioners in the Year 1776 Inlisted in the Cont[l] Service under the Command of Captains Durkee & Ransom by Special Order of the Continental Congress for the Defence of this Place and the frontiers but Contrary to our Expectations were in a few months after our Engagements Call'd away to Join the Cont[l] Army under his Excellency General Washington where we Continued Almost two years which was so great Trouble to us in Leaving our families Exposed to be ravaged by the Savages that one half of our Companies Died in the Service. in the time of our Being in the Cont[l] Army the enemy made Incursions and in a Most Barbarous and inhuman Manner Killd Numbers of our Parents and friends and Destroyd all our Effects and left our wives, families, friends and Parents in the Most Distressed situation. His Excellency General Washington Knowing of the Indians

From Joseph Plumb Martin. *A Narrative of Some of the Adventures, Dangers and Sufferings of a Revolutionary Soldier* (Hallowell, ME: 1830), 96–97.

From Petition of the Westmoreland [Town] Militia to the General Assembly of the State of Connecticut, January 23, 1781. Reprinted in *The Susquehannah Company Papers,* ed. Robert J. Taylor (Ithaca, NY: Cornell U. P., 1969), VII, 79–80.

being on the Frontiers ordered us back to this Place where the enemy were in Actual Possession. When we marched in on the 3ᵈ of August 1778 (same time we could get no troops to assist us) attacked the enemy and drove them off where we have Continued since through a Series of Troubles on Account of Different Incursions from the Indians where we have with our Wages and Some little help from the Continent Supported our families. if we Could Stay here we might Support them without any expence to this State. But we are again Ordered to March out and the Garrison to be relieved with other Troops yet what relief Can we Expect as we must Leave our families exposed to be again Ravaged by the Indians and Probably all Murderd, therefore Your Humble Pititioners Humble Prays a Discharge from the Service or Prays your Honours through your Great Wisdom to Advise some other way to Support them.

Which Your Pititioners is ever Bound to Pray

Dated Westmoreland yᵉ 23ᵈ Janʸ AD 1781

6. Samuel Sutphin, a Black Slave, Tells of His Service in the Revolution (1781–1783) and His Freedom, 1834

At beginning of the War was a slave to Guisbert Bogert of Somerset co. on the Raritan. Caspar Berger of Readington proposed to buy him of Bogert on condition of doing militia duty in Berger's stead during the War. I agreed to the terms, and Bogert sold me to Berger for £92,10, which I believe was paid. Berger had been out one month, and I afterward was to serve in his place. Capt. Matthias Lane commanded the militia co. and Col. Taylor the Regiment. This was the 6th year of the War. Berger bought me in the season of plane (?) seed sowing. Berger went out one month after I went to live with him, in Capt. Lane's Co. Immediately after I had finishing planting 4 acres corn, Co. was [classed?] and I took my turn with others; sometimes 12, sometimes 15 or 20 went at once. I believe Capt. Lane went on my 1st tour; marched thro' Boundbrook and Scotch Plains and Newark to Communipaw, where we were stationed 1 mo.; large militia force was there; a Regt. or more; built breastworks; Col. Abm. Ten Eyck, Major Livin, Col. Hunt, Col. Schamp, Gen. Dickinson, Gen. Blair (?). Staid a month in sight of New York—guard duty.

Second tour in hay and harvest time. Capt. Jacob Ten Eyck stationed at Communipaw; 1 mo. guard duty. The Asia(?) was then in the harbor. British fleet came into N. York harbor whilst on this tour. A large body of militia out. Frelinghuysen and Schamp were out.

Third tour, 1mo. Believes Capt. Lane commanded. Station and duty the same as before. British fleet came into the bay and harbor when on his 2nd tour. Large force of British was out. Was at the Long Island battle in Aug't; and Lane, and Col. Frelinghuysen. Lord Stirling had command of Jersey troops; our comp'y was in the heat of the battle. In the battle and after our defeat we were all dispersed. I found a colored man who took me from L. I. to Staten Isl'd in a skiff with two others of my Co., viz., Wm. Van Syckle and Jacob Johnson, a man of our age. The blk.

From A. Van Doren Honeyman, ed. "The Revolutionary War Record of Samuel Stuphin [sic], Slave," *Somerset County Historical Quarterly* 3 (1914): 186–190.

man piloted us across Staten Isl'd to Eliz'town point, where we crossed to E. T.; came through this town and by Wheatsheaf and Short Hills, Quibbletown and Bound Brook, and so home in about 3 days after the battle. 2 of our co. were taken prisoners in this battle, viz., Peter Low and John Van Campen; they were exchanged some months after and got home. . . .

About corn planting in the same year, as I think, my master was called on to go to the North. Capt. Isaiah Younglove and Lieut. Robt. Robertson were along the branch recruiting men for the northern service. Master Berger order'd me to go with Capt. Younglove for 9 months; this was the term of engagement for all his company. 3 men were furnished by each company for this expedition: 3 from our's, 3 from Ten Eyck's. David Seely from Cumberland Co. was Col. of this regim't. James Ray(?), a free mulatto man and Hendrick Johnson went from our Company. Our Reg't, under Col. Seely, assembled at Cornelius Slack's, Suckasunny plain, after corn planting, about last of May. Marched thro' Sussex Co., and Goshen to N. Windsor, Newburg. At Esopus we fell in with Domine Hardenburg, whom I knew at Somerset. Went to Westpoint first. A chain was fastened to a large rock and stretched across the river to prevent vessels from going up. Thence by Schenectady by Fort Schuyler, now Utica. Here we were for three days. Found here three children massacred by Indians, and had been brought here to repel the Indians who had massacred the whites. A massacre had also been made by the Indians at Cherry Valley, through which we passed on our way to Utica; also at Fort Montgomery. We pursued the Indians through the wilderness as far as Buffalo; had five——pieces. Gen'l Sullivan commanded. When we reached Buffalo it was husking corn time.

It was a week after New Year's before we set out on our return march. The Indians retreated before us as we went onward. We got home about middle of January, returning by the same route, and were discharged after being home about a month. At Westpoint on our return we halted; and, standing sentry one cold night, snow knee deep, a party of Hessians and Highlanders, who had crossed the Hudson on the ice, came on us by surprise. After hailing the first one and he giving no answer, I fired and he fell. The whole guard came out, and all fired and killed sixteen. It was moonlight. The Light Horse soon rallied and came in their rear, and they surrendered prisoners (70). The Highlanders were dressed in woolen blue plaid trousers and armed with broad swords. As soon as I had fired, and repeated the fire twice or thrice, they returned my fire, and I fled till the guard came to my relief. I received a bullet upon the button of my gaiters, which drove the button and ball into my right leg just above the outer ankle bone. The ball and button were both cut out of the leg by Dr. Parrott, the surgeon of our Regiment, next morning. The fight was about at 10 at night. At the same time I received a wound in the tendon of the heel, just opposite the ankle, which seemed to be a cut, and divided the large tendon almost through. [Note: Both wounds or scars yet visible and tangible.] I was two weeks and five days confined at Westpoint by this wound. Dr. Parrott attended me all this time. The Company and Regiment remained there all this time, but [I] hobbled along and kept up with the Regiment homeward. Capt. Younglove was wounded in the thigh this same night with a musket shot—fleshy part of the under side of the thigh. This was my last service.

Henry Vroom, near the Burnt Mills, on the place of Brazer Beekman, was with me on guard at Communipaw under Capt. J. Ten Eyck. [Take his deposition, Enquire of Col. Schamp by letter as to his recollection of Sutphin].

After War ended applied and demanded my freedom of Berger. He sold me to Peter Ten Eyck for £110, a slave for life. Ten Eyck sold me to Rev. John Duryea for £92.10. I lived with him 2½ years, and [he] sold me to Peter Sutphen for the same money. Lived with him and his for two years as slave. Then lived with my mistress for one year. I agreed to pay him [Sutphen?] from the proceeds of my labor £92.10. I paid it and bought my freedom after the additional servitude of 20 years under different masters.

7. Sarah Osborn, a Soldier's Wife, Relates How She Accompanied the Continental Army to Yorktown (1781), 1837

. . . Deponent, accompanied by her said husband and the same forces, returned during the same season to West Point. Deponent recollects no other females in company but the wife of Lieutenant Forman and of Sergeant Lamberson. Deponent was well acquainted with Captain Gregg and repeatedly saw the bare spot on his head where he had been scalped by the Indians. Captain Gregg had turns of being shattered in his mind and at such times would frequently say to deponent, "Sarah, did you ever see where I was scalped?" showing his head at the same time. Captain Gregg informed deponent also of the circumstances of his being scalped: that he and two more went out pigeon hunting and were surprised by the Indians, and that the two men that were with him were killed dead, but that he escaped by reason of the tomahawk glancing on the button of his hat; that when he came to his senses, he crept along and laid his [head near] one of the dead men, and while there, his dog came to his relief, and by means of his dog, [caught the attention of] the two fishermen who were fishing near the fort.

Deponent further says that she and her husband remained at West Point till the departure of the army for the South, a term of perhaps one year and a half, but she cannot be positive as to the length of time. While at West Point, deponent lived at Lieutenant Foot's, who kept a boardinghouse. Deponent was employed in washing and sewing for the soldiers. Her said husband was employed about the camp. . . .

In their march for Philadelphia, they were under command of Generals Washington and Clinton, Colonel Van Schaick, Captain Gregg, Captain Parsons, Lieutenant Forman, Sergeant Lamberson, Ensign Clinton, one of the general's sons. They continued their march to Philadelphia, deponent on horseback through the streets, and arrived at a place towards the Schuylkill where the British had burnt some houses, where they encamped for the afternoon and night. Being out of bread, deponent was employed in baking the afternoon and evening. Deponent recollects no females but Sergeant Lamberson's and Lieutenant Forman's wives and a colored woman by the name of Letta. The Quaker ladies who came round urged deponent to stay, but her said husband said, "No, he could not leave her behind." Accordingly, next day they continued their march from day to day till they arrived at Baltimore, where deponent and her said husband and the forces under command of General Clinton, Captain Gregg, and several other officers, all of whom she

From John C. Dann, ed. *The Revolution Remembered: Eyewitness Accounts of the War for Independence* (Chicago: U. Chicago P., 1980), 242–245.

does not recollect, embarked on board a vessel and sailed down the Chesapeake. There were several vessels along, and deponent was in the foremost. General Washington was not in the vessel with deponent, and she does not know where he was till he arrived at Yorktown, where she again saw him. . . .

. . . Deponent took her stand just back of the American tents, say about a mile from the town, and busied herself washing, mending, and cooking for the soldiers, in which she was assisted by the other females; some men washed their own clothing. She heard the roar of the artillery for a number of days, and the last night the Americans threw up entrenchments, it was a misty, foggy night, rather wet but not rainy. Every soldier threw up for himself, as she understood, and she afterwards saw and went into the entrenchments. Deponent's said husband was there throwing up entrenchments, and deponent cooked and carried in beef, and bread, and coffee (in a gallon pot) to the soldiers in the entrenchment.

On one occasion when deponent was thus employed carrying in provisions, she met General Washington, who asked her if she "was not afraid of the cannon-balls?"

She replied, "No, the bullets would not cheat the gallows," that "It would not do for the men to fight and starve too."

They dug entrenchments nearer and nearer to Yorktown every night or two till the last. While digging that, the enemy fired very heavy till about nine o'clock next morning, then stopped, and the drums from the enemy beat excessively. Deponent was a little way off in Colonel Van Schaick's or the officers' marquee and a number of officers were present, among whom was Captain Gregg, who, on account of infirmities, did not go out much to do duty.

The drums continued beating, and all at once the officers hurrahed and swung their hats, and deponent asked them, "What is the matter now?"

One of them replied, "Are not you soldier enough to know what it means?"

Deponent replied, "No."

They then replied, "The British have surrendered."

Deponent, having provisions ready, carried the same down to the entrenchments that morning, and four of the soldiers whom she was in the habit of cooking for ate their breakfasts.

Deponent stood on one side of the road and the American officers upon the other side when the British officers came out of the town and rode up to the American officers and delivered up [their swords, which the deponent] thinks were returned again, and the British officers rode right on before the army, who marched out beating and playing a melancholy tune, their drums covered with black handkerchiefs and their fifes with black ribbands tied around them, into an old field and there grounded their arms and then returned into town again to await their destiny.

ESSAYS

Mark Lender of Kean College in New Jersey discovered, in his research on the social-economic backgrounds of the enlisted personnel of the New Jersey Brigade in the Continental Army, that most were poor and propertyless men. He became one of the leaders in arguing on the basis of those statistics that, after the enthusiasm of the first year of the Revolutionary War, American soldiers were motivated as much, if not more, by self-interest as by idealism. In direct response to Lender and other revisionists, Charles Royster of Louisiana State University and a veteran of the Vietnam War, rejected such methods and inferences, citing evidence of soldiers continued service despite much physical hardship and impoverishment. The debate continued, but more recently some scholars such as Gregory Knouff of Princeton University and the David Library of the American Revolution have suggested a much greater complexity of motivations, including loyal loyalties and ethnic, racial, and gender identity; in an essay written especially for this volume, Knouff explores the motivations of Pennsylvania soldiers in the Revolution.

Enlistment: Economic Opportunities for the Poor and Working Classes

MARK E. LENDER

In March 1776 Captain Joseph Bloomfield reviewed his new company of the Third New Jersey Regiment. He had recruited the men himself and was immensely proud of them. So was his home county of Cumberland, which had turned out to give them a stirring farewell before they marched to join the Continental army in New York. Be brave, a speaker told them, be patriotic and "virtuous," and die gallantly if necessary. Bloomfield had no doubt that they would measure up to these expectations, for they had enlisted, he assured himself, not out of hopes for personal gain, but "from motives purely to serve their country."

Bloomfield's was a hopeful view; but it was not to last. By the end of the 1776 campaign any ideal of a selfless army seemed far from reality to many. Defeat and privation had discouraged the men, and other officers of the Third New Jersey thought poorly of them. "The profanity and prodigality of our army are amazing," lamented Lieutenant Ebenezer Elmer, "everyone [is] almost striving to outvie each other in wickedness." And in the army generally, the early enthusiasm for the cause had passed. The "noble spirit of patriotism," one Continental doctor felt, "is in a considerable degree extinguished."

In the confusion surrounding the American reverses of 1776 no one really knew what these changes of opinion meant. Clearly troop morale had dropped, but that was a natural consequence of defeat. The more important question was whether or not the soldiery had undergone a permanent change of heart. No patriot could say for certain just what values the men placed on their service in the Revolution, nor what motives would induce them to fight thereafter. This article will assess the attachments of the soldiery to the cause and suggest why the "patriotism" and "virtue" of the army were often less obvious to patriot leadership than to later generations.

The Early War

The War for Independence began with a groundswell of support among the soldiery. Until the defeats in Canada and the retreat across the Delaware destroyed

Mark E. Lender. "The Mind of the Rank and File: Patriotism and Motivation in the Continental Line," in William C. Wright, ed., *New Jersey in the American Revolution,* vol. 3 1976. Permission to reprint this material is courtesy of the New Jersey Historical Commission, a division of the New Jersey Department of State.

American morale, the troops of the Revolution displayed a genuine commitment to the cause. In the New Jersey rank and file, excitement ran high in late 1775 and early 1776. Philip Vickers Fithian, with the Jersey militia in New York City in 1776, wrote home of an army ready to face any test for freedom. Even army food, he proclaimed, was not too much to endure for the cause of "American Liberty." Another Jerseyman on the scene was equally sure of the men's devotion, and reported them "in good Spirits and . . . eager to fight." And in neighboring Pennsylvania, Private Aaron Wright seemed to personify the popular image of the soldier of the early war: he was ardent in the cause and detested strict discipline, arbitrary officers, and the fainthearted. Once, when a junior officer resigned, and then in a change of heart asked for reinstatement, Wright's impatience with slackers boiled over: "You shall not command us," he told him, "for he whose mind can change in an hour, is not fit to command in the field where liberty is contended for."

Excitement about the war generated necessary enlistments, but its most important result was not obvious at first. Amid the enthusiasm of the soldiery grew a distinct American identification. It was a straightforward matter, uncomplicated by talk of the "rights of Englishmen" or of politics. The men simply saw themselves as part of a people apart from the mother country. Sergeant William Young of Pennsylvania, for example, referred naturally to "our American Land" and asked God to scatter the foreign enemy. Other soldiers had similar feelings of separation from the English, talking of "American Liberties" rather than reconciliation with the crown. When Congress formally announced independence, the Jersey militia in New York City applauded it; the response from the Jersey Continentals, encamped in northern New York, was the same. Colonel Elias Dayton of the Third New Jersey, who personally wanted a reconciliation with the king, noted that the troops fully supported the Declaration. They were an American army and they knew it.

The bond between the troops, then, was their nationalism. It was, however, an untheoretical nationalism—a simple love of country—without a commitment to any programs beyond independence. Private Joseph Plumb Martin put the men's position best. He recalled that he had formed "pretty correct ideas for the contest between this country and the mother country . . . I thought I was as warm a patriot as the best of them." He disliked "arbitrary government," and favored independence. But that was the extent of his "correct ideas." He had been only about thirteen years old during the Stamp Act crisis, and he could barely recall the events leading to rebellion. Others were certainly in the same position; if they enlisted at age twenty in 1776, for example, their recollection of the seeds of revolt could have been only hazy memories.

Nationalism, however, was only one characteristic of the early soldiery. Others were less positive. After the defeats of 1776 had demonstrated the harsher aspects of soldiering, the cause alone would no longer keep men in the field. Some now demanded more than the thanks of the republic for their continued service. Many of the men who marched on Canada in 1775, for instance, had already served around Boston; the novelty of war had worn off, and their fight was no longer carried by enthusiasm. One private noted matter-of-factly that his entire company refused to march without advance pay—and then willingly abandoned the expedition when supplies ran low. Indeed, some observers felt that any kind of patriotism now counted for very little in the ranks. The motives of the army were largely selfish, noted a blunt army surgeon. He complained bitterly that if all but those who fought solely for "the cause of Liberty" left ranks, "our army would be reduced to a small number." Captain Joseph Brearley, of a prominent Jersey patriot family, was convinced that instead of more honorable motives, his men were "animated with the pleasing thought of plunder. These men would still fight, but increasingly they wanted the terms of service more to their liking.

Other men no longer cared to serve at all. Once given a taste of combat, cold, and smallpox, troops became markedly less spirited indeed. One group of Continentals actually refused to extend their tours of duty temporarily, even in the face of an enemy attack; they consented to stay on only after being arrested and threatened with flogging. At Fort Ticonderoga in 1776, Private Timothy Tuttle noted that the morale of the Jersey troops had evaporated under the twin blows of the defeat in Canada and the news of the British invasion of New Jersey: they all just wanted to go home. The spirit of the cause was clearly faltering. Sergeant Young, returning home after campaigning in New Jersey in early 1777, was dismayed. "If Salvation comes to our guilty Land it will be through the tender Mercy of our God," he said, "and not through the Virtue of her people." The early enthusiasm for the war was the casualty of 1776.

Despite the flagging zeal of many troops, the cause could still depend on a core of dedicated men. In the darkest days of 1776 some patriots rallied. One Jonathan Holmes, for instance, a Burlington County militiaman, decided that duty was more important than personal welfare. He arranged his will and asked his father to provide for his children if he fell in service. He then announced that "I have this day here joined the Light Horse for I think it dont doe to lie by as an Idle Spectator at this Critical Period." That was in early 1777, and within months Jonathan Holmes was dead. An anonymous Princeton student, hearing an exhortation on the nation's peril from the fiery John Witherspoon, enlisted in the local militia in late 1776. These were both militiamen, though, and their spirited responses were not only unrepresentative in late 1776, but would not in any case have helped fill the regular army for the next campaign.

For most patriot soldiers, then, nationalism was no longer enough to keep the field. It was not that the cause was dead. The men still accepted patriotic appeals "with patience," noted Washington after the 1776 campaign. It was just that those enlisting because of them were "no more than a drop in the Ocean." In this situation, the problem for Whig leadership was that of uniting any patriotic leanings in the men with their desires for personal benefits from service. That is, they must make the army both a patriotic cause and a source of material rewards. As far as Washington could see, there was only one way: "the allowance of a large and extraordinary bounty." In Congress the bounty demands stung some delegates. Although bounties were an accepted part of eighteenth-century warfare, they seemed unbecoming of a republican army. But the commander in chief argued that a love for the cause was not enough of an attraction anymore, and that once initial passions had cooled, Congress would only deceive itself to assume that many "such People, as compose the bulk of an Army . . . are influenced by any other principles than those of Interest. . . ."

Persuaded by Washington, Congress included bounties in recruiting measures for 1777. New soldiers received twenty dollars, a yearly clothing issue, and a hundred acres if they served for the duration. It remained to be seen what impact this appeal would have on the motives of the recruits. Would they be men spurred by financial rewards to join a cause they generally favored anyway? Or would they be a corps of domestic mercenaries fighting only for their bounties and pay?

1777 and After

The sort of men who filled the new battalions of 1777 was unclear to contemporaries. There was no consensus about why men would volunteer for a minimum of three years in a war that everyone now knew would be long and hard. The bounties may have been enough to draw many men with no particular attachment to the cause, and there were observers who said as much. A French officer who thought financial considerations were the chief motive for service saw the men as simple mercenaries. Historian Charles Bolton rejected that view but could not explain the matter satisfactorily himself. Yet despite questions about what kept the men in ranks, there was indeed a pattern in the motives of the rank and file.

The soldiers of the Revolution, with some exceptions, fought because they thought the army offered a better life than the civilian world. This often meant a variety of things. For some, it indeed meant a better financial position because of bounties, army clothing, food, and pay. For others it meant an escape from unpleasant civilian social situations. The common denominator was the hope that they would come out of the army at least a little better off than when they went in.

This does not mean that the men were mercenaries. For most, military service provided a way to combine support for a national cause with self-interest. A recruiting pamphlet demonstrated how the troops could unite the two. It portrayed a meeting of two "friends of the country" in late 1776. One was out of work; after pondering employment prospects, he decided that soldiering would be a fine way "to get my living by." The recruit-to-be then announced that in any case he already supported the cause of "Independency." Enlistment would relieve his unemployment, and attachment to independence—mentioned, perhaps significantly, only after he had decided to enlist for employment—would assure that he fought for Washington, not the English. The entire appeal was a matter-of-fact recognition that recruits were asking not only what they could do for the republic, but also what the republic could do for them in return.

The anonymous author of this tract clearly took his material from life, for the appeal was repeated nationally time and again. A poor woodcutter, for instance, zealous for liberty, enlisted after the first shots of the war. He left the service after the defeats of 1776 and tried to follow a civilian trade: meeting financial "disappointments," he recalled his love for the cause and reenlisted. A farm laborer named Martin, though firm for the cause, saw nothing wrong with taking payment to serve as another's substitute instead of enlisting in his own right. He said that as long as he had decided to fight anyway, he might as well get as much as he could for it. Blacks, as Benjamin Quarles has noted, often found the army better than a civilian life in which they had little stake. Recruiting officers deliberately lured young men without property or social attachments into the ranks with bounty payments and tales of the excitement of war. Many troops, then, did have feelings for the cause—but "pure" patriotism was not their motive. And they in no way viewed enlistment as a personal sacrifice.

New Jersey's soldiers, as a number of cases illustrate, also followed this pattern. Sergeant George Grant, for example, was typical. Poor (there is no evidence of his ever owning anything), he hoped for better times after the war. He apparently wanted to farm. His diary is in fact an agricultural chronicle of his days on Major General John Sullivan's expedition in western New York. He eagerly recorded the quality of the soil and the crops and found what he saw attractive and desirable for the future. And Grant was not alone in this regard. Other Jersey troops, perhaps with an eye to opportunities after the war, also took careful notes on farming conditions. One officer remarked that the Iroquois lands produced crops "such as cannot be equalled in Jersey." And at least some of the soldiery foresaw the postwar occupation of Indian lands by white farmers.

Other Jerseymen also demonstrated a highly personal interest in their service. Groups of Jersey recruits, for example, reported to camp willingly enough but refused to bear arms before collecting their bounties. Men from the lowest reaches of society saw real opportunities in the army. Indentured servants deserted their masters for the chance to work for themselves as soldiers; some free blacks emigrated into the state to serve in the Jersey Brigade. For the escaped servants the army meant freedom, for the blacks and other poor the bounties were more than they would have had otherwise.

But financial concerns were not the only factors in enlistments; self-interest was also defined in social terms. For a few soldiers the army provided a way out of family disputes. Some of them were in delicate situations indeed. One M'Donald Campbell, a Jersey Continental, was in and out of the militia, the Continentals, and British service (in which he afterwards claimed he was an American spy). At one point, he recalled, "I had formed an acquaintance with a young woman in Somerset county, of a very creditable family, with whom I had been too intimate. Her father . . . [sent] for me to come and see him," and Campbell ended up married. But he fled wedlock for the army again. Indeed, the "shotgun marriage" brought more than one man to the Continental recruiter. In 1776 an army doctor treated a soldier who had been "formerly an ordained Minister, but by some misfortune respecting him and his maid he was Dismissed from his congregation, and now Served as a Serjeant in the Continental army."

Family considerations in other cases were not so unusual; but they illustrate how contact with relatives led some men to see the military as a means of improving their personal affairs. In 1780, for instance, a Jersey soldier who himself displayed no warm desire to serve "Volunteered . . . for [the] express purpose of allowing [his] father to remain home, he being upwards of 80, and, though not compelled . . . would go to defend his country." In addition, some young men ran away to the army after family arguments. Occasionally, family loyalties produced soldiers: a New York Continental once argued the patriot cause so effectively against his Tory in-laws that a number of formerly wavering relations followed him into arms. While such family situations were unusual, they brought a trickle of men into the ranks.

Men who had enlisted for such personal reasons and had not rallied in a rush of patriotic emotion seldom expressed enthusiasm for the cause. The meaning of the war beyond the immediate goal of independence stirred only rare comment, and in fact most soldiers' writings emphasized only the tedium of army life. The complaints of a Jersey captain were typical. Leaving for garrison duty in the Mohawk Valley of New York State, he lamented the drudgery of military life. "I am tired of war and war affairs," he wrote. He did not relish serving in garrison with "hoggs horses cows . . . & squalling children," and looked forward to his worst assignment. "In truth," he concluded, "I have a good while felt tired of the situation I am in." None of this alone hints at flagging devotion; it suggests only that patriots could get as bored with army routine as anybody else. But most of the extant diaries and journals are inattentive to the issues at stake, and even aspects of the war that might reasonably have produced "patriotic" responses from the men failed to do so: these facts suggest that soldierly zeal for the contest was something less than later generations have supposed.

Troop reaction to the enemy was a significant case in point. The British represented not only direct personal danger to the soldiers but also the most obvious threat to the Revolution. American leadership tried to build morale and foster dedication to the cause by rallying the army against them. The effect of these efforts seems doubtful, though: collectively, the men did not evince a fervent—and certainly not a political—hatred of their opponents.

Usually, outbursts against the enemy were not generally applied nor political in tone. An occasional soldier was hostile for ideological reasons: to Private Wright the British were "Red Coated Philistines" and "parlimentary tools." But these remarks came in the war's early, emotional days, and were not typical of later periods. Instead, most comments came as responses to particular enemy individuals or actions. Rumors of enemy plots, for example, harassment of private citizens, real and alleged atrocities such as the killing of Hannah Caldwell at Connecticut farms, or unnecessary cruelty on the battlefield could all enrage the Continental soldiers. But in calmer periods attitudes were different. Soldiers who would cut down a foe in battle also could show surprising neutrality, or even a grudging respect for him afterwards. To Private Martin, the English soldiery was "Johnny Bull," who, though cruel at times, was always ready for a good fight. Corporal Lemuel Roberts managed to strike up a conversation with a redcoat he had almost killed in a previous battle, and whose friend he had indeed killed. An enemy in reduced circumstances often received little animosity. Continental troops, who often knew suffering themselves, allowed a bit of sympathy for enemy soldiers in similar distress. There was some genuine sorrow for Hessians killed so far from home and for so little purpose. The plight of General John Burgoyne's men after capture particularly affected Roberts. "The sight of these men," he wrote, "in so undesirable circumstances, gave me . . . serious reflection; while I despised their principles and practices, I could not help feeling for their misfortunes."

There were two notable exceptions to this relative lack of animosity toward the enemy. Feelings took a noticeably belligerent turn when opponents were Indian or Tory. Here the soldiery often expressed genuine hatred. When directed against the Tories, it reflected the intensity of the civil phase of the conflict. Collectively, the Tories were an evil "brood," as one Jersey soldier put it, with no attributes worthy of sympathy. Private Martin once expressed amazement that a patriot woman had escaped unmolested after Loyalist "banditti" had searched her home. In New

Jersey, with its large Tory element, these animosities were extreme. One old soldier was furious, even years after the war: the Tories had "hunted" him "like the hare," he recalled, "and for safety compelled [him] to sleep in his boat on the river . . . with no cover but the canopy of Heaven to protect him." Most striking about the soldiers' reactions to the Loyalists, then, was the virulence of the hatred, a hatred far greater than any anti-British sentiments.

Feelings also ran high toward the Indians, feelings reflecting tensions born of red-white frontier conditions and the severe brand of warfare the Indians waged. To the men, they were mere "Savages" to be hunted and pillaged, against whom any sort of warfare was allowed. On Sullivan's expedition in 1779, for example, the Jerseymen openly enjoyed their work of razing Indian fields and towns: they did it "with the greatest Chearfulness," as one sergeant put it. Enraged when Indians tortured or killed white prisoners, the troops were not above similar tactics. They scalped the Iroquois—and as a Jersey lieutenant recorded, were capable of worse: "At the request of Maj. Piatt," he wrote, "[I] sent out a . . . party to look for some of the dead Indians. . . . They found them and skinned two of them . . . for boot legs . . . for the Major . . . [and] for myself." And except for some isolated regrets over such atrocities, the soldiers' writings dealing with Indian combat make it clear that the army wasted little remorse on nonwhite opponents.

The lack of pronounced feelings against the enemy (with the exceptions just noted) was only one illustration of the soldiers' general lack of zealousness. A disregard for republican standards of "virtue" was another. The fact that the men had little use for Whig morals or patriotic exhortations prompted questions on their resolve. Observers with openly patriotic sympathies complained that army morality was appalling, and that the men were irreligious, profane, vice-ridden, and less than staunch in the cause. One New Jersey private noted that his regiment ignored a "Fast" called by Congress; and the entire Third New Jersey once refused to attend a special exhortation by a patriot minister. Voices in and out of the army consequently demanded more attention "to moral virtue"—which included a warning to a Jersey regiment that anyone not doing his duty bravely would "Instantly be shot down as an Example of Cowardice." Finally, in 1778, Congress itself ordered a crackdown on army "profaneness and vices." Mere military success was not enough to satisfy the Revolution, then; Whigs expected the army of a "virtuous" republic to act the part.

Occasionally, instances of actual disloyalty underscored doubts about soldierly dedication. There were too many draftees, foreigners, and men with apparently weak attachments to the cause to satisfy the firmest Whigs, and too many Continentals who went over to fight for the enemy. Incidents such as the alleged New York plot on Washington's life in 1776 and Benedict Arnold's more spectacular treason in 1780 prompted the patriot command to reserve the most sensitive assignments (like duty in Washington's bodyguard) for picked men of proven loyalty. The harsh fact was that the dedication of many troops simply could not be trusted beyond relatively narrow limits.

The case of Delaware Continental Michael Dougherty exemplifies the loyalties of some of the men and shows the recognition by both sides that the rank and file lacked ideological motivation. Dougherty enlisted in the Delaware regiment in May 1777; he apparently deserted, but he returned in time to be captured at

Brandywine in September. Dougherty, however, was not the kind to sit in jail: "I could never be aisy [easy] within the walls of a prison," he explained. So he joined the British army—and was recaptured by his old Delaware regiment when it stormed Stony Point with Anthony Wayne in 1779. Back with his "ancient comrades" he marched to Camden, South Carolina, where, in General Horatio Gates's debacle, the British took him again—whereupon he enlisted in Banastre Tarleton's Legion. When Tarleton in turn met catastrophe at Cowpens, Dougherty's old Delaware recaptured him again. So Dougherty, man of multiple loyalties, finished the war with his original comrades.

It must be noted that the British often encouraged American prisoners to join them. And many—we do not know how many—did join to escape appalling prison conditions. Fear for survival prompted these conversions, not changing loyalty. Some men enlisted with the king only after despairing of release. Their cases were not similar to Dougherty's, whose fighting spirit was unquestionable, but whose devotion to the cause was so doubtful. One must question too the dedication of those who so quickly forgave his enemy service. And considering the sufferings endured by other prisoners before they succumbed to British recruiters, Dougherty's story (and others like his) probably became amusing to Whigs only in retrospect.

The Matter of "Patriotism"

The Continental soldier, then, was not typically a zealous man. Prone neither to violent hatreds nor enthusiasms, he lacked the fervor of the crusader and the political awareness associated with the so-called "people's armies" of today. In fact, the attitudes of the patriot regulars toward the Revolution apparently differed little from those of later American soldiers toward their wars. Several studies of modern enlisted men (those who served in World War II and in the 1960s) have shown that, like their revolutionary counterparts, twentieth-century troops did not have an openly expressed or politically developed idealism. They were generally unimpressed with patriotic exhortations, and shunned the company of any ideologues in the ranks. Like the Continentals, they expressed their loyalties nonverbally in simple, faithful service, and confined their patriotism to an inarticulate nationalism.

Within this nationalist framework, of course, the Continentals had the immediate goal of independence. This had been the soldier's commitment in 1776, we recall, and so it remained. On the rare occasions during the war when they did verbalize their feelings, they did so in support of the separation from Britain. They toasted the nation on the Fourth of July (although, like most soldiers, they would probably have raised a glass to anything), and sometimes raised a cheer for Congress, the symbol of national unity. But lest any more be read into these activities, it should be noted that the toasting and cheering may have corresponded simply to a royal regiment's cheering after a victory or toasting the king. The writings left by the men do not sustain assumptions that they associated their service with any more fully developed political tenets, concepts of democracy, or social values. They certainly saw themselves less as torchbearers for a rising lower class than as individuals reaching for betterment—"upward mobility"—in the most personal sense.

This concentration on independence was not surprising, for the cause provided few other symbols. The troops cannot have fought for new political institutions or the restructuring of society, simply because such aims did not exist as major political forces. The war began, after all, not as a movement for ideological ends—Whig leaders hardly wanted social revolution—but largely as a spontaneous resistance to actual invasion. A national government and formal military organization came only later, and these provided no ideals to inspire an army in the early days of the war; nor were they much help later. In trying to implement their revolution, Whigs of various persuasions actively disputed the nature of politics and society, and they produced some widely varied state constitutions. Given such diversity among national leaders, it would be unrealistic to expect much unity of opinion on the war among the rank and file. Independence became one of the few available grounds on which to rally patriots.

But the depth of this largely silent nationalism can never be precisely known. Certainly some of the men, as we have seen, were worthy of little trust. And yet events proved the men's basic loyalty. The British never could induce a major portion of them to join the king—even during the mutinies of 1781 the Continentals proclaimed their attachments to America instead of going over to the enemy. And even the men who enlisted for bounties often did so with a belief in independence. Moreover, the acceptance of a bounty tied the soldier to the republic. Had independence failed, Continental pay and bounty monies would have been worthless. Land bounties, perhaps the most valuable to poor men in a farming society, would have lost all validity. So the personal interest of the soldier depended on the success of the cause. It is probably true, then, that for most men who remained under Continental arms, the cause was worth the fight—even if they only expressed their dedication through quiet, loyal service.

Finally, there is reason to believe that America indeed came to accept this inarticulate nationalism as the most she could expect from her troops. When the time came to honor the services of the men who endured the long years of war, the commander in chief himself defined the patriot soldier in terms of simple, uncomplicated loyalty. In August 1782 Washington created the "Badge of Military Merit" to recognize men of "bravery, fidelity, and good conduct." Three years of meritorious service earned a stripe on the left sleeve, and six years, two stripes. "Unusual gallantry," or "extraordinary fidelity and essential service" won a cloth purple heart. No one who had quit the field or "met an ignominious punishment or degradation" was qualified for an award. These, then, were the attributes of soldierly "patriotism": length of service, good conduct, "fidelity"—not zealousness or dedication to any particular political or social tenets. They opened to all, the general said, the "road to glory in a patriot army and a free country."

Enlistment: Patriotic Belief in the Cause of Freedom

CHARLES ROYSTER

In recent years several studies of Continental Army soldiers have drawn upon enlistment rolls, tax records, and similar sources to describe more precisely the social composition of some military units. These studies agree that most soldiers were under twenty-three years old and owned little or no property—conclusions that statistically confirm what Americans said during the Revolutionary War: the Continental Army consisted largely of young, poor men. Going beyond descriptive summaries of their evidence, several authors have also discussed the motivation of Continental soldiers. From their statistical findings, in part, they draw inferences about soldiers' motives for serving in the army. The authors appear to believe that when they have shown the soldiers' poverty, they have also established that men enlisted under the influence of economic need or ambition and not of revolutionary ideals. The most thorough study, by Mark E. Lender, likens the Continental Army to European armies of the eighteenth century. These authors evidently agree with Edward C. Papenfuse and Gregory A. Stiverson that "many, and perhaps most, of Smallwood's recruits enlisted in the army not because of a sense of duty or patriotism, but because Maryland society offered them few other opportunities for employment. Perhaps the most categorical statement comes from John R. Sellers: "I am not impressed by the patriotic fervor of the privates. I think that they acted overwhelmingly out of self-interest. I do not believe that they really fought with a true understanding of independence."

Readers of my book will see the ways in which its interpretation of Continental soldiers differs from the conclusions of these other studies. There is no need to repeat here the discussion in my text or the sources cited in the doctoral dissertation on which this book is based. I can, however, suggest some ways in which these attempts to infer motivation from statistics fail to convince me.

First, the authors set up a misleading dichotomy between self-interest and revolutionary ideals as motives for army service. Having shown that Maryland recruits were poor, Papenfuse and Stiverson go on to argue that "a sense of duty or patriotism" did not influence "many, and perhaps most" of them. Yet none of the authors in question explain the reasoning or the evidence on which they base such an assumption that poverty and revolutionary ideals were mutually exclusive. In fact, to accept this dichotomy would lead one to conclude that the only people capable of serving ideals or making sacrifices were those who had substantial property. Similarly, these scholars suggest that the recruitment of foreign-born soldiers—usually from England or Ireland—contradicts the idea of a revolutionary army moved by patriotism. This reasoning seems to imply that a recent immigrant could respond to no motive except self-interest. We can readily believe that soldiers' service was motivated by the offer of bounties, pay, and land; we need not also assume that no other motives were at work. Lender, in his dissertation and in his Bicentennial pamphlet, and Papenfuse and Stiverson, in their research note, quote Ralph Waldo Emerson's "Concord Hymn" to epitomize the version of the Continental soldier that their findings disprove. The tone of all these studies implies that we are reading tough-minded exposures of harsh, unpleasant truths. However, the authors' recurrent assumption that soldiers must have served either revolutionary ideals or self-interest exclusively is at least as schematic and improbable as the nineteenth-century rhetoric that these scholars have discredited.

Even before we consider the likelihood that men were moved by both self-interest and self-sacrifice, we can see several ways in which the influence of offers of money and land fails to explain adequately the Continental soldiers' conduct. An argument for economic motivation should not only cite the soldiers' peacetime poverty and the army's offer of bounty, pay, food, clothes, and land; it should also explain why soldiers continued to serve when bounty money was gone, pay was rare and depreciated, and food and clothing often were in lower and shoddier supply than almost anywhere in civilian life. When portraying the New Jersey Continentals as deserters and mutineers, Lender says that they "were poorly paid, wretchedly fed and supplied." On the other hand, when portraying the New Jersey Continentals as "like the European armies," he says that they "fought because they thought the army offered a better life than the civilian world. . . . For some, it meant a better financial position because of bounties and army clothing, food, and pay." As Lender's own statements suggest, the facts of Continental soldiers' wartime experiences reveal the difficulty of arguing that their army service always coincided with their material self-interest.

Nor can we assume, in the absence of further evidence, that poverty was measured by tax assessments was equivalent to unemployment. Farm labor was in great, though seasonal, demand during the war years; privateering attracted many men; others opened new lands in Vermont and Kentucky. Even supposing that an unemployed man sought money above all, brief service as a militia substitute frequently offered equal or greater reward for much shorter, less rigorous military service.

Thus, young, poor men faced a more complex situation than choosing between civilian hardship or military betterment. Presumably there were many more young, poor men in Maryland in 1782 than the 308 recruits who joined Smallwood and fell under the scrutiny of Papenfuse and Stiverson. Maryland society offered the same choice to these other men; yet they found in civilian life opportunities preferable to the hardship and disease that Smallwood's recruits sustained. Throughout the war, far fewer men joined the Continental Army than the recruiters sought. And it remains highly probable that the great majority of young, poor men who fit the scholars' composite social portrait of recruits remained outside the Continental Army. In other words, a socioeconomic description of soldiers, although accurate, cannot adequately explain their motivation, especially when the majority of those subject to the same socioeconomic motives did not become Continental soldiers. To understand Continental Army service, we must explain why some young, poor men chose to enlist and stay in the army while others enlisted but did not stay and still others never enlisted at all.

In evaluating the socioeconomic studies of the Continental Line, we must also note that those places where the soldiers' information fails to support their contentions. Both Lender and Robert A. Gross liken the Continentals to European armies. Lender says that continentals came from "the 'dregs of society' " and that the army was "similar to the 'standing armies' of Whig fears." However, when we look at Lender's tables, we find that more than 40 percent of the soldiers owned some land, as measured by tax assessments. This fact does not contradict Lender's general portrait of the soldiers' poverty, but it casts grave doubt on the idea that the Continental Army resembled European armies in its socioeconomic composition. When we turn to the soldiers' attitude toward army service, the analogy between the armies has even less validity. As Lender acknowledges, American soldiers were eager for discharge when the war ended. They evidently did not regard themselves as career soldiers, nor did they prefer military life or its opportunities to a civilian career once peace came. By contrast, the British "dregs" remained professional soldiers.

Papenfuse and Stiverson, Lender, and Sellers all note that Continental soldiers did not fare well economically after the war. Without being explicit, the authors seem to suggest that this information further identifies the soldiers as ne'er-do-well "dregs" who drifted from poverty to army to poverty, prisoners of their economic status. However, the soldiers' willingness to serve in the army, combined with their eagerness to leave it at war's end, shows that they clearly differentiated wartime military duty from peacetime civilian careers. They preferred the latter, and their subsequent economic failures do not imply that they found army life equal to or greater than civilian life in its attractions, material or professional. Whatever their economic status, they evidently had not developed the outlook of European soldiers. Evidence of Continentals' or veterans' poverty does not identify them as a unique group in American society or explain their motivation and conduct or establish a significant similarity to European professional soldiers.

The person who had read only these studies might find it hard to understand how the Continental Army, even with French help, won the war. Lender several times mentions the fighting ability of the New Jersey Brigade. Sellers's doctoral dissertation is a narrative of the Virginia Line's first five years. On what motivation and outlook was this persevering, successful service based? The Continental Army repeatedly failed to provide the material rewards—food, clothes, pay—it had promised to the soldiers; the American officers' use of a modified form of the harsh, corporal discipline current in European armies never consistently managed to intimidate American soldiers. There were three major mutinies and a series of minor ones in the Continental Army throughout the war, while there were no mutinies in the British army's wartime regiments in America. Moreover, as Lender and other scholars demonstrate, desertion from the Continental Army was relatively easy and at certain times frequent; deserters were seldom caught once they escaped the army. The recurrence of adversity and the ease of desertion suggest that some motives other than physical force and material self-interest influenced those Continentals who chose to remain soldiers and became good ones, yet left the army as soon as their discharge was due.

Why, for example, did the "dregs" of America enlist in the American army rather than in the British army, which would have provided more reliably for their physical well-being? Why did most Continentals fail to accept British offers of money for desertion and mutiny? Why did American deserters who, we are told, must have had "few other opportunities" and must have been "the bottom of society" like the British soldiers, desert to their home regions or to Vermont and Kentucky much more often than to the British? In short, with so few Americans willing to fight as regulars and with such degraded, unself-sacrificing American regulars, why could the British not buy off the American soldiers and win the war with money?

Lender alone tries to define motives for the soldiers' service other than self-interest. However, he uses twentieth-century definitions of revolution and studies of modern soldiers to draw an unconvincing distinction between Continentals' "nationalism" or "love of country" and their idealism, the existence of which he doubts. The matter of idealism brings us to the most prevalent and least defensible attribute of these studies. None of the authors ascribes service in the army to motives of self-sacrifice. Gross, although he refrains from drawing explicit conclusions about soldiers' motivation, presents this one-sided description most emphatically: "Most of the ordinary Continental privates from Concord were . . . men with little or nothing to lose by going off to war for three years or more." Gross, like the other scholars, presumably refers to material possessions. A moment's reflection suggests the inadequacy of a materialistic criterion for weighing motives of self-sacrifice, since men "going off to war" stood to lose, above all, their lives. The most recent and most conservative analysis of military mortality in the Revolutionary War finds this war to be second only to the Civil War in its proportion of deaths to population. Short of death, Continental soldiers sustained extremes of adversity that entailed almost all forms of loss and sacrifice possible for men who had no estates to lose. To account for their perseverance by their calculations of material advantage strains credulity.

Perhaps we see this question most clearly in the situation of American prisoners of war held by the British. Whether by policy or by neglect, the conditions under which American prisoners were confined were wretched and lethal. Using the horror of these conditions and the likelihood that men who stayed in prison would die, the British tried to induce Americans to enlist in the British army. An unknown number accepted the inducement. But, rather than serve the king, thousands of American soldiers and sailors chose almost certain death. A recent estimate sets the number of American prisoners who died in British captivity at 8,500. No materialistic explanation of Continental soldiers' motives can adequately account for the diverse and recurrent instances of self-sacrifice in their conduct. Considered as people rather than as socioeconomic entities, soldiers had as much to lose as anyone had; they chose to risk it and, in many instances, to lose it. The student of the American Revolution must go beyond statistics to find out why.

Enlistment: The Complexity of Motivations

GREGORY T. KNOUFF

One of the most vigorous debates about the Revolutionary War regards common soldiers' motives for fighting. At stake is not only our understanding of our first national armies, but also the meaning of the American Revolution itself. Was it a patriotic war fought with equal conviction among Revolutionaries from all levels of society? Or was the conflict carried out by elites who enlisted the help of the lower sort primarily through the promise of bounties, pay, and other material inducements? Charles Royster asserts that the poor men who composed the ranks fought primarily out of principles of self-sacrifice for the new nation. Like their officers, Continental soldiers came to see themselves as the vanguards of republican virtue even when most civilians became apathetic toward the war effort. In contrast, historians such as Mark E. Lender have convincingly demonstrated that most troops in the Continental Army were young, poor, and often propertyless. They

Gregory T. Knouff, "Localism and the Complexity of Motivations: Pennsylvania soldiers as a Case Study." This essay is especially written for this volume by Gregory Knouff based upon his 1996 dissertation, "Class, Race, Masculinity and Locale in Pennsylvania, 1775-1783. Reprinted with the permission of the author.

deduce that because the soldiers came from the humblest ranks of society, they served long terms primarily out of desire for individual gain, not nationalism. Both sides have their compelling points. Royster is correct that poor people are capable of having ideals. His evidence for soldiers' views, however, is based primarily on the writings of officers. He assumes comparable motives among both enlisted men and officers, despite their very different class backgrounds. Lender is persuasive in his assertion that troops were not averse to accepting material reward in exchange for service and that their individual gains do not preclude other motives.

Neither side extensively examines what soldiers actually said about their motivations. A large body of documents, particularly Revolutionary War pension depositions, offers firsthand accounts of why soldiers fought. Using these sources and focusing on Pennsylvania enlisted men as a case study, I argue that localism, defined as an outlook that purposefully emphasized community over national or individual interests, was central to the worldviews of the ordinary early Americans who composed the ranks. Commitment to what poor young men defined as their communities was the primary factor in their decisions to enlist. The varied motives of soldiers become more explicable within this localist context. They fought to protect their homes, improve their families' financial status, assert their public manhood by claiming citizenship, further their class- and region-based ideals, and fight other Americans deemed social outsiders. The rank and file often defined their communities narrowly. They identified with others of similar class, regional, ethnic, and perceived racial backgrounds. Enlisted men's reasons for fighting suggest that the American Revolution was not a singularly national event, but a process composed of many local conflicts. Their motives also challenge assumptions about the centrality of colonial resistance to British policy. Conditions in America often eclipsed or melded with imperial politics.

At the outset of the war, Pennsylvania was a heterogeneous province that had its share of social discord. Boundary disputes with Virginia and Connecticut threatened the holdings of the colony's land claimants on its frontiers. Underrepresented backcountry inhabitants resented the eastern Quaker and Proprietary political establishments who, they believed, did not care about defense against Indian attacks. Western settlers were also coming to see earlier pan-Indian resistance to European-American expansion as harbingers of a coming race war in which frontiersmen, united by a perceived sense of "whiteness," would fight all Indians. Propertyless white men in the province could not claim the status of public manhood and citizenship because they were denied voting rights. Pennsylvania's long history of religious toleration masked deep antipathy among various ethnic and religious groups. Many of these prewar tensions helped determine who took up which side in the coming war. Pennsylvanians followed the debates about British taxation closely, and almost all shared a common Whig vocabulary that stressed a balance of order and liberty. Definition of these terms, however, were influenced by class, regional, and ethnic origins. As a result, the meanings of liberty, equality, and independence meant something very different to soldiers than they did to their officers.

Various local and class-based understandings of Revolutionary ideals among the soldiery congealed early in the war. The ascendance of radicals drawn from the middling sorts to dominance in the state's constitutional convention led to the passage in 1776 of one of the most democratic constitutions that the English-speaking world had yet seen. The state's Committee of Militia Privates was instrumental in undermining the elite-dominated provincial assembly earlier in the year, and they sought to extend the vote to all soldiers who paid taxes. Militiamen were solidly behind the new radical state government that seemed poised to confer the rights of full public manhood on heretofore disenfranchised poor white males. Ordinary soldiers from the city of Philadelphia emphasized the tenet of equality in a cramped urban atmosphere where class disparities were most visible. They declared that common people should be charged with governing and that "rich men will be improper to be trusted." Backcountry soldiers tended to argue for "liberty . . . to do what we please." Their antipathy to central authority and love of liberty regarded Philadelphia as much as London. They sought and received more proportionate representation under the new regime and therefore gained a stake in the state's Revolutionary order. They used their new political voice to argue for self-governance and greater autonomy.

Independence from Britain was declared during this period of social and political change in the state. Ordinary Pennsylvanians linked military service, constitutional change, and the break with the mother country with their own localist political agendas. The internal Revolution in the state thus became intertwined with the larger Revolutionary cause. Furthermore, the concept of independence was an important one to soldiers who came from the lower orders of society. Earlier notions of manhood linked independence with property ownership. By 1776, military service appeared a possible route to citizenship in the new nation. Particularly among the large numbers of indentured servants and apprentices who joined the army, the war seemed to be a way to achieve freedom from servitude as well as an avenue to better their material lots in life. Griffith Smith, for example, left his master to join the militia "immediately after the Declaration of Independence." For Smith and others like him, social, political, and economic independence merged under the rubric of the Revolution.

Serving in combat, however, proved to be entirely different from signing local associations or mustering with the militia. In the matter of fighting, soldiers' intense localism usually was the primary factor. In 1775, Pennsylvanians did not flock in large numbers to the Continental Army. The state sent only one battalion to the encampment outside of Boston, a city that must have seemed a world away for most Pennsylvanians. Far more volunteers, particularly from the vulnerable southeastern part of the state, came forth in 1776, when the main theater of the war shifted to the Middle Atlantic region. The British invasion of New York and New Jersey appeared to endanger southeastern Pennsylvanians' homes, communities, and families. One Philadelphia enlisted man, Jacob Krider, declared that he enlisted during this period because he feared "Howe was marching from New York towards Philadelphia." Other city men such as Thomas Elton enlisted and "immediately on being dismissed, enlisted" again to stall the British advance across neighboring New Jersey. In August of 1776, Bucks County had to form a new militia battalion to accommodate all those moved by the "public spirit." Some men already in the service manifested a desire to go home to protect their communities when they felt they were in danger. Pennsylvania troops in upstate New York wanted to return to their state because "anxiety about their friends in . . . Pennsylvania makes them so impatient to be [led] to the assistance of their countrymen." Significantly, these soldiers defined their "country" as Pennsylvania and more particularly, their region of the state. Others returned home from New York in the midst of British invasion arguing that they were "willing to fight to defend the province we were enlisted for." Patriotic "love of country" for these early Americans was far more localized than our modern understandings of nationalism.

When the British invaded and occupied Philadelphia in 1777–1778, the situation became more dire for common people from the region. Large numbers of men joined the ranks of Revolutionaries for the first time. Many veterans recalled that they specifically enlisted to counter the invasion of their area. Andrew Keen served with the army "while the British remained in Philadelphia." Jacob Sparre "volunteered . . . to oppose the British as they were coming to Philadelphia." Moreover, the presence of the British army operating and foraging in the region served to turn many previously neutral people in the region against them. Suddenly British soldiers, who were largely viewed by common Pennsylvania troops with indifference before and after the invasion of the state, were seen as cruel enemies. Confiscation of local property for the King's forces coupled with acts of violence in the vicinity of the soldiers' homes embittered many. Charles Wallace witnessed British troops kill his elderly father and was subsequently captured. Upon his release, he enlisted in the Continental Army, "moved with a spirit of revenge for the death of his father and barbarous usage while prisoner."

The presence of the British army in the region also spurred many of the area's residents who had been alienated by the Revolutionary regime to act against it. Quakers and other pacifists who refused to take oaths of allegiance to the 1776 constitution or serve in the militia were disenfranchised. Members of these groups, already reproached in the community as "Tory" outsiders, sometimes provided support for the British troops. Others who sought neutrality were so harassed by their Revolutionary neighbors that they ended up seeking refuge in the British army. Wealthy moderate Whigs who opposed the radicals and independence also took up arms against their erstwhile comrades. Royal officials skillfully played other local social divisions to their own advantage. They enlisted a Roman Catholic Corps of Loyalists, successfully mining the states' religious and ethnic tensions. Also, scores of Pennsylvania slaves ran away to join the British army to take advantage of promises of emancipation. What this loose conglomeration of Americans serving with the British had in common was that they were all seen as outsiders within their various Revolutionary-dominated Pennsylvania communities. These "Tories" were often the most detested enemies of common Revolutionaries, who dubbed their American enemies criminal traitors. Many men enlisted specifically to fight against these former neighbors. John Hill, for instance, joined the Bucks County militia to counter "dangerous refugees," declaring his service "entirely voluntary and patriotic."

When the British evacuated the state in 1778, taking most of their local American allies with them, the zeal among southeastern Pennsylvanians for military service waned. Drafts and bounties, used by the state to raise troops throughout the war, became the predominant way of raising recruits to fight the main British army. Bounties and promises of pay were an important material benefit of soldiering. Poor men who could not afford to pay fines or substitutes to serve in their place needed money to replace wages lost in their civilian pursuits. Some men undoubt-edly served with the individualistic motive of financial gain, going from unit to unit collecting enlistment bonuses. Bounty land warrants were especially appeal-ing to poor rural men who saw the army as a vehicle for getting their own farms and status as independent patriarchs. Yet not all material motivations were entirely personal. Poor men who served in the place of others as militia substitutes often re-ceived bounty money. Many, though, went in place of their fathers and brothers. They presumably went for the bounty and served so that patriarchs were able to re-main behind on their farms or in artisan shops. Thus, the most skilled members of the household economy were able to continue to generate income. Their young sons and brothers substituted not for individual gain, but sacrificed for the greater good of their extended families.

Nowhere in the state were bounties, land warrants, and substitution as com-mon a motive for service as they were in the central settled areas. Insulated from Indian attacks by distance from the frontier and spared British invasion, residents of these secure counties rarely felt that their communities were ever endangered. Material inducements to recruits were sometimes not enough to rouse central Pennsylvanians from their apathy toward the war. One state official openly chas-tised "these counties [which have] suffered least by the enemy" for being "the most backward in furnishing their proportions of public duty." Residents of central counties were most likely to volunteer to guard British prisoners in area jails or to suppress local Tories.

The Pennsylvania frontier, in contrast, was the most war-devastated part of the state. From the outbreak of widespread conflict with the majority of local Indian nations in 1777 until after the Revolution ended in 1783, the state's backcountry was a bloody battleground. Once the frontier war commenced, residents from the region lost interest in the main theaters of the war and concentrated on defending their homes and extending their settlements. Men who previously had to be drafted to fight in the East were volunteering en masse to protect their backwoods commu-nities. Both Revolutionaries and Indians carried out guerrilla raids against each other, took scalps, killed women and children, and destroyed property. Revenge for deaths of family and friends was a powerful motivation. John Dougherty stated that "some of my relations and acquaintances had been killed by the Indians." His "readiness to fight the Indians was well known at that time." Peter Keister served to avenge "murders and burnings [by] the Indians of our men." Soldiers were also desirous of opening up the backcountry to European-American settlers and remov-ing Indians. Jacob Leatherman volunteered to "conquer the savages." Continental General William Irvine noted that his frontier troops would not end the war until "the whole of the western tribes are driven over the Mississippi and lakes, entirely beyond American lines."

A racialized view of Indians coalesced among backcountry troops during this war of conquest. Racism spurred enlistments and further brutalized the frontier war. Following what appeared to many settlers as pan-Indian solidarity during Pontiac's War, many Pennsylvanians came to see all Indians as members of a sin-gle racial group. Furthermore, "whiteness" became a common identity among the heterogeneous European-American groups in the region. Indians were seen as non-white and hence could never be members of the soldiers' perceived communities.

Enlisted men's tendencies to discuss the frontier war in the generalized terms of "whites" against "Indians" were pronounced and ominous. John Foster decried how Indians "massacred the whites." John Dougherty remarked that "the Indians were killing the white people wherever they could find them." Andrew Myers stated that "the Indians . . . [were] determined not to yield to the white people." The result of these attitudes was that common soldiers from the region tended to fight all Indians, killing friends and foes alike. Indian groups that fought with the Revolutionaries were often murdered by their supposed allies. The slaughter of neutral Europeanized Moravian Delawares at Gnadenhutten by western Pennsylvania militia demonstrated the culmination of the backcountry soldiers' racial definition of community. Frontier troops believed the Delaware's use of European-made goods was not evidence of cultural similarity, but rather plunder. The soldiers declared that these were "things as were made use of by white people and not by Indians." The conflation of the Revolutionary cause with racism toward Indians had a major impact on definitions of citizenship in the new republic and on the subsequent history of the American West. Indians were seen as obstacles to settlement who could never become true "Americans."

The reality of the frontier war was that it was not simply a war between Indians and whites. As there were a few Indians who fought beside the Revolutionaries, there were also numbers of European Americans who fought with the British-Indian coalition. Most of these backwoods "Tories" chose sides due to land disputes with rival settlers. In the northeastern part of Pennsylvania, claimants favoring Connecticut had long been in conflict with Pennsylvania settlers (Pennamites). The Connecticut settlers began to exert political dominance over the region during the war by labeling their Pennamite opponents Tories. Their attacks on the Pennsylvania settlers were thus prosecuted under the rubric of the Revolution. Many Pennamites joined Loyalist units such as Butler's Rangers and fought alongside Indians primarily to contest their Yankee neighbors. A similar conflict occurred in the southwestern portion of the state where Pennsylvania and Virginia settlers clashed over which state should exert political hegemony. As Pennsylvanians consolidated their control of local government, many Virginians were derided as Tories and "banditti." Hostilities between these groups on the Pennsylvania frontier had little to do with loyalty to the crown or adherence to American independence. As one Pennamite woman stated, her group was "no more Tories than the Yankees were." Like other lower- and middling-sort Pennsylvanians, these backcountry inhabitants took sides according to their definitions of community and against groups believed to be threatening.

Common soldiers did not then simply fight out a nationalist love for an independent United States, nor did they enlist solely for individual gain. They conducted a Revolution that was integrally related to their distinctive notions of community. Their motives varied widely, but were ultimately circumscribed by the localism that predominated ordinary early Americans' outlooks. Men were most likely to volunteer when they felt their communities were endangered. They also fought out of commitment to ideals that were particular to their class, regional, ethnic, and racial status. Understandably, poor men sought some measure of material reward for their service, particularly to buttress their claims to patriarchy or to preserve their families' household economies. In all cases, conditions in America were vitally important from the perspective of common people. The issue of national independence was marginal or secondary to them.

The legacy of soldiers' motivations is mixed. The American Revolution paved the way for the then radical concept of universal white manhood suffrage in the postwar period. Certainly soldiers' equation of military service with entitlement to full citizenship helped achieve this limited democracy. Nonetheless, the veterans' freedom was defined in opposition to those excepted from the new order. Indians and African Americans were not "white." Women could not vote, and their legal identities continued to be subsumed under those of their husbands. Pacifists and other neutrals were stigmatized as Tory traitors. Minority ethnic groups were often pushed out of their communities and into the arms of the British by Revolutionaries who considered them outsiders. Soldiers' localism was predicated upon an exclusive definition of community. Their failure to imagine common interests with people outside their locale or own particular social groups is a problem with which Americans continue to struggle.

♠ *F U R T H E R   R E A D I N G*

Larry G. Bowman, *Captive Americans: Prisoners During the American Revolution* (1976).

Richard Buel, Jr., *Dear Liberty: Connecticut's Mobilization for the Revolutionary War* (1980).

E. Wayne Carp, *To Starve the Army at Pleasure: Continental Army Administration and American Political Culture* (1984).

Colin G. Calloway, *The American Revolution in Indian Country* (1995).

John C. Dann, ed., *The Revolution Remembered: Eyewitness Accounts of the War for Independence* (1980).

John Morgan Dederer, *Making Bricks Without Straw: Nathanael Greene's Southern Campaign and Mao Tse-Tung's Mobile War* (1983).

Linda Grant De Pauw, "Women in Combat: The Revolutionary War Experience," *Armed Forces and Society* 7 (Winter 1981): 209–226.

John E. Ferling, ed., *The World Turned Upside Down: The American Victory in the War of Independence* (1988).

David Hackett Fischer, *Paul Revere's Ride* (1994).

William M. Fowler, Jr., *Rebels Under Sail: The American Navy During the Revolution* (1976).

Lucy Freeman and Alma Bond, *America's First Woman Warrior: The Courage of Deborah Sampson* (1992).

Sylvia R. Frey, *Water from the Rock: Black Resistance in a Revolutionary Age* (1991).

Jeremiah Greenman, *Diary of a Common Soldier in the American Revolution, 1775–1783*. Edited by Robert C. Bray and Paul E. Bushnell (1978).

Robert A. Gross, *The Minutemen and Their World* (1976).

Ira D. Gruber, *The Howe Brothers and the American Revolution* (1972).

Don Higginbotham, *George Washington and the American Military Tradition* (1985).

Ronald Hoffman and Peter J. Albert, eds., *Arms and Independence: The Military Character of the American Revolution* (1984).

James Kirby Martin and Mark Edward Lender, *A Respectable Army: The Military Origins of the Republic, 1763–1789* (1982).

Holly A. Mayer, *Belonging to the Army: Camp Followers and Community during the American Revolution* (1996).

Robert Middlekauff, *The Glorious Cause: The American Revolution, 1763–1789* (1982).

Charles Patrick Neimeyer, *America Goes to War: A Social History of the Continental Army* (1996).

Peter Oliver, *Origin and Progress of the American Rebellion: A Tory View.* Edited by Douglas Adair and John A. Shutz (1961).

Dave R. Palmer, *The Way of the Fox: American Strategy in the War for America, 1775–1783* (1975).

John S. Pancake, *This Destructive War: The British Campaign in the Carolinas, 1780–1782* (1985).

Edwin Papenfuse and Gregory A, Stiverson, *"General Smallwood's Recruits: The Peacetime Career of the Revolutionary War Private," William and Mary Quarterly, 3d ser. 30 (Jan. 1973): 117–132.*

Howard H. Peckman, ed., *The Toll of Independence: Engagements & Battle Casualties of the American Revolution* (1974).

Hugh F. Rankin, *The North Carolina Continentals* (1971).

Steven Rosswurm, *Arms, Country, and Class: The Philadelphia Militia and the "Lower Sort" During the American Revolution* (1987).

Charles Royster, *Light-Horse Harry Lee and the Legacy of the American Revolution* (1981).

————, *A Revolutionary People at War: The Continental Army and the American Character, 1775–1783* (1979).

John Shy, *A People Numerous and Armed: Reflections on the Military Struggle for American Independence* (1976).

James L. Stokesbury, *A Short History of the American Revolution* (1991).

Russell Weigley, *The Partisan War: The South Carolina Campaign of 1780–1782* (1970).

W. J. Wood, *Battles of the Revolutionary War, 1775–1781* (1990).

Robert K. Wright, Jr., *The Continental Army* (1986).

Hiller B. Zobel, *The Boston Massacre* (1970).

The New Nation, the Military, and an American Way of War

The United States was a nation born in war, but many Americans also viewed the republican experiment in self-government as a repudiation of the dynastic conflicts and imperial wars of the Old World. Some hoped that American ideals and material resources could provide an effective foreign and defense policy and that the use of military force, when needed, could be kept limited. America would provide a model of the peaceful and benevolent Republic. Others had a more militant vision, readily accepting the use of force in international affairs and viewing America's wars as the virtuous crusades of a righteous Republic. Scholars debate the views of the founders of the Republic about war and foreign policy, just as they continue to explore the divisions within the founding generation over the relationship of the federal and state governments, including the most appropriate military institutions for the new nation.

▲ D O C U M E N T S

The Articles of Confederation, proposed in 1777 and ratified by 1781, established the first central government for the thirteen former colonies that now formed the United States. The first document, the military provisions, confirms the comparatively limited powers of the confederation government in contrast to those that would later be granted to the national government under the Constitution drafted in 1787. As the victorious commander, General George Washington was asked his views in 1783 on whether the Republic would need a standing army (or rely on the militia) and what kind of military would be most appropriate; the second document is his answer. Four years later, the delegates at Philadelphia wrote a Constitution, document three, that gave the new central government many powers, including authority to raise an army and navy, and to levy taxes to maintain them, but in deference to widespread fears of standing armies and strong central governments as threats to liberty, the federal government's control over the state militias was restricted, and the Bill of Rights, promised by the Federalists in 1787, and adopted in 1791, provided a series of civilian guarantees for restraint of the national military. Evidence of the intensity of Antifederalist sentiments is evident in the fourth document, a 1787 Antifederalist warning against the Constitution in a letter to a New York newspaper. In the fifth document, Secretary of State Thomas Jefferson in a 1793 letter to his friend, Representative James Madison, reflected much Republican and pro-French sentiment when, in the crisis between Revolutionary France and Great Britain, he advocated economic pressures or inducements as alternatives to war. In contrast, in 1798, in response to a mounting diplomatic and maritime crisis with Revolutionary France, New York Federalist leader Alexander Hamilton, a pro-British opponent of France, penned letters to a New York newspaper urging the need to prepare for war by building a strong army and navy. The undeclared war with France involved only a series of limited naval actions. When the United States next declared war, it was against Great Britain in 1812, a conflict the Madison administration entered reluctantly and with limited aims, but that others called enthusiastically a second war of independence from Britain. In the final document, Andrew Jackson, a self-made wealthy planter, and a major general in the Tennessee militia, issues a call upon the declaration of war for volunteers to accompany him on a crusade against British tyranny which, he says, may also lead to the acquisition of Canada.

1. The Articles of Confederation's Provisions on War and the Military, 1777

Article 1.

The stile of this confederacy shall be "The United States of America."

Article 2.

Each State retains its sovereignty, freedom and independence, and every power, jurisdiction, and right, which is not by this confederation expressly delegated to the United States, in Congress assembled.

Article 3.

The said states hereby severally enter into a firm league of friendship with each other for their common defence, the security of their liberties and their mutual and general welfare; binding themselves to assist each other against all force offered to, or attacks made upon them, or any of them, on account of religion, sovereignty, trade, or any other pretence whatever. . . .

[Article 6.]

. . . No vessels of war shall be kept up in time of peace by any State, except such number only as shall be deemed necessary by the United States, in Congress

---

Excerpts on War and the Military from The Articles of Confederation and Perpetual Union (1777).

assembled, for the defence of such State or its trade; nor shall any body of forces be kept up by any State, in time of peace, except such number only as, in the judgment of the United States, in Congress assembled, shall be deemed requisite to garrison the forts necessary for the defence of such State; but every State shall always keep up a well regulated and disciplined militia, sufficiently armed and accoutred, and shall provide, and constantly have ready for use, in public stores, a due number of field pieces and tents, and a proper quantity of arms, ammunition and camp equipage.

No State shall engage in any war without the consent of the United States, in Congress assembled, unless such State be actually invaded by enemies, or shall have received certain advice of a resolution being formed by some nation of Indians to invade such State, and the danger is so imminent as not to admit of a delay till the United States, in Congress assembled, can be consulted. . . .

Article 7.

When land forces are raised by any State for the common defence, all officers of or under the rank of colonel, shall be appointed by the legislature of each State respectively, by whom such forces shall be raised, or in such manner as such State shall direct; and all vacancies shall be filled up by the State which first made the appointment.

Article 8.

All charges of war and all other expences, that shall be incurred for the common defence or general welfare, and allowed by the United States, in Congress assembled, shall be defrayed out of a common treasury, which shall be supplied by the several states, in proportion to the value of all land within each State, granted to or surveyed for any person, as such land and the buildings and improvements thereon shall be estimated according to such mode as the United States, in Congress assembled, shall, from time to time, direct and appoint.

The taxes for paying that proportion shall be laid and levied by the authority and direction of the legislatures of the several states, within the time agreed upon by the United States, in Congress assembled.

Article 9.

The United States, in Congress assembled, shall have the sole and exclusive right and power of determining on peace and war, except in the cases mentioned in the 6th article. . . .

The United States, in Congress assembled, shall also be the last resort on appeal in all disputes and differences now subsisting, or that hereafter may arise between two or more states concerning boundary, jurisdiction or any other cause whatever; . . .

The United States, in Congress assembled, shall also have the sole and exclusive right and power of regulating the alloy and value of coin struck by their own authority, or by that of the respective states; fixing the standard of weights and measures throughout the United States; regulating the trade and managing all affairs with the Indians not members of any of the states; provided that the legislative right of any State within its own limits be not infringed or violated; establishing and regulating post offices from one State to another throughout all the United States, and exacting such postage on the papers passing through the same as may be requisite to defray the expences of the said office; appointing all officers of the land forces in the service of the United States, excepting regimental officers; appointing all the officers of the naval forces, and commisioning all officers whatever in the service of the United States; making rules for the government and regulation of the said land and naval forces, and directing their operations.

The United States, in Congress assembled, shall have authority to appoint a committee to sit in the recess of Congress, to be denominated "a Committee of the States," and to consist of one delegate from each State, and to appoint such other committees and civil officers as may be necessary for managing the general affairs of the United States, under their direction; to appoint one of their number to preside; provided that no person be allowed to serve in the office of president more than one year in any term of three years; to ascertain the necessary sums of money to be raised for the service of the United States, and to appropiate and apply the same for defraying the public expences; to borrow money or emit bills on the credit of the United States, transmitting, every half year, to the respective states, an account of the sums of money so borrowed or emitted; to build and equip a navy; to agree upon the number of land forces, and to make requisitions from each State for its quota, in proportion to the number of white inhabitants in such State; which requisitions shall be binding; and, therupon, the legislature of each State shall appoint the regimental officers, raise the men, and cloathe, arm, and equip them in a soldier-like manner, at the expence of the United States; and the officers and men so cloathed, armed, and equipped, shall march to the place appointed and within the time agreed on by the United States, in Congress assembled; but if the United States, in Congress assembled, shall, on consideration of circumstances, judge proper that any State should not raise men, or should raise a smaller number that its quota, and that any other State should raise a greater number of men than the quota therof, such extra number shall be raised, officered, cloathed, armed, and equipped in the same manner as the quota of such State, unless the legislature of such State shall judge that extra number cannot be safely spared out of the same, in which case they shall raise, officer, cloathe, arm and equip as many of such extra number as they judge can be safely spared. And the officers and men so cloathed, armed, and equipped, shall march to the place appointed and within the time agreed on by the United States, in Congress assembled.

The United States, in Congress assembled, shall never engage in a war, nor grant letters of marque and reprisal in time of peace, nor enter into any treaties or alliances, nor coin money, nor regulate the value thereof, nor ascertain the sums and expences necessary for the defence and welfare of the United States, or any of them: nor emit bills, nor borrow money on the credit of the United States, nor appropriated money, nor agree upon the number of vessels of war to be built or purchased, or the number of land or sea forces to be raised, nor appoint a commander in chief of the army or navy, unless nine states assent to the same; nor shall a question on any other point, except for adjourning from day to day, be determined, unless by the votes of a majority of the United States, in Congress assembled. . . .

Article 10.

The committee of the states, or any nine of them, shall be authorized to execute, in the recess of Congress, such of the powers of Congress as the United States, in Congress assembled, by the consent of nine states, shall, from time to time, think expedient to vest them with; provided, that no power be delegated to the said committee, for the exercise of which, by the articles of confederation, the voice of nine states, in the Congress of the United States assembled, is requisite.

2. General George Washington Calls for a Standing Army, 1783

A Peace Establishment for the United States of America may in my opinion be classed under four different heads Vizt:

First. A regular and standing force, for Garrisoning West Point and such other Posts upon our Northern, Western, and Southern Frontiers, as shall be deemed necessary to awe the Indians, protect our Trade, prevent the encroachment of our Neighbours of Canada and the Floridas, and guard us at least from surprizes; Also for security of our [gunpowder] Magazines.

Secondly. A well organized Militia; upon a Plan that will pervade all the States, and introduce similarity in their Establishment Manœvres, Exercise and Arms.

Thirdly. Establishing Arsenals of all kinds of Military Stores.

Fourthly. Accademies, one or more for the Instruction of the Art Military; particularly those Branches of it which respect Engineering and Artillery, which are highly essential, and the knowledge of which, is most difficult to obtain. Also Manufactories of some kinds of Military Stores.

Upon each of these, and in the order in which they stand, I shall give my sentiments as concisely as I can, and with that freedom which the Committee have authorized.

Altho' a *large* standing Army in time of Peace hath ever been considered dangerous to the liberties of a Country, yet a few Troops, under certain circumstances, are not only safe, but indispensably necessary. Fortunately for us our relative situation requires but few. The same circumstances which so effectually retarded, and in the end conspired to defeat the attempts of Britain to subdue us, will now powerfully tend to render us secure. Our *distance* from the European States in a great degree frees us of apprehension, from their numerous regular forces and the Insults and dangers which are to be dreaded from their Ambition.

But, if our danger from those powers was more imminent, yet we are too poor to maintain a standing Army adequate to our defence, and was our Country more populous and rich, still it could not be done without great oppression of the people. Besides, as soon as we are able to raise funds more than adequate to the discharge of the Debts incurred by the Revolution, it may become a Question worthy of consideration, whether the surplus should not be applied in preparations for building and equipping a Navy, without which, in case of War we could neither protect our Commerce, nor yield that Assistance to each other, which, on such an extent of Sea-Coast, our mutual Safety would require,

From George Washington. "Sentiments on a Peace Establishment," accompanying Washington to Alexander Hamilton, May 2, 1783, reprinted in John C. Fitzgerald, ed. *The Writings of George Washington*, 39 vols. (Washington: GPO, 1931–1944), 26:374–376, 387–390.

Fortifications on the Sea Board may be considered in two points of view, first as part of the general defence, and next, as securities to Dock Yards, and Arsenals for Ship Building, neither of which shall I take into this plan; because the first would be difficult, if not, under our circumstances, impracticable; at any rate amazingly expensive. The other, because it is a matter out of my line, and to which I am by no means competent, as it requires a consideration of many circumstances, to which I have never paid attention. . . .

I come next in the order I have prescribed myself, to treat of the Arrangements necessary for placing the Militia of the Continent on a respectable footing for the defence of the Empire and in speaking of this great Bulwark of our Liberties and independence, I shall claim the indulgence of suggesting whatever general observations may occur from experience and reflection with the greater freedom, from a conviction of the importance of the subject; being persuaded, that the immediate safety and future tranquility of this extensive Continent depend in a great measure upon the peace Establishment now in contemplation; and being convinced at the same time, that the only probable means of preventing insult or hostility for any length of time and from being exempted from the consequent calamities of War, is to put the National Militia in such a condition as that they may appear truly respectable in the Eyes of our Friends and formidable to those who would otherwise become our enemies. . . .

It may be laid down as a primary position, and the basis of our system, that every Citizen who enjoys the protection of a free Government, owes not only a proportion of his property, but even of his personal services to the defence of it, and consequently that the Citizens of America (with a few legal and official exceptions) from 18 to 50 Years of Age should be borne on the Militia Rolls, provided with uniform Arms, and so far accustomed to the use of them, that the Total strength of the Country might be called forth at a Short Notice on any very interesting Emergency. . . .

[T]here are a sufficient proportion of able bodied young Men, between the Age of 18 and 25, who, from a natural fondness for Military parade (which passion is almost ever prevalent at that period of life) might easily be enlisted or drafted to form a Corps in every State, capable of resisting any sudden impression which might be attempted by a foreign Enemy, while the remainder of the National forces would have time to Assemble and make preparations for the Field. I would wish therefore, that the former, being considered as a *denier resort,* reserved for some great occasion, a judicious system might be adopted for forming and placing the latter on the best possible Establishment. And that while the Men of this description shall be viewed as the Van and flower of the American Forces, ever ready for Action and zealous to be employed whenever it may become necessary in the service of their Country; they should meet with such exemptions, privileges or distinctions, as might tend to keep alive a true Military pride, a nice sense of honour, and a patriotic regard for the public. Such sentiments, indeed, ought to be instilled into our Youth, with their earliest years, to be cherished and inculcated as frequently and forcibly as possible. . . .

3. The Constitution's and Bill of Rights' Provisions on War and the Military, 1787, 1791

Military Clauses of the Constitution of the United States

1787

ART. I

... Sec. 8 The Congress shall have Power to lay and collect Taxes, Duties, Imposts and Excises, to pay the Debts and provide for the common Defense and general Welfare of the United States. ...

To declare War, grant letters of Marque and Reprisal, and make Rules concerning Captures on Land and Water;

To raise and support Armies, but no Appropriation of Money to that Use shall be for a longer Term than two Years;

To provide and maintain a Navy;

To make Rules for the Government and Regulation of the land and naval Forces;

To provide for calling forth the Militia to execute the Laws of the Union, suppress Insurrections and repel Invasions;

To provide for organizing, arming, and disciplining the Militia, and for governing such Part of them as may be employed in the Service of the United States, reserving to the States, respectively, the Appointment of the Officers, and the Authority of training the Militia according to the discipline prescribed by Congress;
...

... To make all Laws which shall be necessary and proper for carrying into Execution the foregoing Powers, and all other Powers vested by this Constitution in the Government of the United States, or in any Department or Officer thereof. ...

... Sec. 10. ...

No State shall, without the Consent of Congress, lay any Duty of Tonnage, keep Troops, or Ships of War in time of Peace, enter into any Agreement or Compact with another State, or with a foreign Power, or engage in War, unless actually invaded, or in such imminent Danger as will not admit of delay.

ART. II

Sec. 1. The executive power shall be vested in a President of the United States of America. He shall hold his Office during the Term of four Years. ...

... Sec. 2. The President shall be Commander in Chief of the Army and Navy of the United States, and of the Militia of the several States, when called into the actual Service of the United States. ...

From the United States Constitution, Excerpts from Military Clauses of the Constitution and Bill of Rights (1789–1791).

. . . he shall nominate, and by and with the Advice and Consent of the Senate, shall appoint Ambassadors, other public Ministers and Consuls, Judges of the Supreme Court, and all other Officers of the United States, whose Appointments are not herein otherwise provided for, and which shall be established by Law; but Congress may by Law vest the Appointment of such inferior Officers, as they think proper, in the President alone, in the Courts of Law, or in the Heads of Departments.

ART. IV

. . . Sec. 4. The United States shall guarantee to every State in this Union a Republican Form of Government, and shall protect each of them against Invasion; and on Application of the Legislature, or of the Executive (when the Legislature cannot be convened), against domestic Violation.

Amendment to the Constitution Affecting Military Service

1791

[The first ten amendments, the Bill of Rights, went into effect on November 3, 1791. Among them were the following which are reprinted here from James D. Richardson, ed., *Compilation of the Messages and Papers of the Presidents, 1789–1897* (10 vols., Washington, D.C., 1907), I, pp. 21 ff.]

ART. II

A well-regulated Militia, being necessary to the security of a free State, the right of the people to keep and bear Arms, shall not be infringed.

ART. III

No Soldier shall, in time of peace, be quartered in any house, without the consent of the Owner, nor in time of war, but in a manner to be prescribed by law.

ART. V

No person shall be held to answer for a capital, or otherwise infamous crime, unless on a presentment or indictment of a Grand Jury, except in cases arising in the land or naval forces, or in the Militia, when in actual service in time of War or public danger. . . .

4. Antifederalists Fear a Large Military, 1787

The magistrates in every government must be supported in the execution of the laws, either by an armed force, maintained at the public expence for that purpose; or by the people turning out to aid the magistrate upon his command, in case of resistance.

From "Brutus I." "To the Citizens of the State of New York," in *New York Journal*, October 18, 1787, reprinted in John P. Kaminski and Richard Leffler, eds. *Federalists and Antifederalists* (Madison House: Madison, Wis., 1989), I, 11–13.

In despotic governments, as well as in all the monarchies of Europe, standing armies are kept up to execute the commands of the prince or the magistrate, and are employed for this purpose when occasion requires: But they have always proved the destruction of liberty, and is abhorrent to the spirit of a free republic. In England, where they depend upon the parliament for their annual support, they have always been complained of as oppressive and unconstitutional, and are seldom employed in executing of the laws; never except on extraordinary occasions, and then under the direction of a civil magistrate.

A free republic will never keep a standing army to execute its laws. It must depend upon the support of its citizens. But when a government is to receive its support from the aid of the citizens, it must be so constructed as to have the confidence, respect, and affection of the people. Men who, upon the call of the magistrate, offer themselves to execute the laws, are influenced to do it either by affection to the government, or from fear; where a standing army is at hand to punish offenders, every man is actuated by the latter principle, and therefore, when the magistrate calls, will obey: but, where this is not the case, the government must rest for its support upon the confidence and respect which the people have for their government and laws. The body of the people being attached, the government will always be sufficient to support and execute its laws, and to operate upon the fears of any faction which may be opposed to it, not only to prevent an opposition to the execution of the laws themselves, but also to compel the most of them to aid the magistrate; but the people will not be likely to have such confidence in their rulers, in a republic so extensive as the United States, as necessary for these purposes. The confidence which the people have in their rulers, in a free republic, arises from their knowing them, from their being responsible to them for their conduct, and from the power they have of displacing them when they misbehave: but in a republic of the extent of this continent, the people in general would be acquainted with very few of their rulers: the people at large would know little of their proceedings, and it would be extremely difficult to change them. The people in Georgia and New-Hampshire would not know one another's mind, and therefore could not act in concert to enable them to effect a general change of representatives. The different parts of so extensive a country could not possibly be made acquainted with the conduct of their representatives, nor be informed of the reasons upon which measures were founded. The consequence will be, they will have no confidence in their legislature, suspect them of ambitious views, be jealous of every measure they adopt, and will not support the laws they pass. Hence the government will be nerveless and inefficient, and no way will be left to render it otherwise, but by establishing an armed force to execute the laws at the point of the bayonet—a government of all others the most to be dreaded.

In a republic of such vast extent as the United-States, the legislature cannot attend to the various concerns and wants of its different parts. It cannot be sufficiently numerous to be acquainted with the local condition and wants of the different districts, and if it could, it is impossible it should have sufficient time to attend to and provide for all the variety of cases of this nature, that would be continually arising.

In so extensive a republic, the great officers of government would soon become above the controul of the people, and abuse their power to the purpose of aggrandizing themselves, and oppressing them. The trust committed to the executive offices, in a country of the extent of the United-States, must be various and of magnitude. The command of all the troops and navy of the republic, the appointment of officers, the power of pardoning offences, the collecting of all the public revenues, and the power of expending them, with a number of other powers, must be lodged and exercised in every state, in the hands of a few. When these are attended with great honor and emolument, as they always will be in large states, so as greatly to interest men to pursue them, and to be proper objects for ambitious and designing men, such men will be ever restless in their pursuit after them. They will use the power, when they have acquired it, to the purposes of gratifying their own interest and ambition, and it is scarcely possible, in a very large republic, to call them to account for their misconduct, or to prevent their abuse of power. . . .

5. Thomas Jefferson Advises an Economic Alternative to War, 1793

March 24, 1793

The idea seems to gain credit that the naval powers combined against France will prohibit supplies even of provisions to that country. Should this be formally notified I should suppose Congress would be called, because it is a justifiable cause of war, & as the Executive cannot decide the question of war on the affirmative side, neither ought it to do so on the negative side, by preventing the competent body from deliberating on the question. But I should hope that war would not be their choice. I think it will furnish us a happy opportunity of setting another example to the world, by shewing that nations may be brought to do justice by appeals to their interests as well as by appeals to arms. I should hope that Congress instead of a denunciation of war, would instantly exclude from our ports all the manufactures, produce, vessels & subjects of the nations committing this aggression, during the continuance of the aggression and till full satisfaction made for it. This would work well in many ways, safely in all, & introduce between nations another umpire than arms. It would relieve us too from the risks & the horrors of cutting throats. . . .

6. Alexander Hamilton Urges the Need for Defense and War, 1798

This country has doubtless powerful motives to cultivate peace. It was its policy, for the sake of this object, to go a great way in yielding secondary interests, and to meet injury with patience as long as it could be done without the manifest abandonment of essential rights; without absolute dishonor. But to do more than this is

From Jefferson to James Madison, March 24, 1793, in *Thomas Jefferson: Writings* (New York: Library of America, 1984), 1006–1007.

From [Alexander Hamilton.] "The Stand No. 1," in *The [New York] Commercial Advertiser*, March 30, 1798, reprinted in Harold C. Syrett, ed. *The Papers of Alexander Hamilton* (New York: Columbia U. P., 1974), XXI, 384–387.

suicide in any people who have the least chance of contending with effect. The conduct of our government has corresponded with the cogent inducements to a pacific system. Towards Great Britain it displayed forbearance—towards France it has shown humility. In the case of Great Britain, its moderation was attended with success. But the inexorable arrogance and rapacity of the [five-man Directory of France] barr all the avenues to reconciliation as well as to redress, accumulating upon us injury and insult till there is no choice left between resistance and infamy.

My countrymen! can ye hesitate which to prefer? can ye consent to taste the brutalizing cup of disgrace, to wear the livery of foreign masters, to put on the hateful fetters of foreign bondage? Will it make any difference to you that the badge of your servitude is a *cap* rather than an *epaulet?* Will tyranny be less odious because FIVE instead of ONE inflict the rod? What is there to deter from the manful vindication of your rights and your honor?

With an immense ocean rolling between the United States and France—with ample materials for ship building, and a body of hardy seamen more numerous and more expert than France can boast, with a population exceeding five millions, spread over a wide extent of country, offering no one point, the seizure of which, as of the great capitals of Europe, might deside the issue, with a soil liberal of all the productions that give strength and resource, with the rudiments of the most essential manufactures capable of being developed in proportion to our want, with a numerous and in many quarters well appointed militia, with respectable revenues and a flourishing credit, with many of the principle sources of taxation yet untouched, with considerable arsenals and the means of extending them, with experienced officers ready to form an army under the command of the same illustrious chief who before led them to victory and glory, and who, if the occasion should require it, could not hesitate again to obey the summons of his country—what a striking and encouraging contrast does this situation in many respects form, to that in which we defied the thunder of Britain? what is there in it to excuse or palliate the cowardice and baseness of a tame surrender of our rights to France?

The question is unnecessary. The people of America are neither idiots nor dastards. They did not break one yoke to put on another. Tho a portion of them have been hitherto misled; yet not even these, still less the great body of the nation, can be long unaware of the true situation, or blind to the treacherous arts by which they are attempted to be hood winked. The unfaithful and guilty leaders of a foreign faction, unmasked in all their intrinsic deformity, must quickly shrink from the scene, appalled and confounded. The virtuous whom they have led astray will renounce their exotic standard. Honest men of all parties will unite to maintain and defend the honor and the sovereignty of their country.

The crisis demands it. 'Tis folly to dissemble. The despots of France are waging war against us. Intoxicated with success and the inordinate love of power, they actually threaten our independence. All amicable means have in vain been tried towards accommodation. The Problem now to be solved is whether we will maintain or surrender our sovereignty. To maintain it with firmness is the most sacred of duties, the most glorious of tasks. The happiness of our country, the honor of the American name demands it. The genius of Independence exhorts to it. The secret mourning voice of oppressed millions in the very country whose despots menace us, admonish to it by their suffering example. The offended dignity of man

commands us not to be accessary to its further degradation. Reverence to the
SUPREME GOVERNOR of the universe enjoins us not to bow the knee to the modern
TITANS who erect their impious crests against him and vainly imagine they can sub-
vert his eternal throne.

But 'tis not enough to resist. 'Tis requisite to resist with energy. That will be a
narrow view of our situation which does not contemplate, that we may be called, at
our very doors, to defend our independence and liberty, and which does not provide against it, by bringing into activity and completely organizing all the resources of our country. A respectable naval force, ought to protect our commerce,
and a respectable army ought both to diminish the temptation to invasion, by lessening the apparent chance of success, and to guarantee us, not only against the final success of such an attempt, but against the serious tho partial calamities, which
in that case would certainly await us, if we have to rely on militia alone against the
enterprises of veteran troops, drenched in blood and slaughter and led by a skillful
and daring Chief!   TITUS MANLIUS.

7. Andrew Jackson Proclaims War as a Crusade, 1812

To the 2nd Division

Division orders   March 7th, 1812—
Volunteers to arms!

Citizens! Your government has at least yielded to the impulse of the nation. Your
impatience is no longer restrained. The hour of national vengeance is now at hand.
The eternal enemies of american prosperity are again to be taught to respect your
rights, after having been compelled to feel, once more, the power of your arms.

*War is on the point of breaking out between the united states and the King of
Great Britain! and the martial hosts of america are summoned to the Tented
Fields!*

Citizens! an honourable confidence in your courage and your patriotism has
been displayed by the general government. To raise a force for the protection of
your rights she has not deemed it necessary to recur to the common mode of filling
the ranks of an army.

No drafts or compulsory levies are now to be made.

A simple invitation is given to the young men of the country to arm for their
own and their countries rights. On this invitation 50,000 volunteers, full of martial
ardor, indignant of their Countries wrongs and burning with impatience to illustrate
their names by some signal exploit, are expected to repair to the national standard.

Could it be otherwise? Could the general government deem it necessary to
force *us* to take the field? We, who for so many years have demanded a war with
such clamorous importunity—who, in so many resolutions of town meetings and
legislative assemblies, have offered our lives and fortunes for the defence of our
country—who, so often and so publickly have charged this very government with a

---

From Andrew Jackson. "To the 2nd Division. Division Orders. March 7, 1812. Volunteers to Arms!"
reprinted in Harold D. Moser and Sharon MacPherson, eds. *The Papers of Andrew Jackson* (Knoxville:
U. of Tennessee P., 1984), II, 290–293.

pusillanimous deference to foreign nations, because she had resolved to exhaust the arts of negociation before she made her last appea[l] to the force of arms. No, under such circumstance it was impossible for the government to conceive that compulsion would be wanting to bring us into the field, and shall we now disappoint the expectations which we ourselves have excited? shall we give the lie to the professions which we have so often and so publickly made? Shall we, who have clamoured for war, now skulk into a corner the moment war is about to be declared? Shall we, who for so many years have been tendering our lives and fortunes to the general government, now come out with evasions and pitifull excuses the moment tender is accepted?

But another and a nobler feeling should impell us to action. *Who are we? and for what are we going to fight?* are we the titled Slaves of George the third? the military conscripts of Napoleon the great? or the frozen peasants of the Rusian Czar? No, we are the free born sons of america; the citizens of the only republick now existing in the world; and the only people on Earth who possess rights, liberties, and property which the[y] dare call their own.

For what we are going to fight? To satisfy the revenge or ambition of a corrupt and infatuated Ministry? to place another and another diadem on the head of an apostate republican general? to settle the ballance of power among an assasin tribe of Kings and Emperors? "or to preserve to the prince of Blood, and the grand dignitaries of the empire" their overgrown wealth and exclusive privileges? No: such splendid atchievements as these can form no part of the objects of an american war. But we are going to fight for the reestablishment of our national charector, misunderstood and vilified at home and abroad; for the protection of our maritime citizens, impressed on board British ships of war and compelled to fight the battles of our enemies against ourselves; to vindicate our right to a free trade, and open a market for the productions of our soil, now perishing on our hands, because the *mistress of the ocean* has forbid us to carry them to any foreign nation; in fine, to seek some indemnity for past injuries, some security against future aggressions, by the conquest of all the British dominions upon the continent of North america.

Here then is the true and noble principle on which the energies of the nation should be brought into action: *a free people compelled to reclaim by the power of their arms the rights which god has bestowed upon them, and which an infatuated King has said they shall not enjoy.*

In such a contest will the people shrink from the support of their government; or rather will the shrink from the support of themselves? will the[y] abandon their great imprescriptible rights, and tamely surrender that illustrious national charector which was purchased with so much blood in the war of the Revolution? No: such infamy shall not fall upon us. The advocates of Kingly power shall not enjoy the triumph of seeing a free people desert themselves, and crouch before the slaves of a foreign tyrant. The patriotic tender of voluntary service of the invincible grays Capt. F. Stumps independent company and a correspondent display of patriotism by the voluntary tender of service from the counties of Davidson Sumner Smith and Rutherford, is a sure pledge that the free sons of the west will never *submit to such degradation.*

But the period of youth is the season for martial exploits; and accordingly it is upon the young men of america that the eye of the nation is now fixed. They in a peculiar degree are the proper subjects of a volunteer expedition. To say nothing of the generous courage which distinguishes that period of life, they, from their particular situation, can quit their homes at the shortest notice with the least inconvenience to themselves. Unencumbered with families and free from the embarrassment of domestic concerns they are ready at a moments warning to march to any extremity of the republick.

Should the occupation of the Canadas be resolved upon by the general goverment, how pleasing the prospect that would open to the young volunteer while performing a military *promenade* into a distant country, a succession of new and interesting objects would perpetually fill and delight his imagination the effect of which would be heightened by the war-like appearance, the martial music, and the grand evolutions of an army of fifty thousand men.

To view the stupendous works of nature, exemplified in the falls of Niagara and the cataract of Montmorence; to tread the consecrated spot on which Wolf and Montgomery fell, would of themselves repay the young soldier for a march across the continent. But why should these inducements be held out to the young men of america? They need them not. animated as they are by an ambition to rival the exploits of Rome, they will never prefer an inglorious sloth, a supine inactivity to the honorable toil of carrying the republican standard to the heights of abraham.

In consideration of all which and to carry into effect the object of the general goverment in demanding a voluntary force, to give the valiant young men of the Second Military Division of the state of Tennessee an opportunity to evince their devoted affection to the service of the republic; the Major General of the said division has thereupon ordered

1 That the militia of the second military division of the state of Tennessee be forthwith be mustered by the proper officers.

2 That the act of Congress for raising a volunteer corps of 50,000 men be read at the head of each company.

3 That all persons willing to volunteer under the said act be immediately *enrolled* formed into companies, officered, and reported to the Major Genl

4 The Generals of Brigade, attached to the Second division are charged with the prompt execution of these orders.

Andrew Jackson,
Major Genl. 2 Division

▲ E S S A Y S

Scholars have debated about the dominant attitudes in the early Republic over the role of armed force and the nature of war in the United States. John Shy of the University of Michigan contends that Americans early on came to see wars as crusades for total victory and the elimination of enemy threats. In contrast Reginald Stuart of Dalhousie University in Canada, a historian of the early United States, asserts that, rather than all-out military force, war was seen, at least initially in the Republic, as a rational instrument of policy to be used in limited ways for very specific goals.

American Wars as Crusades for Total Victory

JOHN SHY

An old, yet compelling idea states that international behavior may be best understood in terms of national peculiarities. In other words, a nation's behavior toward the rest of the world cannot be adequately explained as a function of the universal factors of power and interest when its behavior is irrelevant or even detrimental to those factors. And, as the debate over American international behavior has grown increasingly bitter, this idea has moved toward the center of a controversy among those who can agree only in their unhappiness with American foreign and military policy. . . .

Let us begin by dividing almost four centuries of military experience into smaller units of time, according to major changes in the historical situation. The seventeenth and eighteenth centuries appear as the first natural unit: they represent not merely "colonial background," but a formative period of quite serious military troubles which gave rise to considerable anxiety and led to ways of thinking about war, and of acting in war, that set British North America clearly apart from Europe. To call these first centuries an age of survival may seem hyperbolic, but military "survival," at least in a political if not a physical sense, was an important question for American society even to the end of the War of 1812. The second natural period, a golden age, or "age of free security" as [C. Vann] Woodward has called it, was the nineteenth century. There were of course wars and rumors of war in the nineteenth century, and it is possible to argue that the Civil War is the most important single episode in American history. But it is unreasonable to argue, as has recently been tried, that the nineteenth century was almost as full of real and perceived military perils and problems as is our own time. The truth is that for about a century after 1815 American society enjoyed, and was conscious of enjoying, a remarkable freedom from external military threat.

Exactly when the age of free security ended is a complex question, and the answer depends very much on our perspective. Woodward selects 1945; other historians would point to 1898. But the emerging tendencies of the third age, our own age, are clear enough. To call the twentieth century an age of power and insecurity sounds like a textbook cliché, but such a label is an accurate and useful characterization. On the one hand, by the turn of the century there was a growing sense of insecurity, of new threats perceived although the specific dangers could not, and even now cannot, be clearly defined. On the other hand, as American society itself grew in numbers and wealth, there was a growing accumulation of potential military power, with no apparent economic or demographic limits on how much military power it might be possible to accumulate. The limits of American power were thus not seen to be intrinsic, as they were in France, for example, but rather were to be set by the political process, which presumably would establish them on the

John Shy. "The American Military Experience: History and Learning," *Journal of Interdisciplinary History* 1, No. 2 (Winter 1971): 205, 210–218. Reprinted with the permission of the editors of *The Journal of Interdisciplinary History* and The MIT Press, Cambridge Massachusetts. © 1971 by the Massachusetts Institute of Technology and the editors of *The Journal of Interdisciplinary History.*

basis of some strategic calculation. But without clearly defined dangers, such calculations could not be made, at least not convincingly, and any politically established level of military power inevitably seemed arbitrary. These, then, are the principal features of American military experience since the end of the nineteenth century: military insecurity without a clear definition of danger, and military power without any apparent limits—the two constantly interacting to produce a kind of military indeterminacy, and giving a name to our own age of power and insecurity.

With the basic outline of American military experience established, we can now turn to the most important relationships and patterns within this general framework.

The first English colonies were planted in an extraordinarily violent and ideologically polarized period of Western history. It is an obvious point, but one that American historians for some reason have frequently ignored. They have tended instead to treat colonization as a successful flight from European violence and insecurity, as indeed it was seen by many colonists themselves; but to view colonization in that way hardly reduces the historical significance of this particular aspect of the environment in which the colonies originated. The early history of any seventeenth-century colony, even as late as the settlement of Pennsylvania and South Carolina, reveals that these were dangerous times, with violent people and tough leaders who felt the dangers keenly and were ready to use violence themselves. The frightfulness of the Thirty Years War, which coincided with the settlement of Virginia and Massachusetts, had been prefigured in late Elizabethan Ireland, and Irish pacification and early American colonization were closely related in method, problems, and personnel. We should remember, for example, that, while Sir Humphrey Gilbert allegedly prayed aloud when his ship foundered on his last voyage to the New World, he was much better known to contemporaries for the way he had lined the path to his tent with the severed heads of Irish peasants. Gilbert and his numerous English successors knew very well that their ventures in the Western Hemisphere were semi-military, semi-piratical intrusions on the established empire of Spain and the antecedent colonial claims of France. The likelihood of violent consequences was never far from their minds.

The irony is that during most of the seventeenth century these European threats failed to materialize. Instead, the chief threat came from those on whom considerable hopes had been centered. Conversion of Indians to Christianity stood higher among the priorities of early English colonizers, even in Virginia, than is usually recognized, and serious (though ultimately futile) efforts were devoted to that end. But the normal pattern of Anglo-Indian relations became one not of Christian conversion and worship, but of uneasy truce, punctuated by incredibly barbaric warfare, often followed by migration or subjugation. From about 1650 to about 1750, when European states were moving toward forms of military organization, techniques of fighting, goals of foreign policy, and a generally accepted code of military and diplomatic behavior that eliminated or mitigated the worst effects of warfare on society, the English colonists in North America found themselves reenacting on a small scale the horrors of Irish pacification and the Thirty Years War.

There is no need to exaggerate either the frequency of Indian warfare or the vulnerability of colonial society to it, but the difference between American and European military experience in this period is unmistakable and extremely important. The colonies did not have the means to create a hard military shell, composed of specialists, that could protect the soft center of society, composed of the great mass of people, nor would such a shell have been effective against Indian tactics. The colonies, as they become more heavily and densely populated, soon acquired a high military potential, much greater than that of even the strongest Indian tribes, but they never had more than a fairly low capacity for effective self-defense. The distinction between potential strength and defensive capacity is crucial. Moreover, the fighting strength of the colonies was mobilized in wartime only at the price of considerable social disruption caused by the militia system—a general, unspecialized obligation for military service. With great strength but weak defenses, the colonies experienced warfare less in terms of protection, of somehow insulating society against external violence (as was increasingly true of European warfare), than in terms of retribution, of retaliating against violence already committed.

The consequences of this situation would surely have been much less severe if, at the time when hostile Indians were losing their own capacity to do really serious harm to the English settlements, a long period of war between England and France, usually joined by Spain, had not begun. Both sides used Indian auxiliaries against the other, but the English were far more numerous; as a result, the relative weakness of the thinly populated neighboring French and Spanish settlements, plus the costliness and inefficiency of regular troops transported to the Western Hemisphere, forced the French and Spanish to depend heavily on Indian allies, and thus on the forms of Indian warfare. The effect was to perpetuate, and in some areas of English settlement even to intensify, the quality of the seventeenth-century military experience. This effect was further reinforced because these new dangers could be perceived in terms of anti-Catholicism, just at a time when religious antagonism was no longer a major factor in European diplomacy and warfare.

These European wars in America, like the purely Indian wars before them, puzzled and frustrated the English colonists. Invariably war originated in Europe, beyond their reach and even their understanding. Its causes had nothing to do with anything that had happened or been done in the colonies, or so it seemed, but every European war meant inevitable and often horrible death and suffering in the Western Hemisphere. Schemes of neutralization were tried but soon broke down. The delicate territorial adjustments of European diplomacy had no meaning in a wilderness where boundaries were seldom known (even when they could be established) and never respected, just as the elaborate defensive arrangements of forts and lines that suited the Low Countries or the Po Valley were almost completely ineffective where spaces were vast and armies ill-trained and numerically small.

Strong but highly vulnerable, angered and frightened by repeated and ruthless attack, bewildered by the causes of war, disrupted by its effects, and powerless to prevent it, articulate English colonists by the end of the seventeenth century were making extreme proposals for the solution of their military problem. Nothing would do, they wrote, but the complete elimination of French and Spanish power from North America; anything less, it was claimed by those who purported to speak for America, was worse than useless, because it would create a false sense of security. Of course these were fantastic demands by European standards; territorial exchanges and adjustments followed every eighteenth-century war, but the actual conquest and retention of large spaces was too costly militarily and too dangerous diplomatically. When the fortress of Bergen-op-Zoom—a place few colonists could have found on a map—fell to the French in 1747, it became necessary to give Cape Breton Island back to France after Massachusetts had seized it in 1745. These were the rules of the game, but the Americans wanted to change them. Even the Anglicized, judicious, and irenic Benjamin Franklin is found in 1760 reiterating what was by then the classic American demand for a definitive military solution. After recounting the atrocities of the French and Indian wars, he called for the "extirpation" of the French in Canada because of their manifold wickedness. He was writing for the public, to be sure, but there is no evidence to suggest that he did not sincerely believe every word that he wrote.

Several things may be said about this typically American belief that nothing less than a complete solution was required to solve the problem of American military security: One is that it seems a not unreasonable response to difficult military circumstances; another is that it was grossly unrealistic in terms of normal eighteenth-century international relations; a third is that in three great wars, from 1760 to 1815, it was almost completely realized. Precisely how and why an understandable but unrealistic belief which gave rise to a set of fantastic demands was translated into concrete reality is an interesting story; but more important here is the fact of realization itself.

Considered together, from the American point of view, the Seven Years War (1756–63), the Revolutionary War (1775–83), and the War of 1812 reveal a remarkable pattern. In each the very existence of American society was seen to be at stake; invasion and early defeats brought hopes in each of these wars to low ebb. But early setbacks were followed by military recovery, perseverance, and ultimate victory. And the magnitude of victory was the most remarkable and important similarity of all. In 1763, following British naval success so great as to be politically and diplomatically embarrassing, all French and Spanish power on the North American continent east of the Mississippi was actually "extirpated." The British government paid for these extraordinary military and diplomatic results when, twenty years later, isolated by its own success, it was forced by a hostile France, an unfriendly Europe, and rebellious Americans to give to the new United States most of what had been previously won. And thirty years later the United States, caught squarely between Napoleonic France and its strongest enemy, emerged from an unwanted war with a virtual (and within a few years obvious) guarantee that the threat of European military intervention in American affairs was finally at an end.

More might be said about the specific impressions created in the American mind by these great wars. Here it is enough to recognize their impact in a general way. Each war had a rhythm of defeat, despair, endurance, and victory. Each repetition of that rhythm reinforced the impression first made by the Seven Years War. Seen altogether and in conjunction with the earlier colonial experience, these wars repeated on a grand historical scale their own internal rhythmic structure: from the frequent little disasters and occasional despair of colonies that had been beset for a century by ruthless Indians and apparently "implacable" Catholics, to the recovery, total victory, and unique security of a free, successful, and republican nation.

The military experience of these first two centuries was described earlier as formative, and that description seems to be true in a quite literal way. American society entered its age of free security with certain military attitudes which had already been implanted and powerfully reinforced: (1) a deep respect for the kind of military prowess that had become so closely bound up with the very definition of American nationhood, a respect tinged with contempt for military professionalism which was viewed as unnecessary, ineffectual, and thus somehow un-American; (2) a concept of military security that was expressed not in relative but in absolute terms (the society knew both extremes: what had seemed to be total military insecurity, and what now looked like total military security—though opposite, the two were perceptually linked); and, (3) an extraordinary optimism about what, when necessary, could be achieved by the exertion of American military force, as the three wars demonstrated beyond all doubt.

Little happened in the nineteenth century to call any of these attitudes into question, and much to reinforce them still further. In particular, the belief that military security was an absolute value, like chastity or grace, and that American society had been granted it, presumably deserved it, and ought to be able to keep it, was verified simply by the passage of time without the appearance of any perceptible threat. Foreign relations ceased to attract the popular and political attention that they had received for so long. American diplomacy became increasingly freewheeling, even careless and bombastic, but the occasional confrontations with a European Power—with Spain over Florida after the War of 1812, with all the Powers over Latin American independence and recognition in the 1820s, with France over unpaid American claims in the 1830s, with Britain over Oregon in the 1840s, again with France over Mexico in the 1860s, with Germany over Samoa in the 1880s, with Britain and Germany over Venezuela at the end of the century—always ended in what looked very much like a Great Power back-down. And in fact no Great Power could find that its interests were served by pushing disagreement with the inept, unpredictable, but very numerous Americans to the point of war.

The several wars actually fought by the United States during the nineteenth century can be divided into two categories: the Civil War, and all the others. The others—the Mexican War, the Spanish-American War, and the many small wars against various Indian tribes—are a disparate group, but they have essential features in common. The causes of each could be traced back to atrocious behavior by the enemy: the usual murders and mutilation connected with every Indian War, the massacres of the Alamo and Goliad by the Mexicans, and the brutal pacification policies of the Spanish in Cuba. Enemy atrocities were by no means the only or even the main cause of these wars, and in all of them Americans themselves flagrantly broke the rules of civilized warfare—the Illinois militia in the Black Hawk War, Texans at San Jacinto, and the U.S. Army during the Philippine insurrection committed some major atrocities of their own. But the main point is that it was very easy for Americans to explain and justify the outbreak of war in terms of the criminal conduct of an inhuman, perhaps degenerate, foe. And once Americans had been attacked and killed, whether they were a few Western farmers or fur traders, a detachment of soldiers on the Rio Grande, or sailors on a battleship in Havana harbor, other arguments about the causes and the objectives of war came to seem irrelevant.

Each of these nineteenth-century wars also ended in a similar way, with an important extension of American territory and control. A defeated Indian tribe could mean the opening of a future state to American settlement; the Mexican War secured an enormous southwestern territory for the United States; and the war with Spain brought in its wake Hawaii, the Philippines, and new bases in the Pacific and Caribbean. These gains were not the avowed war aims of the United States, nor even the conscious objectives of most war leaders; rather, they seemed, under the circumstances, to be the natural rewards of superior virtue and military skill. . . .

The Early Republic and Limited War

REGINALD C. STUART

The limited-war mentality of the Revolutionary generation dominated American ideas about the origins, application, justice, and objectives of the use of force in world affairs from the mid-eighteenth century to the second decade of the nineteenth century. This mentality gathered elements of thought and experience from Christian precepts, Enlightenment ideals, European statecraft, concepts about the nature of man, historical evidence, views of the nature of international law, convictions about the nature of states, America's own colonial experience, and finally the apparent needs of the United States, which emerged from the imperial crisis of 1763–83 in the old British Empire. This attitude of mind toward war emphasized restraint and the exertion of reason in a realm where human passions normally display great power. Americans discovered that the same forces that had produced the age of limited wars in Europe—the need to gain the consent of parts or the whole of a populace, the costs, the vulnerability to retaliation, the scarcity of resources, the fear of defeat, the moral inhibitions about the use of violence, and the calculation of objectives—acted upon them. The Revolutionary leaders knew that war is a human act, premeditated and purposive, and while fearing its excesses, they employed it in the belief that it could be controlled. There were flaws in their reasoning, and contradictions brought about by the nature of war itself. But regarding European antagonists at least, the Revolutionary leaders assumed that nations in war stood as moral equals, subject to civilized practices. In conducting wars, suffering must be restricted, especially upon the innocent. The possibility of peace being swiftly restored must always be apparent, reprisals must be used sparingly as a deterrent to barbarism, and above all, statesmen must never forget that war is a method of arbitration between sovereign equals defending their self-defined interests, and not a crusade.

Although it is sometimes difficult to weld an amalgam of thought on the one hand to behavior or policy decisions on the other, there is no doubt that the Revolutionary leaders drew upon and applied the precepts of the limited-war mentality

Reginald C. Stuart from *War and American Thought: From the Revolution to the Monroe Doctrine* (Kent, Ohio: Kent State University Press, 1982). Reprinted with the permission of The Kent State University Press as they cultivated the interests of the United States, especially after 1783. In many ways, despite their republicanism and their moral idealism about international relations, they were typical eighteenth-century statesmen. The tenets of the *jus ad bellum* are evident in their foreign policy. The guidelines of the *jus in bello* operated during their conflicts with English, French, and even Indian enemies. Without succumbing to cynicism, they anticipated war in the future, just as they expected a republican democracy to be less aggressive and reluctant to fight, even when provoked. Crusading impulses interwove through the period of this generation's political domination of American affairs, yet these ideals never breached the barricades of restraint when it came to war. To a significant degree, the conflicts of the United States from 1775 to 1823 were limited wars of policy in the eighteenth-century tradition.

Contrasting forces worked against such restraint nevertheless. Human passions emerged in debates over the rights and applications of retaliation. Americans generally distinguished sharply between "civilized" and "savage" warfare as well. Against Indians, the inhibitions of the limited-war mentality exercised less control over American behavior.

And new trends arose which generated illusions about certain aspects of the limited-war mentality, culminating in the American war myth. This lay within eighteenth-century thinking about war and peace, but was dormant until an increasingly self-confident nationalism, combined with a greater sense of national security and self-righteousness regarding national ambitions, gave it shape. The American war myth emerged after 1815 as a developing American philosophy of war.

Another, and more significant point, was the tension which frequently existed between popular conceptions and those of the Revolutionary leaders when cast in their roles as policy-makers. American zeal for the French Revolution led to both popular and congressional opposition to George Washington's policy of strict neutrality in 1793. Building upon fear and suspicion of Great Britain, this enthusiasm contributed to the rise of the first party system, and carried into the Quasi-War with France. After Thomas Jefferson's triumph in 1800, such tensions subsided, but only for a time. They arose again, albeit in partisan form, during the Embargo of 1808 and during James Madison's administration over the policies that preceded the War of 1812 and the decision to fight. And the people disagreed among themselves, as well as with policy-makers, about whether and how force should be used.

These ideas carried beyond 1815, to popular responses to James K. Polk's campaigns to acquire Oregon from Britain and California from Mexico. He exploited the rhetoric of Manifest Destiny so well that he nearly found his country in a confrontation with the British. But diplomacy eased Oregon from partial to full ownership of the United States. Such was not the case with Mexico, and while the west and south supported Polk's limited war of policy for territory, significant segments of opinion in the midwest and northeast did not. Opposition spokesmen employed arguments drawn from the *jus ad bellum* to condemn the Mexican War of 1846 as unjust and immoral, a struggle for conquest and not for national rights.

The elements of the limited-war mentality survived in American thought, a legacy for generations following the Revolution. Albert Gallatin and John

Quincy Adams were still present in 1846 to articulate it in old-fashioned terms. But the significant point is that they reflected a segment of American opinion about the just use of force as an instrument of policy. And despite the power of the antebellum reform movement in the United States, pacifism remained a trivial, if noble, effort in terms of both numbers and influence. Among literary and intellectual circles, a strongly moralistic, even millennial view of war developed, which led to perceptions of the Civil War as a moral crusade and a positive force in the advancement of civilization. Against such convictions, pacifism made little headway, even as it failed to penetrate nationalism. The American war myth convinced many Americans that their system was peaceful, evidence to the contrary notwithstanding.

The influence of the limited-war mentality on the Civil War is less certain than on the conflicts of the Revolutionary generation, but it was nevertheless there. Many of America's leading soldiers and politicians took up arms with an eighteenth-century mentality that resisted crusading impulses. Among soldiers, the writings of the Baron Henri de Jomini had been widely known and absorbed. Jomini's military manual was highly technical, but it contained an underlying philosophy which accepted war as an integral part of civilization subject to control through the application of human reason. Jomini, horrified by the abandon of the Napoleonic struggles, deplored their fanaticism openly, preferring the order, harmony, and restraint of the previous age. Because of Jomini's influence, Civil War strategy betrayed elements of this fundamental perspective. Winfield Scott's anaconda plan, for example, sought to subdue the Confederacy with a minimum loss of life and destruction to property through the application of superior resources, rather than the Napoleonic wastage of superior manpower in furious battle. William Tecumseh Sherman and Philip Sheridan, renowned as practitioners of modern, even total warfare, did not lust for vengeance or view their cause as a crusade. . . .

A study of the attitudes of the Revolutionary generation toward war, and a brief survey of other aspects of the American experience with war in the nineteenth century, suggest that scholars have been working from a legend about the American view of war, rather than with legacies. More detailed study must be done before the legends and the legacies can be unravelled and clarified, but for the early period of its national existence, the United States had a cluster of leaders who had a firm grasp of the role of power in international affairs. And the evidence indicates that they reflected a broad consensus among Americans in which liberal-crusading attitudes played an insignificant part. It is unclear how and when this legend of the liberal-crusading, or anti-Clausewitzian, view of war arose. Although the American war myth suggests tracts of it as early as the period just after 1815, it reflects more a national self-righteousness in combination with ambitions transformed into grants from Heaven. And such attitudes, however they arose, are distinct from the development of total war in the modern world, and from the emergence of distinctive American strategic doctrines.

To say this is not to deny that Americans have ever fought on behalf of liberal principles. Mere defense of their society, which embodies liberalism, is not, however, a contradiction of Clausewitz's doctrine that force is an instrument of policy. The two concepts can coexist without clashing. The many components of the American character suggest that the American view of war is really a collection, and historically therefore a series of collections, of views. For example, the United States has always had a bourgeois character, with a strong emphasis on private ownership and the protection of property. Without accepting economic determinism, this character is reflected in the Revolutionary leaders' efforts to limit the impact of war on private property through strict rules for searches and seizures and later opposition to privateering. To take another example, Americans, although religiously heterogeneous, have been a dissenting, Protestant people, with a strong Calvinistic strain in their view of mankind. It is not surprising, therefore, that the Revolutionary generation frequently saw humanity's flawed nature as a source of war. Finally, Americans have been known as an optimistic people, with high hopes for future progress. Again, the Revolutionary generation's view of war reflects this. Both sectarian and nonsectarian pacifism is an extreme example of this general belief.

The Revolutionary generation drew from the legends and legacies of the past in composing and developing its views of war. In turn, it created legacies, some of which have become so distorted by subsequent generations that they became legends, only tenuously linked with the original thought and experience. The limited-war mentality had clear echoes through the nineteenth century, and even in the modern period with the advent of the Cold War and nuclear weapons. The limited-war mentality, while derivative of a distant time and set of circumstances, retains significance because it suggests the clear possibility of controlling war, although it offers little encouragement toward war's elimination from human affairs. It is the Revolutionary generation's legacy, and not the legend, which must inform our understanding of the American view of war. Only then will the nuances and complexities of mankind's attempts to grapple with the anomalies of armed forces, civilization, and national ambitions in the context of United States history become apparent.

♠ *F U R T H E R   R E A D I N G*

Stephen E. Ambrose, *Undaunted Courage: Meriwether Lewis, Thomas Jefferson, and the Opening of the American West* (1996).

Harrison Bird, *War for the West, 1790–1813* (1971).

Irving Brand, *James Madison: Commander in Chief, 1812–1836* (1961).

Harvey Lewis Carter, *The Life and Times of Little Turtle* (1987).

Edward M. Coffman, *The Old Army: A Portrait of the American Army in Peacetime, 1784–1898* (1986).

Theodore J. Crackel, *Mr. Jefferson's Army: Political and Social Reform of the Military Establishment, 1801–1809* (1987).

Lawrence Delbert Cress, *Citizens in Arms: The Army and Militia in American Society to the War of 1812* (1982).

Alexander DeConde, *The Quasi-War* (1966).

Russell David Edmunds, *Tecumseh and the Quest for Indian Leadership* (1984).

William M. Fowler, Jr., *Jack Tars and Commodores: The American Navy, 1783–1815* (1984).

Donald R. Hickey, *The War of 1812: A Forgotten Conflict* (1989).

Reginald Horsman, *The War of 1812* (1969).

John P. Kaminski and Richard Leffler, eds., *Federalists and Antifederalists: The Debate Over the Ratification of the Constitution* (1989).

Richard C. Knopf, ed., *Anthony Wayne, A Name in Arms: The Wayne-Knox-Pickering-McHenry Correspondence* (1960).

Richard H. Kohn, *Eagle and Sword: The Federalist and the Creation of the Military Establishment in America, 1783–1802* (1975).

____ ed., *The United States Military Under the Constitution of the United States, 1789–1989* (1991).

David Foster Long, *Gold Braid and Foreign Relations: Diplomatic Activities of U.S. Naval Officers, 1798–1883* (1988).

John K. Mahon, *The War of 1812* (1972).

Linda M. Maloney, *The Captain from Connecticut: The Life and Naval Times of Isaac Hull* (1986).

Christopher McKee, *A Gentlemanly and Honorable Profession: The Creation of the U.S. Naval Officer Corps, 1794–1815* (1991).

Paul David Nelson, *Anthony Wayne, Soldier of the Early Republic* (1985).

Frank Lawrence Owsley, Jr. *Struggle for the Gulf Borderlands: The Creek War and the Battle of New Orleans* (1981).

Michael A. Palmer, *Stoddert's War: Naval Operations During the Quasi-War with France, 1798–1801* (1987).

Francis P. Prucha, *The Sword of the Republic: The United States Army on the Frontier, 1783–1846* (1969).

Robert V. Remini, *Andrew Jackson and the Course of American Empire* (1977).

John Shy, "The American Military Experience: History and Learning," *Journal of Interdisciplinary History* 1 (Winter 1971): 205–228.

Marshall Smelser, *The Congress Founds the Navy, 1787–1798* (1959).

Burton Spivak, *Jefferson's English Crisis: Commerce, Embargo, and the Republican Revolution* (1979).

J. C. A. Stagg, *Mr. Madison's War: Politics, Diplomacy, and Warfare in the Early American Republic, 1783–1830* (1983).

Reginald C. Stuart, *War and American Thought: From the Revolution to the Monroe Doctrine* (1982).

Wiley Sword, *President Washington's Indian War: The Struggle for the Old Northwest, 1790–1795* (1985).

Craig L. Symonds, *Navalists and Antinavalists: The Naval Policy Debate in the United States, 1785–1827* (1980).

Glenn Tucker, *Dawn Like Thunder: The Barbary Wars and the Birth of the United States Navy* (1963).

Ernest Lee Tuveson, *Redeemer Nation: The Idea of America's Millennial Role* (1968).

Steven Watts, *The Republic Reborn: War and the Making of Liberal America* (1987).

A. B. C. Whipple, *To the Shores of Tripoli: The Birth of the U.S. Navy and Marines* (1991).

C. Vann Woodward, *"The Age of Reinterpretation,"* *American Historical Review 66 (Oct. 1960): 1–19.*

CHAPTER
5

The Army, Professionalism, Jacksonian Democracy, and Manifest Destiny

As one of the primary instruments of expansion, the military played important if various roles in the Age of Manifest Destiny between the Jacksonian Era of the 1830s and the Civil War. The U.S. Army, sometimes accompanied by militia or ad hoc units of the locally raised and federally funded U.S. Volunteers, implemented government policy in helping to extend American territory and settlement through the Seminole Wars, the removal of the Cherokees and other Indians to the trans-Mississippi West, and the Mexican-American War of 1846–1848, in which President James K. Polk sought to obtain the West and Southwest for the United States. Contemporaries were divided over the wisdom and probity of these actions. Historians have continued to debate their necessity and morality, but have also sought to understand them in their historical context and to explore what such actions and justifications tell us about international relations, American society, and military developments. In addition to examining strategy and battle tactics, military historians of the period also ask about internal developments within the military and about the relationship of the military to the major developments of the period.

The antebellum period also saw important changes in the nation's military institutions, particularly the increased professionalization of the regular officer corps and, at least in the North, the replacement of the traditional, compulsory common militia by volunteer state units of the National Guard. The development of a distinct, disciplined, and cohesive military profession in Jacksonian civilian society, which emphasized unrestrained individualism and entrepreneurialism, and cherished egalitarianism, led to heightened tensions. Stressing values of expertise and self-sacrifice for the nation, the officer corps found itself increasingly detached from civil society. Jacksonian Democrats disdained the regular army officer corps as a fledgling aristocracy and a potential threat to democracy and, in the American popular tradition, celebrated the citizen-soldiers over the regulars. While traditional history has emphasized those citizen-soldiers, military historians have become increasingly interested in the origins of this professionalization in the officer corps and its relationship to the era.

♠ D O C U M E N T S

Few Americans were greater champions of westward expansion and Indian removal
than President Andrew Jackson, who in the first document, an excerpt from his annual
message to Congress in 1830, justified the voluntary or coerced removal of the southeastern Indians to the trans-Mississippi West, which he said was for the Indians' own
benefit. The second document, actually two lithographs (illustrations which were
widely circulated) from the 1830s and 1840s, depicts the transformation of the militia,
the first lampooning the common militia or "scarecrow militia," the second touting the
impressive appearance and discipline of the volunteer National Guard, in this case an
artillery unit of the New York National Guard. In the third document, West Point graduate and regular army Lieutenant Joseph R. Smith, in a letter to his wife in 1838, during the Second Seminole War, complains of the lack of understanding and respect
from civilian society for the army officers. Like the nation, the officer corps was divided over the morality of the Seminole Wars and the Mexican-American War. In the
fourth document, excerpts from the diary of Ethan Allen Hitchcock, a regular army officer and descendant of Revolutionary War patriot Ethan Allen, reflected much New
England sentiment when as a major in 1840, he agonized over the Second Seminole
War and as a colonel in 1846, he criticized the U.S. government's policies and the
army's role in initiating the Mexican-American War. (Despite his criticism, he decided
not to resign but to try to reform the army from within; he did eventually help to write
a code of conduct during the Civil War.) In the fifth document, William Tecumseh
Sherman, a West Pointer who was then a first lieutenant, belittles the probability of
war with Mexico in 1844; like an increasing number of military officers, he disdained
any involvement in politics. Despite Sherman's prediction, the United States did, of
course, go to war with Mexico and achieved a number of U.S. military victories,
including General Zachary Taylor's siege and capture of the provincial capital of
Monterrey in northern Mexico in September 1846, an action described in the sixth
document in a letter to a friend by D. L. Goodall, a member of the Tennessee Volunteers, two weeks after the citadel had surrendered. In the peace treaty of Guadalupe
Hidalgo, in addition to acquiring the West and Southwest, the United States agreed to
try to control the Comanches who raided both sides of the new U.S.-Mexican border.
The Second U.S. Cavalry Regiment was subsequently formed for that task, and
Colonel Albert Sidney Johnston, a leading Texas military officer and a veteran of the
battle of Monterrey, was appointed to command the regiment. In the final document,
Eliza Griffin Johnson, the colonel's wife, provides a diary account of a seven hundred-
mile journey of the regiment, along with wives, children, slaves, and servants, from St.
Louis, Missouri, through Indian territory to its headquarters near San Antonio, Texas,
between October 1855 and May 1856.

1. President Andrew Jackson Calls for Removal of the Indians, 1830

. . . It gives me pleasure to announce to Congress that the benevolent policy of the
Government, steadily pursued for nearly thirty years, in relation to the removal of
the Indians beyond the white settlements is approaching to a happy consummation.

From Andrew Jackson. "Second Annual Message to Congress," December 6, 1830, in J. D. Richardson,
ed. *A Compilation of the Messages and Papers of the Presidents* (New York: Bureau of National Literature, 1897), III, 1082–1086.

Two important tribes have accepted the provision made for their removal at the last session of Congress, and it is believed that their example will induce the remaining tribes also to seek the same obvious advantages.

The consequences of a speedy removal will be important to the United States, to individual States, and to the Indians themselves. The pecuniary advantages which it promises to the Government are the least of its recommendations. It puts an end to all possible danger of collision between the authorities of the General and State Governments on account of the Indians. It will place a dense and civilized population in land tracts of country now occupied by a few savage hunters. By opening the whole territory between Tennessee on the north and Louisiana on the south to the settlement of the whites it will incalculably strengthen the southwestern frontier and render the adjacent States strong enough to repel future invasions without remote aid. It will relieve the whole State of Mississippi and the western part of Alabama of Indian occupancy, and enable those States to advance rapidly in population, wealth, and power. It will separate the Indians from immediate contact with settlements of whites; free them from the power of the States; enable them to pursue happiness in their own way and under their own rule institutions; will retard the progress of decay, which is lessening their numbers, and perhaps cause them gradually, under the protection of the Government and through the influence of good counsels, to cast off their savage habits and become an interesting, civilized, and Christian community. These consequences, some of them so certain and the rest so probable, make the complete execution of the plan sanctioned by Congress at their last session an object of much solicitude.

Toward the aborigines of the country no one can indulge a more friendly feeling than myself, or would go further in attempting to reclaim them from their wandering habits and make them a happy, prosperous people. I have endeavored to impress upon them my own solemn convictions of the duties and powers of the General Government in relation to the State authorities. For the justice of the laws passed by the States within the scope of their reserved powers they are not responsible to this Government. As individuals we may entertain and express our opinions of their acts, but as a Government we have as little right to control them as we have to prescribe laws for other nations. . . .

Humanity has often wept over the fate of the aborigines of this country, and Philanthropy has been long busily employed in devising means to avert it, but its progress has never for a moment been arrested, and one by one have many powerful tribes disappeared from the earth. . . . Philanthropy could not wish to see this continent restored to the condition in which it was found by our forefathers. What good man would prefer a country covered with forests and ranged by a few thousand savages to our extensive Republic, studded with cities, towns, and prosperous farms, embellished with all the improvements which art can devise or industry execute, occupied by more than 12,000,000 happy people, and filled with all the blessings of liberty, civilization, and religion?

The present policy of the Government is but a continuation of the same progressive change by a milder process. The tribes which occupied the countries now constituting the Eastern States were annihilated or have melted away to make room for the whites. The waves of population and civilization are rolling to the westward, and we now propose to acquire the countries occupied by the red men of the South and West by a fair exchange, and, at the expense of the United States, to send them to a land where their existence may be prolonged and perhaps made perpetual. Doubtless it will be painful to leave the graves of their fathers; but what do they more than our ancestors did or than our children are now doing? To better their condition in an unknown land our forefathers left all that was dear in earthly objects. . . .

. . . Rightly considered, the policy of the General Government toward the red man is not only liberal, but generous. He is unwilling to submit to the laws of the States and mingle with their population. To save him from this alternative, or perhaps utter annihilation, the General Government kindly offers him a new home, and proposes to pay the whole expense of his removal and settlement. . . .

May we not hope, therefore, that all good citizens, and none more zealously than those who think the Indians oppressed by subjection to the laws of the States, will unite in attempting to open the eyes of those children of the forest to their true condition, and by a speedy removal to relieve them from all the evils, real or imaginary, present or prospective, with which they may be supposed to be threatened. . . .

2. From "Scarecrow Militia" to Volunteer National Guard Units: Contrasting Lithographs (1836, 1843)

A militia muster is the subject of this lithograph by David Claypoole Johnston, ca. 1836. The scene is somewhere in New England, perhaps Boston. The ragged lineup could have been seen almost anywhere in the United States. The only man in uniform is the officer on the right; and he has overdone his finery.

From the Anne S. K. Brown Military Collection, Brown University. Reprinted in Marcus Cunliffe. *Soldiers and Civilians: The Martial Spirit in America, 1775–1865* (Boston: Little, Brown, 1968), 212, 231.

In this lithograph (ca. 1843) members of an elite New York State militia regiment gather for a muster. All volunteer units like the New York 38th restricted their membership by requiring militiamen to supply lavish uniforms or by imposing other requirements.

3. First Lieutenant Joseph R. Smith Bemoans Lack of Civilian Respect, 1838

Ft. Brooke
13 March 1838

. . . I write this from my sick room. Five days since, I was attacked with the dysentary again;—and the Dr. cannot, as yet, control the movements of my bowels. I am writing this letter, supposing it may be the last one I shall write you. For I cannot conceal from myself that I am pretty sick. I have thought much of dying lately, since my sickness. And oh my love, the pang of parting with you and our babes,—is the severest one I meet. . . .

Fort Brooke Fla
[March 1838]

Again I am seated at my desk to write to you. My health, I think, continues to improve,—but I am sure, that with your care, and affectionate attentions, and the northern atmosphere,—and by the blessing of God, I might soon be well. Genl.

First Lieutenant Joseph R. Smith to his wife, March 13 and March 6, 1838, excerpted in John K. Mahon, ed., "Letters from the Second Seminole War," *Florida Historical Quarterly* 36 (April 1958): 339-340. Reprinted with permission.

Jesup has answered my application by saying that as a principal part of my regiment are serving in Florida, I must continue, and do duty with them. I have also made application to the Agt. Genl., if he decides against me, then the Colonel's answer to my letter resigning my adjutantcy;—will be received in about four or five weeks;—if he decides against me I may be compelled to resign rather than sacrifice my health here during the summer. But, oh, what a prospect for me, with a wife and four children, and no means but my present pay and profession. But I desire to put my trust and confidence in God . . . For myself, I could get along very well;—but you and our children;—it grieves me to think of it.

. . . I have just written to sister Louisa by Col. Davenport, of the army . . . I enclosed a $50. U.S. Bank note to her. I hope the time is not very far distant when we can offer her a permanent home. If Henry could help me to anything, by which with application I could support us,—I would willingly quit a profession for which,—I think there is no longer a feeling of respect entertained by the country. . . .

4. General Ethan Allen Hitchcock Agonizes over the Seminole and Mexican Wars, 1840–1848

"June 22. [1840] We are ordered to St. Louis (Jefferson Barracks) and then, after the sickly season, to Florida. I saw the beginning of the Florida campaigns in 1836, and may see the end of them unless they see the end of me. The government is in the wrong, and this is the chief cause of the persevering opposition of the Indians, who have nobly defended their country against our attempt to enforce a fraudulent treaty. The natives used every means to avoid a war, but were forced into it by the tyranny of our government." . . .

[Fort King, Nov. 4, 1840] "The treaty of Payne's Landing was a fraud on the Indians: They never approved of it or signed it. They are right in defending their homes and we ought to let them alone. The country southward is poor for our purposes, but magnificent for the Indians—a fishing and hunting country without agricultural inducements. The climate is against us and is a paradise for them. The army has done all that it could. It has marched all over the upper part of Florida. It has burned all the towns and destroyed all the planted fields. Yet, though the Indians are broken up and scattered, they exist in large numbers, separated, but worse than ever. . . . The chief, Coocoochee, is in the vicinity. It is said that he hates the whites so bitterly that 'he never hears them mentioned without gnashing his teeth.'" . . .

[Nov. 14, 1840] "General Armistead is entirely subdued and broken-spirited. His confidence in his success has been boundless and his letters to Washington have doubtless been written in that temper. I cannot help thinking it is partly his own fault. If he had freely offered the Indians an ample reward to emigrate, or the undisturbed possession of the country south of Tampa Bay, he might have secured peace. I have suggested his making the overture now, but he declines. Not only did he refuse to make the offer he was authorized to make, but at the very time when

From Ethan Allen Hitchcock. *Fifty Years in Camp and Field: Diary of Major-General Ethan Allen Hitchcock, U.S.A.,* edited by William A. Croffutt (New York: G. P. Putnam's Sons, 1909), 120, 122, 129, 200, 203, 212, 224–225.

Halec was here in amicable talk he secretly sent a force into his rear, threatening his people at home. . . . I confess to a very considerable disgust in this service. I remember the cause of the war, and that annoys me. I think of the folly and stupidity with which it has been conducted, particularly of the puerile character of the present commanding general, and I am quite out of patience." . . .

[Letters Hitchcock to Rep. John Bell, Chair of House Indian Affairs Committee, February 1841]

"Our troops, in moving about the country, have scattered the Indians in every direction; to avoid us, they hide in small parties, taking every precaution to prevent discovery—not building fires, even, for fear of disclosing their hiding-places by the smoke. It is almost impossible for them to find each other; while searching for their friends they may be within a few yards and not know of each other's vicinity. . . . To carry on such a war seems an idle, if not a wicked waste of life and treasure. Lately a party of dragoons, moving a hundred and fifty miles and sending out detachments to right and left, sweeping a breadth of country all the way, brought, in as captives, one man, his wife, and five children!

"Not a single war party, after striking a blow, has been captured by us, so far as I know, out of the multitude of instances of pursuit since this war began. Flight with them has become a science. . . .

"The conclusion, then, is this: that the government will actually gain time and save money, lives, and reputation, by conceding something to the Indians under their present prejudices and alarm—acknowledging their possession (by a truce, not a treaty) of as much of the country as will satisfy them; then seeking amicable intercourse with them, dissipating their prejudices, allaying their fears, soothing them, and finally persuading them to go and join their friends in Arkansas by the promise of that justice which was denied them in the insolence of supposed power in the beginning of the war.

"There is now a tendency on the part of the Indians to abstain from acts of war. Let this be fostered by pacific communications. Some will come in and be induced to emigrate. Others will gradually lay aside the rifle, and the war will die a natural death. It may require time to accomplish this amicably; but it is certain that force cannot effect it in a much longer time if at all." . . .

[Mexican War, 1846–1848] [Diary, Sept. 7, 1846]

"General Taylor talks, whether sincerely or not, of going to the Rio Grande. This is singular language from one who originally and till very lately denounced annexation as both injudicious in policy and wicked in fact! The 'claim,' so-called, of the Texans to the Rio Grande, is without foundation." . . .

Diary "2d Nov. 1846 Newspapers all seem to indicate that Mexico will make no movement, and the government is magnanimously bent on taking advantage of it to insist upon 'our claim' as far as the Rio Grande. I hold this to be monstrous and abominable. But now, I see, the United States of America, as a people, are undergoing changes in character, and the real status and principles for which our forefathers fought are fast being lost sight of. If I could by any decent means get a living in retirement, I would abandon a government which I think corrupted by both ambition and avarice to the last degree." . . .

[Diary, March 25, 1846] "Since crossing the Colorado we hear a multitude of reports of the most contradictory character. At one moment we hear of a large force crossing the Rio Grande at Matamoras to destroy us; then we hear that the people are in favor of our approach and everything is quiet. We hear that 700 men are on our rear and have been following us for several days. They have not been anxious to overtake us, for we have moved slowly. I have been very much prostrated in strength—never was so weak and now I can scarcely hold my pencil to write legibly.

"As to the right of this movement, I have said from the first that the United States are the aggressors. We have outraged the Mexican government and people by an arrogance and presumption that deserve to be punished. For ten years we have been encroaching on Mexico and insulting her. The Mexicans have in the whole of this time done but two wrong things: one was the destruction of the Con-stitution of 1824, which would have converted Texas into a mere department of Mexico; this gave Texas the right of revolution, and she established her independ-ence as far west as the Nueces—no further; the other was the cold-blooded and savage murder of Fannin's men at Goliad—an individual piece of barbarity which has deprived the Mexican army of all respect among civilized people. Beyond these, I know of nothing Mexico has done to deserve censure. Her people I con-sider a simple, well disposed, pastoral race, no way inclined to savage usages." . . .

"New Orleans, 21st Apr. [1846] Reached the St. Charles Hotel at about half past 11 last night and was instantly surrounded by a dozen editors and reporters, eager for news. Have been giving them news ever since.

"April 22. Have ordered sixteen boxes of books to St. Louis ahead of me. Have received from the translator a manuscript copy of Spinoza's *Tractatus.*

"29th Apr. Old steamer *Louisiana,* above Natchez. Left New Orleans the 26th. Am reading Humboldt's *Cosmos.* It is very fascinating and full of promise. Physi-cally, I have alarming symptoms of a fistula. I fancy myself going to a Philadelphia surgeon on a horrible mission. Well, I had as soon die there as anywhere. About November last Dr. Kennedy and others urged me strongly to leave Corpus Christi and go north, but in the unsettled state of affairs with Mexico I was unwilling to leave the regiment that was under my command. But I became useless to the regi-ment and the army.

"St Louis, Mo., May 5. Arrived yesterday morning. Warmly welcomed by friends. Gave Dr. Beaumont a detailed account of my twelve or more months of out-of-healthness.

"11th May. There has been at last an actual conflict on the Rio Grande. Cap-tain Thornton and Lieutenant Kane were sent out with fifty or sixty men. Both these officers were killed and the residue taken prisoners. Colonel Cross was also waylaid and murdered not far from our camp.

"St. Louis, 20th May. Have just received the message of President Polk based on the capture of Thornton's party. It occupies two columns in a good-sized news-paper. The President gives a history ('his-story') of our intercourse with Mexico for the last twenty years, in which he would make it appear that we have been the most injured, patient, and forbearing people in the world! Now that war exists, we must prosecute it with vigor, etc., etc. The President says, in effect, that, anticipat-ing the acts of war that have now taken place, he some months since authorized General Taylor to call into his service volunteers, etc. *Why* did he anticipate such conduct? Ans.: Because he himself had provoked it by the most outrageous insults to Mexico—and not only insults but aggression. He ordered our troops a hundred and fifty miles beyond the proper boundary of Texas into Mexican territory, and because the Mexicans presumed to send troops east of the Rio Grande, upon their own rightful soil, he says they are upon 'our territory.' We ought to be scourged for this!

"Sunday, May 24. General Taylor has had two fights between Matamoras and Point Isabel, in which he lost some very valuable men, but successfully cleared the region of Mexicans, capturing their cannon, killing many, and taking many prisoners, among them General Vega. Our Major Ringgold died of his wounds. It is said that Major Brown has also died of wounds received in defending our post opposite Matamoras.

"I am necessarily losing, from a military point of view, all the honors of the field. I was hoping that no collision would take place. . . . My absence from my regiment at such a time as this is a species of death; yet the doctor says I must not think of going south in the hot weather, as he has another surgical operation to perform. If I go back before my constitution is renovated, the disease will return in an aggravated form, so that I shall be of no service, and shall only destroy myself.

"St. Louis, June 5th. The newspapers announce the entrance of General Taylor into Matamoras and the complete dispersion of the Mexican army from that point: . . . I wish I could describe the lovely quiet rustic scenery I have viewed today. What a beautiful world for man to disturb by unjust wars and commotions!

"June 12. Colonel Kearney, 1st Dragoons, now preparing an expedition against Santa Fé, has written and offered me the appointment of inspector-general of his army. I have thanked him but told him I am not in health and had applied for other service in anticipation of returning health." . . .

5. Lieutenant William T. Sherman Disdains Politics, 1844

Fort Moultrie, S. C., September 17, 1844.

. . . Rumor too says that there is a decided war spirit at Washington caused by a late message from Texas and a report that England is supplying Mexico with arms and munitions of war to enable her to capture Texas. Newspapers have been crying war so much that nobody will believe them when there is real danger. Should there be the least foundation for such reports, they will soon be made public, and if any movement of troops is made in consequence, ours will surely go to Galveston. But it is all surmise as yet, and I do not believe there is a shadow of chance for so fortunate a war. War as such is to be deprecated, but if it is necessary for the interests or honor of the country of course I may with perfect propriety rejoice at the opportunity of being able to practice what in peace we can only profess. But I never believe that we are to have a war that costs money. Our Government talks and bullies a good deal, but when they talk of money they are frightened. Without it, war cannot be carried on. No doubt you are in the midst of election excitements and have to grieve at the constant absence of your father. For his sake I do really wish the elections over and that Clay may be our President, but it is my belief that such will

From Lieutenant William Tecumseh Sherman to Ellen Ewing, September 17, 1844. In M. A. DeWolfe Howe, ed. *Home Letters of General Sherman* (New York: Scribner's Sons, 1909), 26–27.

not be the case. I am not very sanguine. The people of this country are truly sovereign and, like such, are fickle in the extreme, varying from one party to the other without rhyme or reason. I call myself a Whig and usually in conversation advocate their claims, for the simple reason that my family and friends belong to that party; but as long as I hold a commission in the service of the government it is my intention and duty to abstain from any active part in political matters and discussions, and for that reason I never permit myself to become interested in the success of either party. Like a veteran of our service who has served and fought under every President once remarked in his native Dutch tongue, "I've fought for every chief magistrate, Washington and all. I've heard all branded as liars and scoundrels, eulogized as patriots and statesmen, but for his part he thought all bad enough for him." Here in Carolina we have no politics except now and then a blow out like Nullification, which ends in smoke. . . .

6. D. L. Goodall, a Tennessee Volunteer, Exults in the Battle of Monterrey, Mexico, 1846

Camp Allen near Monterrey Mexico
October 10. 1846

Dear Cousin,

We arrived here on the 17th Sept and encamped some three miles from Monterrey. It is necessary that I should give you a description of the city it is surrounded on three sides by impassable mountains the east south and west. On Sunday evening Genl Worth marched out with his force to gain a pass that leads into the interior of the country on the south-west. The Volunteers under Genl Butler were to attack the city on the north and Genl Twiggs on the east. On Monday morning we marched out in battle array before the middle of the city. We did not remain long in this position before we heard a heavy firing at the lower fort at the east end of the City. Genl Twiggs had made an attack on it with three small regiments of regulars and the Baltimore battalion. The Tennesseeans and Mississippians under Genl. Quitman were ordered to sustain Genl. Twiggs in his attack. In getting to this fort we were exposed to a very destructive fire from the enemys batteries for they had three of them playing upon us for a mile and a half, as we drew near the fort to our surprise we found that Twiggs command had been repulsed or withdrawn. Now was the time to try the nerve of Tennesseeans. The Mississippians being riflemen could do nothing in a charge, it consequently devolved on Tennessee to take the lead. Thus within one hundred and fifty yards of the fort we were ordered to the charge. The Tennesseeans bravely . . . charged the Cannons mouth and drove the enemy from it and in a few minutes [sic] was seen the first foreign flag that ever was seen floating from the walls of Monterrey. It was the Stars and Stripes of our beloved country planted there by the brave boys of Tennessee though not without the loss of many a noble fellow. We had thirty Killed in our Regiment and

From D. L. Goodall to Noel E. Winston, October 10, 1846. From Garrett Family Collection, East Carolina Manuscript Collection, East Carolina University, Greenville, N.C.

eighty wounded. We had but one Killed dead in our company it was Booker H. Dalton[.] Raphile has since died of his wounds. James M. Vance slightly wounded in the foot. Albert Tomlinson slightly wounded thigh. R. C. Locke badly wounded in the hip and considered dangerous. Crance shot in the leg badly. An Irishman by the name of Kelly right arm broke doubtful whether he will recover. Maj Alexander while rushing bravely to the charge was badly wounded in the abdomen near the right hipbone with a grape shot. He is rapidly recovering. The wounded are getting along badly some one dying every day. We were ordered to camp on Monday evening and Tuesday morning marched back to it and remained there until Wednesday morning. On the morning of the 23rd Genl. Quitman ordered three of the Tennessee Companies and the Mississippi Regiment to charge a fort in the City. Which they did with success this brought on a general engagement which continued till night closed the horrible scene. This was a fatal day to the Mexicans. We drove them from house to house breaking down their doors and shooting them on the housetops and crowding the streets with their dead. This awful and terrific scene the Mexicans could not stand for they were completely surrounded by Worth on the west and south and our m[en] in the east and north. They were cut off entirely from their provision. On the 24th Ampudia sent in a flag for a parley which was received by Genl Taylor. They entered into an armistice for eight weeks. Ampudia was permitted to march out with the honors of war and carry with him all his small arms and six pieces of artillery. So ends this imperfect outline of the battle. We are now encamped in four or five miles of town in a high and healthy country. I have said nothing about our commanders. We were led on by Capt Bennett and Lieut Duffy and I assure you they both behaved cooly and led us on bravely to the charge If you should see John M. Madding give him my warmest respects for he is worthy the respects of all high minded and honorable men for I say to you that there is no man in the army more deserving than him. I got Tom Duffy to Copy my letter as he wrote faster and better. You doubtless have heard of the deaths of Jim Stubblefield and Tom Seawell. Jim died at Point Isabel on the day of Tom died at Camargo on the day of[.]

Capt Bennett Luiet. Duffy and Tom send their best respects. Write often. Don't fail

D L. Goodall

Noel. Tell Harry Lauderdale that he deserves "the deepest anathemas of the human race" for the way he has treated us about writing. Tom Duffy

7. Eliza Johnston, an Army Wife, Reports on an Expedition Through Indian Territory, 1855–1856

Monday Oct 29th 1855

Well here am I soldiering. My gude man appointed Col of *2nd* Reg of Cavalry a new Reg just enlisted, we are on the march with 850 men for the Texas frontier. I have been at Jefferson Barracks for two weeks waiting for transportation to be

From "The Diary of Eliza (Mrs. Albert Sidney) Johnston,: The Second Cavalry Comes to Texas," edited by Charles P. Roland and Richard C. Robbins, *The Southwestern Historical Quarterly* 60, no. 4 (April 1957): 467-468, 478-480, 483-484, 487-488, 492-493, 500. Reprinted courtesy of the Texas State Historical Association, Austin.

supplied which all counted only amounts to 29 waggons the most of the Regimental property has been sent round by sea. My first experience in garrison life has rather disgusted me, the day after my arrival at the Barracks I was shocked and distressed to hear that 6 of my husbands men had been whipped, and were to be drummed out being attracted to the window next morning by music at an unusual hour I saw the poor fellows with shaven heads marched round the garrison to the tune of poor old soldier, surely-surely, some less degrading mode of punishment can be substituted. The Regiment marched on Saturday 27th Oct 1855 having had ague every other day since arriving at the Barracks, I was unable to leave with them on Saturday, it being my chill day, husband waited for me (placing the Reg under Col Hardee), until next day Sunday had a hard march to overtake the Reg, at about 9 oclock at night, where they were camped in a thick woodland, the scene on driving through the camp in the darkness with a thousand camp fires blazing around the white tents with the glimmering fire light shining upon them the soldiers standing around some bending over the Kettles cooking their suppers others seated on their blankets talking over the expected pleasures of the campaign. as a great accommodation and on account of ill health I was permitted to sleep on the floor of an old school house as a cold drizzling rain was falling. Quartermaster Johnson gave us our supper. Tonight I camped with the rest sleeping on the ground in a tent, the little ones enjoying the frolic vastly. our wall tent is just 10 feet square. excellent beef was supplied us today by our butcher with whom a contract is made to supply the Reg through the whole march. A Soldier was so tipsy that he fell from his horse and was killed he was burried on the roadside. . . .

Tuesday Dec 4th

Marched 20 miles saw some very comfortable Indian farms, saw two Indians far off in Prairie lurking about in the high grass. two of the Pioneers unslung their carbines and galloped towards them thinking they were some wild animal, but on closer inspection discovered their mistake Mr Field related an anecdote yesterday of their stealthy movements he another officer & about 30 or 40 men had taken about 20 Indian prisoners men women & children when they had nearly reached their evening camp, they saw an Indian coming in a long trot after them he said they had taken his wife and children and he wished to be taken prisoner with them. that night after placing the prisoners in the centre of the camp with two sentinels watching them, a shot was heard about 2 oclock all the whites were at once on the alert and it was discovered that man with his wife and children had escaped crawling off into the darkness from under the very eyes of the sentinels. after getting them clear his Indian nature would not permit him to go without stealing a white horse which he did successfully. it was then he was discovered but all his family escaped. We crossed the North Canadien today where there is a small Indian village. clear day but cold. The officers continually have difficulties with our beef contractor Saw a larg [*sic*] Lovos on the Prairie. the wolves have been howling around us for several nights, coming up closely to the tents . . .

Thursday Dec 6th

Marched 20 miles over the roughest road we have yet had. yesterday the Genl had at the request of Mr W. to examine into some reports set on foot about him by

Capt T. the latter accused the former of stealing 250 dollars from his room the latter a mean fellow the former a gentleman born and bred. no one respects or believes a word the Capt says so no credit is given the accusation. Mr W will have the Capt courtmartialed for slander and Conduct unbecoming an officer and gentleman in cheating at cards &c. The Capt sent Maggie a Paroquet today which he shot. The road today passed through the territory belonging to the Creek Nation. was thickly covered with sandstone some in the natural state others having the appearance of having been melted and cooled in ripples. Camped on Gains Creek . . .

Saturday 22nd

Marched 15 miles camped at Buffalo Springs Ellen quite sick with dysentary, thought she was going to die last night & made me promise to keep Martin her nephew. at 8 o'clock the coldest norther I ever felt after a delightful spring day. all the fires had to be put out in Camp. and we found it impossible to keep warm. The thermometer 4 degrees below zero.

Sunday 23

Could not march the wind blowing almost a Hurricane and cold bitter cold had to take Ran & Ellen into our tent on account of the cold. they were nearly frozen. George & little Martin crawled into the carriage. so cold we laid in bed till 12 oclock in the day, and fed the children with cold bread & a slice of ham. Got up at 1 oclock but did nothing but try to keep warm and could not succeed. poor little Maggie crying with the cold and impossible to get near the fire the smoke whirling round in eddys nearly puts out our eyes. I sit with Maggie on my knee trying to keep her warm and roll Sid and Clung up in blankets. went to bed at 6 oclock without dinner or supper after giving little ones a few crackers. had a nice piece of antelope sent us by Mr Low yesterday. today it was frozen so hard we could not cut it with an axe. the water frozen and the men cut it out in blocks 6 inches thick, of clear solid ice. setting in a bucket by the fire it freezes so rapidly we can scarcely use it fast enough. . . .

8th Jan.

It has been so cold for 3 days past that I could not write we have still been travelling through a beautiful country, live oak groves fine scenery and good soil. day before yesterday 6*th* Jan. immense quantities of iron ore covered the earth. weather still clear, but cold eating our meals picknick fashion, gypsey style is not so agreeable, with the thermometer at 9 above zero, and the hot coffee at your side freezing before it can be drank on the 7*th* passed the southern boundary of Peters Colony marked by a post on each side the road. today passed the Fort Gates & Austin roads camped at their junction with the Fort Mason road. found here holes of water in the bed of a creek filled with fish of all sizes from 2½ feet down, the holes frozen over and the fish torpid or just moving, the men had a fine feast on them & they sent me enough for a fine fish fry for dinner. I have never seen such prolonged cold weather in Texas we have had but one temperate day since the 22*nd* of Dec. one of the men died this evening though he had complained for several days he was able to ride his horse and walk about, had eaten his supper & smoked his pipe after coming in to camp this evening, and was sitting on a log talking to one of the sick men, when he fell over and said his bowels pained him and died in a few minutes

9th Jan

The poor man was buried on the road side and a cross placed at his head. large logs were heaped over his grave to keep the wolves from digging him up without a coffin. he was buried in his uniform and his military cloak wrapped round him. . . . he was but 21 years old and an excellent soldier. It was a sad thing for his comrades to march by his grave, and leave him in that great solitude I thought as we passed his lonely grave this morning that a poor mother & sisters and brothers perhaps were looking for his success in life and his return in 5 years with laurels. poor mother poor sister you will never see his loved face again . . .

March 30*th* 1856.

A long time has elapsed since last writing in my Journal and many things have transpired. Capt Oaks went on a scout met the Indians, had a fight killed one, and wounded 3 or 4 others he says the killed man fought desperately. two soldiers were wounded & a horse and one horse Killed. the indian whenever a shot missed would shake his bows and arrows and shout defiance the men behaved very bravely one sprang from his horse, finding him wounded and unmanageable, still holding him by the bridle the Indian tried to seize him from the soldier, and as the mans revolvers were all fired off he took to *stoneing* the Indian. trophies were brought in and I secured two arrows stained with blood of the brave warrior. this occurred on 25*th* Feb A short time after this, Capt Brackett was on a scout when he surprised an Indian camp & took all their mules & horses, shields &c. &c. and some papers &c which proved them to be a party which had been down on the Cohial and Killed a white man and boy & robbed their house. he was unfortunate in not killing any as they got off into a rough, rocky, chaporral country where they could not be followed. 4 weeks since my dear husband was taken with cramp in the stomach a disease to which he is subject at long intervals he & I told Dr Smith what it was, when he shook his head and looked grave but said it certainly was not that. he did nothing for 3 days, at the end of that time I found that inflammation had taken place and I insisted he should send for some other physician as he did not seem to know anything of the case. he then sent for Dr Smith at Chadbourne and begun to exert himself and take some interest my husband was in great danger for about 6 days when he begun to recover slowly Dr Smith then arrived, but by a kind Providence & a good constitution my husband got well. the Dr had the sincerity to say well Col I have not the most remote idea what has been the matter with you. this is not the only subject upon which he seems ignorant I have no faith in him. God forbid that any of us should be sick again while he is with us. he certainly knows nothing of his profession. A court martial has been sitting here for the last two weeks to try Capt Travis for slander against Lieut Wood (what I before mentioned as having took place on the road) & conduct unbecoming an officer & gentleman.

May 7th. . . . Recently a Mexican was captured by a Texan. he was taken prisoner by the Indians (Camanches [*sic*]) when a very young child, raised by them as one of their warriors so that he is Indian in every essential except colour he is fair with sandy hair & more like an Irishman than a Mexican he says he was with the band which Capt

Bracket attacked & that 3 Indians were Killed & several wounded. the Capt did not know he killed any but thought he might have done it. We ride out every evening when weather permits.

⬥ *E S S A Y S*

Historians have differed over the nature of Jacksonian America and also over the relationship between expansionism and American society and its predominant attitudes—particularly the roles played by material interests, Anglo-American racialism, and spread-eagle nationalism. Some interpretations of the emergence of professionalism in the U.S. Army Officer Corps have placed it in the second half of the nineteenth century, produced by larger social forces accompanying industrialization. However, in the first essay, William B. Skelton of the University of Wisconsin at Stevens Point contends that this professionalization occurred between the War of 1812 and the Mexican-American War of 1846–1848 and that it stemmed primarily from reforms and changing views emanating from within the officer corps itself, as it responded to Jacksonian society and devoted itself to preparation for major national tasks. In the second essay, Robert E. May of Purdue University provides a cultural analysis of the ambiguous relationship of army officers and other soldiers to the unofficial "filibustering" invasions and other expeditions by private American paramilitary forces into Mexico, Cuba, and Central America, and concludes that these demonstrate the importance of romantic concepts of masculinity as well as visions of Manifest Destiny.

An Officer Corps Responds to an Undisciplined Society by Disciplined Professionalism

WILLIAM B. SKELTON

A seeming paradox of American history in the first half of the nineteenth century was the appearance of a distinct military profession in a society generally considered to be fragmented, fluid, undisciplined, and egalitarian. While military historians have recognized this development dramatically revealed in the comparative performances of the Regular Army in the War of 1812 and in the Mexican War—few have placed it in a broad historical context. Those who have done so have attributed it to one of two basic causes: the unique military interests of the Southern plantation aristocracy, or an ambiguity in American character which at once distrusted a military elite and tolerated it as a reflection of a popular martial spirit. In either case, the Regular Army emerges as a historical aberration an isolated pocket of authority and discipline in an otherwise amorphous, egalitarian social order.

Attention has focused on the efforts of the officer corps to preserve professional cohesion in the face of democratic hostility rather than inquiring about the process that produced such cohesion in the first place. Was military professionalism an isolated phenomenon, explicable solely by internal factors, by the unique character of military service? Or was it part of a more general tendency, the product

Reprinted by permission of Transaction Publishers. "Professionalization in the U.S. Army Officer Corps during the Age of Jackson," by William B. Skelton from *Armed Forces and Society*, 1 (August 1975). Copyright © 1975 by Transaction; all rights reserved.

of general social forces at work in nineteenth-century America? An examination of these questions may lead to a greater understanding of the military profession as an institution. It may also shed light on broader social changes occurring in the Jacksonian Era.

The several characteristics of an occupational group form its "professionalism," and among these is expertise: a systematic body of specialized knowledge transmitted to group members by a formal educational process. Another is social responsibility: a commitment to use professional knowledge to perform functions important to the well-being of society as a whole. A third component is corporateness: a feeling among group members that they constitute a subculture distinct from the rest of society; a high degree of self-government within that subculture, sanctioned by the larger community; and institutions that uphold codes of group behavior, educate aspiring practitioners, and add to the body of professional knowledge. The history of the professions may best be approached in terms of "professionalization"—the process by which professional standards and procedures are applied in fields formerly handled by intuitive or empirical means—rather than in terms of professionalism as an achieved state. Few occupational groups in the nineteenth century would fully incorporate professional characteristics, but the tendency toward such characteristics in various callings has been one of the most important social developments of recent history.

Here I shall try to show that the professionalization of the army officer corps between the War of 1812 and the Mexican War was in large measure self-induced, the product of a reforming elite of young officers who rose to positions of power during the War of 1812. As a result of their wartime experiences and their career aspirations, these men developed a common ideology, centering on the need for a well-organized, educated, and professionalized officer corps capable of directing a future mobilization. The American social environment reinforced their efforts. First, they faced no entrenched feudal aristocracy clinging to traditional, nonprofessional practices as a sign of class privilege. Second, military professionalization coincided with more basic changes in the social order, especially the erosion of the personalized, community-oriented social patterns of the Colonial Era and the transition toward impersonal, centralized, and bureaucratic institutions. Thus military reformers rationalized military administration, instilled regularity into the officer selection process, attained a considerable degree of security in the pursuit of their careers, and cultivated—through West Point and a variety of other institutions—an intellectual, scientific approach to military problems. Ironically, the popular suspicion which the Regular Army attracted in an egalitarian era intensified group awareness and diffused professional attitudes through the officer corps as a whole. A significant outgrowth of these influences was the self-image of the officer corps as an apolitical instrument of public policy. . . .

American officers derived from no particular social level. During the Revolution and for several decades afterward, military service offered a channel of upward mobility for many young men from obscure middle-class origins. Indeed, the absence of a titled nobility freed the American army from one of the principal barriers to professionalization in Europe. During the early national period, however, Americans modeled their behavior on their European counterparts—or rather on what seemed to them accepted conduct for army officers. Military attitudes tended to be aristocratic attitudes: an obsession with personal honor; the pursuit of individual glory in battle; the cultivation, where possible, of a luxurious life style. Military leadership was seen as an "art" to be grasped intuitively by men of genius or, more commonly, as a trade to be acquired through practical experience. Rarely was it defined as a learned science. Nothing reveals the individualistic, preprofessional character of the officer corps as well as the widespread reliance on dueling to settle personal differences, a practice tacitly condoned by the highest authorities.

Even if strong European models had existed, the decentralized nature of American society in the early national period would have retarded professional integration. For most Americans, traditional loyalties to family, community, and state outweighed a national orientation. The size and organization of the army fluctuated greatly, the result of popular distrust, faith in the declining militia system, and the generally unsettled condition of national administration. Aside from the thoughts of individual Federalist leaders, there was no well-defined military role to give focus to the officer corps. The army's principal functions were the immediate, practical problems of frontier defense and Indian control. Troops were scattered in small garrisons along thousands of miles of frontier and coastline. The absence of adequate communication and administrative precedents made it impossible for high commanders, had they been so inclined, to impose uniform standards of conduct on the officer corps.

In this unstructured situation, few officers made a full commitment to a military career. They remained rooted in social elites at home or cultivated civilian ties in the regions where they were stationed. Politics blended with military life as officers took partisan stands and appealed to political friends for redress in professional matters. . . .

. . . Whatever cohesion among officers had developed during the 1790s and early nineteenth century evaporated with the expansion of 1808, which more than tripled the number of officers and brought an influx of citizen appointees directly into the higher ranks.

A Professional Ideology

The War of 1812 marked a major transition in the history of the military profession. The war effort dramatically revealed the basic characteristics of both the society and the military establishment: localism, lack of coordination, and reliance on spontaneity rather than centralized planning. The result was near disaster, as American armies tried ineffectively to invade Canada and British forces descended at will on the exposed coastline. Repeated failure had another effect, however. By discrediting established commanders, in some cases superannuated veterans of the Revolution, it opened channels of upward mobility for young, reform-minded officers. At the end of the war, Generals Jacob Brown, Edmund P. Gaines, Winfield Scott, and Alexander Macomb were still under forty, but had experienced the responsibility of high command. Scores of others had entered the army in the expansions of 1808 and 1812, and had reached the middle levels of the officer corps. . . .

The chaotic practices of the War of 1812 demonstrated the need for standardization. During the conflict, the War Department published the first official set of general regulations in the army's history. . . . Perhaps the best-known attempt to rationalize procedure occurred at West Point after 1817, where Superintendent Sylvanus Thayer standardized the curriculum and the regulations governing the Military Academy.

Closely related to the appearance of uniform regulations was a trend toward centralization and efficiency in the army's administrative structure. As they evolved through the 1820s and 1830s, the General Staff bureaus differed greatly from the support services of the Revolutionary and Federalist eras. While the government had attempted to coordinate supply and personnel matters in the late eighteenth century, offices had overlapped in function and lacked permanent, systematic procedural patterns. In the absence of formal structure, they had relied for their energy on individual incumbents, often civilians. Military administration at the center had been a reflection of the army as a whole—a continually shifting conglomeration of personal fiefdoms, only loosely coordinated by the secretaries of war and the treasury. The Jefferson administration had reduced even this limited bureaucracy. . . .

A Professional Ethos

It is one thing to trace the growth of military bureaucracy, but something else to describe the emergence of professional consciousness. The first is the work of an elite, imposing standards from above; the second involves common attitudes and loyalties among the mass of group members. The two trends were nonetheless closely related in the Jacksonian army. The attempt to infuse discipline and regularity into military administration merged with the evolution of a professional ethos.

This relationship appeared clearly in the officer selection process. Before 1821, no formal standards had existed for officers' appointments aside from an attempt to maintain geographical balance. A West Point education implied a degree of competence, of course, but graduates had comprised only a small percentage of the officer corps and had concentrated in the engineers and artillery. For 11 years after the reduction of 1821, however, with the exception of semi-military branches such as the Pay and Medical departments, the government reserved all new officers' commissions for West Point graduates. The rationale behind this practice is not entirely clear; it may have reflected the patronage functions of Military Academy appointments. But it meshed with the postwar conception of the army as an educational institution, a repository of expertise. The number of West Pointers in the officer corps rose steadily: 82 of 553 (14.8%) in 1817; 183 of 465 (39.7%) in 1823; 333 of 522 (63.8%) in 1830. This temporary monopoly allowed military men, by determining the academy curriculum, to set standards for granting commissions—in effect, to control professional licensing.

As with other professions, the egalitarian surge of the 1830s weakened these controls. Reacting to pressure from Congress and the public, the executive branch appointed citizens directly to the army, especially when new units were added. A small number of enlisted men received commissions. This tendency was partially counterbalanced, however, by more rigid admissions procedures for civilian applicants. In 1832, for example, the Medical Department established a system of examinations for all candidates for appointment or promotion. Beginning in 1837, citizen appointees to other positions were also subjected to examinations, though these necessarily focused on the candidate's "character" and general knowledge rather than on professional expertise. At any rate, West Pointers continued to receive most commissions and by 1860 constituted 75.8% of the officer corps. The overall effect of the tightening of admission standards was to increase the uniformity and degree of self-government within the military profession.

A related development was the rise of the long-term military career. The reduction of 1821 introduced a period of unprecedented stability for the military establishment. There were no drastic cutbacks in the decades that followed, no violent fluctuations of army organization. In fact, the size of the officer corps gradually increased—from 530 in 1821 to 1,108 in 1860. Officers found it possible to pursue their careers in a relatively secure institutional context. At certain times, the mid-1830s in particular, the unpleasant prospects of frontier duty, the absence of promotion opportunities, and the lures of civilian life caused many young officers to resign. In comparison with the past, however, the outstanding characteristic of the officer corps at the time was the continuity of its membership. The turnover in the highest grades was exceedingly slow: as late as 1860, 20 of the 32 men at or above the rank of full colonel had held commissions in the War of 1812, 10 of them as field-grade officers. The trend was similar among their subordinates. A comparative analysis of the army registers of 1797 and 1830 demonstrates that the median career length for officers under the rank of captain on those lists increased from 6 to 17 years. The proportion of such officers who would serve 10 or more years expanded from 35.2% of the total in 1797 to 78.1% in 1830. Those who would serve 20 or more years rose from 6.6% to 44%. In other words, a military career became for an increasing proportion of the officer corps a lifelong commitment. Although difficult to gauge, the fact that officers served together over a prolonged period of time, sharing common experiences and developing institutional loyalties, was probably the most important single factor in creating a corporate identity. . . .

Thus professional attitudes arose originally from the internal dynamics of the military establishment—the conscious efforts of War of 1812 veterans to stabilize military procedure and to prepare for a future war. The relationship between the army and the larger society contributed to the trend. In a basic way, of course, the transportation revolution facilitated the exchange of ideas and eroded, if it did not destroy, officers' feeling of isolation. More direct was the attack on the army during the 1830s and 1840s. As historians have often shown, the numerous attempts to abolish West Point or to reduce the army were a reflection of the egalitarian impulse of the time. Undoubtedly the threat was more apparent than real. The army performed functions considered desirable by large segments of the population. The representation of prominent families in the officer corps deflected the practical impact of the criticism. Through this period, however, officers were subjected to a continuous volley of speeches, pamphlets, resolutions, and editorials denouncing their profession as both undemocratic and useless and extolling the virtues of the military version of the "natural man"—the citizen volunteer or militiaman.

Officers' responses to this assault varied. Some considered resigning rather than continuing to serve a profession for which "there is no longer a feeling of respect entertained by the country." Except for brief periods, however, relatively few took this step. Instead, the main effect of egalitarian criticism was to intensify group awareness. Officers drew together in an effort to define their collective role and to justify the existence of a standing army and a system of military education in the midst of a democratic nation. On one side, they universally denounced the militia and volunteers. Citizen soldiers were politically motivated, undisciplined, ineffective in combat, extravagantly expensive, and given to committing atrocities. There was a basis to these charges, of course, as Indian campaigns and the Mexican War demonstrated. But the frequency and bitterness of the counterattack indicate that regulars used citizen soldiers as a foil for their growing consciousness, a counterimage representing the reverse of the qualities they prized most highly.

In contrast, officers stressed the advantages of military professionalism, defining it in the context of the cadre system. Quartermaster General Thomas S. Jesup thought that the purposes of the army were "to acquire and preserve military knowledge and perfect military discipline; to construct the permanent defences, and organize the matériel necessary in war; to form the stock on which an army competent to the defence of the country may be engrafted." "The rank and file of an army can be obtained at any time," wrote Inspector General John E. Wool, "but not officers, for it requires years of study and reflection to qualify them for command." A correspondent of the *Military and Naval Magazine* echoed these arguments, but noted an additional advantage: "that nationality of feeling which pervades the officers of the army, who, having no interest but in their country's glory and union, are entirely devoid of all sectional partiality and prejudice." A collective image emerged in reports and military journals of a devoted band of brothers, motivated by selfless patriotism, cultivating specialized knowledge for the welfare of an uncaring public. However exaggerated, this image provided an ideological "lowest common denominator" for officers from diverse backgrounds and educational levels. It diffused through the army views confined earlier to a reforming elite. Even the most unreflective Indian fighter had a stake in professional institutions and military science—if nothing else, they distinguished him from citizen soldiers.

Another unlikely factor contributing to the coalescence of professional attitudes was the army's experience with Indian removal. From the 1820s to the early 1840s, the army was involved in this unpleasant business; the "war" in Florida against the Seminoles was the principal military operation between the War of 1812 and the Mexican War. Officers generally disliked Indian removal, as it offered few chances for distinction, detracted from preparedness, and embroiled the army in complex civil military controversies. While assuming removal to be inevitable, many officers had sincere moral doubts about the exploitation of the red man, especially their role as agents of that exploitation.

Officers never fully incorporated Indian relations into their professional self-image. One of the ironies of the army's early history and an indication of its commitment to the preparedness doctrine was its failure to develop a body of thought concerning the most important practical task. In coming to grips with this problem, however, officers increasingly portrayed themselves as detached instruments of the public will, dedicated to the principle of objective service. Such an approach compensated them for the absence of glory and distinction; it also lessened the guilt that many vaguely felt. . . .

A final aspect of professionalization remains to be examined—the relationship of the officer corps to politics. Until at least the Civil War, the interaction between the army and the political arena was both intense and complicated. Officers of all grades cultivated political sponsors and used them to seek appointments, transfers, and similar favors. The nature of frontier service made close contact between military and civil leaders inevitable; post and department commanders often exercised considerable political authority, on occasion serving as Indian agents or even territorial governors. The commanding general and the General Staff officers in Washington mingled in the highest political circles.

Nevertheless, a gradual change occurred in the way that officers viewed politics. In the early nineteenth century, political and military life had formed a continuum. Not all officers were absorbed in political affairs, but there was little effort to distinguish the two fields, to define them as separate realms of endeavor. This relationship, of course, reflected the undifferentiated leadership patterns of early American society. By the 1830s and 1840s, however, officers were becoming more circumspect in their political activities. In part, the stimulus came from above. High administrators tried to weaken officers' political ties in order to promote bureaucratic efficiency. Another factor was the practice, adopted unofficially after the War of 1812, by which congressmen made appointments to West Point. This system did not nullify political interference, but it ensured that the officer corps would not be dominated by a particular party, as had been the case earlier. The principal impetus, however, was the growing self-image of the officer corps as a specialized elite, devoted to the national interest rather than to a faction. Too close an identification with politics would undermine this image; it might also confirm popular fears of military influence.

A sampling of officers' opinion reveals these changing attitudes. "Without questioning the right of any citizen in civil life, and in a state of peace, to act upon party principles," wrote Brigadier General Edmund P. Gaines in 1838, "I contend that whenever we assume the attitude of soldiers, in the national defence, we must take leave of the spirit of party." When approached regarding the vice presidency in 1843, Quartermaster General Thomas S. Jesup disavowed any interest in the office: "So long as I hold a military commission, I cannot consistently with my obligations to the country, and the opinions I entertain of what is due to its institutions, allow my name to be used in connection with that or any other elective office." Lieutenant William T. Sherman considered himself a Whig by family tradition, but stated that it was his "intention and duty to abstain from any active part in political matters and discussions, and for that reason I never permit myself to become interested in the success of either party." While Major General Zachary Taylor reluctantly agreed to stand for the presidency in 1848, he insisted repeatedly that, if elected, he would be "the president of a nation & not of a party." Expressions of this kind frequently included an undercurrent of contempt for the give-and-take world of party politics, especially among young West Point graduates. Few went as far in print as Lieutenant Daniel H. Hill who, in reference to the secretary of war, bemoaned the "melancholy fact, that the *soldier*, who has devoted himself to the science of war from his childhood, can never rise above an inferior grade, whilst the command of the Army is entrusted to a *politician*, who has gained distinction by courting the mob." Such comments were common in private correspondence, however, and officers tended to use the term "demagogue" interchangeably with "politician."

Given the extent of officers' political involvements, their professions of neutrality might be interpreted as hypocritical attempts to allay public suspicion. Although some evidence supports this view, a subtle shift did occur in the nature of these connections. Early in the century, individual officers had intervened freely in civilian matters. They had been especially active in president-making during the Era of Good Feelings. By the 1830s, however, their political actions focused mainly on issues within the service—appointments, promotions, favorable stations—rather than support for civilian candidates or nonmilitary issues. Interest-group tactics became popular. Military men petitioned Congress for higher pay and a retirement system; line officers attempted to limit staff privileges. One of the most politically oriented of the West Point graduates, Lieutenant Isaac I. Stevens, organized a lobbying effort during the early 1850s to push army bills. "It is time for officers having a common purpose to act together, and do something for their profession . . . ," he wrote a friend. "If we act in concert, compare views in a fraternal and generous spirit, merging the *arm* in the *army,* and taking views as large as our country, and occupying the whole ground of the public defense, and thus come to conclusions, we shall be right, and Congress will act accordingly, I care not what opposition be made in interested quarters."

Thus regulars increasingly viewed politics from a professional perspective. No issue drew the officer corps into the political arena as a body; its members knew that such an event would arouse public reaction and threaten their careers. But the trend was toward the exclusive use of political influence to attain professional goals, either personal advancement or the improvement of particular branches of the service. Accompanying this change was the articulation of the opinion that politics and military service formed separate fields of endeavor, each guided by its own set of values, and that the army should remain politically neutral. This view naturally contributed to the image of the officer corps as an objective arm of national policy. . . .

The Mexican War had an important, albeit ambivalent, effect on military professionalism. On one side, it opened opportunities for advancement and distinction, thus stimulating the "heroic" aspects of officership. Each campaign produced bitter quarrels which reinforced the traditional individualism of the officer corps, eroded but never destroyed by the growth of corporate identities. In a more basic way, however, the war provided a test for the preparedness functions of the Regular Army, thus deepening officers' professional consciousness. Captain Philip N. Barbour spoke for the officer corps as a whole when he expressed hope, in April 1846, that Taylor's army would push the enemy back. "This *must* be done before the arrival of volunteers, or the Army is *disgraced.*" Almost without exception, officers' correspondence dwelled on the superiority of regulars to citizen soldiers in discipline and expertise. The war seemed to the officer corps undeniable proof of the value of formal military education and the cadre system. Out of the spectacular victories in Mexico emerged a body of tradition, exaggerated but nonetheless effective, which would fire future generations of officers with institutional pride. In the opinion of one lieutenant, the siege of Vera Cruz was "the most complete victory of science in modern warfare." Another considered the clashes at Contreras and Churubusco "unquestionably the greatest battle that has ever been fought on this continent and the most brilliant."

Conclusion

By the end of the Mexican War, the officer corps was well along in the process of professionalization. The principal stimulus had been the emergence of an elite of young officers during the closing stages of the War of 1812 which shared a common view of the army's role, emphasizing the cadre plan, preparation for a future war, and formal military education. In contrast to the experience of European armies, these men faced little resistance from an aristocratic tradition within the officer corps which would retard professional consolidation. Rather, professionalization meshed with the personal aspirations of American officers—their quest for career security and for public recognition of their superiority to the militia. This emerging professional spirit found institutional expression in the rise of West Point influence, the experiments with schools of practice and military journalism, the interaction with European affairs, and the general tightening of administrative procedure. Egalitarian criticism of the army deepened group awareness and encouraged the gradual separation of the officer corps from party politics. It would be inaccurate, of course, to portray the majority of officers as articulate and fully committed professionals. Only a small portion of them served on military boards, translated European works, wrote professional articles, or otherwise contributed directly to the development of professional knowledge. Their concept of leadership continued to prize such traditional qualities as physical courage, military bearing, and intuitive brilliance. But the inclusion of professional values had begun and would be carried further after the Civil War.

While the emergence of a distinct military profession is obviously important in the history of the U.S. Army, it is also a significant part of the broader evolution of American institutions in the nineteenth century. Military developments of the period must be viewed in the context of massive dislocations brought on by the transportation revolution and rapid economic growth. These changes undermined traditional relationships based on kinship, community, personality, and social deference. At the same time, they opened the way for the development of more "modern" institutions, oriented toward functional specialization, national organization, and impersonal, bureaucratic relationships. For most groups, the Age of Jackson was a time of flux, the disrupting stage of the modernization process. For certain institutions, of which the military profession is a prime example, it was a period of early consolidation. While the officer corps of the 1850s retained elements of its individualistic, unstructured past, it was moving quietly but inexorably in the direction of centralization, uniformity, and efficient management.

An interesting comparison may be made between the role of the American officer corps and that of military elites in the emerging nations of the twentieth century. Because of their discipline, their administrative skills, and their responsiveness to Western technology, military officers often play a role in the transition of "underdeveloped" countries toward industrialism and national unity. As bureaucracies organized along relatively rational lines, armies contribute to overriding the parochialism and cultural conservatism of traditional societies. The American army, of course, did not set the direction of national development. Officers contributed to economic development through engineering, road-building, suppression of the Indians, and exploration, but they did so as agents of a stable government rather than as determiners of national policy. The importance of the officer corps was more representative than causal. As one of the first major institutions to consolidate along functional, bureaucratic lines, it anticipated the course followed by other institutions—professional, governmental, economic, educational—in later years.

An Officer Corps Responds to Opportunities for Expansion with Images of Heroic Expeditions

ROBERT E. MAY

Asked the meaning of the term *filibuster,* modern Americans are likely to conjure up images of politicians rendering long-winded speeches to delay the passage of legislation. Prior to 1900, however, *filibuster* was most frequently applied to American adventurers who raised or participated in private military forces that either invaded or planned to invade foreign countries with which the United States was formally at peace. Although peoples of other countries occasionally filibustered, only the United States gained repute as a filibustering nation.

Filibustering reached its apex before the Civil War, when thousands of Americans risked their lives in expeditions. The most notorious filibuster was William Walker. Walker invaded Mexican Lower California and Sonora in 1853–1854, cast his lot in a Nicaraguan civil war in the spring of 1855, emerged commander-in-chief of the army in a coalition government that October, and had himself inaugurated as president of Nicaragua the following July. However, Walker represented a generation of filibusters. Filibuster activity touched locales other than Mexico and Nicaragua, including Cuba, Ecuador, Canada, Honduras, and Hawaii. "The fever of Filibusterism is on our country. Her pulse beats like a hammer at the wrist, and there's a very high color on her face," noted the *New-York Daily Times* in an editorial that could have been dated any time between the Mexican War and Civil War.

Filibustering defied international law, United States statutes, and presidential proclamations. Though only Walker's Nicaragua expedition achieved even short-term success, and although many of the expeditions met bloody ends, filibustering disrupted United States relations with England, Spain, France, and many of the countries of middle and South America. It interfered with United States efforts to purchase Cuba from Spain, complicated the negotiations with Mexico that eventuated in the Gadsden Treaty, affected Anglo-American efforts to resolve controversies about Central America deriving from the disputed Clayton-Bulwer Treaty of 1850, provoked outbreaks of anti-Americanism in Central America, and had a host of domestic ramifications. Filibustering sparked heated debate in Congress, state legislatures, and southern commercial conventions. References to filibusters

Robert E. May "Young American Males and Filibustering in the Age of Manifest Destiny: The United States Army as a Cultural Mirror," *Journal of American History* 78, no. 3 (December, 1991). Reprinted by permission of the Organization of American Historians.

peppered political party platforms as well as campaign oratory and song. Filibustering helped make and unmake presidents and contributed significantly to the breakdown of sectional relations, which eventuated in the American Civil War.

Although historians have produced a considerable literature about filibustering's impact upon United States diplomacy and sectional politics, they have been slow to address its significance as a mid-nineteenth-century United States cultural phenomenon. This is partly, I suspect, because historians tend to judge filibustering by the number of adventurers who actually arrived in foreign domains, without taking into account their support networks or the persons who joined filibuster units that disbanded prematurely. Since most filibusters left Gulf Coast or California ports, or crossed the boundary of Texas and Mexico, there has also been a tendency in historical scholarship to explain the filibusters as products of the southern martial spirit, the geopolitics of slavery expansionism, and the lawlessness and labor surplus of post–gold rush California. What has been obscured is filibustering's place in American social history, both North and South.

Rather than restrict filibustering to the sideshows of America's pre–Civil War drama, historians need to respect its salience and probe its meaning. Filibustering contributed to the rhythm of antebellum life. Newspapers and periodicals published countless news items and editorials about filibuster plots, battles, and trials. Filibuster rallies, recruiting and bond drives, serenades, lectures, parades, and stage plays touched communities throughout much of the country. Filibustering provided the nation with heroes, martyrs, and villains. While Americans were often embarrassed by filibuster depredations in foreign countries, even opponents of the movement sometimes found themselves in awe of filibuster courage under adversity. A United States naval officer reflected, "I have forgiven the crime & delusion of the invaders for the immeasurable courage & uncomplaining spirit in which they all to a man met their deaths." Filibustering captured the imagination of common folk. "There are but few men now living who occupy so much of the public mind as Gen. William Walker," regretted the *Louisville Daily Courier.* "He is the theme of conversation among men and women, and children. . . . He is, indeed, the hero of the times." Intellectuals also found that filibustering commanded their attention. Washington Irving concluded that the filibusters signaled a "spirit of mischief" at loose in the country. Filibustering even penetrated the nation's subconscious. Americans found themselves applying the term to matters related only tangentially to private invasions of other countries. The *New-York Tribune* referred to proslavery emigrants in the Kansas Territory as "Col. Buford's Kansas filibusters." Lydia Maria Child read the word backward through time to find William the Conqueror a filibuster. In the late antebellum period, filibustering helped define what it meant to be an American. As a cynic put it in *Harper's Weekly,* "The insatiable spirit of filibusterism . . . forms one of the most amiable virtues of our beloved fellow-countrymen."

Above all, historians need to study filibustering's appeal and meaning to America's young males. Though some filibusters were of advanced age, the great number of them, as might be expected in highly dangerous, physically demanding, and illegal ventures, were young. Walker claimed that all the men involved in his Lower California expedition were young. The average age of the eighty-four filibusters taken prisoner in Narciso López's 1851 expedition to Cuba was 25.9 years.

As would happen later in the Civil War, adolescents who had no business soldiering signed up for expeditions. "At the age of fifteen I ran away . . . to join an aggregation of young gentlemen but little older than myself, who enlisted under the banner of General Walker," one of them later recalled, noting that his group was "caught . . . like a bunch of truant kids" while passing down the Mississippi River. John A. Campbell, a Supreme Court justice, observed that filibusters collected together in Mobile were "merely boys."

Perhaps the most telling indication of filibustering's broad appeal to the nation's young males is its impact on the officers and enlisted men of the United States Army. At first glance, the army would seem a most unlikely institution to foster filibustering. The service had a history of antifilibustering responsibilities that dated back to the Washington administration, and the prevention of filibusters emerged as one of the army's most important peacetime missions by the late 1830s. One might well expect the nation's officers and enlisted men to despise their filibuster antagonists. Yet sympathy for filibustering infiltrated army ranks. Some soldiers even resigned commissions and deserted ranks to join filibuster expeditions. While it would be misleading to brush the whole army with the stain of filibustering because of the derelictions and sentiments of a portion of its personnel, it would also be wrong to exempt United States soldiers from filibustering's spell. The army held up a cultural mirror to its nation. To understand the army's place in the story of filibustering is to render more comprehensible the meaning of filibustering to America's civilians. . . .

Before the Civil War, army service and filibustering represented competing career options. That young men chose one over the other often had more to do with circumstance than with preference. When Robert Farquharson contacted [former Mississippi governor John A.] Quitman in February 1855, he asked if Quitman would let him join his Cuba filibuster force or if Quitman would pull strings to get him a lieutenant colonelcy in one of the army's new regiments. Either alternative would have sufficed. Obviously the army played second fiddle in the case of a new officer posted to Fort Leavenworth in 1858: "Mr. [Secretary of War John B.] Floyd has appointed in our regiment a gentleman from Richmond whose connection with Quitman . . . was well known; in fact the gentleman went to Greytown [Nicaragua] last May but was too late Walker having surrendered." Similarly, Theodore O'Hara procured his captain's commission in the Second United States Cavalry in March 1855 only after service with [Narciso López, who twice invaded Cuba,] and collaboration with the abortive Quitman Cuba conspiracy, which fell through the same month that O'Hara joined the army. O'Hara's resignation from the army in December 1856 raises suspicions that he intended to link up with William Walker, whose Nicaraguan regime was in danger of collapse at that time. That O'Hara conceived filibustering as an extension of army service comes out in his assuring Quitman, with whom he had served in the Mexican War as a volunteer captain, that he had the "zeal & anxiety to enter again with you into the tented field."

During the pre–Civil War era, it was by no means clear to young American males aspiring to be soldiers that they would better serve their country or their own interests by joining the army rather than a filibuster cohort. Commissions and promotions were hard to come by in a shrinking army, and peace with foreign nations limited the battlefield experience they might gain to skirmishes against native Americans on the Plains. Small-scale engagements in isolated western regions held little promise for fame or glory. But filibuster commanders such as Walker and Quitman presented themselves as professional soldiers and urged that their ventures be considered as alternatives to army service, while filibuster exploits attracted front-page headlines. Filibuster leaders and recruiters emphasized the possibilities for advancement awaiting filibuster personnel, sometimes pegging pay and rations precisely to army scales. "How would you like to go to Cuba?" one discharged American officer who had fought in Mexico wrote another about a year after hostilities terminated. "There is an expedition on foot and if you will go—just say the word. The inducements are, aside from the glory—two grades higher than you go out; I am authorized to offer you a first Lieutenantcy with two grades higher in the Army of the new Republic—Pay & emoluments same as the Army of the United States." Many men responded instinctively to such incentives. New Yorker Elijah D. Taft, for instance, solicited an officer's slot with Walker, explaining, "I have been fifteen years in commission in the Militia of this State . . . and as I have made that arm of the service my constant study for some years I should like to put in practice in Nicaragua the benefit of these years of study." Filibustering had a similar appeal to graduates of private military academies. Pre–Civil War males who joined the army rather than filibuster expeditions, therefore, may well have previously given filibustering serious consideration.

Filibustering remained a temptation even after young men joined the army, especially once they experienced a dose of dull military routine. Filibusters dropped by army posts from time to time. "Filibuster McMicken of Phil. here," Capt. John Charles Casey noted cryptically in his diary while stationed at Fort Brooke in 1856. More important, soldiers found their newspapers filled with reports and rumors of filibuster doings. "News comes that General Lopez has been hung at Havana by the Spanish governor—result of his second expedition against Cuba," Hitchcock recorded in October 1851. "Newspapers represent that great excitement prevails in the States, and that large numbers are going and preparing to go to Cuba to revolutionize it." Tales of pending filibusters circulated from post to post, perpetually intriguing soldiers who craved more romance in their lives. "I have heard a 'rumor' here that appears . . . to be entitled to more credence than rumors generally are," reported a young dragoon from California in 1859. "It is stated that Gen. William Walker . . . is in California, having smuggled himself in under the name of James Wilson; that he will proceed secretly to the frontiers of Sonora . . . Sonora will then be invaded."

Had the army provided antifilibuster indoctrination or an intellectual barrier to filibuster thoughts, things might have been different. However, America's soldiers shared civilian ideologies of Anglo-American racial superiority and Manifest Destiny. Capt. Joseph H. La Motte reported from Ringgold Barracks that much was being said around the post about "the indomitable energy & perseverance of the Saxon race." Lt. Theodore Talbot announced, "Our 'Manifest destiny' bids fair for fulfillment." Cognizant of the army's conquests in the recent Mexican War, many officers anticipated additional territorial quests ahead. Even before the war ended, Gen. William Jenkins Worth earned press notice for wanting the annexation of Cuba and Central America. Such wish lists echoed through the army's ranks over subsequent years. "We expect to hear of the annexation of Cuba by the coming mail," Lieutenant Talbot reported to his sister from Columbia Barracks, Oregon Territory, in 1851. In 1859 Gen. William S. Harney took a belligerent position regarding the shooting of a Hudson's Bay Company pig on San Juan Island in the Strait of Juan de Fuca, in part from a conviction that the United States would ultimately annex British Columbia. Manifest Destiny convictions made some officers receptive to filibustering. William Tecumseh Sherman must have been sensitive to filibustering's immorality since he wrote that he favored the acquisition of Cuba by "fair means." Yet, he also confessed revealingly that the island promised such benefit to his country that he sometimes found himself hoping that the filibusters would succeed in conquering the Spanish colony.

Nowhere in the army establishment was there more satisfaction about the Mexican War than at the United States Military Academy at West Point. Before the conflict with Mexico, the institution had been subjected to severe civilian criticism. Antagonists contended that the academy engendered aristocracy, that free education at the public's expense was unconstitutional, and that the education was wasted because so many graduates left the military for more remunerative employment in the private sector. Several state legislatures passed resolutions calling for the institution's abolition. However, West Pointers came into their own in the Mexican War, achieving so much recognition that their fame all but eliminated the movement to terminate the academy. Naturally, pride about West Point's contributions to the effort against Mexico waxed intense at the academy throughout the pre–Civil War years. The return of the engineers to the academy at the war's conclusion was forever imprinted on the mind of William Whitman Bailey, who came of age at the Point.

> There was an illumination of the old North and South barracks, and I can see, even now, the word 'Victory,' as it was formed by the lights of the former building. There was a day-time procession, too, in which the cadets bore the trophy flags, which are now draped in the chapel. The band played a Mexican march. At that time and for some years after, there was much talk about the Mexican War.

Following the war mementos from the conflict were put on display. In new cadets entering academy life, the exhibits must have inspired a sense of awe. "Our chapel is a very pretty building, tastefully decorated on the inside and receiving a military aspect from the flags and cannon ranged along the walls, trophies taken in 1812 and in Mexico," observed plebe Thomas Rowland in a letter home in 1859.

Mexican War legend helped mold West Point into a breeding ground for Manifest Destiny apostles. While some cadets and officers at the Point found talk of further expansion repulsive, many coveted more territory for their country. If it took war to effect such growth, so much the better because war would provide opportunities for promotion and fame. Thus one cadet wrote his mother in 1856, in the middle of a national crisis with England, "Hurrah for Canada & a Brevet!" The next year, another cadet fretted that he was to graduate too late to qualify for a spot on the expedition against the Mormons in Utah but predicted that he would have other opportunities, "perhaps in Cuba." On July 4, 1855, Cadet Guilford D. Bailey of New York made territorial expansion the focus of his Independence Day oration. Fellow cadet James H. Wilson noted in disgust, "Mr Cadet Bailey delivered the oration it was nothing but a piece of bombast . . . he is in favor of taking Cuba by force."

From Manifest Destiny West Pointers had to make only a short ideological jump to filibuster destiny. In his July 4, 1859, oration, first classman William W. McCreery expressed his hope that the United States take Cuba by a "fair fight" rather than by filibuster. But he was also quick to reject assertions that "the American filibuster" was a "ruthless pirate" and to explain that most filibusters were simply hotheaded romantics of "generous" intent. Other West Pointers found no need to apologize for filibustering at all. "It was filibuster," plebe Henry A. Du Pont reported to his father about a Texas cadet's oration in the West Point chapel on July 4, 1856. And, once graduated, West Pointers found little cause to put filibuster emotions behind them. "[James E.] Slaughter is here, the 2 Lieutenant of the Company," Ambrose Hill reported home from the Texas frontier in 1852. "He is . . . a terrible Filibuster." Teresa Vielé recalled that many of the officers stationed with her husband at Ringgold Barracks felt a conflict between profilibuster private feelings and their army obligations. When she once alerted some filibusters as to the whereabouts of an army patrol on their track, the officers merely "winked" at her behavior.

For southerners in the army, a sectionalist imperative reinforced filibuster inclinations. While some southern army officers shed their sectional mentality through the process of serving their nation, others clung tightly to their regional affiliation. Army captain Thomas Claiborne told fellow Tennessean John Overton that he hoped that "our people" would "go to work & help Bill Walker" and advised Overton to "help the good cause" while mentioning his own regret at not being in a position to do something tangible for Walker himself. Should Walker maintain his position in Nicaragua, Claiborne asserted, it would "ensure the integrity of the whole South." Similarly, South Carolina native James Longstreet thought filibustering might help Chihuahua secede from Mexico so that it might become a slave state.

Southern officers did not necessarily offend or alienate their Yankee peers with their slave expansion perspective. Some northern-born officers harbored abolitionist sentiments. Many others, however, absorbed the soft stance on slavery of the Democratic party's "doughface" faction. Furthermore, northern officers took advantage of regulations permitting personal servants and often used slaves in that capacity. Cross-sectional friendships linking together northern and southern officers, or what Jeb Stuart identified as "a sentiment of mutual forbearance," supplemented the physical presence of slaves in the army, forging tolerance for southern demands for new territorial acquisitions.

Given the empathy for filibustering within the army, it is not surprising that some army officers ignored the spirit of their orders and provided filibusters with aid and comfort. When a group of destitute, returning Cuba filibusters arrived at Charlotte Harbor on Florida's west coast in 1850, they were pleasantly surprised by the hospitality provided by an army captain, who landed there with a group of soldiers shortly afterwards. The officer drank with them, sympathized with their cause, informed them that he expected orders for their arrest, and intimated that they should depart so that he would not have to commit such a "repugnant" act. The filibusters took this advice and traveled to Tampa, where they encountered another congenial officer, General Twiggs, then at Fort Brooke. "I called this morning to see Gen. Twig, and found him very talkative," one of the filibusters noted in his diary. Twiggs told the filibusters that their decision to flee Cuba was premature, provided them with three days' rations, and advised them to leave town before he would be forced to arrest them. A year later, Twiggs's lethargic response to the planned departure of López's ship, the *Pampero,* from New Orleans helped enable López to launch his final, and fatal, Cuban expedition. . . .

When John Quitman succeeded López as commander of the Cuba filibusters, the connection between the army and filibustering became even more pronounced. One of the nation's most successful generals in the Mexican War, Quitman had earned a reservoir of respect from the army's regular officer corps, even though he served as a volunteer for most of the war and was mustered out of the service at the end of the conflict. Filibusters anticipated that once Quitman joined their ranks, the cream of the United States Army would flock to his standard. Quitman accepted a commission from the Cuban Junta, an organization of Cuban exiles, in August 1853. Subsequently, some of Quitman's favorite wartime comrades, including officers still in the regular army, flocked to the filibuster standard. Cadmus M. Wilcox, assistant instructor of military tactics at West Point, who had fought with Quitman at Chapultepec, requested seventy days' leave to reconnoiter Cuba on Quitman's behalf and gave serious thought to resigning his commission and becoming a filibuster. "I look on Cuba as our future field of glory & usefulness & am almost disposed to wait no longer but to turn Phillibuster at once" he wrote to Quitman in May 1854. "I would like to hear from you on Cuba matters . . . I really think that we ought not to buy it. The sooner we take it the better." Wilcox retained his commission, but others proved bolder. Lt. Gustavus Woodson Smith, a West Point graduate who had been brevetted a captain for his Mexican War accomplishments, was an assistant professor of engineering at the military academy. Upset over poor promotion prospects, Smith also found teaching excruciatingly boring and frustrating: "Nothing of consequence doing here. Quiet, dull, & stupid. Cadets ignorant, & ill natured—resenting, as an affront not to be submitted to, any attempt to teach them. Ain't they going to graduate in 6 weeks." On December 18, 1854, Smith resigned his commission to join Quitman's staff. That very day, Capt. Mansfield Lovell, a classmate of Smith's at West Point who had been Quitman's aide-de-camp for part of the war, took the same step.

The resignations caused a stir in the army establishment. William H. T. Walker, commandant of cadets at the academy, conjectured accurately on January 4, 1855, that Smith and Lovell intended to join Quitman in a "descent upon Cuba." Quitman's intentions, in fact, were such a badly kept secret that there is reason to assume that Smith and Lovell were not the only officers involved in the plot. The *New York Herald* later claimed that "many" army officers would have participated in Quitman's Cuba operation had it ever actually departed for the island.

Only two months separated the cancellation of Quitman's Cuba project in March 1855 and the launching of William Walker's Nicaragua enterprise. For some restless souls in the army, the temptation of an apparently successful filibuster expedition proved irresistible. Nicaragua enticed adventure-craving cadets at the military academy like George D. Bayard. In April 1856, two months prior to his scheduled graduation, Bayard alerted his mother that he might not give active service much of a chance before turning filibuster. . . . Bayard graduated and stuck things out in the service. But other soldiers took the step that Bayard had only contemplated. When naval commodore Hiram Paulding evacuated destitute filibusters from Central America in 1857 after the collapse of Walker's regime, he noted that a filibuster colonel was "late an officer in the U.S. Army." Half a year later, when Paulding forced Walker's surrender at Punta Arenas following the filibuster's reinvasion of Nicaragua, he took into custody the Mexican War hero Thomas Henry, who had served in the regular army until October 1855, as well as other former United States army soldiers. In lodging a complaint with President James Buchanan about Paulding's interference, Walker noted that some of the men apprehended had at one time "led your soldiers across the continent."

Army officers and enlisted men also participated in filibusters to northern Mexico. Teresa Vielé recalled that enlisted men "daily" deserted Ringgold Barracks [, in Texas,] to join [José Maria Jesús] Carvajal during the filibuster's siege of Camargo. So many soldiers defected to Carvajal that Secretary of State Webster informed the United States minister to Mexico that the frontier army's capacity to enforce the neutrality statutes had become seriously curtailed.

The most startling aspect of the army/filibustering story concerns the officers, some of whom became famous Civil War generals, who went to the filibuster brink but never quite made the ultimate commitment. Mention has already been made of Cadmus Wilcox. Several of his peers experienced similar emotions. In 1855, while surveying the Gadsden Purchase, Lt. William H. Emory heard that Chihuahua's elite desired annexation to the United States and seriously contemplated an invitation from a wealthy Chihuahuan to visit the state in pursuit of that end. "I despise underground work and fillibusterism in all its forms and phases," Emory confided to United States Sen. James A. Pearce. But he also affirmed that he would go should he conclude that this would benefit either his own government or the Chihuahuans. Similarly, P. G. T. Beauregard almost provided his talents to Walker's Nicaragua. Bored with his routine as superintending engineer of the customhouse at New Orleans and convinced that Walker intended the "glorious undertaking" of creating a "Central American Republic, based on our own system, & extending from the Isthmus of Panama to the Sierra Madre," Beauregard asked that Quitman (with whom he had served in Mexico) recommend him to Walker for a commission. It was only after Walker sacked the Nicaraguan city of Granada in November 1856 that Beauregard backed off. The filibuster, from Beauregard's perspective, had displayed "a ferocity, & Vandalism, unworthy of the American Character" and no longer deserved support.

Such flirtation with filibustering survived Walker's eviction from Nicaragua in 1857. No sooner did Walker arrive on American soil in May than he started to organize men and matériel for a return to Nicaragua. That summer and fall, four former Mexican War officers and future Civil War generals—Johnson Kelly Duncan (who had resigned his lieutenantcy in 1855), George B. McClellan (who had resigned his lieutenantcy in January 1857 and become chief engineer of the Illinois Central Railroad), Gustavus Smith, and Lovell—corresponded about joining Walker and rescuing the tropics from the "mongrel occupants" who stood in the way of the area's regeneration. "The fact is Mac," Duncan urged McClellan, "if we don't embrace some chance like this, our day and generation will pass amidst the quiets of peace, . . . our lives will be devoted to the accumulation of dollars and cents." Duncan suggested that McClellan might become Walker's highest-ranking subordinate and that the army group might even take control of the movement if Walker faltered. It is difficult to determine how many other army officers were making plans to accompany Walker's next filibuster. One of Walker's principal organizers reported, "We shall have a much better class of men in the next expedition already we have one major, four captains, and eight Lieutenants all in good standing now in the United States army who hold themselves ready to resign and march when the order is given to move." The Duncan-McClellan-Smith-Lovell coterie dropped out of the scheme prior to Walker's departure in November, to the relief of another future Civil War notable, Lt. Col. Joseph Johnston. Johnston had been kept posted on his compeers' preliminary planning but had concluded that Walker was no better than a "robber."

No sooner had the Duncan group turned away from Walker than it trained its sights on Mexico. In early 1858, Lovell and Johnston negotiated with Mexican Liberals about inserting four thousand American filibusters into the Mexican civil war on the Liberals' side. McClellan, promised a leading role in the force, became excited about the prospects of military service "in a righteous cause & with fair prospect of distinction." The project fell through that February due to Mexican suspicions of the plotters' intent. Yet Johnston found it hard to make a clean break. Sent to Mexico by the War Department a year later to investigate United States military transit rights across Mexican territory, Johnston considered "founding a Spanish castle upon the basis of last year." Only upon discovering that Liberal leaders remained unreceptive did Johnston inform McClellan that the scheme was truly hopeless. The "Filibustees," as Johnston referred to his clique in July 1860, would have to exert their energies in other ways. Ironically, at the very time that Johnston called it quits on dreams of Mexican filibustering, another future Confederate military leader decided to filibuster south of the border. Maj. James Longstreet, army paymaster at Albuquerque, New Mexico Territory, informed Congressman William P. Miles in February 1860 that he and "one or two friends" had been "working very hard, for several years past, to get Chihuahua into the U.S." and that the appropriate moment had arrived. Longstreet wanted Miles to lobby President Buchanan to approve his raising a regiment of volunteers. Longstreet promised he would march the volunteers into Chihuahua within forty days after their authorization. Furthermore, the foray would bring extra dividends: "Once we got a foot hold in Chihuahua Sonora, which is more important, will very soon follow."

Without the interruption of the Civil War, army involvement in filibuster machinations would most likely have persisted indefinitely. Perhaps it would have escalated. Even after the conflict, officers and enlisted men continued to make an occasional contribution to filibustering, either through involvement in expeditions or through lax enforcement of legislation. The difference was that the age of Manifest Destiny had dissolved into new forms of expansion, and filibustering itself had a greatly reduced hold on the American scene. . . .

▲ *F U R T H E R   R E A D I N G*

K. Jack Bauer, *The Mexican War, 1846–1848* (1974).

Averam Bender, *The March of Empire: Frontier Defense in the Southwest, 1848–1860* (1952).

Dwight L. Clarke, *Stephen Watts Kearney: Soldier of the West* (1961).

William A. Croffut, ed., *Fifty Years in Camp and Field: Diary of Major-General Ethan Allen Hitchcock, U.S.A.* (1909).

Marcus Cunliffe, *Soldiers and Civilians: The Martial Spirit in America, 1775–1865* (1968).

John S. D. Eisenhower, *So Far From God: The U.S. War with Mexico, 1846–1848* (1989).

Richard N. Ellis, "The Humanitarian Generals," *Western Historical Quarterly* 3 (April 1972): 169–178.

William H. Goetzmann, *Army Exploration in the American West, 1803–1863* (1959).

M. A. DeWolfe Howe, ed., *Home Letters of General Sherman* (1909).

Robert W. Johannsen, *To the Halls of the Montezumas: The Mexican War in the American Imagination* (1985).

Jeff Long, *Duel of the Eagles: The Mexican and U.S. Fight for the Alamo* (1990).

John K. Mahon, *History of the Second Seminole War, 1835–1842* (1967).

_____, "Letters from the Second Seminole War," *Florida Historical Quarterly* 36 (April 1958).

Robert E. May, "Young American Males and Filibustering in the Age of Manifest Destiny: The United States Army as a Cultural Mirror," *Journal of American Military History* 78 (December 1991): 857–886.

James M. McCaffrey, *Army of Manifest Destiny: The American Soldier in the Mexican War, 1846–1848* (1992).

Robert Ryal Miller, *Shamrock and Sword: The Saint Patrick's Battalion in the U.S.-Mexican War* (1989).

James L. Morrison, Jr., *"The Best School in the World": West Point, the Pre-Civil War Years, 1833–1866* (1986).

Sandra L. Myres, "Romance and Reality on the American Frontier: Views of Army Wives," *Western Historical Quarterly* 13 (October 1982): 409–427.

David M. Pletcher, *The Diplomacy of Annexation: Texas, Oregon, and the Mexican War* (1973).

James W. Pohl and Stephen L. Hardin, "The Military History of the Texas Revolution: An Overview," *Southwestern Historical Quarterly* 89 (January 1986): 269–308.

Francis Paul Prucha, *The Sword of the Republic: The United States Army on the Frontier, 1783–1846* (1969).

Norma Baldwin Ricketts, *The Mormon Battalion: U.S. Army of the West, 1846–1848* (1996).

Charles P. Roland and Richard C. Robbins, "The Diary of Eliza (Mrs. Albert Sidney) Johnston: The Second Cavalry Comes to Texas," *Southwestern Historical Quarterly* (April 1957): 463–500.

Ronald N. Satz, *American Indian Policy in the Jacksonian Era* (1975).

John H. Schroeder, *Mr. Polk's War: American Opposition and Dissent, 1846–1848* (1973).

N. Frank Schubert, *Vanguard of Expansion: Army Engineers in the Trans-Mississippi West, 1819–1879* (1991).

Otis A. Singletary, *The Mexican War* (1960).

William B. Skelton, *An American Profession of Arms: The Army Officer Corps, 1784–1861* (1992).

George Winston Smith and Charles Judah, *Chronicles of the Gringos: The U.S. Army in the Mexican War, 1846–1848* (1968).

Merritt Roe Smith, *Harper's Ferry Armory and the New Technology: The Challenge of Change* (1977).

Robert M. Utley, *Frontiersman in Blue: The United States Army and the Indian, 1848–1865* (1967).

CHAPTER
6

Generals, Soldiers, and the Civil War

Ever since the smoke cleared from the battlefields, the Civil War, which pitted Americans against each other, has sparked heated debates among military histori-ans and thousands of others who have studied the dark and bloody ground of America's deadliest conflict. Some controversies involve refighting the war. On one level, the study of command decisions entails the tactical decisions of particular bat-tles. On another level, it pertains to grand strategy—the overall conception of how resources should be used and war waged to achieve the goal. Since the goals of the Confederate government under President Jefferson Davis were to defend its terri-tory and obtain Northern recognition of its independence, the South's grand strat-egy options varied from fortress-like passive defense to offensive operations to break Northern will to continue the war. In the North, the goal of the U.S. government under President Abraham Lincoln was to end the secession and restore the Union. Lincoln sought to do this in various ways, including inducement as well as coer-cion. Ultimately, the Northern strategy was to besiege the South through a naval blockade, defeat the Confederate armies, and conquer and occupy Southern terri-tory. Both sides recognized that in a long war, the substantially larger population and greater material resources of the North would prove decisive, but Confederate leaders hoped that divided Northern opinion would end the war before that hap-pened. Northern military and political leaders initially predicted that the Union Army would produce decisive victories that would convince divided Southern opin-ion that secession was futile. Ultimately, however, Ulysses S. Grant, who assumed command of the Union Army in 1864, concluded that victory would come only through the bloody attrition of the Confederate armies, the destruction of the South's economic resources, and the resulting loss of the Southerners' will to con-tinue the war.

Historians continue to debate the military strategies adopted by each side. Con-cerning the South, one part of that controversy concerns the offensive-defensive strategy chosen by General Robert E. Lee of Virginia, who, emphasizing that Con-federate forces were outnumbered at least two-to-one by the Union Army, stressed the need for taking the offensive and choosing the battle sites for the most favorable position for the South's outnumbered forces. He eventually took the offensive into the North to pressure Northern public opinion into recognizing the Confederacy. When Lee combined his offensive strategy with the tactical offensive on the battle-field, he won a number of brilliant victories, but these cost alarmingly high casual-ties among officers and enlisted men. Confederate President Jefferson Davis, a West Pointer and former U.S. Secretary of War, favored a different strategy, an overall defensive strategy to conserve Confederate resources. In addition, Lieutenant General James Longstreet was more sympathetic to a broad-based defense including the trans-Appalachian West instead of Lee's focus on Virginia, and, given the casualty rates in frontal attacks, was more inclined to recommend defensive tactics on the battlefield. Among the many debates over the military aspects of the Civil War, scholars and other analysts of that conflict have continued to differ particularly and most controversially over the wisdom of Lee's approach.

A more recent debate concerns the degree to which the Civil War was the first modern "total" war. The world wars of the twentieth century brought a new form of war: mass mobilization of human and industrial resources through nationalistic appeals and the coercive power of the state, waging war against the military and civilians in pursuit of total victory. Was the Civil War, with its intense nationalism, mass mobilization, and industrial support, on behalf of uncompromised victory, an early example of modern total war? Part of this debate focuses on the degree of mo-bilization and the coercive power of the state. But another part concerns the degree to which the total-war tendency to blur the distinction between combatants and noncombatants, the willingness to view civilian populations as contributing to the enemy's war effort and therefore legitimate targets, emerged in the Civil War. Here, debate entails ethical questions raised particularly by the policy of Union General William Tecumseh Sherman toward civilians and their property as Sherman's army cut a broad swath of deliberate destruction on its march through Georgia, from Atlanta to the sea, one of the most controversial actions in American military history.

In keeping with the new social and cultural history, military historians have also turned recently to the experience of war by the average soldiers and civilians as well as to an attention on women and minority groups. What was the effect of war on the civilians and on the citizen-soldiers of the North and the South, on Billy Yank and Johnny Reb? What was the effect of the war on the black soldiers who fought for the Union and for the freedom of African Americans throughout the United States? What was the effect on civilians?

⩘ D O C U M E N T S

In an era before bureaucratically generated, detailed war plans, General Robert E. Lee's thoughts about strategy can be seen primarily in specific instructions or observa-tions in his letters, such as those between 1862 and 1863 included as the first docu-ment. As these indicate, Lee's campaign strategy was to divide his forces in order to separate the enemy armies, then to reconcentrate his forces for a daring blow, hoping for battlefield victories that would undermine Northern will. Taking a more conserva-tive view, Confederate President Jefferson Davis, in the second document, a July 1862 letter to John Forsyth, the mayor of Mobile, Alabama, who fought as a colonel under Braxton Bragg that year, defends himself against accusations of pursuing a pas-sive-defensive strategy by asserting rather duplicitously that his strategy had been, whenever possible, to take the offensive, even to the extent of invading the North.

Lieutenant General James Longstreet, a South Carolinian, who became one of Lee's primary lieutenants (commanding the Confederate right wing at Gettysburg), became one of Lee's main critics after the war. In response to criticism that his delay in taking the offensive on the second day at Gettysburg resulted in Southern defeat, Longstreet, in the third document, an excerpt from his memoirs published in 1895, blames the defeat at Gettysburg on Lee himself.

Beginning as a war to preserve the Union, the Civil War also became, with Lincoln's Emancipation Proclamation, a war also to end slavery. As it did so, African Americans flocked to the protection of the Union Army and freedom as the blue-clad soldiers marched into the South. African-American men, who had been prohibited from joining the U.S. Army since 1820, now rushed to enlist. In the fourth document, a Southern woman, H. A. Yellowley of Nash County in northeastern North Carolina, writes to her brother on November 16, 1862, of how the slaves were running away to the "Yankees" and how the Union Army was arming them. In a more systematic manner, Northern states and the federal government formed segregated units of the U.S. Colored Volunteers. In the fifth document, Corporal James Henry Gooding, a free black man from New Bedford and a volunteer in the 54th Massachusetts Infantry Regiment, comprised of black soldiers and noncommissioned officers and white commissioned officers, describes their July 1863 assault on Fort Wagner guarding Charleston Harbor in a letter to his hometown newspaper a few days after the battle.

In the sixth document, Lieutenant General Ulysses S. Grant in a letter June 23, 1864, to Army Chief of Staff Major General Henry W. Halleck, reiterates, after the bloody battles of the Wilderness, Spotsylvania, and Cold Harbor, his commitment to an unrelenting offensive, regardless of the cost, to wear down the Confederacy through attack on Lee's army in Virginia and Joseph Johnston's army in Georgia. Following that view and the belief that the cost of the war should be brought home to the Southern civilians, Major General William Tecumseh Sherman in a proclamation on September 14, 1864, to the mayor and city council of Atlanta, the seventh document, justifies his decision to have Atlanta evacuated as he brings the costs of war to the South.

1. General Robert E. Lee, C.S.A., Puts Forward an Offensive Strategy of Division and Concentration, 1862–1863

To General Thomas J. ("Stonewall") Jackson

April 25, 1862

Richmond

General:

I have received your letter written on the evening of the 23rd referring to a communication from Genl Field to Genl Ewell.

From *The Wartime Papers of R. E. Lee* by Clifford Dowdey & Louis Manarin. Copyright © 1961 by the Commonwealth of Virginia. By permission of Little, Brown and Company.

I have hoped in the present divided condition of the enemy's forces that a successful blow may be dealt them by rapid combination of our troops, before they can strengthen themselves either in their position, or by reinforcements. I do not know what strength Genl Banks shows in your front. As far as I can learn, Genl Augur's division now opposite Fredericksburg has been drawn from the neighborhood of Warrenton. A second division, with which Genl McDowell is said to be, is reported as being directed upon Fredericksburg from the same point. It is certain that the enemy have not yet occupied Fredericksburg, but that several steamers containing troops and towing canal boats laden probably with provisions, and flat boats for the purpose perhaps of forming a bridge across the river, have ascended the Rappahannock, and I think from all indications they are collecting a strong force at that point.

For this purpose, they must weaken other points, and now is the time to concentrate on any that may be exposed within our reach. If Banks is too strong in numbers and position to attempt, cannot a blow be struck at the enemy in the direction of Warrenton, by a combination of your own and Ewell's command? With this view Genl Edward Johnson might be brought nearer to you. The dispersion of the enemy in that quarter would relieve Fredericksburg. But if neither of these movements be advisable, then a combination of Ewell and Field might be advisable, and a direct blow be given to the enemy at Fredericksburg. That you may judge of the practicability of this step I will mention, that in addition to Field's brigade, about 5,000 troops under Genl J. R. Anderson, including two field batteries, have joined him, and 3,000 on their way to him are yet to pass through this city. The blow wherever struck, must, to be successful, be sudden and heavy.

The troops used, must be efficient and light. I cannot pretend at this distance to direct operations depending on circumstances unknown to me and requiring the exercise of discretion and judgment as to time and execution, but submit these suggestions for your consideration.

I am general very respy, your obt servt

R. E. Lee
Genl Comdg

To Mary Lee (Robert E. Lee's Wife)

April 19, 1863

Camp, Fredericksburg

I received dear Mary your letter of the 15th contained in the box sent by Col Corley & a subsequent letter from you without date reached me to day enveloped in the *Churchman*. I am very glad to hear you are better & hope our visit to Shirley may restore you. I am very much obliged to you for the contents of the box. You must thank Mrs. Caskie, Mrs. Booker & dear Cousin Anne for their contributions to my comfort. They are very nice & I believe I enjoy the thought of their kindness even more than the good things they have sent. The jars I fear will be irrevocably lost, as it will be almost impossible to send them back. But I will try. Tell Miss Norvell & Sallie that I was afraid they would be so absorbed in their beaux that I should never get a sight of them, which would be so mortifying as to increase my disease & that I had better keep at a distance. The sight of them would have been very cheering to me I confess, but they are no longer school girls, & I cannot impose on them any more. Tell Miss Nannie she will have to suffer. I am sorry Mr. Caskie thinks I was jesting at his debility. I was hoping he would become stronger & was thinking of adding to his protection. The war will terminate some of these days & we shall all then be at peace. I send you a letter from Mrs. Coderise. Bev[erly Coderise?] is a fine boy & I wish I could do something for him. His mother has tried before to get him out of the service in various ways, but he has so far remained firm. If you see him tell him to write to me & say what I can do for him. I do not think our enemies are so confident of success as they used to be. If we can baffle them in their various designs this year & our people are true to our cause & not so devoted to themselves & their own aggrandisement, I think our success will be certain. We will have to suffer & must suffer to the end. But it will all come right. This year I hope will establish our supplies on a firm basis. On every other point we are strong. If successful this year, next fall there will be a great change in public opinion at the North. The Republicans will be destroyed & I think the friends of peace will become so strong as that the next administration will go in on that basis. We have only therefore to resist manfully. I think you had better not answer Mrs. C[oderise]. Do what you can for Bev, but be silent. You see their feelings & temper. I am better & returned to my camp three days since. I am feeble & worthless & can do but little. Kiss Chass & Agnes for me. Tell the former F[itzhugh] is working hard & is doing nobly. Kind love to all.

Very truly & affly
R. E. Lee

To General John Bell Hood
May 21, 1863

Camp, Fredericksburg

My Dear General:

Upon my return from Richmond I found your letter of the 13th awaiting me. Although separated from me, I have always had you in my eye and thoughts. I wished for you much in the last battle, and believe had I had the whole army with me, General Hooker would have been demolished. But God ordered otherwise.

I grieve much over the death of General Jackson. For our sakes not for his. He is happy and at peace. But his spirit lives with us. I hope it will raise up many Jacksons in our ranks. . . . I rely much upon you. You must so inspire and lead your brave division as that it may accomplish the work of a corps. . . . I agree with you in believing that our army would be invincible if it could be properly organized and officered. There never were such men in an army before. They will go anywhere and do anything if properly led. But there is the difficulty—proper commanders. Where can they be obtained? . . . . Wishing you every health and happiness, and commending you to the care of a kind Providence, I am, now and always your friend

R. E. Lee

To President Jefferson Davis

June 10, 1863

Headquarters, Army of Northern Virginia

Mr. President:

I beg leave to bring to your attention a subject with reference to which I have thought that the course pursued by writers and speakers among us has had a tendency to interfere with our success. I refer to the manner in which the demonstration of a desire for peace at the North has been received in our country.

I think there can be no doubt that journalists and others at the South, to whom the Northern people naturally look for a reflection of our opinions, have met these indications in such wise as to weaken the hands of the advocates of a pacific policy on the part of the Federal Government, and give much encouragement to those who urge a continuance of war.

Recent political movements in the United States, and the comments of influential newspapers upon them, have attracted my attention particularly to this subject, which I deem not unworthy of the consideration of Your Excellency, nor inappropriate to be adverted to by me in view of its connection with the situation of military affairs.

Conceding to our enemies the superiority claimed by them in numbers, resources, and all the means and appliances for carrying on the war, we have no right to look for exemptions from the military consequences of a vigorous use of these advantages, excepting by such deliverance as the mercy of Heaven may accord to the courage of our soldiers, the justice of our cause, and the constancy and prayers of our people. While making the most we can of the means of resistance we possess, and gratefully accepting the measure of success with which God has blessed our efforts as an earnest of His approval and favor, it is nevertheless the part of wisdom to carefully measure and husband our strength, and not to expect from it more than in the ordinary course of affairs it is capable of accomplishing. We should not therefore conceal from ourselves that our resources in men are constantly diminishing, and the disproportion in this respect between us and our enemies, if they continue united in their efforts to subjugate us, is steadily augmenting. The decrease of the aggregate of this army as disclosed by the returns affords an illustration of this fact. Its effective strength varies from time to time, but the falling off in its aggregate shows that its ranks are growing weaker and that its losses are not supplied by recruits.

Under these circumstances we should neglect no honorable means of dividing and weakening our enemies that they may feel some of the difficulties experienced by ourselves. It seems to me that the most effectual mode of accomplishing this object, now within our reach, is to give all the encouragement we can, consistently with truth, to the rising peace party of the North.

Nor do I think we should in this connection make nice distinctions between those who declare for peace unconditionally and those who advocate it as a means of restoring the Union however much we may prefer the former.

We should bear in mind that the friends of peace at the North must make concessions to the earnest desire that exists in the minds of their countrymen for a restoration of the Union, and that to hold out such a result as an inducement is essential to the success of their party.

Should the belief that peace will bring back the Union become general, the war would no longer be supported, and that after all is what we are interested in bringing about. When peace is proposed to us it will be time enough to discuss its terms, and it is not the part of prudence to spurn the proposition in advance, merely because those who wish to make it believe, or affect to believe, that it will result in bringing us back to the Union. We entertain no such apprehensions, nor doubt that the desire of our people for a distinct and independent national existence will prove as steadfast under the influence of peaceful measures as it has shown itself in the midst of war.

If the views I have indicated meet the approval of Your Excellency you will best know how to give effect to them. Should you deem them inexpedient or impracticable, I think you will nevertheless agree with me that we should at least carefully abstain from measures or expressions that tend to discourage any party whose purpose is peace.

With the statement of my own opinion on the subject, the length of which you will excuse, I leave to your better judgment to determine the proper course to be pursued.

I am with great respect, your obt servt
R. E. Lee
Genl

To General Samuel Cooper, November 4, 1863

General: The application of Colonel Hamilton, of South Carolina, for the transfer of the First Regiment South Carolina Volunteers, formerly commanded by him, to that State for duty, has been received. If the regiment could really be recruited in South Carolina, it might be well to transfer it thither, provided, meantime, a good regiment from that department could be sent to this army to take its place, and thus preserve the integrity of McGowan's brigade, to which it belongs. As to the transfer of troops from the Army of Northern Virginia to the Department of South Carolina at this period, I will make a statement of the facts as I conceive them, and leave it to the Department to decide the question. Meade is in our front, gradually advancing and repairing the railroad, having already reached Warrenton Junction. His army, consisting of five corps of infantry and three divisions of cavalry, has been re-enforced to some extent since its late retreat on Washington, and is variously estimated at from 60,000 to 80,000 effective men. To oppose this the Army of Northern Virginia presents an effective total not greatly exceeding that of General Beauregard's army, which has opposed to it, so far as I can learn, one corps of the enemy which will hardly number more than 20,000 men, exclusive of the naval forces engaged in the attack on Charleston.

I believe the troops of this army have been called upon in winter, spring, and summer to do almost as active service as those of any other department, and I do not see that the good of the service will be promoted by scattering its brigades and regiments along all the threatened points of the Confederacy. It is only by the concentration of our troops that we can hope to win any decisive advantage.

I am, very respectfully, your obedient servant,

R. E. Lee,
General.

2. President Jefferson Davis, C.S.A., Defends His Overall Defensive Strategy, 1862

My Dear Sir,

I have the pleasure to acknowledge yours of the 2d Inst. and so far from find-ing any thing to excuse, I have to offer you my thanks for the kind spirit and mani-fest confidence with which you communicate to me the unfavorable impressions you /have/ found to exist in relation to my policy for the conduct of our military operations.

There could be no difference of opinion as to the advantage of invading over being invaded, if we except that class of politicians who feared to excite the hate of our enemies, and the few others who clung to the /delusive/ hope of aid from our old party-allies at the North. My early declared purpose and continued hope was to feed upon the enemy and teach them the blessings of peace by making them feel in its most tangible form the evils of war.

The time and place for invasion has been a question not of will but of power. There have been occasions when it seemed to me possible to make aggressive movements upon detachments of the enemy and they were pointed out to our Gen-erals, but they did not avail themselves of them, and it may be that their caution was wise, at least I have thought it proper to defer much to the opinions of commanders in the field, and have felt the hazard of requiring a General to execute, what he did not favorably entertain. The report to which you refer that I restrained the army after the Battles of [first] Manassas and Leesburg obtained such currency and was doing such injury to our cause, that I asked Genl Johnston, whether I had counselled against pursuit after the battle of Manassas or had at any other time restrained the army from any active operations, which it was possible to attempt. He assured me unqualifiedly in the negative and reiterated his opinion of the impossibility of a pur-suit after the battle of Manassas, adding that it was not even contemplated.

I cite from memory, but his letter was read in the Congress and should have prevented the repetition of the falsehood by those who have been most industrious in circulating it. If I have borne unjust criticism in silence and allowed vain men to shift the responsibilities of their grievous failures upon me, it has not been because I, "spurned public opinion or was obstinately deaf to the councils of my ablest co-laborers in the revolution," but because every feeling was subjected to the purpose of success in our struggle for recognized independence. It has not happened so far as my memory serves, that any true friend of our cause has advised me to a change of policy without being answered to his satisfaction. The difference in the beginning being usually the result of untenable premises. Of course I do not

From Jefferson Davis to John Forsyth, July 18, 1862, reprinted in Lynda Lasswell Crist and Mary Seaton Dix, eds. *The Papers of Jefferson Davis* (Baton Rouge, LSU P., 1995), VIII, 293–295.

include in the term *true friends* that class who make issues for selfish ends and talk for popular effect. My respect for public opinion would have led me, as my personal advantage might have urged me to announce our weakness and want of the munitions of war, but this could not have been done without publishing to the enemy our assailable points, and if I had thus avoided the disapprobation of our people, it would have been a poor exchange for that which I must have acquired, self condemnation. That there should have been much misapprehension as to our ability to achieve what the country desired does not surprise me for the people have generally no measure of military operations and but little oppertunity to obtain correct information. A General reduced to the necessity of standing on the defensive necessarily conceals his weakness from even his own troops. For example, when I visited the Army of the Potomac, last fall, a Brig Genl. serving there and who had joined after the battles, gave to me /his/ opinion that we should advance into the Enemy's country, by turning his works in front of Alexandria and Washington, assuring me that the army was eager to invade. I asked him with what force we could venture to cross the Potomac, he said he would risk the movement with forty thousand men. I then asked him how he would hold the enemy in check in the position from which he then threatened to advance upon Richmond, he said that he believed thirty thousand men would suffice for that, when our army made a demonstration in rear of the enemy's Capital &c. &c. In discussing questions of immediate operations against the Enemy I had that morning called for a report of the effective strength of the Army and it was in round numbers thirty-five thousand. I have remembered the conversation the better, because it has often occurred to me when I have heard of impatience because impossible things were not attempted; and have pitied as much as blamed officers, whose desire to conceal their weakness, led them to the unjustifiable resort of pointing censure against "the Administration" for their own supposed inactivity. Now, Sir, as to the remedy which you propose for existing discontent. Never having preferred defensive to offensive war, but the rather pined for the day when our soil should be free from invasion and our banners float over the fields of the Enemy, with what propriety could I say "we stand upon the defensive no more" and what value would the declaration have unless it was followed by an advance into the enemy's country. And if I could to-night issue orders to an army adequate to the work of invasion, how could I conscientiously gain the public applause by revealing to the enemy the ordeal to which he was about to be subjected, and thus diminishing our chances for success.

I love approbation and will toil on though it be through evil report, [2nd Corinthians, 6:8] to deserve, with the hope that I may gain it. Your friend & fellow citizen

(Signed) Jeffn Davis.

3. General James Longstreet, C.S.A., Criticizes Lee's Generalship (1863–1864), 1895

My impression was, and is, that General Lee, standing under his trenches, would have been stronger against Hooker [at Chancellorsville] than he was in December [at

From James Longstreet. *From Manassas to Appomattox: Memoirs of the Civil War in America* (Philadelphia: Lippincott, 1895; New York: Da Capo Press, 1992), 329–331, 401–406.

Fredericksburg] against Burnside, and that he would have grown stronger every hour of delay, while Hooker would have grown weaker in morale and in confidence of his plan and the confidence of his troops. He had interior lines for defence, while his adversary was divided by two crossings of the river, which made Lee's sixty thousand for defence about equal to the one hundred and thirteen thousand under General Hooker. By the time that the divisions of Pickett and Hood could have joined General Lee, General Hooker would have found that he must march to attack or make a retreat without battle. It seems probable that under the original plan the battle would have given fruits worthy of a general engagement. The Confederates would then have had opportunity, and have been in condition to so follow Hooker as to have compelled his retirement to Washington, and that advantage might have drawn Grant from Vicksburg; whereas General Lee was actually so crippled by his victory that he was a full month restoring his army to condition to take the field. In defensive warfare he was perfect. When the hunt was up, his combativeness was overruling. . . .

The battle [of Chancellorsville] as pitched and as an independent affair was brilliant, and if the war was for glory could be called successful, but, besides putting the cause upon the hazard of a die, it was crippling in resources and of future progress, while the wait of a few days would have given time for concentration and opportunities against Hooker more effective than we experienced with Burnside at Fredericksburg. This was one of the occasions where success was not a just criterion.

After reporting to General Lee, I offered the suggestions made to Secretary [of War] Seddon, in regard to the means that should be adopted for the relief of Vicksburg. I thought that honor, interest, duty, and humanity called us to that service, and asked the aid of his counsels with the War Department, and reinforcements from his army for the West, to that end. I suggested that General Johnston, instead of trying to collect an army against General Grant, should be sent to reinforce General Bragg, then standing against the Union forces under General Rosecrans in Middle Tennessee; that at the same time he should send my divisions, just up from Suffolk, to join Johnston's reinforcements to Bragg's army; that the combination once made should strike immediately in overwhelming force upon Rosecrans, and march for the Ohio River and Cincinnati.

[Lee] recognized the suggestion as of good combination, and giving strong assurance of success, but he was averse to having a part of his army so far beyond his reach. He reflected over the matter one or two days, and then fell upon the plan of invading the Northern soil, and so threatening Washington as to bring about the same hoped-for result. To that end he bent his energies.

His plan or wishes announced, it became useless and improper to offer suggestions leading to a different course. All that I could ask was that the policy of the campaign should be one of defensive tactics; that we should work so as to force the enemy to attack us, in such good position as we might find in his own country, so well adapted to that purpose,—which might assure us of a grand triumph. To this he readily assented as an important and material adjunct to his general plan. His confidence in making moves threatening Washington and the invasion of Maryland and Pennsylvania grew out of the known anxiety of the Washington authorities as to the safety of their capital and of quiet within the Union lines. . . .

It is difficult to reconcile these facts with the reports put out after his death by members of his family and of his staff, and *post-bellum* champions, that indicate his later efforts to find points by which to so work up public opinion as to shift the disaster [at Gettysburg] to my shoulders. . . .

General Lee was on the field from about three o'clock of the afternoon of the first day. Every order given the troops of the First Corps on that field up to its march on the forenoon of the 2d was issued in his presence. If the movements were not satisfactory in time and speed of moving, it was his power, duty, and privilege to apply the remedy, but it was not a part of a commander's duty or privilege to witness things that did not suit him, fail to apply the remedy, and go off and grumble with his staff-officers about it. In their efforts to show culpable delay in the movements of the First Corps on the 2d, some of the Virginia writers endeavor to show that General Lee did not even give me a guide to lead the way to the field from which his battle was to be opened. He certainly failed to go and look at it, and assist in selecting the ground and preparing for action.

Fitzhugh Lee says of the second day, "Longstreet was attacking the Marye's Hill of the position." At Fredericksburg, General Burnside attacked at Marye's Hill in six or more successive assaults with some twenty or thirty thousand against three brigades under McLaws and Ransom and the artillery; he had about four hundred yards to march from his covered ways about Fredericksburg to Marye's Hill. When his last attack was repulsed in the evening, he arranged and gave his orders for the attack to be renewed in the morning, giving notice that he would lead it with the Ninth Corps, but upon reports of his officers abandoned it. General Lee's assaulting columns of fifteen or twenty thousand had a march of a mile to attack double their numbers, better defended than were the three brigades of Confederates at Marye's Hill that drove back Burnside. The enemy on Cemetery Hill was in stronger position than the Confederates at Marye's Hill.

Fitzhugh Lee writes . . . [in *General Lee*],—

> "Over the splendid scene of human courage and human sacrifice at Gettysburg there arises in the South an apparition, like Banquo's ghost at Macbeth's banquet, which says the battle was lost to the Confederates because some one blundered."

Call them Banquo, but their name is Legion. Weird spirits keep midnight watch about the great boulders, while unknown comrades stalk in ghostly ranks through the black fastnesses of Devil's Den, wailing the lament, "Some one blundered at Gettysburg! Woe is me, whose duty was to die!"

Fitzhugh Lee makes his plans, orders, and movements to suit his purpose, and claims that they would have given Gettysburg to the Confederates, but he is not likely to convince any one outside of his coterie that over the heights of Gettysburg was to be found honor for the South.

General Meade said that the suggestion to work towards his line of communication was sound "military sense." That utterance has been approved by subsequent fair judgment, and it is that potent fact that draws the spiteful fire of latter-day knights.

Forty thousand men, unsupported as we were, could not have carried the position at Gettysburg. The enemy was there. Officers and men knew their advantage, and were resolved to stay until the hills came down over them. It is simply out of the question for a lesser force to march over broad, open fields and carry a fortified front occupied by a greater force of seasoned troops. . . .

Even Napoleon Bonaparte, the first in the science and greatest in the execution of the art of war, finally lost grasp of his grandest thought:

"In war men are nothing; a man is everything."

The Confederate chief at Gettysburg looked something like Napoleon at Waterloo.

Fitzhugh Lee quotes evidence of Governor Carroll, of Maryland, that General Lee said, "Longstreet is the hardest man to move in my army."

It does not look like generalship to lose a battle and a cause and then lay the responsibility upon others. He held command and was supported by his government. If his army did not suit him, his word could have changed it in a minute. If he failed to apply the remedy, it was his fault. Some claim that his only fault as a general was his tender, generous heart. But a heart in the right place looks more to the cause intrusted to its care than for hidden ways by which to shift its responsibility to the shoulders of those whose lives hang upon his word.

4. H. A. Yellowley, a Southern White Woman Tells of Slaves Running off to Join the Yankees Who Armed Them, 1862

Oak Grove Nash Co. Nov 16 1862

My Dear Brother

Mr. Patrick left here this morning he came up last night with Feriby and her children and Louis, Daniel returned with him to bring up the others as soon as the crop is housed. They had to take back the mules, he sold them to Mr. Caring without his seeing them, on the reccomendation of Mr. Albritton and Mr. Howell, Mr. C become dissatisfied and to [prevent] a suit, he took them back. The negroes are all well. Nancy is at home no one would permit her to stay on there plantation she behaves so badly. Mr. P says she maid an attempt to go to the Yankees but was prevented by Sylas. I would not have her I would get some one to sell her, negroes are bringing fine prices, a great many have gone to the Yankees, the Yankees ware at Greenville last Sunday they remained but a short time, one of our pickets shot and killed one of them, they set the Bridge on fire to revenge his death; after finding it was'nt any of the inhabitants of the Town they allowed it to be put out, it was'nt injured very materially. When leaving the warf they gave a general invitation to all the negroes to go with them, none left at that time there Artillery was drawn through the Streets by negroes those that left Greenville the negroes ware all in Uniform belts Swords and Pistols around them. They carried of 10 of[f] the Citizans they remained all night in the bank all returned next day but one, Mr. Cobb was detained because he has been in service. The negroes ware all well pleased at the sight of the Yankees, they ware unmanageble for several day after there departure but sobered down again to there old habits. I met Mr. Atkinson and Murry in the road last Wednesday with a part of his negroes 30 of his have left him 5 of Dr. Gormans his two Carpenters and House servant. Cousin Louisa and all of her negroes are in Nashvelle, Mr. Joe Biggs and Caden Biggs have bought lots in

---

H. A. Yellowley to her Brother, November 16, 1862 from the Henry T. King Collection, East Carolina Manuscript Collection. East Carolina University, Greenville, N. C.

Hilliardston, the neighborhood is crowded with Refugees and negroes. A great many people have left Greenville and are still mooveing. What is to become of us all I know not. I heard from Jimmie last week, he was quite, well and wanted money to take him from school the last of this month poor little fellow he has no home to go to Mr. Patrick handid me 252 dollars belonging to you, I gave him a receipt for it, what must I do with it? Cousin Jo was to see you the day after you left Camp, he carried the books you wanted some Apples onions and a pair of Socks in the small Carpet bag. he left them and a letter in the care of one of your men his name is Harris, he carried for Eddy one blanket, Overcoat, two flannel Shirts, apples and potatoes the potatoes ware to be divided with you Mr. Patrick wrote to you a few days ago, and gave you all the particulars about Home. I hope this letter will find you in Camp. I hope you all got back safe and in health, I have been greatly troubled about you; the weather has been so bad for the last two weeks. Not long since we ware informed of the death of poor Charlton he was wounded on the 14 of Sept at the South Mountain M D. was taken prisoner and carried to the hospittle at Frederic, he died the first of October; poor fellow he suffered much he was wounded in the leg and thigh so high up that it would not admit of an amputation, he leaves a wife and 4 little Children. I fear that Sylas will not be willing to leave his wife to come up here I think Nancy will be a great trouble to you it will be imposs- to keep her in a home she sent to Mr. C. for Lydia to take of with her, she and Dr. Browns Nancy ware going off together. The Yankees say they intend taking possession of the Town when they come up again. They ware met by a good many white persons male and female. Joe Dany Hodges, Hoell, Tyce, Cobb, B. Albritton, Bob Greene, Allen Tice, Jim Forbs, A. Forbs, Bill Stocks, was arrested I believe I have told you all that I can think of. I hope you will let me hear from you soon. Tell Eddy Bob says he must write to him and let him know whare he is, he wants to visit him. Joe health is restored he will return to his Regiment next week. Dorsey and Jimmie are near Winchester we heard from them yesterday both ware well. Accept of my warmest love and write soon to your affectionate sister,

H. A. Yellowley

5. Private James Henry Gooding, a Northern Black Soldier, Fights for Freedom and the Union, 1863

[*Mercury,* August 1, 1863]

Morris Island, July 20, 1863

Messrs. Editors:—At last we have something stirring to record. The 54th, the past week, has proved itself twice in battle. The first was on James Island on the morning of the 16th. There were four companies of the 54th on picket duty at the time; our picket lines extending to the right of the rebel battery, which commands the approach to Charleston through the Edisto river. About 3 o'clock in the morning, the rebels began harassing our pickets on the right, intending, no doubt, to drive them

---

From James Henry Gooding, July 20, 1863, to *The Mercury* [New Bedford, MA], reprinted in James Henry Gooding. *On the Altar of Freedom: A Black Soldier's Civil War Letters from the Front,* edited by Virginia Matzke Adams (Amherst: U. Mass. P., 1991), 36–39.

in, so that by daylight the coast would be clear to rush their main force down on us, and take us by surprise. They did not suppose we had any considerable force to the rear of our pickets on the right, as Gen. Stevenson's brigade was plain in sight on the left; and their plan, I suppose, was to rush down and cut Gen. Stevenson off. They made a mistake—instead of returning fire, the officer in charge of the pickets directed the men to lie down under cover of a hedge, rightly expecting the rebels to advance by degrees toward our lines. As he expected, at daylight they were within 600 yards of the picket line, when our men rose and poured a volley into them. That was something the rebels didn't expect—their line of skirmishers was completely broken; our men then began to fall back gradually on our line of battle, as the rebels were advancing their main force on to them. On they came, with six pieces of artillery and four thousand infantry, leaving a heavy force to drive Gen. Stevenson on the left. As their force advanced on our right, the boys held them in check like veterans; but of course they were falling back all the time, and fighting too. After the officers saw there was no chance for their men, they ordered them to move on to a creek under cover of the gunboats. When the rebels got within 900 yards of our line of battle, the right wing of Gen. Terry's brigade gave them three volleys, which checked their advance. They then made a stand with their artillery and began shelling us, but it had no effect on our forces, as the rebels fired too high. The 6th Connecticut battery then opened fire on them from the right, the John Adams and May Flower from the creek between James and Cole Islands, and the Pawnee and a mortar schooner from the Edisto [i.e., Stono], when the rebels began a hasty retreat. It was a warmer reception than they had expected. Our loss in the skirmishing before the battle, so far as we can ascertain, was nine killed, 13 wounded, and 17 missing, either killed or taken prisoners; but more probably they were driven into the creek and drowned. Sergeant Wilson, of Co. H, was called upon to surrender, but would not; he shot four men before he was taken. After he was taken they ordered him to give up his pistol which he refused to do, when he was shot through the head.

The men of the 54th behaved gallantly on the occasion—so the Generals say. It is not for us to blow our horn; but when a regiment of white men gave us three cheers as we were passing them, it shows that we did our duty as men should.

I shall pass over the incidents of that day, as regards individuals, to speak of a greater and more terrible ordeal the 54th regiment has passed through. I shall say nothing now of how we came from James to Morris Island; suffice it to say, on Saturday afternoon we were marched up past our batteries, amid the cheers of the officers and soldiers. We wondered what they were all cheering for, but we soon found out. Gen. Strong rode up, and we halted. Well, you had better believe there was some guessing what we were to do. Gen. Strong asked us if we would follow him into Fort Wagner. Every man said, yes—we were ready to follow wherever we were led. You may all know Fort Wagner is the Sebastopol of the rebels; but we went at it, over the ditch and on to the parapet through a deadly fire; but we could not get into the fort. We met the foe on the parapet of Wagner with the bayonet— we were exposed to a murderous fire from the batteries of the fort, from our Monitors and our land batteries, as they did not cease firing soon enough. Mortal men could not stand such a fire, and the assault on Wagner was a failure. The 9th Me., 10th Conn., 63d Ohio, 48th and 100th N.Y. were to support us in the assault; but after we made the first charge, everything was in such confusion that we could hardly tell where the reserve was. At the first charge the 54th rushed to within twenty yards of the ditches, and, as might be expected of raw recruits, wavered— but at the second advance they gained the parapet. The color bearer of the State colors was killed on the parapet. Col. Shaw seized the staff when the standard bearer fell, and in less than a minute after, the Colonel fell himself. When the men saw their gallant leader fall, they made a desperate effort to get him out, but they were either shot down, or reeled in the ditch below. One man succeeded in getting hold of the State color staff, but the color was completely torn to pieces.

I have no more paper here at present, as all our baggage is at St. Helena yet; so I cannot further particularize in this letter. Lieut. Grace was knocked down by a piece of shell, but he is not injured. He showed himself a great deal braver and cooler than any line officer.

J. H. G.

6. General Ulysses S. Grant, U.S.A., Commits the Union Army to Relentless Offensive, 1864

City Point, Va. June 23d 1864.

Maj. Gen. H. W. Halleck
Chief of Staff of the Army,
General,

The siege of Richmond bids fare to be tedious, and in consequence of the very extended lines we must have, a much larger force will be necessary than would be required in ordinary sieges against the same force that now opposes us. With my present force I feel perfectly safe against Lee's Army, and acting defensively would still fèel so against Lee and Johnston combined. But we want to act offensively. In my opinion to do this, effectively we should concentrate our whole energy against the two principal Armies of the enemy. In other words nothing should be attempted except in Georgia and here, that is not directly in co-operation with these moves. West of the Miss. I would not attempt any thing until the rebellion East of it is entirely subdued. I would then direct Canby to leave Smith unmolested where he is; to make no move except such as is necessary to protect what he now holds. All the troops he can spare should be sent here at once. In my opinion the white troops of the 19th Corps can all come together, with many of the colored troops.

I wish you would place this matter before the Sec. of War and urge that no offensive operations West of the Miss. be allowed to commence until matters here are settled. Send the 19th Corps and such other troops as you can, from the Dept. of the Gulf, to me.

Very respectfully
your obt. svt.
U. S. Grant
Lt. Gen.

Gen. U. S. Grant to Gen. Henry W. Halleck, June 23, 1864, in John Y. Simon, ed., *The Papers of Ulysses S. Grant* (Carbondale: Southern Illinois University Press, 1984), vol. 11, pp. 111–112. Copyright © 1984 by The Ulysses S. Grant Association, reprinted by permission of the publisher, Southern Illinois University Press.

7. General William T. Sherman, U.S.A., Justifies Taking War to the Civilians, 1864

Headquarters Military Division of the Mississippi, in the Field,
Atlanta, Georgia, September 12, 1864.

James M. Calhoun, Mayor, E. E. Rawson
and S. C. Wells, representing City Council of Atlanta.

Gentlemen: I have your letter of the 11th, in the nature of a petition to revoke my orders removing all the inhabitants from Atlanta. I have read it carefully, and give full credit to your statements of the distress that will be occasioned, and yet shall not revoke my orders, because they were not designed to meet the humanities of the case, but to prepare for the future struggles in which millions of good people outside of Atlanta have a deep interest. We must have peace, not only at Atlanta, but in all America. To secure this, we must stop the war that now desolates our once happy and favored country. To stop war, we must defeat the rebel armies which are arrayed against the laws and Constitution that all must respect and obey. To defeat those armies, we must prepare the way to reach them in their recesses, provided with the arms and instruments which enable us to accomplish our purpose. Now, I know the vindictive nature of our enemy, that we may have many years of military operations from this quarter; and, therefore, deem it wise and prudent to prepare in time. The use of Atlanta for warlike purposes is inconsistent with its character as a home for families. There will be no manufactures, commerce, or agriculture here, for the maintenance of families, and sooner or later want will compel the inhabitants to go. Why not go now, when all the arrangements are completed for the transfer, instead of waiting till the plunging shot of contending armies will renew the scenes of the past month? Of course, I do not apprehend any such thing at this moment, but you do not suppose this army will be here until the war is over. I cannot discuss this subject with you fairly, because I cannot impart to you what we propose to do, but I assert that our military plans make it necessary for the inhabitants to go away, and I can only renew my offer of services to make their exodus in any direction as easy and comfortable as possible.

You cannot qualify war in harsher terms than I will. War is cruelty, and you cannot refine it; and those who brought war into our country deserve all the curses and maledictions a people can pour out. I know I had no hand in making this war, and I know I will make more sacrifices to-day than any of you to secure peace. But you cannot have peace and a division of our country. If the United States submits to a division now, it will not stop, but will go on until we reap the fate of Mexico, which is eternal war. The United States does and must assert its authority, wherever it once had power; for, if it relaxes one bit to pressure, it is gone, and I believe that such is the national feeling. This feeling assumes various shapes, but always comes back to that of Union. Once admit the Union, once more acknowledge the authority of the national Government, and, instead of devoting your houses and streets and roads to the dread uses of war, I and this army become at once your

From William T. Sherman. Response to the Mayor and City Council of Atlanta, September 12, 1864, reprinted in *William Tecumseh Sherman: The Memoirs of General W. T. Sherman* (New York: Library of America, 1990), 600–602.

protectors and supporters, shielding you from danger, let it come from what quarter it may. I know that a few individuals cannot resist a torrent of error and passion, such as swept the South into rebellion, but you can point out, so that we may know those who desire a government, and those who insist on war and its desolation.

You might as well appeal against the thunder-storm as against these terrible hardships of war. They are inevitable, and the only way the people of Atlanta can hope once more to live in peace and quiet at home, is to stop the war, which can only be done by admitting that it began in error and is perpetuated in pride.

We don't want your negroes, or your horses, or your houses, or your lands, or any thing you have, but we do want and will have a just obedience to the laws of the United States. That we will have, and, if it involves the destruction of your improvements, we cannot help it.

You have heretofore read public sentiment in your newspapers, that live by falsehood and excitement; and the quicker you seek for truth in other quarters, the better. I repeat then that, by the original compact of Government, the United States had certain rights in Georgia, which have never been relinquished and never will be; that the South began war by seizing forts, arsenals, mints, customhouses, etc., etc., long before Mr. Lincoln was installed, and before the South had one jot or tittle of provocation. I myself have seen in Missouri, Kentucky, Tennessee, and Mississippi, hundreds and thousands of women and children fleeing from your armies and desperadoes, hungry and with bleeding feet. In Memphis, Vicksburg, and Mississippi, we fed thousands upon thousands of the families of rebel soldiers left on our hands, and whom we could not see starve. Now that war comes home to you, you feel very different. You deprecate its horrors, but did not feel them when you sent car-loads of soldiers and ammunition, and moulded shells and shot, to carry war into Kentucky and Tennessee, to desolate the homes of hundreds and thousands of good people who only asked to live in peace at their old homes, and under the Government of their inheritance. But these comparisons are idle. I want peace, and believe it can only be reached through union and war, and I will ever conduct war with a view to perfect and early success.

But, my dear sirs, when peace does come, you may call on me for any thing. Then will I share with you the last cracker, and watch with you to shield your homes and families against danger from every quarter.

Now you must go, and take with you the old and feeble, feed and nurse them, and build for them, in more quiet places, proper habitations to shield them against the weather until the mad passions of men cool down, and allow the Union and peace once more to settle over your old homes at Atlanta. Yours in haste,

W. T. Sherman, Major-General commanding.

⚟ E S S A Y S

Robert E. Lee, one of the most celebrated figures in American military history, also remains one of the most controversial. After his death in 1870, his friends consciously stressed his strengths and minimized his failings, as they constructed an image of him as the Southern hero par excellence, a "marble man" in the phrase of historian Thomas

L. Connelly, who traced Lee's apotheosis. The debate continues, however, over Lee's generalship. Was he a brilliant general or a flawed commander? In the first essay, Douglass Southall Freeman, a native Virginian, former editor of the Richmond *News Leader,* authority on the Civil War and recipient of the 1935 Pulitzer Prize for his four-volume biography of Robert E. Lee, summarizes Lee's greatness as a military commander. In contrast, Albert T. Nolan, a Harvard Law School graduate, Indianapolis attorney, Fellow of the Company of Military Historians, member of the Indianapolis Civil War Round Table, and author of several publications about the war, sees Lee as a flawed general. The third essay deals with the controversy over whether the Civil War was the first modern "total" war; Mark E. Neely, Jr., director of the Lincoln Museum in Fort Wayne, Indiana, and author of several books on the Civil War, offers a number of reasons why it was not.

Robert E. Lee: A Brilliant Commander

DOUGLASS SOUTHALL FREEMAN

No scratch was on the sword that General Lee laid away that April day in Richmond on his return from Appomattox. His weapon had never been raised except in salute. Rarely had it been even drawn from its scabbard. Yet it was the symbol of a four-year war, the symbol of an army and of a cause. . . .

Had his sense of duty held him to the Union, as it held Winfield Scott and George H. Thomas, how much easier his course would have been! Never, then, after the first mobilization, would he have lacked for troops or been compelled to count the cost of any move. He would not have agonized over men who shivered in their nakedness or dyed the road with shoeless, bleeding feet. Well clad they would have been, and well fed, too. They would not have been brought down to the uncertain ration of a pint of meal and a quarter of a pound of Nassau bacon. The superior artillery would have been his, not his adversary's. On his order new locomotives and stout cars would have rolled to the front, swiftly to carry his army where the feeble engines and the groaning trains of the Confederacy could not deliver men. He would have enjoyed the command of the sea; so that he could have advanced his base a hundred miles, or two hundred, without the anguish of a single, choking march. If one jaded horse succumbed on a raid, the teeming prairies would have supplied two. His simplicity, his tact, his ability, and his self-abnegation would have won the confidence of Lincoln that McClellan lost and neither Pope, Burnside, nor Hooker ever possessed. He would, in all human probability, have won the war, and now he would be preparing to ride up Pennsylvania Avenue, as was Grant, at the head of a victorious army, on his way to the White House.

But, after the manner of the Lees, he had held unhesitatingly to the older allegiance, and had found it the way of difficulty. Always the odds had been against him, three to two in this campaign, two to one in that. Not once, in a major engagement, had he met the Federals on even terms; not once, after a victory, had his army been strong enough to follow it up. . . . Always, within this exposed territory, his prime mission had been that of defending a capital close to the frontier. With poverty he had faced abundance; with individualism his people had opposed nationalism.

Desperate as his country's disadvantage had been, it had been darkened by mistakes, financial, political, and military. Of some of these he had not been cognizant, and of others he had not spoken because they lay beyond a line his sense of a soldier's duty forbade his passing. Against other errors he had protested to no purpose. From the first shot at Sumter he had realized that the South could only hope to win its independence by exerting itself to the utmost; yet he had not been able to arouse the people from the overconfidence born at Bull Run. Vainly he had pleaded for the strict enforcement of the conscription laws, exempting no able-bodied man. Times unnumbered he had pointed out that concentration could only be met by like concentration, and that the less important points must be exposed that the more important might be saved. On the strategy of particular campaigns he had been heard and heeded often; on the larger strategy of full preparation, his influence had not been great, except as respected the first conscription act. Regarding the commissary he might as well not have spoken at all, because Mr. Davis held to Northrop until it was too late to save the army from the despair that hunger always breeds.

Lee had himself made mistakes. Perhaps no one could have saved Western Virginia in 1861, but he had failed to recover it. With it the Confederacy had lost the shortest road to the Union railway communications between East and West. In his operations on that front and during the Seven Days, he had demanded professional efficiency of an amateur staff and had essayed a strategy his subordinates had been incapable of executing tactically. After Second Manassas he had overestimated the endurance of his men, and in Maryland he had miscalculated the time required for the reduction of Harpers Ferry. Longstreet had been permitted to idle away in front of Suffolk the days that might have been spent in bringing his two divisions back to Chancellorsville to crush the baffled Hooker. In reorganizing the army after the death of Jackson, Lee had erred in giving corps command to Ewell. Apart from the blunders of that officer and the sulking of Longstreet at Gettysburg, he had lost the Pennsylvania campaign because his confidence in his troops had led him to assume the offensive in the enemy's country before his remodelled machine had been adjusted to his direction. At Rappahannock Bridge he had misread the movements of the Federals, and in the Wilderness, on the night of May 5–6, 1864, he had left Wilcox and Heth in a position too exposed for their weary divisions to hold. Wrongly he had acquiesced in the occupation of the Bloody Angle at Spotsylvania. Incautiously, that blusterous 11th of May he had withdrawn his artillery from Johnson's position. The detachment of Hampton and of Early, however necessary, had crippled him in coping with Grant when the Army of the Potomac crossed the James. He had strangely underestimated Sheridan's strength in the Shenandoah Valley, and he had failed to escape from Petersburg. Until the final retreat, none of these errors or failures, unless it was that of invading Pennsylvania so soon after the reorganization of the army, affected the outcome of the war, but together they exacted of the South some of its bravest blood.

Deeper still had been the defect of Lee's excessive amiability. . . . His consideration for others, the virtue of the gentleman, had been his vice as a soldier.

Perhaps to this defect may be added a mistaken theory of the function of the high command. As he explained to Scheibert, he believed that the general-in-chief should strive to bring his troops together at the right time and place and that he should leave combat to the generals of brigade and division. To this theory, which he had learned from Scott, Lee steadfastly held from his opening campaign through the battle of the Wilderness. It was for this reason, almost as much as because of his consideration for the feelings of another, that he deferred to Longstreet at Second Manassas and did not himself direct the attacks of the Confederate right on July 2 and 3 at Gettysburg. Who may say whether, when his campaigns are viewed as a whole, adherence to this theory of his function cost the army more than it won for the South? If this policy failed with Longstreet, it was gloriously successful with Jackson. If the failure at Gettysburg was partly chargeable to it, the victory at Chancellorsville was in large measure the result of its application. Not properly applicable to a small army or in an open country, this theory of command may have justified itself when Lee's troops were too numerous to be directed by one man in the tangled terrain where Lee usually fought. Once adopted where woods obscured operations, Lee's method could not easily be recast for employment in the fields of Pennsylvania.

When Lee's inordinate consideration for his subordinates is given its gloomiest appraisal, when his theory of command is disputed, when his mistakes are written red, when the remorseless audit of history discounts the odds he faced in men and resources, and when the court of time writes up the advantage he enjoyed in fighting on inner lines in his own country, the balance to the credit of his generalship is clear and absolute.

In three fast-moving months he mobilized Virginia and so secured her defense that the war had been in progress a year before the Unionists were within fifty miles of Richmond. Finding the Federals, when he took command of the Army of Northern Virginia on June 1, 1862, almost under the shadow of the city's steeples, he saved the capital from almost certain capture and the Confederate cause from probable collapse. He repulsed four major offensives against Richmond and by his invasion of Pennsylvania he delayed the fifth for ten months. Ere the Federals were back on the Richmond line again—two years to the day from the time he had succeeded Johnston—Lee had fought ten major battles: Gaines's Mill, Frayser's Farm, Malvern Hill, Second Manassas, Sharpsburg, Fredericksburg, Chancellorsville, Gettysburg, the Wilderness, and Spotsylvania. Six of these he had indisputably won. At Frayser's Farm he had gained the field but had not enveloped the enemy as he had planned. Success had not been his at Malvern Hill and at Sharpsburg, but only at Gettysburg had he met with definite defeat, and even there he clouded the title of his adversary to a clear-cut victory. During the twenty-four months when he had been free to employ open manœuvre, a period that had ended with Cold Harbor, he had sustained approximately 103,000 casualties and had inflicted 145,000. Holding, as he usually had, to the offensive, his combat losses had been greater in proportion to his numbers than those of the Federals, but he had demonstrated how strategy may increase an opponent's casualties, for his losses included only 16,000 prisoners, whereas he had taken 38,000. Chained at length to the Richmond defenses, he had saved the capital from capture for ten months. All this he had done in the face of repeated defeats for the Southern troops in nearly every other part of the Confederacy. In explanation of the inability of the South to capitalize its successes, one British visitor quoted Lee as saying: "The more [the Confederates] followed up the victory against one portion of the enemy's line the more did they lay themselves open to be surrounded by the remainder of the enemy." Lee "likened the operation to a man breasting a wave of sea, who, as rapidly as he clears a way before him, is enveloped by the very water he has displaced." These difficulties of the South would have been even worse had not the Army of Northern Virginia occupied so much of the thought and armed strength of the North. Lee is to be judged, in fact, not merely by what he accomplished with his own troops but by what he prevented the hosts of the Union from doing sooner elsewhere.

The accurate reasoning of a trained and precise mind is the prime explanation of all these achievements. Lee was preeminently a strategist, and a strategist because he was a sound military logician. It is well enough to speak of his splendid presence on the field of battle, his poise, his cheer, and his manner with his men, but essentially he was an intellect, with a developed aptitude for the difficult synthesis of war. The incidental never obscured the fundamental. The trivial never distracted. He had the ability—who can say how or why?—to visualize his fundamental problem as though it had been worked out in a model and set before his eyes. In Richmond, during May, 1862, to cite but one instance, he saw clearly where others saw but dimly, if at all, that Jackson's little army in the Valley was the pawn with which to save the castle of Richmond.

Once his problem was thus made graphic, he projected himself mentally across the lines to the position of his adversary. What was the logical thing—not the desirable thing from the Confederate point of view—for his opponent to do? Assuming that the Federals had intelligent leadership, he said, "It is proper for us to expect [the enemy] to do what he ought to do." After he had studied the probabilities, he would turn to his intelligence reports. Prisoners' statements, captured correspondence, newspapers, information from his spies, dispatches from the cavalry outposts—all these he studied carefully, and often at first hand. Every stir of his enemy along the line he canvassed both for its direct meaning and for its relation to other movements.

In assembling this information he was not more adept than many another capable general, and in studying it he was not more diligent, but in interpreting it he excelled. Always critical of the news that came from spies, few of whom he trusted, he was cautious in accepting newspaper reports until he learned which correspondents were close-mouthed or ill-informed and which were reckless or well-furnished with fact. . . . If Lee's strategy was built, in large part, on his interpretation of his intelligence reports, that interpretation was facilitated more by Stuart and Stuart's scouts than by anything else.

Lee did not rely so much as has been supposed upon his knowledge of his adversaries. He knew that McClellan would be meticulous in preparation, and that Meade, making few mistakes himself, would be quick to take advantage of those of which he might be guilty. But these were the only Federal generals-in-chief with whom he had been closely associated before the war. The others, save Grant, were in command for periods so brief that he scarcely knew them before they were gone. Grant's bludgeoning tactics and flank shifts he quickly fathomed, but he was progressively less able to combat them as his own strength declined. . . .

Having decided what the enemy most reasonably would attempt, Lee's strategy was postulated, in most instances, on a speedy offensive. "We can only act upon probabilities," he said, "and endeavor to avoid greater evils," but he voiced his theory of war even more fully when he wrote, ". . . we must decide between the positive loss of inactivity and the risk of action." His larger strategy, from the very nature of the war, was offensive-defensive, but his policy was to seize the initiative wherever practicable and to force his adversary to adapt his plans thereto. If a "fog of war" was to exist, he chose to create it and to leave his opponent to fathom it or to dissipate it.

Once he determined upon an offensive, Lee took unbounded pains to execute it from the most favorable position he could occupy. As far as the records show, he never read Bourcet, but no soldier more fully exemplified what that master taught of the importance of position. The student can well picture Lee in his tent, his map spread on his table before him, tracing every road, studying the location of every town and hamlet in relation to every other and choosing at last the line of march that would facilitate the initial offensive and prepare the way for another. . . .

His patient synthesis of military intelligence, his understanding employment of the offensive, his sense of position and his logistics were supplemented in the making of his strategy by his audacity. Superficial critics, puzzled by his success and unwilling to examine the reasons for it, have sometimes assumed that he frequently defied the rules of war, yet rarely sustained disaster in doing so because he was confronted by mediocrity. Without raising the disputable question of the capacity of certain of his opponents, it may be said that respect for the strength of his adversaries, rather than contempt for their abilities, made him daring. Necessity, not choice, explains this quality. . . .

These five qualities, then, gave eminence to his strategy—his interpretation of military intelligence, his wise devotion to the offensive, his careful choice of position, the exactness of his logistics, and his well-considered daring. Midway between strategy and tactics stood four other qualities of generalship that no student of war can disdain. The first was his sharpened sense of the power of resistance and of attack of a given body of men; the second was his ability to effect adequate concentration at the point of attack, even when his force was inferior; the third was his careful choice of commanders and of troops for specific duties; the fourth was his employment of field fortification. . . .

The final major reason for Lee's success in the face of bewildering odds . . . was his ability to maintain the hope and the fighting spirit of the South. The confidence aroused by the first victory at Manassas sustained the South until the disasters at Fort Henry and Fort Donelson. Thereafter, for a season, the belief was strong that Europe's need of cotton would bring recognition and intervention. As months passed with no hopeful news from France or from England, while the Union forces tightened their noose on the Confederacy, the Southern people looked to their own armies, and to them alone, to win independence. Vicksburg fell; the Confederacy was cut in twain. The expectations raised by the victory at Chickamauga were not realized. The Army of Tennessee failed to halt the slow partition of the seceded states. Gradually the South came to fix its faith on the Army of Northern Virginia and on its commander. Elsewhere there was bickering and division; in Virginia there was harmony and united resistance. The unconquered territory was daily reduced in area, but on the Rapidan and the Rappahannock there was still defiance in the flapping of each battle flag. The Southern people remembered that Washington had lost New York and New England, Georgia and South Carolina, and still had triumphed. Lee, they believed, would do no less than the great American he most resembled. As long as he could keep the field, the South could keep its heart. So, when the despairing were ready to make peace and the cowardly hid in the swamps or the mountains to escape the conscript officer, the loyal Confederate took his last horse from the stable for his trooper-son, and emptied his barn of corn in order that "Lee's army" might not starve. Morale behind the line, not less than on the front of action, was sustained by Lee. Conversely, he could count upon a measure of popular support that neither the President, the Congress, nor any other field commander could elicit.

The qualities that created this confidence were essentially those that assured Lee the unflagging aid of the President, the loyalty of his lieutenants, and the enthusiastic devotion of his men. But the order in which these qualities were esteemed by the civil population was somewhat different. Mr. Davis and the corps commanders knew that Lee was better able than any other Southern soldier to anticipate and to overthrow the plans of the enemy; the men in the ranks were satisfied he would shape his strategy to defeat the enemy with the least loss to them. The people in the Southern towns and on the farms of the Confederate states saw, in contrast, a series of military successes they were not capable of interpreting in terms of strategy or of tactics. They understood little of all the subtle factors that entered into army administration and into the relations of commander with President and with soldiers. But for them the war had taken on a deeper spiritual significance than it had for some of those who faced the bloody realities of slaughter. In the eyes of the evangelicals of the South, theirs was a contest of righteousness against greed, a struggle to be won by prayers not less than by combat. They saw in Lee the embodiment of the faith and piety they believed a just Heaven would favor. A war that would make a partisan of God works other changes no less amazing to the religious concepts of a nation, and among the Southern people, during the last year of the struggle, it lacked little of lifting Lee to be the mediator for his nation. The army, seeing him in battle, put his ability first and his character second. The civilian population, observing him from afar, rated his character even above his ability.

These, then, would seem to be the signal reasons why Lee so long was able to maintain the unequal struggle of a Confederacy that may have been foredoomed to defeat and extinction. To recapitulate, the foundation stone of his military career was intellect of a very high order, with a developed aptitude for war. On that foundation his strategy was built in comprehensive courses. Visualizing a military problem with clarity, he studied every report that would aid in its solution. If it were possible, he put his solution in terms of the offensive. With care he would select his position; with skill he would reconnoitre it; with precision of logistics he would bring his troops to it, and with daring he would engage them. For every action he sought to concentrate adequately, and for every task he endeavored to utilize the lieutenant best suited. In combat, however excellent his constantly improving tactics, he begrudged the life of each soldier he had to expose, yet he hurled his whole army into the charge, sparing not a man, when his daring gave him an opening for a major blow. As his numbers diminished and he was forced to the defensive, he perfected a system of field fortification that had a strategic no less than a protective value. A diligent army administrator, self-controlled and disciplined in his dealings with his superiors, he chose his subordinates wisely and treated them with a justice that Washington himself could not have excelled. He had, besides, a personality and a probity that combined with his repeated victories to gain for him the unshakable confidence of his troops and of the civil population. The tactics he employed in the 1860's belong to the yesterday of war, but the reasons for his success remain valid for any soldier who must bear a like burden of responsibility, whether in a cause as desperate or where the limitless resources of a puissant government are his to command.

Robert E. Lee: A Flawed General

ALAN T. NOLAN

[T]his book accepts the fact that Lee's campaign and battle strategy and his tactical performance were largely, although not invariably, brilliant. Granting this brilliance, there nevertheless are grounds for questioning his generalship. The questions are in reference to the grand strategy of the war from the Confederacy's standpoint. In order to evaluate Lee's performance as a general, it is imperative that we distinguish between military *tactics* and military *strategy*. . . .

In evaluating Lee or any army commander, however, the key consideration is not the brilliance or boldness of his performance in a tactical or operationally strategic sense. These are surely matters of interest and importance, but the key consideration must be whether the general's actions helped or hurt the cause of his government in view of that government's grand strategy. In short, the appropriate inquiry is to ask whether the general's actions related positively or negatively to the war objectives and national policy of his government.

The issue addressed is not, therefore, Lee's tactics and operational strategy in any given campaign or battle. His brilliant direction of his forces during the fighting at Antietam and what happened at Gettysburg are not the point. At Gettysburg he suffered a decisive defeat, a defeat that did not alone decide the war but in which his losses, on the heels of other casualties, were so great that his army's subsequent ability to maneuver was severely restricted. The reference-book evaluations of Lee include the traditional view that this defeat was the fault of his subordinates. Contemporary students of the battle disagree on this point. Some persuasively contend that Lee's subordinates, especially Longstreet, are unfairly blamed for the Gettysburg loss. But, whatever may be said about the factors that determined the outcome of this or any battle, the issue here is more profound than explaining Lee's campaign or battle failures or successes. The issue is to understand the grand strategy of the Confederacy and to appreciate Lee's contribution to the larger success or failure of that strategy. . . .

Lee believed that the South's grand strategic role was offensive. He had consistently planned and advocated the offensive. He had told President Davis that the way to peace was to drive the opposing army from the field, and this is what he sought to accomplish. Thus, [Louis H.] Manarin asserts that "Lee never seems to have forgotten that although on the defensive the only way to win was by attacking and driving the enemy." And [Thomas L.] Connelly and [Archer] Jones conclude that "Lee's frequent offensive thrusts and his almost invariable assumption of the offensive in battle" suggest that he believed the war was to be won by "annihilation of the enemy army."

There was a profound problem with Lee's grand strategy of the offensive: it was not feasible to defeat the North militarily as distinguished from prolonging the contest until the North gave it up. And indeed to attempt an outright defeat of the Federal army was counterproductive in terms of the Confederacy's "objects of war." Curiously, that Lee's attack grand strategy was misplaced is suggested by his own awareness of factors that argued against it.

The primary factor that made the attack grand strategy counterproductive was numbers, and Lee was sensitive to the South's manpower disadvantage and the implications of that disadvantage. . . .

The Confederacy faced a constant dilemma concerning the deployment of its limited manpower between its eastern and western armies. Connelly and Jones provide casualty statistics that graphically address this tension: "Lee's losses in the Seven Days' exceeded the number of effectives in the Army of Tennessee the previous autumn. In the Gettysburg campaign, Lee lost more men . . . than Braxton Bragg had in his Army of Tennessee in October of 1862. At Chancellorsville, Lee's casualties almost equaled those of the combined Confederate surrenders of Forts Henry and Donelson. In fact, during his first four months as commander of the Army of Northern Virginia, . . . Lee lost almost fifty thousand troops. Such a number far exceeded the total troop strength of the Army of Tennessee . . . during the same time span."

Because Lee's biographers seem to overlook the point, it is necessary to emphasize that there was a profound difference between Federal casualties and Lee's casualties. Federal casualties could be, and were in fact, made up with additional manpower. Lee's were irreplaceable, including the severe losses, even prior to Gettysburg, in field-grade officers and other mid-level commanders. As Robert K. Krick has noted, these leadership casualties were especially crippling for the Army of Northern Virginia. Writers like Freeman would impress us with statements of Federal losses that on occasion exceeded Lee's in absolute numbers. They miss the point that the losses were of very different significance for the two antagonists because of the replacement factor. As his own correspondence indicates, Lee realized this difference and said so. His advocates disregard it.

Lee was conscious of another problem related to numbers as well, namely, the consequences to his army of a siege. He consistently expressed the view that his army's being besieged in the Richmond defenses was bound to result in its defeat.

Writing in the Southern Historical Society Papers, General Henry Heth quoted Lee as having said this regarding his 1863 situation: "I considered the problem in every possible phase, and to my mind it resolved itself into a choice of one of two things—either to retire on Richmond and stand a siege, which must ultimately have ended in surrender, or to invade Pennsylvania." . . .

Finally, Lee also seems to have had intimations that the outcome of the war depended on the North's political reaction and will rather than on military defeat of the North. A letter to his son Custis on February 28, 1863, expresses the view that a "revolution" among the Northern people was the only check on the intent of the "present administration" vigorously to prosecute the war against the South. A more comprehensive statement of this thinking appears in a letter to Mrs. Lee written on April 19, 1863. . . .

In sum, there were at least four aspects of Lee's own assessment of his army's situation that ran counter to the logic of his grand strategy of the offensive. He was aware of his numerical disadvantage, believed a siege would assure his defeat, and thought it critical for the South to keep its armies in the field. Yet his offensives consistently produced high casualty rates, and these casualties exacerbated the manpower differential, made a siege more likely, and reduced the Confederacy's ability to maintain an effective fighting force. In addition, he saw the loss of Northern support for the war as "what we are interested in bringing about." He nevertheless did not abandon his offensive campaigns until 1864, by which time they were practically impossible. Lee pursued the war with what Colonel [George A.] Bruce calls "that spirit of aggression, which remained permanently his most prominent characteristic as a soldier." . . .

Was there an alternative to Lee's glorious campaign leading to total defeat? A perimeter defense or war of position was not feasible. Johnston's apparently entirely defensive policy in Georgia did not have promise. But there was another option: a defensive grand strategy, within the context of which Lee could on occasion have undertaken offensive thrusts, appropriate operationally strategic and tactical offensives, while avoiding the costly pattern of offensive warfare that he pursued in 1862 and 1863.

Of course, there is no guarantee that a defensive grand strategy would necessarily have succeeded. In terms of negatives, it could have involved the loss of Confederate territory, but so did the offensive grand strategy that Lee adopted. It could have risked dampening home front morale among a civilian population that craved victorious offensives, but so did Lee's offensive grand strategy. When he was ultimately forced to resort to the defensive in 1864, that strategy was effective even though his army and its leadership by that time had been grievously reduced by the casualties that resulted from his prior offensives. Had Lee adopted this defensive approach during the two years that he spent on the offensive, he could have had available a fair proportion of the more than 100,000 of his soldiers and officers who went down during the offensive years. With these additional numbers, he could have maintained mobility and avoided a siege. Maneuvers like Early's 1864 movement down the Valley could have been undertaken with sufficient numbers. The Union, on the offensive, could have suffered for an earlier or longer period the ceaseless Federal casualties that began in May 1864. The war could have been prolonged and the Northern people could have abandoned their political support of the war. All of these things are conjectural, but they arise reasonably from the fact that there was an alternative. The truth is that in 1864 Lee himself demonstrated the alternative to his earlier offensive strategy and tactics. In the process he demonstrated the feasibility of the grand strategy of the defense.

When compared to the defensive, Lee's offensive grand strategy, because of the losses entailed, led inexorably, to use his words, to the "natural military consequences of the enemy's numerical superiority," that is, surrender. That superiority was enhanced by Federal reinforcements, but it was also heightened by Lee's heavy and irreplaceable losses. The grand strategy of defense would have muted these "natural military consequences" because it would have slowed the increase in the enemy's numerical superiority insofar as that numerical superiority arose from Lee's heavy and disproportionate losses. Further, because of the strategic and tactical advantages of the defense, that numerical superiority would have been less significant had Lee assumed the defensive in 1862–63. Lee proved this when massively outnumbered on the defensive in 1864–65. In 1864, Lee's defense, in Porter Alexander's words, exacted "a price in blood" that significantly threatened "the enthusiasm of [the North's] population." Adopted earlier, this defensive policy might have worn the North out. The grand strategy of the defense was therefore not only a feasible alternative; it was also more likely to have led to victory.

The Generalship of Grant and Sherman: Was the Civil War a Modern "Total" War? A Dissenting View

MARK E. NEELY, JR.

In a recent article, Charles Strozier, a Lincoln biographer and co-director of the Center on Violence and Human Survival, argues that the United States' demand for unconditional surrender in World War II, and ultimately the use of two atomic bombs on Japan, found antecedents in President Lincoln's surrender terms in the Civil War. . . .

The assertion that the United States insisted on unconditional surrender in the Civil War can be quickly proven wrong. . . .

The attribution of the concept of unconditional surrender to Lincoln has gained prominence only recently in serious historical writing, but the idea in which it is rooted, that of the Civil War as a total war, has been around a long while. In fact, it might be said to constitute the regnant interpretation of the nature of the great American conflict. Its appeal transcends the sections in Civil War debates, and the idea lies at the heart of most modern interpretations of the war by the most respected and artful writers.

The idea of total war was first applied to the Civil War in an article about William T. Sherman published in the *Journal of Southern History* in 1948: John B. Walters's "General William T. Sherman and Total War." After this initial use of the

From Mark E. Neely, Jr. "Was the Civil War a Total War?" *Civil War History* 37, No. 1 (1991): excerpts from 5, 7–14, 16–20, 22–28. Reprinted with the permission of Kent State University.

term, it was quickly adopted by T. Harry Williams, whose influential book *Lincoln and His Generals,* published in 1952, began with this memorable sentence: "The Civil War was the first of the modern total wars, and the American democracy was almost totally unready to fight it." Among the more popular Civil War writers, the idea also fared well. Bruce Catton, for example, wrote in a 1964 essay on "The Generalship of Ulysses S. Grant" that "He was fighting . . . a total war, and in a total war the enemy's economy is to be undermined in any way possible." Scholarly writers continued to use the term as well. In his masterful *Battle Cry of Freedom: The Civil War Era,* Princeton University's James M. McPherson writes, "By 1863, Lincoln's remarkable abilities gave him a wide edge over Davis as a war leader, while in Grant and Sherman the North acquired commanders with a concept of total war and the necessary determination to make it succeed." Professor McPherson's book forms part of the prestigious Oxford History of the United States. In another landmark volume, *"A People's Contest": The Union and the Civil War* (Harper & Row's New American Nation series), historian Phillip Shaw Paludan writes, "Grant's war making has come to stand for the American way of war. For one thing, that image is one of total war demanding unconditional surrender."

Surely any idea about the military conduct of the Civil War that has been championed by Williams, Catton, McPherson, and Paludan, that is embodied in the Oxford History of the United States and in the New American Nation series, can fairly be called accepted wisdom on the subject. Most writers on the military history of the war, if forced to articulate a brief general description of the nature of that conflict, would now say, as McPherson has, that the Civil War began in 1861 with a purpose in the North "to suppress this insurrection and restore loyal Unionists to control of the southern states. The conflict was therefore a limited war . . . with the limited goal of restoring the status quo ante bellum, not an unlimited war to destroy an enemy nation and reshape its society." Gradually, or as McPherson puts it, "willy-nilly," the war became "a total war rather than a limited one." Eventually, "Union generals William Tecumseh Sherman and Philip Sheridan saw more clearly than anyone else the nature of modern, total war, a war between peoples rather than simply between armies, a war in which the fighting left nothing untouched or unchanged." President Lincoln came to realize the nature of the military contest and "sanctioned this policy of 'being terrible' on the enemy." Finally, "when the Civil War became a total war, the invading army intentionally destroyed the economic capacity of the South to wage war." Northern victory resulted from this gradual realization and the subsequent application of new and harsh doctrines in the war's later phase.

The idea of total war embodies a rare quality among interpretations of the American Civil War: it is without sectional bias. Walters, after all, was a Southerner; he saw in Sherman's doctrines the breeding ground of a counter-productive hatred at odds with the North's mission to heal the nation after the war. Williams and Catton were both Northerners, and James McPherson and Phillip Paludan might fairly be termed neo-abolitionist in their interpretations of the war. Yet all agree that it was a total war. Modern writers on the Confederacy also remain ready to regard the war as a total war. Indeed, the idea provides the key to historian Emory M. Thomas's book, *The Confederacy as a Revolutionary Experience,* which argued that "by 1865, under the pressure of total war, the Confederate South had surrendered most of its cherished way of life."

Northerner and Southerner alike have come to agree on the use of this term, total war, but what does it mean exactly? It was never used in the Civil War itself. Where does it come from?

The roots of the term are instructive. It was coined in 1921 by Giulio Douhet, the pioneering Italian advocate of air power, when he wrote: "The prevailing forms of social organization have given war a character of national totality—that is, the entire population and all the resources of a nation are sucked into the maw of war. And, since society is now definitely evolving along this line, it is within the power of human foresight to see now that future wars will be total in character and scope." Such ideas were rife in the 1920s among military thinkers who had witnessed the appalling slaughter on the Western Front in the Great War, and who fancied how much better it would be to vault over the stalemated trenches and attack the enemy's industries and centers of population remote from their armies. . . .

Unfortunately, like many parts of everyday vocabulary, total war is a loose term with several meanings. Since World War II, it has come to mean, in part, a war requiring the full economic mobilization of a society. From the start, it meant the obverse of that idea as well: making war on the economic resources of the enemy rather than directly on its armed forces alone. Yet there was nothing really new about attacking an enemy's economic resources; that was the very essence of naval blockades and they long predated the Civil War. The crucial and terrible new aspect of the notion of total war was embodied in the following idea, part of a definition of the term cited in the *Oxford English Dictionary:* "Every citizen is in a sense a combatant and also the object of attack." Every systematic definition of the term embodies the concept of destroying the ages-old distinction between civilians and soldiers, whatever other ideas may be present. . . .

Close application of this twentieth-century term, the product of the age of strategic bombing and blitzkrieg and powerful totalitarian governments capable of mobilizing science and psychology, to the Civil War seems fraught with difficulty. Surely no one believes, for example, that the Civil War was fought "without any scruple or limitations." From the ten thousand plus pages of documents in the eight full volumes of the *Official Records* dealing with prisoners of war, to the many copies of General Orders No. 100, a brief code of the laws of war distributed throughout the Union army in 1863, evidence abounds that this war knew careful limitation and conscientious scruple. Even World War II followed the rules bearing on prisoners of war. Any assessment of the Civil War's nearness to being a total war can be no more than that: an assertion that it *approached* total war in some ways. By no definition of the term can it be said to *be* a total war.

Occasionally, the term total war approximates the meaning of *modernity.* T. Harry Williams used the terms interchangeably, as in this passage from a later work in which he hedged a bit on calling the Civil War a total war: "Trite it may be to say that the Civil War was the first of the modern wars, but this is a truth that needs to be repeated. If the Civil War was not quite total, it missed totality by only a narrow margin."

Modernity is not a very useful concept in military history. Surely, every war is thought to be modern by its participants—save possibly those fought by Japan in the strange era when firearms were consciously rejected. As a historian's term, modern when applied to warfare has a widely accepted meaning different from total. Modern warfare generally connotes wars fought after the French Revolution by large citizen armies equipped with the products of the Industrial Revolution and motivated more by ideology than the lash or strictly mercenary considerations. The Civil War certainly was a modern war in that sense, but it was not a total war in the sense that civilians were commonly thought of as legitimate military targets.

. . . Seeing how often that fragile barrier broke in the Civil War will tell how nearly it approached being a total war. All such matters of degree contain dangers for the historian trying to answer the question; the risk of sinking under a mass of piecemeal objections raised afterward by critics is very high. . . .

Leaving aside similar isolated instances caused by temporary rage, can a historian seeking to describe the war's direction toward or away from total war examine larger aspects of the war where the "fragile barriers" between soldiers and civilians may have broken down? Since the conscious application of a new doctrine in warfare forms part of the total war interpretation, can a historian focus on certain figures in high command who held such doctrines, and applied them to the enemy in the Civil War? Throughout, can the historian keep an eye on the dictionary definition of total war to measure the proximity of the Civil War to it? Surely this can be done, and short of a study of the Civil War day by day, there can hardly be any other test.

William T. Sherman, Ulysses S. Grant, and Philip H. Sheridan are the obvious figures for study, with particular emphasis on the March to the Sea and the campaign in the Carolinas from 1864 to 1865, and actions in northern Virginia in 1864. Likewise, some attention to President Lincoln's views would also fit the traditions of the literature on this subject.

Sherman is the Civil War soldier most often quoted on the subject of total war. An article about him gave rise to this interpretation of the Civil War, and indeed it is now widely held that, as historian John F. Marszalek has expressed it, William T. Sherman was the "Inventor of Total Warfare." "We are not only fighting hostile armies, but a hostile people, and must make old and young, rich and poor, feel the hard hand of war, as well as their organized armies," Sherman told Gen. Henry W. Halleck on Christmas Eve, 1864. As early as October 1862 he said, "We cannot change the hearts of these people of the South, but we can make war so terrible . . . [and] make them so sick of war that generations would pass away before they would again appeal to it."

The gift of sounding like a twentieth-century man was peculiarly Sherman's. Nearly every other Civil War general sounds ancient by comparison, but many historians may have allowed themselves to be fooled by his style while ignoring the substance of his campaigns.

Historians, moreover, quote Sherman selectively. In fact, he said many things and when gathered together they do not add up to any coherent "total-war philosophy," as one historian describes it. Sherman was not a philosopher; he was a general and a garrulous one at that. . . .

Though not a systematic military thinker, General Sherman did compose a letter addressing the problem of noncombatants in the Civil War, and it described his actual policies better than his frequently quoted statements of a more sensational nature. He sent the letter to Maj. R. M. Sawyer, whom Sherman left behind to manage Huntsville, Alabama, when he departed for Meridian, Mississippi, early in 1864. Sherman also sent a copy to his brother, Republican Senator John Sherman, with an eye to possible publication: . . .

> When men take up arms to resist a rightful authority, we are compelled to use like force. . . . When the provisions, forage, horses, mules, wagons, etc., are used by our enemy, it is clearly our duty and right to take them also, because otherwise they might be used against us. In like manner all houses left vacant by an inimical people are clearly our right, and as such are needed as storehouses, hospitals, and quarters. But the question arises as to dwellings used by women, children and non-combatants. So long as non-combatants remain in their houses and keep to their accustomed peaceful business, their opinions and prejudices can in no wise influence the war, and therefore should not be noticed; but if any one comes out into the public streets and creates disorder, he or she should be punished, restrained, or banished. . . . If the people, or any of them, keep up a correspondence with parties in hostility, they are spies, and can be punished according to law with death or minor punishment. These are well-established principles of war, and the people of the South having appealed to war, are barred from appealing for protection to our constitution, which they have practically and publicly defied. They have appealed to war, and must abide its rules and laws. . . .

Excepting incidents of retaliation, Sherman by and large lived by these "principles of war." . . .

Sherman's purposes in the Georgia and Carolinas campaigns, usually pointed to as the epitome of total war in the Civil War, are obscured by two months of the general's letters to other generals describing his desire to cut loose from Atlanta and his long, thin line of supply to march to the sea. From mid-September to mid-November 1864, Sherman worried the idea, and his superiors, explaining it in several ways. At first, he argued from his knowledge of the political disputes between Jefferson Davis and Georgia Governor Joseph E. Brown that the march would sever the state from the Confederacy. "They may stand the fall of Richmond," Sherman told Grant on September 20, "but not of all Georgia." At the same time he belittled the effects of mere destruction: ". . . the more I study the game the more I am convinced that it would be wrong for me to penetrate much farther into Georgia without an objective beyond. It would not be productive of much good. I can start east and make a circuit south and back, *doing vast damage to the State* [italics added], but resulting in no permanent good. . . ."

Less than three weeks later, Sherman gave a rather different explanation to Grant: "Until we can repopulate Georgia, it is useless to occupy it, but the utter destruction of its roads, houses, and people will cripple their military resources. By attempting to hold the roads we will lose 1,000 men monthly, and will gain no result. I can make the march, and make Georgia howl."

Ten days after that, he more or less combined his different arguments in a letter to General Halleck. "This movement is not purely military or strategic," he now said, "but it will illustrate the vulnerability of the South." Only when Sherman's armies arrived and "fences and corn and hogs and sheep" vanished would "the rich planters of the Oconee and Savannah" know "what war means." He spoke more tersely to his subordinates. "I want to prepare for my big raid," he explained on October 19 to a colonel in charge of supply, and with that Sherman arranged to send his impedimenta to the rear.

With plans set, more or less, Sherman explained to Gen. George Thomas, who would be left to deal with Confederate Gen. John Bell Hood's army, "I propose to demonstrate the vulnerability of the South, and make its inhabitants feel that war and individual ruin are synonymous terms." Delays ensued and Sherman decided to remain in place until after election day. On the twelfth, he cut his telegraph lines and the confusing explanations of the campaign ceased pouring out of Georgia.

Sherman did not attempt the "utter destruction" of Georgia's "people." He did not really attack noncombatants directly or make any serious attempt to destroy "the economic capacity of the south to wage war," as one historian has described his purpose. After capturing Atlanta, for example, Sherman moved to capture Savannah and then attacked the symbolic capital of secession, South Carolina. He did not attack Augusta, Georgia, which he knew to contain "the only powder mills and factories remaining in the South." Though he did systematically destroy railroad lines, Sherman otherwise had little conception of eliminating essential industries. Indeed, there were few to eliminate, for the South, in comparison with the North, was a premodern, underdeveloped, agrarian region where determined men with rifles were the real problem—not the ability of the area's industries to manufacture high-technology weapons. Despite scorching a sixty-mile-wide swath through the Confederacy, Sherman was never going to starve this agrarian economy into submission, either. He had remarked in the past on how well fed and even shod the Confederate armies were despite their backward economy.

What Sherman was doing embodied traditional geopolitical objectives in a civil war: convincing the enemy's people and the world that the Confederate government and upper classes were too weak to maintain nationhood. He did this with a "big raid." "If we can march a well-appointed army right through his [Jefferson Davis's] territory," Sherman told Grant on November 6, 1864, "it is a demonstration to the world, foreign and domestic, that we have a power which Davis cannot resist." . . .

If Sherman had his politic moments, there was hardly a more politically astute general in the Northern armies than his military superior and friend, Gen. Ulysses S. Grant. To depict Grant as an advocate of total war is to take him at his word when he spoke in temporary anger and frustration, and, more important, to make him appear a clumsy and brutal slugger, whereas he was really a deftly political puncher.

Of course, the doctrine of total war has its political side, but the point here is that no general as politic as Grant was going to embark on a singleminded strategy for the war that was certain to offend Victorian sensibilities throughout the world and make permanent enemies of all persons in the South. Grant, therefore, did not make as many "mad" remarks as Sherman did about killing "millions." He was a more reticent man. Nevertheless, the logic of military conscription and the frustrations of guerrilla or partisan warfare could drive even Grant to make statements well beyond the accepted bounds of warfare in the middle of the nineteenth century. . . .

Ulysses S. Grant never applied a unitary military philosophy to the South, not total war or any other doctrine. Rounding up civilians and destroying the crops and livestock by which a local army could live—these were strategies Grant ordered only in bitterly disloyal areas infested with guerrillas. Where the political complexion of the local populace appeared different, Grant's orders took a different tone. After Vicksburg's fall in 1863, for example, he issued a general order counseling restraint on the part of U.S. forces, which now controlled the western third of Mississippi. He called upon the people of the state "to pursue their peaceful avocations in obedience to the laws of the United States," and assured them that if they did so the occupying forces would be "prohibited from molesting in any way the citizens of the country." "In all cases," he added, "where it becomes necessary to take private property for public use a detail will be made, under a Commissioned officer, to take specified property, and none other." . . .

Grant was not growing soft; he always believed that commanders ought to be tailored for the districts commanded. Thus, he thought Benjamin F. Butler worthless as a soldier, but in "taking charge of a Dept.mt where there are no great battles to be fought, but a dissatisfied element to controll no one could manage it better than he." As late as the summer of 1864, Grant contemplated a restructuring of military districts that would put Butler in command of Kentucky or Missouri. These areas Grant had seen himself, and he regarded them as more difficult to control than Mississippi. Butler, whose notorious treatment of civilians in occupied New Orleans earned him the nickname "beast" and made him an outlaw in the Confederacy, seemed to Grant ideal for the intractable western border states. General Grant adapted his policies to the situation at hand, but he remained always "within the bounds of civilized warfare." . . .

. . . Total war may describe certain isolated and uncharacteristic aspects of the Civil War, but is at most a partial view.

The point is not merely semantic. The use of the idea of total war prevents historians from understanding the era properly. Taking the notion, for example, that total war hitches science to the military cause, one can see the inappropriateness of applying this idea to the Civil War. As Robert V. Bruce notes in *The Launching of American Science, 1846–1876,* there was no Civil War Manhattan Project [for building an obliterating weapon—the atomic bomb]. The war, in fact, mainly hampered science by killing young men who might have become scientists later. Neither Yankee ingenuity nor Confederate desperation, as Bruce shrewdly reveals, caused technological breakthroughs of significance for the battlefield. And the great symbol of American science in the era, the Smithsonian Institution, flew no national flag during the Civil War. Science remained neutral, though individual scientists enlisted as their sectional preferences dictated.

Likewise, the economic aspect of total war is misleading when used to describe characteristics of the Civil War reputedly more forward-looking than naval blockades. The ideas of economic planning and control from World War II cannot be applied to the Civil War. Hardly anyone then thought in such macro-economic terms. Abraham Lincoln did calculate the total daily cost of the war, but he did not do so to aid long-range economic planning for the Union war effort. Instead, he used the figure to show how relatively inexpensive it would be for the U.S. government to purchase the freedom of all the slaves in the border states through compensated emancipation. At $400 a head, the $2 million daily war expenditure would buy every slave in Delaware at "less than one half-day's cost," and "less than eighty seven days cost of this war would, at the same price, pay for all in Delaware, Maryland, District of Columbia, Kentucky, and Missouri."

From the Confederate perspective, the economic insight seems ironically somewhat more appropriate. The blockade induced scarcities on which almost all

Confederate civilian diarists commented—coffee, shoe leather, and needles were sorely missed. The Confederate government's attempts to supply scarce war necessities led some historians to call the resulting system "state socialism" or a "revolutionary experience." Yet these were the outcome less of deliberate Northern military strategy (the blockade aside) than of the circumstance that the South was agrarian and the North more industrialized.

For its part, the North did little to mobilize its resources—little, that is, that would resemble the centralized planning and state intervention typical of twentieth-century economies in war. There was no rationing, North or South, and the Yankees' society knew only the sacrifice of men, not of materials. . . .

The *essential* aspect of any definition of total war asserts that it breaks down the distinction between soldiers and civilians, combatants and noncombatants, and this no one in the Civil War did systematically, including William T. Sherman. He and his fellow generals waged war the same way most Victorian gentlemen did, and other Victorian gentlemen in the world knew it. That is one reason why British, French, and Prussian observers failed to comment on any startling developments seen in the American war: there was little new to report. The conservative monarchies of the old world surely would have seized with delight on any evidence that warfare in the New World was degenerating to the level of starving and killing civilians. Their observers encountered no such spectacle. It required airplanes and tanks and heartless twentieth-century ideas born in the hopeless trenches of World War I to break down distinctions adhered to in practice by almost all Civil War generals. Their war did little to usher in the shock of the new in the twentieth century.

FURTHER READING

Virginia Matzke Adams, ed., *On the Altar of Freedom: A Black Soldier's Civil War Letters from the Front* (1991).

Ira Berlin, et al., eds., *The Black Military Experience,* Series II, *Freedom: A Documentary History of Emancipation, 1861–1867* (1982).

Richard E. Beringer, Herman Hattaway, Archer Jones, and William N. Still, Jr., *Why the South Lost the Civil War* (1986).

Gabor S. Borit, *Lincoln, the War President: The Gettysburg Lectures* (1992).

Bruce Catton, *Grant Moves South* (1960).

_____, *Grant Takes Command* (1969).

Edwin B. Coddington, *The Gettysburg Campaign* (1968).

Thomas L. Connelly, "Robert E. Lee and the Western Confederacy: A Criticism of Lee's Strategic Ability," *Civil War History* 15 (1969): 116–132.

_____, *The Marble Man: Robert E. Lee and His Image in American Society* (1977).

Clifford Dowdey and Louis H. Manarin, eds., *The Wartime Papers of R. E. Lee* (1961).

Drew G. Faust, *Mothers of Invention: Women of the Slaveholding South in the American Civil War* (1996).

Michael Fellman, *Inside War: The Guerrilla Conflict in Missouri During the American Civil War* (1989).

William M. Fowler, *Under Two Flags: The American Navy in the Civil War* (1990).

Douglas S. Freeman, *Robert E. Lee,* 4 vols. (1934–1935).

J.F.C. Fuller, *Grant and Lee: A Study in Personality and Leadership* (1957 ed.).

Gary W. Gallagher, ed., *Lee: The Soldier* (1996).

Joseph T. Glatthaar, *Forged in Battle: The Civil War Alliance of Black Soldiers and White Officers* (1990).

_____, *The March to the Sea and Beyond: Sherman's Troops in the Savannah and Carolinas Campaigns* (1985).

Mark Grimsley, *The Hard Hand of War: Union Military Policy toward Southern Civilians, 1861–1865* (1995).

Edward Hagerman, *The American Civil War and the Origins of Modern Warfare* (1988).

Herman Hattaway and Archer Jones, *How the North Won: A Military History of the Civil War* (1983).

Lee Kennett, *Marching Through Georgia: The Story of Soldiers and Civilians During Sherman's Campaign* (1995).

Elizabeth D. Leonard, *Yankee Women: Gender Battles in the Civil War* (1994).

Gerald F. Linderman, *Embattled Courage: The Experience of Combat in the American Civil War* (1987).

James Longstreet, *From Manassas to Appomattox: Memoirs of the Civil War in America* (1895, reprint 1992).

John F. Marszalek, *Sherman: A Soldier's Passion for Order* (1993).

William S. McFeely, *Grant: A Biography* (1981).

James M. McPherson, *Battle Cry of Freedom: The Civil War Era* (1988).

_____, *For Cause and Comrades: Why New Men Fought in the Civil War* (1997).

Reid Mitchell, *Civil War Soldiers* (1988).

_____, *The Vacant Chair: The Northern Soldier Leaves Home* (1993).

Mark E. Neely, Jr., "Was the Civil War a Total War?" *Civil War History* 37 (March 1991): 5–28.

Allan Nevins, *The War for the Union*, 4 vols. (1959–1971).

Alan T. Nolan, *Lee Considered: General Robert E. Lee and Civil War History* (1991).

Stephen B. Oates, *A Woman of Valor: Clara Barton and the Civil War* (1994).

Geoffrey Perret, *Ulysses S. Grant: Soldier and President* (1997).

Harry W. Pfanz, *Gettysburg: The Second Day* (1987).

William G. Piston, *Lee's Tarnished Lieutenant: James Longstreet and His Place in Southern History* (1987).

John M. Priest, *Antietam: The Soldier's Battle* (1994).

Carol Reardon, *Pickett's Charge in History and Memory* (1997).

Rowena Reed, *Combined Operations in the Civil War* (1978).

James I. Robertson, Jr., *Soldiers Blue and Gray* (1988).

Charles Royster, *The Destructive War: William Tecumseh Sherman, Stonewall Jackson, and the Americans* (1991).

Stephen W. Sears, *George B. McClellan: The Young Napoleon* (1988).

William L. Shea and Earl J. Hess, *Pea Ridge: Civil War Campaign in the West* (1992).

William Tecumseh Sherman, *The Memoirs of General W. T. Sherman*, 2nd ed. (1886, reprint, 1990).

Brooks D. Simpson, *Let Us Have Peace: Ulysses S. Grant and the Politics of War and Reconstruction, 1861–1868* (1991).

Steven E. Woodworth, *Jefferson Davis and His Generals: The Failure of Confederate Command in the West* (1990).

CHAPTER
7

Indian Wars
on the Great Plains

As the United States resumed its westward expansion after the Civil War, it confronted the nomadic Indians of the Great Plains. A half dozen great Indian nations, such as the Cheyenne, Sioux/Lahota, Arapahos, Kiowas, and Comanches roamed the vast grasslands and the mountain ranges. They soon faced the advancing miners, ranchers, farmers, westward emigrants, and soldiers. The U.S. Army had exercised constabulary duty on the Indian frontier since the establishment of the Republic. But now instead of eastern woodland Indians, it was faced with the mounted warriors of the Great Plains. The army's primary mission was to protect U.S. citizens in the westward expansion by enforcing the restrictions that the U.S. government placed on the indigenous peoples. This role was complicated by the government's unwillingness to control American citizens in their westward movement and by the fact that although the army had responsibility for returning Indians to their reservations, the management (often mismanagement) of the reservations was done by politically appointed civilian agents of the Bureau of Indian Affairs. As it had been since the founding of the Republic, the fundamental policy of the government, and the army, of course, was to prevent the Indians from obstructing the development of the land and its resources by Americans. The questions of whether the government's specific actions were warranted or justifiable have come under increasing criticism and whether alternatives would have been preferable are debated.

In military terms, the U.S. Army was confronted with controlling warriors who used nontraditional methods of warfare. It also used Indian allies in scout units, particularly the Crow who were traditional enemies of the Cheyenne and the Sioux/Lahota. The army and other military groups in the West, such as local militia or volunteer units, sometimes unleashed violence against entire peoples, not simply the warriors, raising important ethical as well as military and political questions. Army officers and Indian leaders were divided over their attitudes towards each other; some hated and some respected their adversaries. With the clash of interests and cultures involved in such a confrontation, some violence was probably inevitable, but how much violence there had to be remains an open question. While the number of those killed in the battles of the Plains Indian Wars has been greatly exaggerated in popular literature and motion pictures, there certainly were

bloody battles and massacres on both sides. The number of major engagements be-
tween soldiers and Indian warriors between 1864 and 1890 was limited; the most
famous battles number little more than a dozen. Among these, none is more de-
bated than the battle in the Little Big Horn Mountains of Montana in June 1876
in which a detachment of 264 men of the Seventh Cavalry Regiment, including
Colonel George Armstrong Custer, was overwhelmed and annihilated by a force of
Cheyenne and Sioux/Lahota in what was seen as one of the most disastrous defeats
in U.S. military history. Historians and others continue to debate the reasons for
Custer's defeat and its meaning as a symbol of the tragic warfare between Ameri-
cans and Native Americans.

▲ D O C U M E N T S

In the first document, George Brent, a member of the Southern Cheyenne, in an interview sometime between 1905 and 1918, recounted the Sand Creek massacre. During
the Cheyenne-Arapaho War in 1864, caused by an influx of miners, a unit of Colorado
militia volunteers under Colonel J. M. Chivington mistakenly attacked an encampment of peaceful Cheyenne under Black Kettle, killing more than two hundred men,
women, and children. The second document is an official report, dated January 3,
1867, by Colonel Henry B. Carrington of Fort Phil Kearney in the Dakota Territory. It
describes the destruction of a force of 79 soldiers, including their commander, Lieutenant William Fetterman, and two other officers, and the mutilation of some of their
bodies by Cheyenne warriors of Red Cloud's tribe in the First Sioux War. The Indians
sought to block the Army's expansion of forts along the Bozeman Trail deep into
Sioux territory. In the Treaty of Medicine Lodge Creek in 1867, the army agreed to
abandon its posts along the Bozeman Trail, and the Indians agreed to relinquish their
rights off the reservations in return for government annuities. But Congress delayed
funding, and Indian warriors launched new raids.

General William Tecumseh Sherman, commanding general in the West, and his
chief subordinate Major General Philip H. Sheridan, launched a three-pronged winter
offensive against the Indians in October 1868. Lieutenant Colonel George Armstrong
Custer, leading the Seventh Cavalry Regiment, divided his command and ordered a
dawn assault, on November 27, 1868, upon an Indian village along the Washita River.
The Cheyenne village was headed by Chief Black Kettle, who had escaped the Sand
Creek massacre in 1864 and who had tried to return to the reservation. A number of his
followers, however, had remained on the warpath, as confirmed by the four white captives and assorted spoils found afterwards in the village. As the Indians scattered,
Custer's men killed more than one hundred of them—men, women, and children. Like
Custer and Sheridan, General Sherman had little sympathy for the Indians, as he
makes clear in the third document, a December 23, 1868, letter to Sheridan and his
subordinates. Eight years later, the Cheyenne, together with the Sioux/Lahota, got
their revenge against Custer and the Seventh Cavalry at the Battle of the Little Big
Horn on June 25, 1876. The fourth document is a scrawled letter from Lieutenant
Colonel Frederick W. Benteen, to his wife, written on July 4, only eleven days after
the battle. Benteen, commander of one of the units that Custer detached as he made his
advance, explains what happened. In the fifth document, a 1932 oral history recollection (to John G. Neihardt/Flaming Rainbow), Iron Hawk, who had been a fourteen-
year-old Hunkpapa Sioux/Lahota youth in 1876, describes what he did and saw in one
of the war parties that overwhelmed Custer, his unit, and its Crow Indian scouts.

During the Indian Wars, some army officers felt compassion and even admiration for the Indians, among them Brigadier General George Crook, who had negotiated with and fought Indians for three decades and Apaches in the Southwest since the Apache War began in 1871. In the sixth document, he demonstrates his sympathy for his adversaries in a July 1884 letter to *Harper's Weekly.* In the seventh document, Frederic Remington, then a 28-year-old illustrator, reports for *Century Magazine* on his journey with a patrol from the Tenth U.S. Cavalry Regiment composed of white officers and black enlisted men, whom the Indians called the "Buffalo Soldiers," as they patrolled the Arizona territory for renegade Indians in 1889, three years after the Apache War ended with the capture of Geronimo in 1886.

1. George Bent, Cheyenne Indian, Decries the Massacre of Native Americans by the Colorado Militia at Sand Creek (1864), 1905–1918

When the fight opened, my friend Little Bear was in the thick of it. He tells the story in this way: "I got up before daylight to go out to where my brother-in-law Tomahawk had left our pony herd the evening before. He told me where he had left the ponies and said he did not think they would stray far from that place. As soon as I was dressed I went out of the lodge and crossed the creek; but as I was going up on the hill I saw Kingfisher running back toward the camp. He shouted to me that white men were driving off the herds. I looked toward the Fort Lyon Trail and saw a long line of little black objects to the south, moving toward the camp across the bare brown plain. There was some snow on the ground, but only in the hollows. I ran back to the camp as fast as I could, but soldiers had already come up on the other side of the creek and were firing in among the lodges. As I came into camp the people were running up the creek. As I passed Black Kettle's lodge I saw that he had a flag tied to the end of the pole and was standing there holding the pole. I ran to our lodge to get my bow, quiver, shield, and war bonnet. My father, Bear Tongue, had just recently given me these things. I was very young then and had just become a warrior.

"By this time the soldiers were shooting into the camp from two sides, and as I put on my war bonnet and took up my shield and weapons, the bullets were hitting the lodge cover with heavy thumps like big hailstones. When I went out again I ran behind the lodges, so that the troops could not get good shots at me. I jumped over the bank into the creek bed and found Big Head, Crow Neck, Cut-Lip-Bear, and Smoke standing there under the high bank. I joined these young men. The people were all running up the creek; the soldiers sat on their horses, lined up on both banks and firing into the camps, but they soon saw that the lodges were now nearly empty, so they began to advance up the creek, firing on the fleeing people. Our party was at the west end of the camps, not one hundred yards from the lodges. At this point the creek made a bend, coming from the north and turning toward the southeast just at the upper end of the village. As the soldiers began to advance, we ran across to the west side of the creek to get under another high bank over there, but just as we reached this bank another body of cavalry came up and opened fire on us. We hardly knew what way to turn, but Big Head and the rest soon decided to go on. They ran on toward the west, but passing over a hill they ran into another body of troops just beyond and were surrounded and all killed.

"After leaving the others, I started to run up the creek bed in the direction taken by most of the fleeing people, but I had not gone far when a party of about twenty cavalrymen got into the dry bed of the stream behind me. They chased me up the creek for about two miles, very close behind me and firing on me all the time. Nearly all the feathers were shot out of my war bonnet, and some balls passed through my shield; but I was not touched. I passed many women and children, dead and dying, lying in the creek bed. The soldiers had not scalped them yet, as they were busy chasing those that were yet alive. After the fight I came back down the creek and saw these dead bodies all cut up, and even the wounded scalped and slashed. I saw one old woman wandering about; her whole scalp had been taken off and the blood was running down into her eyes so that she could not see where to go.

"I ran up the creek about two miles and came to the place where a large party of the people had taken refuge in holes dug in the sand up against the sides of the high banks. I stayed here until the soldiers withdrew. They were on both sides, firing down on us, but not many of us were killed. All who failed to reach these pits in the sand were shot down."

When the soldiers first appeared, Black Kettle and White Antelope, who had both been to Washington in 1863 and were firm friends of the whites, would not believe that an attack was about to be made on the camps. These two chiefs stood in front of their lodges and called to their people not to be afraid and not to run away; but while they were still trying to quiet the frightened women and children, the soldiers opened fire on the camps. Black Kettle still stood in front of his lodge, holding the lodgepole with the big American flag tied to its top. White Antelope, when he saw the soldiers shooting into the lodges, made up his mind not to live any longer. He had been telling the Cheyennes for months that the whites were good people and that peace was going to be made; he had induced many people to come to this camp, telling them that the camp was under the protection of Fort Lyon and that no harm could come to them; and now he saw the soldiers shooting the people, and he did not wish to live any longer. He stood in front of his lodge with his arms folded across his breast, singing the death song:

> "Nothing lives long,
> "Only the earth and the mountains."

while everyone was fleeing from the camp. At length the soldiers shot him and he fell dead in front of his lodge. Black Kettle stood in his camp until nearly everyone had gone, then took his wife and started up the creek after the rest of the people. Soldiers kept firing at them, and after a while Black Kettle's wife fell. He turned and looked at her, but she seemed to be dead; so he left her and ran on up the creek until he came to the place where the people were hiding in the pits. After the soldiers had withdrawn about dark, the chief went back down the creek to find the body of his wife, but he found her still alive, although wounded in many places. He took her on his back and carried her up the creek to where the rest of us were waiting. Her story was that after she had fallen and her husband had left her, soldiers rode up and shot her several times as she lay helpless on the sand. At the peace council in 1865 her story was told to the peace commissioners and they counted her wounds, nine in all, I believe.

2. Colonel Henry Carrington Details the Destruction and Mutilation of Lieutenant Colonel William Fetterman's Unit (1866), 1867

[Jan. 3, 1867]

On the morning of the 21st ultimo [of last month], at about eleven o'clock, my picket on Pilot Hill reported the wood-train [the wagons to gather wood for fuel] corralled and threatened by Indians on Sullivant Hills, about a mile and a half from the fort.

A few shots were heard. Indians also appeared in the brush at the crossing of Peney by the Virginia City road.

Upon tendering to Brevet Major Powell the command of Company C, U. S. Cavalry, then without an officer, but which he had been drilling, Brevet Lieutenant-Colonel Fetterman claimed by rank to go out. I acquiesced, giving him the men of his own company that were for duty, and a portion of Company C, 2d Battalion, 18th U. S. Infantry. Lieutenant G. W. Grummond, who had commanded the mounted Infantry, requested to take out the Cavalry. He did so.

In the previous skirmish, Lieutenant Grummond was barely saved from the disaster that befell Lieutenant Bingham by timely aid.

Brevet Lieutenant-Colonel Fetterman also was well admonished, as well as myself, that we were fighting brave and desperate enemies, who had sought to make up, by cunning and deceit, all the advantage which the white man gains by intelligence and better arms.

My instructions were therefore peremptory and explicit. I knew the ambition of each to win honor, but being unprepared for large aggressive action through want of adequate force, now fully demonstrated, I looked to continuance of timber supplies, to prepare for more troops, as the one practical duty; hence, two days before, Major Powell, sent out to cover the [wood] train under similar circumstances, simply did that duty, when he could have had a fight to any extent.

The day before, viz., the 20th ultimo [of last month], I went myself to the pinery, and built a bridge of forty-five feet span, to expedite the passage of wagons from the woods into open ground. Hence my instructions to Brevet Lieutenant-Colonel Fetterman, viz.: "Support the wood-train, relieve it, and report to me. Do not engage or pursue Indians at its expense; under no circumstances pursue over the Ridge, viz.: Lodge trail Ridge, as per map in your possession."

To Lieutenant Grummond I gave orders to "report to Brevet Lieutenant-Colonel Fetterman, implicitly obey orders, and not leave him."

Before the command left, I instructed Lieutenant A. II. Wands, my Regimental Quartermaster and acting Adjutant, to repeat these orders. He did so.

From Colonel Henry Carrington. *Official Report.* U.S. War Department, Secretary of War, *Annual Report* (1866–1867): 21–22, 62.

Fearing still that the spirit of ambition might over-ride prudence, as my refusal to permit sixty mounted men and forty citizens to go for several days down Tongue River valley after villages had been unfavorably regarded by Brevet Lieutenant-Colonel Fetterman and Captain Brown, I crossed the parade, and from a sentry platform halted the Cavalry, and again repeated my precise orders. I knew that the Indians had, for some days, returned each time with increased numbers, to feel our strength and decoy detachments to their sacrifice, and believed that to foil their purpose was actual victory, until reinforcements should arrive and my preparations were complete. I was right.

Just as the command left, five Indians reappeared at the crossing. The [spy] glass [telescope] revealed others in the thicket, having the apparent object of determining the watchfulness of the garrison, or cutting off any small party that should move out. A case shot dismounted one and developed nearly thirty, who broke for the hills and ravines to the North.

In half an hour the picket reported that the wood-train had broken corral and moved onto the pinery. No report came from the detachment. It was composed of eighty-one officers and men, including two citizens, all well armed; the Cavalry having the new carbine, while the detachment of Infantry was of choice men, the pride of their companies.

At twelve o'clock firing was heard toward Peno Creek, beyond Lodge Trail Ridge. A few shots were followed by constant shots, not to be counted. Captain Ten Eyck was immediately dispatched with Infantry, and the remaining Cavalry, and two wagons, and orders to join Colonel Fetterman at all hazards. The men moved promptly and on the run, but within little more than half an hour from the first shot, and just as the supporting party reached the hill overlooking the scene of action, all firing ceased.

Captain Ten Eyck sent a mounted orderly back with the report, that he could see or hear nothing of Fetterman, but that a body of Indians on the road below him were challenging him to come down, while larger bodies were in all the valleys for several miles around. Moving cautiously forward with the wagons (evidently supposed by the enemy to be guns, as mounted men were in advance), he rescued from the spot where the enemy had been nearest, forty-nine bodies, including those of Brevet Lieutenant-Colonel Fetterman and Captain F. H. Brown. The latter went out without my consent or knowledge, fearless to fight Indians with any adverse odds, and determined to kill one at least before joining his Company.

Captain Ten Eyck fell back slowly, followed, but not pressed by the enemy, reaching the Post without loss. The following day, finding general doubt as to the success of an attempt to recover other bodies, but believing that failure to rescue them would dishearten the command and encourage the Indians, who are so particular in this regard, I took eighty men and went to the scene of action, leaving a picket to advise me of any movement in the rear, and to keep signal communication with the garrison.

The scene of action told its own story.

The road on the little ridge where the final stand took place, was strewn with arrows, arrow-heads, scalp-poles, and broken shafts of spears. The arrows that were spent harmlessly, from all directions, show that the command was suddenly overwhelmed, surrounded, and cut off in retreat. Not an officer or man survived! A few bodies were found at the north end of the divide over which the road runs, just beyond Lodge Trail Ridge.

Nearly all were heaped near four rocks, at the point nearest the Fort, these rocks, enclosing a space about six feet square, having been the last refuge for defence. Here were also a few unexpected rounds of Spencer cartridge.

Fetterman and Brown had each a revolver-shot in the left temple. As Brown always declared that he would reserve a shot for himself, as a last resort, so I am convinced that these two brave men fell, each by the other's hand, rather than undergo the slow torture inflicted upon others.

Lieutenant Grummond's body was on the road between the two extremes, with a few others. This was not far from five miles from the fort, and nearly as far from the wood-train. Neither its own guard nor the detachment could by any possibility have helped each other, and the train was incidentally saved by the fierceness of the fight, in the brave but rash impulse of pursuit.

The officers, who fell, believed that no Indian force could overwhelm that number of troops, well held in hand.

Their terrible massacre bore marks of great valor, and has demonstrated the force and character of the foe; but no valor could have saved them.

Pools of blood on the road and sloping sides of the narrow divide showed where Indians bled fatally; but their bodies were carried off. I counted sixty-five such pools in the space of an acre, and three, within ten feet of Lieutenant Grummond's body. Eleven American horses and nine Indian ponies were on the road, or near the line of bodies; others, crippled, were in the valleys.

At the northwest or farther point, between two rocks, and apparently where the command first fell back from the valley, realizing their danger, I found citizens James S. Wheatley and Isaac Fisher, of Blue Springs, Nebraska, who, with "Henry Rifles," felt invincible, but fell, one having one hundred and five arrows in his naked body. The widow and family of Wheatley are here.

The cartridge shells about them told how well they fought. Before closing this report, I wish to say that every man, officer, soldier, or citizens who fell received burial, with such record as to identify each.

Fetterman, Brown, and Grummond lie in one grave; the remainder also share one tomb, buried, as they fought, together: but the cases in which they were laid are duly placed and numbered.

I ask the General Commanding to give my report, in the absence of the Division Commander, an access to the eye and ear of the General-in-Chief. The Department Commander must have more troops; and I declare this, my judgment, solemnly, and for the general public good, without one spark of personal ambition other than to do my duty daily as it comes; and whether I seem to speak too plainly or not, ever with the purpose to declare the whole truth, and with proper respect to my superior officers, who are entitled to the facts, as to scenes remote from their own immediate notice. I was asked to "*send all the bad news.*" I do it, so far, as far as I can.

I give some of the facts as to my men, whose bodies I found just at dark, resolved to bring all in, viz.:

Mutilations.

Eyes torn out and laid on the rocks.

Noses cut off.

Ears cut off.

Chins hewn off.

Teeth chopped out.

Joints of fingers cut off.

Brains taken out and placed on rocks, with members of the body.

Entrails taken out and exposed.

Hands cut off.

Feet cut off.

Arms taken out from socket.

Private parts severed, and indecently placed on the person.

Eyes, ears, mouth, and arms penetrated with spear-heads, sticks, and arrows.

Ribs slashed to separation, with knives; skulls severed in every form, from chin to crown.

Muscles of calves, thighs, stomach, breast, back, arms, and cheek taken out.

Punctures upon every sensitive part of the body, even to the soles of the feet and palms of the hand.

All this does not approximate the whole truth. Every Medical Officer was faithful, aided by a large force of men, and all were not buried until Wednesday after the fight.

The great real fact is, that these Indians take alive when possible, and slowly torture. It is the opinion of Dr. S. M. Horton, Post Surgeon, that not more than six were killed by [musket or rifle] balls. Of course the whole arrows, hundreds of which were removed from naked bodies, were all used after the removal of the clothing.

General William T. Sherman Approves Wiping out the Hostiles, 1868

My last date from General Sheridan is December 7, at Camp Supply on the point of starting for Fort Cobb. My last from General Hazen is November 30, at Fort Cobb, giving the localities of the various camps of the Indians, and the first account of the Battle of November 27, and the last General Grierson is of December 7th at Fort Gibson, when he was on the point of going to Fort Cobb with the two companies called for by General Hazen.

From General William T. Sherman to Major General P. H. Sheridan, Major General Hazen, and Brevert General Grierson, December 23, 1868, William T. Sherman Papers, Container 25, Reel 14, Library of Congress, Washington, D. C.

I have promptly furnished copies of these to the War Department, to meet the cry, raised by, Co., Tappan, Taylor and Co., to the effect that Black Kettle's was a friendly camp, and that Custer's battle was a second Sand Creek affair.

I have also furnished parts to the Press to counteract the effects of their bold and marked assertions. This you know is a free country, and people have the lawful right to misrepresent as much as they please, and to print them, but the great mass of our people cannot be humbugged into the belief that Black Kettle's camp was friendly, with its captive women and children, its herds of stolen horses, its stolen mail, arms, powder, [e]tc., trophies of war. I am well satisfied with Custer's attack and would not have wept if he could have served Satanta's and Bull Bear's bands in the same styles. I want you all to go ahead, kill and punish the hostile, rescue the captive white women and children, capture and destroy the ponies, lances, carbines, [e]tc., [e]tc., of the Cheyennes, Arapahoes and Kionas, mark out the spots where they must stay, and then systematize the whole (friendly and hostile) into camps with a view to economical support, until we can try and get them to be self-supporting, like the Cherokees and Choctaws. They must clearly understand that they must never again hunt outside the limits of the Territory defined as General Hazen's District, and that they must not enter Texas at all, much less for the purpose of stealing horses, and capturing women & children. If the game of the Indian Territory do not suffice for their support, the United States must feed them till they can tame cattle, sheep and hogs, and until they can raise patches of corn, potatoes, pumpkins, [e]tc. Bearing these general principals in view, I will be responsible for your acts, and risk all consequences.

Wm. T. Sherman

4. Lieutenant Frederick Benteen Depicts the Battle of the Little Big Horn, 1876

July 4th 1876, Montana
Camp 7th Cavalry, Yellowstone River,
Opposite mouth of Big Horn River.

My . . . . Darling,

. . . I will commence this letter by sending a copy of the last lines Cooke ever wrote, which was an order to me to this effect.

Benteen. Come on. Big village. Be quick, bring packs.

W. W. Cooke (P. S. Bring pac-s)

He left out the k in last packs.

I have the original, but it is badly torn and it should be preserved. So keep this letter, as the matter may be of interest hereafter, likewise of use. This note was brought back to me by Trumpeter Martin of my Co. (which fact saved his life.) When I received it I was five or six miles from the village, perhaps more, and the

---

Lt. Frederick W. Benteen to his wife, July 4, 1876, describing the Battle of the Little Big Horn (June 25, 1876), originally published in Col. W. A. Graham (U.S. Army-Ret.), "The Lost is Found: Custer's Last Message Comes to Light!" *The Cavalry Journal* (July-August 1942): 62–66. Also reprinted in W. A. Graham, comp. *The Custer Myth: A Source Book of Custeriana* (NY: Bonanza Books, 1953), 297–300.

packs at least that distance in my rear. I did not go back for the packs but kept on a stiff trot for the village. When getting at top of hill so that the valley could be seen—I saw an immense number of Indians on the plain, mounted of course and charging down on some dismounted men of Reno's command; the balance of R's command were mounted, and flying for dear life to the bluffs on the same side of river that I was. I then marched my 3 Co's. to them and a more delighted lot of folks you never saw. To commence—On the 22d of June—Custer, with the 7th Cavalry left the Steamer "Far West," Genl. Terry and Genl. Gibbon's command (which latter was then in on the side of river and in same camp in which we now are) and moved up the Rosebud, marching 12 miles—the next day we marched 35 miles up the same stream. The next day we marched 35 more miles up same stream and went into bivouac, remaining until 12 o'clock P.M. We then marched until about daylight, making about 10 miles; about half past five we started again—and after going 6 or 7 miles we halted and officers' call was sounded. We were asked how many men of the companies were with the Co. Packs and instructed that only six could remain with them—and the discourse wound up with—that we should see that the men were supplied with the quantity of ammunition as had been specified in orders and that the 1st Co. that reported itself in readiness should be the advance Co. I knew that my Co. was in the desired condition and it being near the point of Assembly I went to it, assured myself of same, then announced to Genl. Custer that "H" Co. was ready; he replied the Advance is yours, [Lieutenant] Col. Benteen. We then moved four or five miles and halted between the slopes of two hills and the Regt. was divided into Battalions—Reno getting Co's. "A. G. and M." I getting "D. H. K." From that point I was ordered with my Battn. to go over the immense hills to the left, in search of the valley, which was supposed to be very near by and to pitch into anything I came across—and to inform Custer at once if I found anything worthy of same. Well, I suppose I went up and down those hills for 10 miles—and still no valley anywhere in sight, the horses were fast giving out from steady climbing—and as my orders had been fulfilled I struck diagonally for the trail the command had marched on, getting to it just before the Pack train got there—or on the trail just ahead of it. I then marched rapidly and after about 6 or 7 miles came upon a burning tepee—in which was the body of an indian on a scaffold, arrayed gorgeously—None of the command was in sight at this time. The ground from this to the valley was descending but very rough. I kept up my trot and when I reached a point very near the ford which was crossed by Reno's Battn. I got my first sight of the Valley and river—and Reno's command in full flight for the bluffs to the side I was then on—Of course I joined them at once. The ground where Reno charged on was a plain 5 or 6 miles or 10 miles long and about one mile or more wide; Custer sent him in there and promised to support him—after Reno started in, Custer with his five Co's instead of crossing the ford went to the right—around some high bluffs—with the intention—as is supposed—of striking the rear of the village; from the bluff on which he got he had his first glimpse of the whole of it—and I can tell you 'twas an immense one. From that point Cooke sent the note to me by Martin, which I have quoted on 1st page. I suppose after the five Co's had closed up somewhat Custer started down for the village, all throats bursting themselves with cheering (So says Martin). He had 3½ or 4 miles to go before he got to a ford—as the Village was on the plain on opposite side to Custer's column. So, when he got over those 4 miles of rough country and reached the ford, the indians had availed themselves of the timely information given by the cheering— as to the whereabouts and intentions of that column, and had arrangements completed to receive it. Whether the indians allowed Custer's column to cross at all, is a mooted question, but I am of the opinion that nearly—if not all of the five companies got into the village—but were driven out immediately—flying in great disorder and crossing by two instead of the one ford by which they entered. "E" Co. going by the left and "F. I. and L." by the same one they crossed. What became of "C" Co. no one knows—they must have charged there below the village, gotten away—or have been killed in the bluffs on the village side of stream—as very few of "C" Co. horses are found. Jack Sturgis and Porter's clothes were found in the Village. After the indians had driven them across, it was a regular buffalo hunt for them and not a man escaped. We buried 203 of the bodies of Custer's command the 2d day after fight—The bodies were as recognizable as if they were in life. With Custer—was Keogh, Yates and Tom Custer (3 Captains) 1st Lieut's. Cooke, A. E. Smith, Porter, Calhoun (4) 2d Lieuts. Harrington, Sturgis, Riley and Crittenden (J. J. of 20th Inf.) Asst. Surgeon Lord was along—but his body was not recognized. Neither was Porter's nor Sturgis' nor Harrington's.

McIntosh and Hodgson were killed at Reno's end of line—in attempting to get back to bluffs. DeRudio was supposed to have been lost, but the same night the indians left their village he came sauntering in dismounted, accompanied by McIntosh's cook. They had hidden away in the woods. He had a thrilling romantic story made out already—embellished, you bet! The stories of O'Neill (the man who was with him) and De R's of course, couldn't be expected to agree, but far more of truth, I am inclined to think, will be found in the narrative of O'Neill; at any rate, it is not at all colored—as he is a cool, level-headed fellow—and tells it plainly *and the same way all the time*—which is a big thing towards convincing one of the truth of a story.

I must now tell you what we did—When I found Reno's command. We halted for the packs to come up—and then moved along the line of bluffs towards the direction Custer was supposed to have gone in. Weir's Company was sent out to communicate with Custer, but it was driven back. We then showed our full force on the hills with Guidons flying, that Custer might see us—but we could see nothing of him, couldn't hear much firing, but could see immense body of Indians coming to attack us from both sides of the river. We withdrew to a saucer like hill, putting our horses and packs in the bottom of saucer and threw all of our force dismounted around this corral; the animals could be riddled from only one point—but we had not men enough to extend our line to that—so we could not get it—therefore the indians amused themselves by shooting at our stock, ditto, men—but they, the men, could cover themselves. Both of my horses (U. S. horses) were wounded. Well they pounded at us all of what was left of the 1st day and the whole of the 2d day—withdrawing their line with the withdrawal of their village, which was at dusk the 2d day. Corporal Loll, Meador and Jones were killed; Sergt. Pahl, both of the Bishops, Phillips, Windolph, Black, Severs, Cooper, etc. (21 altogether) wounded. I got a slight scratch on my right thumb, which, as you see, doesn't prevent me from writing you this long scrawl. As this goes via Fort Ellis it will be a long time reaching you. Genl. Terry, with Genl. Gibbon's command—came up the morning of the 3d day, about 10 o'clock. Indians had all gone the night before. Had

Custer carried out the orders he got from Genl. Terry, the commands would have formed a junction exactly at the village, and have captured the whole outfit of te-pees, etc. and probably any quantity of squaws, pappooses, etc. but Custer dis-obeyed orders from the fact of not wanting any other command—or body to have a finger in the pie—and thereby lost his life. (3000 warriors were there).

Margin:

. . . Boston Custer and young Mr. Reed, a nephew of Genl. Custer, were killed, also Kellogg, the reporter. . . .

This is a long scrawl—but not so much in it after all—and I am about getting to the end of my tether. Reno has assumed command and Wallace is Adjutant. Edgerly, Qr. Mr. By the death of our Captains, Nowlan, Bell and Jackson, 3 "coffee-coolers" are made Captains and Godfrey is Senior 1st Lt., Mathey 2d, Gibson, 3d. Quick promotion. I am inclined to think that had McIntosh divested himself of that slow poking way which was his peculiar characteristic, he might have been left in the land of the living. A Crow indian, one of our scouts who got in the village, reported that our men killed a great many of them—quite as many, if not more, than was killed of ours. The indians during the night got to fighting among themselves and killed each other—so the Crow said—he also said as soon as he got possession of a Sioux blanket, not the slightest attention was paid to him. There was among them Cheyennes, Arrapahoes, Kiowa and representatives proba-bly from every Agency on the Mo. River. A host of them there sure.

The latest and probably correct account of the battle is that none of Custer's command got into the village at all. We may not be back before winter, think so very strongly.

Well—Wifey, Darling, I think this will do for a letter, so with oceans of love to you and Fred and kisses innumerable, I am devotedly,

Your husband
Fred Benteen.

5. Iron Hawk, a Hunkpapa Sioux/Lahota Warrior, Recalls the Battle of the Little Big Horn (1876), 1932

I went into our tepee and got dressed for war as fast as I could; but I could hear bul-lets whizzing outside, and I was so shaky that it took me a long time to braid an ea-gle feather into my hair. Also, I had to hold my pony's rope all the time, and he kept jerking me and trying to get away. While I was doing this, crowds of warriors on horses were roaring by up stream, yelling: "Hoka hey!" Then I rubbed red paint all over my face and took my bow and arrows and got on my horse. I did not have a gun, only a bow and arrows.

When I was on my horse, the fight up stream seemed to be over, because everybody was starting back downstream and yelling: "It's a good day to die!" Soldiers were coming at the other end of the village, and nobody knew how many there were down there.

A man by the name of Little Bear rode up to me on a pinto horse, and he had a very pretty saddle blanket. He said: "Take courage, boy! The earth is all that lasts!" So I rode fast with him and the others downstream, and many of us Hunkpapas gathered on the east side of the river at the foot of a gulch that led back up the hill where the second soldier band was. There was a very brave Shyela with us, and I heard someone say: "He is going!" I looked, and it was this Shyela. He had on a spotted war bonnet and a spotted robe made of some animal's skin and this was fastened with a spotted belt. He was going up the hill alone and we all followed part way. There were soldiers along the ridge up there and they were on foot holding their horses. The Shyela rode right close to them in a circle several times and all the soldiers shot at him. Then he rode back to where we had stopped at the head of the gulch. He was saying: "Ah, ah!" Someone said: "Shyela friend, what is the matter?" He began undoing his spotted belt, and when he shook it, bullets dropped out. He was very sacred and the soldiers could not hurt him. He was a fine looking man.

We stayed there awhile waiting for something and there was shooting everywhere. Then I heard a voice crying: "Now they are going, they are going!" We looked up and saw the cavalry horses stampeding. These were all gray horses.

I saw Little Bear's horse rear and race up hill toward the soldiers. When he got close, his horse was shot out from under him, and he got up limping because the bullet went through his leg; and he started hobbling back to us with the soldiers shooting at him. His brother-friend, Elk Nation, went up there on his horse and took Little Bear behind him and rode back safe with bullets striking all around him. It was his duty to go to his brother-friend even if he knew he would be killed.

By now a big cry was going up all around the soldiers up there and the warriors were coming from everywhere and it was getting dark with dust and smoke.

We saw soldiers start running down hill right towards us. Nearly all of them were afoot, and I think they were so scared that they didn't know what they were doing. They were making their arms go as though they were running very fast, but they were only walking. Some of them shot their guns in the air. We all yelled "Hoka hey!" and charged toward them, riding all around them in the twilight that had fallen on us.

I met a soldier on horseback, and I let him have it. The arrow went through from side to side under his ribs and it stuck out on both sides. He screamed and took hold of his saddle horn and hung on, wobbling, with his head hanging down. I kept along beside him, and I took my heavy bow and struck him across the back of the neck. He fell from his saddle, and I got off and beat him to death with my bow. I kept on beating him awhile after he was dead, and every time I hit him I said "Hownh!" I was mad, because I was thinking of the women and little children running down there, all scared and out of breath. These Wasichus wanted it, and they came to get it, and we gave it to them. I did not see much more. I saw Brings Plenty kill a soldier with a war club. I saw Red Horn Buffalo fall. There was a Lakota riding along the edge of the gulch, and he was yelling to look out, that there was a soldier hiding in there. I saw him charge in and kill the soldier and begin slashing him with a knife.

Then we began to go towards the river, and the dust was lifting so that we could see the women and children coming over to us from across the river. The soldiers were all rubbed out there and scattered around.

The women swarmed up the hill and began stripping the soldiers. They were yelling and laughing and singing now. I saw something funny. Two fat old women were stripping a soldier, who was wounded and playing dead. When they had him naked, they began to cut something off that he had, and he jumped up and began fighting with the two fat women. He was swinging one of them around, while the other was trying to stab him with her knife. After awhile, another woman rushed up and shoved her knife into him and he died really dead. It was funny to see the naked Wasichu fighting with the fat women.

By now we saw that our warriors were all charging on some soldiers that had come from the hill up river to help the second band that we had rubbed out. They ran back and we followed, chasing them up on their hill again where they had their pack mules. We could not hurt them much there, because they had been digging to hide themselves and they were lying behind saddles and other things. I was down by the river and I saw some soldiers come down there with buckets. They had no guns, just buckets. Some boys were down there, and they came out of the brush and threw mud and rocks in the soldiers' faces and chased them into the river. I guess they got enough to drink, for they are drinking yet. We killed them in the water.

Afterwhile it was nearly sundown, and I went home with many others to eat, while some others stayed to watch the soldiers on the hill. I hadn't eaten all day, because the trouble started just when I was beginning to eat my first meal.

6. General George Crook Defends the Indians, 1884

Head-Quarters Department of Arizona,
Whipple Barracks, Prescott, July 16, 1884.

My Dear Mr. Welsh,—The best answer to the questions contained in your communication of the 23d ult. would be found in a recital of the facts which careful and impartial investigation could not fail to develop in regard to the Chiracahua and other Apaches. Until such an investigation, deep, systematic, and perfectly unbiassed, can be made by yourself or some other member of your association, I ask that some consideration be given to the few remarks I wish to make in their behalf.

It is not to be denied that the Apache is the fiercest and most formidable of all our Indians when upon the war-path. Opinions may differ as to the place in the scale of intelligence the Apache should occupy, but there is no diversity of sentiment—at least not among army officers—as to the skill and cunning with which this Indian conducts all warlike operations. Speaking for myself, after a somewhat extended experience of over thirty-two years' duration with the various Indian tribes from British America to Mexico, from the Missouri River to the Pacific Ocean, I do not hesitate to put the Apache at the very head for natural intelligence and discernment. He knows his rights and is not afraid to maintain them. Were he a

From General George Crook to Herbert Welsh, *Harper's Weekly* 28 (August 30, 1884): 565.

Greek or a Roman, we should read with pride and enthusiasm of his determination to die rather than suffer wrong; but looking at him as a native of our own soil, and as the feeble barrier which stands between ourselves and the silver mines or coal measures supposed to exist on his reservation, it is not always possible to do justice to his virtues, or to consider his faults as identical with those of which we ourselves should be guilty under similar provocation. . . .

Upon being re-assigned to command the Department of Arizona I found that all that had been accomplished with so much patient labor had been destroyed, and almost all trace of it had been obliterated. From the simple, pathetic story of the Apaches I gathered that they had been systematically and outrageously plundered by a gang of sharks thinly disguised as Indian agents and others. The Indians had about lost all confidence in our government, and were on the brink of an outbreak, which would have cost us heavily in the losses we should have had to suffer, and still more heavily in the taxes we should have had to pay for its suppression. In this exigency there was only one thing to be done. I personally visited the various bands, including those already on the war-path, and assured them that the people of the United States were not in sympathy with the rascals of whom they complained, but were sincerely desirous of doing full justice to the Indians, and I asked them, if they had any confidence left in me, and if they believed that I would act toward them just exactly as if they were white men, to remain at peace until an adjustment of their wrongs could be effected.

7. Western Artist Frederic Remington Covers Black Troopers Chasing Apaches Through the Arizona Territory, 1889

Up the ascent of the mountain we toiled, now winding among trees and brush, scrambling up the precipitous slopes, picking a way across a field of shattered rock, or steadying our horses over the smooth surface of some boulder, till it seemed to my uninitiated mind that cavalry was not equal to the emergencies of such a country. In the light of subsequent experiences, however, I feel confident that any cavalry officer who has ever chased Apaches would not hesitate a moment to lead a command up the Bunker Hill Monument. The slopes of the Sierra Bonitas are very steep, and as the air became more rarified as we toiled upward I found that I was panting for breath. My horse—a veteran mountaineer—grunted in his efforts and drew his breath in a long and labored blowing; consequently I felt as though I was not doing anything unusual in puffing and blowing myself. The resolutions of the previous night needed considerable nursing, and though they were kept alive, at times I reviled myself for being such a fool as to do this sort of thing under the delusion that it was an enjoyable experience. On the trail ahead I saw the lieutenant throw himself on the ground. I followed his example, for I was nearly "done for." I never had felt a rock that was as soft as the one I sat on. It was literally down. The old troop-horse heaved a great sigh, and dropping his head went fast asleep, as

Frederic Remington, "A Scout with the Buffalo Soldiers." Reprinted in John M. Carroll, ed. *The Black Military Experience in the American West,* shorter ed. (New York: Liveright, 1973), 130–131, 139–141.

every good soldier should do when he finds the opportunity. The lieutenant and I discussed the climb, and my voice was rather loud in pronouncing it "beastly." My companion gave me no comfort, for he was a "soldier, and unapt to weep," though I thought he might have used his official prerogative to grumble. The Negro troopers sat about, their black skins shining with perspiration, and took no interest in the matter in hand. They occupied such time in joking and in merriment as seemed fitted for growling. They may be tired and they may be hungry, but they do not see fit to augment their misery by finding fault with everybody and everything. In this particular they are charming men with whom to serve. Officers have often confessed to me that when they are on long and monotonous field service and are troubled with a depression of spirits, they have only to go about the campfires of the Negro soldier in order to be amused and cheered by the clever absurdities of the men. Personal relations can be much closer between white officers and colored soldiers than in the white regiments without breaking the barriers which are necessary to army discipline. The men look up to a good soldier, rely on him in trouble, and even seek him for advise in their small personal affairs. In barracks no soldier is allowed by his fellows to "cuss out" a just and respected superior. As to their bravery, I am often asked, "Will they fight?" That is easily answered. They have fought many, many times. The old sergeant sitting near me, as calm of feature as a bronze statue, once deliberately walked over a Cheyenne rifle-pit and killed his man. One little fellow near him once took charge of a lot of stampeded cavalry-horses when Apache bullets were flying loose and no one knew from what point to expect them next. These little episodes prove the sometimes doubted self-reliance of the Negro. . . .

That night we were forced to make a "dry camp"; that is, one where no water is to be found. There is such an amount of misery locked up in the thought of a dry camp that I refuse to dwell upon it. We were glad enough to get upon the trail in the morning, and in time found a nice running mountain-brook. The command wallowed in it. We drank as much as we could hold and then sat down. We arose and drank some more, and yet we drank again, and still once more, until we were literally water-logged. Lieutenant Jim became uneasy, so we took up our march. We were always resuming the march when all nature called aloud for rest. We climbed straight up impossible places. The air grew chill, and in a gorge a cold wind blew briskly down to supply the hot air rising from sands of the mesa far below. That night we made a camp, and the only place where I could make my bed was on a great flat rock. We were now among the pines, which towered above us. The horses were constantly losing one another in the timber in their search for grass, in consequence of which they whinnied, while the mules brayed, and made the mountain hideous with sound.

By another long climb we reached the extreme peaks of the Pinal range, and there before us spread a view which was grand enough to compensate us for the labor. Beginning in "gray reds," range after range of mountains, overlapping each other, grow purple and finally lose themselves in pale blues. We sat on a ledge and gazed. The soldiers were interested, though their remarks about the scenery somehow did not seem to express an appreciation of the grandeur of the view which impressed itself strongly upon us. Finally one fellow, less aesthetic than his mates, broke the spell by a request for chewing tobacco, so we left off dreaming and started on.

That day Lieutenant Jim lost his bearings, and called upon that instinct which he had acquired in his life among the Indians. He "cut the signs" of old Indian trails and felt the course to be in a certain direction—which was undoubtedly correct, but it took us over the highest points of the Mescal range. My shoes were beginning to give out, and the troop-boots of several soldiers threatened to disintegrate. One soldier, more ingenious than the rest, took out some horse-shoe nails and cleverly mended his boot-gear. At times we wound around great slopes where a loose stone or the giving way of bad ground would have precipitated horse and rider a thousand feet below. Only the courage of the horses brings one safely through. The mules suffered badly, and our weary horses punched very hard with their foreparts as they went down hill. We made the descent of the Mescals through a long canyon where the sun gets one in chancery, as it were. At least we reached the Gila, and early downed a pack-mule and two troopers in a quicksand. We began to pass Indian huts, and saw them gathering wheat in river bottoms, while they paused to gaze at us and doubtless wondered for what purpose the buffalo soldiers were abroad in the land. The cantonment appeared, and I was duly gratified when we reached it. I hobbled up to the "Grand Hotel" of my host the captain, who laughed heartily at my floundering movements and observed my nose and cheeks, from which the sun had peeled the skin, with evident relish at the thought of how I had been used by his lieutenant. At his suggestion I was made an honorary member of the cavalry, and duly admonished "not to trifle again with the Tenth Nubian Horse if I expected any mercy."

In due time the march continued without particular incident, and at last the scout "pulled in" to the home post, and I again sat in my easychair behind the lattice-work, firm in the conviction that soldiers, like other men, find more hard work than glory in their calling.

⚜ E S S A Y S

George Armstrong Custer was a brash and handsome cavalry officer, who became a Northern hero in the Civil War, but became a contested figure because of his actions on the Great Plains. He remains one of the most controversial commanders in American history, his place in history fixed by his disaster at the Little Big Horn. Historians and others continue to debate the reasons for Custer's defeat. In the first essay taken from a contrasting dual biography of Crazy Horse and George Armstrong Custer written in 1975, Stephen E. Ambrose, military historian, biographer, and former director of the Eisenhower Center at the University of New Orleans, chastises the commander of the Seventh Cavalry as not simply being outnumbered but also outgeneraled by the Indians. Taking a contrasting view, the second essay, written by Robert M. Utley, former chief historian of the National Park Service and author of numerous books on the Indian Wars, continues to celebrate Custer as one of the Army's great battle leaders, concluding that in the end, he lost because he was simply overwhelmed by superior numbers of highly motivated Indian warriors. Custer's famous luck finally ran out, but in his battlefield death he became immortal.

George Armstrong Custer: A Reckless Commander Brought Down by His Own Mistakes

STEPHEN E. AMBROSE

The Little Bighorn is a sparklingly delightful stream. Its water is clear, nicely cool in late June, a pleasure to drink. Anywhere from ten to forty yards wide, it has a strong current. Numerous rocks break the flow of the river and cause it to gurgle constantly. The rocks are smooth, the bottom mostly gravel, and the depth seldom over five feet, making it altogether a perfect river for swimming. On the morning of June 25, 1876, hundreds of Sioux and Cheyenne children were bobbing up and down in the Little Bighorn, letting the current carry them along, laughing and splashing, choking when they swallowed too much water. Occasionally a teen-aged girl would cry out to the little ones to be careful, but they paid no attention. Here and there a fisherman tried his luck with a grasshopper for bait. Swallows darted through the surrounding cottonwoods and over the creek—the valley was filled with the birds.

Up on the west bank—and it was a high bank—the children's mothers and fathers went about their business. There was still sufficient grass on the tableland above their camp to feed the ponies for a couple of days, and there was plenty of food in the camp, so the women didn't have any pressing work. Many of them toiled together on hides, chatting about recent events, wondering when the soldiers would come. Some were arguing with their ten-year-olds, telling them they were too young to fight. Most boys of around that age, however, were up on the tableland, keeping watch on the gigantic pony herd. Other women were helping their men prepare for battle. A few just lazed under the abundant cottonwoods, escaping the already hot rays of the morning sun. Black Elk, a brave Sioux warrior, was out with some women gathering wild turnips.

"It seemed that peace and happiness were prevailing all over the world," a Cheyenne warrior later recalled, "and nowhere was any man planning to lift his hand against his fellow man." Few of the Indians knew much about Custer's approach.

But their leaders knew. The lodges of men like Crazy Horse, Gall and Sitting Bull of the Hunkpapas, Two Moons of the Cheyennes and others became small command posts, with scouts riding in every few minutes to report. The scouts were hanging around Custer's flanks, knew where he was and where he was headed. The only things they didn't know were exactly where, how, and when he would attack the village. But the leaders absolutely expected an attack and even wanted it to come, to fulfill Sitting Bull's vision of soldiers falling into camp. Indeed, on at least two occasions small groups of scouts tried the old decoy trick, hoping to draw Custer into a pell-mell charge into the village. Custer didn't take the bait, although the evidence indicates that the action of the decoys reinforced his *idée fixe* that the Sioux were attempting to escape.

It may be that the single most important fact about the battle of the Little Bighorn was that Custer was doing exactly what the Indians expected and wanted him to do. In any event, as Custer moved to the attack (knowing almost nothing about his enemy's force or position), Crazy Horse stuck to his command post, refusing to commit his men until he knew exactly where, when, and how Custer would make his charge.

Of the four parts of Custer's divided command, Benteen was on the left, Reno in the center, Custer on the right, with the ammunition train following. "You could tell that the plan was to strike the Indian camp at three places," a sergeant in the 7th Cavalry later wrote. About noon, Custer came to the site of a recently abandoned village. One lodge—immortalized today as the Lone Tipi—was still standing, a warrior's body inside—he had just died from wounds received a week earlier on the Rosebud. Custer ordered the tipi burned, and evidently decided that the main body of Indians were on the run. The abandoned village had been the site of the full Sitting Bull-Crazy Horse encampment a couple of days earlier, so from the plentiful tracks it was natural for Custer to assume that they had just fled in panic. Bluffs and trees cut off his view of the new campsite.

A scout rode forward to a knoll about fifty yards beyond the tipi, saw great clouds of dust (probably created by the normal activity in the village), and called out, "There go your Indians, running like devils." Custer may have thought, "And there goes the White House with them, if I don't catch them soon." He ordered Benteen to march south, feeling constantly to his left until he reached the Little Bighorn, to make certain that the Indians didn't escape in that direction. He then sent his adjutant, Cooke, to Reno, with verbal orders to "move forward at as rapid a gait as he thought prudent, and charge the village afterward, and the whole outfit would support him."

Custer himself, with his five troops, turned to the north, behind the last line of bluffs (which were thus between him and the camp), with the evident intention of turning the Indians' flank or of preventing their escape down the Little Bighorn. He believed, it appears, that the Indians would fight a rear guard action against Reno while the women and children fled and that Reno's attack would require the warriors' full attention. With the bluff hiding his column from the hostiles, Custer must have thought that his tactics would restore the element of surprise, lost that morning when the Sioux scouts spotted his columns, and that he would be able to pitch into the retreating Indians unexpectedly.

Actually, the reverse was true. The hostiles knew all about Custer—but had failed to see Reno break off. Thus Reno's move was the real surprise. Crazy Horse had kept his warriors in hand to meet Custer. Reno crossed the Little Bighorn and came up on the south end of the village. He had open ground in front of him, perfect terrain for a cavalry charge, and his orders were positive and peremptory— charge the enemy. But in sight of the tipis, Reno stopped, dismounted his men, and engaged in some long-range and fruitless firing at the Sioux who were beginning to ride out to meet him.

It was a critical moment. Crazy Horse organized a blocking force—his main concern continued to be Custer's flanking march toward the northern, or lower, end of the village. According to Billy Garnett, who got his information from the Oglalas, "when Reno attacked the village the Indians were almost uncontrollable, so great was their eagerness to press a counterattack, but Crazy Horse rode up and down in front of his men talking calmly to them and telling them to restrain their ardor till the right time." But other Indian accounts suggest that Crazy Horse was still in his lodge when Reno appeared. Short Bull said he and others had Reno's men on the run back across the Little Bighorn when Crazy Horse rode up with his men.

"Too late! You've missed the fight!" Short Bull called out to Crazy Horse.

"Sorry to miss this fight," Crazy Horse laughed. "But there's a good fight coming over the hill. That's where the big fight is going to be. We'll not miss that one." He was not a bit excited, Short Bull said. "He made a joke of it." But Lieutenant William H. Clark, who in 1877 got to know Crazy Horse as well as any white man . . . and who based his information on interviews with Crazy Horse and other Oglala participants, reported: "Crazy Horse rode with the greatest daring up and down in front of Col. Reno's skirmish line, and as soon as these troops were driven across the river, he went at once to Genl. Custer's front and there became the leading spirit." It is impossible, in short, to make a definitive statement about Crazy Horse's actions versus Reno, in sharp contrast to his abundantly documented activities versus Custer at the other end of the field.

As Reno's men were dismounting, Custer and his staff rode to the top of the bluffs. From that point he could see Reno and a part of the village, although not all of it—the lower, or northern, end being hidden by cottonwood trees. At this moment he must have realized that everything he had done up until now had been based on a faulty assumption. The Indians were not running; indeed, Custer could see normal activity going on in the camp. He had sent Benteen off on a wild goose chase. But he was not discouraged. Reno was—he thought—preparing to charge the upper end of the village. All the warriors would be drawn to Reno's front. Meanwhile, he and his five troops could slip around to the lower end and attack the women and children, causing a general stampede. It would be like the Washita.

"We've caught them napping," Custer called out. Turning in his saddle, he waved his broad-brimmed hat for his men on the east side of the bluff to see, shouting, "We've got them!" Riding down to his five companies, he turned to trumpeter John Martini, an Italian immigrant just learning English, and said, "I want you to take a message to Captain Benteen.[†] Ride as fast as you can, and tell him to hurry. Tell him it's a big village, and I want him to be quick, and to bring the ammunition packs." Shifting in his saddle to face his men, Custer called out, "As soon as we get through, we will go back to our station"—that is, Fort Abraham Lincoln.

As Martini prepared to ride off on his mission, Adjutant Cooke stopped the trooper and gave him a written order, scrawled on a notebook pad: "Benteen: Come on. Big village. Be quick. Bring packs. W. W. Cooke. P.S. Bring Packs."

Custer and his five troops rode north, behind the bluffs. On his way to Benteen, Martini passed Boston Custer, who had left the pack train and was going to join his brother. "Where's the general?" Boston snapped. Martini pointed to the north, and Boston put his spurs to his tired horse.

Reno and his men saw Custer wave his hat up on the bluff and thought he was cheering them on. Crazy Horse may have seen Custer too, and it was apparently at

---

[†]Benteen had decided there were no Indians to the south, so on his own he had decided to turn to his right. He joined Reno that afternoon.

this point that he made his own battle plan—i.e., after he knew his enemy's strength, position, and intentions. He would outflank Custer, who was attempting to outflank him. First, however, Reno had to be stopped.

That task proved easy enough. Reno never did attack. The chief reason was that his men were exhausted. It would be impossible to overstate the extent of their weariness, after days of marching with little or no sleep. Sitting Bull expressed it best. "They were brave men," he said, "but they were too tired. When they rode up, their horses were tired and they were tired. When they got off from their horses they could not stand firmly on their feet. They swayed to and fro—so my young men have told me—like the limbs of cypresses in a great wind. Some of them staggered under the weight of their guns."

Reno, having lost one man, ordered a retreat into some cottonwoods along the bank of the Little Bighorn. The Indians did not press him, but they did fire in his direction, and one lucky bullet hit Bloody Knife in the head and splattered his brains all over Reno's face. Reno lost his nerve (remember that he was as exhausted as his men, and a tired commander doesn't think clearly). He ordered a further retreat, back across the Little Bighorn and up into the bluffs, where he could make a defensive stand, and he took off at the head of his men, without making certain that his orders were passed on. It was a rout, not a retreat, and Reno suffered his first serious casualties when his column was getting over the river and up the bluffs. He abandoned sixteen men and one officer in the cottonwoods, but the Indians left them alone and Reno too after he got to the high ground. The Indians had more important business elsewhere; only a few stayed to harass Reno. The whole affair took about thirty minutes.

Custer meanwhile was pushing north, on exhausted horses, hidden by the bluffs. Crazy Horse called to his men, "Ho-ka hey! It is a good day to fight! It is a good day to die! Strong hearts, brave hearts, to the front! Weak hearts and cowards to the rear." He then led them, at a gallop, through the camp, planning to get beyond Custer, ford the Little Bighorn, and hit the 7th Cavalry in the right flank and rear. The Indian force picked up reinforcements as it tore through the camp, until there were as many as one thousand men following Crazy Horse, mainly Oglalas and Cheyennes.

It must have been a sight, that dash through the village on fresh ponies, the animals just as excited as their riders, knocking over tipis, cooking pots, dogs and small children who got in the way, the women screaming out the names of the brave ones. But what was most impressive was that Crazy Horse was getting the warriors to ride *away* from the scene of action, something no one had ever been able to get them to do before.

When Custer reached Medicine Trail Coulee, which cut through the east bank of the river, he must have thought he had reached the lower end of the village. He turned to his left and rode down the coulee, planning to ford the river and attack the hostile rear. But Gall, who had already crossed to the north side of the river, had gathered together some 1,500 Hunkpapas and blocked Custer's path. Custer turned again, to his right, toward the line of bluffs. Gall's warriors pressed him hard, attacking in force.

At this point Custer realized, probably, that he was no longer on the offensive. Suddenly he was in a fight for survival. He had to get to the high ground, dig in, and wait for Benteen (or Gibbon, way to his rear but due the next day) to come to his rescue. The highest ground was in front of him, a hill at the northern end of the bluffs (called Custer Hill today). At the head of his column, he set out for it, Gall and about one thousand warriors pressing him in the rear.

Custer's command got stretched out, Lieutenant Calhoun's company in the rear. Custer was almost on top of the hill. Once there he could set up a defensive perimeter (as Reno had now done four miles to the south) and wait for help. With more than two hundred carbine-carrying troopers, he figured to be able to hold a hilltop indefinitely against almost any force of warriors. He may have realized that although he had lost the victory and thus the presidency, he had not yet lost his command or his life. At that instant, Crazy Horse, who had forded the Little Bighorn beyond Custer's position and come up on the north side of the hill, appeared on its top.

When a group of men on horseback reach the top of a hill after a hard gallop, there is a natural pause; the men want to look around and they pull up, which suits the horses just fine, because they too want to see what's ahead before plunging on. Thus it is likely that when Crazy Horse, his thousand warriors following close behind, reached the top of the hill after a difficult ascent, their horses slightly out of breath and gasping just a little, there was a pause, an instant in which the action was frozen.

What a sight it must have been, especially for George Armstrong Custer, who was—probably—at that instant leading his men toward the spot on which Crazy Horse stood. Behind Crazy Horse, Custer would have seen the thousand warriors, all painted, many with war bonnets, some holding spears high in the air, their glistening points aimed right at Custer. Many braves, as many as one out of five, were brandishing Winchesters or other rifles. Half or more of the Indians held bows and fistfuls of arrows, often with shields in the other hand—they guided their ponies with their knees. The ponies were painted too, with streaks and zigzags and other designs, and with their new coats, sleek sides, and plenty of fat from the spring grass, the animals looked magnificent. They snorted and pranced, caught their second wind, and were ready for battle.

Crazy Horse would have been in front, alone, standing out in that kaleidoscope of shifting color by his apparent plainness. He would have worn only his breechcloth and a single hawk's feather in his hair. Almost surely he had his pebble behind his ear, another under his arm, and had thrown some dust over himself and his pony after painting zigzag marks on his body and some lightning streaks on his pony. He carried his Winchester lightly. His eyes must have sparkled; certainly he must have been proud—of himself, of his warriors, of all the Oglalas, all the Sioux and Cheyennes. Together they had achieved something never before accomplished—an armed mass of Indians, a thousand or more strong, was about to descend from an unexpected direction upon less than 225 regular Army troopers. The warriors had the smell of victory in their nostrils, a smell Custer had known so well, and as Custer also knew, once fighting men begin to smell victory, they are unbeatable.

As at the Yellowstone three years earlier, did Custer and Crazy Horse see each other? We do not and cannot know. It was certainly possible that they did catch each other's eye, although it is unlikely that they would have recognized one another. Custer might have heard from scouts about the way Crazy Horse dressed for battle, but Crazy Horse could hardly have recognized Custer, whom he knew as "Long Hair," because Custer had cropped his hair for this campaign.

What Crazy Horse saw before him was a long slope with a few more than 200 soldiers on it. With their backs to the top of the hill, they were fighting for their lives, most of them horseless by now, many wounded, hard pressed by Gall's force. The troopers were badly strung out. Hot, tired, dusty, thirsty, afraid, they were slowly working their way up the hill, trying meanwhile to maintain a steady volume of fire in order to hold back Gall's warriors. Just below Crazy Horse there was a small knot of men. Tom Custer was there, and Bos, and most of Custer's staff. Custer was at their head, not much more than twenty yards away from Crazy Horse. The officers were making their way to the top, probably looking in that direction, so it is possible that Crazy Horse and Custer looked into each other's eyes.

If so, it was only for an instant. Crazy Horse and his men, making the air fearful with their battle cries, came sweeping down the hill. They crushed everything in their path. They swarmed among Custer's soldiers, killing them with arrows, clubs, lances, and bullets. Gall was simultaneously attacking Calhoun and the troopers on the lower end of the hill. "The country was alive with Indians going in all directions," an Oglala brave later recalled, "like myriads of swallows, yet the great body all the time moving down on Custer." It was almost like hunting buffalo.

Yellow Horse said that "Custer fought and Reno did not; Custer went in to die, and his fighting was superb; I never saw a man fight as Custer did; he was conspicuous in the battle . . . directing his men." An Arapaho brave who was with Crazy Horse said, "Crazy Horse, the Sioux Chief, was the bravest man I ever saw. He rode closest to the soldiers, yelling to his warriors. All the soldiers were shooting at him, but he was never hit."

Two Moons, the Cheyenne leader, recalled that after he topped the hill, following Crazy Horse, "the shooting was quick, quick. Pop—pop—pop very fast. Some of the soldiers were down on their knees, some standing. The smoke was like a great cloud, and everywhere the Sioux went the dust rose like smoke. We circled all around them—swirling like water round a stone. We shoot, we ride fast, we shoot again. Soldiers drop, and horses fall on them. Soldiers in line drop, but one man rides up and down the line, all the time shouting. . . . I don't know who he was. He was a brave man."

In twenty minutes, perhaps less, it was over. Custer and his 225 soldiers were dead. Around Custer's body—which lay just short of the crest of the hill he so desperately needed to gain and which Crazy Horse had denied him—lay his closest comrades—Tom and Boston Custer, Autie Reed, Calhoun a little ways off.

There are many versions of Custer's death. The one that sounds most authentic is Sitting Bull's, who freely admitted that he was not there, but who got an immediate after-action report from some young Hunkpapas. Sitting Bull passed the account on to a reporter for the New York *Herald* in 1877.

Sitting Bull: Up there where the last fight took place, where the last stand was made, the Long Hair stood like a sheaf of corn with all the ears fallen around him.
Reporter: Not wounded?
Sitting Bull: No.
Reporter: How many stood by him?
Sitting Bull: A few.
Reporter: When did he fall?
Sitting Bull: He killed a man when he fell. He laughed.
Reporter: You mean he cried out.
Sitting Bull: No, he laughed. He had fired his last shot.

If his life flashed in front of him, as is sometimes said to happen on the verge of sudden death, no wonder Custer laughed. If he did flash back, he had many achievements to be proud of—his West Point appointment and graduation, his general officer's commission, his string of successful charges in the Civil War, his key role at Appomattox, the Washita, opening the Black Hills—and much to recall of the good life in Washington, New York, on the frontier posts. And of course, most of all, Libbie. He had turned down numerous offers that would have made him a rich man, choosing instead to live the life he loved. He had lived big, thought big, had only big ambitions. He had nothing to regret.

Not even on this last day. The attack had been a gamble, but so had all his attacks. It was a good plan. It could have worked. If only that damn Reno would have charged the camp when he first came upon it! Anyway, one doesn't get to live in the White House without taking some risks. Custer had gambled all his life, and although he usually lost in card games or horse races, he always won on the battlefield. Like all confirmed gamblers, however, he knew that someday he would have to lose. At least, when he lost, all the chips were on the table. It was a winner-take-all game, and Custer would have played it again if given the chance.

He laughed. Then he died.

The world hardly needs another analysis of the battle of the Little Bighorn, but the temptation to comment is too strong to resist. Custer's mistakes, in order of importance, were as follows:

First, he refused to accept Terry's offer of four troops of the 2nd Cavalry. If Reno had had two more troops with him, he might have had sufficient momentum to make a successful charge when he first came upon the Sioux camp. Had Custer had two more troops with him, he might have made it up the hill. But he wanted all the glory for the 7th Cavalry, and it must be said that he managed to make it for generations the most famous outfit in the history of the United States Army.

Second, Custer badly underestimated his enemy, not so much in terms of numbers (where his guess of 1,500 was not a fatal underestimate) as in terms of fighting capability, where he was disastrously wrong. Splitting his force four ways was thus a major error. The point is this: Custer had more than six hundred men. He often boasted that with that force he could whip all the Indians "in the Northwest," and he wasn't far wrong. But he never got a chance to prove it, because of his own overconfidence and inept tactics. Had he kept the regiment together he would have faced three thousand warriors with six hundred-plus well-armed and disciplined troopers, and under those circumstances he should have won. But because he divided his column, and because Crazy Horse and Gall kept their forces close together, Custer faced 2,500 warriors with 225 soldiers. In the first case, the odds would have been five to one against him; in the second case, the odds were ten to one, the crucial difference.

Custer's third mistake was assuming that his men could do what he could do; to put it another way, he attacked too soon. He should have spent June 25 resting, then attacked the next day, when Gibbon could have, on urgent request, reinforced him. All Indian accounts agree that Custer's men and horses, like Reno's, were so exhausted that their legs trembled. It was a hot day, which further cut the troopers' efficiency. A fourth mistake was to commit his command when he did not know his enemies' position, strength, or location. He also lost the element of surprise—his enemies knew more about where he was, in what strength, and with what intentions, than he knew about them. Yet he attacked.

Finally, when Custer lost the initiative, he failed to gain the high ground and dig in, although here one should perhaps blame Custer less and praise Crazy Horse more.

How did Crazy Horse know to swing around the flank? This was not a simple circling maneuver of a small unit caught on the open prairie; it was an intricate series of movements over difficult terrain, planned in advance, requiring exact timing. Crazy Horse had learned the lesson from the Wagon Box Fight of 1867, when he had led an attack up a ravine with all the warriors crowded in on each other, masking their own fire. This time he realized that the way to use his manpower effectively was to spread it out. He had learned, in addition, one of the most basic combat lessons—never attack your enemy directly when you can outflank him. In an Indian-versus-Indian battle, flanking was not necessary, in fact, it did not fit into the scheme of things, as the object in an Indian fight was to win honors, not kill enemies. But if you are involved in an Indian-versus-white soldier fight, Crazy Horse had learned, you damn well better start maneuvering your warriors and striking the flanks. In military affairs it is exceedingly difficult to outflank a flanking force, but when it is achieved it is usually spectacularly successful.

It is even possible to speculate (I would not want to push this too far, but much of the fun of studying this battle is the free rein it gives to the imagination) that if Crazy Horse had not swung around Custer's flank and hit him from an unexpected direction, the 7th Cavalry could have survived the battle of the Little Bighorn. With only enemies in the front to worry about, it would seem that it should have been possible for Custer to make it to the top of the hill, not just near its crest where Crazy Horse caught him. Once on top Custer could have held the high ground, and although the Indians would have attacked in great numbers, Custer should have been able to hold them off. Custer might have been able to rally his troopers and hold Custer Hill long enough to be rescued by Benteen and Reno or by Gibbon. Doubtful, certainly, but it was his best chance, what he almost surely must have had in mind.

Crazy Horse ruined it all. At the supreme moment of his career, Crazy Horse took in the situation with a glance, then acted with great decisiveness. He fought with his usual reckless bravery on Custer Hill, providing as always an example for the other warriors to admire, draw courage from, and emulate, but his real contribution to this greatest of all Indian victories was mental, not physical. For the first time in his life, Crazy Horse's presence was decisive on the battlefield not because of his courage, but because of his brain. But one fed on the other. His outstanding generalship had brought him at the head of a ferocious body of warriors to the critical point at the critical moment. Then with his courage he took advantage of the situation to sweep down on Custer and stamp his name, and that of Custer, indelibly on the pages of the nation's history.

There is some intriguing postfight speculation about this battle. What if Reno had charged, as Custer ordered and expected? He might have put the Indians on the run but that seems unlikely; more probably he would have pinned down Crazy Horse's blocking force and that could have been important. But Crazy Horse had planned for and expected just such a maneuver (the soldiers always tried to hit from at least two directions at once, he had learned through experience). He still, probably, could have outflanked Custer.

What if Custer had followed Reno and supported his attack? Certainly that would have given him a better chance, but his horses and men just didn't have sufficient energy to press home a charge. With a rested command, it might have worked.

What if Benteen had obeyed orders and come quick with the packs? That would have helped only if Custer had gained the high ground. As it was, Crazy Horse had rubbed Custer out long before Benteen could have gotten there (if he ever could have made it). As to the charges that Benteen and Reno, who each hated Custer, deliberately abandoned him, such charges are a wholly unjustified slur on them and on the officer corps of the United States Army. These men were professional soldiers who did their best under trying conditions. Of course they made mistakes—who hasn't in a combat situation?—but they were neither cowards nor traitors to their commander. They were hot, sweaty, hungry, thirsty, absolutely spent men, whose mistakes were in large measure a result of the positions Custer had placed them in. They thought (and so did their men) that Custer had abandoned *them,* but they did not abandon him.

The conclusion is inescapable. At the Little Bighorn, Custer was not only outnumbered; he was also outgeneraled.

All that followed the battle on Custer Hill was anticlimax. The Indians besieged Reno and Benteen, but as always they lacked the killer instinct. Enough had been done. The next day, when Sioux scouts reported to Crazy Horse Gibbon's advance from the north, the great camp—possibly the largest Indian village ever seen in the Great Plains—retired to the south, toward the Bighorn Mountains.

The battle of the Little Bighorn had been a supreme moment in the life of the Sioux nation. Never before had the Sioux people been so united, nor would they be again. Never before had the Sioux warriors been so ably led, nor would they be again.

As the Sioux nation dispersed, Crazy Horse counted up the losses. Forty men dead, or thereabouts. He mourned for them, of course, but not too deeply, because it had been a good day to die.

George Armstrong Custer:
A Great Commander Overwhelmed by a Larger Force

ROBERT M. UTLEY

How could it have happened? What flagrant blunders produced so awful a debacle? How could a commander and a regiment widely perceived as the best on the frontier succumb so spectacularly to a mob of untrained, unlettered natives?

The simplest answer, usually overlooked, is that the army lost largely because the Indians won. To ascribe defeat entirely to military failings is to devalue Indian strength and leadership. The Sioux and Cheyennes were strong, confident, united, well led, well armed, outraged by the government's war aims, and ready to fight if pressed. Rarely had the army encountered such a mighty combination in an Indian adversary. Perhaps no strategy or tactics could have prevailed against Sitting Bull's power.

But this explanation exonerates all the military chiefs and yields no scapegoat in blue. George Armstrong Custer is the favored candidate. Driven to win a great victory and wipe out the humiliation inflicted by President Grant [who had threatened to relieve Custer from command of the expedition in retaliation for the impetuous cavalryman's cooperation with House Democrats seeking to impeach Grant's Secretary of War William Belknap], he rushed up the Rosebud and plunged into battle before the cooperating units could get in place. He disobeyed Terry's orders by taking a direct rather than a circuitous route to his destination. He attacked a day early, with an exhausted command and without adequate reconnaissance. Violating an elementary military maxim, he divided his force in the face of a superior enemy and then lost control of all but the element retained under his personal direction, and perhaps, in the end, even of that.

Analysis of this indictment must take account of the character of the evidence on which it rests. No sooner had Custer's body been buried on Custer Hill than all the principals—Terry, Gibbon, Brisbin, Reno, Benteen—began to recompose the history of recent events. Eager to explain the calamity and avert any culpability of their own, they conveniently forgot some things that had happened and remembered some things that had not happened. Their efforts freighted the historical record with firsthand evidence that threw the blame on Custer and powerfully influenced historical interpretation for generations to come.

This self-serving evidence is not without historical value. But only by rigorously comparing it with evidence dating from before the fatal last hour on Battle Ridge can a true understanding of the dynamics of the disaster be reached. A vital step in such an analysis is to strike out of the equation any facts, however plain now, unknown to Custer then. At each critical decision point the test is what he knew and what he could reasonably be expected to foresee.

In such a comparison and analysis most of the charges against Custer collapse. Undoubtedly he hoped to win a great victory for himself and the Seventh Cavalry.

But he did not rush up the Rosebud any faster than had been planned on the *Far West*. He did not disobey Terry's orders; they were entirely discretionary and, because of the uncertain location of the Indians, could not have been otherwise. He did not precipitate battle a day before Terry intended, for Terry did not and could not fix any day for the attack; Custer's mission was to attack the Indians whenever and wherever he found them. Custer did not take an exhausted regiment into battle; the men were tired, as soldiers in the field usually are, but no more so than normal on campaign.

That Terry intended Custer to use his own judgment in finding and striking the Indians is made abundantly clear by the written orders, by evidence of what occurred in the conference on the *Far West*, and by the simple logic of what was and was not known to the strategists on June 21.

In addition there is the much-debated affidavit of Mary Adams, Custer's black cook. Until recently most students thought this affidavit spurious because they did not believe that Mary Adams accompanied the expedition. Now she is known to have been with Custer. According to the affidavit she executed in 1878, either on the night of June 21 or the next morning Terry came to Custer's bivouac, and she overheard their conversation. "Custer," said Terry, "I do not know what to say for the last." "Say whatever you want to say," replied Custer. "Use your own judgment and do what you think best if you strike the trail," said Terry. "And whatever you do, Custer, hold on to your wounded."

Custer's first critical decision was to follow the Indian trail over the Rosebud Divide instead of continuing up the Rosebud, as suggested in his orders from Terry. The sudden freshness of the trail on the afternoon of June 24 was all the justification he needed. Plainly, Indians were just over the mountain, a day's march away. His assignment was to find and attack them. The surest and quickest way was to follow the trail.

The fresh Indian sign provided persuasive rationale for what he probably would have done anyway. The judgment to which Terry deferred would likely have kept him on the trail until he overhauled the Indians, wherever they were. A circuit up the Rosebud would have heightened the chances of striking the quarry from the south and driving them toward Gibbon. But it may be doubted that Custer, secure in the conviction that the Seventh alone could handle the enemy, gave much thought to a role for Gibbon or much cared whether he struck from the north or the south. Had the Indians continued their movement up the Little Bighorn, as the chiefs had planned, the attack would indeed have come from the north. Only the chance discovery of antelope herds, prompting the return of the village down the valley, brought Custer in from the south.

The fresh trail also held implications for enemy strength, which Custer failed to note. By the evening of June 24 the Crow and Ree scouts knew that there were more Indians across the Rosebud Divide than anyone suspected. They dropped enough clues that Custer might have taken their worries more seriously and might have questioned them intently in order to bring into the open what they thought and why.

But Custer was not concerned with how many Indians he would encounter, only with preventing their flight. Knowledge of their actual strength would not have changed his dispositions. He had total confidence in the capability of the Seventh Cavalry to whip any number of Indians.

So did all the other generals, from Sheridan down. Most experience with Indian warfare showed that a charge into a village, however large, wrought panic and fleeing Indians, as at the Washita. But this year the Indians were not only numerous but full of fight, as Crook had discovered when hundreds of warriors uncharacteristically attacked him in open battle. News of Crook's defeat on the Rosebud had not reached the Yellowstone, however, and Custer cannot be severely faulted for a mindset shared with his fellow commanders.

It was a mindset, indeed, shared with all his fellow citizens and thus in large part derived from them. That the generals had such contempt for the fighting prowess of their foe as to care little for their numbers was but one symptom of society's attitudes toward Indians. The cultural and racial arrogance of the American people found expression in their generals. Combined with the personal conceit of Custer, this was a deadly mixture. Unquestionably, Custer underestimated his opponents.

Much of what went wrong stemmed from the decision to attack on June 25 instead of the next day, as Custer intended until Sioux were spotted in the vicinity of the command. This decision forced battle before reconnaissance had developed the location of the enemy and the nature of the terrain on which the fight would take place. It prompted Benteen's scout to the left, which would not have been needed had the absence of Indians on the upper Little Bighorn already been established. It led to an afternoon attack rather than the preferred dawn attack. And it decreed a battle plan that had to unfold as information and circumstances unfolded, rather than one conceived in advance.

Despite the consequences, the decision to attack on June 25 was sound. Custer had ample reason to suppose himself discovered and to expect that the village would bolt as soon as alerted. This did not happen because the Indians who observed him continued eastward toward the agencies or were on the way from the agencies to the village. That afternoon the village on the Little Bighorn had perhaps half an hour's warning of the approach of soldiers. Had he known the truth, Custer might still have hidden the regiment, reconnoitered, and struck at dawn on June 26.

Custer drew reproach for dividing the regiment in the face of superior strength. That he faced superior strength, of course, he neither knew nor cared. He formed battalions because of the need to advance in a reconnaissance in force and doubtless also because of his intention, if possible, to attack from more than one direction.

The division of the regiment entailed unavoidable consequences for the impending battle. Because of their seniority Custer had to give battalion commands to Reno and Benteen. Within limits of personal ability they could be expected to do their duty, but not with the enthusiastic, unquestioning loyalty of the favorites in the "royal family." Custer compounded the problem by keeping the most reliable officers with him. Of his inner circle only Weir and Moylan rode with the other battalions.

Custer's decision to order Benteen to the left was sensible. He had to assure himself that the upper Little Bighorn contained no Indians who might fall on his rear in battle or escape southward, as Terry feared. Had the Indians continued up the valley as intended, Benteen would probably have spotted them. If not, the trail would have led to them, and another battle altogether would have resulted.

As it turned out, the scout to the left counted Benteen and three companies out of the critical stage of the battle. It need not have. Benteen counted himself out, as timing factors show. When he came back to the main trail, he was about half an hour behind Custer and Reno. When he neared the mouth of Reno Creek, he was one hour and twenty minutes behind. Had he moved at the same pace as Custer, and had he responded to the message brought by Martin with the swiftness that Custer expected, Benteen might well have fought with Custer. He and his battalion might have perished with Custer, too, but that does not excuse the laggard pace that kept one-fourth of the regiment out of the fight at a decisive moment.

Benteen's course is hard to understand. A possible explanation is distrust of Custer coupled with a rising suspicion that Custer, hoping to keep him out of the fight, had sent him on a useless errand. Keogh or Yates would have signaled a gallop as soon as they received Sergeant Kanipe's report.

Reno also failed Custer, as well as every test of leadership. His retreat freed large numbers of Indians to concentrate on Custer just as he reached the mouth of Medicine Tail Coulee. Had Reno continued to fight in the valley, the pressure on Custer would have been lessened, perhaps decisively. What cannot be known is whether such a course would have awarded Reno the same fate as Custer. Significantly, those who followed Reno into the valley did not condemn the decision to withdraw, only the execution. Some, however, did think that he could have stood firm in the timber, a belief shared by some of the Indian combatants.

Likewise vulnerable is Reno's management of the hilltop operation. He should have rushed to Custer's aid no matter what the odds and even at the risk of disaster to his own companies. The written orders to Benteen, now Reno's by virtue of superior rank, explicitly required such a move. In addition, some of his officers urged this course on him. In fact, Reno made no decision, and his indecision freed subordinates to go off on their own and in the end endangered the entire command. Thereafter, through a night and day of defensive action, he failed to exert effective command. Indeed, there is evidence that he proposed to pull out altogether, abandoning the wounded, a proposition that Benteen indignantly rejected. In fact, no one doubted that Benteen functioned as the true commander. His strong leadership and cool bravery contributed greatly to the successful defense.

On the Custer battlefield itself, nagging questions of leadership arise. Can Indian numbers alone account for Yates's quick repulse from the ford at the mouth of Medicine Tail Coulee? This movement shifted the initiative from the cavalry to the Indians and forced the battle into terrain inhospitable to mounted action. The retreat of both battalions to Battle Ridge also allowed warriors to thrust up Medicine Tail Coulee in strength and thus cut them off from the rest of the regiment.

On Battle Ridge, how to account for patterns of fallen bodies that suggest only one pocket of organized defense—L Company on Calhoun Hill? And how further to account for the concentration of company commanders on Custer Hill? George Yates, Tom Custer, and Algernon Smith fell here. Much of Yates's Company F appears to have died here, but most of C and E perished on other parts of the field.

Whatever Armstrong Custer's failings, combat leadership was not one. Did he take one or two mortal wounds at the Medicine Tail ford? Did that so demoralize Yates's men that they too readily allowed themselves to be driven back from the ford? This move, in turn, led Keogh to yield his position on the heights and fight his way northward to join them on Calhoun Hill. The dead Custer finally came to rest on Custer Hill. Either mortally wounded or dead, he could have been borne there from as far away as Medicine Tail Coulee. No one can ever know, but such a theory would account for much that is puzzling about the fighting on the Custer battlefield.

On the other hand, Adjutant Cooke fell near Custer rather than with Keogh, to the east. Had Custer ceased to function, command would have devolved on Keogh, and Cooke's place would have been with him. Also, there is some indication that expended shells from Custer's Remington sporting rifle were found near his body.

Even more compelling, this theory would force the American people to relinquish the glorious image of Custer's Last Stand that is indelibly burned into their collective memory. That renunciation is as unthinkable as it is impossible.

Could Custer have won? It is a question destined to be forever debated and never settled. Even against the Sioux and Cheyennes in all their numbers and power, however, good arguments support a conclusion that he could have won.

Crucial to this conclusion is the fact that Custer came close to surprising the Indians. The men had little time to prepare for battle. Most of the ponies grazed on the benchland. Several hundred warriors managed to mobilize to meet Reno, but most of the fighters in the village were not ready. Had there been warning, the men would surely have engaged Custer before he got close enough to endanger their families.

In such circumstances Indians usually panicked. Suddenly confronted with soldiers among their tipis, each man turned instinctively to the safety of his family. Thus distracted, the fighting strength could not offer organized resistance, and the village exploded in fleeing family groups. This could be expected to happen even when the Indians enjoyed superiority of numbers.

At the Little Bighorn several scenarios held the possibility of producing such a panic.

First, and most simply, a charge by the eight companies of Custer and Reno into the upper end of the village would almost certainly have stampeded the Indians. The force and momentum of a mounted charge by nearly 350 cavalrymen would have carried into the very heart of the village, striking consternation and chaos and preventing the formation of effective defenses. The attackers would have taken severe casualties, and most of the Indians would have escaped to the north, but Custer would have been left in possession of the village and possibly of much of the pony herd. Benteen and the packtrain would have come up in time to fortify the victors.

Even the two-pronged attack that Custer must have visualized might have worked had Reno not lost his nerve. To continue his charge into the village with 112 men required a fortitude and blind loyalty to Custer that Reno, unlike Keogh or Yates, did not possess. Such an assault, however, could have created enough momentary confusion to win success *if* Custer had driven into the village at the

Medicine Tail ford before the Indians could recover and swallow Reno's small command. To achieve this feat, Custer would have had to cover more than three miles, from the bluffs where he overlooked the valley to the mouth of Medicine Tail Coulee, before the Indians crushed Reno. The possibilities of this formula seem slim.

More plausible is Reno holding the timber long enough for Custer to get into the village at the Medicine Tail ford. Although control was difficult in the timber, Reno had taken few casualties when he ordered the retreat. In forming the skirmish line, two horses had bolted and carried their riders into the Sioux. One man had died on the skirmish line and two in the timber. One of the latter was the Ree scout Bloody Knife, sitting his horse beside Reno. A bullet struck his head and spattered blood and brains into Reno's face, an unnerving experience that contributed to the decision to get out of the timber. Had Reno's force remained in place, the warriors here could not have left for Medicine Tail without exposing their families. As it happened, Reno's withdrawal freed them to concentrate on Custer in a strength that forced him back from the river into unfriendly terrain.

Could Benteen have altered the outcome? A swift march on Custer's trail upon receiving Kanipe's report probably would have brought him to Medicine Tail while the action still centered there. His presence might at least have allowed Custer to extricate himself and consolidate the entire regiment on Reno Hill. Had Reno held in the valley, Benteen's timely appearance on Medicine Tail would have given Custer eight companies with which to storm into the village and perhaps carry the day.

The fourth scenario is less a prescription for victory than a remote possibility of staving off defeat. Had Reno and Benteen corralled the packtrain and the wounded on the bluff tops and boldly rushed six companies to the sound of the firing, could they have saved Custer? With a brand of leadership neither had yet displayed, they might have averted the total annihilation of Custer's command. But they would have been badly mauled themselves, perhaps even wiped out. This course should have been tested more promptly and vigorously than it was, but a favorable outcome seems improbable.

Besides the Seventh Cavalry's officers, other campaign leaders are open to criticism but have remained largely immune because of the storm swirling around Custer. Neither before nor after the Little Bighorn did Terry, Gibbon, or Crook gather and use intelligence in a thoughtful way. Gibbon let opportunity slip from his grasp and failed to keep Terry even minimally informed. Crook mismanaged both his March and June offensives, withdrawing on both occasions with dubious justification. The second withdrawal, after the Rosebud, stopped his movement into the very country that Custer entered less than a week later. Had Crook continued his advance, he could not have failed to alter the result of Custer's offensive. Privately, General Sherman believed that Crook bore large responsibility for the failure of the campaign.

And yet, in dissecting strategy and tactics from the perspective of a century later, it is easy to do injustice to the responsible commanders. One cannot know all the circumstances of enemy, weather, terrain, troops, weapons, and a host of other factors great and trivial (Gibbon had a bad stomachache) that influenced judgment and sometimes decisively shaped the final outcome.

But one conclusion seems plain. George Armstrong Custer does not deserve the indictment that history has imposed on him for his actions at the Little Bighorn. Given what he knew at each decision point and what he had every reason to expect of his subordinates, one is hard pressed to say what he ought to have done differently. In truth, at the Little Bighorn "Custer's Luck" simply ran out. Although the failures of subordinates may have contributed and the strength and prowess of the foe certainly contributed, Custer died the victim less of bad judgment than of bad luck.

♠ *F U R T H E R   R E A D I N G*

Constance W. Altshuler, *Chains of Command: Arizona and the Army, 1856–1875* (1981).

Stephen E. Ambrose, *Crazy Horse and Custer: The Parallel Lives of Two American Warriors* (1975).

Robert G. Athearn, *William Tecumseh Sherman and the Settlement of the West* (1956).

John W. Bailey, *Pacifying the Plains: General Alfred Terry and the Decline of the Sioux, 1866–1890* (1979).

Monroe Lee Billington, *New Mexico's Buffalo Soldiers, 1866–1900* (1991).

Dee Brown, *Bury My Heart at Wounded Knee: An Indian History of the American West* (1970).

Colin G. Calloway, ed., *Our Hearts Fell to the Ground: Plains Indians Views of How the West Was Lost* (1996).

John M. Carroll, ed. *The Black Military Experience in the American West* (1973).

Evan S. Connell, *Son of the Morning Star: Custer and The Little Bighorn* (1984).

Thomas W. Dunlay, *Wolves for the Blue Soldiers: Indian Scouts and Auxiliaries with the United States Army, 1860–1890* (1982).

Odie B. Faulk, *The Geronimo Campaign* (1969).

W. A. Graham, comp., *The Custer Myth: A Source Book of Custeriana* (1953).

John S. Gray, *Custer's Last Campaign: Mitch Boyer and the Little Bighorn Reconstructed* (1991).

Jerome A. Greene, *Yellowstone Command: Colonel Nelson A. Miles and the Great Sioux War, 1876–1877* (1991).

James L. Haley, *The Buffalo War: The History of the Red River Indian Uprising of 1874* (1976).

Stan Hoig, *The Battle of Washita: The Sheridan-Custer Indian Campaign of 1867–69* (1976).

Paul Andrew Hutton, *Phil Sheridan and His Army* (1985).

_____, ed., *The Custer Reader* (1992).

George E. Hyde, *Life of George Bent: Written From His Letters* (1968).

Richard E. Jensen, R. Eli Paul, and John E. Carter, *Eyewitness at Wounded Knee* (1991).

Alvin M. Josephy, Jr., *The Nez Perce Indians and the Opening of the Northwest* (1965).

Oliver Knight, *Life and Manners in the Frontier Army* (1978).

David Lavender, *Let Me Be Free: The Nez Perce Tragedy* (1992).

William H. Leckie, *The Buffalo Soldiers: A Narrative of the Negro Cavalry in the West* (1967).

Thomas C. Leonard, "Red, White and the Army Blue: Empathy and Anger in the American West," *American Quarterly* 26 (May 1974): 176–190.

Brigham D. Madsen, *The Shoshoni Frontier and the Bear River Massacre* (1985).

John G. Neihardt, *Black Elk Speaks: Being the Life Story of a Holy Man of the Oglala Sioux* (1932).

Charles E. Rankin, ed., *Legacy: New Perspectives on the Battle of the Little Bighorn* (1996).

Don Russell, *Campaigning with King: Charles King, Chronicler of the Old Army* (1991).

Frank N. Schubert, *Buffalo Soldiers, Braves, and the Brass: The Story of Fort Robinson, Nebraska* (1993).

Sherry Lynn Smith, *The View from Officers' Row: Army Perceptions of Western Indians* (1990).

Robert M. Utley, *Cavalier in Buckskin: George Armstrong Custer and the Western Military Frontier* (1988).

_____, *The Lance and the Shield: The Life and Times of Sitting Bull* (1993).

Philip Weeks, *Farewell, My Nation: The American Indian and the United States, 1820–1890* (1990).

Frederick Whittaker, *A Complete Life of General George A. Custer*, 2 vols. (1993).

Robert A. Wooster, *The Military and United States Indian Policy, 1865–1903* (1988).

CHAPTER
8

Armed Forces and
an Expanding World Power

With the end of the Indian Wars and the simultaneous emergence of an industrial-izing America as a world power, the American military turned to new outward roles. Technological, political, and military developments were transforming armed forces and weaponry around the globe. The land powers on the European conti-nent and in Asia created mass conscription armies based upon systems of universal military training, while maritime nations developed immense new fleets, centered on modern, steam-powered, steel-hulled, big-gun battleships. Because of the con-tinued belief in the protection offered by the Atlantic and Pacific Oceans and the balance of power in Europe, the American public retained a sense of natural secu-rity, even while it debated whether the nation's new overseas expansion should take the form of European-style colonies or what a later historian would call an "informal empire" of American trade and ideas. For its military needs, the United States continued to rely primarily upon the citizen soldiers of the National Guard and, if necessary, ad hoc wartime U.S. Volunteers. Proposals from regular army officers such as Emory Upton, a protégé of General Sherman's and a professor at West Point, for a European-style, mass national army and powerful general staff got nowhere. The public and many of the policy-making elites were more receptive, however, to calls for a modern navy to protect the United States and its expanding interests and to symbolize its new international status. Most prominent among the publicists of sea power was Captain (later Admiral) Alfred Thayer Mahan, a pro-fessor at the new Naval War College, who joined civilian navalists like Theodore Roosevelt and Henry Cabot Lodge in advocating a fleet of modern battleships, even though there were some who saw other kinds of weaponry—torpedo boats, sub-marines, floating mines, and harbor fortifications for example—as more effective than battleships for coastal defense. Military historians too continue to debate Mahan's prescriptions.

The American military's role in the overseas expansion became most dramatic through the Spanish-American War of 1898, the public highlight of which was the capture of San Juan Heights, the commanding ridge overlooking the city of Santi-ago in Spanish Cuba. Although the military importance of the "Rough Riders" (the volunteer cavalry regiment of eastern elites and western cowboys led by

Theodore Roosevelt, a New York patrician and former assistant secretary of the navy) has been contested, particularly in contrast to the role of regular army units of Gatling guns and dismounted cavalry, the political importance is undeniable. The publicity given to Lieutenant Colonel Roosevelt and his citizen-soldiers gave a boost to his political fortunes, which helped him win the governorship of New York and subsequently the vice-presidency and presidency of the United States. The successful war against Spain brought the United States an island empire, from Puerto Rico to the Philippines. Historians continue to debate the nature of the American military and civic action in the Philippines after Spain relinquished it to the United States in 1899. Subsequent fighting between Filipino nationalists and the U.S. Army and U.S. Volunteers continued from 1899 to 1902. After the Americans defeated the insurgent units in conventional battles during the first year, the Filipino revolutionaries shifted to guerrilla-style warfare against American soldiers and the Filipinos who supported them. Atrocities followed on both sides. Filipino guerrillas surprised and hacked to death 42 soldiers of Company C of the Ninth U.S. Infantry Regiment at Balangiga on September 28, 1901, and in counterguerrilla action, U.S. forces engaged in a number of brutal "pacification" campaigns against guerrillas and civilians, particularly on Samar and Batangas in the final months of the war. Historians continue to debate the nature, extent, and causes of such atrocities. The 1899–1902 conflict, known by the U.S. Army as the Philippine Insurrection and by Filipinos as the Philippine-American War, remains controversial to the present day.

⚑ D O C U M E N T S

As the U.S. Army debated the proper form of military institutions for the nation's expanding world role, Brevet General Emory Upton's *The Military Policy of the United States,* circulated in manuscript form among the officer corps beginning in 1880 (although it was not published until 1904). In the excerpt included in the first document, Upton attacks traditional American volunteer forces of citizen-soldiers as untrained, undisciplined, and poorly led, and calls instead for a more European-style national army. In the second document, a selection from the introduction to the highly influential book, *The Influence of Sea Power Upon History,* first published in 1890, Captain (later Admiral) Alfred Thayer Mahan links sea power with prosperity and national greatness and argues in favor of an offensive-oriented high seas battleship fleet rather than America's traditional reliance upon coastal defense and commerce-raiding frigates and cruisers. The Spanish-American War was the last American war fought with units of the traditional U.S. Volunteers; in the third document, Theodore Roosevelt in an 1899 memoir, entitled *The Rough Riders,* celebrates the achievement of his unit, officially the 1st U.S. Volunteer Cavalry Regiment, in taking the San Juan Heights on July 1, 1898. A strikingly different picture of the same attack is provided in the fourth document, an account originally published in 1899, by 22-year-old Sgt. William Payne, E Troop, 10th U.S. Cavalry Regiment, a black trooper in one of the Regular Army's units composed of African-American soldiers and white commissioned officers. The war in the Philippines offers an example of even more contrasting documents, the ones reprinted here pertaining to an incident involving an army unit and a Filipino village in late December 1901. In the fifth document, Private Frederick Presher from New Jersey, stationed in Banan, located in Batangas province, south of Manila, writes in his diary of December 26 to 28, 1901, of the U.S. Army's abuse of civilians in a nearby village. In contrast, the commander of Presher's unit, Captain

J. Hartman, filed a much different official account of the same incident to the adjutant general of his brigade on December 26, 1901. The contrast between these two documents demonstrates why it is important for students of history to locate and assess accounts of the same events by different witnesses as they seek to reconstruct and interpret the past.

1. General Emory Upton Urges a European Style Army (1880), 1904

All of our wars have been prolonged for want of judicious and economical preparation, and often when the people have impatiently awaited the tidings of victory, those of humiliating defeat have plunged the nation into mourning.

The cause of all this is obvious to the soldier and should be no less obvious to the statesman. It lies partly in the unfounded jealousy of not a large, but even a small standing army; in the persistent use of raw troops; in the want of an expansive organization, adequate for every prospective emergency; in short and voluntary enlistments, carrying with them large bounties; and in a variety of other defects which need not here be stated. In treating this subject, I am aware that I tread on delicate ground and that every volunteer and militiaman who has patriotically responded to the call of his country, in the hour of danger, may possibly regard himself as unjustly attacked.

To such I can only reply, that where they have enlisted for the period of three months, and, as at Bladensburg and on many other fields, have been hurled against veteran troops, they should not hold me responsible for the facts of history, which I have sought impartially to present. . . .

The same prejudice has led our people to another false conclusion. If standing armies are dangerous to liberty, then it ought to follow that officers of the army should be inimical to republican institutions. But here again, if the lessons of history be read and accepted, it will be admitted that of all forms of government the republican, or democratic, is most favorable to the soldier. There is not a well-read officer in our service who does not know that monarchy sets a limit to military ambition, while in republics military fame is frequently rewarded with the highest civic honors. . . .

In every civilized country success in war depends upon the organization and application of its military resources. The resources themselves consist of men, material, and money. Their organization is wholly within the province of the statesman. Under our Constitution Congress has the power to raise and support armies, and, subject to the supervision of the President, only professional soldiers should command them.

In time of war the civilian as much as the soldier is responsible for defeat and disaster. Battles are not lost alone on the field; they may be lost beneath the Dome of the Capitol, they may be lost in the Cabinet, or they may be lost in the private office of the Secretary of War. Wherever they may be lost, it is the people who suffer and the soldiers who die, with the knowledge and the conviction that our military

From Emory Upton. *The Military Policy of the United States from 1775* (Washington, D.C.: Government Printing Office 1904), viii, ix, xi, xiii–xiv.

policy is a crime against life, a crime against property, and a crime against liberty. The author has availed himself of his privileges as a citizen to expose to our people a system which, if not abandoned, may sooner or later prove fatal. The time when some one should do this has arrived. . . .

Looking at the example of every pioneer, as well as the prosperous man of business, the statesman could have informed the Senator that the military policy of an agricultural nation of 3,000,000 people just emerging from the forest, was no policy for a nation extending from ocean to ocean and now numbering more than fifty millions. But bad as is our system it would be unpatriotic to attack it if at the same time no remedy could be suggested. In order that this work may not be mis-judged we will first indicate to the reader that the chief causes of weakness of our present system, and next will outline the system which ought to replace it.

The causes of the weakness are as follows:

First. The employment of militia and undisciplined troops commanded by generals and officers utterly ignorant of the military art.

Second. Short enlistments from three months to three years, instead of for or during the war.

Third. Reliance upon voluntary enlistments, instead of voluntary enlistments coupled with conscription.

Fourth. The intrusion of the States in military affairs and the consequent wag-ing of all our wars on the theory that we are a confederacy instead of a nation.

Fifth. Confusing volunteers with militia and surrendering to the States the right to commission officers of volunteers the same as officers of militia.

Sixth. The bounty—a national consequence of voluntary enlistments.

Seventh. The failure to appreciate military education, and to distribute trained officers as battalion, regimental, and higher commanders in our volunteer armies.

Eighth. The want of territorial recruitment and regimental depots.

Ninth. The want of post-graduate schools to educate our officers in strategy and the higher principles of the art of war.

Tenth. The assumption of command by the Secretary of War.

The main features of the proposed system are as follows:

First. In time of peace and war the military forces of the country to consist of—

The Regular Army.

The National Volunteers, and

The Militia.

The Regular Army in time of peace to be organized on the expansive principle and in proportion to the population, not to exceed one thousand in one million.

The National Volunteers to be officered and supported by the Government, to be organized on the expansive principle and to consist in time of peace of one bat-talion of two hundred men to each Congressional district.

The Militia to be supported exclusively by the States and as a last resort to be used only as intended by the Constitution, namely, to execute the laws, suppress insurrections, and repel invasions.

The author is well aware that in suggesting this system he will be accused of favoring centralization and strong government. This is a charge which he would neither covet nor deny. No soldier in battle ever witnessed the flight of an undisciplined army without wishing for a strong government, but a government no stronger than was designed by the fathers of the Republic.

2. Admiral Mahan Champions Sea Power Through Battleships, 1890

To turn now from the particular lessons drawn from the history of the past to the general question of the influence of government upon the sea career of its people, it is seen that that influence can work in two distinct but closely related ways.

First, in peace: The government by its policy can favor the natural growth of a people's industries and its tendencies to seek adventure and gain by way of the sea; or it can try to develop such industries and such sea-going bent, when they do not naturally exist; or, on the other hand, the government may by mistaken action check and fetter the progress which the people left to themselves would make. In any one of these ways the influence of the government will be felt, making or marring the sea power of the country in the matter of peaceful commerce; upon which alone, it cannot be too often insisted, a thoroughly strong navy can be based.

Secondly, for war: The influence of the government will be felt in its most legitimate manner in maintaining an armed navy, of a size commensurate with the growth of its shipping and the importance of the interests connected with it. More important even than the size of the navy is the question of its institutions, favoring a healthful spirit and activity, and providing for rapid development in time of war by an adequate reserve of men and of ships and by measures for drawing out that general reserve power which has before been pointed to, when considering the character and pursuits of the people. Undoubtedly under this second head of warlike preparation must come the maintenance of suitable naval stations, in those distant parts of the world to which the armed shipping must follow the peaceful vessels of commerce. . . .

Colonies attached to the mother-country afford, therefore, the surest means of supporting abroad the sea power of a country. . . .

Such colonies the United States has not and is not likely to have. . . . Having therefore no foreign establishments, either colonial or military, the ships of war of the United States, in war, will be like land birds, unable to fly far from their own shores. To provide resting-places for them, where they can coal and repair, would be one of the first duties of a government proposing to itself the development of the power of the nation at sea. . . .

The question is eminently one in which the influence of the government should make itself felt, to build up for the nation a navy which, if not capable of reaching distant countries, shall at least be able to keep clear the chief approaches to its own. The eyes of the country have for a quarter of a century been turned from the sea; the results of such a policy and of its opposite will be shown in the instance of France and of England. Without asserting a narrow parallelism between the case of the United States and either of these, it may safely be said that it is essential to

Alfred Thayer Mahan. *The Influence of Sea Power Upon History* (Boston: Little, Brown, 1890), 82–83, 87, 89.

the welfare of the whole country that the conditions of trade and commerce should remain, as far as possible, unaffected by an external war. In order to do this, the enemy must be kept not only out of our ports, but far away from our coasts.

. . . "Naval strategy has for its end to found, support, and increase, as well in peace as in war, the sea power of a country."

3. Colonel Theodore Roosevelt Boasts of His "Rough Riders" at San Juan Hill (1898), 1899

The instant I received the order I sprang on my horse and then my "crowded hour" began. The guerillas had been shooting at us from the edges of the jungle and from their perches in the leafy trees, and as they used smokeless powder, it was almost impossible to see them, though a few of my men had from time to time responded. We had also suffered from the hill on our right front, which was held chiefly by guerillas, although there were also some Spanish regulars with them, for we found their dead. I formed my men in column of troops, each troop extended in open skirmishing order, the right resting on the wire fences which bordered the sunken lane. Captain Jenkins led the first squadron, his eyes literally dancing with joyous excitement.

I started in the rear of the regiment, the position in which the colonel should theoretically stay. Captain Mills and Captain McCormick were both with me as aides; but I speedily had to send them off on special duty in getting the different bodies of men forward. I had intended to go into action on foot as at Las Guasimas, but the heat was so oppressive that I found I should be quite unable to run up and down the line and superintend matters unless I was mounted; and, moreover, when on horseback, I could see the men better and they could see me better.

A curious incident happened as I was getting the men started forward. Always when men have been lying down under cover for some time, and are required to advance, there is a little hesitation, each looking to see whether the others are going forward. As I rode down the line, calling to the troopers to go forward, and rasping brief directions to the captains and lieutenants, I came upon a man lying behind a little bush, and I ordered him to jump up. I do not think he understood that we were making a forward move, and he looked up at me for a moment with hesitation, and I again bade him rise, jeering him and saying: "Are you afraid to stand up when I am on horseback?" As I spoke, he suddenly fell forward on his face, a bullet having struck him and gone through him lengthwise. I suppose the bullet had been aimed at me; at any rate, I, who was on horseback in the open, was unhurt, and the man lying flat on the ground in the cover beside me was killed. There were several pairs of brothers with us; of the two Nortons one was killed; of the two McCurdys one was wounded.

I soon found that I could get that line, behind which I personally was, faster forward than the one immediately in front of it, with the result that the two rearmost lines of the regiment began to crowd together; so I rode through them both,

---

From Theodore Roosevelt. *The Rough Riders* (New York: Scribner's, 1924; orig. American Historical Press, 1899), 95–101.

the better to move on the one in front. This happened with every line in succession, until I found myself at the head of the regiment.

Both lieutenants of B Troop from Arizona had been exerting themselves greatly, and both were overcome by the heat; but Sergeants Campbell and Davidson took it forward in splendid shape. Some of the men from this troop and from the other Arizona troop (Bucky O'Neill's) joined me as a kind of fighting tail.

The Ninth Regiment was immediately in front of me, and the First on my left, and these went up Kettle Hill with my regiment. The Third, Sixth, and Tenth went partly up Kettle Hill (following the Rough Riders and the Ninth and First), and partly between that and the blockhouse hill, which the infantry were assailing. General Sumner in person gave the Tenth the order to charge the hills; and it went forward at a rapid gait. The three regiments went forward more or less intermingled, advancing steadily and keeping up a heavy fire. Up Kettle Hill Sergeant George Berry, of the Tenth, bore not only his own regimental colors but those of the Third, the color-sergeant of the Third having been shot down; he kept shouting, "Dress on the colors, boys, dress on the colors!" as he followed Captain Ayres, who was running in advance of his men, shouting and waving his hat. The Tenth Cavalry lost a greater proportion of its officers than any other regiment in the battle—eleven out of twenty-two.

By the time I had come to the head of the regiment we ran into the left wing of the Ninth Regulars, and some of the First Regulars, who were lying down; that is, the troopers were lying down, while the officers were walking to and fro. The officers of the white and colored regiments alike took the greatest pride in seeing that the men more than did their duty; and the mortality among them was great.

I spoke to the captain in command of the rear platoons, saying that I had been ordered to support the regulars in the attack upon the hills, and that in my judgment we could not take these hills by firing at them, and that we must rush them. He answered that his orders were to keep his men lying where they were, and that he could not charge without orders. I asked where the colonel was, and as he was not in sight, said, "Then I am the ranking officer here and I give the order to charge"— for I did not want to keep the men longer in the open suffering under a fire which they could not effectively return. Naturally the captain hesitated to obey this order when no word had been received from his own colonel. So I said, "Then let my men through, sir," and rode on through the lines, followed by the grinning Rough Riders, whose attention had been completely taken off the Spanish bullets, partly by my dialogue with the regulars, and partly by the language I had been using to themselves as I got the lines forward, for I had been joking with some and swearing at others, as the exigencies of the case seemed to demand. When we started to go through, however, it proved too much for the regulars, and they jumped up and came along, their officers and troops mingling with mine, all being delighted at the chance. When I got to where the head of the left wing of the Ninth was lying, through the courtesy of Lieutenant Hartwick, two of whose colored troopers threw down the fence, I was enabled to get back into the lane, at the same time waving my hat, and giving the order to charge the hill on our right front. Out of my sight, over on the right, Captains McBlain and Taylor, of the Ninth, made up their minds independently to charge at just about this time; and at almost the same moment Colonels Carroll and Hamilton, who were off, I believe, to my left, where we could see neither them nor their men, gave the order to advance. But of all this I knew nothing at the time. The whole line, tired of waiting, and eager to close with the enemy, was straining to go forward; and it seems that different parts slipped the leash at almost the same moment. The First Cavalry came up the hill just behind, and partly mixed with my regiment and the Ninth. As already said, portions of the Third, Sixth, and Tenth followed, while the rest of the members of these three regiments kept more in touch with the infantry on our left.

By this time we were all in the spirit of the thing and greatly excited by the charge, the men cheering and running forward between shots, while the delighted faces of the foremost officers, like Captain C. J. Stevens, of the Ninth, as they ran at the heads of their troops, will always stay in my mind. As soon as I was in the line I galloped forward a few yards until I saw that the men were well started, and then galloped back to help Goodrich, who was in command of his troop, get his men across the road so as to attack the hill from that side. Captain Mills had already thrown three of the other troops of the regiment across this road for the same purpose. Wheeling around, I then again galloped toward the hill, passing the shouting, cheering, firing men, and went up the lane, splashing through a small stream; when I got abreast of the ranch buildings on the top of Kettle Hill, I turned and went up the slope. Being on horseback I was, of course, able to get ahead of the men on foot, excepting my orderly, Henry Bardshar, who had run ahead very fast in order to get better shots at the Spaniards, who were now running out of the ranch buildings. Sergeant Campbell and a number of the Arizona men, and Dudley Dean, among others, were very close behind. Stevens, with his platoon of the Ninth, was abreast of us; so were McNamee and Hartwick. Some forty yards from the top I ran into a wire fence and jumped off little Texas, turning him loose. He had been scraped by a couple of bullets, one of which nicked my elbow, and I never expected to see him again. As I ran up to the hill, Bardshar stopped to shoot, and two Spaniards fell as he emptied his magazine. These were the only Spaniards I actually saw fall to aimed shots by any one of my men, with the exception of two guerillas in trees.

Almost immediately afterward the hill was covered by the troops, both Rough Riders and the colored troopers of the Ninth, and some men of the First. There was the usual confusion, and afterward there was much discussion as to exactly who had been on the hill first. The first guidons planted there were those of the three New Mexican troops, G, E, and F, of my regiment, under their captains, Llewellen, Luna, and Muller, but on the extreme right of the hill, at the opposite end from where we struck it, Captains Taylor and McBlain and their men of the Ninth were first up. Each of the five captains was firm in the belief that his troop was first up. As for the individual men, each of whom honestly thought he was first on the summit, their name was legion. One Spaniard was captured in the buildings, another was shot as he tried to hide himself, and a few others were killed as they ran.

Among the many deeds of conspicuous gallantry here performed, two, both to the credit of the First Cavalry, may be mentioned as examples of the others, not as exceptions. Sergeant Charles Karsten, while close beside Captain Tutherly, the squadron commander, was hit by a shrapnel bullet. He continued on the line, firing until his arm grew numb; and he then refused to go to the rear, and devoted himself to taking care of the wounded, utterly unmoved by the heavy fire. Trooper Hugo Brittain, when wounded, brought the regimental standard forward, waving it to and fro, to cheer the men.

4. Sergeant William Payne, a Black Trooper, Portrays Black Regulars Helping to Take San Juan Hill (1898), 1899

About 6 A.M., July 1st, the battle started. I remarked: "Boys, we are in for it." Later in the day we received orders to advance. As we did so we stopped for the balloon to pass; after it passed we again resumed the march. Just as the front troop crossed San Juan River the enemy opened fire on us and the balloon. We all threw off our blanket-rolls and knapsacks then, prepared for action. At this place Private Henry McCormick, of my troop, was wounded through the left leg and right foot.

We remained at San Juan River about three hours. Then came the advance for the bloody charge up San Juan Hill, which we did in good order. This was the second time we came to the rescue of the Rough Riders. After we drove the enemy from their stronghold we deployed our skirmish line on the hill and awaited orders to commence firing. During this time our brave commander, Captain Charles G. Ayres, had to be begged and finally ordered to kneel or lie down out of danger, for shot and shell were falling all around him. He is the coolest man I ever saw in action. Shortly afterward we were again ordered to the brow of the hill and the command was, at seven hundred yards, fire one volley. When the men fired that one volley it was all the officers could do to stop them from firing long enough to change the sights on their guns. We had been firing about a half-hour this time, which was about 6:30 P.M. I was wounded in the left arm, causing a complete compound fracture. I tried to carry my gun from the line but could not, as I had to support the broken arm with the good one. Two men were detailed to go to the hospital with me, but I did not want them to go. However, they started with me and on the way to the hospital I met Lieutenant Willard of my regiment who asked me if he could have one of the men to help carry rations to the regiment. I gave my consent and left one of them with him. I had gone about half a mile when the American guard stopped me, took my belt and pistol, and ordered the man with me to return to his troop. This left me alone. While traveling alone I was fired at several times by Spanish sharpshooters. But none of them hit me. Finally, I reached the hospital about 12 o'clock midnight. The doctors set my arm and dressed it. I was then sent about two hundred yards from the hospital to sleep in the grass. I had nothing to lie on and only the sky for a cover; but I could not stay in the hospital for the sharpshooters fired on it all night.

The next morning, July 2d, being wet with my own blood and the heavy dew that fell during the night, I naturally felt miserable. I was quite anxious to be in another engagement to get my revenge.

From Herschel V. Cashin, et. al., *Under Fire with the 10th U.S. Cavalry* (New York: F. Tennyson Neely, 1899; rep. New York: Bellwether Publishing Co., 1976), 222–223.

5. Private Frederick Presher Describes the U.S. Army's Abuse of Noncombatants in a Filipino Village, 1901

December 25th [1901]:   A couple of detachments went out to-day, one under Captain Hartmann and the other with Lieutenant Arnold in charge. I was with Capt. Hartmann's detachment When we started out from BAUAN about 50 of the most prominent hombres of the town all mounted on ponies, went along with us. Our detachment went towards the peninsula with the long line of hombres stringing along behind us. Our objective was a deep ravine near DURANGAO in which a great number of rifles was supposed to be hidden and although the ravine and the surrounding terrain was thoroughly searched, the native volunteers assisting, nary a rifle was found. We did find the place where they had been hidden however, but they had been recently removed. We also found a insurgent camp, recently vacated and also the place where their putpost had been located. Finally some of the outfit found one lone gugu hiding in the tall grass near one of the trails that we were following. He was taken before the Captain for questioning but he could not or would not tell the Captain a thing so after awhile the Captain told Sergt. Eufeld, Private Baylor and myself to take him away and see if *we* couldn't get him to talk. The Sergeant with us two "bucks" following took the hombre down to the bottom of the ravine where there was a pool of very dirty and very stagnant water and dumped Mr. Gugu in. "No habla["] talk, so he was ducked again and again holding him under water until he nearly strangled. Every time he came up foe air the sergeant would inquire "Quiere habla? and the answer was always the same "Inde habla" (No talk) Down he would go again and "Quiere habla" when he came up—"Inde habla" and down he would go again.

After a while the gugu couldn't even sputter so he was let up. Beating him brought the same response "Inde Habla" so finally the sergeant headed him up the ravine and with a few swift kicks where it would do the most good yelled "Vamous". Gugu understood that all right and he sure did get away from there in no seconds flat. After a few yards start the sergeant fired a shot or two in the air to hurry him along—and he even beat his former pace. Soon the troop went on over in the direction of SAN LUIS DE TAAL and shortly after those "prominent and respected" citizens of the Pueblo of BAUAN begin to get busy. They first looted and then burned every shack in sight and shortly the ponies had a much heavier load than they started out with for as fast as a native gathered his loot he tied it to his pony, chickens, rice, clothing, blankets, pictures, in fact, everything they could lay their hands on or carry away. Some of the ponies were so heavily laden that their owners had to walk all the way back to BAUAN leading them. What they could not carry a[wa]y they destroyed. Lieutenant Arnold's detachment had better luck than our detachment for on the further, or south east end of the peninsula, near MONTE SOLLA, they found a Mauser and 5 Remington rifles in excellent condition.

December 27th. On kitchen Police. A couple of detachments went out at different times during the day but only for escort duty.

From Private Frederick Presher. Diary entries of 26 December to 28 December 1901, Frederick M. Presher Papers, Army Historical Collection, Carlisle, Pa.

Wrote a letter to Pvt. D. F. Thewlis, of "F" troop, stationed at Fort Yellowstone.

December 28th: On fatigue duty nearly all day, getting out troop equipment from the store room and sorting it over. The Inspector General Major F. K. Ward was on hand and inspected all the equipment belonging to the troop. What was still servicable was returned to the storehouse and the unservicable equipment piled up in the middle of the street and burned, that is, all the stuff that would burn. All articles that could not be destroyed by burning such as currycombs, canteens, mess-kits, tin cups, knives, forks, spoons, tools, bits and other metal articles were smashed to bits with an axe. A detachment of the troop went out in the afternoon accomplied by another mob of "leading citizens" who looted and burned BOLOGBOG. In this case however, all the rice found in the barrio was confisacated by the Government who stored it in Storehouse #2. On guard again.

6. Captain J. Hartman Submits an Official Account of the Same Incident, 1901

Telegram. Barran P.I. Dec. 26 1901

Lieut. P.W. Arnold 1 Cav. with 6 men Troop K captured 1 serviceable Mauser [rifle] and 4 Remingtons and 1 unserviceable Remington [rifle] with 260 rounds ammunition near Mt. Solo today. Many uniforms, bolt of uniform cloth, and 3 seal stamps pertaining to Col. Dimacalangan, were captured. Presidente, Chief of Police, Treasurer and numerous other natives accompanied expedition.

> Hartman
> Comdg [Commanding]

▲ E S S A Y S

Although Admiral Mahan became the prophet and guiding light for the navies of the United States and most other nations for more than half a century, his analysis and prescriptions may have been dated and in error; so at least is the interpretation of Russell F. Weigley, military historian from Temple University in Philadelphia, in a provocative 1973 essay reprinted here. The next two essays provide differing perspectives on the U.S. Army in the Philippines. In the second essay, a historian of the U.S. Army's role in the Philippines, Stuart Creighton Miller of San Francisco State University, rejecting what he considers false analogies with American attitudes in the Vietnam War, concluded in 1984 that in the Philippines at the turn of the century, the U.S. Army did engage in racist and lawless acts in a "dirty" guerrilla, but it never lost its patriotism and sense of purpose. In the third essay, John M. Gates, a historian at the College of Wooster in Ohio and also a student of the U.S. Army in the Philippines, offered a comparison in 1983 between the army's experience in confronting insurgency by Plains Indians and later by Filipinos. Gates notes that there are inherent problems

---

From Captain J. Hartman to Adjutant General, 3rd Separate Brigade, December 26, 1901. File 3089, Letters Sent, RG395 Records of U.S. Army Overseas Operations and Commands, 1898–1942, National Archives, Washington, D.C.

faced by regular military units when they encounter irregular forces resisting conquest of their homelands, but he concludes that, influenced by its experiences in the Mexican and Civil Wars, the U.S. Army tried to fight an anti-guerrilla war in the Philippines within a set of legal and moral constraints.

Mahan Planned for the Wrong Kind of War and the Wrong Kind of Ships

RUSSELL F. WEIGLEY

Needless to say, the Jomini whom Luce found was Captain Alfred Thayer Mahan. This Mahan was the son of West Point's Dennis Hart Mahan. He chose a naval career against his father's wishes and graduated from the Naval Academy in 1859. To the time in 1884 when Luce invited him to lecture at the Naval War College his naval career was not outstanding, and in fact he possessed only middling talents in seamanship and had developed an aversion to sea duty. . . .

In the course of preparing his lectures for the Naval War College, Mahan somehow found himself, rose above a career which until now he himself acknowledged had been nearly wasted, and exceeded Luce's expectations by developing his famous trilogy to inaugurate a philosophical study of naval history: *The Influence of Sea Power upon History, 1660–1783* (1890); *The Influence of Sea Power upon the French Revolution and Empire, 1793–1812* (1892); and *Sea Power in Its Relation to the War of 1812* (1905). The first of these three books won Mahan an international reputation as indeed the Jomini of naval strategy. . . .

Sea power confers control of maritime communications in general, but in a contest between rival naval powers control of favorable lines of communication in the more specialized strategic sense is a major goal. In naval war as on land, a principal desideratum of strategy is control of the interior lines, because the possessor of interior lines will be able to threaten the enemy upon several fronts and to concentrate his forces more quickly than the enemy upon any one of them. Certain geographic points are strategic points for naval war because they command interior lines. Certain places on the globe are strategic points of lasting worldwide importance, such as Suez, on the interior line from Europe to the East as opposed to the exterior line via the Cape of Good Hope, and Panama, which especially with the building of an isthmian canal would represent an interior line connecting the Atlantic and the Pacific. The possession of such strategic points affords great advantage in any contest between rival naval powers. In naval strategy as on land, a strategic point should possess intrinsic strength and access to military resources as well as a favorable geographic location. In naval strategy as on land, the strategist seeks to throw the greatest possible concentration of his own force against the enemy's vital points. The principle of concentration most emphatically carries over from land to maritime war. . . .

The purpose of naval strategy is to gain control of the sea. "Naval strategy has for its end to found, support, and increase, as well in peace as in war, the sea power of a country." To control the sea in war it is necessary first to destroy the enemy's fleet. The destruction of the enemy fleet is the first task of a navy in war. Everything else is a sideshow. Once the enemy fleet is destroyed, the victorious navy can exploit its resulting control of the sea for any further purpose that is desirable. In particular, having won control of the sea a navy can advance its nation's economic power by keeping open its access to the resources of the world, while correspondingly strangling the enemy economy by depriving it of such access. Ultimately, Mahan believed, "War is not fighting, but business." But control of the sea must come first, and that could be achieved only by a great navy which could overthrow the enemy navy. . . .

Mahan's main purpose clearly was to provide the rationale for an enlargement of his service, the Navy, and in particular for the transformation of the commerce-raiding Navy into a battleship navy. He wrote at the right time. When his books began appearing during the 1890s, his ideas soon received the acceptance of thoughts whose hour had struck. . . .

Nevertheless, Mahan was deficient in the role for which Stephen Luce had cast him, that of a maritime Jomini. He was better as a propagandist for a policy of sea power than as a strategist. Perhaps Mahan was also too much the historian to be all Luce might have hoped for in a strategist. Not only were his strategic precepts scattered unsystematically through his histories—an arrangement which concealed inconsistencies—but they were uniformly conservative, more appropriate to the age of wood and sail than that of steel and steam.

They were also too much bound up with Great Britain's special geographic position. While Mahan acknowledged that geography contributed much to British naval predominance, he did not make fully clear how much of what the Royal Navy accomplished was possible only because of Britain's geography. . . . In the heyday of British sea power, however, there had existed no effective naval power outside Europe. Therefore by concentrating her fleet in home waters, in her favored position astride the European routes to the outside world, Britain was able to keep in check all the navies that counted and to protect her possessions everywhere. The United States enjoyed no such favored geographical position. No American bases in which the United States fleet could concentrate could afford naval security for both American coastlines, let alone the overseas interests of the United States. . . .

This dispersal of world sea power complicated and indeed undermined Mahan's strategic prescriptions for the United States. He insisted that the American fleet should be kept concentrated; the essence of sea power was a concentrated battle fleet able to assume the primary strategic task of confronting and defeating an enemy battle fleet in order to assert control of the sea. At the same time, he said that American sea power demanded an isthmian canal—to assist concentration—and bases on both its eastern and western approaches to protect the canal, with outlying bases and coaling stations to permit patrolling to protect the first bases. But in a period witnessing the development of several centers of sea power, the canal and its outlying defenses could be given a semblance of protection only by dispersing, not concentrating, the American fleet. No concentration in home waters in the traditional British fashion could meet the needs of the United States.

Apart from the difficulties for the United States in maintaining a concentrated battle fleet, the battle fleet was losing its ability to command the strategic results which Mahan described from the past. Technological developments occurring while Mahan wrote were making it possible for a battle fleet to destroy the enemy's rival battle line and yet not be able to exercise full control of the sea in order to bring economic pressures against the enemy homeland. These developments included the explosive floating mine, its offspring the self-propelled torpedo, and a new instrument for carrying the torpedo, the submarine. With these devices a defeated or otherwise inferior navy might render at least the waters adjacent to its own coast so precarious that control of the sea might be diluted beyond meaning and recognition. . . .

In yet another way he failed to appreciate the possible strategic importance of the torpedo and the submarine. Mahan may have been unduly contemptuous of the possibilities of a strategy of commerce raiding even in the past. . . . Mahan also ignored the greatly enhanced possibilities for commerce raiding implicit in the torpedo and the submarine. . . .

The United States Navy must not be the greatest in the world in order to be worth building, but it must be a battleship navy. Mahan's major books had not yet been published and he was not yet famous when President Benjamin Harrison's Secretary of the Navy, Benjamin F. Tracy—in a Republican administration with expansionist tendencies—issued his annual report for 1889; but Mahan's ideas and echoes of his phrasing are evident in the report, which called for a fleet of twenty armored battleships "to raise blockades," to "beat off the enemy's fleet on its approach" to the American coast, and to divert him from the American coast "by threatening his own, for a war, though defensive in principle, may be conducted most effectively by being offensive in operations." . . .

Mahan's conception of sea power and Theodore Roosevelt's application of it gave the United States a fleet of "capital ships"—to use the term that came into vogue about 1909—more than capable of controlling the waters of the Western Hemisphere. Roosevelt set in motion the building of an American-controlled isthmian canal to ease the single most difficult problem of American naval strategy, and he saw to it that the battleships became welded into a fleet, not remaining a mere aggregation of vessels. . . .

But none of these achievements solved the strategic puzzles most evident in the problem of defending the Philippines but underlying, even undermining, the whole naval program. The concentrated battle fleet as the essence of sea power simply could not do for the United States what it had done for Great Britain in another era and from a far different geographical base. Mahan's emphasis on the battle fleet and his deprecation of any kind of naval war except the contest of first-line ships for control of the sea had combined with the difficulties of extracting from Congress even the later battleships to create an unbalanced fleet. Roosevelt got most of the battleships he wanted, but the Navy did not have enough cruisers or auxiliary vessels, and especially it did not have enough ships for a fleet train to support the battle fleet on long voyages. For the cruise around the world, foreign merchant ships had to be hired to assist in supporting the fleet. This imbalance obviously aggravated the already severe difficulty of naval defense of the distant possessions.

Alfred Thayer Mahan published his books when the strategic problems of the United States were changing from those merely of protecting the continental domain to those of providing military means to sustain the projection of American interests overseas. The means clearly had to be in part naval; therefore Mahan's theory of sea power seemed to appear at precisely the appropriate moment, and Mahan became a figure of tremendous influence and prestige. But the kind of sea power that Mahan described from the historic experience of Great Britain proved inadequate to the requirements of the new American empire. Pressure brought by sea power against lines of maritime commerce was no longer capable of serving any nation so well as it had served Great Britain in the past, except in the limited situations when it was applied against one of the specialized maritime powers themselves, Britain or Japan. But beyond that shortcoming in Mahan's conceptions, the American empire was to be the projection overseas of the interests not of a maritime and primarily commercial state but of a continental land mass, and the appropriate military instrument for it was to prove to be not merely a battle fleet on the British model but a more amphibious form of military power, combining warships with a capacity to place on foreign shores and support over oceanic distances large numbers of soldiers. . . .

. . . [W]hen the United States eventually entered the World War, the Navy Department and everyone else proved to have neglected both the possibilities of the submarine and the other principal American naval problem of the war, the one to which Commander Sears had referred, how to transport an army of a million men and more across the Atlantic with all its equipment and to keep it supplied. . . .

. . . Still, Mahan's books and articles provided the belaying pin by which the Navy had fastened its ambitions to the popular national mood and the expansionist policies of the Spanish War and the Rooseveltian era; the Navy was committed to him irretrievably. Even as younger and more progressive officers came to recognize the shortcomings of Mahanian strategic thought, the Navy had to pay homage to Mahan because its public and political image depended on him. Thus his ideas survived the criticism they encountered in his later years, and after his death in 1914 he gained renewed stature as the high priest of American navalism, whose strategic teachings were its holy writ. . . .

Among the many reasons for the vogue of Mahan, one surely was that he promised a way to relatively anesthetic victory in war. However terrible a climactic battle at sea might be, with hundreds or even thousands of men consumed in the fiery explosions of warship magazines or suffocated in ironclad tombs, Mahan promised that such an event might swiftly and abruptly ensure the outcome of a war, and it was a more inviting prospect than a repetition of Grant's costly battering campaign against the Confederate armies in 1864–65. Once command of the sea was achieved, the naval siege of a blockaded foe still more excelled in attractiveness a Grant-style campaign to destroy enemy armies. Those who cast themselves in the role of blockaders could readily overlook prospective deprivation and even starvation among an enemy people while contemplating the painless course to victory that Mahan seemed to offer for themselves. . . .

By the time the United States entered the World War in April, 1917, the intermediate objective of command of the sea had in a conventional sense been achieved. The Royal Navy had the German High Seas Fleet securely bottled up in German coastal waters. Unfortunately, when the United States entered the war the German submarine campaign was making conventional command of the sea appear a very bad joke. William S. Sims, now a rear admiral, arrived in London soon after the American declaration of war to learn from the Admiralty's statistics that Great Britain was within measurable distance of strangulation. The submarines were sinking one ship of every four that left England, and the British were able to replace only one ship in ten. With the submarine and the self-propelled torpedo employed against a vulnerable maritime nation, the *guerre de course,* the commerce-raiding war, was becoming an immense German success, Mahan to the contrary notwithstanding. Indeed, one of the principal mistakes the Germans had made was to have paid too much heed to Mahan and to have built too many battleships and not enough submarines before the war. . . .

American Racism and Lawlessness in the Philippines

STUART CREIGHTON MILLER

The recent intervention in Vietnam has rekindled considerable interest in an earlier, almost forgotten war fought in Asia by Americans to suppress the national aspirations of Filipinos. Similarities between the two wars have invited historians to construct some historical analogies. Both conflicts degenerated into "dirty" guerrilla-style struggles that soon blurred any distinction between enemy soldier and civilians. Both struggles bitterly divided the American people over the issues of imperialism and the nature of warfare. War critics forced debate on these issues in domestic elections, though with far less success in 1900 and 1904 than was realized seven decades later. But the analogy also breaks down in many ways, most dramatically in the vastly different attitudes of the men who fought the two wars.

A surprising number of private and public letters, diaries, marching songs, camp newspapers, and an occasional literary effort from the Philippine campaign have survived the vagaries of time. While not a "sample" in any technical sense, there is sufficient evidence to support some conclusions about the Americans who served in the Philippines. Volunteers for the most part, and recruited largely from western and southern states, these men were lured to combat by both patriotism and a desire to escape dull routines on the farm. While the reality of guerrilla warfare dulled any romantic illusions about combat, it never diminished their ardent patriotism.

From *Reappraising an Empire: New Perspectives on Philippine-American History,* ed. Peter W. Stanley (Cambridge: Harvard University Press, 1984). Reprinted by permission of the History Department of Harvard University.

The Occupation of Manila

There were abundant complaints, to be sure, aimed at army life, the conduct of war, the natives, and the Islands in general. But they sound much like those common to all wars, and heard, no doubt, by Leonidas at Thermopylae. Rather than expressing qualms over the "dirty" war being waged, the soldiers complained most commonly about the lack of significant combat to relieve the boredom of garrison duty in the "boondocks." They had signed up to fight a war, and to cover themselves with glory before returning to the farm. There was no glory in fighting mosquitos, or in chasing an unseen foe, who sporadically fired a few badly aimed shots before disappearing into the jungle.

Even before the war began on 4 February 1899, there were standard gripes about the quality of the food, the necessity of wearing dress whites, difficulties in finding accommodating females, and, above all, insults endured from Filipino soldiers on a line that encircled the American positions at Manila. These volunteers were bitter that they had missed all the action in Cuba. The assault on Manila in August lasted a few hours, and was too transparently rigged to be satisfying. If there was to be no showdown with their Filipino tormenters, they wanted to be relieved by regulars and returned in time for spring planting. Of course, they vowed repeatedly that they were "just itching to get at the niggers" before leaving "these damned islands." Their officers were equally eager. Lt. Frederick Sladen, the young aide to Governor General Elwell S. Otis, wondered just what it would take to get these "insolent natives to fight," following a series of provocative American maneuvers and demands designed to incite the Filipinos to warfare. "The fun begins now. Will the Aguinaldo party come off the perch or will they wait for us to take them off?" Sladen wondered.

Contrary to official accounts, American soldiers did not "grin and bear the insult and abuse heaped upon them" by their native counterparts. A more sensitive American observed that "almost without exception soldiers, and also many officers, refer to the natives in their presence as 'niggers' and the natives are beginning to understand what 'nigger' means." Filipino soldiers crossing American lines into Manila were knocked down with the butt of a sentry's Springfield merely for seeming "surly." A Minnesota sentry shot a civilian just for "looking suspicious." A Filipino captain was gunned down without warning for approaching a sentry while armed, even though his sidearm was safely strapped into its holster. A native woman and child were "accidentally shot," Otis reported. Pvt. William Christner of the "Pennsy Vols" wrote to his father before the war: "We killed a few to learn them a lesson and you bet they learned it." During this same period, one American was killed and two wounded in a single incident behind Filipino lines. General Emilio Aguinaldo explained to his outraged American counterpart that the three soldiers had shot each other in a drunken argument over cards. Otis apparently accepted this explanation and dropped the matter.

The Scramble for Glory

The "glorious Montana yell" and a "fearless Nebraska charge" on the morning of 5 February wiped out all the petty whining, at least temporarily. But, once they were unleashed, the volunteers refused to halt their wild scramble for glory. During most of the preceding night, they had demonstrated a total lack of fire discipline, shooting "wildly into the night and wasting ammunition," a regular officer complained of the "green Dakotans." Major William Kobbe, who commanded the only regular outfit in the northern sector where it all began, had retired early, believing "it was another false alarm brought about by the excited confusion of the volunteers." Only when his 3rd Artillery was ordered to join Dewey's naval batteries in softening up the Filipino lines as the first light silhouetted them did Kobbe realize that the war had begun. American artillery was so effective that the charging volunteers found mostly dead Filipinos in the conquered trenches, so they simply continued on after the retreating enemy. Colonel Frederick Funston led the Kansans so swiftly past their assigned objective on the coast that he came under fire from the USS *Charleston*. By the day's end, the American line was "so greatly extended that any civilized foe could break it," Sladen recorded with contempt.

Over the next few weeks, the letters home were euphoric. "With a good old Pennsylvania yell, we charged up the hill," Christner recounted. "I hardly think that I was born to be killed by a nigger," he reassured his parents. A cavalry unit pierced the line so fast that it crossed the Pasig River ahead of the retreating Filipinos in the only boats available. This trapped swimming enemy soldiers in a murderous crossfire by the Washington and Idaho regiments. "From then on the fun was fast and furious," with the native dead piling up "thicker than Buffalo chips," Sladen wrote. One jubilant lad confessed that picking off Filipinos in the water was "more fun than a turkey shoot."

The mood changed with the realization that, although there would be no more pitched battles, the war was far from being over. "Well, I guess the niggers are whipped at last," Pvt. Hugh Clapp bragged that February. By April, he was complaining that "you have niggers you can't see shoot at you until you get close enough to shoot at them and then Mr. Nigger tears off to another good place and shoots again." Equipped for more traditional combat, the Americans could not keep pace with the lightly armed and lightly clad Filipino. When trapped, the Filipinos buried their weapons and blended with the local peasantry—a "cowardly" ploy that infuriated the over-eager volunteers. Finally Clapp's dream of one final battle was shattered along with his leg by an unseen sniper. His last letter from a hospital was bitter—not because he had been ordered to fight an unjust war, but because he was returning to Nebraska with little glory and no victory.

One shocking characteristic of these soldiers—especially the volunteers—was their lawlessness. Military leaders tried to pass off looting and senseless destruction as "souvenir hunting." Since officers, sometimes ranking ones, were involved, discipline in the ranks was out of the question. Colonel Funston helped loot a Catholic church, and personally desecrated its sacred precincts to amuse his men from the Bible Belt. Funston may have set the lawless tone before the Kansas Regiment ever left San Francisco. Leading his men down Market Street in a July 4th parade, Funston charged, and narrowly missed with his sword, a spectator, who had thrown a firecracker under his horse.

Some soldiers complained of the behavior of their comrades. D. M. Mickle of the Tennessee outfit wrote: "You have no idea what a mania for destruction the average man has when the fear of the law is removed. I have seen them . . . knock chandeliers and plate glass mirrors to pieces just because they couldn't carry them off. It is such a pity." Another soldier observed of his regiment: "Talk of the natives plundering towns: I don't think they are in it with the 51st Iowa." But many others bragged about their loot and wanton destruction. Captain Albert Otis entered a house in Santa Ana that contained five pianos: "I couldn't take them, so I put a big grand piano out of a second-story window. You can guess its finish." San Franciscans got a taste of this lawlessness when some drunken Wyoming Volunteers at the Presidio used a schooner entering the bay for target practice. Thereafter the volunteers were disarmed before leaving the Philippines.

This lawlessness made it easier for soldiers to commit atrocities against natives, who had already been dehumanized by racial hatred. On top of this, widespread stories of Filipino mutilation of American captives helped raise the soldiers' blood lust. "They cut their ———— off and put them in their mouths. That is the kind of people they have here," Hambleton reported to his brother. For every soldier who protested that "we came here to help, not to slaughter, these natives," there were dozens who justified atrocities; many professed to enjoy committing them:

> Soon we had orders to advance, and we . . . started across the creek in mud and water up to our waists. However, we did not mind it a bit, our fighting blood was up, and we all wanted to kill "niggers." This shooting human beings is a "hot game," and beats rabbit hunting all to pieces. We charged them, and such a slaughter you never saw. We killed them like rabbits; hundreds, yes thousands of them. Every one was crazy. . . . No more prisoners.

Another soldier explained that, "when we find one that is not dead, we have our bayonets." Because the Filipino "is so treacherous," even "when badly wounded," he has to be killed, Sgt. Leman insisted, asking, "Can you blame us?" One soldier thought it hilarious when some "Tennessee boys" were ordered to escort "thirty niggers" to a hospital, and "got there with about a hundred chickens and no prisoners."

Again, officers set the example. Funston not only ordered the Kansans to take no prisoners, but bragged to reporters of personally stringing up 35 civilian suspects without a trial. He even offered to repeat the chore for leading war critics in the United States. Corporal Richard O'Brien testified that Captain Fred McDonald ordered every native killed in La Nog, save a beautiful mestizo mother, whom the officers repeatedly raped, before turning her over to enlisted men. Major Edwin Glenn did not even deny the charge that he had 47 prisoners kneel and "repent of their sins" before he ordered them bayoneted and clubbed to death. The court-martial acquitted Glenn of murder when he cited the orders of General Adna Chaffee to elicit information from natives, "no matter what measures have to be adopted." It is an error, however, to believe that American soldiers reluctantly obeyed unlawful orders, as some anti-imperialists argued. Sgt. A. A. Barnes reflected the sentiments of too many of his comrades when he described the slaughter of "1,000 men, women and children" after "one of our boys was found shot and his stomach cut open," and confessed, "I am probably growing hard-hearted, for I am in my glory when I can sight my gun on some dark skin and pull the trigger." A Utah volunteer testified that such feeling was widespread:

The boys will say that no cruelty is too severe for these brainless monkeys, who can appreciate no sense of honor, kindness or justice. . . . With an enemy like this to fight, it is not surprising that the boys should soon adopt "no quarter" as a motto, and fill the blacks full of lead before finding out whether they are friends or enemies.

The most damning evidence that the enemy wounded were being murdered came from the official reports of Otis and his successor, General Arthur MacArthur, claiming 15 Filipinos killed for every one wounded. In the American Civil War, the ratio had been 5 wounded for every soldier killed, which is close to the historical norm. Otis attempted to explain this anomaly by the superior marksmanship of rural southerners and westerners who had hunted all their lives. MacArthur added a racial twist, asserting that Anglo-Saxons do not succumb to wounds as easily as do men of "the inferior races." . . .

In the final analysis, the American soldier fought this "dirty" colonial war as readily as did his British counterpart in India or South Africa. It was for both, of course, an era of intense nationalism. But possibly there is another more peculiarly American explanation as well. The proponents of imperialism had hailed the Philippine Islands as "America's new frontier," and, appropriately, the volunteers brought with them a frontier spirit steeped in an individualism that easily degenerated into lawlessness. Virtually every member of America's high command in the Philippines had spent most of his career chasing Apaches, Comanches, Kiowas, and the Sioux. Some of them had taken part in the massacre at Wounded Knee. It was easy for these commanders to order similar tactics in the Philippines when faced with the frustrations of guerrilla warfare. But their young charges, many of whom were descendants of old Indian fighters, carried out such orders with amazing, if not surprising, alacrity.

Inherent Problems in Counter-Guerilla Warfare

JOHN M. GATES

Both during the Vietnam War and after, students of 19th-century American military history frequently claimed to see important similarities between whatever campaign they happened to be surveying and the conflict in Indochina. In his 1976 Harmon Memorial lecture, Robert M. Utley, a distinguished historian of the Indian-fighting Army, drew attention to the "parallels with frontier warfare" in the so-called "limited wars" of the nuclear age. Jack Bauer, in his study of the Mexican War, implied much the same thing in a reference to General Scott's operation to secure his line of supply from attack by Mexican guerrillas. Scott's problems, wrote Bauer, were "as complex and difficult as any faced by modern American soldiers who think the problem unique to mainland Asia." I concluded my own book with the observation that a study of the Army's Philippine campaign might provide insight into the solution of similar problems in the 20th century. Underlying all such

Abridged text from John M. Gates, "Indians and Insurrectos: The U.S. Army Experience with Insurgency," *Parameters: Journal of the U.S. Army War College*, 13 (March 1983): 59, 61–64, 66–68. Reprinted by permission of the publisher.

observations seems to be a belief that the Army had failed to learn as much as it could or should have from its 19th-century counterinsurgency experience. . . .

When Indians fought against the Army they fought as warriors. Although tactically they fought as guerrillas, and often displayed tremendous skill in the process, strategically they were not guerrillas. They were not attempting to wear down the enemy by harassment, nor were they in a position to create secure base areas or win over the civilian population living in the heartland of the Army they confronted. They fought as they did because it was the only way they knew to fight, and their success in keeping in the field as long as they did resulted as much from the Army's meager size as from the Indians' prowess as warriors.

Much of the Army's work on the frontier was that of a constabulary. It served eviction notices on Indians and then forcibly removed them when required. If "imprisoned" Indians "broke out" of the reservations, the Army found them and coerced them back. Failing in the latter, it would attempt the equivalent of an arrest, an armed attack to force the Indians to surrender. Indians who raided white settlers, Army posts, or peaceful reservation-Indians engaged in criminal activity, in white eyes at least; and the Army's task was that of the police officer, to track down the guilty parties and bring them back for punishment. Because of the numbers involved those activities sometimes looked like war, and in a few instances, when entire tribes rose up in arms to fight against the intrusion of the white, it was. Most of the time, however, it was routine though difficult police work.

As the US Army's only military activity between the 19th century's infrequent real wars, the so-called Indian Wars have received far more attention than they deserve. At best, except for a few significant successes, such as that against Custer at the Little Big Horn, the Indians were little more than a nuisance. . . .

The Army's confrontation with guerrillas in the Philippines differed markedly from all its previous experiences, being much more comparable to the guerrilla wars of national liberation waged after World War II than to any of the Army's earlier campaigns. Unlike the Mexican or the Civil War, the war's outcome would not be decided by the clash of regular forces, and the outcome was not, as in the Indian conflicts, certain from the start. In the Philippines, the United States was engaged in a war of conquest, although Americans both at the time and later have seen fit to hide their actions by referring to the enemy as insurgents, or worse. There could be no insurrection, however, because the United States did not control the Islands when the Philippine-American War began in 1899. The fighting that ensued took place between two organized forces, one representing the government of the United States and the other representing the revolutionary government of the Philippine Republic under the leadership of Emilio Aguinaldo. The conflict began as a conventional war, pitting American regulars and volunteers against the Philippine army that had seized control of the Islands from Spain. Although beginning as a guerrilla force, the army surrounding the Americans in Manila had adopted conventional organization and tactics, planning to engage the American forces in regular combat and hoping to gain international recognition for the Philippine Republic as a result.

When their attempts at regular warfare ended in disaster, the Filipinos shifted to a guerrilla strategy aimed at making an occupation of the Philippines too costly for the Americans and achieving by a political solution what they had failed to achieve through a more conventional military approach. The problems presented by the Filipino strategy were greater than any faced by the Army in its previous confrontations with Indians or true guerrillas. Bent on conquest of the entire Philippines, the United States could not achieve peace and accomplish withdrawal by arranging a partial cession of territory as it had done in Mexico. And because the value of the Islands as a colony resided, at least in part, in the population, policies of removal or extermination were also inappropriate, even had they been acceptable on moral grounds—and, of course, they were not. Filipino numbers and the colonial nature of the conflict thus precluded a solution based on the experience of the Indian Wars. Finally, the Filipino leadership, unlike that of the South in the Civil War, had no reservations about calling their followers into the field in a people's war of prolonged guerrilla struggle. From the Army's point of view, however, the Philippine situation, like that of the Civil War, demanded that the war be fought and ended in a way that would help create a lasting peace.

The tremendous differences in the contexts of the Army's guerrilla war experiences make generalizations difficult, but not impossible. Some uniformities can be discerned, although frequently they are not nearly so important as the differences, a point to be doubly emphasized when one attempts to compare any of the Army's guerrilla war experiences with the war in Vietnam.

The most obvious uniformity is that of guerrilla technique; General George Crook's observation that Apaches "only fight with regular soldiers when they choose and when the advantages are all on their side" might just as easily have been made about Mexican, Confederate, or Philippine guerrillas. . . . Whether in Mexico, the Shenandoah Valley, the Great Plains, or the Philippines, guerrillas behaved much the same: fleeing from strength, attacking weakness, preying upon small isolated garrisons and poorly defended supply trains, killing the lone sentry or the unwary patrol, living off the land with the aid of their people—and terrorizing those who refused to cooperate or joined with the enemy.

A second uniformity, only slightly less obvious than the first, can be seen in the Army's response to the threat posed by Indian and guerrilla bands. The actions taken to counter them were remarkably similar from place to place over time. Whether the enemy was Mexican, Confederate, Indian, or Filipino, the Army responded eventually with many of the same general techniques of counterguerrilla warfare. To protect supply lines, commanders increased the size of the guard assigned to supply trains and strengthened garrisons along their routes of march. To facilitate operations against marauding bands and to provide security to populated areas, commanders garrisoned towns and built forts. To hunt down enemy units and force them to disband or be destroyed, the Army sent highly mobile, self-contained units into the field to pursue them relentlessly. Often at a disadvantage because of their unfamiliarity with the terrain or the local population, Army officers enlisted the support of indigenous inhabitants whenever possible. In Mexico, for example, Lieutenant Colonel Ethan Hitchcock obtained the aid of robber Manuel Dominguez and his band, and in the American southwest General George Crook formed units of friendly Apaches to help him find and fight renegades such as Geronimo. In perhaps the most celebrated use of indigenous collaborators,

Frederick Funston used a force of Filipino scouts to capture Aguinaldo in his own headquarters in 1901.

The Army was relatively successful in developing methods to deal with the problems presented by hostile Indians and guerrilla bands in the field. A more difficult set of problems emerged, however, regarding the treatment to be accorded guerrilla combatants who had been captured, particularly part-time guerrillas, and the noncombatant population from which the guerrillas derived support. Throughout the 19th century one sees tension between two general policies, one rooted in severity and the other more humane. The frustrations of guerrilla warfare, the ease with which guerrilla bands eluded regular troops when aided by a friendly population, the atrocities committed by irregulars, and a common assumption that guerrillas were not legitimate combatants all worked to push commanders in the field toward a policy of reprisal. But recognition by these officers that their enemies were frequently doing nothing that they themselves would not do in a similar situation, the need to fight and terminate conflicts in a fashion that would bring a lasting peace, and the desire to keep one's humanity even in the midst of barbarous war all supported policies of conciliation aimed at winning over the opposition by good works rather than fear.

Nineteenth-century customs and laws of war reflected, rather than resolved, these tensions. Although the United States had yet to promulgate any official statement on the laws of war to guide officers during the Mexican War and the early years of the Civil War, by February 1863 Professor Francis Lieber, a noted authority on international law, had drafted a code that was summarized and distributed to the Army on 24 April of that year as General Order No. 100, "Instructions for the Government of Armies of the United States in the Field." It became the cornerstone of the growing body of international law upon which current practices rest, and by the time of the Philippine-American War it had become the final word for American Army officers on the laws of war.

General Order 100 manifested the tension between the two different approaches to pacification. On the assumption that "sharp wars are brief," the order asserted that "the more vigorously wars are pursued the better it is for humanity." In an 1862 commentary written for General Halleck on the status of guerrilla parties in the laws and customs of war, Lieber concluded that "armed bands" rising "in a district fairly occupied by military force, or in the rear of an army," were "universally considered" to be "brigands, and not prisoners of war" when captured. He also observed that such groups were "particularly dangerous because they could easily evade pursuit, and by laying down their arms become insidious enemies." His negative view of guerrillas was carried over into General Order 100. Although item 81 of the order stated that properly uniformed "partisans" were entitled to be treated as true prisoners of war, item 82 stated that guerrillas who fought without commissions or on a part-time basis, returning intermittently to their homes to hide among the civilian population, were to be treated "summarily as highway robbers or pirates." Similarly, so-called "armed prowlers" were also denied the privileges of prisoners of war, and all who rose up against a conquering army were "*war rebels,*" subject to death if captured. As item 4 noted, "To save the country is paramount to all other considerations."

At the same time that it condemned the guerrilla and sanctioned reprisals, however, General Order 100 also recognized that the conduct of officers administering martial law should "be strictly guided by the principles of justice, honor, and humanity." Although military necessity might justify destruction, even of innocent civilians, it did not sanction "cruelty . . . revenge . . . [or] torture." General Order 100 reminded officers that men who took up arms did not cease "to be moral beings, responsible to one another and to God." Unarmed citizens were "to be spared in person, property, and honor as much as the exigencies of war will admit." Retaliation, deemed "the sternest feature of war," was to be used with care, "only as a means of protective retribution" and "never . . . as a measure of mere revenge." As item 28 observed:

> Unjust or inconsiderate retaliation removes the belligerents farther and farther from the mitigating rules of regular war, and by rapid steps leads them nearer to the internecine wars of savages.

Lieber knew that in war the barrier between civilization and barbarism was exceedingly thin, and he provided few opportunities for conscientious soldiers to breach it. . . .

The pattern in the Philippines at the century's end had much in common with events both in Mexico and in the Civil War. Many of the officers in the islands—such as General Elwell S. Otis, in command when the war began, and General Arthur MacArthur, his successor—were convinced that the swiftest way to end the war and pacify the population was to demonstrate the benefits of American colonial government; and the Army put considerable effort into establishing municipal governments, schools, and public works projects. Rejecting the concept of total war implied in Sherman's March to the Sea, most officers in the Philippines, at least initially, seemed to accept the idea put forth by Captain John Bigelow, Jr., in his *Principles of Strategy* that "the maintenance of a military despotism in the rear of an invading army must generally prove a waste of power."

As the frustrations of the guerrilla war increased, however, officers began to either urge upon their superiors in Manila a policy of greater severity or engage in harsh reprisals without waiting for official sanction. As Colonel Robert L. Bullard wrote in his diary in August 1900:

> It seems that ultimately we shall be driven to the Spanish method of dreadful general punishments on a whole community for the acts of its outlaws which the community systematically shields and hides.

A few months later General Lloyd Wheaton urged "swift methods of destruction" to bring a "speedy termination to all resistance," claiming it was "no use going with a sword in one hand, a pacifist pamphlet in the other hand and trailing the model of a schoolhouse after." Fortunately, General MacArthur recognized the value of the reform programs being implemented by the Army as well as the efforts being made to prevent excesses in the campaign against the guerrillas. Even he was frustrated, however, and, by the end of 1900, sanctioned the enforcement of the most severe sections of General Order 100. In areas where guerrillas and their supporters proved most intransigent, such as Batangas Province, the Army even resorted to population relocation and a scorched-earth policy comparable to that of General Ewing in western Missouri. On the island of Samar the line between retaliation and revenge became blurred beyond recognition for some soldiers.

Atrocities have taken place in virtually all wars, but the frustrations of guerrilla warfare, in which the enemy's acts of terror and brutality often add to the anger generated by the difficulty of campaigning, create an environment particularly conducive to the commission of war crimes. In almost all such wars one can discover numerous incidents in which counterinsurgents resorted to acts of counterterror, punishment, or revenge that fell clearly outside the relatively severe actions sanctioned by 19th-century laws of war.

During the Civil War, reprisals sometimes went well beyond those sanctioned by the laws of warfare. Robert Gould Shaw, for example, witnessed the "wanton destruction" of Darien, Georgia, in 1863, an act that made him ashamed to be an officer of the Union force that committed the act. According to Shaw, the city was destroyed for no apparent reason other than his commander's desire to subject the Southerners to the hardships of war. As described by Shaw, it was an act of pure revenge and a war crime. In other instances, when the enemy was perceived as savage, the Army's actions could be even more severe, as exemplified by Custer's 1868 attack of Black Kettle's Cheyenne camp on the bank of the Washita. The men of the 7th Cavalry destroyed numerous Indians (including women and children), the camp's tepees (thus denying the survivors food and winter robes), and 875 Indian ponies.

Stories of atrocities would become the hallmark of the Philippine campaign. No history of that war is complete without a description of the "water cure," in which unwilling suspects were seized and their stomachs forcibly filled with water until they revealed the hiding place of guerrillas, of supplies, or of arms—or, as happened on occasion, until they died. The more frustrating the campaign became, the more frequently the Americans crossed the line separating the harsh reprisals sanctioned by General Order 100 from such crimes of war as torture and wanton destruction.

Although often quite harsh, the Army's 19th-century response to problems of guerrilla warfare was, in general, based upon the existing laws of war. Widely publicized, of course, have been the deviations from those laws that took place. In virtually every conflict, officers and men alike committed atrocities, such as shooting prisoners or noncombatants, or torturing people suspected of withholding information. Significantly, despite the tendency of those committing such acts and of their supporters to plead the extenuating circumstances of barbarous guerrilla war as a defense, few people accepted their argument that no crime or breach of the laws of war had been committed.

The conclusion that American soldiers in the 19th century made an effort to fight guerrillas within the context of a set of legal and moral restraints would not be particularly significant were it not for the tremendous contrast presented by current [in 1983] counterinsurgency campaigns. In places as remote from each other as El Salvador and Afghanistan, one sees an acceptance of widespread and seemingly indiscriminate terror against civilians as a primary technique for dealing not only with insurgents and their supporters, but with the uncommitted as well. At present, the laws of war are frequently ignored, and war against potential as well as actual insurgents is fought with a barbarity associated more than with the likes of Attila the Hun than the soldiers of supposedly civilized nations.

For American soldiers not yet directly involved in this wholesale assault on the laws of war and humanity, the contrast between the attitude of many American officers in the 19th century and that evident in a number of foreign armies at present, particularly in Latin America, highlights a moral problem of immense proportions. That American officers are not unaware of the problem has been demonstrated by events such as the 1980 West Point symposium on "War and Morality." At that gathering, Professor Michael Walzer spoke of "two kinds of military responsibility," and his approach to the subject had much more in common with the views held by most 19th-century military officers than those exhibited by many of the world's soldiers currently engaged in counterguerrilla warfare. In language that Francis Lieber would have readily endorsed, Walzer observed that the military officer "as a moral agent" has a responsibility beyond that upward to the officers over him and downward to the soldiers under him. He also has a responsibility "outward—to all those people whose lives his activities affect." In the 19th century, Walzer's second kind of military responsibility was accepted by American officers as they attempted to defeat guerrillas without sinking to the level of barbarity that is now deemed "indispensable."

Today, if US Army officers fail to give careful attention to the moral problems inherent in warfare against determined guerrilla forces, they may find themselves drawn more into the inhumane form of contemporary counterinsurgency practiced by communists and capitalists alike. To avoid such a fate, they must continue to ask themselves what at first glance seems to be a very 19th-century question. In countering insurgents, they must ask—in the moral sense of these words (a sense not commonly brought to bear in gauging the potential effectiveness of military operations)—what response is *right, good,* and *proper.* To do less is to risk the loss of their humanity as well as any claim to be defending a government based upon the rule of law.

FURTHER READING

John D. Alden, *The American Steel Navy* (1972).

Stephen E. Ambrose, *Upton and the Army* (1964).

James C. Bradford, ed., *Crucible of Empire: The Spanish-American War and Its Aftermath* (1993).

Henry W. Brands, *The Last Romantic* (1997).

Herschel V. Cashin, et. al., *Under Fire With The 10th U.S. Cavalry* (1899; reprint 1970).

Richard D. Challener, *Admirals, Generals, and American Foreign Policy: 1898–1914* (1973).

Garna L. Christian, *Black Soldiers in Jim Crow Texas, 1899–1917* (1995).

B. Franklin Cooling, *Grey Steel and Blue Water Navy: The Formative Years of America's Military-Industrial Complex, 1881–1917* (1979).

Graham A. Cosmas, *An Army for Empire: The United States Army in the Spanish-American War* (1971).

Marvin Fletcher, *The Black Soldier and Officer in the United States Army, 1891–1917* (1974).

John M. Gates, "Indians and Insurrectos: The U.S. Army's Experience with Insurgency," *Parameters* 13 (March 1983): 59–68.

_____, *Schoolbooks and Krags: The United States Army in the Philippines, 1898–1902* (1973).

Willard B. Gatewood, Jr., "Black Americans and the Quest for Empire, 1898–1903," *Journal of Southern History* 38 (November 1972): 545–566.

Kenneth J. Hagan, *American Gunboat Diplomacy and the Old Navy, 1877–1889* (1973).

Virgil C. Jones, *Roosevelt's Rough Riders* (1971).

Peter Karsten, *The Naval Aristocracy: The Golden Age of Annapolis and the Emergence of Modern American Navalism* (1972).

Paul A. C. Koistinen, *Mobilizing for Modern War: The Political Economy of American Warfare, 1865–1919* (1997).

Gerald F. Linderman, *The Mirror of War: American Society and the Spanish-American War* (1974).

Brian M. Linn, *The U.S. Army and Counterinsurgency in the Philippine War, 1899–1902* (1989).

William E. Livezey, *Mahan on Sea Power* (1947).

Alfred Thayer Mahan, *The Influence of Sea Power upon History: 1660–1783* (1890).

Ernest R. May, *Imperial Democracy: The Emergence of America as a Great Power* (1961).

Glenn Anthony May, *Battle for Batangas: A Philippine Province at War* (1991).

Stuart C. Miller, *"Benevolent Assimilation": The American Conquest of the Philippines, 1899–1903* (1983).

Allan R. Millett, *The Politics of Intervention: The Military Occupation of Cuba, 1906–1909* (1968).

Timothy K. Nenninger, *The Leavenworth Schools and the Old Army* (1978).

Robert L. O'Connell, *The Cult of the Battleship and the Rise of the U.S. Navy* (1991).

G. J. A. O'Toole, *The Spanish War: An American Epic, 1898* (1984).

Louis A. Perez, Jr., *The War of 1898: The United States and Cuba in History and Historiography*, (1998).

Carol Reardon, *Soldiers and Scholars: The U.S. Army and the Uses of Military History, 1865–1920* (1990).

Hyman G. Rickover, *How the Battleship* Maine *Was Destroyed* (1976).

Theodore Roosevelt, *The Rough Riders* (1899).

Robert Seager II, *Alfred Thayer Mahan: The Man and His Letters* (1977).

Jack Shulimson, *The Marine Corps' Search for a Mission, 1880–1898* (1993).

Mark Russell Shulman, *Navalism and the Emergence of American Seapower, 1882–1893* (1995).

Ronald H. Spector, *Professors of War: The Naval War College and the Development of the Naval Profession* (1977).

Peter W. Stanley, *Reappraising an Empire: New Perspectives on Philippine-American History* (1984).

William N. Still, Jr., *American Sea Power in the Old World: The United States Navy in European and Near Eastern Waters, 1865–1917* (1980).

David R. Sturtevant, *Popular Uprisings in the Philippines, 1840–1940* (1976).

David F. Trask, *The War with Spain in 1898* (1981).

Richard W. Turk, *The Ambiguous Relationship: Theodore Roosevelt and Alfred Thayer Mahan* (1987).

Emory Upton, *The Military Policy of the United States* (1904).

Richard E. Welch, Jr., *Response to Imperialism: The United States and the Philippine-American War, 1899–1902* (1979).

CHAPTER
9

World War I:
The Challenge of Modern War

Guarded by a troop of cavalry, President Woodrow Wilson drove to Capitol Hill on April 2, 1917, and asked Congress to declare that a state of war existed with Imperial Germany. Berlin's submarine campaign, he declared, was "warfare against mankind." "The world must be made safe for democracy." On April 6, Congress adopted the war resolution, and the United States joined the war that the Allies and the Central Powers had been fighting since August 1914. This was the first modern war that Americans fought against a major foreign power. But although the United States soon adopted national conscription and ultimately sent a mass army to France, America's war experience, because of its differing circumstances and traditions, diverged significantly from those of the other belligerents. Some of the American experiences in World War I concerned decisions that continue to remain controversial, for example, those involving the issues of conscription versus a volunteer force, an entirely independent U.S. Army in France as opposed to integrated training and unit deployment within the veteran Allied armies, and the American emphasis on open-field tactics rather than trench warfare.

When the traditional American wartime system of ad hoc units of the U.S. Volunteers was abandoned in 1917 and national conscription adopted, it was not the highly centralized permanent system of universal military training of continental nations, but a particular American form of a draft—temporary wartime Selective Service implemented in a decentralized manner by draft boards composed of local civilians, not the military. By the armistice on November 11, 1918, the American Expeditionary Force (AEF) in France, numbered more than two million "doughboys," and included volunteers in the Regular Army, National Guard, and Marines, as well as the conscripts in the so-called National Army. During the war, General John J. Pershing, the AEF commander, and President Wilson had resisted Allied efforts to amalgamate the doughboys into veteran British and French units, and had insisted on a separate and independent U.S. Army in France. Furthermore, believing that the Europeans were bogged down in a trench-warfare mentality and considering the mobility and initiative of American soldiers to be one of their greatest assets, Pershing continually refused to emphasize trench-warfare training. Instead, he stressed open-field tactics for the American Expeditionary

Force. These decisions by Pershing have remained controversial, some historians and other analysts claiming that they unduly increased U.S. casualties, while others assert that they helped win the war.

▲ D O C U M E N T S

Facing considerable opposition to his decision at the beginning of the war to abandon the tradition of the U.S. Volunteer units, President Woodrow Wilson puts forward his justification for primary reliance upon a selective wartime draft in a public letter, April 19, 1917, to Representative Guy T. Helvering of Kansas, a fellow Democrat. One of the congressional leaders of the opposition to the draft and to U.S. intervention in the war, Senator Robert M. LaFollette of Wisconsin, a leading progressive, Republican reformer, declares his objections in the second document, a speech in the Senate on April 27, 1917, during the lengthy debate on the administration's proposed selective draft law.

The majority of doughboys did not arrive in France until 1918. The first American action there occurred when units of the AEF helped block the spring offensive organized by German General Erich Ludendorff. Behind these Americans were the first of several thousand army and Red Cross nurses. One of them, Laura Frost, from Boston, Massachusetts, assigned to Evacuation Hospital No. 5 (Evac 5), just behind the front, recalls in the third document (excerpts from letters to her family, an unpublished memoir, and interviews after 1988) some of the U.S. actions at Belleau Wood and Cantigny that spring, as well as her unit's subsequent deployment to Villers Cotterets on the Oise-Aisne front and eventually to a village near Ypres on the Belgian front. General Pershing's decision to maintain an independent American army in France came under continual attack by the Allies, but that criticism reached its height in August 1918, when French Marshal Ferdinand Foch, coordinator of the Allied effort on the Western Front, launched a series of counteroffensives that would win the war. The fourth document, the transcribed notes taken by one of General Pershing's aides-de-camp at a meeting between Pershing and Foch (and French General Maxime Weygand) on August 30, 1918, shows the intensity of feelings between the two commanders as Foch tried to integrate the newly created U.S. First Army into his major Oise-Aisne region offensive (the largest Allied effort), while Pershing insisted on a separate, if more limited, American action in Woevre (the St. Mihiel salient, on the far right of the Allied line). Pershing remained firm; the attack on St. Mihiel, September 12–16, was the first distinctively U.S. offensive; subsequently, between September 26 and November 11, the U.S. forces embarked on the Meuse-Argonne offensive. The fifth document, a copy of the *Combat Instructions* issued by AEF Headquarters on September 5, 1918, the eve of the U.S. offensive, formalized Pershing's distinctions between trench warfare and open-field tactics. Among the 550,000 "doughboys" engaged in the St. Mihiel offensive was Sergeant Theodore K. Jones, a former Woolworth sales clerk from Yonkers, New York, now in charge of a field artillery gun crew with the AEF. In the sixth document, an unpublished memoir, he describes the arrival of his horse-drawn artillery unit at the front and the onset of the St. Mihiel offensive on September 12, as well as the beginning of the Meuse-Argonne Offensive on September 26. General Pershing never wavered in his adherence to his decisions. After the war, when writing his memoirs in 1930, he asked his most brilliant wartime aide, George C. Marshall, to review the manuscript; in the seventh document, the comments of Marshall, then a lieutenant colonel, reflected, if even in a gentle way, some of the criticism of the AEF's performance.

1. President Woodrow Wilson Wants a Drafted Army, Not the U.S. Volunteers, 1917

From Guy Tresillian Helvering

My dear Mr. President,   Washington, D.C. April 19, 1917.

The next few weeks—possibly days—will decide as to the policy which the country will adopt in securing the necessary forces which will be needed to protect the interests of the country.

Of course I am aware that you favor what is familiarly termed a "selective draft," but that term is not generally understood by the people and I feel that if you would but express your views, as clearly as you have on many other occasions, so that all may understand, much of the doubt would disappear and we would be able to get together for the common good much more readily.

I trust that you will realize that in writing you I am doing so in no captious spirit. We are all aiming for a common goal and I believe with the same earnestness of purpose, but we cannot overlook the fact that a great many of our people have a decided objection to anything which could be construed as "conscription" or "draft" and I am certain that a statement from you to the country would quickly clear away much of the misunderstanding which is now in existence.

Sincerely yours, Guy T. Helvering

To Guy Tresillian Helvering

My dear Mr. Helvering: [The White House] 19 April, 1917

I welcome the inquiry of your letter of April nineteenth because I have realized the truth of what you say from my own observation, namely, that what is meant to be understood by the selective draft is not generally understood throughout the country.

The process of the draft is, I think, very clearly set forth in the bill drafted by the War Department and which I so earnestly hope the Congress will adopt, but it is worth while to state the idea which underlies the bill a little more fully.

I took occasion the other day in an address to the people of the country to point out the many forms of patriotic service that were open to them and to emphasize the fact that the military part of the service was by no means the only part, and perhaps, all things considered, not the most vital part. Our object is a mobilization of all the productive and active forces of the nation and their development to the highest point of cooperation and efficiency, and the idea of the selective draft is that those should be chosen for service in the Army who can be most readily spared from the prosecution of the other activities which the country must engage in and to which it must devote a great deal of its best energy and capacity.

From Guy T. Helvering to Woodrow Wilson, April 19, 1917, and Woodrow Wilson to Guy T. Helvering, April 19, 1917. Reprinted in Arthur S. Link, et al., eds. *Papers of Woodrow Wilson*, 69 vols. (Princeton: Princeton U. P. (1983), XLII, 96–98.

The volunteer system does not do this. When men choose themselves, they sometimes choose without due regard to their other responsibilities. Men may come from the farms or from the mines or from the factories or centers of business who ought not to come but ought to stand back of the armies in the field and see that they get everything that they need and that people of the country are sustained in the meantime.

The principle of the selective draft, in short, has at its heart this idea, that there is a universal obligation to serve and that a public authority should choose those upon whom the obligation of military service shall rest, and also in a sense choose those who shall do the rest of the nation's work. The bill if adopted will do more, I believe, than any other single instrumentality to create the impression of universal service in the Army and out of it, and if properly administered will be a great source of stimulation.

Those who feel that we are turning away altogether from the voluntary principle seem to forget that some 600,000 men will be needed to fill the ranks of the Regular Army and the National Guard and that a very great field of individual enthusiasm lies there wide open.

Cordially and sincerely yours, Woodrow Wilson

2. Senator Robert LaFollette Opposes the Draft, 1917

Mr. President, however uncertain the meaning of some portions of this bill may be, its main purpose is clear. About that there is no dispute. The main purpose of this bill is to clothe one man with power, acting through agents appointed by him, to enter at will every home in our country, at any hour of the day or night, using all the force necessary to effect the entry, and violently lay hold of 1,000,000 of our finest and healthiest and strongest boys, ranging in age from 19 to 25 years, and against their will, and against the will and wishes of their parents or family, deport them across the seas to a foreign land three thousand and more miles away, and to require them, under penalty of death if they refuse, to wound and kill other young boys just like themselves and toward whom they feel no hostility and have cause to feel none.

Briefly told, and in as plain language as I can command, that is the purpose of this bill. That is what the draft means. I have not overstated—indeed, no one can overstate—the horror it is proposed to perpetrate by this bill, nor the insult which it conveys to the intelligence and patriotism of the people of this country. Anyone who would have prophesied one short month ago that this body would seriously consider, under existing circumstances, such a measure as this would have raised a question as to his sanity. . . .

. . . If newspaper reports are correct, the representatives of the allied nations from over the seas, who are visiting here at present and who may be supposed to

From Senator Robert LaFollette, *Congressional Record,* 65th Cong., 1st Sess. (April 27, 1917), 1354–1358, 1360.

speak with some knowledge of the question, suggest that 5,000,000 of our soldiers will be necessary to complete the job.

That our boys will enter upon the actual killing and being killed only after some months of training designed to fit them peculiarly for the atrocious task does not mitigate but rather increases the horrors of the bloody work proposed just in proportion as it increases their efficiency. That the killing will be done by the enginery and in the formations of regular warfare certainly does not make it more humane or less horrible. Killing such as we propose our boys shall engage in, either to kill or be killed, by machine guns, by bursting bombs, by poison gas and tearing shrapnel is the most horrible, and is deliberately designed to be the most horrible, killing that can be devised. . . .

Committee Held No Public Hearings Upon This Bill

It seems to me a little strange that the committee having this bill in charge should in its consideration have departed from the universal custom of holding public hearings on bills of great importance and general interest, such as this. . . .

The Congress was assembled in special session. The demand was made for an unconditional declaration of war. While I opposed that declaration and urged that the momentous question should be first submitted to the people, I appreciate the point of view of the majority of both Houses of the Congress, which lead them to make the required declaration of war without submitting it to the people.

But upon this question, sir, scarcely less vital to the people than the declaration of war itself, I purpose to urge as strongly as I can that the voters shall have an opportunity to express themselves by an advisory vote. As I hope to show a little later, under the amendment I have offered that vote can be taken without delaying by one moment the plans for the war, and with practically no expense.

The war will end some time. I pray it may be soon. But the iniquitous system of draft which this bill proposes and the military domination which must attend upon it, if once fastened upon the country may perpetuate itself forever. Arm the executive branch of the Government with the power that this bill purposes, to select the men to constitute the Army of which the President is Commander in Chief, and it marks the beginning of the end of our constitutional government. Its forms may be for a time preserved, but the substance of government will be transferred to the Executive. . . .

The senior Senator from Idaho spoke feelingly, eloquently, in this Chamber on the day that war was declared, of his sympathy for the 8,000,000 Germans and 2,000,000 Austrians who are a no less integral part of our national life than the citizens of Scandinavian, Irish, Italian, Russian, or English origin, and who have contributed in the same spirit to our national unity, prosperity, and progress.

The fact that we are made up of peoples of many nationalities, most of whom feel very intensely on this subject of draft, should in itself be an impelling reason why Congress should insist on a volunteer army to fight on foreign soil.

The draft is the corollary of militarism and militarism spells death to democracy. No war can be successfully prosecuted that has not the spontaneous support of the men who do the fighting. There is not the shadow of an excuse for pressing men into involuntary military servitude for the conduct of this war.

In face of all the reasons why we should adopt the volunteer plan for the conduct of this war, it will be a black page in the history of Congress, if we pass the draft provisions of this bill.

The feature of compulsory overseas service in foreign lands embodied in this bill, for the first time in the history of civilized government, I believe, distinguishes this measure from any draft law of which I have knowledge. It distinguishes it certainly from any adopted by any country in a situation similar to our own. . . .

What the Selective Draft Means

It has been said that the obligation to serve the country as a soldier is a universal obligation, like that of paying taxes, to support the Government. In my opinion there is no analogy between the two; but, even if there were, the analogy between the selective draft of this bill and the obligation to pay taxes would mean that it would be left to the judgment of some "public authority" to decide who would pay taxes and who should not. . . .

. . . Under the selective draft, the sports and bloods, whom some friend thought would make officers, or who had a pull, would not get into the trenches. It would be just plain Jimmie Jones and Johnnie Smith who would be taken for that work, and the sportsmen and the politicians' sons and the boys whose fathers had influence would be held back as "material for officers." So the selective draft will choose not only who shall go but where they shall go, whether to be shot or to be brevetted, whether to be kicked and cuffed, "jacked up," and "bawled out" as a private soldier, or whether they shall receive such soft berths as parental pull may provide for them. All this in the name of democracy!

3. Laura Frost, a U.S. Army Nurse, Recalls Her Experiences at the Front in France (1918), 1918–1997

"If it hadn't been the amputation ward, maybe the shock wouldn't have been so devastating, but helping dress those quivering stumps and hearing the men's laughter and jokes in spite of their misfortune, was too much for me and I cried all that first day." . . .

. . . "Meanwhile, the Americans were fighting their first big action [the Aisne-Marne offensive], trying to turn back the German advance on Paris." . . .

> We heard that the fighting was intense and that a French general had ordered the Marines to retreat. . . . An American officer responded, "Retreat? Hell, no, we just got here." It was then that our troops snatched the initiative from the Germans at Chateau Thierry, and it was here that Evac 5 came into the picture. We set up our first mobile

Published in Lettie Gavin, *American Women in World War I: They Also Served* (Niwot, CO: University Press of Colorado, 1997), pp. 50–52. Reprinted by permission.

tent hospital near the ruins of a town on the River Marne, with a total of about forty nurses in our unit.

When the wounded began to come in, the stretchers were laid on the ground and the corpsmen stripped them of their muddy clothes and deloused them, usually before we received them in the operating tent. I can still hear the sound of a leg being sawed off and remember the boy who had one side of his face blown away, asking: "Do I look bad?"

We worked eight hours on and eight hours off, around the clock. By the time we got up and got into bed, it was more like six hours off in the twenty-four. The patients were given only necessary operations in our evacuation hospital, and then were sent back to the base hospitals as soon as they could be moved. It was a long way back to the base on a jolting train, but it was the first leg of their journey home for some. . . .

We nurses lived in tents. They were large, each one with room for twenty of us. Our lockers fit under each cot, with a box between our beds to keep our things. A cone-shaped stove called a Sibley [used during the U.S. Civil War] was in the middle of the tent. It took off some of the chill. A wooden floor kept us out of the mud, for it rained a lot and there were many tramping feet. We had to walk everywhere outside on slippery duckboards laid down over the muck.

The operating tents were covered with khaki blankets to keep the lights from showing at night, and we couldn't have any light showing in our own tents, which made it hard to find our way back and crawl into bed. One nurse used to make herself a cup of tea on her little alcohol lamp when she came off duty. She kept a small pail of water under her cot, also another pail in case she had to get up in the night. One late night we were awakened by her cussing—she had mistakenly used the wrong bucket for her tea.

For washing and bathing, when a big push was over, we used a basin and pitcher of hot water that we heated over a bonfire in a big can. The only real bath we had was when we were taken back to Rest and Rehabilitation.

. . . "One of the officers loaned me a suit, so I accomplished one ambition and incidentally, a bath. The bath was no small part of the swim, either. Do you know, you don't mind being dirty over here. It is quite the thing, and if you wash too much, you are considered odd." . . .

. . . "The trains were so slow you could get off at each village and go shopping," . . . "To pass the time, we sang all the popular songs of the time, 'Pack Up Your Troubles,' 'Long, Long Trail,' and our own twist to the lyrics to 'The Rose of No Man's Land'—'Mid the war's great curse, stands the Cross Red Nurse. She's the rose of no man's land.' " . . .

. . . "The Germans were getting desperate and using more and more mustard gas," . . .

Our casualties were 20 and 30 percent gassed. It caused huge blisters on the men, and they suffered painfully. . . . We became very fond of one of our patients, a young fellow with a bullet hole right in the middle of his forehead. We kept trying to get him to talk. All he could say was "glass," but he wasn't paralyzed. When he wanted something, we would keep asking him until we hit the right thing and he would nod his head. One day Margaret sang "Over There" to him and he followed along, saying all the words. That was a great day for us. When he was evacuated, we went to the train with him and sat by his litter until the train pulled out.

4. General John J. Pershing Insists on a Separate American Army in France, 1918

HS Secret File: Fldr. F-2: Record

Discussion of Proposed Operations

FIRST ARMY, A. E. F.,
Ligny-en-Barrois, August 30, 1918.

NOTES ON CONVERSATION BETWEEN GENERAL PERSHING AND MARSHAL FOCH AT LIGNY-EN-BARROIS

Present at the conversation were also General Weygand, Col. Boyd and Captain de Marenches.

Marshal Foch began the conversation by stating that the German Army is in complete disorder and that we must not allow them an opportunity to reorganize. He stated that the British propose to continue their attack in the direction of Cambrai and St-Quentin; that the French will continue their push in the vicinity of Mesnil. He then outlines the plan. . . .

General Pershing stated that another thought was that this arrangement would cause a separation of the American forces, leaving some Americans in the Woevre, then the French Second Army with some Americans on its left; then some French; then some Americans on the Aisne and then the French. That this destroys the thing we have been trying so long to form—that is, an American Army. . . .

. . . He stated that he did not want to appear difficult, but that the American people and the American Government expect that the American Army shall act as such and shall not be dispersed here and there along the Western Front. Each time that we are on the point of accomplishing this organization, some proposition is presented to break it up.

Marshal Foch asked very plainly: "Do you wish to take part in the battle?" (Voulez-vous aller à la battaille?)

General Pershing replied: "Most assuredly, but as an American Army."

Marshal Foch replied, that means it will take a month. . . .

The Marshal stated that there are many details to be considered in this connection; that the American Army would not be in a very fit plight if put altogether without any assistance from the French. . . .

Marshal Foch replied that it is now August 30; that we must start the battle on the 15th [of September]; that it is a question of time; that he is quite at General Pershing's disposition to listen to any proposition, but that we must act on September 15.

General Pershing stated that he is quite ready to take all the divisions we will not need here in the Woevre and send them to the west of the Argonne as an American Army; that all extra divisions should be put there; that he did not approve of putting American divisions in the French Second Army.

The Marshal replied that in that event the French have not enough divisions to attack. . . .

From "Notes on Conversation [about amalgamation] between General Pershing and Marshal Foch at Ligny-en-Barrois," August 30, 1918. Reprinted in Center of Military History, U.S. Army, *United States Army in the World War* (Washington, D.C.: GPO, 1990), VIII, 36, 38–40.

Marshal Foch then withdrew with General Weygand and completed the memorandum referred to in the beginning of this paper, which he then handed to General Pershing and asked him if he had any observations to make on it.

General Pershing replied that he had none except those he had already made. He stated that he had always depended on the Marshal to assist him in carrying out the organization of the American Army; that the American people, the American Government, Secretary of War and President, insisted that the American Army shall fight as such; that the Government, from the President down, and General Pershing himself have been criticized for parcelling out American troops here and there among the Allies; that the President had sent a message to the embassies stating that the American Army should fight as such and that the battle for us would be on the Western Front.

5. American Expeditionary Force (AEF) Combat Instructions Stress Open-Field Tactics, Not Trench Warfare, 1918

September 5, 1918.

1. The principles enunciated in Bulletin No. 30, May 23, 1918; Memorandum for Corps and Division Commanders, August 5, 1918, and Notes on Recent Operations, No. 1, August 7, 1918, are not yet receiving due application. Attack formations of platoons, companies, and battalions are everywhere too dense and follow too rigidly the illustrations contained in the Offensive Combat of Small Units. Waves are too close together; individuals therein have too little interval. Lines are frequently seen with the men almost elbow to elbow, and seldom with intervals greater than two or three paces. Columns, when used, are too long; in first line companies they should rarely have a greater depth than ten files. All formations are habitually lacking in elasticity; there is almost never any attempt to maneuver, that is, to throw supports and reserves to the flanks for envelopment. Scouts, if used, are frequently only a few yards in front of the leading waves, where the only purpose they can serve is to blanket or to receive the fire of the men behind them. Subordinate officers display little appreciation of the assumed situation and how best to meet its requirements. It is necessary, therefore, to repeat once more a few fundamental principles which must be impressed upon all concerned.

2. The essential difference between open and trench warfare, so far as effect upon formations is concerned, is characterized by the presence or absence of the rolling barrage ahead of the infantry. From a tactical point of view, the method of combat in trench warfare presents a marked contrast to that employed in open warfare, and the attempt by assaulting infantry to use trench warfare methods in an open warfare combat will be successful only at great cost. Trench warfare is marked by uniform formations, the regulation of space and time by higher command down to the smallest details, absence of scouts preceding the first wave, fixed distances and intervals between units and individuals, voluminous orders, careful rehearsal, little initiative upon the part of the individual soldier. Open war-

---

From AEF Document No. 1348, *Combat Instructions* GHQ, AEF, 5 September 1918, 3–5. Box 11, G-5 A.F. Documents, Records of the American Expeditionary Forces (World War I), RG 120, Military National Archives, Washington, D.C.

fare is marked by scouts who precede the first wave, irregularity of formations, comparatively little regulation of space and time by the higher command, the greatest possible use of the infantry's own fire power to enable it to get forward, variable distances and intervals between units and individuals, use of every form of cover and accident of the ground during the advance, brief orders, and the greatest possible use of individual initiative by all troops engaged in the action.

3. The following principles deal chiefly with warfare in the open. In a trench-to-trench attack, where a moving barrage is to be followed closely, uniform formations are generally expedient until the enemy's first line trenches have been entered. Thereafter, the principles outlined below should be applied.

4. *Scouts.* When closely following a moving barrage, there is seldom room for scouts. When the barrage has been lost or does not exist, as is ordinarily the case in the open field, scouts should precede the first line companies. They should deploy at wide and irregular intervals, 10 to 50 paces, to present a poor target to hostile machine guns. They should take every possible advantage of the ground to obtain cover, provided their advance is not thereby unduly delayed. Exposed ground should be crossed at a run. Their distance in front of the main bodies of their platoons should follow no set rule, but should constantly vary with the ground and with the anticipated position of the enemy. One moment they may be 500 meters ahead of their platoons, a few minutes later they may be absorbed therein. Their purpose is to compel the enemy machine guns to open fire and so disclose their location or be run over by the scouts. When the hostile machine guns have been located, the scouts should at once open fire.

5. *Platoons.* . . . . As soon as the scouts have located the machine gun, the rifle grenadiers assist the advance of everyone by heavy fire from suitable positions behind the first line. The ability of the platoon leader is displayed by prompt reconnaissance of the ground, by a rapid estimate of what it offers toward facilitating the advance of his men, and by immediate decision upon a simple plan for the use of his combined weapons and of the ground to enable him to close with the enemy. His plan should habitually include pinning the enemy to the ground by frontal and flanking fire, under cover of which some portions of the platoon, usually those sent against the hostile flanks, can close by short rushes with the enemy. The training and discipline of the platoon are shown by the skill with which the men carry out the plan of the leader. A platoon should by itself be able to capture one, or even a pair, of hostile machine guns.

6. Theodore Jones, an AEF Artilleryman, Recounts His First Exposure to Combat, 1918

We have to dig our gun pits about 1000 yards in the rear of the infantry front lines and are in the depths of the wood. We have pitched shelter tents quite some distance

Theodore Jones, Diary excerpts, September 1918, from an EAF artilleryman in France, Theodore K. Jones Papers, Box 1, Acc. No. 69–250, Georgia State Archives, Atlanta, GA (original document for this collection). Typed transcription, excerpts from pages 110–113, 120, 123–124.

in the rear of our new positions right in the thich of the wood. There are numbers of rustic houses built by the French troops who have held this position since the beginning of the war. Of course our bunch was not lucky enough to get one as they were mostly used by the infantry, but as the ground was nice and soft we did not mind it very much. Our daily program is that every morning we start out from our tents to the new gun pits and stay there all day and work at digging our trail holes and getting the guns in position to fire when the orders are given. . . .

One of the experiences that sticks out with the most prominence is that one of hearing my first shell exploding near us and knowing it was intended for us. Could hear it coming through the air and thought sure that it had me but it broke about a hundred yards away in the deep woods. The whistling of the shell as it approached before it struck sounded like an express train approaching at top speed and then the tremendous explosion throwing branches into the air, for it had struck a tree. Later we got to judge nearly the exact place that it would explode but it was some time before this was realized. At first the natural tendancy is to bend forward but later you overcome this to a certain degree but still there is a natural inclination to bend the head forward. . . .

All the time we were in this position Hun aeroplanes flew over us and we used to watch them through the camaflage and hope they did not spot us. One day saw a German aeroplane brought down by one of our planes. We all stopped work and watched the battle. The German was ringed about with black puffs of exploding anti aircraft shells and glistened like a star in the suns rays. The American plan[e] flew right in back of it and we could hear the faint putput of its machine guns in action. Finally when it was quite some distance away, the German plan did a nose dive and burst into flames. No doubt a shell hit the gas tank. . . .

On the morning of September 12th, at 1:15 a.m. we opened our first barage on the enemy and believe me it was a wonder. I never knew that there were so many guns in the whole world as were in our hearing, and all going at the same time. My gun fired an enormous amount of shells for the empty cassings made an awful heap in the rear of the gun where they had been thrown by the crew. Some of us stripped to our waists as the rate of fire at first was two or three shells to the minute and consisted of three high expl[o]ding shells to one gas shell.

We had been receiving shells for the past week every night and what with our digging all day and unloading shells at night our time was well taken up. The rate that we sent over the barrage was not the rate of speed that we were supposed to fire but we became excited and gave the Germans all that we could send. I am sure that we gave more gas shells than were ordered for we all wanted our boys when they went over the top to have as little opposition as possible, and from all that I hear they didnt have hardly any at all.

We were firing on and off till noon that day and all that we had to eat was coffee and some bread that we took in between the different times we were at the guns. Talk about tired when it was over, we were all in.

I never knew that the French had a lot of guns right near us and they were also going at full blast all the time that we were firing. Talk about the fourth of July selebrations. It was a picknick in comparison to the noise that we all made. The flares lit the entire sky line and the shells flying through the air sounded like ceaseless taps of drums. The whole sky was lit with the flashes of the shells exploding and the roars of all the guns mixed with the explosions made us all deaf for some time. You couldnt tell which way the shells were going and we were all so busy we never had time to think that perhaps some of the noise was the sound of the Germans sending shells at us. . . .

When we finally did halt the battery devided with the guns and cassions [caissons] going forward and the wagons going to the rear. We then moved forward and after a little ride on the road turned off and into the fields. It was getting dark by now and we did not enjoy the trip at all with the darkness and not knowing where we were going. Here accured [occured] my first close experience with dead men and this is how it accured. We had made frequent stops to allow the officers to find out where we were and at the halts we had all fallen out to rest. I saw a nice log in the darkness and had made my way to sit on it and rest. Imagine my surprise to find the log to be soft and on putting my hand down to investigate I found that my hand touched a cold and clammy dead mans face. I did not sit on the log for long as you can imagine when I found out what it was. . . .

October V. Woke up at 5, finished digging in and prepaired to fire. The barrage started at little after 5 oclock, just at break at day. It was a slow barrage but kept us busy enough for the few minutes we were firing and took our mind off our surroundings which was a good thing. The fields surrounding the brush where we were situated was literly covered with dead Americans and Germans. The brush was the only cover to be seen and the bare hills stretched back for about a mile. It was rolling country and the poor infantry had had to advance in the face of terrible machine gun fire from the brush where we were now located. Most of the men near us were from the 23 Infantry and must have lost an awful slew of men.

We were firing on and off till 1 oclock and by this I mean that we would no longer get our guns cleaned up than the orders would come back to begin again. During a pause in the firing and as soon as we got chance we buried a dead American that was in the same place where the gun was located and interfered with the placing and pointing of the gun. He was lying with his face towards the brush and with his hands outstretched in front of him. Right across his chest and on his outstretched left arm were the wounds of at least eight machine gun bullets and on his right arm was a luminus wrist watch. This watch gleamed at us all the night previous. We only had time to dig a small hole to put him in and stood a rifle at its head with his "dog tag" on for the berrial squad to identify the remains. . . .

Oct. 8. Drizzling all the night and also today. Not very good chow, so we are getting a touch of real warfare. Fired a barrage for the infantry from 6 oclock untill 9. We did not fire very fast, only about two shots per minute on and off till 9. The coffee which we are getting tasted good when you are all cold and damp. It was still dark when we started the barrage at 6 oclock and the rain didnt help any.

As soon as we had stopped firing we had to bail out our gun pit as the rain all night had filled it nearly to the brim and the man who puts the shells in the gun had had to stand in the cold water over his shoe tops. The spad of the gun had sunk out of sight and when ever we fired the gun the recoil of the gun had shot the water into the air and we were all covered with mud and water. The mud around the gun is also terrible as the constant tramping of a number of men over the soft ground had made the mud deep all over everywhere.

7. General George Marshall Describes
Some Inadequacies of the AEF (1918), 1930

To General John J. Pershing   October 24, 1930
                                                              Fort Benning, Georgia

Dear General, . . .

Certain things about the A.E.F. I think are open to stricture, yet have never been touched upon. All I have in mind were directly incident to the hard driving tactics which won the war—therefore excusable. But I think it well to have them in mind so that your treatment of the period or events connected with them may be handled accordingly.

The most severe criticism I could launch pertains to the opening of the Meuse-Argonne battle. We refer to it as our greatest and one of the greatest battles in history, determining in winning the war. We point to the great strength of the German position, describe your offer to undertake this most difficult task with fresh young American troops. We dwell on the fact that we had to make the opening fight with but partially trained, and in some instances, wholly inexperienced divisions.

Yet, knowing all this, the staffs of these inexperienced divisions were absolutely scalped a *few* days before the assault, in several cases I believe the day before—*in order that the next class at Langres might start on scheduled time.* The amount of confusion and mismanagement resulting from this was tremendous. A delay of ten days at Langres would have permitted the machine to get well under way—even a week would have helped immeasurably. Students and instructors were demanded and secured.

I always thought General Fox Conner, Hugh Drum and General Nolan should had [sic] determinedly opposed General Fisk at this moment, particularly Conner and Nolan. I always thought General McAndrew should have represented the matter to you in strong terms.

No one has ever leveled this criticism at the A.E.F. control, and I have never breathed it to any one. But I think it could be made, especially, by some of the divisions that were seriously mismanaged.

It is rather odd to send you two such contrasting papers as this and the attached memorandum. But I wanted you to be on your guard.

Possibly, probably you do not agree with me in this matter. But I would hate to have some one, with hostile intent, seize upon it.

I hope you can arrange to send me the manuscript. I will go over it immediately on its receipt, and give you my frankest reaction. Affectionately yours,

G. C. Marshall, Jr.

George C. Marshall to John J. Pershing, October 24, 1930, reprinted in Larry I. Bland, ed., *The Papers of George Catlett Marshall*, vol. 1, *"The Soldierly Spirit" December 1880–June 1939* (Baltimore: The Johns Hopkins University Press, 1981), pp. 360–361. Reprinted by permission of the publisher.

▲ E S S A Y S

Reflecting two different perspectives on General Pershing's insistence on an independent U.S. Army rather than amalgamating American detachments into veteran Allied units, the late Donald Smythe of John Carroll University in Cleveland and author of a sympathetic biography of Pershing, argued in 1976 that Pershing made the right choice; while David F. Trask, former chief historian of the U.S. Army, in a 1993 volume on the AEF and coalition warfare, chastises Pershing as a flawed commander and faults his decisions for leading to increased American casualties and to the lack of a decisive U.S. military victory over the German Army.

The Wisdom of a Separate American Army

DONALD SMYTHE

There was much to be said for the idea [of amalgamation]. The Allies had the existing staffs of divisions, corps and field armies; they lacked men to fill them. America had the men, but lacked the higher organisations. By the time she created them the war could well be lost under the impact of the massive German assaults expected for the spring and summer of 1918.

As far as the Allies were concerned, amalgamation—at least temporarily—made sense, even from the viewpoint of America. Raw recruits would train better and faster if associated with veterans; consequently American casualties would be lower. Amalgamation would also eliminate the need to develop AEF higher staffs; hence America's weight could more quickly be brought to bear and the war could be ended sooner, which was to America's interest. Finally, amalgamation would relieve the tonnage problem, since it would not be necessary for America to bring over the support troops and impedimenta to sustain full divisions, corps and armies.

Always, in treating of amalgamation, the Allies spoke of an *eventual* American army. Only for the moment, only *pro tem,* would smaller units be trained and fought in larger Allied units. Later, after they were "bloodied" and proficient, American regiments would be gathered into their own divisions, American divisions into their own corps, and American corps into their own army. The advantage of this was that it was organic; it permitted the development of larger American units after they had grown to proficiency as smaller ones. In the meantime they would have the benefit of Allied tutelage and experience. How much better this would be, they contended, than to commit a whole American army, virtually untried and untested, to a separate portion of the front. The Germans would surely tear it apart.

These were good arguments, irrefutable in the eyes of the Allies. Even so staunch a Pershing partisan as James G. Harbord, his Chief of Staff, admitted that were he French or English, "my views on amalgamation would have been the same as theirs."

Donald Smythe, "General of the Armies John J. Pershing" in *The War Lords: Military Commanders of the Twentieth Century* (George Weidenfeld and Nicolson Ltd., 1976). Reprinted by permission of the publisher.

Pershing himself admitted that had massive German offensives occurred during the fall and winter of 1917, instead of during the following spring and summer, he would have had no choice but to accede to amalgamation. But he was always suspicious of Allied talk about a separate and independent American army in the future, while clamouring for immediate amalgamation in the present. Such talk he considered so much "camouflage," a "downright piece of impudence." He observed that with rare exceptions the British had never thought to amalgamate Australians, Canadians or Indians into British units, nor had the French attempted it with their Senegalese, Moroccans or other colonials.

The Allies might point out however that the Canadians and Australians had had time—three years of war—to develop their organisations organically. Furthermore, in their formation and development, they had not been confronted with the crisis that loomed up now on the western front: a projected 60 per cent manpower disadvantage during the coming German offensives.

Accordingly in December the Allies began strong attempts to amalgamate American units, becoming increasingly persistent throughout the ensuing months. British or American ships would bring over surplus American companies or battalions for temporary incorporation into Allied units, with the understanding that when the emergency was over they could be recalled for American divisions. As surplus troops, they contended, their temporary incorporation would not interfere with American plans for forming a separate army. Lloyd George, the British Prime Minister, warned Washington in mid-December that the Germans were planning "a knock-out blow to the Allies before a fully trained American Army is fit. . . ."

Alarmed, President Wilson talked the matter over with Secretary of War Newton D. Baker and instructed him to cable Pershing as follows on 24 December: "We do not desire loss of identity of our forces *but regard that as secondary* to the meeting of any critical situation by the most helpful use possible of the troops at your command." This was Pershing's basic position also, although Lloyd George, frustrated in dealing with him, came to believe that the general preferred building a separate American army to winning the war.

The crucial phrase in Baker's cablegram was "critical situation." How critical must a situation be, and who was to decide? The answer was: Pershing, to whom Baker's cablegram gave "full authority to use the forces at your command as you deem wise. . . '."

In effect then the United States placed in the hands of its field commander the ultimate decision as to whether to amalgamate, and if so, under what circumstances. The effect was to focus and bring to bear enormous pressures on Pershing, the Allies knowing that if he could be persuaded, cajoled, intimidated, or in some manner won over, the deed was done. Washington, feeling that Pershing was on the spot and knew the situation firsthand, would concur in his decision.

With the exception of Lord Northcliffe, a newspaper publisher, and Marshal Joffre, a sidelined general, the Europeans presented a united front against Pershing on this question. Prime ministers, chiefs of staff, army commanders, ambassadors—all made their pressure felt during the ensuing months, attempting to wear him down.

Pershing resisted them all. If American troops went into Allied ranks, "very few of them would ever come out," he predicted. Furthermore, "no people with a grain of national pride would consent to furnish men to build up the army of another nation." His basic stand, held unswervingly throughout the coming months, was summed up in the declaration: "We cannot permit our men to serve under another flag except in an extreme emergency and then only temporarily."

He ran a great risk, for the Allies might well be right. Nobody maintained that the Americans were incapable, given time, of providing skilled leaders and staffs. But time was what was lacking. An inexperienced, untrained American army was a gamble and if the Germans tore it apart, as they were to do experienced Allied armies in the coming months, the results could be disaster. Harbord well said of Pershing: "He risked the chance of being cursed to the latest generation if, through his failure to co-operate, the War were lost."

Replying to Baker's message of 24 December, putting authority into his hands, Pershing cabled on 1 January 1918: "Do not think emergency now exists that would warrant our putting companies or battalions into British or French divisions, and would not do so except in grave crisis." This was his basic position, maintained steadfastly in the months to come.

His objections were the loss of national identity, the problem of reclaiming contingents without disrupting Allied divisions, language difficulties with the French, hard feelings if American casualties resulted from Allied mistakes, and differences in training methods. Specifically Pershing objected to the Allied emphasis on training for trench rather than open warfare.

Trench warfare was as the name implies: static, subterranean, oriented toward the taking and holding of trenches. In an attack the artillery laid down a tremendous barrage on the enemy's trenches, caving them in, destroying barbed wire, and disrupting communications. At a signal the infantry crossed no-man's-land, captured the enemy's front trenches, then repeated the process for as long as momentum lasted, after which they burrowed into the ground like moles, fortifying the trenches captured. It was frontal assault warfare, of limited objectives, and it had not moved the lines more than about 10 miles in either direction since late 1914. It had also heaped up casualties by the millions.

In contrast open warfare was fluid. Open-ended, flexible, oriented to the earth's surface rather than its bowels, it inclined to go around strongpoints rather than into them. Infantrymen hugged the ground, as they must always do, but only temporarily until, momentum regained, the lines swept forward again, probing, enfilading, encircling, cutting off defenders from the side and rear. It was this type of warfare for which Pershing felt Americans had a special genius and in which he desired them trained, especially in America where vast spaces permitted sweeping movements. With men trained to fight *on* the earth rather than within it, he hoped to break open the front and win the war. Victory could be won, he maintained, only "by driving the enemy out into the open and engaging him in war of movement."

To Pershing's dismay French instructors sent to America to aid in training taught not open warfare but trench warfare—probably not surprising, as it was the only warfare they knew. At Waco, Texas, after a month of instruction devoted exclusively to trench warfare, an American asked one of the French instructors, "How shall we know what to do if we should ever have the Germans on the run?"

"This war will be fought out in the trenches," was the reply; "in this respect, it has been different, and will be different, from all previous wars."

This was typical. An American assigned to translate French training documents said that he "never once saw any mention of open warfare."

Pershing felt he was being undercut in the United States by French instructors and by a complacent War Department which deferred to their experience. He asked repeatedly that training in open warfare be the principal instruction given before embarkation.

The dispute over training methods was epitomised in the rifle. In trench warfare it was not that important, since artillery did the preliminary work, while grenades and satchel charges did the mopping up. Pershing actually heard of cases where Allied soldiers were so habituated to using grenades that encountering the enemy in the open they instinctively threw grenades at them, rather than shot.

In open warfare however the rifle would be the weapon *par excellence,* as the infantrymen moved forward, hugged the ground, isolated strongpoints, and killed at a distance. Significantly French target ranges were short, under 100 metres. Pershing insisted that Americans be trained to shoot up to at least 600 metres.

To him the rifle was the essential infantry weapon and he complained repeatedly that it was not sufficiently stressed in training at home. A flow of "teach them to shoot straight" cables went to the War Department, followed by complaints that they were not being complied with.

For their part the French regarded the Americans as a people who had not fired a shot in anger until October 1917 and who surely were foolish if they did not follow French practice, based as it was on three years of hard-fought combat. "If the Americans do not permit the French to teach them," said Clemenceau ruefully, "the Germans will do so. . . ."

[The dispute over the independence or amalgamation of the American Army in France continued well into 1918. In the end, it was not Allied pressure, but events themselves which determined the fate of a separate American army. As long as the Germans were pushing the Allies back, U.S. forces would have to be sent piecemeal into the lines to help stave off defeat, but if Allies blocked the German offensives, French General Ferdinand Foch, the overall commander, could build up reserves for an Allied counteroffensive, and this would mean a separate U.S. Army.]

[T]he German offensive was grinding to a halt, in part because of an heroic stand made by the US 2nd Division, which planted itself across the Paris Highway, blocking further advance. Looking back on the event, American writers have tended to make much of the 2nd's gallant stand, and rightly so, but its importance must not be overestimated. In its sixth day when the 2nd Division deployed, the German offensive had in many ways "shot its bolt." All First World War offensives tended to peter out after a week because of difficulties of getting men and matériel forward across devastated terrain in sufficient quantities and speed to keep the offensive moving. Then too the French, while giving way at the centre, had held firm at the shoulders of the salient, at Rheims on the right and west of Soissons on the left. Holding at the shoulders necessarily limited advance in the centre and would eventually make the salient very vulnerable.

None the less frequently in life it is not what the situation actually is that is important, but what it seems to be. French troops, fleeing the Germans, cried "*La guerre finie"* to advancing Americans as they passed. The fact remains, as Harbord later pointed out, that when the 2nd Division went into line on the afternoon of 1 June on both sides of the Paris-Metz highway, "the French had been retiring along the whole Rheims-Soissons front from one to ten miles a day for five days. No unit along the whole front had stood against the German masses. The first unit to stand was the Second Division and it not only stood but went forward."

The advance began on 6 June. "Come on, you sons of bitches," yelled Sergeant Dan Daly, "Do you want to live forever?" Apparently some 1,087 of them did not, for the Marine Brigade of the 2nd Division suffered the most casualties that day in its history, not to be exceeded until bloody Tarawa twenty-five years later.

The next nineteen days around Belleau Wood were pure hell. Long, almost unbroken lines of ambulances headed back along the Paris road, carrying men racked by disease, diarrhoea, thirst, exhaustion, weather, wounds and gas. The gas casualties were particularly pitiable; many were delirious, nearly all were blind, crying, moaning and thrashing about.

The struggle for Belleau Wood was neither strategical nor tactical, but psychological. General Böhm, commanding one of the German divisions opposite the Americans, pinpointed the issue: "It is not a question of the possession or nonpossession of this or that village or woods, insignificant in itself; it is a question whether the Anglo-American claim that the American Army is equal or even the superior of the German Army is to be made good."

It was a test of wills. Even Ludendorff recognised the consequences when on 8 June he ordered that any American units encountered "should be hit particularly hard in order to render difficult the formation of an American Army."

The Germans did their best, but on 25 June, after an all-day artillery barrage, the Americans drove into Belleau Wood and came out the other side. "Woods now U.S. Marine Corps entirely," read the message to headquarters. The cost was some 5200 casualties, over 50 per cent of the Marine Brigade of the 2nd Division.

Meanwhile American troops began pouring into Europe, more than 300,000 in July, helping to convert a 324,000 Allied rifleman deficiency in March to a 627,000 superiority in November. On 18 July the US 1st and 2nd divisions, together with the Moroccans, spearheaded the Allied attack on the Château-Thierry salient, while some 300,000 other American troops participated in the difficult follow-up drive there in late July and August. On 12 September the American First Army, operational since 10 August and deploying 550,000 men, overwhelmed the vulnerable St Mihiel salient just as the Germans were getting ready to withdraw from it. Two weeks later, on 26 September, it launched a difficult assault on the Meuse-Argonne front, commencing a bitter forty-seven-day battle involving 1,200,000 men, which was only intermittently successful. Finally, on 1 November, it achieved a breakthrough. Ten days later hostilities ceased.

Pershing felt the armistice was a mistake.

We shouldn't have done it [he commented shortly afterwards]. If they had given us another ten days we could have rounded up the entire German army, captured it, humiliated it. . . . The German troops today are marching back into Germany announcing that they have never been defeated . . . What I dread is that Germany doesn't know that she was licked. Had they given us another week, we'd have *taught* them.

He was correct about the German attitude. On Armistice Day General von Einem, commander of the German Third Army, told his troops, "Firing has ceased. Undefeated . . . you are terminating the war in enemy country." A decade later Adolf Hitler was preaching the same error.

A few days after the armistice Pershing encountered Clemenceau, with whom he had contended furiously over the amalgamation issue. "We fell into each other's arms, choked up and had to wipe our eyes," he wrote in the very last sentence of his memoirs. "We had no differences to discuss that day."

Commented Harbord: "The armistice thus ended two wars for us—the one with our friends, the other with our enemies."

After the war Pershing served as Chief of Staff from 1921 to 1924, when he retired. His later years were devoted to work as chairman of the American Battle Monuments Commission, which supervised American memorials and cemeteries in Europe, and to his memoirs, *My Experiences in the World War,* which were published in 1931 and won a Pulitzer prize. He died in Walter Reed Hospital in Washington on 15 July 1948.

How to evaluate Pershing?

A careful rather than brilliant or great commander, he worked hard in planning an army on a scale sufficient to tip the balance. Captain B. H. Liddell Hart, an Englishman whom Pershing thought prejudiced against him, wrote in *Reputations Ten Years After:* "There was perhaps no other man who would or could have built the structure of the American army on the scale he planned. And without that army the war could hardly have been saved and could not have been won."

In the amalgamation controversy he took great risks. A man who throughout life had stressed preparedness and the fact that in modern war one could not improvise overnight, he none the less seemed impervious to Allied arguments concerning the need for priority shipments of infantry and machine-gun units in the face of expected German attacks during the spring and summer of 1918. As Pershing admitted he was willing to take the risk of the British being pushed into the sea and the French driven back beyond the Loire. History has been kind to him, in that he ran the risk successfully. But he was like a man playing Russian roulette. He lived through it, but he was lucky he did not blow his head off.

On the other hand, even conceding that he might at times have been unnecessarily obstinate and failed to see the gravity of successive crises, he none the less guessed correctly in estimating that they were not as severe as the Allies represented them and that the Germans would not in fact break through and win the war before an American army could be trained and fielded. He may have been saved by luck from being "cursed to the latest generation," but the fact is that he guessed correctly. The Allies did not need as many priority shipments of American infantry and machine-gun units as they said they did.

In the controversy about rifle training for open warfare he was on less sure ground. Frederick Palmer, who liked Pershing and wrote his biography, said later:

> On Salisbury field and at Aldershot in 1914, I heard the same talk about the value of the rifle that I heard later in our training camps in Lorraine; and I saw it put in practice not only by the Canadians, who are our neighbors in western individualism and frontier

marksmanship, and by the Australians, but by the British themselves, without being able to go through the trench line to open warfare.

Harvey A. DeWeerd, an American military writer, felt that the secret of advancing against multiple defensive lines lay not in rifle markmanship, but in a combination of artillery, tanks and innovative infiltration methods, such as the Germans had used at Riga and at Caporetto.

For all Pershing's talk about the advantage of open warfare training and his indictment of the Allies for their defensive mentality and stress on trench warfare, the fact remains that during the last five months of the war, when the Germans were gradually pushed back all along the front, the British advanced farther and faster than the Americans. In addition they captured three times as many prisoners.

Confronted with this fact the AEF staff would later argue that the Americans were pushing against the most sensitive part of the German line, the pivot that the enemy had to hold lest we cut vital rail communications to his armies in the northwest, compelling him to withdraw all along the line. There is something to be said for this, which is why the argument still goes on.

None the less Liddell Hart was probably right when he said of Pershing's stress on the rifle, open warfare and the offensive: "He thought that he was spreading a new gospel of faith when actually it was an old faith exploded . . . He omitted but one factor from his calculations—German machine guns—and was right in all his calculations but one—their effect."

The key weapon in the First World War was not the rifle, but the machine gun, which killed many, and artillery, which killed more. Against them the American infantryman pitted raw courage, enthusiasm, inexperience, guts, some support from his own auxiliary arms, and his own blood. "The A.E.F. learned to fight through bitter experience," said DeWeerd, "not through any legerdemain with the rifle."

In America's greatest battle, the Meuse-Argonne, it is questionable how much the AEF engaged in open warfare. Day after day the First Army butted its head against stubborn German resistance, inching its way ahead from 26 September to 1 November until, under Hunter Liggett, who had replaced Pershing as First Army commander, it finally achieved a breakthrough. In truth it might be argued that the war was eventually won, not by the introduction of any tactic like open warfare, but simply by attrition, by the fact that one side became exhausted before the other. At the armistice the Germans had not one division left in reserve; every one was in line. They had simply run out of men and matériel. Had they not, the war might still have gone on, with Pershing, like Nivelle, removed from command for ordering foolhardy assaults entirely incommensurate with the ground gained.

A Separate American Army Impeded a Decisive Blow

DAVID F. TRASK

Leading histories of the American Expeditionary Forces (AEF), like those of Edward Coffman and Harvey DeWeerd written a generation ago, reflect the views of

David F. Trask, *The AEF and Coalition Warmaking, 1917–1918* (Lawrence: University Press of Kansas, 1993), pp. 1–2, 168–177. Reprinted by permission of the University Press of Kansas.

Gen. John J. Pershing as expressed in his final report of 1919 and his memoirs of 1931. According to its commander, the operations of the AEF decided the First World War. It assured victory to the Allied and Associated Powers after both belligerent coalitions had endured over four years of the most terrible sacrifices. The task was difficult because of a bumbling War Department at home and perverse interference from the Allies abroad, who opposed independent American operations, but the superior qualities of the AEF overcame all obstacles.

Pershing's account did not give sufficient attention to certain developments during 1917–1918 that greatly affected the operations of the AEF. The unpreparedness of the United States ensured that its army could not fight independently at full efficiency until 1919 or 1920, two or three years after the intervention of April 1917, but an unexpected crisis during 1918 forced premature commitment of the AEF. In March, the German High Command dominated by First Quartermaster General Erich Ludendorff, deeply alarmed because of the imminent appearance of the AEF in France, launched a powerful offensive on the western front. It was designed to end the war before General Pershing could affect the outcome. The German push, which continued until the middle of July, forced Pershing to permit the employment of some of his divisions on the western front under French or British command. They served mostly as replacements for Allied divisions in quiet sectors. Some American divisions were drawn into battle. When Ferdinand Foch, the French generalissimo of the Allied and Associated Powers, stemmed the German surge and regained the initiative, he launched powerful counteroffensives. Foch's projects of July and after forced Pershing to undertake operations, this time on a large scale, before the AEF was fully prepared to fight on its own in France.

How well did the Americans fight, and how much did they contribute to the victory of November 1918? Full consideration of two influences, the prolonged American mobilization and the great 1918 battle, suggests an evaluation of the AEF that differs from that of Pershing and historians who have accepted his views. . . .

In one fundamental respect President Wilson's strategy diverged from the wishes of the Allies. He decided that the United States would mobilize an independent army that would fight under its own flag and in its own sector of the western front, according to its own doctrine, with its own commanders, staffs, and services of supply. When in position, the independent American army would strike a decisive blow, giving Woodrow Wilson the leverage needed to dictate the terms of peace. The United States rejected the alternative urged by the Allies, which was to deploy troops to Europe organized in divisions or even smaller organizations for service in the French and British armies. This scheme, which became known as "amalgamation," would bring American fighting power to bear on the western front in a short time because it would be unnecessary to train higher-level commanders, to provide support troops, and to build logistical facilities.

The decision to field an independent army, a consequence mainly of political considerations, meant postponement of full-scale American operations until 1919 at the earliest, since it would take at least two years to mobilize a large army that could deal with the German army. General Pershing was sent overseas to create the American Expeditionary Forces and mould them into a powerful army. He enjoyed unusually strong support from his civilian superiors, who gave him the time and freedom of action needed to complete his task.

The decision to form an independent army entailed substantial risk because the Central Powers might prevail before the United States could influence the outcome, but neither the War Department nor the president gave serious thought to any other course. Various considerations influenced this decision. Amalgamation would prove enormously unpopular among the American people; the army itself would object for reasons of pride; technical difficulties would arise given organizational, doctrinal, and other types of asymmetry between American and European practice; and above all, an independent army that forced victory would ensure Wilson's domination of the postwar peace negotiations.

Despite the strenuous efforts of the War Department and the commander of the AEF, only a few American divisions arrived in France by January 1918. None were ready for combat, a cause of great concern because the war had gone badly for the Allied and Associated Powers in 1917, and prospects were dim for 1918. The helter-skelter American mobilization necessarily produced considerable confusion and delay, enough to stimulate a serious congressional inquiry. Fortunately the home government attained much improved efficiency by the summer of 1918. There was, to be sure, one important inter-Allied achievement in 1917. Germany's attempt to gain victory at sea was frustrated, although the U-boats sank millions of tons of merchant shipping, because the adoption of the convoy system kept losses within manageable limits. On land the Central Powers defended themselves well, rebuffing powerful offensives launched by the French, the British, and the Russians. Besides, they won two great victories: Russia was knocked out of the war, and Italy almost collapsed after a catastrophic defeat at Caporetto. Germany's triumph on the eastern front released many experienced divisions for service in the west. The maritime strategy having failed in 1917, the German High Command composed of Field Marshal Hindenburg and First Quartermaster General Ludendorff decided to stake everything on a great land offensive in 1918. They intended to destroy the British and French armies on the western front before the United States could dispatch sufficient reinforcements to decide the outcome.

Germany's purpose, which became apparent late in 1917, stimulated various responses on the Allied side. The necessity for improved inter-Allied cooperation forced the Allied and Associated Powers to form a Supreme War Council and several other coordinating agencies to make the most of their remaining resources. Also, the Allies revived proposals for the amalgamation of American troops into their armies to cope with the expected German offensive. General Pershing, who continued to receive firm support from his government, strongly resisted this course. He was prepared to permit temporary service by American divisions in quiet sectors of the French and British fronts primarily for training. He viewed this measure as a part of the process by which he would create an independent force to conduct separate operations at the earliest possible time. Pershing opposed combat service by American divisions under British and French commanders not only because of his divergent views on training and doctrine but because he believed that, if committed to battle, his troops would be so weakened that they would become unfit for service in an independent American army. He relaxed his resistance only to obtain British shipping needed to transport American divisions to Europe. In return he condoned severely limited forms of temporary amalgamation.

Unfortunately for Pershing and his troops, the German offensive, which began late in March 1918, severely disrupted plans to field an independent army. Ludendorff directed five powerful strikes against the British and French armies and created a desperate emergency, retaining the initiative until July. In March and April, British forces on the Somme River in Picardy and the Lys River in Flanders endured a terrible beating, and the French suffered similarly during offensives in May and June against the Chemin des Dames ridge and the line between Montdidier and Noyon. Pershing was forced to condone temporary amalgamation of some American divisions not only for training but for combat. He was also compelled to accept Allied proposals that the United States send to France only combat soldiers, infantrymen, and machine gunners, in return for needed shipping. This expedient delayed the arrival of supporting elements such as artillery and engineers. The Allies promised to make up these deficiencies from their resources, and they did so during the concluding months of combat.

On 15 July, Ludendorff launched the last of his offensives, but it was quickly contained, and the Allied generalissimo, Ferdinand Foch, immediately recaptured the initiative. During July, August, and September, he conducted a series of limited counteroffensives against the salients that the Germans had driven into the Allied lines. These attacks were intended to restore the elan of his troops, improve rail communications, consume the German reserves, and secure positions from which to launch a general offensive. Offensive operations became possible because, by July, American troops had arrived in sufficient numbers to give Foch a narrow but constantly growing superiority in manpower. The German command committed most of its available reserves between March and July, and those remaining were soon sacrificed in efforts to defend against Foch's limited counteroffensives.

Foch organized a French counterattack on the Marne during July, a British offensive on the Somme River in August, and operations on the German flanks in Belgium and Lorraine during September. He hoped to prevent Ludendorff from shifting troops to threatened points. Petain attacked on 18 July between the Aisne and the Marne and reached the Vesle River by 6 August. On 8 August, Haig inflicted a devastating defeat on the Germans at Amiens, the most impressive of the limited offensives, which led to German discussions about ending the war. Anticipating an Allied attack in Flanders, Ludendorff decided to refuse battle there, withdrawing eastward and shortening the front to conserve his dwindling manpower.

Meanwhile General Pershing finally forced Foch to allow the formation of the initial independent American force, the First Army. It was assigned as its first task the last limited counteroffensive, reduction of the St. Mihiel salient in Lorraine. Ever since his early months in France, Pershing had planned independent operations in Lorraine, which was at the right of the active western front. He built up his services of supply with operations in this sector in mind. Hoping to strike a decisive blow intended to win the war, he proposed to drive toward Metz and interdict the lateral railway that supplied the bulk of the German army located to the west. This achievement would force the German army to withdraw from the occupied territories and would move the struggle across the German border. Pershing envisioned as the first step in this operational design the reduction of the St. Mihiel salient, which had been created in 1914 and had long been a quiet sector. At the last minute Foch decided that Pershing should undertake as his main effort an attack with the French Fourth Army northward from positions west of the Meuse River toward Mezieres, another location on the lateral railroad. This thrust would be one pincer of a mighty converging attack on Ludendorff's depleted forces that Foch wished to make late in September.

When the commander of the German Composite Army C, which held the St. Mihiel salient, realized that an American attack was imminent, he ordered his forces to withdraw to the Michel Stellung, a line of fortifications at the base of the salient. This movement was only in its initial stages when, on 12 September, the First Army attacked in overwhelming force. Pershing's blow confused the German withdrawal and also accelerated it. The First Army captured only about 16,000 prisoners, not having cut off most of the retreating enemy because of inexperience, but it was a solid victory that improved Allied morale. Pershing gained control of the railroad between Nancy and the west and eliminated a threat to the rear of the Allied forces operating west of the Meuse.

Foch then prepared a general inter-Allied offensive, hoping to expel the German army from France and Belgium and to seize good positions from which to force a decision in 1919. He chose to attack both faces of the huge salient that had been driven into France and Belgium, aiming to interdict a section of the lateral railroad that ran behind the German lines between Lille and Strasbourg. Haig's troops would attack the west face of the salient in the direction of Cambrai and Maubeuge, seeking to cut the railroad at Aulnoye. Simultaneously a Franco-American force would launch another powerful attack against the south face of the salient aimed at Mezieres. Two other attacks would prevent Ludendorff from maneuvering his reserves to block the move against the Aulnoye-Mezieres region. One of these would come in Belgium on the line of the Lys River where the Group of Armies of Flanders commanded by Albert, king of the Belgians, would move on Ghent. The French in the center of the Allied lines would advance toward Laon against the nose of the salient.

The American First Army was assigned the task of penetrating a strong section of the Hindenburg line, the Kriemhilde Stellung, located between the Meuse River and the Argonne forest, while west of the Argonne the French Fourth Army advanced against the line of the Aisne toward Mezieres. Pershing was forced to move his divisions into line in the short space of ten days. Initially he had to rely almost entirely on inexperienced troops, having committed his veterans at St. Mihiel. Pershing drew heavily on the French and British armies for artillery, aircraft, armor, and many types of support troops. His operational plans prescribed a quick penetration of three distinct German bastions located in difficult terrain, including the Kriemhilde Stellung, during the first two days of battle. He depended on surprise and spirit to break through before German reinforcements appeared in strength.

On 26 September, the First Army with nine divisions in the front line attacked between the Meuse River and the Argonne forest, only to encounter stubborn resistance from five weak enemy divisions. Well-sited machine-gun and artillery positions on high ground repulsed the American frontal attacks short of the Kriemhilde Stellung. The French Fourth Army west of the Argonne forest also advanced slowly. Neither the French nor the Americans moved more than a few miles toward

Mezieres during the initial phases of Foch's great converging operation. Again, American inexperience contributed to what amounted to a check in the Meuse-Argonne sector. Both civil and military leaders of the Allies voiced considerable criticism of Pershing because of the AEF's failure to breach the German position.

Meanwhile, on 27 September Haig assaulted the Hindenburg line between the Sensee River and Villers-Guilain, and this attack gained immediate success. In three days the British reached the outskirts of Cambrai. On 29 September, another British attack farther south also penetrated the Hindenburg line, making excellent progress across the St. Quentin Canal. Haig had originated the plan to have the Americans attack north toward Mezieres instead of east toward Metz so that Ludendorff would have to transfer troops from the British sector to the Meuse-Argonne, but the British Army gained its main purpose before the German High Command could take such action.

As the British and Franco-American forces carried out converging operations against the German salient, the Group of Armies of Flanders attacked in Belgium, and a Franco-British force in the center of the line moved toward La Fere-Peronne. Everywhere from Dixmude in Flanders to the Meuse River in Lorraine, Foch kept his armies on the move, straining Ludendorff's depleted resources along a front of about 250 miles.

At this juncture, the German High Command, recognizing that the war was lost, pressed the civil government to seek an armistice and arrange for peace negotiations. The British success against the Hindenburg line forced Ludendorff's hand, although the collapse of Bulgaria and intimations of Austrian and Turkish breakdowns also influenced him. During October, a new German chancellor, the liberal-minded Prince Max of Baden, conducted a bilateral correspondence with President Wilson. He sought to end the war based on the least onerous enemy statements of war aims, the American Fourteen Points and associated pronouncements. These negotiations, from which the Allies were purposefully excluded, ended on 23 October, when Wilson accepted Prince Max's proposal to negotiate peace based on the American war aims. Meanwhile Foch prepared the terms of an armistice, a separate matter properly delegated to the military. Representatives of the Allies and the United States then met in Paris, sitting as the Supreme War Council, to decide whether to endorse Wilson's arrangements with Prince Max and Foch's military, naval, and air terms of armistice. Colonel House, Wilson's delegate, forced the reluctant Allies to accept the American program for the peace settlement with but two modifications when he announced that otherwise the United States would withdraw its army from the war. The Supreme War Council also acquiesced in the onerous armistice terms that Foch had drawn up after consulting with Haig, Petain, Pershing, and the Belgians.

Thus operations during the last six weeks of the war unfolded while the German government moved rapidly toward peace negotiations, a circumstance that lifted the morale of Foch's armies and depressed those of the Central Powers. However, the German army offered stubborn resistance in all sectors. The dispirited Ludendorff recovered his balance sufficiently to attempt a fighting withdrawal to a line between Antwerp and the Meuse River from which he hoped to hold out through the winter. This desperate effort, which proved unacceptable in Berlin, led to his forced retirement on 26 October.

The American First Army sustained its costly frontal attacks against the Kriemhilde Stellung throughout the first three weeks of October. Finally it managed to penetrate the German defenses and to gain favorable positions for future operations, although it suffered over 100,000 casualties. By this time, Pershing had become commander of an American army group. He relinquished command of the First Army to General Liggett and established the American Second Army under General Bullard. During the last two weeks of October, Liggett devoted himself to resting and reorganizing the First Army while planning a resumption of the offensive.

On 1 November, the First Army launched an attack coordinated with others on the western front that immediately proved successful. Liggett routed the enemy and outflanked the Hindenburg fortifications before the French Fourth Army to the west. The Germans then began a general withdrawal from the line of the Aisne to the Antwerp-Meuse line. Accordingly the American First Army engaged in a pursuit during the remaining days of the war.

Pershing, upset by his failure to gain a brilliant victory, vented his frustration in two ways. First, he advocated unconditional surrender instead of a negotiated armistice, sending an unauthorized letter to the Supreme War Council urging this course. Colonel House quickly neutralized this insubordinate initiative, and Pershing escaped a reprimand. Next, during the last days of the war, the AEF commander authorized the capture of Sedan, scene of the great French disaster of 1870. This action would deprive the French army of this honor. Fortunately General Liggett put a stop to this misconceived enterprise, an operational and political monstrosity.

The war ended on 11 November at the eleventh hour. Foch's general offensive had succeeded far beyond its author's expectations, showing the validity of his aphorism that nothing gives wings to an army like victory. His coordinated and sustained attacks imposed terrible attrition on the German army, which used its last reserves in the defense of the Hindenburg line. He did not force a general breakthrough and envelopment, but the unrelenting operations of July–November finally broke the will of the German army, the German people, and the German leadership. At the end, resistance simply melted away.

The AEF conducted itself as might have been expected of an army that lacked experience and was thrown into battle prematurely. The decision to create an independent army and conduct separate operations ensured that Pershing's command could not fight efficiently on a large scale until at least two years after the intervention of April 1917. The emergency that developed on the western front during March–July 1918, when Ludendorff sought a decision through massive offensives, forced premature employment of American troops, an unavoidable change of plan. This unexpected outcome led initially to temporary amalgamation of some American divisions into the Allied armies, mostly in quiet sectors for training. Some of these brigaded units entered combat, acquitting themselves well under French and British command after undergoing bruising baptisms of fire.

The performance of the American First Army, created only three months before the armistice, was less impressive than those of the amalgamated divisions. During the Meuse-Argonne offensive, this organization, only a rudimentary version

of what had been planned, suffered from incomplete organization, inadequate training, unsound logistical support, and inexperienced commanders and staffs. In many
ways, the difficulties that the AEF encountered during its brief interlude of service
in 1918 paralleled those of the European armies in the first stages of the war. The
improvement of the First Army during the bloody Meuse-Argonne campaign, especially after Liggett assumed command, suggests that it would have fought with
growing confidence and success, if the struggle had carried over into 1919.

The AEF never fulfilled the mission established for it in 1917, the delivery of a
decisive blow to assure Wilson of a dominant position at the postwar peace conference, but it contributed significantly with the French, British, and Belgian armies
to Foch's huge joint offensive that finally broke the German army. In the end, the
most important service of the AEF was to appear in France. Its presence allowed
release of veteran Allied divisions from quiet sectors and gave Foch the superiority
in manpower he needed to make a success of his coordinated and sustained operations. Although Pershing never struck a knockout punch, the AEF's achievements
were more than sufficient to guarantee President Wilson's control of the postwar
peace negotiations, the purpose for which the AEF fought in France. When the
Germans decided to end the war, the Allies were unable to prevent Wilson from
committing both the Central Powers and themselves to a settlement based on the
American war aims and peace proposals.

As in most American wars, the overwhelming military reality was the unpreparedness of the United States Army. Delay in committing American divisions to
battle and the brevity of American operations tended to obscure the bitter truth of
the dubious victory in the Meuse-Argonne sector, one that was long deferred and
most costly. The sudden end of the war headed off what might have become serious criticism of the AEF. Pershing's inflated claims of success have been too often
accepted without careful study.

Pershing was surely a flawed commander. If the war had continued into 1919,
he might well have fallen from grace. No American theater commander ever received more support from his civilian superiors. President Wilson and Secretary
Baker backed him unswervingly during the long controversy over amalgamation.
Pershing's stubborn self-righteousness, his unwillingness to correct initial miscon-
ceptions such as those that marred the doctrine and training of the AEF, and his
stormy relationships with Allied military and civilian leaders hurt the AEF.

Pershing considered his sustained resistance to amalgamation a great achievement, but his intransigence is open to criticism. Given the extent of the emergency
in 1918, he ought to have considered extensive brigading of American divisions
and corps on a temporary basis for both training and combat. The experience
gained from this exposure would have greatly benefited the AEF, when organized
for independent operations. General Bliss, the most judicious American soldier in
France during 1918, privately held this view but did not choose to undermine the
commander-in-chief. Pershing should not have accepted long-term amalgamation,
but no one ever proposed that he do so. His conviction that combat service by
amalgamated divisions would render them unfit for future operations under American command was in error. Organizations such as the 1st, 2d, 28th, and 42d Divisions absorbed rough treatment during tours in other armies but emerged with
considerable experience that was put to excellent use during later service in the

American First Army. Despite postwar accolades conferred on Pershing, close study of the controversy over the shipment and employment of American troops during 1918 reveals that Baker and Wilson had begun to sense some of the general's limitations, which accounts for proposals made in July 1918 to confine his responsibilities to field command. Pershing's personal shortcomings were revealed briefly during the last days of the war. He overstepped his military authority in advocating unconditional surrender and foolishly attempted to deprive the French army of the honor of occupying Sedan. The unexpected victory of November 1918 masked these transgressions. What reason was there to dwell on such matters in the glow of Foch's great victory? Pershing railed at what he considered the premature end of the war. He wanted to fight on so that the AEF could prove with deeds the excellence that he had claimed for it, but it seems probable that the armistice spared him growing difficulties later.

Marshal Foch served superbly as generalissimo in 1918. He realized that the key to victory was attrition instead of maneuver. He was able not only to coordinate an ultimately successful containment of Ludendorff's tremendous attacks but to organize limited counteroffensives and eventually a general counteroffensive that imposed irreplaceable losses of men and material on the German army and finally broke its will and that of the German people. He made effective use of all the national contingents under his authority, including the American Expeditionary Forces, despite the difficulties that arose in dealings with the timorous Petain, the unimaginative Haig, and the stubborn Pershing.

In measuring the American contribution of 1918 to the defeat of Germany it is well to bear in mind comparisons such as one made by John Terraine. Between 18 July and 11 November, the armies under Foch captured enemy troops and guns as follows:

British Army	188,700 prisoners	2,840 guns
French Army	139,000 prisoners	1,880 guns
American Army	43,000 prisoners	1,421 guns
Belgian Army	14,500 prisoners	474 guns

As these statistics suggest, the most important American contribution in 1918 was not combat operations, although the inexperienced AEF for the most part fought bravely. The principal American offering was to provide the margin in manpower and material that allowed Foch to wage his war of attrition successfully during the last four months of the war.

Gen. Frederick Maurice, a perspicacious British observer who wrote a cogent postwar analysis of Foch's remarkable campaign, thought it idle to dispute about who won the war. He argued correctly that no one army, leader, or event decided the outcome. "Germany could not have been beaten in the field, as she was beaten, without the intimate cooperation of all the Allied armies on the Western Front directed by a great leader, nor without the coordination for a common purpose of all the resources of the Allies,—naval, military, industrial, and economic." The prime lesson of 1918 is that coalition warfare is a most difficult enterprise. Victory comes to allies who persevere in the trying but essential effort to cooperate effectively in the common cause despite inevitable conflicts of interest and outlook.

▲ *F U R T H E R   R E A D I N G*

Dean C. Allard, "Admiral William S. Sims and United States Naval Policy in World War I," *American Neptune* 35 (April 1975): 97–110.

Arthur E. Barbeau and Florette Henri, *The Unknown Soldiers: Black American Troops in World War I* (1974).

Daniel R. Beaver, *Newton D. Baker and the American War Effort, 1917–1919* (1967).

Paul F. Braim, *The Test of Battle: The American Expeditionary Forces in the Meuse-Argonne Campaign* (1987).

John Whiteclay Chambers II, *To Raise an Army: The Draft Comes to Modern America* (1987).

J. Garry Clifford, *The Citizen Soldiers: The Plattsburg Training Camp Movement, 1913–1920* (1972).

Edward M. Coffman, *The War to End All Wars: The American Military Experience in World War I* (1968).

James J. Cooke, *Pershing and His Generals: Command and Staff in The AEF* (1997).

Harvey A. DeWeerd, *President Wilson Fights His War: World War I and the American Intervention* (1968).

John Ellis, *Eye-Deep in Hell: Trench Warfare in World War I* (1976).

Robert H. Ferrell, *Woodrow Wilson and World War I, 1917–1921* (1985).

John P. Finnegan, *Against the Specter of a Dragon: The Campaign for American Military Preparedness, 1914–1917* (1974).

David S. Foglesong, *America's Secret War against Bolshevism: U.S. Intervention in the Russian Civil War, 1917–1920* (1995).

Frank Freidel, ed., *Over There: The Story of America's First Great Overseas Crusade* (1964).

Lettie Gavin, *American Women in World War I: They Also Served* (1997).

David M. Kennedy, *Over Here: The First World War and American Society* (1980).

Lee Kennett, *The First Air War 1914–1918* (1991).

Arthur S. Link, *Woodrow Wilson: Revolution, War and Peace* (1979).

Bullitt Lowry, *Armistice 1918* (1996).

Allan R. Millett and Williamson Murray, eds., *Military Effectiveness. Vol. I: The First World War* (1988).

Timothy K. Nenninger, "Tactical Dysfunction in the AEF, 1917–1918" *Military Affairs* 51 (October 1987): 177–181.

John H. Morrow, Jr., *The Great War in the Air: Military Aviation from 1909 to 1921* (1993).

John J. Pershing, *My Experiences in the World War,* 2 vols. (1931).

Forrest C. Pogue, *George C. Marshall: Education of a General, 1880–1939* (1963).

James W. Rainey, "Ambivalent Warfare: The Tactical Doctrine of the AEF in World War I," *Parameters* 13 (September 1983): 34–46.

Dorothy and Carl J. Schneider, *Into the Breach: American Women Overseas in World War I* (1991).

Gene Smith, *Until the Last Trumpet Sounds: The Life of General of the Armies John J. Pershing* (1998).

Donald Smythe, *Pershing: General of the Armies* (1986).

Ronald Spector, "You're Not Going to Send Soldiers Over There Are You!: The American Search for an Alternative to the Western Front 1916–1917," *Military Affairs* 36 (February 1972): 1–4.

Laurence Stallings, *The Doughboys: The Story of the AEF, 1917–1918* (1963).

David F. Trask, *The AEF and Coalition Warfare, 1917–1918* (1993).

_____, *Captains and Cabinets: Anglo-American Naval Relations, 1917–1918* (1972).

Frank E. Vandiver, *Black Jack: The Life and Times of John J. Pershing,* 2 vols. (1977).

Dale E. Wilson, *Treat 'em Rough! The Birth of American Armor, 1917–1920* (1989).

David R. Woodward, *Trial by Friendship: Anglo-American Relations, 1917–1918* (1993).

Phyllis A. Zimmerman, *The Neck of the Bottle: George W. Goethals and the Reorganization of the U.S. Army Supply System, 1917–1918* (1992).

CHAPTER
10

Innovation

in the Interwar Years

Antiwar sentiments and slashed federal budgets contributed to major arms reductions in the interwar years, before the buildup that began in the late 1930s. Within those constraints, the military sought to assess the lessons of World War I and develop technological, structural, and doctrinal means to restore mobility and decisiveness to warfare. For land warfare, the development in the closing years of the war of a mobile, armed, and armored vehicle—the tank—offered important new possibilities, but American military officers disagreed over its potential use. Former cavalrymen tended to urge that army tanks and armored scout cars be used in massed formations, replacing cavalry, with the shock power to smash enemy lines in frontal or flanking attacks. But infantry officers remained paramount, and they dictated that tanks be dispersed to infantry units to help the soldiers move forward against enemy fire. What was the most effective use of armored vehicles, and what kind of tanks would be most effective?

The airplane was the most dramatic new weapon to emerge from the World War, but how should aircraft be used? The foremost American champion of air power was Brigadier General William ("Billy") Mitchell, who had commanded the Army Air Service in France. Back in the United States, he drew media and public attention by sinking captured German battleships off the Virginia Coast with his fragile little planes in 1921 and by his court-martial for insubordination in 1925, the result, in part, of his outspoken crusade for a large and independent air force. Mitchell's theories and methods have remained controversial ever since, with some portraying him as a martyred prophet of modern warfare, and others denouncing him as egotistical at best and, at worst, immoral in ultimately espousing terror bombing of urban populations.

Even among the theorists of land-based airpower, there was a debate over the relative importance of tactical versus strategic airpower. This was a debate won in America in the interwar years by the champions of long-range strategic bombing, defined doctrinally as daylight, precision bombing. A much less flamboyant and doctrinaire approach to air power than Mitchell's was that of the leading proponent of naval aviation in the interwar period, Rear Admiral William Moffett. Bureaucratically and successfully, Moffett battled Mitchell's desire to downgrade the naval aviators and bring them under his control and also the desire of senior naval officers to restrict naval aviation and the construction of aircraft carriers in order to protect the primacy of their Mahanian fleet of battleships.

Despite continued intra- and interservice rivalry, the armed forces managed an unprecedented degree of joint planning in the 1920s and 1930s. Although established in 1903, the Joint Army and Navy Board did not function effectively until the new strategic environment of the interwar period. Beginning in the early 1920s, it developed a series of detailed war plans with potential adversaries designated by individual colors. PLAN ORANGE was for war against Japan. It presumed that the war would commence with a Japanese surprise attack, as in the Russo-Japanese War of 1904–1905. The U.S. forces in the Philippines and Guam were to try to hold out while the American fleet battled its way across the Pacific (the Marines would seize island bases along the way), until it met and defeated the Japanese fleet in a climactic Mahanian-style battle. Thereafter, the Americans would relieve the Philippines and mount a naval blockade of the Japanese home islands. The Joint Board produced versions of PLAN ORANGE in 1924, 1928, and 1938, despite the fact that during the 1920s war against Japan was politically improbable and that by the late 1930s Washington viewed Nazi Germany as the greater menace. In actuality, the planners doubted that the American forces on Guam and the Philippines could hold out long enough to be rescued by the fleet; nevertheless, both services prepared to implement PLAN ORANGE. Despite the flaws of PLAN ORANGE, which became evident during World War II, the development of joint, detailed war planning represented an innovation that was much more fully developed during and after the Second World War and which continues to the present.

The Marine Corps also proved innovative in the interwar era. After the repulse of the 1915 landing of British imperial forces on the Gallipoli peninsula by the Turks, amphibious invasions of heavily defended enemy territory were widely deemed to be impossible. Under the leadership of Major General John A. Lejeune, however, the U.S. Marine Corps began to develop the doctrine, organization, and technology for amphibious warfare in order to seize the forward bases required to project U.S. naval power across the Pacific in a war against Japan. The Marine Corps accomplished that mission in World War II, although extremely heavy casualties taking Tarawa in the Gilbert Islands in November 1943, led to modifications in doctrine and equipment that were implemented in the invasion of such fortified islands as Kwajalein, Eniwetok, Peleliu, Saipan, Okinawa, and Iwo Jima.

▲ D O C U M E N T S

Brigadier General William ("Billy") Mitchell, in the first document, an article for a prestigious popular magazine in September 1920, calls for a unified, independent air force and asserts the primary importance of strategic bombing as the key to victory. In the second document, Rear Admiral William A. Moffett, chief of the Navy's Bureau of Aeronautics, carefully disputes many of Mitchell's assertions in the admiral's testimony in September 1925, before the Morrow Board, which had been appointed by President Calvin Coolidge to examine Mitchell's criticism and policy recommendations. In the 1930s, the Air Corps Tactical School (ACTS) at Maxwell Field in Alabama began to augment Mitchell's strategic bombing doctrine with another, albeit subsidiary, role for military aviation, one emphasized by World War I aviator General Claire Chennault. The third document, an ACTS memorandum of 1931–1932, emphasizes developments in attack aviation (what would later be called close-air tactical support of ground operations).

In the fourth document, a 1922 memorandum to the Naval General Board after the Washington Naval Arms Limitation Conference, Major General John A. Lejeune, commandant of the Marine Corps, asserts that in a future war with Japan, the Marines will have the vital role of seizing forward bases the Navy would need as it battled across the Pacific—the origin of the Marines' amphibious warfare mission and doctrine. The fifth document, an excerpt from the Joint Army and Navy Board's WAR PLAN ORANGE, version of June 14, 1928, envisions a primarily naval war against Japan with expeditionary forces from the army and Marine Corps. The 1928 plan anticipated ultimate mobilization of some 380,000 soldiers and 40,000 Marines and a two-year campaign before the war could be brought to the immediate vicinity of the Japanese home islands. The actual war against Japan, 1941–1945, took much greater effort than the planners had envisioned in the interwar period.

After World War I, George S. Patton, Jr., a cavalryman who had commanded a tank battalion in the AEF, argued unsuccessfully for a separate Tank Corps, and then returned to the cavalry. By the 1930s, however, he was advocating armored scout cars as a form of mechanized cavalry. Nevertheless, in December 1936, when he typed up his thoughts on mechanized warfare in the sixth document included here, Patton cautioned about some of the limitations of Armored Fighting Vehicles (AFVs), in regard to terrain for instance, even while speculating on their ability to deliver a knockout blow to the enemy. Historians continue to explore and seek to explain the divisions and indecision within the U.S. Army in the interwar period over the future of armored warfare.

1. General William ("Billy") Mitchell, Army Air Service, Calls for a Unified Air Force and Declares Strategic Airpower the Key to Victory, 1920

It is necessary to organize an Air Service into different branches, with proper proportions of each branch to the other. For instance, in Europe 70 per cent. of offensive aviation was pursuit. Consequently, as we had no pursuit aviation, we were completely in the hands of any foe that might attack us. . . .

The forces that actually come in contact with and fight with the enemy are called tactical units. The air tactical unit of aviation is the group of one hundred airplanes, divided into four squadrons of twenty-five planes each. This corresponds in a way to the infantry battalion, and is the fighting unit of aviation. . . .

Pursuit aviation, whose mission is to gain control of the air, fights in groups, wings, and brigades. . . . It is armed with .30-caliber machine guns, .50-caliber machine guns, and 37-mm. cannon. The speed of the pursuit plane is from 150 miles an hour up. It climbs to 20,000 feet in twenty minutes or less. It can out-maneuver any existing aircraft of other branches of the Air Service; consequently, pursuit aviation can bring an enveloping and surrounding attack in three dimensions against other aircraft, which is decisive. . . .

Bombardment aviation is organized similarly to pursuit aviation. . . . Its mission is to drop explosive projectiles on enemy targets. Whenever an attack of a

From William Mitchell, "Our Army's Air Service," *The American Review of Reviews* 62 (September 1920): 283–285, 287–290.

military object depends on an explosive, an aerial bomb attack is the most efficient, because air projectiles carry a far greater proportion of explosives than any other missile (roughly, one-half their weight). A 500-pound bomb carries 250 pounds of explosive, . . . and a 3000-pound bomb holds 1500 pounds of explosive. . . . The 16-inch armor-piercing cannon projectile, weighing more than one ton, carries only about 55 pounds of explosive. . . . Water torpedoes range from about 200 pounds of explosive with a 1500-pound torpedo. . . .

The accuracy of bombing depends entirely upon the distance to the target. If hostile aviation and anti-aircraft defense can be subdued by the action of pursuit and attack aviation, objects on the water or on the ground can be hit with great accuracy. A projectile from a cannon is limited to something like 60,000 yards, and in the case of a torpedo to about one-tenth of that distance. A modern bombardment airplane can go out 200 miles and come back again with its load, and still have a reserve of 200 or more miles of flight. The Army has recently tested an airplane which shows that it can carry 5000 pounds of bombs with a flying capacity of about 800 miles.

As to expense, the present bombardment airplane, with all its accessories, would cost less than $80,000. Compared to this, the present 16-inch gun, with its mount, costs $500,000. The present battleship, with its accessories, costs about $45,000,000. It is believed that a single 1000-pound bomb, striking in the water within thirty feet of a battleship, will greatly injure it or put it out of line so that it will become an easy object for attack. This is entirely independent of any hits on the battleship itself. There are many other new aerial projectiles in development for attack on navies. . . .

Attack aviation is organized like bombardment aviation. . . . Its mission is to attack at low altitude with gunfire and lightweight bombs. On land it is directed against personnel, military trains, tanks, railroad trains, anti-aircraft posts, searchlight posts, hostile airdromes, and any target susceptible of fire attack. On water it attacks all classes of vessels capable of being destroyed single-handed by means of fire attack; against heavily armored ships its object is to distract the attention or destroy the personnel, the equipment, the anti-aircraft defense cannon, searchlights, and machine guns, to attack the observation posts on such vessels, drop parachute flares at night, and take measures for covering the attack of bombardment airplanes.

The type of airplanes devised for this purpose at present is covered with quarter-inch armor over the space for its personnel and motors. It is built in sections of three everywhere, so that at least two members at any one place must be shot off in order to bring down the plane. It is armed with 37-mm. cannon and seven machine guns.

Anti-aircraft artillery, machine guns, searchlight defenses, balloon barrages, liaison systems, a meteorological system, and a system of airways are auxiliary to an air force. An air force can now be handled in the air itself by means of radio telegraphy and telephony.

It is believed that, in the future air force, lines of communication will be supplied by airships. This remains to be proved, however, and is one of the important developments of lighter-than-air craft at the present time. Recent experiments have been very successful.

An air force, judged by results in the European war, will contain about 70 per cent. pursuit aviation. It would appear that the proportion for this arm in the United States, in a future great war, might be 60 per cent. pursuit, 20 per cent. bombardment, and 20 per cent. attack aviation. . . .

The question now is, What shall be done in the future? Congress this year allowed a force of 1520 officers and 16,000 men for the Air Service, and an appropriation sufficient to equip the air units now in the service with modern airplanes. These, as mentioned above, constitute about three hundred and fifty airplanes with the squadrons. France, for instance, has ten times this number in her army at present, or three thousand airplanes. Practically all the flying personnel in every service advocate the unification of activities under one central control, in order to cut out the overheads that now exist with aviation divided among Army, Navy, Marines, and Coast Guard, Post Office, and all sorts of different places. Such unification would, it is believed, secure an economical administration looking essentially to the development of the air as a main issue and not as one secondary to something else. . . .

What is needed is a comprehensive study of the problem which will assign to an air force a definite place as a defensive arm of the United States. What the airmen recommend at the present time is that the navy constitute the first line of defense, that the air force constitute the second line, and that the army constitute the third line of defense. As soon as the air force is provided with suitable floating airdromes having sufficient speed to keep away from naval vessels, and supplied by airships, we believe the air force will be the first line of defense and that surface navies, at least, will disappear. . . .

In case of any operation involving defense of the coast (which presupposes the elimination of our navy), an offensive war on foreign soil, or any operation involving an army, the first element to enter into combat with the enemy will be the air force. If an initial advantage is gained by an enemy, it is a question whether the air force or the country will ever recover from it. In other words, the most important battle will be the first air battle. Therefore, our Air Service should be so organized that one part of it will be permanently stationed behind the Atlantic coast, one part of it behind the Pacific coast, each sufficient to act defensively against the first echelons of an enemy air force, and that there should be stationed midway between these a reserve force or air mass of maneuver which could be thrown in either direction and be sufficiently large to master the enemy air forces. In addition to these, the reserve units, means of production, and training capabilities should be so organized that they can be developed in accordance with the problem that faces us. . . .

It is interesting to note that the maximum distance over water from Europe to the United States is only about three hundred miles, if the route is taken via Canada, Greenland, Iceland, and the islands north of Great Britain. The distance across Behring Strait from Siberia to Alaska is only twenty-one miles. In the future air forces coming by these routes may be supplied completely by airships, even if they have no vessels on the water to supply them; or, if they have a combination of both, the matter is facilitated just so much.

A British airship has already crossed the Atlantic, and Germany, as is well known, had some ready to do so if the war had lasted longer. . . .

We are convinced that aviation can only be put on its feet in this country through the unification of all air activities, so as to obtain an economical administration of this most important element under persons who are actually familiar with flying and the things that go with it.

2. Admiral William Moffett, Naval Aviation Chief, Criticizes Mitchell, 1925

. . . [I]t was shown that the present law as it first passed the House contained the proviso "that the Army Air Service shall control all aerial operations from land bases and naval aviation all aerial operations attached to a fleet."

If the wording quoted had become law it would practically have wiped out naval aviation development and would, had war come meanwhile, have seriously crippled the fleet. Fortunately, the Navy Department discovered the existence of this legislation as a rider on an Army appropriation bill in time, and after energetic protests on the part of the Secretaries of War and Navy the legislation was amended in conference by members of Congress who appreciated its far-reaching effect.

The law, as amended, and passed in the act making appropriations for the Army Air Service for the fiscal year 1922, reads:

> *And provided further,* That hereafter the Army Air Service shall control all aerial operations from land bases, and naval aviation shall have control of all aerial operations attached to a fleet, including shore stations whose maintenance is necessary for operations with the fleet, for construction and experimentation, and for the training of personnel.

The fleet includes patrol and district and convoy vessels, as well as the high-seas fleet.

While presumably this should be satisfactory, it appears that in some quarters it has been, and in the future is likely to be, invoked to restrict and hamper the development of naval aviation, and I am in favor of its repeal. . . .

I recommend repeal of the existing legislation quoted above in order to make conflict of ideas and ambiguity impossible; and to this recommendation, I would add another, namely, that the functions of the Army and Navy, including Army Air Service and naval aviation, be determined in the future by the joint board, as is now provided. If legislation is necessary to define these functions, I recommend it be enacted only after recommendation by the joint board.

Our whole program of aircraft types, functions, etc., is based on the present rules approved by the Secretary of War and Secretary of the Navy, and this procedure should govern in future.

We have all heard statements to the effect that our coast can be bombed by aircraft from foreign shores. In my original statement I told you that there was no plane in existence at the present time, and none in sight, which could fly in one flight from

From William A. Moffett, testimony, September 22, 1925. In U.S. President's Aircraft Board *Hearings before the President's Aircraft Board,* 4 vols. (Washington: GPO, 1925), I, 993–996.

Europe to our coast with a military load. I do not think that statement can be refuted. In order for aircraft to operate against our coast, from foreign-owned lands, such as Bermuda, Jamaica, Canada, and other near-by foreign possessions, bases must be established and aircraft provided. To do this the materials for bases and the aircraft must be brought from foreign shores in ships. If the number of subsurface, surface [ships], and aircraft in the United States is maintained in accordance with the 5–5–3 ratio [for the U.S., U.K., and Japan], the bases will never be established and the aircraft will never reach our coast. The greatest assurance against such an attack is a Navy second to none under the sea, on the sea, and over the sea. . . .

Following the World War, the United States Navy was confronted with the stupendous problem of adapting aircraft to the needs of the Navy. During the World War naval aircraft was used only for patrol purposes. The actual use of aircraft on battleships and the development of aircraft carriers were not considered. For the past four years the Naval Bureau of Aeronautics has been concentrating on the problem of developing aviation with the fleet. This not only includes the development and equipment of aircraft carriers, but also the supplying of aircraft for every type of floating craft, from the battleship to the submarine. The past four years might be called years of experimentation in the development of the proper type of aircraft for naval aviation. . . .

In regard to the Navy Department Budget, I believe that the Navy must be not only the treaty Navy but have its full quota of aviation. Aviation will settle the next naval war, because the fleet without its full quota of aviation, and the best aviation, will be defeated. I therefore say aviation is of transcendent importance to a navy—to our Navy. An army may get along without it—witness the Riffs [in Morocco]—but a fleet, never. . . .

I claim that aviation is a gun, a bomb, a torpedo, a mine, a spotter, and a scout, all in one, fragile it is true comparatively, and at present limited in its operation but with infinite possibilities. I claim that as long as our fleet is not evenly balanced as to its aviation, both in matériel and personnel, it is as if the fleet were short of guns, torpedoes, mines, and men, and that until this shortage is made up more money should be allotted to aviation and less to surface ships—if money for both can not be obtained—I am for ships, surface and subsurface, but the ships without their aviation will be crippled or lost, our fleet defeated and the war lost.

3. Air Corps Tactical School Argues for Tactical as Well as Strategic Airpower, 1931–1932

Attack aviation is the latest member to gain recognition in the family of military aviation.

From the time in the early days of the World War when military airplanes first carried weapons, the crews of observation planes scouring the enemy domain for information were wont to use their rifles, pistols, machine guns or hand grenades

From Air Corps Tactical School, Maxwell Field, Alabama. "Present Status of Attack Aviation and its Trend of Development," 1931–1932. USAF Historical Resource Agency, Air University, Maxwell AFB, AL. 248.222-55E. pp 1–3, 4–5, 6–7.

to attack such hostile troops as were discovered during the course of a reconnaissance, and pursuit pilots returning from an uneventful search for enemy planes aloft would descend on their way home to empty their machine guns against enemy soldiers in bivouacs, on roads or in trenches. The effect of these incidental assaults by observation and pursuit pilots on enemy personnel were without important effect on ground operations, at first, but they lead [sic] the Germans first to give serious thought to their possibilities and later to organize, train and equip in 1917 sites of squadrons for the exclusive employment against ground tactical units in the combat zone. So great was their success that the British and French soon followed their example and at the close of the war both sides had realized the importance of making direct attacks on various classes of personnel . . . units on the ground and to a greater or lesser extent had organized air units and developed tactics primarily for this kind of employment.

The primary function of attack aviation as a branch, the function which justifies its existence as a separate branch and which should dominate the development of its equipment and tactics is the delay, disorganization and destruction of tactical units on the ground or sea through the demoralization and destruction of their personnel. Tactical advantage and victory by one military force over another are gained largely by the ability of the former to concentrate and move its personnel so as to exert a greater fire power at the critical place and time in an operation, whether that operation be a skirmish of small units or a decisive battle on a broad front. The modern military machine possessed the facilities in marching or mechanical transport for affecting the necessary concentrations and movements without serious opposition by the weapons possessed by enemy ground forces. Aviation alone has the power through destruction of necessary roads, railroads, bridges, terminal facilities, vehicles, supplies and other necessary elements, to decisively affect such movements by the enemy. With the development of motorization and the ability of ground forces to move at increasing speeds, on broad fronts, and across country, the destruction of combat personnel and tactical units will become increasingly important. For this destruction attack aviation is preeminently fitted, by virtue of its equipment and tactical employment against targets on the ground between attack aviation on one hand and bombardment or pursuit aviation carrying small bombs and using machine guns on the other. . . .

These changes in conditions with regard to the enemy [their greater ground firepower] has [sic] led to the development of attack airplanes of greater speed, greater volume of offensive and defensive machine gun fire, greater number and efficiency of bombs, and greater endurance and range. The fragmentation bomb superseded the machine gun as the most important weapon in the arsenal of attack aviation. The increase in the effectiveness of the bomb and the training of hostile ground troops to return effective fire created the necessity for attack aviation to modify its tactics by making the assault at higher altitudes. To overcome the danger from its own bombs, attack aviation has sought to develop bombs with delay fuzes, parachutes and other devices, and thus permit a return to its hedge-hopping tactics. Thus far no permanent solution of the problem has been achieved.

The most recent as well as probably the most important development in the offensive power of attack aviation is the adaptation of the airplane to the employment of toxic chemicals in the form of spray. Treaties to the contrary notwithstanding, all world powers are developing various means for the use of gas, offensively as well as defensively. . . . Because of its primary function of attacking personnel because of its normal low altitude tactics, and because of the great superiority in efficiency of sprayed chemical over chemical carried in bombs, the task of using chemicals offensively by aviation has been chiefly delegated to attack aviation. The tactics of employing gas by aircraft are still in the early stages of development. . . .

. . . The function assigned to attack aviation and the organization and equipment developed for performing that function permits of a very wide selection of objectives. Personnel and tactical units, subject to attack operations, exist all the way from the front lines to locations deep in the communications zone. Moreover, the airplane and offensive armament of attack aviation make it suitable for employment for many other missions, such as the destruction of enemy air units on the ground (thus supplementing the work of friendly pursuit), the direct attack of hostile antiaircraft defenses (thus supporting the operation of friendly air forces in general and bombardment in particular), and the destruction of railroad tracks, terminal facilities and rolling stock, light bridges of all kinds, highways, small shipping and harbor facilities, motor transportation, and similar material targets (thus supplementing or infringing the work of bombardment aviation). The selection of the objectives and the assignment of missions of attack aviation is generally admitted to be the responsibility of higher air force commanders and subject to the influence of the tactical and strategical ground situation. . . .

Attack aviation had its origin in the crushing moral and physical effect it could produce in the battle between ground forces. The improvement of attack materiel and the development of attack organizations and tactics have increased this effect. Ground forces fear hostile attack from the air and have come to rely upon the timely and proper employment of friendly attack units. Any employment of attack forces which diverts the energies and results of attack aviation from its primary function may be resorted to only when the situation clearly justifies and demands this diversion. The employment of well trained attack aviation in its true role will be one of the most effective ways in which military aviation can contribute to the ultimate success of the military forces as a whole.

4. Major General John A. Lejeune, Commandant, U.S. Marine Corps, Proposes a New Mission for the Marines, 1922

II. Discussion:

1. The strength and organization of the Marine Corps should be determined by the following considerations:
   (a) The duties it is required to perform in time of peace;
   (b) Its missions in time of war.

From Major General Commandant John A. Lejeune, Memorandum for the [Navy] General Board, "Future Policy of the Marine Corps as Influenced by the Conference on Limitation of Armament," February 11, 1922. File 432, Records of the [Navy] General Board. General Records of the Department of the Navy (RG #80). National Archives, Washington, D.C.

2. The duties which the Marine Corps is required to perform in time of peace are as follows:
   (a) As marine detachments on board the vessels of the Fleet in full commission.
   (b) As guards for navy yards, naval stations, ammunition depots, naval prisons, etc., at home and abroad.
   (c) As garrisons for Haiti, Santo Domingo, Virgin Islands, Guam, Peking, Managua, etc.
   (d) As a mobile force in training for use on expeditionary duty abroad for the purpose of carrying out the foreign policy of our Government, or for emergency use at home.
   (e) As detachments necessary for the recruiting service, for training recruits, and for administrative purposes.
3. The primary war mission of the Marine Corps is to supply a mobile force to accompany the Fleet for operations on shore in support of the Fleet: This force should be of such size, organization, armament and equipment as may be required by the plan of Naval Operations. Also, it should be further utilized in conjunction with Army operations on shore, when the active naval operations reach such a stage as to permit its temporary detachment from the Navy.
4. (a) The secondary mission of the Marine Corps in time of war is to continue the performance of its peace time duties, as outlined in Paragraph 2, immediately above.
   (b) The continuance in war of these duties, exclusive of expeditionary forces, with the Fleet, would require a minimum increase of 100 per cent over peace time requirements. This statement is based on the experience of the last war, when large increases were made in all detachments assigned to duty as guards of Navy Yards, Ammunition Depots, etc., and in 1917 an expeditionary force was organized and sent to Cuba, where it served throughout the war, and an additional force was held at Galveston, Texas, in readiness for service in Mexico.
   (c) War would necessitate a large increase in the number of Marines required for duty as a mobile force with the Fleet. About 25,000 Marines are considered necessary with the advance elements of the Fleet for the purpose of seizing naval bases, and other service on shore in conjunction with the fleet. In addition, a supporting force of large strength would be necessary to fortify and hold bases thus seized, until this supporting force could be relieved by the Army.
   (d) The Second Division, American Expeditionary Forces, required approximately 150% replacements during about nine (9) months of active service against the enemy. This fact indicates the necessity of a large number of replacement units, especially as in future wars the casualties would probably be even heavier than in the last war.
5. Whereas the Conference on the Limitation of Armament has restricted the immediate material means (navies) for waging war on sea, there is no restriction on the size of the mobile forces which may be attached to, or be held in readiness for service with the Fleet.

6. Obviously it will be contrary to our agreement to increase the number of naval vessels. The only other outlet for progress in efficiency will be the general development in the Navy and Marine Corps: . . .

8. In regard to a policy of providing Marine Corps garrisons for the adequate defense of U.S. Naval Bases, and Marine Corps mobile forces adequate to conduct offensive operations on land in support of the Navy, there is no doubt that such a policy would expedite the success of naval operations.

9. The situation in the Pacific is the most conspicuous example of the need for distant Naval Bases. Between Honolulu and Manila, the United States has no developed Naval Base. In war such a base would be necessary. The loss of Guam under this situation would be most serious and its recapture would be necessary to the conduct of successful naval operations in the Pacific.

10. It is obvious that the loss of Guam could be avoided by maintaining there a mobile force adequate to prevent a hostile landing. However, it is probable that an increase in the garrison would be considered a violation of the spirit of the Treaties arising out of the Conference.

11. The advantage of having immediately available a mobile Marine Corps force adequate to conduct offensive land operations against hostile Naval Bases is apparent.

12. There can be no doubt that the immediate availability of Guam as a Naval Base and a suitable mobile Marine Corps force would materially speed the successful progress of a campaign in the Pacific.

13. The duty of the Marine Corps, according to law, is to serve with the Army or Navy, or anywhere, as the President may direct. For this reason the sphere of activity of the Marine Corps is large. . . .

15. The present strength of 21,000 is not adequate to carry out Marine Corps peace-time missions. Normally, only about 3,000 men can be kept in readiness for expeditionary service. There should be at least nine thousand Marines in training, divided between the East and West Coast, as a nucleus for the mobile force to accompany the Fleet in war, and as an expeditionary force for emergencies at home or abroad.

16. The authorized strength of 27,400 would supply present peace-time requirements, and make possible some preparations for the future. With that strength proper attention could be given to Schooling and Training of personnel. Present indications point to the great need of such instruction. The Marine Corps lost during the War many of its valuable old-time noncommissioned officers. Some were appointed officers, many were casualties, and many have left the service for one reason or another. The large influx of new personnel since the War makes necessary a greater amount of systematic instruction for officers and men than was the case heretofore, when comparatively few such replacements were made.

III. Recommended: . . .

7. A Naval Policy of maintaining a Marine Corps of such strength that it will be able in every emergency to adequately support the Navy in accomplishing its missions.

/s/ John A. Lejeune

5. Joint Army and Navy Board Plans
for War with Japan, 1928

Directive

1. This JOINT ARMY AND NAVY BASIC WAR PLAN—ORANGE shall constitute the basis upon which all Army Plans—Orange, all Navy Plans—Orange, and all Joint Plans—Orange, shall be formulated and developed. . . .

General Assumptions

1. Any war in the PACIFIC involving the UNITED STATES, in so far as can be foreseen, will be with ORANGE.

2. In the event of such a war, if ORANGE has no European Allies, the UNITED STATES will have to achieve success in the WESTERN PACIFIC.

3. War with ORANGE will be precipitated without notice.

4. Conditions as they may exist upon such sudden entry into war must be the basis for estimating the time required for Mobilization of Armed Forces. . . .

Concept of the War

. . . An offensive war of long duration, primarily Naval throughout, unless large Army Forces are employed in major land operations in the WESTERN PACIFIC, directed toward the isolation and exhaustion of ORANGE through control of her vital sea communications and through offensive operations against her Armed Forces and her Economic Life. . . .

Missions

1. *National Mission:* To impose the will of the UNITED STATES upon OR-ANGE by destroying ORANGE Armed Forces and by disrupting ORANGE Economic Life, while protecting AMERICAN Interests at home and abroad.

2. *Mission for the Armed Forces:* To gain and to exercise command of the sea, and as necessary of the air, and to operate offensively against ORANGE Armed Forces, Bases of Operation, and Economic Life, in order to isolate, exhaust and subdue ORANGE, while protecting AMERICAN Territory and AMERICAN Interests.

　　a. *Mission for the Navy:* To gain and to exercise command of the sea, and with the Army, to operate offensively against ORANGE Armed Forces, Bases of Operations, and Economic Life, especially War Industries.

　　b. *Mission for the Army:* To provide for the defense of UNITED STATES Territory; to support the Navy in operations to gain and to exercise command of the sea; and with the Navy, to operate offensively against ORANGE Armed Forces, Bases of Operations, and Economic Life, especially War Industries.

From Steven T. Ross, ed. *American War Plans, 1919–1941,* 5 vols. (New York: Garland Pub. Inc., 1992), II, 36–37, 39, 150–151.

3. *Mission for the Civil Power:* To support the Armed Forces in their operations; to prevent ORANGE from obtaining any means of waging war from Neutral Countries and to destroy ORANGE credit in order to accomplish the economic exhaustion of ORANGE. . . .

Joint Decisions and Operations Required Thereunder

1. TO ESTABLISH, AT THE EARLIEST PRACTICABLE DATE, UNITED STATES NAVAL POWER IN THE WESTERN PACIFIC IN STRENGTH SUPERIOR TO THAT OF ORANGE AND TO OPERATE OFFENSIVELY IN THAT AREA.

2. The operations required to carry out this decision will include:

a. The concentration in the PACIFIC of available vessels and aircraft of the UNITED STATES FLEET;

b. The organization and concentration of Expeditionary Forces of Army and Marine Corps troops for the support of the FLEET;

c. The movement to the WESTERN PACIFIC of a combined Naval and Military Expedition as soon after the outbreak of war as possible, and the seizure of an Advanced Fleet Base in that area. The Naval Forces in this initial movement must be superior to the Naval Forces available to ORANGE, and the Expeditionary Forces should be of sufficient strength to overcome all anticipated hostile resistance.

d. The establishment of an Advanced Fleet Base at MANILA BAY, or at some other location.

e. The organization and earliest possible development of the Advanced Fleet Base, or bases, for defense, and for the maintenance and supply of the UNITED STATES Forces in the Principal Theater of Operations;

f. The establishment and maintenance of secure Lines of Communication between the UNITED STATES and the Advanced Fleet Base, including the seizure, occupation and defense of Subsidiary Bases;

g. The establishment and maintenance of an adequate Communication System throughout the areas occupied by our Forces.

3. TO HOLD THE MANILA BAY AREA AS LONG AS POSSIBLE WITH THE MILITARY AND NAVAL FORCES IN THE WESTERN PACIFIC AT THE OUTBREAK OF WAR AND TO DENY THIS AREA TO ORANGE AS A NAVAL BASE IN CASE WE CANNOT USE IT OURSELVES. . . .

Estimate of Possible Progress of Operations.

OPERATION	FROM	TO
Prepare first concentration	M day	M plus 30
M plus 30 Group to Western Base	M plus 30	M plus 60
Seizure and occupation of Western Base	M plus 60	M plus 90
Reinforcement of Corregidor	M plus 60	M plus 90
Organize and equip Western Base	M plus 60	M plus 600
Operations against Japanese fleet	M plus 60	End
Operations against Japanese commerce	M plus 60	End
Air attacks against Japanese main islands	M plus 60	End
M plus 60 Group to Western Base	M plus 60	M plus 90

Seizure and occupation of Malampaya Sound	M plus 90	M plus 120
M plus 90 Group to Western Base	M plus 90	M plus 120
Seizure and occupation of Marshall Islands	M plus 105	M plus 135
Seizure and occupation of Sakishima Islands	M plus 120	M plus 150
Seizure and occupation of Pescadores Islands	M plus 150	M plus 180
Operations in Carolines and Marianas	M plus 180	M plus 240
Seizure and occupation of Koolung	M plus 240	M plus 300
Seizure and occupation of Okinawa Islands	M plus 300	M plus 360
Air attacks upon Amami Oshima	M plus 390	M plus 450
Seizure and occupation of Amami Oshima	M plus 450	M plus 540
Seizure and occupation of Osumi Islands	M plus 540	M plus 570
Intensive air attacks upon Japanese Home Is.	M plus 540	End
Seizure and occupation of Goto Islands	M plus 570	M plus 600
Operations against Tsushima Islands	M plus 600	M plus 690
Operations for complete control of sea in immediate vicinity of Japanese Main Is.	M plus 690	End.

6. Colonel George Patton Speculates on the Future of Armored Vehicles, 1936

Schools of Thought:

Initially there are two very opposed schools of thought concerning the employment of Armored Fighting Vehicles (A.F.V.'s). This divergence of opinion is inherent in two concepts of war.

Those who envision the next war as a repetition of 1918 affirm that A.F.V.'s will retain their pristine role as assault machines; a sort of cross between an infantryman and a barrage.

On the other hand those who hope for a resumption of movement think of mechanized units as a modernized heavy cavalry. . . .

The Objectives to Be Sought:

One school adheres to the belief that the A.F.V.'s should drive right ahead through the outpost, delaying and [*sic*] main battle positions into the artillery zone and having reached this happy hunting ground, less whatever losses mud, A.T. weapons and infantry have inflicted, they will there cruise about destroying with wanton abandon whatever comes within ken of their eye slits.

A second group maintains that since machine guns stop infantry and that an unsupported break through by machines is futile the proper mission of the A.F.V.'s is the machine guns and anti-tank weapons. They further state that if by chance the unsupported machines get into the artillery it is they and not the guns which will be destroyed because owing to dispersion in depth the guns will be able to render each other such mutual support as to insure the destruction of the tanks.

Finally, there is a school, doubtless the lineal descendants of a certain Alladin of the famous lamp, who overcome all resistance by the simple insertion of the

From George S. Patton, "Current Thoughts on Mechanization," December 15, 1936. In Box No. 53, 1937 file, George S. Patton, Jr. Papers, Library of Congress, Washington, D.C..

phrase: "A sufficient number of machines" and then go on to say that in this happy land of "Never was" the light machines and the leading wave of the heavies will assault the guns while succeeding waves of heavies will chaperon the infantry and chivy the machine guns.

Comment:

Since, unlike Peter Pan, I do not believe in Fairy Godmothers and hence cannot picture a situation in which there will ever be "A sufficient number" of anything, especially tanks, I pass without further remark this otherwise excellent plan.

Laboring, as I do, under the disadvantage of vivid memories, I find myself inclined to side with the school of opinion which allots to the A.F.V.'s the destruction of the machine guns and A.T. weapons.

Finally, I am wholly opposed to the launching of a tank attack against a prepared position. The act is analogous to that of sending battleships to attack seacoast forts; you might win but the odds are against you and the price is too high. . . .

Advance Guards:

There is quite a strong sentiment for the use of A.F.V.'s in advance guards with the idea of sweeping away minor resistance and of rapidly developing the situation.

Comment:

Undoubtedly such an employment of machines would be most effective, but before adhering fully to such a system we should weigh the advantages against the drawbacks. In other words will the evident advantages to be gained out-weigh the wastage which will be inevitable? If one can picture a practically unlimited supply of machines the answer is yes, but will such a situation ever occur? In my opinion certainly not in the initial stages of a war. It is, I think, evident that considering the fire-power of his day Napoleon could have facilitated the march of his advance guards by placing Currassiers with them. The fact that he did not was due to his fear of dissipating a force which in the crisis of a general battle would possibly prove invaluable. The same considerations apply to heavy A.F.V.'s. Armored cars of course will be invaluable to advance guards and in a pursuit, the value of time may even justify using tanks and combat cars. After Jena, Murat rode his heavy cavalry to exhaustion. It is all a question of the importance of the ends sought.

Delaying Actions:

So far as I know hardly any emphasis has been placed on the great value of A.F.V.'s in delaying actions, yet I believe that here their capacity is even greater than on the offensive while circumstances under which they can be employed will make their . . . casualties negligible. In such operations armored cars will generally suffice. It is however probable that at night they must be relieved by other troops.

General Comments on the Use of A.F.V.'s:

In my opinion that due to the high susceptibility of A.F.V.'s to circumstances of terrain the scope of their employment is more limited than is sometimes assumed. While this fact does prevent the organization of wholly mechanized armies, it does not detract from the power and importance of mechanization when circumstances permit its use.

⚐ *E S S A Y S*

The debate over "Billy" Mitchell's concepts of air power and his methods of promoting it continues to the present day. In the first essay, one written especially for this volume, Michael L. Grumelli, a former Air Force officer with a doctorate in history and a professor at the Air Command and Staff College, Maxwell Air Force Base, while somewhat critical of Mitchell's rigidity, places his broad vision within both airpower theory and the larger early twentieth-century American fascination with aviators and aviation. In the second essay, William F. Trimble of Auburn University, in a sympathetic biography of Admiral William Moffett in 1994, contrasts the naval aviation chief's quiet, bureaucratic efforts to fend off the flamboyant and dogmatic Mitchell and his idea of a unified Air Service on one hand and on the other to maneuver between the impatient young Turks and the conservative shellbacks in the navy. In the third essay, William J. Woolley, a historian at Ripon College in Wisconsin, emphasizes the degree to which George S. Patton, Jr., remained guided by traditionalist and pre-industrial attitudes even as he moved gradually to adopt the new view of mechanization and the decisive use of armored warfare.

"Billy" Mitchell Espouses
a Broad Vision of Airpower

MICHAEL L. GRUMELLI

William "Billy" Lendrum Mitchell has been primarily defined, in the literature scrutinizing the role of the armed forces in the United States, within the context of his strident dissent from military orthodoxy in the early interwar period. His 1925 court-martial for conduct prejudicial to good order and discipline held the nation's attention for 51 days; it remains one of the most sensational trial extravaganzas of a decade noted for extraordinary courtroom dramas. Indeed, the tremendous public fascination with the trial and defendant suggests much about America's need for individualistic heroes in an age of mass society, and the airman's ability to meet that need.

Military aviators, like Billy Mitchell, met an important cultural need by representing a successful union between modern technology and traditional regard for the near mythical individualism of America's pre-industrial past. This powerful

Original paper written for this volume by Michael L. Grumelli, Professor of War Theory and Campaign History at the USAF Air Command and Staff College, Maxwell AFB, AL.

combination of pilot, flying machine and "rugged individualism" first caught the country's attention during the Great War. Although pursuit pilots like Eddie Ricken-backer captured the lion's share of attention through romantic newspaper accounts of air fighting above the dismal slaughter in the trenches, America's premier air combat commander, Brigadier General William L. Mitchell, also gained national recognition and an inescapable public allure for his service at the front. . . .

Mitchell arrived in France [as a major and chief of the Signal Corps Aviation Section] only four days after the United States declared war on Germany and her allies. He was dispatched to Europe to review wartime aeronautical developments and make recommendations for the creation of an American air service. Once there, however, Billy Mitchell concentrated on the operational nature of air fighting. He examined doctrinal concepts with allied air leaders, became especially taken with Major General Hugh Trenchard's command of the Royal Flying Corps, flew as an observer on British and French combat missions, and began to formulate ideas about the proper employment of aircraft in support of a ground campaign as well as in the overall scheme of modern warfare.

Energetic, knowledgeable, and able to express clearly his views on the future of American aviation at the front, Billy Mitchell gained the attention of Major General John J. Pershing, Commander of the American Expeditionary Force (AEF), in June of 1917. Pershing made him a member of his staff, which also carried a promotion to the rank of lieutenant colonel. Mitchell spent the next year jockeying for position with other talented aviation officers in the expanding Air Service of the AEF. It was a period marked by often bitter organizational disputes over areas of responsibility, control of resources, and command. Concerned by the growing intensity of this intramural conflict and cognizant of the need to provide his aviators with strong decisive leadership, General Pershing reorganized the Army air arm under the overall command of Colonel Mason Patrick, a West Point classmate. He also gave Billy Mitchell command of all American air units on the front line—euphemistically termed the "zone of advance."

Although volatile at times, Mitchell's firm grasp of aerial warfare and inspirational leadership held an inexperienced, as well as technologically inferior, American air brigade together during the crucial battle of Chateau-Thierry in July and August of 1918. By the time Pershing's First American Army was prepared to eliminate German positions in the St. Mihiel salient, a prelude to a major thrust into the Meuse-Argonne region, Billy Mitchell had become the accepted American air combat leader. At St. Mihiel he led a coalition force of more than fourteen hundred American, British, French, and Italian airmen. It was the single largest concentration of air power in World War I, and it marked him as one of the leading air commanders of the entire conflict. By the end of the war, Billy Mitchell had risen to the rank of brigadier general, and was directing the operations of 45 frontline squadrons.

After the war, the inevitable debate over Army reorganization was ignited. In addition to traditional concerns about personnel levels, equipment requirements, and adequate funding, a new element was injected into the discussion with an intensity that could not be ignored. This fresh point of contention involved the subject of determining a proper organizational format for United States military aviation. This issue, first publicly raised by the civilian aeronautical elite, gained increasing force as returning airmen joined the debate and stridently began to dissent from the institutional schemes put forth by the proponents of military or-thodoxy—the subordination of aviation within a defense structure dominated by surface forces. Convinced that the course of the next war would be increasingly determined by a nation's aerial strength, flying officers in the United States Army strove to bring about a peacetime military establishment conducive to the future development of American air power. Motivated by their hopes for a better state of affairs for aviation than had existed during the war, and distrust of the General Staff, army airmen demonstrated an amazing willingness to advance positions that conflicted with War Department policy at congressional hearings convened to de-termine legislative action on the topic of aeronautics. In truth, reform-minded avi-ators like Billy Mitchell, Benjamin Foulois, Hap Arnold, Hiram Bingham, and Fiorello La Guardia derived the concept of airmindedness from the established tenets of the gospel of efficiency, which touted the benefits of expertise, scientific management, technology, and proper organization in public life. Although progres-sive thought formed the mind of this embryonic reform movement, its passion stemmed from wartime frustrations with the pace of United States military avia-tion progress and a nurtured sense of betrayal surrounding the quality of aircraft provided by the War Department for service at the front. For Billy Mitchell, the "Great War in the Air" was more often than not a frantic search for airmen and air-craft to keep squadrons at the front, especially bombardment units, in the fight. A situation made worse in his estimation by a lack of preparedness during peacetime and organizational disarray in the United States Air Service once war came. In essence, wartime performance in the air had been limited primarily because airminded individuals had not overseen its employment and development. These beliefs were fully reflected in an article that appeared in the September 1920 issue of *The American Review of Reviews* entitled "Our Army's Air Service." The concluding paragraph was a mixture of adumbration and summation: "We are con-vinced that aviation can only be put on its feet in this country through the unifica-tion of all air activities . . . under persons who are actually familiar with flying and the things that go with it."

As a result, Mitchell and most army aviators spurned Secretary of War Newton Baker's plea for unity of purpose in approaching the question of postwar reorgani-zation and went their own way. In September 1919, Newton Baker urged all of his officers to reaffirm their commitment to discipline and the service by adhering to the principles established by former Secretary of War Elihu Root. Baker re-minded his audience that Root thought it best to "fight out our quarrels among our-selves . . . and when we go to the Congress, or to the people, let us present a solid front, which having determined a wise course for the Nation, insist as a unit to back that determination." In war the singleness of purpose required to achieve vic-tory can act to regulate the intensity of internal conflict within a military organiza-tion and such was generally the case with the United States Army in the First World War. However, with the restoration of peace in November of 1918, any sem-blance of the unity gained while serving in France under General John J. Pershing was quickly discarded in the rush of demobilization.

Perhaps the returning soldiers and airmen simply caught the growing mood of resentment in postwar America. This shift in public spirit was propelled, in part, by the painful process of industrial reconversion and rapid demobilization of the armed forces. It also represented an emerging national indifference to Wilsonian idealism. Or perhaps their restlessness was generated by the realization that there would be little opportunity in the service after the war to employ adequately the talented professionals that wartime demanded. In either case, the attitude of many military members reflected the increasingly popular disenchantment with an administration that seemed to be out of touch and ineffective.

Officers associated with flying were not the only ones marching to the beat of a different drum during the Army reorganization battles of 1919 and 1920. Rebelliousness and dissent manifested itself in the Quartermaster Corps and Chemical Service. Even such normally bucolic and unwarlike sections as Finance, Transportation, and Construction attempted to influence legislation in order to achieve an end quite different from the official position advanced by the General Staff and Secretary of War. What made the airmen different from their other service brothers was the war itself. It nourished an elitist attitude that spilled over into peacetime and led them to discount the more significant contribution made by the ground forces and to dismiss as irrelevant the history of the art of war before 1914. More importantly, what set aviators apart from the rest was the degree to which their dissent drew even more strength from their fixed belief that air power would make them the final arbiters in any future war. In the foreword to his 1921 book, *Our Air Force,* Mitchell argues: "The first battles of any future war will be air battles. The nation winning them is practically certain to win the whole war, because the victorious air service will be able to operate and increase without hindrance."

The legislative battle to secure a separate organizational format for American military aeronautics began in earnest when, during the fall of 1919, army aviators started to challenge the accepted policies, doctrine, and traditional leadership role of the Army and Navy departments before Congress. At issue was the possibility of securing positive legislative action for aviation interests through passage of bills introduced in late July by Representative Charles Curry of California and Senator Harry S. New of Indiana, calling for the creation of a separate department of aeronautics to administer all civil and military aviation activities in the United States and its foreign possessions. During the numerous hearings on defense reorganization, military aviation, and War Department expenditures held by the 66th Congress, the principal rationale for air power dissent was established.

First, the future of the nation's security now rested primarily on a powerful independent air arm. Ignoring the operational limitations imposed by the present state of aviation technology, Billy Mitchell and other army aviators argued that the airplane was capable of conducting strategic air operations over vast distances. Moreover, they maintained that the next war would be decided in the air, and therefore it was absolutely essential that ground and naval surface forces give way in matters of national defense to the new air weapon. Next, the public interest would be best served by the creation of an executive-level department (with its own cabinet-level secretary) capable of directing all aeronautical travel, training, operations, and development. Most importantly, such an organization must be controlled by individuals with special expertise in aviation. . . .

Although most aviators agreed there must be a new bureaucratic scheme for aviation, they disagreed over the form that organization should take. Mitchell and his followers clung tenaciously to the proposition that the only acceptable solution was the creation of a super department of aeronautics with its own secretary; separate budget; final authority over the development of all military, civil, and commercial aviation; its own training academy (similar to West Point and Annapolis); and a unified combatant air force to constitute the nation's first line of defense. Other military aviators thought the time for complete independence was still in the future and suggested instead that a semi-independent air corps be established. Civil aviation proponents resisted any attempt to meld their activities with defense-oriented aeronautics. Most naval aviators were devoted to maintaining their link with the fleet and chose to work within their service. They argued not for independence, but urged congressional leaders to provide the navy with an effective bureau of aeronautics instead.

The 66th Congress considered no less than eight separate measures aimed at establishing an independent organizational format for air power during its fifteen-month deliberation on defense reorganization, but all came to naught. The Army Reorganization Act of 1920 did not create an air force or even free aviators from the control of general staff officers. After months of rising expectations, many army aviators viewed the act's passage as a crushing defeat. Nevertheless, the act did provide the airmen with a distinct legislative identity, enhanced organizational prestige equal to the army's traditional combat arms branches, and a personnel strength (on paper) of fifteen hundred officers and sixteen thousand men. It also created two general officer billets, a major general to serve as Chief of the Air Service and a brigadier for an assistant. The act limited the number of non-flying officers to no more than 10 percent of all officers assigned in the grades below general and provided a 50 percent increase in base pay for all officers and enlisted men participating "regularly and frequently in aerial flights." Moreover, flying units would be commanded solely by flying officers; a clear victory for the organizational progressive spirit within aviation.

In many ways, the airmen fared much better than the other branch of the service called forth by the internal combustion engine's contribution to twentieth-century warfare. The Army Reorganization Act of 1920 simply abolished the Tank Corps and reassigned its personnel to the infantry. Funding for tank research development was practically nonexistent in the early interwar years, and talented armor officers like George S. Patton left for their old career fields, in his case the cavalry. Even though the Air Service remained under the Army's General Staff, the airmen had not done badly, and there was also the possibility that they might do better the next time they went before Congress.

Billy Mitchell sensed early in 1920 that his optimism and plans for accommodating a bold and broad vision for air power within a unified and independent organizational format were premature. Nonetheless, he remained undaunted and told the airmen that chose to rally around his leadership and vision that next year "the prospects for favorable Air Service legislation look much brighter than for any other branch of the service." It was always going to happen next year.

Admiral Moffett Adheres to a Cautious Approach

WILLIAM F. TRIMBLE

More than any other person, Rear Adm. William A. Moffett shaped naval aviation during the critical, formative years of the twenties and early thirties. He was the consummate professional, the dedicated officer who in all his thoughts and actions demonstrated an abiding loyalty to his service and its role as the nation's first line of defense. Out of Annapolis, he served in more than twenty ships ranging from old windjammers to the most modern and powerful superdreadnoughts. He retraced the well-worn path that other officers had followed to senior rank, leaving few clues in his early service record to hint at his later commitment to aviation.

At first glance it appears odd that a battleship officer like Moffett would eventually devote his career and his life to such a new and visionary element as aviation. One would think that it clashed with his sense of traditionalism. But the apparently confusing dichotomy vanishes in the realization that Moffett saw aviation as an integral, organic part of the fleet. To Moffett the airplane and the airship had utility only in how they contributed to the overall effectiveness of the Navy, its ships, and its personnel. This was not a rationalization or an intentional accommodation to the extremists on both sides of the question. It was a deeply held conviction. Moffett comprehended the tactical, strategic, and political implications of naval aviation, and he was willing to dedicate his career as a flag officer first to bringing aviation into the fleet and then to guaranteeing its role as a powerful arm of the modern Navy. . . .

Moffett played a key role in the formation and initial operation of the Bureau of Aeronautics in 1921. Those who supported the creation of the bureau did so largely based on assurances that Moffett would become its first chief. As director of Naval Aviation in 1921, he actively lobbied for the new bureau, and as its chief he personally created its organizational structure, selected its personnel, and assigned them to their duties. He was an unusually effective administrator who delegated authority to subordinates and encouraged independence, initiative, and innovation. Loyal to those under him in the bureau and expecting loyalty in return, Moffett knew he could always count on the bureau's junior officers. But in demanding absolute loyalty and tolerating little or no dissent, Moffett ran the risk of surrounding himself with amiable cronies and yes-men, thereby losing perspective on vital questions where there could be legitimate contrary opinion. Some particularly strong and opinionated officers, notably Capt. Ernest J. King, found they could not work with Moffett under such circumstances. In stressing loyalty, commitment, and consensus within the Bureau of Aeronautics, Moffett conveyed an impression of confidence and assurance that what he advocated was right both for the Navy and for the country. On the occasions when his tactics of persuasion failed, he knew exactly when to call on friends for help and, most important, how

William F. Trimble, *Admiral William A. Moffett: Architect of Naval Aviation* (Washington, D.C.: Smithsonian Institution Press, 1994). Reprinted by permission of Smithsonian Institution Press.

to make them feel that in assisting him they were also contributing in a material way to the benefit of the service. . . .

Moffett had an impeccable sense of timing. When it came to using special investigatory committees and boards, he knew that too often personalities became enmeshed in highly controversial issues, obscuring the fundamentals and preventing their solution. But panels of experts, seemingly removed from the baggage of personality and emotions, could often accomplish what he wanted and do so in a constructive, noncontroversial manner. Moreover, boards fit well into the institutional structure and seemed less threatening than strident cries for change or a long series of clashes between highly placed individuals. The success of Moffett's tactics can be measured in the incremental growth of naval aviation during a decade generally characterized by fiscal economy and reduced military appropriations. Moffett knew how to manipulate the system.

Moffett's mastery of politics enabled him to fight and win a three-front war in Washington. He had first to confront the aviators within his own service. John Rodgers, Richard E. Byrd, Henry C. Mustin, John H. Towers, Bruce Leighton, and Kenneth Whiting were among some of the lower-ranking officers who had become true believers, ardent converts to aviation and unswerving in their certainty that the airplane would revolutionize naval warfare. Some of them demanded the establishment of a separate aviation corps within the Navy, which Moffett adamantly opposed because he was convinced it would pull officers out of the mainstream of general line service and prevent the full integration of aviation into the fleet. At least part of his problem with those aviators stemmed from Moffett's own place within the Navy's administrative structure. Nominally head of a material bureau, he could only make recommendations regarding operations or the development of tactics to those responsible for aviation with the fleet. Normal procedure dictated that his channels to the operational side pass through the offices of the secretary of the Navy or the chief of Naval Operations. Thus circumscribed, Moffett faced the constant difficulty of maintaining two-way communication with the aviators and ran the risk of insulating himself from their special requirements, demands, and ideas. Moffett overcame the obstacle by establishing and maintaining close, informal contacts with operating personnel and creating a rotation system whereby aviators interspersed tours at the bureau with their flying duties.

At the opposite end of the spectrum from the aviators were the entrenched conservatives, mostly high-ranking officers desperately clinging to their turf and defending it against all usurpations, real or imagined. Led by Admirals Charles F. Hughes and Samuel S. Robison, both commanders in chief of the U.S. Fleet, and including such other senior officers as Rear Admirals William R. Shoemaker and Richard H. Leigh of the Bureau of Navigation, the group appeared intolerant of change and incapable of accommodating something as revolutionary as what the aviators advocated. The airmen derisively labeled the conservatives "battleship admirals" or scorned them as members of the Navy's "gun club." Captain Joseph Mason Reeves (later a rear admiral), a convert to aviation in the twenties, referred to them as "those old coots who command battleships." Aviation advocates and historians have sometimes dismissed these officers as hopelessly narrow-minded and irrationally Luddite in their opposition to the airplane. Yet following the Washington Conference, which suspended capital ship construction for a decade, American officers for the most part were less concerned with the battleship than they were with the airplane and the aircraft carrier. Generally they wanted, along with Moffett, to incorporate aviation into the fleet and to determine how to maximize the potential of the new technology. Moffett's struggle with the conservatives was not so much with a crusty group of battleship admirals or members of the exclusive gun club as it was a conflict with senior bureau chiefs in Washington. These men deeply resented Moffett's authority and influence and perceived the new Bureau of Aeronautics as a threat to their long-established prerogatives and a drain on the Navy's limited manpower and resources. When it was created, the bureau drew a large number of people away from the Bureau of Construction and Repair and the Bureau of Steam Engineering and took lesser numbers from some of the other established bureaus. Few raised objections, but when Moffett reached out to exercise control over aviation personnel, he came into conflict with the all-powerful Bureau of Navigation, which had a virtual stranglehold on personnel selection, assignment, and promotion. Moffett deftly wielded his multiple weapons of leadership, political know-how, and force of personality in the confrontation with the conservative bureaucrats within the service.

Finally, there was the third front, the believers in air power, exemplified by colorful, controversial, and flamboyant General William ("Billy") Mitchell. Mitchell saw aviation in altogether different terms from Moffett's. To him, the airplane and, to a lesser extent, the airship brought an entirely new dimension to warfare. Aviation alone could fight and win wars between nations and peoples. The long-range bomber had such enormous destructive capacity that neither navies nor armies could resist it. To realize the full potential of air power, the United States, Mitchell believed, had to establish an independent air force supplied with the most up-to-date equipment, flown by trained air personnel, and led by officers who were unencumbered by ties to either the Army or the Navy. Mitchell's views were antipathetic to Moffett, who saw aviation as a dependent force within the Navy, but in many ways Mitchell was easier to deal with than the young Turks or the old shellbacks within Moffett's service. Mitchell thrived on controversy and attracted charges like a lightning rod. Moffett knew that all he had to do was wait until Mitchell's intemperance led to his own undoing. Moffett often referred to disloyalty during the height of the Mitchell controversy during the twenties, but he rarely mentioned Mitchell's name in public. He did not have to. Moffett won the war with Mitchell using an astute combination of carefully worded jabs in the news media and the support of fiscally conservative Republican administrations that did not want to add another military service to the already existing layers of Washington bureaucracy.

Mitchellite propaganda tried to give the impression that aviation was neglected during the twenties. Nothing could be farther from the truth. Official Washington and both military services devoted an enormous amount of time and effort to the aviation question. During the decade, there were at least fifteen major investigations and numerous Navy General Board hearings dealing with aviation. The probes grappled with the problems presented in defining the federal regulatory role, keeping the aviation industry reasonably competitive and profitable, developing aviation as an offensive striking force, and determining the quantity and quality of military airplanes within coordinated, long-range procurement programs. Aviation was a major budgetary item for the Navy throughout the twenties and thirties, on an annual basis consuming ever larger portions of naval appropriations. Equally important, a number of senior naval officers had become aviation advocates by the early thirties, foremost in the flag rank being (besides Moffett) Joseph Mason Reeves, William V. Pratt, Ernest J. King, and Frank Brooks Upham. There may have been indecision, misdirection, opposition, and controversy, but aviation was not neglected.

The Mitchell-Moffett drama played itself out on all levels, but the most decisive battles took place in the field of public relations. The twenties saw the emergence of the modern mass media. The high-speed rotary press and access to international wire services gave the metropolitan newspaper unprecedented power to inform and mold opinion. Where the newspaper left off, the radio picked up, bringing an immediacy to news reporting unmatched by the press. For visual effect, nothing at the time compared with the motion picture, which after 1927 acquired the added attraction of sound. Traditionally, the Navy was the silent service and shied away from publicity, but Moffett saw great opportunities in adroitly handled public relations to promote naval aviation. In his hands the modern mass media became powerful instruments for change. Mitchell, too, recognized and exploited the power of publicity, but he failed to see beyond its immediate dramatic effect and, unlike Moffett, never understood its subtleties.

Aviation issues were central to Moffett's life and career after the creation of the Bureau of Aeronautics. The early bureau bore his personal imprint. Its people were a mix taken from the older, established bureaus; many of them were civilians. Moffett was a no-nonsense officer who ran what everyone considered a tight ship, and he molded a diverse group into a cohesive, efficient, and creative unit. Part of the success of the Bureau of Aeronautics was due to its relatively small size and informality, but it was due also to a dynamic interaction of people and their implicit belief and trust in the bureau's purpose. Jerome C. Hunsaker, head of the bureau's Plans Section in the early twenties, recalled that his relationship with Moffett was "one of great confidence." There was a pervasive feeling on the third floor of Main Navy in the twenties and early thirties that everyone was cooperating toward a common goal.

Like no other single figure in the Navy at the time, Moffett carved out a personal empire. Determined not to be in charge of just another material agency, he put his personal imprint on the institutional identity of the Bureau of Aeronautics and molded it into a superbureau. Under Moffett, the bureau assumed control over the design, procurement, and testing of aircraft and engines, took responsibility for all budgetary and fiscal matters concerning aviation, and established considerable authority over personnel assigned to aviation duties. Moffett resolutely defended the bureau against all challenges both from within and without the naval bureaucracy. In his most serious confrontation—with the Bureau of Navigation—he established control over the training and assignment of naval aviation personnel. . . .

In Congress, Moffett quickly identified and befriended key representatives and senators and learned how to manipulate the legislative process, especially when it came to securing the money needed for aircraft procurement. At the same time, he recognized his responsibilities as a public official to secure the best products at the most reasonable cost. Under most circumstances he and his staff made dispassionate judgments about the material requirements of aviation and got the most out of the companies under contract to provide aircraft and aviation equipment. That procurement policy remained muddled at the time of Moffett's death could be attributed more to congressional shortsightedness and inaction than to any administrative or political failures on his part.

Moffett actively promoted qualitative as well as quantitative changes in naval aviation. Possibly most important was the introduction of the aircraft carrier. Moffett saw the carrier as the principal means of taking the airplane to sea, although initially he was circumspect about the carrier's limited offensive role in support of the battleship's striking power. Largely through Moffett's efforts, the Navy completed the conversion of *Langley* in 1922 and received appropriations for the conversion of the large carriers *Saratoga* and *Lexington,* which joined the fleet in 1927. With those vessels the United States gained valuable experience in carrier design, construction, and operations. By Moffett's second term there was a not-so-subtle change in his thinking about the offensive capabilities of the carrier. More confident of his position in the Navy bureaucracy and with a steady stream of new aircraft coming into service as a result of the 1926 five-year program, Moffett was more outspoken about the potential of the aircraft carrier as a powerful strike weapon in its own right. In the late twenties he advocated the introduction of bombing and torpedo aircraft into fleet air squadrons and closely followed the transformation of carrier tactics wrought by Rear Admiral Reeves. . . .

In retrospect, it is easy to see that the rigid airship, the flying-deck cruiser, and the small aircraft carrier diverted Moffett and the Navy from what proved to be more fruitful areas of naval aviation. But with technology in a state of flux and with carrier tactics still evolving in the early thirties, it is understandable that Moffett and others should be sidetracked into less promising fields. More remarkable, perhaps, is that there were so few instances in which Moffett lost sight of the principal goals he had set for naval aviation and how successful he was in achieving those objectives. For Moffett, naval aviation was not just the aircraft carrier, the flying boat, the airship, or the flying-deck cruiser; it was also a complex matrix of technologies and people and organizations, all of which had to be molded into a coordinated whole. Moffett had a far more sophisticated, pluralistic vision of naval aviation than most of his contemporaries. . . .

To a certain extent the findings of the Navy's court of inquiry [1933] and the congressional investigation into airship disasters amounted to posthumous recognition of Moffett's key role in lighter-than-air development and brought to a close the last chapter in the admiral's controversial tenure as chief of the Bureau of Aeronautics. With Moffett's name already linked to the airship, Moffett's death in the crash of *Akron* fixed his reputation in the public mind as the uncompromising defender of lighter-than-air in the Navy. The association is unfortunate, for Moffett saw the rigid airship as only one component of a complex, powerful naval air force. His advocacy of the rigid airship tended to obscure less spectacular but, in the long run, more important contributions he made in integrating aviation with the fleet. Rather than being thought of only for his enthusiasm for the airship, Moffett should be remembered as the proponent of fleet aviation.

Viewing Moffett's accomplishments in a broader perspective reveals how much he did to bring about the realization of a true air navy during the interwar years. Through persistence and tireless effort, Moffett made the aircraft carrier an indispensable component of the fleet, and he saw to it that there were enough up-to-date airplanes to fly from those carriers. After the 1921 law creating the Bureau of Aeronautics, the 1926 five-year aircraft program was the most important legislation affecting the naval aviation establishment. Not only did it provide for the numbers of aircraft needed by an expanding naval air arm, but it also rescued manufacturers from almost certain doom by guaranteeing orders over an extended period. He did not overcome congressional opposition to more flexible aircraft contracting procedures, but he did establish a rational procurement policy that met the needs of both the industry and the Navy. Moreover, Moffett's commitment to advancing technological change ensured that American naval aviators flew some of the best airplanes available to any service in the world.

Moffett had an innate sense of what was possible and what was not possible in times of rapid technological change. Though a traditional line officer with little background in engineering, he appreciated the problems of the specialist officer and had some understanding of how aircraft and engines and their ancillary equipment worked. He understood the limits of technology, as well, and strove to ensure that the Navy did not expend large sums on projects that offered only limited potential for success. That was one of the reasons why he, influenced by Henry Mustin, insisted on limiting the bureau's planning to five-year cycles. Beyond that span of time, it was impossible to make reasonable predictions about the technology or to determine accurately the Navy's requirements for new material. To him, the Army's ten-year procurement plans seemed absurd, pie-in-the-sky dreams.

That Moffett accomplished this during an era of restricted budgets and limited enthusiasm for the military was even more remarkable. His political perspicacity was the reason for his success. He quickly learned his way around the civilian and military bureaucracy in Washington and, as he was blooded in the bureaucratic wars, knew how to get what he wanted. The results speak for themselves. In the process, however, he carved out a personal empire and gained considerable celebrity. Fortunately for the Navy and the nation, he never allowed the celebration of the individual to obscure what the individual stood for or to overshadow the importance of institutional goals. Admiral Hyman G. Rickover had a similar influence in the creation of the modern nuclear navy, but Rickover's organization, despite its effectiveness, bore the unmistakable stamp of his tyrannical personality. Moffett, instead, maintained the delicate balance of personal and organizational priorities better than any other military officer of his generation. . . .

Moffett at the time of his death had already done more than anyone before or since to secure the place of naval aviation in the military establishment. His tireless efforts laid the foundation for the modern air navy and created the organization and infrastructure on which naval aviation built during World War II. For that alone he deserves acknowledgment and praise for a job well done.

Colonel George Patton Only Slowly Embraces Modern Mechanized Warfare

WILLIAM J. WOOLLEY

Coming to terms with the industrial revolution caused a crisis of some sort in nearly every modern army. For most, the crisis was introduced by the machine gun, which mechanized the production of firepower. The resultant increase in the power of the defense overturned most of the Napoleonic tactical principles that had been so laboriously worked out during the previous century. But the mechanization of movement made possible by the gradual military adaptation of the principles of automotive transport threatened to revolutionize all aspects of warfare. As a result, during the decades separating the two world wars, the major source of military controversy in nearly every modern army was the issue of introducing the internal combustion engine into warfare on the ground and in the air.

On the ground the debate centered on the tank. At issue was not whether tanks should be used in warfare—all doubt on that question had vanished during the war—but how they were to be used. In nearly all major armies this controversy was ignited by the claims of a radical minority that warfare should be revolutionized by supplanting the traditional combat arms with totally new mechanized forces designed to fight the innovative mobile and strategic forms of warfare described in the works of J. F. C. Fuller and Basil Liddell Hart. These claims, in turn, aroused the opposition of a larger group which generally would allow mechanized weapons no more than a supportive and tactical role within the traditional combat arms, which were expected to fight war in a conventional manner.

In the United States Army the traditionalist outlook remained particularly dominant throughout the interwar period. This dominance was not due to a repressive conservatism imposed from above: The American Army was too fragmented in its structure to allow this, and its command leadership depended more on consensus than on coercion in exercising control. The problem lay, rather, in the institutional and intellectual obstacles that stood in the way of effecting change within the Army. Given the continued disaggregated structure of the Army, significant change could not be made without the mobilization of some degree of consensus among the officer corps. While the Army had the communications networks necessary for such a mobilization (professional journals and schools reinforced by widespread webs of private correspondence), it was also necessary that officers be receptive to change and adaptive in their thinking. While most American officers in this period saw themselves as professional and progressive students of warfare, there were still many aspects of their mental outlook that made accommodation to rapid or far-reaching change difficult. A study of the changing attitudes of one officer in this period, George S. Patton, Jr., toward the issue of mechanized warfare illuminates some of the problems faced by many of the others in making the adaptations it demanded.

Abridged text from William J. Woolley, "Patton and the Concept of Mechanized Warfare," *Parameters: Journal of the U.S. Army War College* 15, no. 3 (Autumn 1985), pages 71–72, 74–78. Reprinted with permission of the publisher.

Actually, Patton might appear to have been a unique case in this regard. He had more exposure to tanks than almost any other American officer of his time. During the First World War he organized the American Tank School in France and then led the first American tank units in battle. In the interwar period he continued to read extensively about mechanized warfare and wrote and spoke on the subject often. In 1940 he was among the first officers chosen to command a major mechanized unit in the two armored divisions finally being formed. Yet, despite the fact that he had an exposure to tanks that was longer and more extensive than that of almost any of his peers, his attitudes toward mechanization were basically traditionalist. During the 1920s and early 1930s he was one of the most outspoken defenders of the traditionalist military outlook and one of the most caustic and popular critics of the concept of mechanization. And while, by 1940, he had come to accept many of the ideas of the mechanizationists, this adaptation was a slow one which involved a complex interplay between traditionalist values and professional appraisals of the changing nature of warfare. Thus, in coming to terms with mechanization Patton was different from most of his fellow officers only in that he was somewhat more successful in making the mental adaptations necessary and much more vocal in doing so, leaving behind a wealth of articles, lecture notes, letters, and reports to mark the trail of his evolution. . . .

Patton began that career by establishing himself firmly within the traditionalist camp, though he also demonstrated his capacity to see outside of it. Within his first four years of service he had already made a name for himself by participating successfully in the 1912 Olympics and by redesigning the cavalry saber to improve its qualities as an offensive weapon. . . .

It was initially a concern for his career, however, rather than an interest in automobiles that led Patton to join the nascent Tank Corps as it was being formed in France in late 1917. Patton then was desperately seeking an escape from staff duty, which he found boring and without career potential. While he considered shifting branches in order to get command of an infantry battalion, he decided that greater chances for promotion lay with the tanks. Yet once associated with tanks, Patton developed an attachment for them that transcended career concerns, and he began early to accommodate them intellectually into his traditionalist world. Not only was the introduction of tanks legitimized by association with Alexander the Great, but Patton also developed the habit of referring to them in animalistic terms, and in his attempts at poetry he tried to give the tank service the same aura of romantic respectability enjoyed by cavalry. All this culminated for Patton in several opportunities to lead his tanks in combat, an experience which he found to be "thrilling" and which allowed him sufficient opportunity for traditional heroism to win the Distinguished Service Cross.

Thrilling and fulfilling as this wartime experience with tanks may have been, Patton's view of their role in combat remained unabashedly traditional. Shortly after the war he noted that "immense as the influence of mechanical devices may be, they can never of themselves decide a campaign. Their true [role] is that of assisting the infantry man. . . . They can never replace him." The dreams of the enthusiasts about mechanical armies he derided as "absurd." This traditionalist vision was, perhaps, reinforced by a vague fear that tanks could lead to an industrialization of warfare. . . .

Patton's attachment to the tanks kept him in the Tank Corps for nearly two years after the end of the war, during which time he campaigned actively in favor of granting the corps status as an independent combat arm. This position, which was quite at variance with his wartime orthodoxy, was apparently adopted by Patton more out of expediency than from a real shift in attitude. It was the line being taken by his commanding officer and other officers in the corps, and an independent status for the corps offered Patton his best chance for promotion. His arguments along this line, however, contained little that would appeal to professionals, and he abandoned them afterward.

Patton left the Tank Corps in October 1920 in a mood of increasing pessimism regarding the future of both the country and the Army. The National Defense Act of 1920 had not only ended the independent status of the Tank Corps (and the career prospects Patton had earlier associated with service in the Tank Corps), but had also gutted the Army, indicating a rapidly developing public disaffection with its armed forces. Patton explained this development to himself in terms of the Carthaginian tendency of American society, and like many of his colleagues he turned his attention to the preservation of the professional integrity of the Army. For the next eight years, his interest in tanks and mechanized warfare diminished considerably. His principal concern, instead, was the problem of command and his perception that a rapid invasion of civilian attitudes was undermining the traditional heroic model of military leadership. Not only were officers becoming too concerned with their own personal security in combat, but they were being taught that a scholarly approach to leadership was superior to a moral one, that "brains outrank guts." In this mood, he tended to view the Army's interest in mechanization as another form of the civilian invasion of the military world. . . . Patton's response was a volley of arguments emphasizing the actual limitations of existing military vehicles and reiterating the idea that war was made by men, not machines.

The year 1928 proved to be something of a turning point both for mechanization in the United States and for Patton. The successful development of several fast tank prototypes that year provided the vehicles needed by the theories of the mechanizationists, while a successful summer maneuver by an independent mechanized unit in Great Britain seemed to vindicate those theories and led the Secretary of War to commit the American Army to the development of its own experimental mechanized force. Meanwhile, in May 1928 Patton was transferred to the Office of the Chief of Cavalry as head of the Plans and Training Division. The Office of the Chief of Cavalry was then much concerned with mechanization but in an ambivalent way. On the one hand the office was the political and intellectual citadel of traditionalism within the cavalry. It published *Cavalry Journal* and coordinated all lobbying efforts on behalf of the cavalry. Its major concern in this area was to counter mounting pressures in favor of supplanting horse cavalry with armored vehicles. On the other hand, the chief's office was mandated by law and by the expectations of military professionals to develop the weapons and doctrines needed by the cavalry to meet new situations.

Patton's position in the office was particularly ambiguous, since he was expected to head both enterprises. His initial response to this was to seek a middle ground that would allow the cavalry the appearance and some of the advantages of mechanization without diluting its traditional character. Several years earlier he had supported the idea of attaching several troops of armored cars to a cavalry division to act in cooperation with horse units. By late 1928 the cavalry was ready to accept this limited mechanization. . . .

Patton initially defended this modest concession as representing the limit of mechanization necessary, supporting his position with more articles and lectures on the continued value of horse cavalry. Nevertheless, by the spring of 1930 his evaluation of developments in other armies convinced him that in almost any future combat situation American cavalry could expect to encounter hostile armored vehicles. A mechanization limited to armored cars capable of operating only on roads would obviously be an inadequate response to such a situation. While he agreed that the problem might be met temporarily by developing mobile .50-caliber machine guns for horse pack as antitank weapons, he was rapidly becoming convinced that a more far-reaching solution was called for and that this solution involved the tank.

Earlier Patton had argued that there was no place for the tank in the cavalry, since "at present there is no tank . . . which can keep up with Cavalry." However, the appearance of the new fast tank prototypes in 1928, and particularly the model developed by J. Walter Christie, caused him to reconsider. The Christie prototype was capable of rapid maneuver on either wheels or tracks, so that it seemed to offer the advantages of both the armored car and the tank. . . . By early 1931 [Patton] was arguing that the cavalry could not hope to counter expected enemy armored vehicles unless it possessed armored vehicles of its own. While Patton cautiously referred to such vehicles as "heavy armored cars," it is clear that he had Christie tanks in mind. At the same time, in his historical references the tank was increasingly referred to as the modern descendent [*sic*] of the armored knight, or chariot warfare. . . .

Contact with the reality of current military trends was not, however, the most important force that pushed Patton toward accepting the tank. Efforts over ten years to defend traditional horse cavalry had caused him to refine considerably his traditionalist attitudes, leading him to a vision of warfare that was more mobile, strategic, and mechanized. Repeated emphasis of the cavalry's critical role in reconnaissance led Patton from his earlier tactical and battle-centered vision of war to a conception that was more campaign-oriented and strategic. Similar efforts to dissociate American cavalry from the failures of European cavalry during the First World War on the grounds that Americans belonged to the dragoon rather than the cuirassier tradition of cavalry led Patton to envision cavalry less as a unit capable of shock action in battle and more as a self-contained organization that emphasized maneuver and firepower.

Finally, and most important, for over ten years Patton and others had argued that one could make no judgment about the future of cavalry on the basis that it had not been used in the First World War, since that war had been of a unique character unlikely to be seen again. For Patton this argument was not a matter of expediency but represented a genuine and deeply troubling sentiment. Within a short time of his arrival in France in 1917, Patton came to feel that the conflict there was not real war. Ever since he had first encountered warfare in history, real war had meant to him movement and decisiveness. West Point and his experience in Mexico had reinforced that view, so that he saw the static and indecisive trench warfare that he found in France in 1917 as an unhealthy aberration. . . .

Patton's aristocratic upbringing, his classic and heroic value structure, and his ambition for preeminence left him little capacity to accept democratic values or institutions. By the time he had left West Point, Patton was a full-fledged Uptonian in his conviction that only professional military organizations were of any value. Contact with reserve officers in subsequent years tended to reinforce these views. In the late 1920s Patton became deeply interested in the writing of Ardant du Picq and in that of current French and German military figures who extolled the values of the professional army. This reading helped Patton to clarify his earlier views and led him to argue in 1930 and 1931 that while the huge conscript armies raised in 1914 and thereafter had been relatively easy to supply over Europe's magnificent transportation network, they were too massive and ill-trained to maneuver. As a result, the conflict in Europe had quickly stabilized along extended parallel lines so that war became a matter of attrition rather than movement. For Patton, attrition degraded warfare from a form of human conflict into an industrial process in which "the inert human masses became fodder for their equally inert masses of machines."

In Patton's mind, the obvious solution to this problem was to reject the wrong turn taken toward mass industrial warfare in 1914 and to return to the traditional warfare of maneuver, to be fought now by small, highly mobile, and fully professional armies. He spelled out this idea in great detail in his major student paper at the Army War College in 1932, giving it a broad historical introduction, and it remained fundamental to his thinking during the rest of the decade. For a while he continued to claim that horse cavalry would play a number of major roles in such a force, arguing that mobility meant flexible speed, which could be gained only by a force made up of horse and machine units working in complementary fashion. Later, however, he began to drop that argument, and the roles assigned to horse units in his imagined force began to diminish.

Thus, during the four years spent in the Office of the Chief of Cavalry and at the Army War College, Patton had come to accept a vision of warfare involving armored vehicles organized as self-contained units operating on a strategic as well as a tactical basis, a vision not too far removed from that of the mechanizationists. Yet he got there principally by means of a reactionary line of thought, to the degree that he was still able to see himself as a defender of tradition. As such, he continued to criticize the "pure mechanizationists" vigorously and to point out repeatedly the limitations of armored vehicles. Thus, while there may have been a significant convergence between Patton and the mechanizationists in regard to the arms and doctrines both advocated, they were still as far apart as ever on the philosophic bases on which their ideas were founded. What the mechanizationists had proposed as a revolutionary means to overthrow an outworn traditional system of warfare, Patton had finally come to accept as an evolutionary means to restore it.

Patton's subsequent assignments during the 1930s brought him into contact with other problems, and for a number of years his interest in mechanization faded.

Later, the Spanish Civil War . . . and the [1936–39] feeling that a new European war was imminent rekindled that interest to some extent, leading to some refinement in his ideas. Patton was now willing to give significant reconnaissance and even tactical roles to aircraft and almost none to horse units. At the same time he continued to attack mechanizationists for their lack of realism and for pandering to the public's craving for security from a draft.

In July 1940 the Army committed itself to the creation of a mechanized force. Brigadier General Adna R. Chaffee, who had been one of the leaders of the mechanizationist movement since 1928 and who was now slated to head the new armored force, invited Patton to take command of a brigade in the new Second Armored Division. Patton accepted eagerly and threw himself immediately into training his unit. Gathering his unit for a lecture in early September, he explained, among other things, that the key to German success in this war was the fact that "they did not use weapons because they were new, but because through their use, age-old military tasks could be better accomplished." Patton had joined the mechanizationists; yet he remained a traditionalist.

It would seem that at least two conclusions could be drawn from this brief survey of the development of Patton's vision of mechanized warfare. First, by the late 1930s Patton had developed a rather perceptive insight into the nature of the warfare that would emerge in the opening stages of the Second World War. Doing so required a major transformation in Patton's thinking on how tanks were to be used in combat. Giving them initially a role strictly subordinate to the traditional combat arms, he gradually came to accept a view of mechanized warfare similar to that of the mechanizationists. Yet this transformation in thinking was episodic in its development, with most changes taking place when Patton had responsibilities directly linked to tanks. At other times, interests created by other assignments and the inhibitions arising from his traditionalist vision of the nature of war and of legitimate change all but halted any development in his thinking in this area. These latter circumstances were common to many other officers in the Army, which may help explain the slowness of the Army in accepting the ideas of mechanization.

Second, while Patton came to adopt much of the mechanizationists' style of warfare and even to make himself a master of it, he did so by incorporating it into his own traditional outlook, so that the latter survived the transformation intact. The fact that Patton and many of his fellow officers could modernize their style of fighting without disturbing their traditionalist outlook may partially explain their ability to maintain a sense of stability and self-assurance within the confusion of a new kind of warfare. It may also help explain why the Second World War so quickly assumed a traditional character.

♠ F U R T H E R   R E A D I N G

Merrill L. Bartlett, *Lejeune: A Marine's Life, 1867–1942* (1991).
Larry I. Bland, et. al., *The Papers of George Catlett Marshall*, vol. 1 (1981).
Martin Blumenson, ed., *The Patton Papers, 1885–1940*, vol. 1 (1972).

Lester H. Brune, *The Origins of American National Security Policy: Sea Power, Air Power, and Foreign Policy, 1900–1941* (1981).

Thomas H. Buckley, *The United States and the Washington Conference, 1921–1922* (1970).

Paolo E. Coletta, "Prelude to War: Japan, the United States, and the Aircraft Carrier, 1919–1945," *Prologue* 23 (1991) 343–359.

Robert L. Daugherty, *Weathering the Peace: The Ohio National Guard in the Interwar Years* (1992).

Joel Davidson, *The Unsinkable Fleet: The Politics of U.S. Navy Expansion in World War II* (1996).

Carlo D'Este, *Patton: A Genius for War* (1995).

Jeffrey M. Dorwart, *Conflict of Duty: The U.S. Navy's Intelligence Dilemma, 1919–1945* (1983).

J. F. C. Fullet, *On Future Warfare* (1928).

Robert F. Futrell, *Ideas, Concepts, Doctrine: A History of Basic Thinking in the United States Air Force, 1907–1964* (1971).

Mildred H. Gillie, *Forging the Thunderbolt: A History of the Development of the Armored Force* (1947).

Thomas H. Greer, *The Development of Air Doctrine in the Army Air Arm, 1917–1941* (1955).

Richard P. Hallion, *Strike from the Sky: The History of Battlefield Air Attack, 1911–1945* (1989).

Frederick S. Harrod, *Manning the New Navy: The Development of a Modern Naval Enlisted Force, 1899–1940* (1978).

Alfred F. Hurley, *Billy Mitchell: Crusader for Air Power* (1975).

Robert J. Jakeman, *The Divided Skies: Establishing Segregated Flight Training at Tuskegee, Alabama, 1934–1942* (1992).

Charles Johnson, Jr., *African American Soldiers in the National Guard* (1992).

Basil Liddell Hart, *A History of the World War, 1914–1918* (1934).

John W. Killigrew, *The Impact of the Great Depression on the Army* (1979).

Paul A. C. Koistinen, "The 'Industrial-Military Complex' in Historical Perspective: The Interwar Years," *Journal of American History* 56 (March 1970): 819–839.

Brian McAllister Linn, *Guardians of Empire: The U.S. Army and the Pacific, 1902–1940* (1997).

Donald J. Lisio, *The President and Protest: Hoover, Conspiracy, and the Bonus Riot* (1974).

Charles M. Melhorn, *Two-Block Fox: The Rise of the Aircraft Carrier, 1911–1929* (1974).

Allan R. Millett, *In Many a Strife: General Gerald C. Thomas and the U.S. Marine Corps, 1917–1956* (1993).

Williamson Murray and Allan R. Millett, eds., *Military Innovation in the Interwar Period* (1996).

Clark G. Reynolds, *The Fast Carriers: The Forging of an Air Navy* (1968).

William F. Trimble, *Admiral William A. Moffett: Architect of Naval Aviation* (1994).

Lucian K. Truscott, Jr., *The Twilight of the U.S. Cavalry: Life in the Old Army, 1917–1942* (1989).

Michael Vlahos, *The Blue Sword: The Naval War College and the American Mission, 1919–1941* (1980).

Gerald E. Wheeler, *Prelude to Pearl Harbor: The United States Navy and the Far East, 1921–1931* (1963).

Robert H. Williams, *The Old Corps: A Portrait of the U.S. Marine Corps Between the Wars* (1982).

William J. Woolley, "Patton and the Concept of Mechanized Warfare," *Parameters* 15 (Autumn 1985): 71–80.

CHAPTER
11

World War II: Ground Combat
in Europe and the Pacific

The United States entered World War II on December 7, 1941, at least two years after most of the other Allies, but it nevertheless contributed significantly to the defeat
of the Axis powers: Germany, Italy, and Japan. More than 16 million Americans
served in the armed forces during the war, 11 million in the army and Army Air
Forces, 4 million in the navy, 670,000 in the Marines, and 330,000 in women's
military units. It was the most massive war effort in the nation's history; Americans fought in the Atlantic, North Africa, Europe, the Pacific, and Asia. Historians
continue to debate many aspects of the war, including military operations, international relations, and diverse human experiences. As part of the new social and cultural history, scholars recently have become particularly interested in the memories
of common service people for what they indicate about the variety of war experience
as well as about combat motivation. Indeed, part of the debate among American
military historians has concerned the combat effectiveness of the average G.I. In a
1947 book, Men against Fire, Brigadier General S. L. A. Marshall, a former
journalist and military historian, claimed to have interviewed some 400 American
soldiers after battles in the Central Pacific and Europe, and he asserted that only
one out of four soldiers had fired their weapons when they were in combat. Marshall's assertions were highly controversial and remain so to the present day, but
they led the army to alter its training to increase the rate of fire of the average rifle
squad. An even broader and more recent debate involves comparing the performance of entire national armies in World War II. Some military historians have
asserted that the German Army was superior to the U.S. Army in discipline, leadership, and virtually every aspect except quantity of material. Others, however,
have contended that the individualism and democratic values of America made its
army more than a match for Hitler's vaunted Wehrmacht.

▲ D O C U M E N T S

E. B. Sledge was a freshman at Marion Military College in Alabama when he enlisted
in the Marines in December 1942; two years later, the 21-year-old private stormed

310

ashore with the First Marine Division on the tiny, heavily fortified island of Peleliu in the western Carolines on September 15, 1944, the first day of a month-long action in which 1,300 Marines were killed; in the first document, his memoir published in 1981, Sledge recalls his baptism of fire. J. Robert Slaughter of Roanoke, Virginia, was a 19-year-old heavy weapons sergeant in the Twenty-ninth (National Guard) Division, which along with the regular army's 1st Infantry Division, made the initial assault against Omaha beach on the Normandy Coast of France on D-Day, June 6, 1944. In 1993, he recounted his experience at "Bloody Omaha," where the Germans nearly prevented the Americans from gaining a foothold. By December, the Allies had liberated France and had pushed eastward to the German border, when Hitler launched a surprise counteroffensive December 16, 1944, through the Ardennes Forest (the Battle of the Bulge), killing many G.I.s, taking thousands of prisoners, and temporarily surrounding pockets of American troops. In the third document, Private Franklin ("Frank") Kneller of New Jersey reminisces in a 1994 oral history interview about his experience as a young replacement in the 101st Airborne Division, serving in the snow-covered Ardennes Forest when he learned that the Germans were attacking. Gertrude Pearson, a New York bank teller, joined the Women's Army Corps (WACs) in January 1943 at 21; as a cryptographic technician operating coding machines, she relates in 1995, in the fourth document, how she and two dozen other WACs in a Signal Corps mobile communications unit, assigned to the First Tactical Air Force, arrived in late October 1944 in Vittel, south of Nancy, France, close behind the front lines of George Patton's Third U.S. Army only two months before the Battle of the Bulge. One of the debates about combat motivation concerns whether soldiers are motivated more by ideology or by unit cohesion, that is, fighting to protect one another. The fifth document, the results of interviews and questionnaires by U.S. Army psychologists of combat soldiers in Europe and the Pacific in 1944 as to how combat units maintained themselves psychologically, suggests that a number of factors influenced unit cohesion and combat effectiveness, including concepts of masculinity, loyalty to buddies, and a desire to defeat the enemy and return home. In the sixth document, a philosophy professor, J. Glenn Gray, a counter-intelligence officer with American infantry divisions in the campaigns in Italy, southern France, and Germany between 1943 and 1945, reflects in 1959 about the nature of the combat experience, which he says includes fear, hatred, and guilt, but also what he calls the "enduring appeals of battle."

1. Private E. B. Sledge, U.S.M.C., Remembers Heavy Fighting at Peleliu (1944), 1981

"Hit the beach!" yelled an NCO moments before the machine lurched to a stop.

The men piled over the sides as fast as they could. I followed Snafu, climbed up, and planted both feet firmly on the left side so as to leap as far away from it as possible. At that instant a burst of machine-gun fire with white-hot tracers snapped through the air at eye level, almost grazing my face. I pulled my head back like a turtle, lost my balance, and fell awkwardly forward down onto the sand in a tangle of ammo bag, pack, helmet, carbine, gas mask, cartridge belt, and flopping canteens. "Get off the beach! Get off the beach!" raced through my mind.

Once I felt land under my feet, I wasn't as scared as I had been coming across the reef. My legs dug up the sand as I tried to rise. A firm hand gripped my shoulder. "Oh god, I thought, it's a Nip who's come out of a pillbox!" I couldn't reach my kabar—fortunately, because as I got my face out of the sand and looked up, there was the worried face of a Marine bending over me. He thought the machine-gun burst had hit me, and he had crawled over to help. When he saw I was unhurt, he spun around and started crawling rapidly off the beach. I scuttled after him.

Shells crashed all around. Fragments tore and whirred, slapping on the sand and splashing into the water a few yards behind us. The Japanese were recovering from the shock of our prelanding bombardment. Their machine gun and rifle fire got thicker, snapping viciously overhead in increasing volume.

Our amtrac spun around and headed back out as I reached the edge of the beach and flattened on the deck. The world was a nightmare of flashes, violent explosions, and snapping bullets. Most of what I saw blurred. My mind was benumbed by the shock of it.

I glanced back across the beach and saw a DUKW (rubber-tired amphibious truck) roll up on the sand at a point near where we had just landed. The instant the DUKW stopped, it was engulfed in thick, dirty black smoke as a shell scored a direct hit on it. Bits of debris flew into the air. I watched with that odd, detached fascination peculiar to men under fire, as a flat metal panel about two feet square spun high into the air then splashed into shallow water like a big pancake. I didn't see any men get out of the DUKW.

Up and down the beach and out on the reef, a number of amtracs and DUKWs were burning. Japanese machine-gun bursts made long splashes on the water as though flaying it with some giant whip. The geysers belched up relentlessly where the mortar and artillery shells hit. I caught a fleeting glimpse of a group of Marines leaving a smoking amtrac on the reef. Some fell as bullets and fragments splashed among them. Their buddies tried to help them as they struggled in the knee-deep water.

I shuddered and choked. A wild desperate feeling of anger, frustration, and pity gripped me. It was an emotion that always would torture my mind when I saw men trapped and was unable to do anything but watch as they were hit. My own plight forgotten momentarily, I felt sickened to the depths of my soul. I asked God, "Why, why, why?" I turned my face away and wished that I were imagining it all. I had tasted the bitterest essence of war, the sight of helpless comrades being slaughtered, and it filled me with disgust.

I got up. Crouching low, I raced up the sloping beach into a defilade. Reaching the inland edge of the sand just beyond the high-water mark, I glanced down and saw the nose of a huge black and yellow bomb protruding from the sand. A metal plate attached to the top served as a pressure trigger. My foot had missed it by only inches.

I hit the deck again just inside the defilade. On the sand immediately in front of me was a dead snake about eighteen inches long. It was colorful, somewhat like American species I had kept as pets when a boy. It was the only snake I saw on Peleliu.

Momentarily I was out of the heavy fire hitting on the beach. A strong smell of chemicals and exploding shells filled the air. Patches of coral and sand around me were yellowed from the powder from shell blasts. A large white post about four feet high stood at the edge of the defilade. Japanese writing was painted on the side facing the beach. To me, it appeared as though a chicken with muddy feet had walked up and down the post. I felt a sense of pride that this was enemy territory and that we were capturing it for our country to help win the war.

One of our NCOs signaled us to move to our right, out of the shallow defilade. I was glad, because the Japanese probably would pour mortar fire into it to prevent it being used for shelter. At the moment, however, the gunners seemed to be concentrating on the beach and the incoming waves of Marines.

I ran over to where one of our veterans stood looking to our front and flopped down at his feet. "You'd better get down," I yelled as bullets snapped and cracked all around.

"Them slugs are high, they're hittin' in the leaves, Sledgehammer," he said nonchalantly without looking at me.

"Leaves, hell! Where are the trees?" I yelled back at him.

Startled, he looked right and left. Down the beach, barely visible, was a shattered palm. Nothing near us stood over knee high. He hit the deck.

"I must be crackin' up, Sledgehammer. Them slugs sound just like they did in the jungle at Gloucester, and I figured they were hittin' leaves," he said with chagrin.

"Somebody gimme a cigarette," I yelled to my squad mates nearby.

Snafu was jubilant. "I toldja you'd start smokin', didn't I, Sledgehammer?"

A buddy handed me a smoke, and with trembling hands we got it lit. They really kidded me about going back on all my previous refusals to smoke.

I kept looking to our right, expecting to see men from the 3rd Battalion, 7th Marines (3/7), which was supposed to be there. But I saw only the familiar faces of Marines from my own company as we moved off the beach. Marines began to come in behind us in increasing numbers, but none were visible on our right flank.

Unfamiliar officers and NCOs yelled and shouted orders, "K Company, first platoon, move over here," or "K Company, mortar section, over here." Considerable confusion prevailed for about fifteen minutes as our officers and the leaders from our namesake company in the 7th Marines straightened out the two units. . . .

We started to move inland. We had gone only a few yards when an enemy machine gun opened up from a scrub thicket to our right. Japanese 81mm and 90mm mortars then opened up on us. Everyone hit the deck; I dove into a shallow crater. The company was completely pinned down. All movement ceased. The shells fell faster, until I couldn't make out individual explosions, just continuous, crashing rumbles with an occasional ripping sound of shrapnel tearing low through the air overhead amid the roar. The air was murky with smoke and dust. Every muscle in my body was as tight as a piano wire. I shuddered and shook as though I were having a mild convulsion. Sweat flowed profusely. I prayed, clenched my teeth, squeezed my carbine stock, and cursed the Japanese. Our lieutenant, a Cape Gloucester veteran who was nearby, seemed to be in about the same shape. From the meager protection of my shallow crater I pitied him, or anyone, out on that flat coral.

The heavy mortar barrage went on without slackening. I thought it would never stop. I was terrified by the big shells arching down all around us. One was bound to fall directly into my hole, I thought.

If any orders were passed along, or if anyone yelled for a corpsman, I never heard it in all the noise. It was as though I was out there on the battlefield all by myself, utterly forlorn and helpless in a tempest of violent explosions. All any man could do was sweat it out and pray for survival. It would have been sure suicide to stand up in that fire storm.

Under my first barrage since the fast-moving events of hitting the beach, I learned a new sensation: utter and absolute helplessness. The shelling lifted in about half an hour, although it seemed to me to have crashed on for hours. Time had no meaning to me. (This was particularly true when under a heavy shelling. I never could judge how long it lasted.) Orders then came to move out and I got up, covered by a layer of coral dust. I felt like jelly and couldn't believe any of us had survived that barrage.

The walking wounded began coming past us on their way to the beach where they would board amtracs to be taken out to one of the ships. An NCO who was a particular friend of mine hurried by, holding a bloody battle dressing over his upper left arm.

"Hit bad?" I yelled.

His face lit up in a broad grin, and he said jauntily, "Don't feel sorry for me, Sledgehammer. I got the million-dollar wound. It's all over for me."

We waved as he hurried on out of the war.

We had to be alert constantly as we moved through the thick sniper-infested scrub. We received orders to halt in an open area as I came upon the first enemy dead I had ever seen, a dead Japanese medical corpsman and two riflemen. The medic apparently had been trying to administer aid when he was killed by one of our shells. His medical chest lay open beside him, and the various bandages and medicines were arranged neatly in compartments. The corpsman was on his back, his abdominal cavity laid bare. I stared in horror, shocked at the glistening viscera bespecked with fine coral dust. This can't have been a human being, I agonized. It looked more like the guts of one of the many rabbits or squirrels I had cleaned on hunting trips as a boy. I felt sick as I stared at the corpses.

A sweating, dusty Company K veteran came up, looked first at the dead, and then at me. He slung his M1 rifle over his shoulder and leaned over the bodies. With the thumb and forefinger of one hand, he deftly plucked a pair of hornrimmed glasses from the face of the corpsman. This was done as casually as a guest plucking an hors d'oeuvre from a tray at a cocktail party.

"Sledgehammer," he said reproachfully, "don't stand there with your mouth open when there's all these good souvenirs laying around." He held the glasses for me to see and added, "Look how thick that glass is. These sonsabitches must be half blind, but it don't seem to mess up their marksmanship any."

He then removed a Nambu pistol, slipped the belt off the corpse, and took the leather holster. He pulled off the steel helmet, reached inside, and took out a neatly folded Japanese flag covered with writing. The veteran pitched the helmet on the coral where it clanked and rattled, rolled the corpse over, and started pawing through the combat pack.

The veteran's buddy came up and started stripping the other Japanese corpses. His take was a flag and other items. He then removed the bolts from the Japanese rifles and broke the stocks against the coral to render them useless to infiltrators. The first veteran said, "See you, Sledgehammer. Don't take any wooden nickels." He and his buddy moved on.

I hadn't budged an inch or said a word, just stood glued to the spot almost in a trance. The corpses were sprawled where the veterans had dragged them around to get into their packs and pockets. Would I become this casual and calloused about enemy dead? I wondered. Would the war dehumanize me so that I, too, could "field strip" enemy dead with such nonchalance? The time soon came when it didn't bother me a bit.

Within a few yards of this scene, one of our hospital corpsmen worked in a small, shallow defile treating Marine wounded. I went over and sat on the hot coral by him. The corpsman was on his knees bending over a young Marine who had just died on a stretcher. A blood-soaked battle dressing was on the side of the dead man's neck. His fine, handsome, boyish face was ashen. "What a pitiful waste," I thought. "He can't be a day over seventeen years old." I thanked God his mother couldn't see him. The corpsman held the dead Marine's chin tenderly between the thumb and fingers of his left hand and made the sign of the cross with his right hand. Tears streamed down his dusty, tanned, grief-contorted face while he sobbed quietly.

The wounded who had received morphine sat or lay around like zombies and patiently awaited the "doc's" attention. Shells roared overhead in both directions, an occasional one falling nearby, and machine guns rattled incessantly like chattering demons.

We moved inland. The scrub may have slowed the company, but it concealed us from the heavy enemy shelling that was holding up other companies facing the open airfield. I could hear the deep rumble of the shelling and dreaded that we might move into it. . . .

As I passed the different units and exchanged greetings with friends, I was astonished at their faces. When I tried to smile at a comment a buddy made, my face felt as tight as a drumhead. My facial muscles were so tensed from the strain that I actually felt it was impossible to smile. With a shock I realized that the faces of my squad mates and everyone around me looked masklike and unfamiliar. . . .

About a dozen Company K riflemen commenced firing at Japanese soldiers wading along the reef several hundred yards away at the mouth of the bay. Other Marines joined us. The enemy were moving out from a narrow extension of the mangrove swamp on the left toward the southeastern promontory on our right. About a dozen enemy soldiers were alternately swimming and running along the reef. Some of the time only their heads were above the water as my buddies sent rifle fire into their midst. Most of the running enemy went down with a splash.

2. Sergeant Robert Slaughter, U.S. Army, Recalls Struggling Across Omaha Beach in the D-Day Invasion (1944), 1993

"My thinking, as we approached the beach, was that if this boat didn't hurry up and get us in I would die from seasickness. This was my first encounter with this

Account of Sgt. J. Robert Slaughter, U.S. Army, reprinted in Robin Neillands and Roderick de Normann. *D-Day, 1944: Voices From Normandy* (London: Weidenfeld & Nicolson, 1993), pp. 143–145. Reprinted by permission.

malady. Wooziness became stomach sickness and then vomiting. At this point death is not so dreadful. I used the first thing at hand—my steel helmet. I didn't care what the Germans had to offer, I wanted to get on dry land. Nothing is worse than motion sickness, except maybe 88mm's and MG-42 machine-guns.

About 200 or 300 yards from shore we encountered the first enemy artillery fire. Near misses sent water skyward, and then it rained back on us. The British coxswain shouted to step back, he was going to lower the ramp and we were to dis-embark quickly. I was stationed near the front of the boat and heard Sergeant Nor-fleet counter, 'These men have heavy equipment and *you will take them all the way in.*' The coxswain begged, 'But we'll all be killed!' and Norfleet unholstered his .45 Colt pistol, put it to the sailor's head and ordered, 'All the way in!' The craft proceeded ashore, ploughing through the choppy water until the bow scraped the sandy bottom.

About 150 yards from shore I raised my head despite the warning from some-one to 'Keep your heads down!' I could see the craft to our right taking a terrific licking from small arms. Tracer bullets were bounding and skipping off the ramp and sides as they zero'd in on the boat, which touched down a few minutes before we did. Had we not delayed a few minutes to pick up the survivors from a sunken craft, we might have taken the concentration of fire that boat took. Great plumes of water from enemy artillery and mortars kept spouting close by.

We knew then that this was not going to be a walk-in. No one thought that the enemy would give us this kind of opposition on the water's edge. We expected 'A' and 'B' Companies to have the beach secured by the time we landed. The reality was that no one else had set foot in the sector where we touched down. This turned the boys into men. Some would be very brave men, others would soon be dead men, but all of those who survived would be frightened men. Some wet their breeches, others cried unashamedly, and many just had to find it within themselves to get the job done. This is where the discipline and training took over.

As we approached the beach the ramp was lowered. Mortar and artillery shells exploded on land and in the water. Unseen snipers concealed in the cliffs were shooting down at individuals, but most havoc was from automatic weapons. The water was turning red from the blood. Explosions from artillery gunfire, the rapid-fire rattle from nearby MG-42s, and naval gunfire firing inland was frightening.

I was stationed on the left side of the craft and about fifth from the front. Nor-fleet was leading the right side. The ramp was in the surf and the front of the steel craft was bucking violently up and down. As my turn came to exit, I sat on the edge of the bucking ramp, trying to time my leap on the down cycle. I sat there too long, causing a bottleneck and endangering myself as well as the men who fol-lowed. The one-inch steel ramp was going up and down in the surf, rising as much as 6 or 7 ft. I was afraid it would slam me in the head. One of our men was crushed by the door, killing him instantly. There were dead men in the water and there were live men as well. The Germans couldn't tell which was which. It was ex-tremely hard to shed the heavy equipment, and if one were a weak swimmer, he could drown before inflating his Mae-West. I had to inflate mine to get in, even though I was a good swimmer. I remember helping Private Ernest McCanless, who was struggling to get closer in, so he wouldn't drown under all the weight. He still had one box of precious 30 cal. One of the dead, Mae-West inflated, had turned a dark colour.

There were dead men floating in the water and there were live men acting dead, letting the tide take them in. I was crouched down to chin-deep in the water when mortar shells began falling at the water's edge. Sand began to kick up from small-arms fire from the bluffs. It became apparent that it was past time to get the hell away from that killing zone and across the beach. I don't know how long we were in the water before the move was made to go. I tried to take cover behind one of the heavy timbers, and then noticed an innocent-looking mine tied to the top, so I made the decision to go for it. Getting across the beach became an obsession. The decision not to try never entered my mind.

While lying half in and half out of the water, behind one of the log poles, I noticed a GI running from right to left, trying to get across the beach. He was weighted with equipment and looked as though he was having a difficult time running. He was probably from the craft that touched down about 50 yards to our right. An enemy gunner shot him as he stumbled for cover. He screamed for a medic. One of the aid men moved quickly to help him, and he also was shot. I will never forget seeing that medic lying next to that wounded GI and both of them screaming. They died in minutes.

The tide was rushing in, and later waves of men were due, so we had to get across. I believe I was the first in my group, telling Pfc Walfred Williams, my Number One gunner, to follow. He still had his 51-pound machine-gun tripod. I had my rifle ready to fire, safety off, and had also fixed the bayonet before disembarking.

I gathered my courage and started running as fast as my long legs would carry me. I ran as low as I could to lessen the target, and since I am 6ft 5ins I still presented a good one. I had a long way to run—I would say a good 100 yards or more. We were loaded down with gear and all our clothes were soaking wet. Can you imagine running with shoes full of water and wet wool clothing? As I ran through a tidal pool with about six or eight inches of water, I began to stumble. I finally caught my balance and accidentally fired my rifle, barely missing my foot. I continued on to the sea wall. This is the first time I have admitted the embarrassment of inadvertently almost shooting myself!

Upon reaching the sea wall I looked back for the first time and got a glimpse of the armada out in the Channel. It was an awesome sight to behold. I also saw that Williams, Private Sal Augeri and Private Ernest McCanless were right behind. I didn't see Norfleet until later. Augeri had lost the machine-gun receiver in the water and I had got sand in my rifle. We still had one box of MG ammo but I don't believe we had a weapon that would fire. The first thing I did was to take off my assault jacket and spread my raincoat so I could clean my rifle. It was then I saw bullet holes in my raincoat. I didn't realize until then that I had been targeted. I lit my first cigarette. They were wrapped in plastic, as were the matches. I had to rest and compose myself because I had become weak in the knees. It was a couple of days before I had enough appetite to eat a K-ration. . . .

3. Private Franklin J. Kneller, a G.I., Reminisces About Near Disaster at the Battle of the Bulge (1944), 1994

. . . On December 18th, [1944] we were shaken out of bed, [to] get ready to leave. Of course, we didn't have complete equipment. We didn't know what was going on, just the Germans were coming through. They [the American supply units] drove trucks down the street, throwing out equipment. So you took whatever equipment you could find. That afternoon, it was the fastest, theoretically, well actually, it was the fastest organization any division had ever activated, in a couple hours. [They announced,] Get ready to move from rest time, without equipment really. We had rifles and some ammunition, and we got in the trucks, 100 men to a truck. . . . [On our way to Bastogne] I [will] always remember passing the trenches from World War I, . . . they're not deep, they're about [four inches], filled in. You could see the outline.

. . . We arrived at Bastogne and saw the 82nd [Airborne Division] pulling out, and we started in. . . . We were up all night, or half . . . [asleep]. We didn't even stop for a toilet break, . . . because we were hurrying so fast. Then we dug in a while, moved, dug-in, moved, dug-in, you know, one of those deals. Then they at last found a place to dig-in, and then the Germans came in, it was about five or ten hours later. Oh, I . . . [remember]. We spent another night dug in and then the Germans came in that morning, . . . the 18th [or] 19th of December. . . .

I felt [I] was well trained, but not experienced. . . . I was frightened when we were hit. . . . Once the big shells came in, they came up with the tanks and things, I was frightened. Of course, what do I get but a troop carrier to try to protect . . . my squad. . . . That attracts everything. [The Germans had their artillery on it.] . . . I was extremely frightened. . . . [But] . . . the joke was: "Where am I gonna run, we're surrounded." . . .

We had gone through Bastogne and settled outside of [a nearby place] Foy, which I'd been in and out so many times I thought I knew the place. . . .

I spent days being so frightened, and then all of a sudden it turned . . . [around], and then I thought nothing could hurt me. You know, from being ready to maybe shoot yourself . . . to thinking nothing's gonna happen to me. . . .

Another, . . . [incident]. . . . During the '30s . . . [I saw a World War I movie] *Balalaika* with Nelson Eddie. Nelson Eddie was a Cossack. He sang "Silent Night" in English to the Germans and the Germans sang back to him "Silent Night" in German. So those things stick with you, if you're ever in battle on Christmas. So, I sang "Silent Night." . . . Another guy's standing beside me, you know, talking, and I finished singing it and we heard "zing." I said, "that came in my left ear," he said, "that came in my right ear." It came between us. So I got really mad, so I called up for some [artillery] fire, 'cause they had the grids on the Germans.

Napalm. Now I didn't know what napalm was. . . . It could have been napalm, because it got a couple of Germans [and] they were running around screaming,

Franklin J. Kneller, Unpublished Oral History Memoir, October 6, 1994, in the Rutgers Oral History Archives of World War II, pp. 22–27. Reprinted with the permisson of the author. Available on http://history.rutgers.edu/oralhistory/or /lhom.htm website.

their backs on fire. Of course, I got the worst sense of guilt. It was only recently that I found out, I thought it was phosphorus or something. . . . I didn't realize we had napalm during that war. But then they . . . must have dropped the napalm or phosphorus, they dropped a lot of stuff the Friday before Christmas. So they had dropped that stuff, and artillery shot it over. I'll always remember that. Jeez, I felt guilt . . . [in doing] that. . . .

When they [the officers] say death tomorrow, you die or something, [the Germans are] . . . gonna send the tanks in, you want to dig a foxhole near a tree, because you don't want a goddamn tank to get on top of you. . . . At night sometimes, we'd move fast [to] . . . where they were attacking, and I tell you it was so cold and, of course, they didn't have body bags. . . . So they stacked up the bodies three across, three one way, three the other way. . . . Affected me, I didn't like running into a battle area passing those stiff bodies. . . .

I did not know what the casualty situation was, but we had about 65 in the platoon and I think I was one of the last two, left . . . [alive and unwounded]. . . . My feet were frozen black.

4. Private Gertrude Pearson, an Army WAC, Remembers Her Experiences Near the Front in the Ardennes (1944), 1995

When we arrived we could clearly hear the artillery guns ahead of us—the front was about twenty-five to thirty miles away, and judging from the noise of weaponry, the fighting was still going on in the mountains and hills around us. Shortly after our arrival, we had a security lecture by an intelligence officer—there were spies in Vittel. We were forbidden to discuss the content of our work, or what we did (which we never did anyway). Later, we were to find that strangers often sat or stood close to us in the shops. We never did find out whether they were Allied intelligence personnel or spies. . . .

When von Rundstedt broke through our lines, signaling the Battle of the Bulge [in December], the WACs were told by our CO that we had become a target of enemy agents because of our work. She told us spies had and were parachuting into the forests and had infiltrated Vittel.

One night we heard gunshots outside our house—the guards had apprehended and shot an enemy agent. Another time, a female agent arrived, saying that she had had plane trouble and was looking for a place to stay. She said she was a member of a British organization. She was clothed in British clothes, but I noticed her shoes were not or did not look British. I mentioned this to my first sergeant. The woman's room was searched and she was subsequently taken away by the military police.

One of the larger hotels became the Twenty-third General Hospital. Soldiers were brought here from the field hospitals. Our room faced the railroad station, and for days on end during the Battle of the Bulge train after train pulled into the

From *They Also Served: American Women in World War II* by, Olga Gruzhit-Hoyt. Copyright © 1995 Olga Gruzhit-Hoyt. Published by arrangement with Carol Publishing Group. A Birch Lane Press Book.

station filled with wounded. Medics on the train unloaded the soldiers on their litters to the platform, where they waited in long lines to be placed in one of the never-ending fleet of ambulances. It was bitterly cold and some had no blankets. When they arrived at the hospital—because they were arriving in such large numbers—they were again placed in long lines on their litters on the sidewalk leading to the entrance of the hospital. I saw this when I went to the hospital to donate blood. It upset me to see them lying wounded, waiting patiently in the cold for medical attention.

At this time the overworked nurses asked for WAC volunteers to help the soldiers. Many volunteered. We wrote letters for them, read to them, wrapped and mailed packages, and if they were too weak to talk, we just sat by their beds for a short time, in the hope that our presence would give them comfort. Both men and women of our First TACAF gave blood whenever it was needed, on a regular basis.

Here in Vittel we had seen the ravages of war—destroyed buildings, discarded German equipment, smashed and bloody German helmets, pierced by bullets, left along the roads as the enemy raced in retreat. But seeing our wounded men and the extent of some of their injuries was the worst. The fact that I could walk into a wardroom filled with soldiers and barely hear a murmur left a lasting impression. Sometimes we were requested to leave because a soldier required surgery in the ward because there wasn't room in the ORs! I shall never forget the white bed linens and their pale faces, almost as white, and the silence in those rooms. . . .

One day we woke up to find three army trucks parked in the backyard of our house. Our CO explained that the trucks were there to evacuate us to Mirecourt Airport, where a plane was stationed to take us to safety, if the enemy came too close. It was sobering. We continued our work as usual around the clock, coping with the snow and a diet of C and K rations and Spam and powdered eggs for breakfast. When we were off-duty we volunteered at the hospital; other times we walked to the village.

The winter of 1944 and 1945 in Vittel was an important time in our military careers. We had been accepted into the First TACAF against the wishes of some who felt women belonged in the rear areas and were unsuitable for the type of work assigned to us. They felt that women were incapable of enduring the hardships and rough conditions of a combat area. However, our success and outstanding work changed many attitudes. We had remained reliable and stable while on duty under stressful conditions. It was the roughest winter any of us had experienced, and we were eager to go on.

5. American Soldiers Explain Their Views Towards Combat (1944), 1949

The codes according to which a combat unit judged the behavior of its members, and in terms of which conformity was enforced, differed in their generality.

Perhaps the most general was one drawn largely from civilian culture but given its special interpretation in the combat situation: Be a man. Conceptions of masculinity vary among different American groups, but there is a core which is common to most: courage, endurance and toughness, lack of squeamishness when confronted with shocking or distasteful stimuli, avoidance of display of weakness in general, reticence about emotional or idealistic matters, and sexual competency. The conditions in which the code is applied also vary. For example, it seems not to have been invoked in the same way in the recent war as in World War I. In World War II there was much less community pressure on the young men to get into the Army. There were few real counterparts to the white feather, painting homes yellow, use of the epithet "slacker." The general attitude was that everyone should do what he was assigned as well as he could, but it was *not* considered essential that the individual "stick his neck out." To oversimplify, it might be said that in World War I the test of social manhood began much farther from actual fighting than in World War II. In the First World War, a man was more severely censured for failing to enter the armed services; this time, the test was more nearly whether he adequately filled his role once placed in the combat situation.

Combat posed a challenge for a man to prove himself to himself and others. Combat was a dare. One never knew for sure that he could take it until he had demonstrated that he could. Most soldiers facing the prospect of combat service had to deal with a heavy charge of anticipatory anxiety. The more they heard about how tough the fighting was, the greater the anxiety and the insecurity that came from doubt as to whether they could handle the anxiety. Thus, combat might actually come almost as a relief—it joined the issue and broke the strain of doubt and waiting.

A code as universal as "being a man" is very likely to have been deeply internalized. So the fear of failure in the role, as by showing cowardice in battle, could bring not only fear of social censure on this point as such, but also more central and strongly established fears related to sex-typing. To fail to measure up as a soldier in courage and endurance was to risk the charge of not being a man. ("Whatsa matter, bud—got lace on your drawers?" "Christ, he's acting like an old maid.") If one were not socially defined as a man, there was a strong likelihood of being branded a "woman," a dangerous threat to the contemporary male personality. The generally permissive attitude toward expression of fear that will be described in a later chapter mitigated the fear of failure in manliness, but by no means obviated it. A man could show and admit fear without necessarily being branded a "weak sister," but only so long as it was clear that he had done his utmost.

The generalized code of masculinity serves as a context for various more specific codes that may be isolated more or less arbitrarily. The prescribed avoidance to claims of idealistic motivation will be considered later. The most direct application of the masculinity code was to the social role of the combat soldier. In fact, the code of the combat soldier can be summarized by saying that behavior in combat was recognized as a test of being a man. When this code was internalized, or enforced by playing on an internalized code of manliness, a man once in combat had to fight in order to keep his own self-respect: "Hell, I'm a soldier." . . .

The pride in being a combat man may be illustrated by an account told to an interviewer at the front in Europe by a sergeant in a veteran Infantry battalion. He had been wounded and later returned to his outfit through the chain of replacement depots. His account of this revealed that he was indifferent to the physical conditions encountered, but like many combat men of similar experience he was very bitter about the treatment of combat veterans by the permanent personnel of the replacement depots. He complained that the cadre were indifferent to the welfare of replacements, "showed no respect for what the combat men had been through," tried to "shove people around," and so on through a long list. When asked for an example, he told of a corporal who was in charge of a group of veteran combat replacements:

> He kept ordering us around and putting combat men on kitchen details. Finally I got fed up. I told him: "Look here, damn you—you stay out of here. There are *men* in here, and I don't want them contaminated." . . .

Some Miscellaneous Goals

In the course of our discussion of combat motivation, we have touched in one way or another on several incentives which could be considered as goals of combat behavior—such objectives as to show one's masculinity, to stick up for one's buddies and win their approval, to preserve our way of life, to wreak vengeance on the enemy. Certain other goals, not considered thus far, deserve mention. Some of them raise problems on which direct evidence is not available but which appear to warrant at least passing mention to avoid serious gaps in the total picture.

First is a goal which should certainly not be neglected—the desire to get the job over with, to go home and get out of the Army. . . .

A victory for a soldier in combat had a meaning very different from that enjoyed by his countrymen at home. For most situations, Waller is quite right when he says, "For the soldiers victory or defeat meant just another battle with an enemy who was still full of fight." When the end of the war was still not in view, one more victory may simply have meant the necessity to attack again tomorrow, and again the next day and so on into the seemingly endless bleak future with no hope of escape other than a good clean wound. . . .

With all this, there did still remain rewards in local victories. "Every hill taken means that we are that much nearer home": captured positions and enemies out of action carried a promise of ultimate victory and a quicker end to the war. In periods of very rapid advance, combat troops sometimes exhibited an almost "civilian" degree of high spirits. The period of late August and early September in 1944 when the American armies were pursuing the retreating Wehrmacht through France and Belgium is a large-scale example. Even here, however, victory was not a cause for unmixed feelings. Combat soldiers had a pessimism, a caution ingrained from bitter experience, which checked the exuberance of wish projection. And when, as happened in that instance, infantrymen walked until completely exhausted—in one case observed by Research Branch interviewers, a regiment advanced forty miles in twenty-four hours—the factor of sheer fatigue temporarily overshadowed the psychological rewards of victory. And always, there were comrades being killed and wounded.

6. Lieutenant J. Glenn Gray Reflects on Men in Battle (1943–1945), 1959

The feeling of belonging together that men in battle often find a cementing force needs first to be awakened by an external reason for fighting, but the feeling is by no means dependent on this reason. The cause that calls comradeship into being may be the defense of one's country, the propagation of the one true religious faith, or a passionate political ideology; it may be the maintenance of honor or the recovery of a Helen of Troy. So long as there is a cause, the hoped-for objective may be relatively unimportant in itself. When, through military reverses or the fatiguing and often horrible experiences of combat, the original purpose becomes obscured, the fighter is often sustained solely by the determination not to let down his comrades. . . .

Many veterans who are honest with themselves will admit, I believe, that the experience of communal effort in battle, even under the altered conditions of modern war, has been a high point in their lives. Despite the horror, the weariness, the grime, and the hatred, participation with others in the chances of battle had its unforgettable side, which they would not want to have missed. For anyone who has not experienced it himself, the feeling is hard to comprehend, and, for the participant, hard to explain to anyone else. Probably the feeling of liberation is nearly basic. It is this feeling that explains the curious combination of earnestness and lightheartedness so often noted in men in battle.

Many of us can experience freedom as a thrilling reality, something both serious and joyous, only when we are acting in unison with others for a concrete goal that costs something absolute for its attainment. Individual freedom to do what we will with our lives and our talents, the freedom of self-determination, appears to us most of the time as frivolous or burdensome. Such freedom leaves us empty and alone, feeling undirected and insignificant. Only comparatively few of us know how to make this individual freedom productive and joyous. But communal freedom can pervade nearly everyone and carry everything before it. This elemental fact about freedom the opponents of democracy have learned well, and it constitutes for them a large initial advantage.

The lightheartedness that communal participation brings has little of the sensuous or merely pleasant about it, just as the earnestness has little of the calculating or rational. Both derive instead from a consciousness of power that is supraindividual. We feel earnest and gay at such moments because we are liberated from our individual impotence and are drunk with the power that union with our fellows brings. In moments like these many have a vague awareness of how isolated and separate their lives have hitherto been and how much they have missed by living in the narrow circle of family or a few friends. With the boundaries of the self expanded, they sense a kinship never known before. Their "I" passes insensibly into a "we," "my" becomes "our," and individual fate loses its central importance.

At its height, this sense of comradeship is an ecstasy not unlike the aesthetic ecstasy previously described, though occasioned by different forces. In most of us there is a genuine longing for community with our human species, and at the same time an awkwardness and helplessness about finding the way to achieve it. Some extreme experience—mortal danger or the threat of destruction—is necessary to bring us fully together with our comrades or with nature. This is a great pity, for there are surely alternative ways more creative and less dreadful, if men would only seek them out. Until now, war has appealed because we discover some of the mysteries of communal joy in its forbidden depths. Comradeship reaches its peak in battle.

The secret of comradeship has not been exhausted, however, in the feeling of freedom and power instilled in us by communal effort in combat. There is something more and equally important. The sense of power and liberation that comes over men at such moments stems from a source beyond the union of men. I believe it is nothing less than the assurance of immortality that makes self-sacrifice at these moments so relatively easy. Men are true comrades only when each is ready to give up his life for the other, without reflection and without thought of personal loss. Who can doubt that every war, the two world wars no less than former ones, has produced true comradeship like this?

Such sacrifice seems hard and heroic to those who have never felt communal ecstasy. In fact, it is not nearly so difficult as many less absolute acts in peacetime and in civilian life, for death becomes in a measure unreal and unbelievable to one who is sharing his life with his companions. Immortality is not something remote and otherworldly, possibly or probably true and real; on the contrary, it becomes a present and self-evident fact.

Nothing is further from the truth than the insistence of certain existentialist philosophers that each person must die his own death and experience it unsharably. If that were so, how many lives would have been spared on the battlefield! But in fact, death for men united with each other can be shared as few other of life's great moments can be. To be sure, it is not death as we know it usually in civilian life. In the German language men never die in battle. They *fall*. The term is exact for the expression of self-sacrifice when it is motivated by the feeling of comradeship. I may fall, but I do not die, for that which is real in me goes forward and lives on in the comrades for whom I gave up my physical life.

Let me not be misunderstood. It is unquestionably true that thousands of soldiers die in battle, miserable, alone, and embittered, without any conviction of self-sacrifice and without any other satisfactions. I suspect the percentage of such soldiers has increased markedly in recent wars. But for those who in every battle are seized by the passion for self-sacrifice, dying has lost its terrors because its reality has vanished.

There must be a similarity between this willingness of soldier-comrades for self-sacrifice and the willingness of saints and martyrs to die for their religious faith. It is probably no accident that the religions of the West have not cast away their military terminology or even their militant character—"Onward, Christian soldiers! Marching as to war . . ." nor that our wars are defended in terms of devotion and salvation. The true believer must be ready to give up his life for the faith.

And if he is a genuine saint he will regard this sacrifice as no loss, for the self has become indestructible in being united with a supreme reality. There are, of course, important differences. The reality for which the martyr sacrifices himself is not visible and intimate like the soldier's. The martyr usually dies alone, scorned by the multitude. In this sense his lot is infinitely harder. It is hardly surprising that few men are capable of dying joyfully as martyrs whereas thousands are capable of self-sacrifice in wartime. Nevertheless, a basic point of resemblance remains, namely, that death has lost not only its sting but its reality, too, for the self that dies is little in comparison with that which survives and triumphs.

This is the mystical element of war that has been mentioned by nearly all serious writers on the subject. William James spoke of it as a sacrament, and once remarked that "society would rot without the mystical blood payment." And G. F. Nicolai, in his book *The Biology of War,* is persuaded that "the boundless capacity for self-sacrifice" is what is intoxicating and great about war. It is this that occasions frequent doubt in lovers of peace whether men will ever give up warfare, and, at times, the vagrant question whether it is desirable that they should. This capacity for self-sacrifice is what all defenders of war (in our day grown few) use as their final argument for the necessity and ultimate morality of war. Since men can only be brought by such extreme means to a recognition of their true nature and their essential relationships, these defenders tell us, it is folly to seek to abolish war, because it would be to abolish death itself.

Many humanists and humanitarians, on the other hand, attack the impulse to self-sacrifice as the very core of moral evil. It offends their whole rational image of the distinctively human. And the more forthright do not hesitate to express their abhorrence for the Christian faith insofar as it is founded on the theme of self-sacrifice. . . .

It is true that we in the West are frequently infatuated with the idea of sacrifice, particularly self-sacrifice. Why are some people so strongly repelled and others again and again attracted by the impulse to self-sacrifice? Or why do both attraction and repulsion have place in the same breast at different moments? As moralists, we are repelled, I suspect, because the impulse to sacrifice is not subject to rational judgment and control. It takes hold of us and forces us against our will, later claiming justification from some higher authority than the human. As often as not, it puts itself at the service of an evil cause, perhaps more frequently than in the service of the good. The mysterious power that such leaders as Napoleon, Hitler, and Stalin had in their being that enabled them to create a love for self-sacrifice perplexes us endlessly. We cannot condemn it with full conviction, since it seems likely that both leaders and led were in large degree powerless to prevent the impulses that dominated them.

Yet such power is appalling beyond measure and from a rational viewpoint deserving of the deepest condemnation. The limits of free will and morality are transgressed, and man is forced to seek religious and metaphysical justification for self-sacrifice, even when committed in an evil cause. As in the aesthetic appeal of war, when we reach the impulse of the sublime, so in the communal appeal of comradeship, when we reach the impulse to self-sacrifice, we are confronted with contradictions that are deeply embedded in our culture, if not in human nature itself.

What our moral self tells us is abhorrent, our religious self and our aesthetic self yearn for as the ultimate good. This is part of the riddle of war.

If we are truly wise, perhaps we should not want to alter these capacities of our human nature, even though we suffer from them immeasurably and may yet succumb to their threat. For the willingness to sacrifice self, like the attraction of the sublime, is what makes possible the higher reaches of the spirit into the realms of poetry, philosophy, and genuine religion. They prevent our best men from losing interest in and hope for our species. They stand in the way of discouragement and cynicism. As moralists, we can condemn Saint Paul and Saint Augustine for their mystical conviction that without sacrifice no purgation from sin is possible. But we should be cautious in so doing, for they were convinced that without the supramoral act, we human beings are not able to lead even a normally moral existence. Though they were not disposed to believe that God was without moral qualities, they were quite certain that there was more in His universe than the determinations of good and evil. For them the "I am" preceded logically and in time the "I ought." And vast numbers of people have agreed with them that the religious order is superior to the moral, though they continue to be confused about how the two are related.

Are we not right in honoring the fighter's impulse to sacrifice himself for a comrade, even though it be done, as it so frequently is, in an evil cause? I think so. It is some kind of world historical pathos that the striving for union and for immortality must again and again be consummated while men are in the service of destruction. I do not doubt for a moment that wars are made many times more deadly because of this striving and this impulse. Yet I would not want to be without the assurance their existence gives me that our species has a different destiny than is granted to other animals. Though we often sink below them, we can at moments rise above them, too.

ESSAYS

In the first essay, Martin van Creveld, a military historian from Hebrew University in Jerusalem, in a 1982 comparison of the performance of the German and American armies in World War II, concludes that the U.S. Army emphasized increased weaponry and firepower and efficient centralized administration over the physical and morale needs of its soldiers and that the rapidity of the U.S. mobilization resulted in many problems, among the most important of which were deficiencies in the training and ability of America's wartime officer corps. In direct rebuttal of some of the main points of S.L.A. Marshall and van Creveld, the author of the second essay, Michael D. Doubler, a military historian from the Ohio State University who has taught at West Point and serves in the U.S. Army's National Guard Bureau, asserts in a 1994 book on the G.I.s in Europe that American soldiers had the ability to adapt and innovate; that they used a collective, decentralized approach to problem solving that proved effective; that Americans efficiently allocated their resources; and that the reliance upon equipment, weapons, and firepower was not a deficiency but a major strength of the American army in the European Theater of Operations (ETO).

The German Wehrmacht Was Superior to the U.S. Army

MARTIN VAN CREVELD

Between 1940 and 1945 the U.S. Army grew from 243,000 officers and men into a force numbering over 8 million. With eighty-nine divisions, made up of men who had shortly before been civilians in one of the world's less militarized nations, it crossed the oceans and played a decisive role in the defeat of two of the most highly militarized powers the world has ever known. It is doubtful whether any other nation would have been capable of such feats: not for nothing, indeed, has General [George] Marshall been called "the organizer of victory."

Many of the U.S. Army's shortcomings were the direct result of overrapid expansion. Other objective factors also played their part: long lines of communications, for example, prevented American officers from being trained as German ones were, that is, by service at the front, and were also partly responsible for the enormous divisional slices. There was, too, a desperate shortage of cadres. This helps explain why the system had to be so centralized, and why, in consequence, mechanical methods of administration had to be employed to the extent that they were.

Inexperience, too, played a role in shaping the American Army; yet inexperience as an explanation has its limitations. No amount of inexperience can excuse a cruel replacement system under which individual replacements were allowed to travel, without comrades or commanders, from one depot to the next and then to enter battle without even their names being known to the men around them. No amount of inexperience can excuse a system under which it was those officers whose lives were least endangered that got the fastest promotions. No inexperience can excuse (given the first-class experience that was available from World War I) the way in which the whole question of psychiatric casualties was handled. Not inexperience but bureaucratic inefficiency pure and simple can explain the slowness of the decoration system. Not inexperience but a laxness intolerable in war—however admirable it may be in times of peace—can explain a justice system that treated military offenses committed by servicemen as if they were matters of no consequence.

A point to be noted about each of the above factors is the fact that they did not involve "mechanical" performance, in which respect the U.S. Army was for the most part as good as, and often vastly superior to, the German one. We saw, for example, that American divisions did not contain significantly more fat than did their German equivalents; that the U.S. Army developed logistic capabilities that the Germans could only dream about hardly requires mentioning. It was not here, but in the dearth of attention paid to the most elementary psychological needs of the soldier (combined, paradoxically, with a far-reaching readiness to accept "psychology" as an excuse) that the weakness lay. A case in point was the system under

Martin van Creveld, *Fighting Power: German and U.S. Army Performance, 1939–1945* (Westport, Ct: Greenwood Press, © 1982 Martin van Creveld), pp. 166–169. Reproduced with permission of Greenwood Publishing Group, Inc., Westport, CT.

which technical NCOs, but not leadership-type ones, received special training. An even more glaring one was the treatment of the wounded; while the American medical services were considerably better at saving lives than were the German ones, the morale effect of this fact was counteracted by the way these men were handled after recovery.

Coming now to the true core of things, it would appear that the U.S. Army, backed by a gigantic productive engine and possibly looking across its shoulder at the organization of an automobile factory, chose to regard war not so much as a struggle between opposing troops but rather as one whose outcome would be decided largely by machines. Rather than concentrating on fighting power, therefore, it aimed at confronting the enemy with the greatest possible firepower. Not attention to the needs of the soldier, but scientific management and the optimum distribution and deployment of resources became the name of the game. Not a single-minded concentration on *operativ* (the very word, incidentally, has no exact English equivalent) aspects of war but a balanced organization aimed at coordination and control was the result. This approach tended to turn men into adjuncts of their machines and largely explains the gulf between the army's "mechanical" efficiency and the scant attention it paid to social and psychological problems.

To deploy all resources as well as possible, to put every man and screw in their proper place, a highly centralized organization and vast amounts of detailed information were needed. Information being superabundant, mechanical means to process it were needed. Business machines being available, any- and everything had to be shaped in such a way as to enable them to process this information as efficiently as possible. Conversely, anything that could not be processed by mechanical means did not exist; and this, unfortunately, included precisely those *seelische* (psychical—the expression, once again, is difficult to translate) attitudes that constitute the core of fighting power.

These considerations, which ultimately derive from the peculiar American balance between men and machines, may explain why wounded and replacements were handled as they were; why units were put together without regard to geographic origins; and why men were allowed to enter combat without knowing either their commanders or their comrades. They also explain much about the way in which the divisions operated and the absence of a unit rotation system. From a purely managerial point of view aiming at the optimal coordination of available resources, a system which treats men as if they were interchangeable cogs undoubtedly IS the most efficient. Again, the haste with which the army was organized probably played a role in this; equally important, however, was the determination of headquarters at all levels to put administrative efficiency above all else.

The addiction to information also had further unfortunate results. Since knowledge—as extensive and complete as possible—was regarded as the key to victory, the best and the brightest were, not unnaturally, put to the task of producing, procuring, and processing it. The number of—frequently commissioned—pen pushers in the rear was enormous, whereas the fighting arms were starved of high-quality manpower. The fact that Class I and II men were proportionally least numerous in the arms that suffered the most casualties, and the definitely low number of ground officers killed, leaves little doubt that the American democracy fought World War II primarily at the expense of the "tired, the poor, the huddled masses."

If it is indeed true, as is so often said, that the officer corps counts for everything in war, then the American officer corps of World War II was less than mediocre. Owing partly no doubt to pressure of time, the methods used to select and train officers were none too successful. Far too many officers had soft jobs in the rear, far too few commanded at the front. Those who did command at the front were, as the official history frankly admits and the casualty figures confirm, often guilty of bad leadership. Between them and their German opposite numbers there simply is no comparison possible.

Yet when all is said and done, the fact remains that the American GI did win World War II. He did so, moreover, without assaulting, raping, and otherwise molesting too many people. Wherever he came—even within Germany itself—he was received with relief, or at any rate without fear. To him, no greater tribute than this is conceivable.

The Superiority of American GIs

MICHAEL D. DOUBLER

The U.S. army's process of managing change reflects several predominant characteristics of American society. The fact that ideas for change came from a wide number of sources reflects the American values of individual freedom, free speech, and the entrepreneurial spirit. Coming from a society that tends to resist centralized control, it was natural for American soldiers to use a collective, decentralized approach to problem solving. The army's permissive attitude toward changes in established doctrine reflects the values of a society that often questions higher authority. The adaptations that took place also suggest that Americans are a people who respect innovation and are comfortable with change. The great number of technical improvements in the use of weapons and equipment reflects the particularly American aptitude for operating and repairing machines. While Yankee ingenuity is a hallmark of U.S. commercial production and manufacturing, it is an American trademark that also accompanies soldiers to the battlefield. . . .

In *Fighting Power,* Martin van Creveld presents his findings on the relative combat performance of the German and American armies in World War II. He argues that the American army regarded war not as a struggle between opposing forces, but as a contest in which machines and firepower would largely determine the outcome. To Creveld, the army viewed soldiers as little more than adjuncts of machines, overlooked their most elementary psychological needs, and placed bureaucratic efficiency ahead of troop morale or unit cohesion. *Fighting Power* maintains that the U.S. personnel replacement system, with its tendency to treat soldiers like spare parts, and insufficient numbers of combat divisions were serious deficiencies that greatly inhibited the army's fighting ability.

Many of Creveld's evaluations of the U.S. army's performance have substantial merit but fail to measure the improvements the army made on the battlefield.

From Michael D. Doubler. *Closing with the Enemy: How GIs Fought the War in Europe, 1944–1945* (Lawrence: University Press of Kansas, 1994), pp. 281–82, 287–94. Reprinted by permission of the University of Kansas.

Certainly, the military's key decision to field only ninety divisions resulted in an inadequate number of fighting units. The army had planned for a force of 213 divisions, but American policymakers whittled down that number to ninety based on optimistic estimates that Allied air power and the Russian army would gravely weaken the Germans. Fewer major formations meant that divisions had to stay on the front lines longer with no prospect of relief. Generals were forced to fight without reserves, and vast numbers of casualties reduced the fighting power of American divisions at an alarming rate. The decision to field only ninety divisions was influenced by other huge, competing demands on U.S. manpower. The Soviets and Germans fielded hundreds of army divisions, but only the United States had to form a global army, a two-ocean navy, and multiple strategic and tactical air forces. The shortage of American manpower required women to enter the workplace on the production lines. Criticisms of the lack of U.S. ground forces often neglect the fact that America successfully distributed its human resources to create a global, joint military organization backed by enormous manufacturing facilities.

Creveld's critical views on the army's soldier replacement system are more than justified. The policy of providing standing divisions with replacements rather than raising new divisions was a concept carried to extremes. Although the replacement system made good bureaucratic sense and promoted efficient management, it is hard to imagine a system more detrimental to the individual soldier's discipline, morale, and training. Replacements were the army's lost orphans, and they personified a tremendous waste of combat power. The army's handling of personnel matters was perhaps its greatest institutional blunder in World War II. However, it is inaccurate to conclude that the army was content with the replacement system; the army was aware of the deficiencies in the replacement system and tried to make improvements. Depots and transportation systems became more hospitable and comfortable, and replacements received refresher training. The greatest change was that by war's end replacements moved to the front in ad hoc squads and platoons where they joined divisions as a group. While it may be difficult to measure the results of these reforms, they do indicate that American commanders were aware of existing problems in the replacement system and made efforts to improve conditions.

Fighting Power argues that the American army ignored the needs of its soldiers and placed too much emphasis on the use of weapons and machinery. However, a study of combined arms operations in the ETO shows that the army was aware of its manpower deficiencies and decided to maximize the use of weapons, firepower, and machinery. The full use and integration of firepower compensated for shortcomings in the personnel system. The technical and tactical adaptations that took place throughout the ETO best illustrate American superiority in employing weapons and equipment. Americans had a special flair for bringing their resources to bear in devastating land and air attacks. Reliance on special equipment, weapons, and firepower was not a major American deficiency but a great strength.

Adaptations in air-ground operations best illustrate the American military's superior aptitude for using its machines and weapons. Tactical and technical innovations permitted the air-ground battle team to generate a tremendous amount of coordinated combat power. Americans found ways to solve target acquisition problems and to prevent the attack of friendly troops by supporting aircraft. The development of tank-mounted air controllers and improvements in the HORSEFLY system resulted in some of the best air-ground cooperation ever conducted. Army and air leaders eventually discovered effective techniques for integrating the tremendous weight of heavy bombers into the ground battle. Aviators and soldiers learned to coordinate their efforts against enemy positions under varying conditions. Great progress occurred in the use of tactical air reconnaissance. The full synchronization of bombers, fighter-bombers, massed artillery, and the organic weapons of forward units during overwhelming preparatory bombardments best displays American superiority in the employment and coordination of weaponry. The adaptations airmen and soldiers invented and implemented to make air power part of the combined arms team shows the extraordinary ability of Americans to make the best use of their weapons and equipment.

A survey of combined arms battles in Europe reveals that too much has been made over the notion that Americans did not shoot enough. S. L. A. Marshall's findings in *Men against Fire* were accepted as gospel at one time, but veterans and historians have called Marshall to task in recent years. Marshall's findings resulted from intuitive and subjective means rather than quantitative or scientific methods. Because of a lack of hard data, his conclusions can be neither proven nor disproven, and his personal style often included bluster and hyperbole as he tried to drive home the force of his convictions to listeners and readers. A close survey of after-action reports and training memoranda from the ETO does reveal that volume of fire was a problem in many units. But Marshall's belief and grave concern that only 15–25 percent of soldiers fired their weapons does not appear among the voluminous reports and writings of the participants. An exhaustive review of anecdotal evidence, unit after-action reports, and training literature suggests that Marshall's figures on the numbers of active firers are too conservative and that many more soldiers were pulling the trigger. Furthermore, it is hard to believe that an army attacking prepared defenses for the better part of an entire year could have accomplished much of anything with only one quarter of its soldiers firing their weapons. While many soldiers probably never did fire their weapons, the problem was perhaps not as great as Marshall believed.

If Americans did not fire their weapons, it was because of training inadequacies rather than some innate inability or lack of courage. Many infantrymen believed that marksmanship training under controlled conditions on known-distance rifle ranges taught soldiers little about firing in combat, where fear and confusion reigned and the enemy was hard to spot. It should come as no surprise that new soldiers forced through an impersonal replacement system or other troops hastily retrained as infantrymen may have had problems firing their weapons. After the war, infantrymen took a long, hard look at their marksmanship training. One article in the *Infantry Journal* told readers that "a soldier experienced in combat knows that such marksmanship training has nothing to do with combat training." The army's success with marching fire and Marshall's own advocacy of better training methods convinced the army to implement more realistic marksmanship programs that required firers to acquire obscure and fleeting targets and to estimate ranges.

A strange parallel exists between soldiers' understanding of S. L. A. Marshall's main themes and the other training deficiencies identified in the ETO. Too many professional soldiers and historians have forgotten most of Marshall's other main points. In addition to his views on small arms firepower, Marshall observed that unit cohesion keeps soldiers present and functioning on the battlefield, that fatigue breeds fear, and that excessive loads of equipment and ammunition drain soldiers' physical stamina and courage. In the same way, commanders in the ETO saw many training deficiencies they considered just as damaging as the lack of infantry firepower. Troops bunching together under fire, freezing upon initial enemy contact, failing to follow artillery barrages close enough or not moving out from underneath enemy shell fire, and not digging deep enough all had grave consequences. A comprehensive picture of the problems of soldier performance on the battlefield must include all of these points rather than concentrating solely on why soldiers may not have fired their weapons enough.

Writers and historians have recently assaulted S. L. A. Marshall's honesty regarding his own career and historical findings, and a tendency has developed to discredit his arguments along with his integrity. Professional historians and soldiers must remember that the broader questions Marshall raised are probably more significant than any facts about his personal career. Disciplined thinkers must separate the man from his arguments and perform critical analyses of Marshall's ideas based solely on their own merits and available evidence. On balance, it appears as though Marshall's writings about the broad experience of men under fire are much more often right than wrong. To forget or disregard Marshall's main theses solely because of concerns over his personal integrity is to throw the baby out with the bath water. And in Marshall's case, the issues contained in the bath water may be far more significant than questions about the infant's personal integrity.

While historians are quick to point out the army's reliance on vast firepower, soldiers in Europe were more struck with the limits of firepower than with its omnipotence. The army learned that vast amounts of ordnance could hurt, demoralize, and disrupt the Germans, but that firepower alone was not decisive. No matter how many bombs and shells were unleashed, riflemen and tankers still had to root the Germans out of their prepared positions. Firepower served as a catalyst to help keep units moving forward but was not powerful enough to let American troops merely step over the enemy's broken remnants. The COBRA bombardment and the subsequent ground attack is probably the most dramatic example of the effectiveness of massed firepower and ground units working in concert. Firepower had a terrible effect when Americans mistakenly opened fire on other Americans. Artillery battalions had good reputations for fire discipline despite the occasional shelling of friendly units, and improvements in target identification kept bombers and fighter-bombers off the backs of friendly ground units. Ironically, the COBRA bombardment [July, 1944] caused the enemy the most harm but also produced perhaps the largest single incident of American casualties to friendly fire in all of World War II.

Two aspects of the use of firepower are little known. Units in Europe quickly discovered the effectiveness of heavy-caliber fire delivered at point-blank range, and commanders had no reservations in using tank and TD main guns as well as self-propelled artillery to batter German strongholds into submission. Heavy-caliber weapons used at close quarters physically dismantled German defenses and greatly bolstered soldiers' morale. Tanks and TDs wrecked pillboxes as well as hedgerow, forest, and urban strongholds, while direct fire artillery blasted away at heavy fortifications. Soldiers also discovered a number of creative ways to use explosives. Demolitions gapped hedgerows, blew passageways through buildings, and fractured steel and concrete defenses. Americans used close-quarters firepower without restraint or any regard for humanitarian considerations rather than risking their own lives. To average soldiers, blasting the enemy into oblivion at point-blank range was one of the best ways to minimize casualties and to get the fighting over with as quickly as possible.

Combat zone training programs that increased soldier's capabilities and proficiency are one of the army's unsung success stories of World War II. A variety of training activities helped improve and sustain combat power. The ETO as a whole mustered resources to run an extensive retraining program for soldiers newly reassigned to combat duties. Divisions trained during lulls in the fighting to prepare for specific battlefield challenges, to hone skills dulled due to heavy losses, and to provide replacements with refresher training. One of the most significant functions of training was to introduce soldiers to new organizations and equipment. Companies and platoons reorganized into assault and support teams and rehearsed new tactics and techniques devised for attacking through hedgerows and forests, down city streets, and against fortifications. Combat zone training programs repaired many of the problems of tank-infantry coordination and air-ground cooperation. Soldiers learned how to use bangalore torpedoes, bazookas, and flame throwers. Units rehearsed for specific operations in the days just before the actual attack, while units new to the theater used training sessions to familiarize themselves with lessons other units had already learned. The best way to assimilate new troops was through tough training before battle. The army did not recognize the need for these training functions before the war, but everyone came to realize the importance of training conducted in the combat zone.

Training programs near the front lines taught commanders two important lessons. Prewar doctrine often spoke of the need for "special units" or "special troops armed with unique equipment" for certain types of operations. Officers facing the formidable tasks of attacking stubborn defenses realized that special troops and equipment were a mirage. They had to attack with only the troops and equipment readily available. Training permitted regular units to learn and sharpen the special skills required for urban combat, the attack of fortifications, and a number of other unique operations. Second, leaders learned that combat zone training is a legitimate requirement that must be anticipated in peacetime. Armies cannot believe that they train to peak proficiency before war and then expend their expertise in battle, or that training ceases with the beginning of hostilities. The need to maintain readiness extends into wartime, so commanders and trainers must think about how to hone soldiers' skills, teach troops new techniques, and assimilate replacement troops with combat zone training programs.

It did not take long for commanders to realize that the best peacetime training programs have distinct limits in preparing soldiers for battle. No matter how thorough or rigorous, training could not simulate battlefield conditions realistically. Soldiers under fire for the first time were struck with the sense of fear, confusion, and helplessness that shelling and direct, heavy fire induced. Commanders and leaders had to learn how to maintain command, control, and communications, while keeping their soldiers moving despite the paralyses of fear and confusion and a hail of enemy shot and shell. The noises of battle are all new to unseasoned troops. The sights and sounds of the dead and wounded and the notion that soldiers had to kill or be killed could not be a part of training programs, yet these factors had a profound, emotional impact on most soldiers. No peacetime army can come to believe its training methods fully approximate battle. In a world where lasers and electronics make battle simulations more realistic, commanders and trainers must resist the tendency to think their mock battles are just about the same as real war. No matter how hard an army prepares for war, the physical and emotional shocks of the sights and sounds of battle are challenges soldiers cannot confront and overcome until their first fight.

Combat was far different from what many soldiers had expected. In peacetime exercises groups of soldiers moved together rapidly in mock attacks, but the opposite was true in battle. The tempo of combat was much slower, with single attacks often taking hours rather than minutes. A myriad of tasks slowed units in battle: gathering intelligence, coordinating direct and indirect fires, evacuating casualties, and handling PWs. Even in small unit actions, detailed planning achieved success more effectively than élan or adrenaline. The battlefield was a lonely place that tended to isolate rather than unify soldiers. Fear and confusion were more prevalent than anyone had expected and tended to hold units back. Much more combat took place at close quarters than on open terrain, and the combat arms had to work much closer together than in peacetime. Commanders discovered that combined arms attacks not only increased their combat power but improved soldiers' morale and confidence. Infantrymen felt better with tanks and TDs nearby, while artillery barrages and air strikes gave footsoldiers confidence. The numbers and types of casualties took commanders by surprise. Hypothetically, a twelve-man infantry squad eliminated in combat would suffer two soldiers killed, five wounded, one missing, two evacuated for trench foot, and two others incapacitated by combat exhaustion.

Junior officers faced two significant leadership challenges in Europe. The U.S. army was a mass conscript force drawn from a liberal, democratic society, and the first problem facing officers was the fundamental conflict between the need for military discipline and draftees' desire to retain some form of individual freedom. Officers felt compelled to instill discipline through tough training, inspections, punishment, and military courtesy while remaining somewhat aloof from the troops. On the other hand, soldiers felt that discipline was almost a vice and desired more familiarity with their officers. The incongruence in values between a professional officer corps and a mass conscript army has always existed, and the American army in Europe was no exception. When it came to the problems of leading conscripts into battle, young officers had much in common with their professional forebears in the Civil War and World War I.

Company grade officers learned not to accept at face value the simplistic battlefield leadership style in the cry "Follow me!" They had to lead by example but also had to exercise common sense and judgment in how to influence tactical situations. Officers who led from the front with a reckless disregard for their own safety quickly became casualties, and battalions and companies that lost their leaders in the early stages of battle became bogged down and confused. Yet junior officers knew that at crucial times mission accomplishment came before their own personal safety. Many captains and lieutenants grabbed their carbines and led the way against German defenses; some survived, most did not. Officers came to understand that their troops did not expect them always to lead from the front. In fact, most soldiers felt better knowing that their officers were alive and doing all they could to control the fight and to bring the other combat arms to bear. . . .

Despite significant changes in warfare since 1945, the U.S. military's recent war in the Persian Gulf has many close parallels with World War II and suggests the timeliness of a number of the attitudes and characteristics of the American way of war. The 1941 edition of FM 100-5 had served as a broad guide for the conduct of operations in the ETO, and fifty years later the new FM 100-5 outlined the principles of AirLand Battle, which proved effective in the open desert of Southwest Asia. U.S. troops in Saudi Arabia wanted to get the fighting over with and go home as quickly as possible while defeating the enemy and suffering as few casualties as possible, and American soldiers attacking Omaha Beach, crossing the Moselle River, or breaching the Siegfried Line had said the exact same things. In both wars, soldiers at all levels displayed a flair for devising innovative ways to use their weapons. The adaptations devised by U.S. troops to help breach Iraqi defenses beg comparison with similar developments that occurred in the bocage a half a century earlier. The army again displayed a capacity to collect and disseminate lessons learned, to coordinate the use of overwhelming firepower, and to conduct combined arms operations. Once deployed to Saudi Arabia, combat zone training programs gave soldiers confidence in living and fighting in the desert and imparted them with a number of new skills in much the same way divisional training centers had done in Europe. In both campaigns, air power helped hasten the enemy's defeat by attacking both rear areas and forward combat units. The pilots and FACs of DESERT STORM could trace the historical roots of air-ground cooperation back to the Normandy campaign and the HORSEFLY air control system. Once the ground war began the attack scenario was not unfamiliar: the U.S. VII Corps conducted the main attack, assisted by tremendous fire support and aircraft from the U.S. Ninth Air Force, just as General [J. Lawton] Collins's VII Corps had tackled German formations in the ETO. Perhaps the most ironic of all these similarities was that American troops, for the first time since World War II, were fighting the forces of an authoritarian dictator whom many compared to Adolf Hitler.

The legacy of the fighting in Europe, reinforced by the recent DESERT STORM experience, points to several characteristics of the American way of war that may become prevalent in future conflicts. Within the bounds of political objectives and constraints, the American war machine is relentless in achieving its goals. Commanders stay on the offensive to destroy their opponents even if it means fighting the enemy under disadvantageous conditions. The army prefers to maneuver but does not shirk from plodding battles of attrition. Americans concentrate overwhelming combat power to win quickly and to keep casualties to a minimum, and firepower will remain a key ingredient to success. Massed artillery and air power will bleed the enemy and help keep ground units moving forward. Modern battlefield technologies, such as enhanced sensors and communications, precision-guided munitions, night vision equipment, and a host of other improvements, will help commanders destroy the enemy even faster with fewer friendly losses. However, the tremendous effects of firepower and technology still will not relieve ground troops of the burden of closing with the enemy. On the offensive and the defensive, American units will employ the most effective combined arms tactics possible. Training in the combat zone will improve morale and make soldiers more confident and proficient.

The greatest single trait of Americans in any future conflict may once again be their ability to adapt and innovate on the battlefield. The pattern of problem solving and adaptation that occurred in the ETO is likely to repeat itself during extended operations. Americans will revise doctrine, invent new combined arms tactics, and innovate changes in weapons and equipment in order to respond to varying conditions of terrain, technology, enemy defenses, and weather. Ideas will come from a wide number of sources and spread among units through both formal and informal channels. Soldiers will have success in finding techniques to improve their performance and survivability and will improvise quick remedies to manageable problems. More significant challenges may defy easy solution, and commanders and small unit leaders must have the competence and expertise to identify and find solutions to unexpected challenges without major involvement from higher staffs. Senior commanders will hold subordinates responsible for the results of battlefield adaptation.

The notion that a successful army must be capable of making adjustments in its tactics and methods after the shooting starts was not lost on the combatants in the ETO. The veterans of one unit reflected back on their experience and remembered, "K Company's war was far different from the one we'd been trained to fight . . . some things had definitely changed. Gone was the blind faith in the manuals, in the infinite wisdom of senior officers. What counted instead was experience, sheer bloody experience." Soldiers of all ranks relied on their experience, training, and judgment to find better ways of bridging the gaps between theory and practice and training and fighting. Innovations in tactics and the use of weapons and equipment helped soldiers take objectives easier with fewer casualties.

In the immediate aftermath of World War II, the army clearly recognized the importance of critical analysis and the need to adapt in battle. In reflecting on the successes in Europe, the theater's General Board challenged America's future military leaders:

> While operations in the Western European campaign have indicated no necessity for changes in our present tactical doctrines, it can be expected that these doctrines will require modification with the future development of improved weapons and equipment. . . . The tactics and techniques of the various arms, and of the combined arms, must be reviewed constantly in the light of new developments. . . . Only by this means can we hope to be fully prepared for the next war.

Perhaps the greatest lesson the army learned in World War II was that the learning process itself is an integral part of any conflict and can spell the difference between victory and defeat. It is a lesson contemporary American soldiers should never forget.

⬥ *F U R T H E R   R E A D I N G*

Stephen E. Ambrose, *Band of Brothers: E Company, 506th Regiment, 101st Airborne: From Normandy to Hitler's Eagle's Nest* (1992).

_____, *D-Day, June 6, 1944: The Climactic Battle of World War II* (1994).

_____, *Citizen Soldiers: The U.S. Army from the Normandy Beaches to the Bulge to the Surrender of Germany* (1997).

Eric Bergerud, *Touched with Fire: The Land War in the South Pacific* (1996).

Alison R. Bernstein, *American Indians and World War II: Toward a New Era in Indian Affairs* (1991).

John Sloan Brown, *Draftee Division* (1986).

Craig M. Cameron, *American Samurai: Myth, Imagination, and the Conduct of Battle in the First Marine Division, 1941–1951* (1994).

D'Ann Campbell, *Women at War with America: Private Lives in a Patriotic Era* (1984).

_____, "Women in Combat: The World War II Experience in the United States, Great Britain, Germany, and the Soviet Union," *Journal of Military History* 57 (1993) 301–323.

Lewis H. Carlson, *We Were Each Other's Prisoners: An Oral History of World War II American and German Prisoners of War* (1997).

Jeffrey J. Clarke and Robert Ross Smith, *Riviera to the Rhine* (1993).

Albert E. Cowdrey, *Fighting for Life: American Military Medicine in World War II* (1994).

Carlo D'Este, *World War II in the Mediterranean, 1942–1945* (1990).

Michael D. Doubler, *Closing with the Enemy: How GIs Fought the War in Europe, 1944–1945* (1994).

John W. Dower, *War Without Mercy: Race and Power in the Pacific War* (1986).

Charity Adams Earley, *One Woman's Army: A Black Officer Remembers the WAC* (1989).

Marvin E. Fletcher, *America's First Black General: Benjamin O. Davis, Sr., 1880–1970* (1989).

George Q. Flynn, *The Draft, 1940–1973* (1993).

J. Glenn Gray, *The Warriors: Reflections on Men in Battle* (1959).

Olga Gruhzit-Hoyt, *They Also Served: American Women in World War II* (1995).

Gwendolyn Midlo Hall, ed., *Love, War, and the 96th Engineers (Colored): The World War II New Guinea Diaries of Captain Hyman Samuelson* (1995).

Max Hastings, *Overlord: D-Day and the Battle for Normandy* (1984).

John Keegan, *Six Armies in Normandy: From D-Day to the Liberation of Paris* (1984).

Lee Kennett, *GI: The American Soldier in World War II* (1987).

Gerald F. Linderman, *The World Within War: America's Combat Experience in World War II* (1997).

Lamont Lindstrom and Geoffrey M. White, *Island Encounters: Black and White Memories of the Pacific War* (1990).

Charles B. MacDonald and Sidney T. Mathews, *Three Battles: Arnaville, Altuzzo, and Schmidt* (1952).

John Douglas Marshall, *Reconciliation Road: A Family Odyssey of War and Honor* (1993).

S. L. A. Marshall, *Men Against Fire* (1947).

John Miller, Jr., *Guadalcanal: The First Offensive* (1949).

Brenda L. Moore, *To Serve My Country, To Serve My Race: The Story of the Only African American WACs Stationed Overseas during World War II* (1996).

Eric Morris, *Salerno: A Military Fiasco* (1983).

Robin Neillands and Roderick de Normann, *D-Day, 1944: Voices from Normandy* (1993).

George H. Roeder, Jr., *The Censored War: American Visual Experience During World War II* (1993).

Cornelius Ryan, *The Longest Day: June 6, 1944* (1959).

E. B. Sledge, *With the Old Breed at Peleliu and Okinawa* (1981).

Ronald H. Spector, *Eagle Against the Sun: The American War with Japan* (1985).

Roger J. Spiller, "S.L.A. Marshall and the Ratio of Fire," *Royal United Services Institute Journal* 133 (Winter 1988): 63–71.

Richard M. Stannard, *Infantry: An Oral History of a World War II American Infantry Battalion* (1993).

Samuel A. Stouffer, et al., *The American Soldier: Combat and Its Aftermath*, vol. 2 (1949).

Barbara Tomblin, *G.I. Nightingales: The Army Nurse Corps in World War II* (1996).

Mattie E. Treadwell, *The Women's Army Corps* (1954).

Martin van Creveld, *Fighting Power: German and U.S. Army Performance, 1939–1945* (1982).

Russell F. Weigley, *Eisenhower's Lieutenants: The Campaign of France and Germany, 1944–1945* (1981).

World War II: Strategic Bombing in Europe and Asia

The rise of American air power as a major force, using conventional munitions and ultimately atomic weapons, raised questions of the military effectiveness of strategic bombing and of the morality of area bombing of civilian population centers. The Army Air Corps had committed itself in the 1930s to the doctrine of precision bombing of military and industrial targets as a war-winning strategy. To implement that doctrine, it had developed well-armed, four-engine, long-range, heavy bombers: the B-17 "Flying Fortress" (beginning in 1935), and the B-24 "Liberator" (beginning in 1939); and ultimately the longer-range, very heavy bomber, B-29 "Superfortress" (beginning in 1944). In 1941, as President Franklin Roosevelt committed the United States to the defense of the Allies and preparation for U.S. entry into the war, U.S. and British military planners mapped out Anglo-American grand strategy in a War Plan code-named RAINBOW 5, which made the primary mission the defeat of Nazi Germany. For such a task, the U.S. Army's "Victory Program" completed in September 1941, envisioned a wartime ground force of 6.7 million troops, and an army air force of 2 million. While the army planners imagined an air force primarily supporting the ground units, the planners of the Army Air Corps (soon renamed the U.S. Army Air Forces, USAAF) concluded that U.S. strategic bombers flying from Britain and the Mediterranean could perform a vital and perhaps decisive role in defeating Germany. While Britain's Bomber Command planned its own air offensive, the U.S. Air Corps' War Plans Division in August 1941 drafted its own supplement to the Army's RAINBOW 5; it was known as AWPD-1. The goals of the projected American air offensive against Germany were, without unacceptable losses, to disrupt the electrical power system and the railroad network, destroy the oil and petroleum facilities, and undermine German civilian morale by attack upon "civil concentrations." Most immediately the air offensive was designed to neutralize the German air force by attacking its bases and the aircraft and aluminum factories that supplied it. From 1943 to 1945, while the British engaged in night-time area bombing, the U.S. Army Air Forces, with increasing numbers of

bombers, launched high-altitude daylight raids against a wide variety of targets—from ball bearing factories to railroad yards, aircraft plants, and petrochemical complexes. The bomber losses among the B-17s and B-24s and their crews were among the highest ratios in the American armed forces (29,000 crewmen killed and 8,000 bombers lost), particularly before the arrival of long-range fighter escorts in 1944.

The effectiveness of the bombing of Germany by the U.S. and British air forces has remained the subject of debate to the present day. German industry continued to produce war material until the end of the war, but the Allied air offensive destroyed the Luftwaffe *and petrochemical and transportation systems. Allied bombing also killed some 600,000 German civilians. The Army Air Forces' bombing of Japanese cities by B-29s, beginning in 1944, and the transition from precision to area bombing and from regular munitions, first to incendiary bombs, and finally to nuclear weapons, led to an ongoing debate over the morality of terror bombing and the use of weapons of indiscriminate, mass destruction. Although the efficacy and morality of strategic bombing was debated after World War II, it is clear that ideas about the effectiveness of air power, and the relationship between technology and strategy, continued to influence the manner in which the United States subsequently waged war in Korea, Vietnam, and the Persian Gulf. Such ideas also contributed to the primary American reliance upon nuclear strategy to deter the Soviet Union during the Cold War.*

▲ D O C U M E N T S

The first document, an excerpt from the U.S. Army Air Corps' AWDP-1, prepared in August 1941 under a team headed by Major (later Major General) Haywood S. Hansell, Jr., provides the basic war plan for the air offensive against Germany. In the second document, an excerpt from the diary of Nazi Propaganda Minister Joseph Goebbels, after the British firebombing raid on Hamburg on Sunday, July 25, 1943, in which 40,000 persons were killed, Goebbels predicts the disastrous effect on German morale and industry of the Allied bombing campaign. The bombing raids also took a tremendous toll among the air crews, as is made clear in the third document, a previously unpublished diary account of a B-17 raid on a synthetic oil plant in Merseburg, near Leipzig, Germany, by one of the pilots, First Lieutenant Chester ("Chet") Szarawarski of Garfield, New Jersey. For an independent assessment of the effectiveness of strategic bombing, President Roosevelt established the U.S. Strategic Bombing Survey, which included among its dozen officers such subsequently famous statesmen as John Kenneth Galbraith, George W. Ball, and Paul H. Nitze. In the fourth document, from the Survey's September 1945 *Summary Report* on the European Theater of Operations, the group noted some qualified accomplishments as well as some tremendous successes, concluding that Allied air power was decisive in the war in western Europe. In the air war against Japan, the Army Air Forces eventually abandoned attempts at daylight precision bombing and turned to area bombing at night, using incendiary bombs. Just after midnight on the night of March 9–10, 1945, more than 300 B-29s firebombed Tokyo, creating a firestorm that killed an estimated 84,000 persons. The firestorm was recalled in the late 1980s in an interview by American historians Theodore Cook and Haruko Taya Cook, with two Japanese survivors who had worked at the telephone company, Tomizawa Kimi, 80, a former switchboard operator, and Kobayashi Hiroyasu, 70, a maintenance technician. The sixth document, a special restricted report published in April 1947 by the U.S. Strategic Bombing Survey on the effects of incendiary bomb attacks on eight Japanese cities examined by Survey representatives in late 1945, concludes that the fire raids were devastatingly effective in terms of curtailing production. Yet the authors also noted that more Japanese civilians had died in the fire raids (approximately 160,000 persons) than Japanese military personnel had been killed by the American armed forces. Although not cited in the report, more than one million civilians were killed by American air raids on the cities of Japan.

1. U.S. Army Air Corps Puts Forward a Strategic Bombing Plan Against Germany, 1941

2. Air Mission:

a. To wage a sustained air offensive against German military power, supplemented by air offensives against other regions under enemy control which contribute toward that power . . .
b. To support a final offensive, if it becomes necessary to invade the continent.
c. In addition, to conduct effective air operations in connection with Hemisphere Defense and a strategic defensive in the Far East. . . .

3. Situation . . .

d. . . . The basic conception on which this plan is based lies in the application of air power for the breakdown of the industrial and economic structure of Germany. This conception involves the selection of a system of objectives vital to continued German war effort, and to the means of livelihood of the German people, and tenaciously *concentrating all bombing* toward the destruction of those objectives. The most effective manner of conducting such a decisive offensive is by the destruction of precise objectives, at least initially. As German morale begins to crack, area bombing of civil concentrations may be effective.
e. It is improbable that a land invasion can be carried out against Germany proper within the next three years. If the air offensive is successful, a land offensive may not be necessary. Our air bases in England and elsewhere must be made secure, primarily by ground forces, and the lines of communication by sea must also be made secure.

4.

a. *Possible Lines of Action.* Based on an analysis of military and economic factors, the following lines of action for an air offensive can be set up for consideration.
   (1) *Lines of action whose accomplishment will accomplish the air mission in Europe.*

U.S. Army Air Corps, Air War Plans Division, AWPD-1, August 1941, reprinted in Maj. Gen. Haywood S. Hansell, Jr., *The Air Plan That Defeated Hitler* (Reproduced by the U.S. Air Force from Atlanta, GA: Higgins-McArthur, 1972; copyright H.S. Hansell, Jr. 1972), pp. 298–300, 304–305, 307–309.

(a) Disruption of a major portion of the Electric Power System of Germany.
(b) Disruption of the German transportation system.
(c) Destruction of the German oil and petroleum system.
(d) Undermining of German morale by air attack of civil concentrations.

(2) *Lines of action representing intermediate objectives, whose accomplishment may be essential to the accomplishment of the principal objectives listed above.*

(a) Neutralization of the German Air Force.
   (1) By attack of its bases.
   (2) By attack of aircraft factories. (engine and airframe) . . .
(3) By attack of aluminum and magnesium factories, . . .

f. *Morale.* Timeliness of attack is most important in the conduct of air operations directly against civil morale. If the morale of the people is already low because of sustained suffering and deprivation and because the people are losing faith in the ability of the armed forces to win a favorable decision, then heavy and sustained bombing of cities may crush that morale entirely. However, if these conditions do not exist, then area bombing of cities may actually stiffen the resistance of the population, especially if the attacks are weak and sporadic. Hence, no specific number of targets is set up for this task. Rather it is believed that the entire bombing effort might be applied toward this purpose when it becomes apparent that the proper psychological conditions exist.

2. Beneath the Bombs:
Nazi Propaganda Minister Joseph Goebbels
Bemoans the Impact of the Allied Air Campaign
on German Morale and Industry, 1943

[July 26, 1943]

During the night an extraordinarily heavy air raid on Hamburg occurred, one which will have very severe consequences both for Hamburg's civilian population as well for armaments production. With this raid all illusions regarding the effectiveness of the enemy's air operations will finally be shattered. Unfortunately we shot down embarrassingly few enemy planes—all told, twelve. That hardly compares with the nearly 500 planes which attacked us. As bad luck would have it, just two days before Commanding General [Generaloberst Hubert] Weise transferred the heavy antiaircraft guns from Hamburg to Italy. That's all we needed. One can imagine how furiously the enemy planes struck Hamburg. The eastern section of [neighboring] Altona was particularly hard-hit. Here a real catastrophe occurred. The civilian populace endured extraordinary damage. The number killed is not yet known. Estimates for those without homes range from 150,000 to 200,000. At the moment I do not know how we will solve these problems. . . .

A translation of Nazi Propaganda Minister Joseph Goebbels' diary entry, July 26, 1943 from a photocopy of the original manuscript obtained from the Russian archives in Moscow by John Chambers. Also reprinted in Elke Froehlich, ed. *Die Tagebuecher von Joseph Goebbels* (Munich: K.G. Saur, 1993), Part II, Volume 9, pp. 162–163. Translated from the German by Professor David Culbert, Department of History, Louisiana State University.

[State Secretary Leopold] Gutterer meets me at the train station in Berlin. He gives me the first report about Hamburg. Things there have gone most tragically. The air war is our most vulnerable point. At the moment we have our hands full simply trying to clear away the worst destruction in Hamburg. We have ordered fire trucks from nearby major cities to Hamburg, at least to bring the raging fires under control by evening. . . . I hope to get at least one or two hours of sleep before departing [for Hitler's headquarters in the East].

3. Lieutenant Chester ("Chet") Szarawarski, an American Bomber Pilot Recounts a B-17 Bomber Raid, 1944

August 24, 1944

Awakened before three o'clock—breakfast as usual—2 eggs coffee, fruit juices bread & butter, etc. Had to hurry to get to Briefing on time. Doors to the briefing room didn't open until after four. (Gunners were not briefed at all.) and there was no need to hurry at all.

Target—Merseberg, [*sic*] Germany—I. G. Farben Chemical Co's large synthetic oil plant (one of the largest if not the largest in the country)

Secondary = P.F.F. target, smaller synthetic oil plant in Leipzig.

Last resort target = Marshalling yards

Gas load = 2780 gal.

Bomb load = 10 five hundred pound demolition bombs.

Twelve wings going into the same area from the 1st Div. We were the ten wing over the coast. 2nd & 3rd division also had targets in the same area.

Close to 10/10 cloud coverage over England. Visibility very good over Germany. High clouds above 30,000 ft over target. Our group flew at 23,000.

Our position was supposed to be No. 6 in the low Squadron. No. 4 aborted, No. 5 moved into the number 4 position and we moved into the No. 5 position. The stand by ship filled in the spot we left vacant.

The leader of the second element was out of position all the way into the target. He was too high and too far back. If he had moved closer to the lead ship, dropped lower and stayed to the right of him instead of directly behind him we would not have had to wallow around and fight prop wash all the way. No. 2 ship also lagged behind behind.

We couldn't fly in our proper position off the right wing of No 4 ship so as long as we had to be out of position it should not have mattered where we flew. Kastie insisted on flying almost behind the No. 4 ship, practically in trail with him. He'd keep fighting the prop wash, rolling and diving when it became severe but was too stubborn to try getting out wider and pulling up further abreast the other ship. I never want to go into heavily defended Germany again flying as tail end Charlie when it should have been a fairly safe and easy position to fly.

Unpublished Diary/Journal/Notes of Chester ("Chet") Szarawarski, of bombing raid of August 24, 1944. Reprinted by permission of Helen Szarawarski.

Fighter protection to the target was good even though the planes were so far out they couldn't be identified as freind [sic] or foe. The gunners were all on the ball and kept calling them out.

The flak bursts could be seen for miles around the target long before we reached it. Several wings must have gone over before us for the city below was blanketed by huge billowing clouds of dark grey smoke. Before we reached the target flak began popping all around us. Some of it was so close you could hear the "Womp" and feel the ship bounce as though hit. Over the target it was still worse and from the squadron before us I saw for the first time a B-17 catch fire (#4 engine) spiral out of formation, snap roll, spiral down again, chandelle out as though he was going to level out again then fall off on its wing and explode. From the explosion a few large pieces like flaps and ailerons seemed to fall, the rest of it looked like a heap of dust the fragments not larger than coins. And back in the states B-17 pilots used to speak of B-24s exploding. They had never heard of a 17 explode, but it happens often. C. V. Cooke the ball turret gunner of our former crew was said to be flying in that ship.

We flew over the target without dropping bombs. I thought we were going on to the secondary when we got out into the clear; but Hell No! we turned right into it again. It was Col. Norman's last mission and I guess he wanted to make it a good [one]. It was on the second run that they got his ship. The major who was supposed to replace him as sqdn. C.O. went down too in the same ship. J. Geissler a boy who was in the same sqdn. with me at Maxwell Field and went through the same cadet schools as I was tail gunner. His usual position is co-pilot. I don't know why they carry co-pilots in the lead ships as tail gunners.

Several other ships went down and amid all the flak one lone enemy ship appeared—a small jet propelled . . . job. I only got one glimpse of him before he disappeared. A small fuselage with bat shaped wings and no visible tail. The ball turret gunner got several good shots at him and may have damaged him.

All the formations broke up and planes straggled all over the sky. On the way out of the target area the No. 2 ship in our formation dropped out and we took his place. It was smooth flying from then on. He appeared again about a half hour later. After we landed we found that the pilot was hit in the arm.

It was raining in England when we got back. One ship without brakes could be seen on the road below after it ran off the runway. Another, the one that was No. 2 in our squadron was off the runway with one of it's [sic] landing gear buckled and foam all over the ground and No. 2 engine nacelle where a fire had just been put out. The elevators were shot up too. A third one had a tire torn off the rim.

In all six ships were missing, one, Arnold's ship, landed on the coast, Plenty were damaged.

The afternoon before, we met a bunch of enlisted men who were supposed to become our crew. However half of the men on the crew we flew with were new to me. I don't know just how well each man knew his specific duties but they all seemed to be pretty good.

The mission lasted over ten hours. We were in flak about 35 minutes. The E.T.A. was delayed by the second run on the target and the late landing was caused by crippled ships on the runway. The formation must have circled close to an hour before we were cleared to land.

4. U.S. Strategic Bombing Survey Appraises the Bombing Offensive Against Germany, 1945

Some Signposts

1. The German experience suggests that even a first class military power—rugged and resilient as Germany was—cannot live long under full-scale and free exploitation of air weapons over the heart of its territory. By the beginning of 1945, before the invasion of the homeland itself, Germany was reaching a state of helplessness. Her armament production was falling irretrievably, orderliness in effort was disappearing, and total disruption and disintegration were well along. Her armies were still in the field. But with the impending collapse of the support-ing economy, the indications are convincing that they would have had to cease fighting—any effective fighting—within a few months. Germany was mortally wounded.

2. The significance of full domination of the air over the enemy—both over its armed forces and over its sustaining economy—must be emphasized. That dom-ination of the air was essential. Without it, attacks on the basic economy of the en-emy could not have been delivered in sufficient force and with sufficient freedom to bring effective and lasting results.

3. As the air offensive gained in tempo, the Germans were unable to prevent the decline and eventual collapse of their economy. Nevertheless, the recuperative and defensive powers of Germany were immense; the speed and ingenuity with which they rebuilt and maintained essential war industries in operation clearly sur-passed Allied expectations. Germany resorted to almost every means an ingenious people could devise to avoid the attacks upon her economy and to minimize their effects. Camouflage, smoke screens, shadow plants, dispersal, underground facto-ries, were all employed. In some measure all were helpful, but without control of the air, none was really effective. Dispersal brought a measure of immediate relief, but eventually served only to add to the many problems caused by the attacks on the transportation system. Underground installations prevented direct damage, but they, too, were often victims of disrupted transportation and other services. In any case, Germany never succeeded in placing any substantial portion of her war pro-duction underground—the effort was largely limited to certain types of aircraft, their components, and the V weapons. The practicability of going underground as the escape from full and free exploitation of the air is highly questionable; it was so considered by the Germans themselves. Such passive defenses may be worth while and important, but it may be doubted if there is any escape from air domination by an enemy.

4. The mental reaction of the German people to air attack is significant. Under ruthless Nazi control they showed surprising resistance to the terror and hardships of repeated air attack, to the destruction of their homes and belongings, and to the conditions under which they were reduced to live. Their morale, their belief in

From U.S. Strategic Bombing Survey. *Summary Report (European War)* (Washington, D.C. U.S. Strategic Bombing Survey, 1945), 16–17.

ultimate victory or satisfactory compromise, and their confidence in their leaders declined, but they continued to work efficiently as long as the physical means of production remained. The power of a police state over its people cannot be underestimated.

5. The importance of careful selection of targets for air attack is emphasized by the German experience. The Germans were far more concerned over attacks on one or more of their basic industries and services—their oil, chemical, or steel industries or their power or transportation networks—than they were over attacks on their armament industry or the city areas. The most serious attacks were those which destroyed the industry or service which most indispensably served other industries. The Germans found it clearly more important to devise measures for the protection of basic industries and services than for the protection of factories turning out finished products.

6. The German experience showed that, whatever the target system, no indispensable industry was permanently put out of commission by a single attack. Persistent re-attack was necessary.

7. In the field of strategic intelligence, there was an important need for further and more accurate information, especially before and during the early phases of the war. The information on the German economy available to the United States Air Forces at the outset of the war was inadequate. And there was no established machinery for coordination between military and other governmental and private organizations. Such machinery was developed during the war. The experience suggests the wisdom of establishing such arrangements on a continuing basis.

8. Among the most significant of the other factors which contributed to the success of the air effort was the extraordinary progress during the war of Allied research, development, and production. As a result of this progress, the air forces eventually brought to the attack superiority in both numbers and quality of crews, aircraft, and equipment. Constant and unending effort was required, however, to overcome the initial advantages of the enemy and later to keep pace with his research and technology. It was fortunate that the leaders of the German Air Force relied too heavily on their initial advantage. For this reason they failed to develop, in time, weapons, such as their jet-propelled planes, that might have substantially improved their position. There was hazard, on the other hand, in the fact that the Allies were behind the Germans in the development of jet-propelled aircraft. The German development of the V weapons, especially the V-2, is also noteworthy.

9. The achievements of Allied air power were attained only with difficulty and great cost in men, material, and effort. Its success depended on the courage, fortitude, and gallant action of the officers and men of the air crews and commands. It depended also on a superiority in leadership, ability, and basic strength. These led to a timely and careful training of pilots and crews in volume; to the production of planes, weapons, and supplies in great numbers and of high quality; to the securing of adequate bases and supply routes; to speed and ingenuity in development; and to cooperation with strong and faithful Allies. The failure of any one of these might have seriously narrowed and even eliminated the margin.

5. Beneath the Bombs: Tomizawa Kimi and Kobayashi Hiroyasu, Japanese Civilians, Shudder over the Firebombing of Tokyo (1945), 1992

Kobayashi: March 9, 1945. I was there. Air-raid warnings came every day, so we weren't particularly shaken when we saw red spots far away, but soon the airplanes were flying above us. Places near us were turning red. Over there, it's red. Here, it's red! Some were still at the switchboards. The others were trying to extinguish the flames after the building caught fire. Outside, huge telephone poles, set against the building and meant to protect the windows and withstand any bomb blast, became like kindling under the incendiary bombs. When the poles started burning, there were still some working the phone lines.

Tomizawa: Our place had communication lines to the antiaircraft batteries and the fire-fighting units for the whole Shitamachi area. There weren't any wireless communications in use then, so crucial government lines passed through our switchboard. Until the last second, many operators were still working, plugging lines into the jacks.

Kobayashi: Parts of the building were still made of wood. The windowframes, for instance, and the rest areas. Wood, covered with stucco. Up on the roof, there was a water tank. Through pipes, it was supposed to lay down a curtain of water over the whole building. But the water in the tank, when it was released, was soon exhausted. We opened up fire plugs, and though water poured out fast at first, everyone was using them, too, so it soon trickled to a stop. We had a small pond, maybe two meters long. It had goldfish we kept for fun. We drained that water, throwing it onto the windows to cool them down. The glass shattered, *"Ping!"* because of the heat. I remember those kids carrying buckets. Helter-skelter. Even the water in the teakettle was used up.

Outside, the world was ablaze. We had no more water. It was all gone. That was it. The operators and the night supervisor, Matsumoto Shūji, were there. Mr. Matsumoto was found dead in the shelter. Burned to death. He was a marathon runner, but he was responsible for them. According to a survivor, Miss Tanaka, they finally did try to leave the building. "Get out, get out!" they were told, but the flames were too strong. They couldn't flee.

Tomizawa: Only four of them survived. Fortunate to escape that dangerous situation. The remaining thirty-one all perished.

Kobayashi: When we left, we men thought we were the last ones. We couldn't really get the gate open, so we climbed over the side wall. The bridge over the Arakawa was jammed. People coming this way from the far side, and trying to go there from this side. They packed together in the middle and couldn't move. People are greedy. Even at times like that, people are carrying things. Our phone cable was next to the bridge, partially submerged in the water. We took a chance. There was no other way. We hung on to it and moved across hand over hand, our bodies in the water. All the way across the river to escape the burning air. It was like a circus act.

If there'd still been water, water coming from the hydrants, we probably wouldn't have made it. But there was no water. No way to fight the fire. Besides, our line of command was separate from that of the girls. We were later questioned. "Why did only the men flee?" They wanted to know why we didn't take more girls with us. But when they investigated, they found that even the coin boxes on the public phones had melted completely. Then they understood.

Not even a single line was still operational. When I returned the next day, where the thick cables went in, they had melted down. There were no window-frames. All the metallic things had melted in the heat and were bowing down, all bent over. The switchboards, anything made of wood, all burned. Gone.

Tomizawa: The interior cables were still hanging in the empty concrete box. A chill went through me.

Kobayashi: Some people could be identified. By their stomach wraps. Where it had been tight against their skin a name could be found written on it. It wasn't burned. To tell you the truth, I couldn't tell if they were men or women. They weren't even full skeletons. Piled on top of each other. The bottom of the pile, all stuck together. A few bits of clothing could be found on them. The underpants of Mr. Matsumoto were left. Touching the wall of the shelter. When Matsumoto-san's wife came, nobody could bear to tell her that her husband was not there anymore. "You have to tell her," everyone told me. "You were on night duty together." There's nothing more painful than that. His wife confirmed that they were her husband's underwear.

Even after all the bones were buried, when it rained, a blue flame burned. From the phosphorus. Soldiers stationed there used to say, "Maybe they'll come out tonight," thinking of the ghosts and the blue flames.

I wonder what war is. I wonder why we did it. I'm not talking about victory or loss. I merely feel heartbroken for those who died. Its not an issue of whether I hate the enemy or not. However much you're glorified, if you're dead, that's it. Young kids worked so hard. Without complaint. It makes me seethe. Burning flames, huge planes flying over, dropping bombs. My feeling of hatred—"You bastards! Bastards!" you shout. But there was no sense that you're capable of doing anything about it. If you win, you're the victors. You can justify anything. It's all right if the ones who have rifles are killed. That's OK. But these kids didn't have weapons, they had only their breasts. Those are the ones whose end was tragic.

I wonder, does war bring happiness to anyone? The ones who perished here on duty were merely promoted two ranks. They got a medal from the Emperor. A long time afterwards. Their parents didn't even get their pensions. Only the men with stars are enshrined in Yasukuni. But where are those who perished here? Girls of fifteen and sixteen. Who did their best. [*His voice breaks.*] People even ask, "Why didn't they escape earlier? They should have fled earlier."

Tomizawa: They are the ones who should be enshrined.

Kobayashi: No! Not that! Their parents want them back!

6. U.S. Strategic Bombing Survey Assesses the Incendiary Bombing of Tokyo and Seven Other Japanese Cities, 1947

I. Introduction

1. The fire studies of eight Japanese cities contained in this report were made to determine the extent of fire damage and the effectiveness of bombs. Some consideration has also been given to the effectiveness of precautionary measures.

2. Of the eight cities, the two largest were selected because they were subjected to multiple attacks, and represented the most and least successful extremes; four were chosen because only one type of weapon in each case was used in attacks; one was significant because it was attacked by one type of incendiary bomb plus high explosives; and one small city was included because the attack on it was believed to have been highly ineffective. . . .

9. One of the subjects treated briefly is the effect of fire on the population. This subject is important to everyone, for it is recorded that fire killed more persons than any other cause or weapon. The number of civilian deaths in Japan greatly *exceeded* the number of strictly military deaths inflicted on the Japanese in combat by the armed forces of the United States. This statement is pregnant with significance, for if there still be a doubt that the emphasis in warfare has shifted from military forces to the civilian populations, then this fact should dissipate all uncertainty.

a. The results of the air attacks were erratic. The number of persons killed in one attack on Tokyo (9–10 March 1945) was equal to the number killed in all other major attacks on Japanese cities. In this particular case, it is probable that more persons were killed in one 6-hour period by the least expenditure of bombs than in any other recorded attack of any kind. Only at Dresden, Germany, was the number of dead greater, and that was so because of the population's having been swollen by the influx of refugees and the prolonged attack having covered a large area. Hamburg, Germany, sustained the next greatest number of casualties: 41,800 known dead, and an estimated 37,500 seriously injured. Some 280,000 persons were made homeless in an area of 4.5 square miles of total damage and 12 square miles of heavy damage for an expenditure of 2,360 tons of bombs. By comparison, during the 10 March 1945 attack on Tokyo, 83,793 persons lost their lives, 41,000 were injured, and 1,000,000 were made homeless in 15.8 square miles of totally damaged area for an expenditure of 1,667 tons of bombs.

10. The high vulnerability of Japanese cities to fire made them ideal targets for incendiary attack; typical buildings of inflammable light-frame construction, density of urban areas with their narrow, congested streets and the widespread accumulation of combustible materials in and around both residential and commercial structure combined to create a constant invitation to disaster by fire.

U.S. Strategic Bombing Survey. *Effects of Incendiary Bomb Attacks on Japan: A Report on Eight Cities* (Washington, D.C.: U.S. Strategic Bombing Survey, 1947), 1–4.

11. The Japanese had given some thought to the protection of their cities and had taken certain precautions against the time when they would be subjected to aerial bombardment and incendiary attack, but their preparations, based upon assurances of the military that they would never be attacked in force, were woefully inadequate even when they had emerged from the planning stage which was often not the case.

12. Several results of the lack of thorough preparation were apparent. The people had been lulled into a feeling of false security and thus had no realization of the need for urgency or of the necessity of preparing elaborate passive defense; modern fire-fighting equipment was lacking and such as existed was generally of poor quality; there was no modern, efficient training program for either the paid firemen or the civilian-defense organizations; the lack of facilities to utilize the usually adequate water supply was especially striking; and procrastination in providing safe shelters for the populace and essential equipment proved disastrous when the crisis came. Also, firebreaks and fire lanes failed to fulfill their primary purpose, that of stopping the spread of fire, when incendiaries were dropped on both sides of lanes. . . .

17. The weapons used in the incendiary attacks described in this report were the M47, 100-pound, oil-gel bomb; the M69, 6-pound, gelled-gasoline bomb; the M47, 10-pound, magnesium-gasoline and white phosphorus bomb; and the M50, 4-pound magnesium bomb. These bombs were especially effective in the densely built-up areas of cities where the flimsy construction and abundance of combustible material facilitated the spread and merging of numerous fires into huge conflagrations of terrifying and destructive magnitude. Virtually all combustible structures in the fire areas were consumed. Buildings of noncombustible construction suffered damage in direct ratio to the combustibility of their contents. Many fire-resistive buildings were gutted or were damaged to varying degrees by exposure fires. In several instances important factory installations and government buildings were saved from total damage at the expense of less vital buildings by the concentration of fire-fighting equipment and personnel.

18. The incendiary bombs were generally effective against industrial plants having thin roofs and moderately combustible contents. They did not perforate heavy reinforced-concrete roofs. The M50 incendiary had too much penetration for the average light-frame construction typical of Japanese dwellings; its high penetration, however, achieved unusual, if unexpected, success by breaking buried water mains in unpaved streets, thereby reducing the supply of water available for fire fighting.

19. The incendiary attacks on Japanese cities were highly effective in causing widespread damage. In several instances, it was considered that the bomb load was excessive for the target area, and that a smaller bomb load would have achieved the same proportion of damage. Variable factors, however, such as weather conditions, active opposition, and the obscuring of target by smoke, enter into this matter. It was likewise found at some of the targets that the density within the bomb-fall area was not uniform; many bombs fell into areas already ignited or into sparsely built-up districts; and, on one target at least, it was considered that greater damage would have been caused had the fall of the bomb been compressed into a shorter

period of time. The effectiveness of the incendiary weapons lay to a large extent in the larger number dropped and the wide area covered, which nullified the protection of firebreaks and created an insuperable task for firefighting and civilian-defense organizations.

20. It was found that when subsequent incendiary attacks were made on the two largest cities the resulting damage by fire was generally lower in proportion to the tonnage of bombs dropped or, conversely, a greater bomb load was required to cause an equal amount of damage. This fact was accounted for by a part of the bomb load's falling on burned-out areas or those partly burned; by the probability that there was a lower concentration of combustible material to facilitate rapid fire spread; and by the fact that many of the larger burned areas served as firebreaks. It is believed that a series of attacks on a given target becomes more effective if the attacks are closely spaced within a period of not more than several days, which prevents repair of protective facilities and recuperation of defense agencies.

21. Production in cities hit by large-scale incendiary attacks was drastically reduced. This effect was brought about, first, because many plants were heavily or totally damaged by fires, either as a result of direct bomb strikes or by fire spread. Second, normal plant operations were curtailed by (1) plant employees being rendered homeless by fires; (2) damage to facilities supplying the plants, such as water, electricity, gas and transportation; (3) damage to the plants' own facilities; (4) loss of innumerable home workshops which supplied parts to the plants; (5) loss of raw materials; (6) damage to finished parts and (7) deaths and injuries among employees. In many cases, the production loss was greater than the percentage of damage sustained by a plant would seem to warrant.

22. This report covers damage by fire in the following target cities: Imabari, Oita, Tokyo, Aomori, Akashi, Hachioji, Ube and Nagoya.

▲ E S S A Y S

In the continuing debate over the efficacy and morality of the U.S. strategic bombing campaigns in World War II, Ronald Schaffer of California State University at Northridge in Los Angeles, in the first essay, criticizes the bombing of cities as immoral and argues that contrary to their public pronouncements about morality, senior officers of the U.S. Army Air Forces believed that bombing enemy population centers was not immoral and was justified as a means to victory. Arguing to the contrary, in the second essay, Lieutenant Colonel Conrad C. Crane, a professor at the U.S. Military Academy at West Point, contends that leaders of the U.S. Army Air Forces tried to maintain a moral stance and the air power doctrine retained its emphasis on precision bombing of specific military-industrial targets even though a variety of factors led the Americans to move, particularly in the war against Japan, to the devastation of cities. In the third essay, Paul Fussell, a scholar of war literature, who was in the summer of 1945 a young combat veteran in Europe reluctantly about to be transported to the Pacific for the anticipated invasion of Japan, tells of his relief at hearing the news of the atom bomb and Japan's surrender. Disagreeing with Fussell is philosopher Michael Walzer of the Institute for Advanced Study in Princeton, who contends that the United States was not justified in using nuclear weapons against Japan.

U.S. Strategic Bombing Was Immoral

RONALD SCHAFFER

During World War II the United States Army Air Forces (AAF) enunciated a policy of avoiding indiscriminate attacks against German civilians. According to this policy, American airmen were to make selective strikes against precise military and industrial targets, avoiding direct attacks on the populace. Although some noncombatants would inevitably be killed or wounded, these casualties would be the result of accidents of war, not of intention. The AAF policy appears as a noteworthy phenomenon in a savage, atrocity-filled war. It seems to distinguish the United States from such nations as Japan, Germany, and Great Britain, which intentionally attacked civilian-populated areas. It also seems to tell something about the ethical codes of American air force leaders, for official historians of the United States armed forces strongly suggest that those men agreed with the policy for moral reasons. According to the official AAF history, General Carl Spaatz, commander of the United States Strategic Air Forces in Europe, consistently opposed recommendations "frankly aimed at breaking the morale of the German people." Spaatz repeatedly "raised the moral issue" involved in bombing enemy civilians and was strongly supported, when he did so, by AAF headquarters in Washington. Another AAF commander, General Ira C. Eaker, stated that "we should never allow the history of this war to convict us of throwing the strategic bomber at the man in the street." Citing the official AAF history, army historian Kent R. Greenfield contended that "the Americans not only believed [selective bombing] to be more effective: they were opposed to the mass bombing of civilians." The views of AAF leaders in World War II appear to provide a standard against which to measure the ethics of military professionals.

Yet when the evidence is examined closely, it is clear that the ethical codes of these men did little to discourage air attacks on German civilians. Prewar American air plans and doctrine and the development of operations during the war reveal that official policy against indiscriminate bombing was so broadly interpreted and so frequently breached as to become almost meaningless. Statements of air commanders that supposedly indicate abhorrence of terror bombing, when analyzed in context, mean something very different. In the end, both the policy and the apparent ethical support for it among AAF leaders turn out to be myths; while they contain elements of truth, they are substantially fictitious or misleading. How did these particular myths arise? What were the actual views of AAF leaders on the morality of bombing civilians? How does a more accurate reconstruction of moral attitudes in the war against Germany affect understanding of the history of American military ethics? . . .

At first glance the record of early AAF actions in Europe seems to uphold the view that American air force commanders wished to avoid bombing enemy civil-

Ronald Schaffer. "American Military Ethics in World War II: the Bombing of German Civilians," *Journal of American History,* 67 (September 1980). Reprinted by permission of the Organization of American Historians.

ians. It shows that they dispatched their planes in daylight to hit precise military and industrial targets and that when the British asked them to join in night raids on urban residential areas they refused. The Royal Air Force (RAF) was committed to urban area bombing. It had tried precision raids but found that its own losses far outweighed the damage inflicted on the enemy. Unable to bomb German factories effectively, the British decided to attack residential districts, hoping to "dehouse" and otherwise incapacitate factory workers, striking at the German economy through its labor force and demoralizing the enemy population. Prime Minister Winston Churchill and British military leaders thought the U.S. Eighth Air Force should send some of its planes on night saturation raids, but at the Casablanca Conference of January 1943 the AAF persuaded the Allied leaders to let its precision daylight raids continue. "We had won a major victory," [Gen. H. H.] Arnold [AAF Chief of Staff] wrote about this agreement, "for we would bomb in accordance with American principles, using methods for which our planes were designed."

These principles did not include moral objections to bombing the residents of German cities, a fact that emerges from the arguments that Eaker, then commander of the Eighth Air Force, used to persuade Churchill to agree to continued American day attacks. American heavy bombers, Eaker observed, were designed for daylight operations and were equipped with precision bombsights that worked correctly only when the target could be seen. American crews, who were trained for precision bombing, could hit small but important installations. When they flew in daylight they would draw out and destroy enemy day fighters. Attacking by day, while the British bombed at night, they would, in Eaker's words, "give the devils no rest."

Every one of Eaker's arguments was pragmatic. None implied any solicitude for the welfare of German civilians. Indeed, Eaker told an Air Force historian after the war that his colleagues in the AAF never objected on moral grounds to bombing the people of Germany. "I never felt there was any moral sentiment among leaders of the AAF," he explained. "A military man has to be trained and inured to do the job. . . . The business of sentiment never enters into it at all."

After the Casablanca Conference, Arnold made it clear that he did not intend to exempt German civilians from American air attacks. In April 1943 he told a logistics officer that the Eighth Air Force was going to use incendiary bombs to burn densely built-up sections of towns and cities in daylight raids. Shortly afterward, he had an aide inform members of the Air Staff in Washington that "this is a brutal war and . . . the way to stop the killing of civilians is to cause so much damage and destruction and death that the civilians will demand that their government cease fighting. This doesn't mean that we are making civilians or civilian institutions a war objective, but we cannot 'pull our punches' because some of them may get killed."

The meaning of Arnold's last point was brought home to German civilians when American planes bombed outside the target area—something that happened frequently when weather was poor or enemy opposition was strong and that occasionally occurred when there was no opposition at all. Sometimes the killing of civilians was not entirely accidental. On October 10, 1943, 236 Eighth Air Force planes bombed Münster in clear weather, using the center of the town as their aiming point. At a conference eleven days later, some of the officers involved explained that houses as well as factories were good aiming points because they enabled airmen to "put down enough bombs to destroy the town." This made it unnecessary to go back and hit the target again.

As a direct attack on a civilian area in good weather, the Münster raid was an exception to AAF practice at this stage of the war. But shortly after it took place, the Americans began a series of bombings through cloud cover that were tantamount to urban area attacks. European weather was unusually foul in the fall of 1943, and AAF planners felt they would have to abandon the strategic bombing offensive if their planes could only attack in clear skies. They chose instead to guide the bombers toward their objectives with radar. Since radar could not distinguish targets precisely at that time, the result was the killing and wounding of large numbers of noncombatants.

This lack of precision looked like a virtue to some American officers who wanted to find a way to launch massive direct attacks on civilians. Colonel Henry A. Berliner, an intelligence officer on Arnold's staff, thought that radar-assisted attacks on German cities would disperse Luftwaffe fighter defenses, weaken enemy morale, and by driving civilians from their homes in wintertime, force the Nazi government to use up resources caring for the victims of bombardment. He believed that, without diminishing the precision bombing offensive, the AAF could stage at least one raid a month like the Hamburg operation—a series of joint British-American attacks in the summer of 1943 that had killed at least 60,000 Germans and incinerated a large part of the city. Eaker also thought radar bombing should be used to erode enemy morale when weather prevented raids on higher priority precision objectives. "We learn from enemy reaction from secret sources," he told another officer, "and from his squealing and press and propaganda, that he abhors these attacks on his cities. They cause great gloom in Germany." On November 1, 1943, Arnold directed that when daytime precision raids were impossible, heavy bombardment units should attack area targets in Germany using radar.

A few weeks after Arnold issued this order, AAF planners began to consider a further step: making civilian morale an explicit target system. Officers appointed to study bombing programs for the next phase in the war examined this possibility but concluded that morale would not be a suitable objective. They believed that bombing might actually strengthen civilian determination to fight. But even if it were possible to destroy civilian morale, they thought that the feelings of the populace could not bring an early end to the war since no group or combination of groups in Germany was strong enough to overcome Nazi control. One member of the committee, told that morale was bad in Berlin, remarked that the "only morale worth considering now is the morale of the people in high places—the people in power, the High Command."

While none of these officers raised anything but pragmatic objections to morale bombing, other persons, outside the armed forces, had begun to criticize area attacks as immoral, and their complaints had an important effect on the AAF. In March 1944 twenty-eight noted clergymen and antiwar activists signed an introduction to an article in *Fellowship,* the journal of the pacifist organization Fellowship of Reconciliation, stating, among other things, that "Christian people should be moved to examine themselves concerning their participation in this carnival of death." The *New York Times* printed a front page story about the incident and a flurry of controversy followed in religious and secular media.

This show of dissent alarmed officials in the War Department and the AAF. Undersecretary of War Robert P. Patterson publicly denounced the protestors, claiming that they were encouraging the enemy. Robert A. Lovett, the assistant secretary of war for air, visited AAF leaders in Europe and briefed them on the problem of adverse publicity at home. Shortly after D-Day, he informed Spaatz at the headquarters of the United States Strategic Air Forces in Europe (USSTAF), that there was genuine feeling in the country and in Congress about the inhumanity of indiscriminate bombing and advised utmost caution in pursuing such a program. Lovett predicted serious trouble if indiscriminate attacks became the announced policy of the AAF.

Lovett touched on an issue of the highest importance to air commanders—the public image of the AAF. During the years between the wars, officers like Spaatz, Eaker, and William L. ("Billy") Mitchell had worked diligently to develop a favorable image, testifying at congressional hearings, staging exhibitions of flight endurance and bombing demonstrations, and cultivating journalists who could help them make the American people feel positively about the air corps and the doctrine of strategic air power. After Pearl Harbor public relations was just as important to the air commanders, for not only did they want to contribute as much as possible to the winning of the war, but they hoped that by making a massive display of effective strategic bombing they would insure their preeminence in the postwar military establishment as an independent air force. As Arnold told Eaker in June 1943, "We want the people to understand and have faith in *our way of making war.*"

Eaker was so concerned about public perceptions of the AAF that he sought to control the way its history would be written. He warned an officer in Arnold's headquarters that no criticism of the conduct of the war in any theater of operations should appear in official correspondence without clearance from the "war chiefs." To General Clayton L. Bissell, the assistant chief of air staff for intelligence, Eaker wrote: "We have got a mass of historians at both ends watching all this correspondence and these things cannot but creep into the official documents unless we are all on guard."

Even before Lovett's warning, AAF leaders had begun to fear that area bombing might jeopardize the reputation of their service at home. Large numbers of Americans did not appear to hate the German people, even after the Nazi government declared war. There were, of course, millions of German-Americans in the United States and many citizens, regardless of ancestry, felt their country should not have become involved in war with Germany in the first place. AAF generals knew about these attitudes, felt that making war against civilians conflicted with national ideals, and worried about the way Americans might react to stories of American attacks on German women and children.

It was this concern for the image of the AAF, together with reluctance to divert resources from the precision bombing offensive, that led Spaatz, in summer 1944, to turn down proposals for morale bombing. Some of these originated with the British, while others were developed in Spaatz's own headquarters where the deputy director of intelligence, Colonel Lowell P. Weicker, promoted a psychological warfare bombing plan. Weicker wanted to broadcast warnings that particular German towns and cities were about to be destroyed, then issue black propaganda, purporting to originate with the Nazi government, that would tell the inhabitants that the Americans could not harm them. Finally, American planes would bomb the designated places, showing the German people that their government could no longer defend them. . . .

The AAF had started working, meanwhile, on other programs which offer additional proof that the official policy did not conform to practice. One of these was the War Weary Bomber project, designed to take hundreds of worn-out bombers, fill them with explosives, and aim them at enemy targets. After the crews bailed out over friendly territory, automatic devices would direct the winged bombs toward their objectives. This project was America's response to the German V-1 and V-2 missiles, which were falling indiscriminately on the English. The robot planes were intended to blow up industrial targets and military installations, such as the V-1 launching sites. AAF leaders also hoped they would disrupt the German economy, force the enemy to mobilize large numbers of people for defense, and reduce the German will to resist. They could serve, in addition, as prototypes for guided missiles to be used against Japan.

It was obvious to air force commanders that the employment of robot bombers was really indiscriminate air warfare, and it is equally evident that the generals had no moral objection to using them. "I can see very little difference," Arnold wrote Spaatz in November 1944, "between the British night area bombing and our taking a war weary airplane, launching it, at say, 50 or 60 miles away from Cologne and letting it fall somewhere in the city limits." Arnold then suggested turning the robot planes loose all over Germany so the Germans would be as afraid of them, not knowing where they would hit, as the English were of V-1s and V-2s. "I think that the psychological effect on the morale of the German people would be much greater this way." Spaatz replied that war-weary aircraft would have the greatest chance of success if directed against reasonably large, undefended towns. While he did not think they would affect the outcome of the war significantly, he saw no reason for not attacking those towns with robot planes if they had military or industrial targets "associated with them."

Early models of war-weary bombers were so inaccurate that Leahy described their use as an "inhumanized and barbarous type of warfare with which the United States should not be associated." Even after the AAF equipped the experimental robot planes with radar guidance late in the war with Germany, they were estimated likely to hit somewhere within a mile and a half of their targets, leading the War Department to wonder if they did not violate the official policy against indiscriminate bombing. Arnold's staff was able to allay this concern by redefining indiscriminate bombing. It notified the War Department that robot aircraft were more accurate than radar bombing (which the AAF had employed on a large scale since the fall of 1943), and since robot bombers were bound to affect enemy productions when they exploded within large industrial targets, they would not be indiscriminate. Reassured that the weapon was accurate enough to use in Germany, the War Department approved its employment.

Only a few of the robot planes ever flew, for the British government feared that the Germans would retaliate against London with robot bombers of their own and induced the military chiefs to delay the project until the last few days of the war. [A]nother program, even more deadly to civilians, did go into effect: operation CLARION, which sent American fighters and bombers all over Germany to attack targets in small towns and villages. Its purpose was to persuade the German people that they were defenseless against air attacks and that additional resistance was futile—in other words, to break civilian morale.

Air planners set to work on this project in earnest during the late summer of 1944. In September, Colonel Charles G. Williamson, a USSTAF planning officer, told General Laurence Kuter, chief of plans at AAF headquarters, about the kind of attacks Williamson's group had in mind. The targets should be in "relatively virgin areas" and should include transportation facilities in small towns, small machine shops, and other targets, no matter how small, "resembling known industrial establishments." A few days later, at a meeting with Kuter and Williamson, Arnold proposed that planning begin for attacks lasting six or seven days against widespread German targets. Arnold felt that if these raids were carried out at the right time they might decide the war. He stated that they were not to be obliteration attacks aimed at the people of Germany. Rather, groups of roving fighters and bombers should hit numerous types of military objectives throughout Germany "to give every citizen an opportunity to see positive proof of Allied air power."

Given the probable accuracy of the attacking planes, this distinction meant virtually nothing, for there was no way that the attackers could avoid obliterating villages or parts of larger communities if they struck at small machine shops or at railroad stations and other transportation targets. Spaatz and others had made exactly this point before the D-Day invasion, arguing against proposals to hit transportation facilities in French and Belgian towns because too many civilians would be killed and wounded. Furthermore, AAF planners had long regarded transportation bombing as a form of antimorale warfare because of its effects on nearby civilians.

Nevertheless, in response to Arnold's wishes, USSTAF developed the CLARION plan, giving it the euphemistic subtitle: GENERAL PLAN FOR MAXIMUM EFFORT ATTACK AGAINST TRANSPORTATION OBJECTIVES. AAF commanders had no difficulty understanding what was really being prepared, and several of them protested. General James H. Doolittle, who then commanded the Eighth Air Force, warned Spaatz that widespread strafing of German civilians behind the battle lines might so enrage the enemy populace that they would retaliate against Allied prisoners of war. German propagandists would use CLARION to justify Nazi brutality, and if the operation led to substantial Allied losses, the American people might begin to ask why the AAF had changed its strategy. The commander of the Fifteenth Air Force, General Nathan F. Twining, added his own cautions, warning of potential heavy losses for the attackers and urging Spaatz to consider how the enemy and the American people would react to the inevitable civilian casualties.

Eaker offered the most vehement objections. In a letter for Spaatz's eyes only, he predicted that CLARION would absolutely convince the Germans "that we are the barbarians they say we are, for it would be perfectly obvious to them that this is primarily a large scale attack on civilians, as, in fact, it of course will be." Eaker reminded Spaatz that CLARION was completely contrary to what Lovett had said about sticking to military targets and added that it entailed an inefficient and excessively risky employment of strategic bombers. Eaker wrote:

> If the time ever comes when we want to attack the civilian populace with a view to breaking civil morale, such a plan . . . is probably the way to do it. I personally, however, have become completely convinced that you and Bob Lovett are right and we should never allow the history of this war to convict us of throwing the strategic bomber at the man in the street. I think there is a better way we can do our share toward the defeat of the enemy, but if we are to attack the civilian population I am certain we should wait until its morale is much nearer [the]breaking point and until the weather favors the operation more than it will at any time in the winter or early spring.

It should be noted that each of these arguments was pragmatic. Eaker worried about German propaganda and excessive risks and losses. He expressed, not moral objections to bombing civilians, but concern over the shifting of resources from more efficient modes of warfare, over the timing of the operation, and over the way CLARION would make the AAF appear in the history of the war. In fact, Eaker explicitly denied, several years later, that he had meant to indicate in this letter that he opposed bombing that endangered enemy civilians. The civilian who supported national leaders in war, he contended, was just as responsible as the military man.

While Spaatz seemed hesitant about carrying out CLARION, there was considerable enthusiasm at higher levels for sending United States planes against large and small German targets in a series of widespread sweeps. Secretary of War Henry L. Stimson and Assistant Secretary John McCloy found the idea, in Stimson's words, "intriguing." Chief of Staff George C. Marshall declared that he wanted to see attacks all over Germany. And on January 9, 1945, Lovett himself urged Arnold to begin the operation. "If the power of the German people to resist is to be further reduced," Lovett explained, "it seems likely that we must spread the destruction of industry into the smaller cities and towns now being used for production under the German system of dispersal."

Eisenhower's headquarters finally ordered CLARION to proceed. On February 22 and in the early morning hours of February 23, thousands of bombers and fighters of the Eighth, Ninth, and Fifteenth Air Forces, joined by RAF units, ranged over Germany, bombing and strafing transportation objectives and targets of opportunity.

CLARION was only one of a series of operations in 1945 officially described as attacks on transportation but really aimed largely at reducing civilian morale. General Haywood S. Hansell, one of the designers of the pre-Pearl Harbor plan AWPD/1, observed that during the last weeks of the war, the strategic air forces dropped great quantities of bombs on German marshalling yards and stations, some of them in cities, although the German rail system was already wrecked. In reality, Hansell observed, the marshalling yards were area bombing targets. By this time the conditions for area bombing that Arnold, Eaker, and Hansell had predicated before the war had been met. Since bombers were available in greater numbers than were required to eliminate the remaining important precision targets, they could be used against civilians with no loss of efficiency. The German industrial system was so devastated that the AAF could devote a substantial part of its resources to breaking civilian morale.

The most publicized instances of the now fully formed program of American area bombing were the raids, early in 1945, on Berlin, Dresden, and other east German cities. Substantial impetus for these raids came from a Russian offensive into Germany that began the second week of January. Added to the hope of ending the war by breaking enemy morale and destroying Nazi administrative centers was a belief that AAF and RAF bombers could assist the Soviet advance. By battering the remnants of German transportation and by dislocating the German rear, American and British aircraft could make it harder for the Germans to bring up supplies and reinforcements to resist the Red Army. . . .

After some hesitation Spaatz proceeded with the bombing of Berlin, arranging for it to occur as a radar-guided, blind-bombing operation. He also had his staff prepare for the attack on Munich that Marshall had requested. Following Spaatz's instructions, nearly a thousand B-17s blasted targets in Berlin on February 3, 1945. Although American bombardiers were able to do visual bombing through holes in the clouds and hit several military targets, perhaps 25,000 civilians were killed.

Other raids on east German cities followed, climaxing February 13 and 14 in an attack on Dresden, where British planes created a vast firestorm that swept across the city. Then more than three hundred American bombers roared high over the still flaming ruins, aiming through dense clouds at the marshalling yards, while American fighters strafed moving targets down below.

The east German raids, particularly the attack on Dresden, produced just the kind of publicity that Spaatz and Doolittle wished to avoid. . . . Anderson [Spaatz's deputy commander for operations] informed Washington on Spaatz's behalf, that while the bombing of Berlin had not been expected to be precise, it was justified by the city's military significance and that the same was true of Dresden and the other cities in eastern Germany. "It has always been my policy," he told Arnold (in Spaatz's name), "that civilian populations are not suitable military objectives." Anderson did not say what Spaatz's practice had been—which was to permit indiscriminate bombing of German civilians when his superiors required him to.

We are now in a position to explain how the myth arose of an AAF policy against indiscriminate bombing. There was a policy—on paper. Sometimes it was adhered to; often it was not, or it was so broadly reinterpreted as to become meaningless. High-ranking officers sent official messages to one another which caused the record to suggest that AAF practice fitted with the official policy. Yet these officers knew this was not the case. . . .

Whatever restraints there were did not arise out of the consciences of the men who ran the AAF, for the record provides no indication that they objected on moral grounds to radar bombing, inaccurate robot plane attacks, sweeps against small towns and villages, or the devastation of cities calculated to break morale. While these men did prefer precision bombing to area attacks, at least until the last weeks of the war, it was not for reasons of conscience. Rather, it was because they considered selective bombing more efficient militarily, better suited to the image they wished to project, more likely to verify their theory of strategic air power and, for all these reasons, a more effective way of establishing the preeminence of their service after the war. When Spaatz and his colleagues "raised the moral issue," they were expressing not personal repugnance to the bombing of noncombatants, but apprehension over the way others would regard the actions of the AAF. Their approach to the business of war was essentially pragmatic.

This does not mean that they never thought about the ethical implications of air warfare. Certainly Arnold did. In June 1943 he sent a memorandum to his combat commanders in which he warned that bombing was bound to add to the horrors of war and likely to intensify feelings of hatred in the "victim populations" that could poison international relations after the war ended. As a "spur to conscience," he reminded the commanders that increased accuracy of bombing meant lives saved (though whether he meant enemy or American lives is not clear). The bomber, he observed, when used with the proper degree of understanding . . . becomes, in effect, the most humane of all weapons" and, depending on how it was employed, could be either "the savior or the scourge of humanity."

These sentiments appear to conflict with Arnold's willingness to burn down enemy cities, his desire to see robot bombers fall indiscriminately among the German people, and his acceptance of morale attacks. Yet they are more than lip service or words for the historical record. They represent a moral attitude inherent in air power theory, a position that goes back to World War I—the idea that bombing is a way of preserving lives by ending wars quickly and by providing a substitute for the kind of ground warfare that had killed so many soldiers a quarter century earlier. Anderson reflected this view when he wrote, in July 1943, that his Eighth Bomber Command would so devastate the German economy that there would be no necessity of an invasion of the continent "with the consequent loss of thousands and possibly millions of lives." Eventually, American airmen were sent to attack German civilians and the German economy as a way of rapidly ending the war (and saving the lives of those who would otherwise be killed).

Despite his claim that AAF leaders never evinced moral sentiments, Eaker himself defended area bombing with a moral argument—that civilians could legitimately be killed in air attacks because they supported the enemy's war effort. As Eaker put it, the man who builds a weapon is as responsible for its use as the man who carries it into battle. Eaker also contended that the avoidance of a greater evil justified endangering civilians, for he regarded the entire conflict with Nazi Germany as a war against evil in which it was necessary to attack bad people in order to save the good, the righteous, and the just. While Eaker offered these arguments long after the end of the war, there is no reason to doubt that something like the same sentiments occurred to him while it was going on. If so, then he, like other AAF leaders held moral attitudes about the bombing of civilians, attitudes that did not forbid such bombing but rather made it permissible.

This reinterpretation of World War II bombing policy and moral attitudes has several consequences for the history of American military ethics. It makes it somewhat harder to distinguish the ethical conduct of the United States in World War II from its conduct in Vietnam and in other wars and from the morality of other nations that practiced terror bombing. It raises the question whether feelings for the welfare of enemy civilians can ever be compatible with military success. And it invites us to scan the history of American warfare to see what other myths affect our perception of the role of moral constraints.

The Air Force Struggled to Maintain a Moral Stance

CONRAD C. CRANE

Allied strategic bombing during World War II has generated considerable controversy among historians, regarding both results and motivations. Perhaps the most heated debate has focused on the intentional bombardment of civilians to break their morale, a practice called "morale bombing" or "terror bombing." Basil Liddell Hart, the noted British military historian, called the practice of indiscriminate Allied area bombing of cities "the most uncivilized method of warfare the world has known since the Mongol devastations." An American counterpart, Walter Millis, termed such tactics "unbridled savagery." Many American historians have perceived a difference between the practices of the Royal Air Force (RAF) and the United States Army Air Forces (AAF), however, especially in the European theater. While the British enthusiastically embraced a policy of indiscriminate night area bombing, the Americans pursued daylight aerial offensives against well-selected military and industrial targets that were justified by both "strategic judgment and morality."

During World War II, the United States Army Air Forces did enunciate a policy of pinpoint assaults on key industrial or military targets, avoiding indiscriminate attacks on population centers. This seems to differentiate U.S. policy from those of Germany, Great Britain, and Japan, all of which resorted to intentional terror attacks on enemy cities during the war. Scholars who have cited the official AAF history emphasize the intention of American leaders to resist bombing noncombatants in Europe for both military and ethical reasons. Many of these writers contend that U.S. airmen regarded civilian casualties as an unintentional and regrettable side effect of bombs dropped on military or industrial objectives; in contrast, the Royal Air Force campaign to destroy the cities themselves and kill or dislocate their inhabitants was a deliberate strategy.

A few British writers, such as Max Hastings, have for some time criticized the claimed ethical superiority of AAF strategic bombing as "moral hair-splitting." Most recently, however, the tar of morale bombing that Spaatz feared has been applied by American historians such as Ronald Schaffer and Michael Sherry. In a groundbreaking 1980 article, Schaffer analyzed the statements of AAF leaders as well as numerous wartime bombing documents in Europe and concluded that ethical codes "did little to discourage air attacks on German civilians." In fact, "official policy against indiscriminate bombing was so broadly interpreted and so frequently breached as to become almost meaningless." He argued that both the policy against terror bombing and ethical support for that policy among AAF leaders were "myths." In his most recent work, *Wings of Judgment,* which also discusses strategic bombing in the Pacific, Schaffer examines the issue in more detail. He has softened his harsh judgment somewhat, but he still concludes that although "virtually every major figure concerned with American bombing expressed some

From Conrad C. Crane. *Bombs, Cities, and Civilians: American Airpower Strategy in World War II* (University Press of Kansas, 1993), pp. 1–11, 158–162. Reprinted by permission of the University Press of Kansas.

views about the moral issue . . . moral constraints almost invariably bowed to what people described as military necessity," another disputed concept.

Sherry's award-winning book focuses on the development of American air-power, which ultimately led to the use of the atomic bomb. He concentrates on the bombing campaign against Japan and contends that strategists adopted the policy of indiscriminate firebombing of cities after precision bombing against military and industrial targets proved only marginally effective in 1944. Though racism made such tactics easier to adopt against Japan, firebombing was the inadvertent but inevitable product of an anonymous "technological fanaticism" of Allied bombing and airpower. The assumption that using everything available would lead to eventual victory was key in the decisions to firebomb and eventually to use the atomic bomb. The American press and public at the time accepted such measures as retribution for war crimes or as preparation for invasion. Since 1945 concerned Americans have focused on the decision to use the atomic bomb as "the moment of supreme moral choice"; Sherry argues that the whole bombing campaign was the product of "a slow accretion of large fears, thoughtless assumptions, and incremental decisions."

Doctrine, Command and Control, and Operations

Certainly AAF leaders had varying motivations and opinions about terror bomb-ing. But a sophisticated understanding of military processes, particularly of doctri-nal development, command and control, and operational execution, is needed to evaluate American strategic bombing. Both Schaffer and Sherry contend that the AAF failed to live up to the letter and spirit of precision bombing doctrine. Sherry is especially critical because doctrine was not inspired and shaped to a greater de-gree by technology. Because of the limitations of the bombers of the 1930s, when precision bombing was developed, he argues, wartime technology was "more demonstrably than usual . . . the offspring, not the parent, of doctrine," leading to vague and unrealistic assumptions about the potential of pinpoint strategic bom-bardment and diminishing utility and support of the doctrine as the war went on.

Doctrine, however, is supposed to be developed to meet national goals, per-form battlefield missions, or counter a perceived threat, and technology is then designed to implement the doctrine. Technological developments may force modi-fications in doctrine; ideally they should not drive it. Otherwise, the result is some-thing like the Army's rejected Sergeant York Air Defense Gun, an expensive piece of sophisticated equipment whose capabilities were shaped more by technological possibilities than by an accurate appraisal of the evolving threat of enemy aircraft. The entire family of U.S. armor and antiarmor weapons in World War II illustrates the problem of allowing current technology to define tactical doctrine. Developed by technical experts to be light and mobile, American tanks and tank destroyers were employed to maximize mobility. But they could not support the army's over-all strategy and doctrine of firepower and direct assault, which was required by the conditions of European combat. This flaw affected U.S. ground operations throughout the war.

Allowing current technology to define doctrine can also limit the scope of doctrine without providing guidance or flexibility for later developments. A study of the evolution of military doctrine in the three decades after World War II by the U.S. Army's Combat Studies Institute (CSI) concludes that "the great value of doctrine is less the final answers it provides than the impetus it creates toward developing innovative and creative solutions" for future problems. Air Forces Chief of Staff Gen. Henry "Hap" Arnold understood this process. In his final report to the secretary of war in 1945 he emphasized, "National safety would be endangered by an Air Force whose doctrines and techniques are tied solely to the equipment and processes of the moment." The Air Force must keep "its doctrines ahead of its equipment, and its vision far into the future."

It can be argued that the technology for precision bombing really did not exist until the "smart bombs" of the Vietnam War. The destruction of the French Embassy during the 1986 air strike on Libya, however, as well as the few televised misses with guided munitions and admitted poor accuracy with unguided weapons during DESERT STORM, demonstrates that the ideal of perfect pinpoint accuracy under all combat conditions has still not been reached. Yet the pursuit of accurate bombing remained a primary goal throughout World War II, influencing American tactics and technology during that conflict and setting precedents for later wars, including DESERT STORM, in which the U.S. Air Force gave an impressive demonstration of advances in precision methods and munitions. And when examined in comparison with the bombing results of other air forces in World War II, the intent, if not always the effect, of American air attacks, was consistently to achieve the most precise and effective bombardment possible. Wartime improvements in bombing accuracy demonstrate that such a goal was realistic, not a dream always to be abandoned in favor of military expediency. Changing conditions influencing combat effectiveness in the European and Pacific theaters did lead to the Army Air Forces' acceptance of greater risks for enemy civilians by 1945, but in Europe at least the operational record shows that the avoidance of noncombatant casualties in accordance with precision doctrine remained a component of American bombing.

Military doctrine is simply a condensed expression of an accepted approach to campaigns, major operations, and battles. The general purposes of doctrine during and after World War II remained basically the same: "to provide guides for action or to suggest methods that would probably work best" and to facilitate communication between different elements by defining terms and providing concepts. Historically, American field commanders have felt free to interpret doctrinal guidance generally as they pleased. Indeed the Soviets taught that "one of the serious problems in planning against American doctrine is that the Americans do not read their manuals nor do they feel any obligation to follow their doctrines." This is certainly an exaggeration, but field commanders have rightly assumed that doctrine is basically a set of guidelines that permits much situational leeway. And traditionally these same field commanders have been given considerable freedom from strict command and control, far in the rear. Even the official AAF history of World War II admits that "air force commanders actually enjoyed great latitude in waging the air war and sometimes paid scant attention" to directives from higher up.

This means that the attitudes of leaders in Washington do not always determine operations in far-flung theaters of war. As Schaffer and Sherry have pointed out, the leader in Washington most concerned about moral issues, Secretary of War Henry L. Stimson, was either ineffective or isolated. His position was basically administrative, and unlike the president or the chiefs of staff, he was not deeply involved in making strategy. And whatever their public pronouncements to the contrary, neither Roosevelt nor Arnold had any aversion to terror bombing when it suited their purposes. But the extent of their control over commanders in the field should not be overstated. At times Arnold's shifts in commanders had considerable influence on bombing policies, such as when he replaced Lt. Gen. Ira Eaker with Maj. Gen. Jimmy Doolittle and Brig. Gen. Haywood Hansell, Jr., with Maj. Gen. Curtis LeMay. In addition, Arnold's consuming desire to justify an independent air service put pressure on AAF combat leaders to produce decisive bombing results. Yet whether because of distance, heart trouble, or the complexity of the war, Arnold rarely wielded a great deal of direct influence, especially in key operations late in the conflict. Sherry's contention that he consistently exercised particularly strong direction of American strategic-bombing operations and units is not supported by the operational record.

This loose doctrinal and command direction resulted in a bombing policy that was shaped by the operational and tactical commanders who actually dropped the bombs. To understand fully American strategic bombing, we must look at day-to-day planning and operations in the field, not just policy papers in the Pentagon. In his exemplary study of the escalating air war between Germany and Great Britain in 1940, F. M. Sallagar notes that "changes crept in as solutions to operational problems rather than as the consequences of considered policy decisions. In fact, they occurred almost independently of the formal decision making process." In that case, the operational solutions always led toward terror bombing; the same is not true for the AAF. An examination of the actual execution of operations in Europe, such as CLARION, THUNDERCLAP, and the War-Weary Bomber project, reveals that American air commanders there consciously tried to avoid terror bombing even when superiors were encouraging it. Some, like Carl Spaatz, seemed to have genuine moral concerns about such bombing; others, like Ira Eaker, were apparently more concerned with public opinion against such tactics or believed they were ineffective or inefficient. AAF operations in Europe contrast starkly with the American strategic bombing of Japan, where the destruction of cities by firebombing was adopted. Yet this decision also was made by the commander on the scene, Curtis LeMay, without real direction from Washington. Bombing policy in each theater was shaped by the "military necessity" of combat, but it was also affected by the individual personality of each commander, who defined that necessity. Air campaigns were also influenced by command relationships. In Europe, U.S. Strategic Air Forces (USSTAF) Commander Spaatz worked closely with the theater commander, General Eisenhower, to synchronize air and ground operations. The Pacific theater had no such unified command, nor such a unified strategy.

Certainly air operations in the European and Pacific theaters had come to accept more risks for noncombatants by 1945. In both cases, this evolution came about as planners and commanders in the field interpreted doctrine and searched for optimum bombing strategies. In Europe, the change resulted from an increasing resort to attacks on transportation targets as higher-priority industrial objectives were destroyed. Such operations assisted ground advances by restricting the movement of reinforcements and supplies, by putting extra burdens on a transport system already strained by the destruction of oil targets, and by facilitating widespread attacks that used the increased air assets present in the theater. Large transportation objectives could also be discerned by radar used for nonvisual bombing through overcast, a technique that allowed American bombers to increase their missions significantly during German winter weather but that also contributed to an acceptance of less accurate bombing results. Precision doctrine recognized the validity of transportation targets as a means to weaken the enemy's economy, but attacks on marshaling yards in cities were bound to increase the number of noncombatant casualties from errant bombs. In the Pacific, the evolution toward total war went much further. The strategic air campaign targeted factories and military facilities, but normal precision tactics did not seem to work. In order to destroy these objectives, LeMay resorted to incendiary attacks on urban areas that were bound to kill thousands of civilians. If European air commanders were showing less concern for noncombatant casualties in 1945, Pacific air leaders were demonstrating none at all. Proponents of precision bombing had long argued that it was both the most efficient and humane way to fight a war. But once LeMay became convinced that pinpoint tactics were no longer effective, morality alone was not enough to prevent the firebombing of Tokyo.

Other Influences on Commanders

It is usually difficult to pinpoint moral considerations in the decision making of key U.S. commanders in World War II. Their primary objective was to win the war in the shortest time with the most efficient use of resources and the fewest possible American casualties. Mission requirements usually prevented any sense of morality from being "an overriding criterion" on aerial operations, although one planner stated that his group "took some comfort that our proposals would be much less costly in terms of the lives of civilians." The need for Allied cooperation also tended to mute ethical arguments because the British so strongly supported attacks on civilian morale and the Americans did not want to cause a rift or aid German propaganda. Although it is hard to determine moral positions from official records and correspondence, it is probably true that ethical restraints were not the most important limitations on terror bombing by United States Strategic Air Forces. Such considerations, however, cannot be completely discounted.

At the same time, it must be noted that psychological effects have always been an important part of air warfare. Like the bayonet or the tank, the airplane has a shock effect that is intended to unnerve an enemy and break the will to resist. Unlike those other weapons, however, the long range of the airplane encompasses vast regions of the enemy's rear area, inhabited mainly by civilians. Once factories became acceptable bombing targets as part of the enemy's capacity for making war, factory workers could no longer be seen as noncombatants. Once the trend to recognize some civilians as belligerents began, it was only a matter of time until the justification would be made, as in Japan, that everyone supported the war effort in some way. And the temptation to exploit and magnify the psychological effects of bombing civilians would also be hard to resist. American airmen, even those most devoted to precision doctrine or morally opposed to bombing any civilians, expected that the destruction of economic and industrial targets would have a significant effect on enemy civilian morale. Yet at least in the European theater AAF leaders were not willing to achieve the same goal by intentionally killing women and children or burning down their homes. Even LeMay's first fire raids had the destruction of industrial targets as the primary objective. But once a campaign of psychological warfare was launched to terrorize the rest of Japan with the threat of more conflagrations, there was no longer any major difference between this American air campaign and RAF Bomber Command's area raids on German cities or the Luftwaffe's Blitz against London.

Other influences on air commanders also affected their decisions. Pressures from various levels of command and perceptions of public opinion helped shape planning and operations. Any mission includes implied tasks to fight, win, and return with honor intact, but these elements have different weight, depending on where the soldiers are on the battlefield. Although Arnold hoped to achieve an independent air force with "Victory through Airpower," B-17 crewmen were more concerned with doing the best job they could and surviving. Operational and tactical commanders were caught in the middle; they had to be loyal to the goals of their organization and to the welfare of their men. A quick and overwhelming victory served both purposes and was also in keeping with the "Airpower Ethic" by preventing long and bloody land combat. The lure of achieving the Allies' stated aim of winning the war "as decisively and speedily as possible" through technological solutions or by a single operation to produce a deathblow became especially strong after the success of Operation OVERLORD in Europe and as the invasion of Japan approached. With the exception of some officers like LeMay, devotion to precision-bombing doctrine remained strong in the field, especially with those officers who had helped develop it, though its applications changed as the military situation evolved. Contrary to many American doctrines in our military history, this one was uniformly known, understood, and believed by most of the soldiers who were supposed to follow it. Indeed it often seems that precision bombing was better understood in the field than in Washington. In his recent book, *Wartime,* Paul Fussell claims that "precision bombing became a comical oxymoron relished by bomber crews with a sense of black humor" although he provides no real evidence to back up this statement about American strategic bombing. In reality, aircrews and their leaders were convinced of the effectiveness and appropriateness of their pinpoint tactics and missions and were quick to express dissatisfaction with any perceived deviations from proven and accepted methods and operations.

This continuity in doctrine is not really evident unless one focuses on day-to-day operations. Though archival sources such as the papers of Spaatz or Arnold provide invaluable topical information, letters or documents are grouped by subject more than by time period, and even unit histories can be narrow in focus. The best source for a full understanding of the milieu of air operations is the daily operational diaries of Frederick L. Anderson, U.S. Strategic Air Forces deputy commander for operations. Each daily file contains bound packets of correspondence that passed in and out of USSTAF headquarters, including letters from Arnold and Spaatz, press releases, and battle reports from the field. This concentrated operational and tactical level documentation describes the course of the air war in great detail and shows the continuity and persistence of precision-bombing doctrine even while temptations to use terror bombing increased.

Yet in the Pacific theater, a unique combination of military problems and an innovative commander less committed to prescribed doctrine produced a far different response to these temptations. This contrast makes the European record even more remarkable, especially when one considers the need to cooperate with an ally dedicated to terror bombing. Though adverse weather, technological limitations, or enemy countermeasures such as flak or smoke-screens often made it difficult to achieve the standards of precision-bombing doctrine, most AAF airmen did live up to the spirit of it. Moreover, in the Pacific theater, Brig. Gen. Haywood Hansell, LeMay's predecessor, was replaced because he would not swerve from the tenets he had helped develop.

Most critics of precision bombing have been asking the wrong question since it is impossible to determine accurately the specific ethical motivations for strategic bombing from the documentation available. On the narrower issue of the application of precision-bombing practices in the field, an impartial observer must conclude that in general most American airmen did the best they could to win the war with consistent application of a doctrine that favored military and industrial targeting over terror bombing. Their intent was to spare noncombatants, and they succeeded better than many historians are willing to concede.

Perhaps the survivors of strategic bombing attacks understood this better than the historians. As one German who lived through the American bombing and the RAF-induced firestorms in Hamburg commented, "The Americans were regarded by us as *soldiers*. Their attacks were during the daytime and were nearly always directed on military targets, even if the civilian population sometimes suffered heavy casualties because of them. They flew in good visibility and risked the aimed fire of our Flak. Hence [we had] a certain respect for the 'Amis' as we called them."

Yet it is undeniable that for a number of reasons strategic-bombing principles and precedents from Europe contributed to "the slide to total war" in the bombing of Japan. Military conditions were different in the Pacific theater, as were perceptions of the enemy; command and control was much looser also. According to the official history of the Joint Chiefs of Staff, "The division of the Pacific Theater between two major commands [Nimitz and MacArthur] complicated the problems of war and undoubtedly reduced the efficiency with which the war was fought." And as the Army and Navy pursued competing strategies, the AAF also mounted an essentially independent campaign. Perhaps the most important difference from the European theater was that in the Pacific, the air commander who instituted the firebombing campaign had not been involved in the development of strategic-bombing doctrine, had learned "not much" when he attended the Air Corps Tactical School (ACTS), and "was always more practical than theoretical." Once LeMay decided on the burning of Japanese cities as the solution to his operational problems and the practice became accepted by leaders in Washington and in the field, the next step in the escalation to total war, dropping the atomic bomb on Hiroshima, was indeed, to use Sherry's words, only an "incremental decision."

An ironic legacy of strategic bombing in World War II, evident in more limited conflicts such as the war in Vietnam and in the recent campaign against Iraq, is that even though public opinion tends to focus on the image of the mushroom cloud destroying cities or on B-52s carpet bombing enemy populations, the American military ideal in both doctrine and wars has remained the pursuit of precision bombing.

The military ethics and accuracy espoused in doctrinal literature on air operations today and demonstrated so convincingly during Operation DESERT STORM have evolved directly from the effort and intent of the experience in World War II.

A Defense of the Atomic Bomb and a Dissent

PAUL FUSSELL AND MICHAEL WALZER

Paul Fussell

The dramatic postwar Japanese success at hustling and merchandising and tourism has (happily, in many ways) effaced for most people important elements of the assault context in which Hiroshima should be viewed. It is easy to forget what Japan was like before it was first destroyed and then humiliated, tamed, and constitutionalized by the West. "Implacable, treacherous, barbaric"—those were Admiral Halsey's characterizations of the enemy, and at the time few facing the Japanese would deny that they fit to a T. One remembers the captured American airmen locked for years in packing-crates, the prisoners decapitated, the gleeful use of bayonets on civilians. The degree to which Americans register shock and extraordinary shame about the Hiroshima bomb correlates closely with lack of information about the war.

And the savagery was not just on one side. There was much sadism and brutality—undeniably racist—on ours. No Marine was fully persuaded of his manly adequacy who didn't have a well-washed Japanese skull to caress and who didn't have a go at treating surrendering Japs as rifle targets. Herman Wouk remembers it correctly while analyzing Ensign Keith in *The Caine Mutiny:* "Like most of the naval executioners of Kwajalein, he seemed to regard the enemy as a species of animal pest." And the enemy felt the same way about us: "From the grim and desperate taciturnity with which the Japanese died, they seemed on their side to believe they were contending with an invasion of large armed ants." Hiroshima seems to follow in natural sequence: "This obliviousness on both sides to the fact that the opponents were human beings may perhaps be cited as the key to the many massacres of the Pacific war." Since the Japanese resisted so madly, let's pour gasoline into their emplacements and light it and shoot the people afire who try to get out. Why not? Why not blow them all up? Why not, indeed, drop a new kind of big bomb on them? Why allow one more American high school kid to see his intestines blown out of his body and spread before him in the dirt while he screams when we can end the whole thing just like that?

On Okinawa, only weeks before Hiroshima, 123,000 Japanese and Americans *killed* each other. "Just awful" was the comment not of some pacifist but of MacArthur. One million American casualties was his estimate of the cost of the forthcoming invasion. And that invasion was not just a hypothetical threat, as some theorists have argued. It was genuinely in train, as I know because I was to be in it.

Paul Fussell, "Thank God for the Atom Bomb. Hiroshima: A Soldier's View," *The New Republic* (August 26 and 29, 1981), pp. 28–30; and Michael Walzer's response, ibid., (Sept. 23, 1981), pp. 13–14. Reprinted by permission of *The New Republic*, © 1981, The New Republic, Inc.

When the bomb ended the war I was in the 45th Infantry Division, which had been through the European war to the degree that it had needed to be reconstituted two or three times. We were in a staging area near Reims, ready to be shipped across the United States for final preparation in the Philippines. My division was to take part in the invasion of Honshu in March 1946. (The earlier invasion of Kyushu was to be carried out by 700,000 infantry already in the Pacific.) I was a 21-year-old second lieutenant leading a rifle platoon. Although still officially in one piece, in the German war I had already been wounded in the leg and back severely enough to be adjudged, after the war, 40 percent disabled. But even if my legs buckled whenever I jumped out of the back of the truck, my condition was held to be satisfactory for whatever lay ahead. When the bombs dropped and news began to circulate that "Operation Olympic" would not, after all, take place, that we would not be obliged to run up the beaches near Tokyo assault-firing while being mortared and shelled, for all the fake manliness of our facades we cried with relief and joy. We were going to live. We were going to grow up to adulthood after all. When the *Enola Gay* dropped its package, "There were cheers," says John Toland, "over the intercom; it meant the end of the war."

Those who cried and cheered are very different from high-minded, guilt-ridden GIs we're told about by the late J. Glenn Gray in *The Warriors* (1959). During the war in Europe Gray was an interrogator in the Counter Intelligence Corps, and in that capacity he underwent the war at division level. After the war he became a professor of philosophy at Colorado College (never, I've thought, the venue of very much reality) and a distinguished editor of Heidegger. There's no doubt that Gray's outlook on everything was noble and elevated. But *The Warriors,* his meditation on modern soldiering, gives every sign of remoteness from experience. Division headquarters is miles behind the places where the soldiers experience terror and madness and relieve these pressures by sadism. "When the news of the atomic bombing of Hiroshima and Nagasaki came," Gray asks us to believe, "many an American soldier felt shocked and ashamed." But why, we ask? Because we'd bombed civilians? We'd been doing that for years and, besides the two bombs, wiped out 10,000 Japanese troops, not now often mentioned, John Hersey's kindly physicians and Jesuit priests being more touching. Were Gray's soldiers shocked and ashamed because we'd obliterated whole towns? We'd done that plenty of times. If at division headquarters some felt shocked and ashamed, down in the rifle companies none did, although Gray says they did:

> The combat soldier knew better than did Americans at home what those bombs meant in suffering and injustice. The man of conscience realized intuitively that the vast majority of Japanese in both cities were no more, if no less, guilty of the war than were his own parents, sisters, or brothers.

I find this canting nonsense: the purpose of dropping the bombs was not to "punish" people but to stop the war. To intensify the shame he insists we feel, Gray seems willing to fiddle the facts. The Hiroshima bomb, he says, was dropped "without any warning." But actually, two days before, 720,000 leaflets were dropped on the city urging everyone to get out and indicating that the place was going to be obliterated. Of course few left.

Experience whispers that the pity is not that we used the bomb to end the Japanese war but that it wasn't ready earlier to end the German one. If only it could have been rushed into production faster and dropped at the right moment on the Reich chancellery or Berchtesgaden or Hitler's military headquarters in East Prussia or—Wagnerian *coup de théâtre*—at Rommel's phony state funeral, most of the Nazi hierarchy could have been pulverized immediately, saving not just the embarrassment of the Nuremburg trials but the lives of about four million Jews, Poles, Slavs, gypsies, and other "subhumans," not to mention the lives and limbs of millions of Allied and Axis soldiers. If the bomb could have been ready even as late as July 1944, it could have reinforced the Von Stauffenberg plot and ended the war then and there. If the bomb had only been ready in time, the men of my infantry platoon would not have been killed and maimed. . . .

The predictable stupidity, parochialism, and greed in the postwar international mismanagement of the whole nuclear problem should not tempt us to mis-imagine the circumstances of the bomb's first "use." Nor should our well-justified fears and suspicions occasioned by the capture of the nuclear business by the mendacious classes (cf. Three Mile Island) tempt us to infer retrospectively extraordinary corruption, cruelty, and swinishness in those who decided to drop the bomb. Times change. Harry Truman was not a fascist, but a democrat. He was as close to a real egalitarian as we've seen in high office for a very long time. He is the only president in my lifetime who ever had the experience of commanding a small unit of ground troops obliged to kill people. He knew better than his subsequent critics what he was doing. The past, which as always did not know the future, acted in ways that ask to be imagined before they are condemned. Or even before they are simplified.

Michael Walzer

Paul Fussell's defense of the bombing of Hiroshima (*TNR,* August 22 & 29) is written, as he tells us repeatedly, from the standpoint of the ordinary GI. And that standpoint is human, all too human: let anyone die but me! There are no humanitarians in the foxholes. I can almost believe that. But Fussell's recital does remind me a little uneasily of the speech of that Conradian villain Gentleman Brown (in *Lord Jim*): "When it came to saving one's life in the dark, one didn't care who else went—three, thirty, three hundred people. . . ." And Brown went on to boast, very much as Fussell wants to do, that he made Jim wince with this "despairing frankness": "He very soon left off coming the righteous over me. . . ."

But we shouldn't be intimidated, and we shouldn't leave off, but accept the risks of righteousness. After all, Fussell's argument isn't only the argument of ordinary soldiers. It is also and more importantly the argument of ordinary generals—best expressed, I think, by the Prussian general von Moltke in 1880: "The greatest kindness in war is to bring it to a speedy conclusion. It should be allowable, with that end in view, to employ all means save those that are absolutely objectionable." But von Moltke, a stolid professional, probably still believed that the wholesale slaughter of civilians was "absolutely objectionable." With Fussell, it seems, there are no limits at all; anything goes, so long as it helps to bring the boys home.

Nor is this the argument only of GIs and generals. The bombing of Hiroshima was an act of terrorism; its purpose was political, not military. The goal was to kill enough civilians to shake the Japanese government and force it to surrender. And this is the goal of every terrorist campaign. Happily, none of today's terrorist movements have yet been able to kill on the scale of the modern state, and so they have not enjoyed successes as dramatic as the one Fussell describes. But their ordinary members, the terrorists in the foxholes, as it were, must think much as he does: if only we could kill enough people, not a dozen here and there, in a pub, a bus station, or a supermarket, but a whole city full, we could end the struggle once and for all, liberate our land, get the British out of Ireland, force the Israelis to accept a PLO state, and so on. To the boys of the IRA, to young Palestinians in Lebanon, that argument is surely as attractive as it was to the young Paul Fussell on his way to the Pacific in 1945. It is the same argument.

What is wrong with it? If war is indeed a tragedy, if its suffering is inevitable, then nothing is wrong with it. War is war, and what happens, happens. In fact, however, war imposes choices on officers and enlisted men alike. "There wasn't a single soldier," says an Israeli officer who fought in the Six-Day War," who didn't at some stage have to decide, to choose, to make a moral decision. . . ." Fussell, who has written so beautifully about the literature of war, must know this to be true. And he must also know that there is a moral argument, different from his own argument, that shapes these military choices. Perhaps that argument is most often expounded by those professors far from the battlefield for whom he has such contempt. But it is an argument as old as war itself and one that many soldiers have believed and struggled to live by. It holds, most simply, that combat should be a struggle between combatants, and that noncombatants—civilian men, women, and children—should be protected as far as possible against its cruelties. "The soldier, be he friend or foe," wrote Douglas MacArthur, "is charged with the protection of the weak and the unarmed. It is the very essence and reason of his being . . . a sacred trust." Like policemen, firemen, and sailors at sea, soldiers have a responsibility to accept risks themselves rather than impose risks on ordinary citizens. That is a hard requirement when the soldiers are conscripts. Still, they are trained and armed for war and ordinary citizens are not; and that is a practical difference that makes a moral difference.

Consider how the risks of police work might be reduced, and how many more criminals might be caught, if we permitted the police to ignore the rights of ordinary citizens, to fire indiscriminately into crowds, to punish the innocent relatives of criminals, and so on. But we don't grant such permissions. Nor are soldiers permitted comparable acts, even if they carry with them the promise of success.

There is a code. It is no doubt often broken, particularly in the heat of battle. But honorable men live by it while they can. Hiroshima was a violation of that code. So was the earlier terror bombing of cities—Hamburg, Dresden, Tokyo—but Hiroshima was worse because it was even more terrifying. Its long-term effects were literally unknowable by the men who decided to impose them. And the effects were not imposed, any more than those of the earlier bombing, in the heat of battle, face-to-face with enemy soldiers who aim to kill and have already killed comrades and friends. Though there were soldiers in Hiroshima, they were not the targets of the attack (or else we would have attacked a military base); the city was the target and all its inhabitants.

Fussell writes (again) as a democrat, on behalf of "the low and humble, the quintessentially democratic huddled masses—the conscripted enlisted men manning the fated invasion divisions." Given that standpoint, one might have expected him to question the US demand for unconditional surrender that made the invasion of the Japanese islands seem absolutely necessary. There were people in the US government in 1945 who thought a negotiated settlement possible without an invasion and without the use of the atomic bomb. Surely some attempt should have been made—not only for the sake of our own soldiers, but also for those other "huddled masses," the civilian inhabitants of Hiroshima (and Nagasaki too). Why don't they figure in Fussell's democratic reckoning! If Harry Truman's first responsibility was to American soldiers, he was not without responsibility elsewhere; no man is. And if one is reckoning, what about all the future victims of a politics and warfare from which restraint has been banished? Given the state of our political and moral order, with which Hiroshima probably has something to do, aren't we all more likely to be the victims than the beneficiaries of terrorist attacks?

▲ *F U R T H E R   R E A D I N G*

Thomas B. Allen and Norman Polmar, *Code-name Downfall: The Secret Plan to Invade Japan—and Why Truman Dropped the Bomb* (1995).

Earl R. Beck, *Under the Bombs: The German Home Front, 1942–1945* (1986).

Thomas M. Coffey, *Iron Eagle: The Turbulent Life of General Curtis LeMay* (1986).

Haruko Taya Cook and Theodore F. Cook, *Japan at War: An Oral History* (1992).

Conrad C. Crane, *Bombs, Cities, and Civilians: American Airpower Strategy in World War II* (1993).

Wesley Frank Craven and James Lea Cate, eds., *The Army Air Forces in World War II*, 7 vols. (1948–1953).

Richard G. Davis, *Carl A. Spaatz and the Air War In Europe* (1992).

Daniel Ford, *Flying Tigers: Claire Chennault and the American Volunteer Group* (1991).

Paul Fussell, *Wartime: Understanding and Behavior in the Second World War* (1989).

Donald M. Goldstein and Katherine V. Dillon, *The Pearl Harbor Papers: Inside the Japanese Plans* (1993).

R. Cargill Hall, ed., *Lightning Over Bougainville: The Yamamoto Mission Reconsidered* (1991).

John Hersey, *Hiroshima* (1946).

Michael J. Hogan, ed., *Hiroshima in History and Memory* (1996).

Thomas Alexander Hughes, *Over Lord: General Pete Quesada and the Triumph of Tactical Air Power in World War II* (1995).

Alvin Kernan, *Crossing the Line: A Bluejacket's World War II Odyssey* (1994).

Stuart Leuthner and Oliver Jensen, *High Honor: Recollections by Men and Women of World War II Aviation* (1989).

Stephen L. McFarland and Wesley Phillips Newton, *To Command the Sky: The Battle for Air Superiority Over Germany, 1942–1944* (1991).

Jacob Vander Meulen, *Building the B-29* (1995).

Leroy W. Newby, *Target Ploesti: View from a Bombsight* (1983).

R. J. Overy, *The Air War, 1939–1945* (1980).

Melvyn R. Paisley, *ACE! Autobiograhy of a Fighter Pilot, World War II* (1992).

Geoffrey Perret, *Winged Victory: The Army Air Forces in World War II* (1993).

Gordon W. Prange, *Miracle at Midway* (1982).

Clark G. Reynolds, *The Fast Carriers: the Forging of an Air Navy* (1968).

Stanley Sandler, *Segregated Skies: All-Black Combat Squadrons of World War II* (1992).

Ronald Schaffer, *Wings of Judgment: American Bombing in World War II* (1985).

Max Schoenfeld, *Stalking the U-Boat: USAAF Offensive Antisubmarine Operations in World War II* (1994).

Michael S. Sherry, *The Rise of American Air power: The Creation of Armageddon* (1987).

Martin J. Sherwin, *A World Destroyed: Hiroshima and the Origins of the Arms Race* (1987).

John Ray Skates, *The Invasion of Japan: Alternative to the Bomb* (1994).

Mark K. Wells, *Courage and Air Warfare: The Allied Aircrew Experience in the Second World War* (1995).

CHAPTER
13

The Korean War and MacArthur's Leadership

In public memory, no military officer is more linked to the Korean War than General Douglas MacArthur, a commander who reversed the tide of battle from the brink of defeat to nearly complete victory, only to suffer new military losses and finally to be relieved of command by the president of the United States. It was a monumental drama involving a larger-than-life character; for Douglas MacArthur, one of the towering military figures in America, is also one of its most controversial generals—for political as well as military reasons. In addition, the Korean conflict was the first of a new kind of war for the United States, a limited war for limited goals, a deviation from what had become the traditional American way of war: the pursuit of total victory.

Born in 1880, the son of a top-ranking U.S. Army general, Douglas MacArthur was a leader in his West Point class of 1903. Almost from the beginning the political and military strands of his career were intertwined. As a young officer, he served as military aide to his father's friend, Republican President Theodore Roosevelt. During World War I, he served as chief of staff of the 42nd (Rainbow) Infantry Division and afterwards headed the U.S. Military Academy. Appointed first by Republican President Herbert Hoover, MacArthur was chief of staff of the U.S. Army from 1930 to 1935, including his controversial part in using the army to drive unemployed veterans from the nation's capital in 1932. Democratic President Franklin Roosevelt later sent him to prepare a defense of the Philippines. To avoid capture by the Japanese in early 1942, MacArthur fled to Australia. He subsequently led the U.S. ground offensive in the southwest Pacific, liberating New Guinea and the Philippines, and in September 1945, accepting the Japanese surrender on the U.S.S. Missouri. He directed the Allied occupation of Japan until 1951. Particularly popular with the conservative, Far-Eastern-oriented wing of the Republican party, MacArthur was seriously considered for the G.O.P. presidential nomination in 1948, but his candidacy ended with his defeat in the Wisconsin primary election.

In June 1950, when North Korea invaded South Korea, MacArthur was appointed commander of the forces of the UN military coalition. A daring amphibious invasion by U.S. Marines at Inchon near Seoul, ordered by MacArthur, led to a

*quick envelment and capture of many North Korean soldiers, while others raced
back across the 38th parallel that divided North and South Korea. With authorization from the UN Assembly and U.S. President Harry S Truman, MacArthur
advanced north to North Korea's border with the People's Republic of China, persuading Truman that the Chinese would not intervene. When the Chinese did intervene in the frigid winter of 1950–1951, the UN forces were driven back into
South Korea. In April 1951, MacArthur recommended expanding the war to
mainland China, including bombing Chinese bases in Manchuria, with conventional and if necessary, atomic bombs and helping the Nationalist Chinese Army in
Taiwan launch an amphibious invasion of Communist China. When Truman and
the Allies rejected MacArthur's suggestions as a dangerous enlargement of the war
in an area of secondary importance to Europe, the main cockpit of the Cold War,
MacArthur went public through the Republican leadership in the Congress. Irate
over such insubordination, the president, on April 11, 1951, relieved the general of
all of his commands in the Far East. Frustrated with the apparent stalemate of the
war and the high number of U.S. casualties, the American public gave MacArthur
a hero's welcome as he returned to the United States for the first time since World
War II. But after the Democratic-controlled Senate held hearings into the situation
in May, and the State and Defense Departments put forward their views, the majority of the American public swung against MacArthur and his proposals for expanding the war directly against China. A final attempt by MacArthur's supporters to gain him the presidential nomination failed in 1952 when the
Europe-oriented wing of the Republican party nominated General Dwight D.
Eisenhower for president.*

*Historians continue to debate many aspects both of MacArthur's long career
and of the Korean War itself (such as its underlying causes, the role of the Soviet
Union, the failure of U.S. intelligence operations to predict the war or the subsequent Chinese intervention, as well as the conduct of particular units and the effectiveness of particular battles and campaigns). No issue, however, has been of such
continuing interest as the controversy between MacArthur and Truman, between
the commanding general and the president. For in addition to the personal conflict
between these two men, the dispute involved vital issues of the nature of limited
war and civilian control of the military.*

▲ D O C U M E N T S

The Korean War resulted in significant changes in the U.S. Army, not simply in the
replacement of the senior theater commander but also in the end of the racially segregated units that had characterized the army since the Civil War. In the first document,
Lieutenant Beverly Scott, a black officer, recalls in 1993 the desegregation of the army
at the front, as traditional black units such as the 24th Regiment of the 25th Infantry
Division were broken up and their soldiers transferred to other units; Scott also remembers the nature of the hilltop fighting so common in the Korean War. In the second document, William S. Boldenweck of San Francisco, in a 1997 memoir, recreates
his feelings in September 1950, when as an 18-year-old Marine private, he found himself crammed into a navy landing ship heading for the beach at Inchon. Although the
Inchon landing succeeded thoroughly, the massive Chinese intervention three months
later led MacArthur to advocate a wider war, first privately, and then publicly in a letter read on the floor of the House of Representatives on April 5, 1951, by Republican

Minority Leader Joseph W. Martin of Massachusetts, reprinted here as the third document. In the fourth document, President Truman announces on April 11 that he has relieved MacArthur of all his Far Eastern commands. The most influential testimony given at the Senate Foreign Relations Committee hearings was that of General Omar Bradley, chairman of the Joint Chiefs of Staff, on May 21, 1951, who, in the fifth document, faces cross-examination by Republican Senator Wayne Morse of Oregon, a critic of MacArthur, and by Senator Harry P. Cain, a Republican from Washington and a supporter of MacArthur. As MacArthur's successor, Truman appointed Lieutenant General Matthew Ridgway, a paratroop leader in World War II, who in 1951 was field commander of the U.S. Eighth Army in Korea. In the sixth document, an excerpt from Ridgway's 1967 history of the war, the general recounts his first thoughts upon taking over as commander of the UN forces in Korea and his instructions to his subordinates. These reflected his orders not to extend the war and his cautious operational approach designed to reduce the risk of catastrophic surprise (a Chinese offensive into the Imjin River Valley to menace Seoul) and hold down UN casualties, while allowing the UN firepower to ravage the Chinese and North Korean forces.

1. Lieutenant Beverly Scott, a Black Infantry Officer, Portrays Desegregation and Combat (1951–1952), 1993

I want to make something clear from the beginning. From the first day I went in the army I had no thought of getting out. I saw the army as something I could do extremely well. I fitted in. The army offered everything I like in life. I like order, I like structure, I like organization, I like discipline, I like judgment on the basis of performance.

And it was honorable. There was no better institution in American life, no better one anywhere, than the army for the black man in the forties and fifties. Things weren't perfect, but they were better than any civilian institution. You had more leverage in the army. You always had somebody you could go to and complain about bad treatment. A black man couldn't do that in civilian life. Especially in the South.

From almost my first day in the army I planned to go to officer candidate school. I got my orders for OCS around Christmas of 1945. Graduated in July 1946. A nineteen-year-old second lieutenant.

OCS was my first experience with living in an integrated society. There were no all-black officer candidate schools. Most of my bunkmates were white, and that was my first experience with meeting white people on a person-to-person basis. Previous to that all my experience with whites had been adversarial. Growing up in rural North Carolina, I'd done all kinds of menial jobs as a boy, and I was always subjected to insults and names. We had white neighbors living across the creek from our house, and all us kids did was fight.

OCS was the first time I'd ever competed with guys who had gone to Yale and Harvard and the various prep schools. It was a very enlightening experience.

Lt. Beverly Scott, "One Man's War," in Rudy Tomedi, *No Bugles, No Drums: An Oral History of the Korean War.* Copyright 1993. Reprinted by permission of John Wiley & Sons, Inc.

Frankly, it set the tone for the rest of my life, because OCS taught me that I could successfully compete with these people.

When the war in Korea broke out I was at Fort Knox, Kentucky, helping train black troops. I was an infantry officer, always had been. But in Korea they immediately began experiencing severe communications problems, because the men over there didn't know how to handle their radios or lay wire properly. They told us they needed school-trained communications officers. That became one of the army's highest priorities. So I was sent to Fort Benning, Georgia, to learn communications.

I graduated from Benning in December 1950, and a month later I was in Korea as a commo officer with the 25th Infantry Division. . . .

I was transferred to the 14th, and right away I experienced some problems. People in the 14th didn't want anybody from the 24th. I was a technically qualified communications officer, which the 14th said they needed very badly, but when I got there, suddenly they didn't need any commo officers.

Then their executive officer said, "We got a rifle platoon for you. Think you can handle a rifle platoon?"

What the hell do you mean, can I handle a rifle platoon? I was also trained as an infantry officer. He knew that. I was a first lieutenant, been in the army six years, almost all that time in the infantry. If I had been coming in as a white first lieutenant the question never would have been asked.

In any case, I became the first black platoon leader in the 14th Regiment. I was the only black officer in the battalion. I never had any problems with my men; they were mostly Hispanics, and when they saw that I knew what I was doing, and wasn't going to get them killed or shot up unnecessarily, they relaxed and accepted me.

My relationship with the other officers was cool. Especially with the company commander. For a while I wasn't talked to. I was watched very closely. I should have been made the executive officer of the company, since I outranked all the other lieutenants, and it was customary to have the second-highest in rank as the company exec. But I wasn't given the job.

I saw right away it was going to be pretty tough for me.

It was now the fall of 1951. We'd just moved to the Iron Triangle area. Three towns arranged in a triangle around a long valley, the valley surrounded by steep hills.

That valley had been one of the main invasion corridors to the south, but the truce talks had started, and now they were digging in. Every morning we'd see fresh piles of dirt on the ridges. You never saw the Chinese, but you saw the dirt. They were always digging, and they churned out that dirt like worms.

We were digging in too, until what you had were two armies facing each other from opposing trenchlines. Between the two trenchlines there was maybe five hundred or six hundred yards of no man's land. And what the war came down to for us was patrolling that no man's land.

It was a miserable time. Just a miserable, miserable time. We lost men almost every day, killed or wounded, and it was hard to see the point. The lines stayed exactly where they were.

After we'd been in our positions for about a month, word came down that we were going to make this big attack. We were going to attack all the way up the Iron

Triangle to Pyongyang, to straighten out the line, and I'll tell you, we truly believed that was going to be our last action of the war. We were absolutely convinced we would never survive an attack like that. The Chinese were not going to be dislodged on those hill masses. It would have been impossible to get them out of there. We'd been patrolling those hills for a month, and we'd never gotten more than halfway up any one of them before taking heavy fire and a lot of casualties.

But the order came down that we were going to attack. We were pulled back off the line, re-outfitted, issued fresh ammunition, we recalibrated our weapons, we spent about two days—cold, wet, miserable days—rehearsing the attack. And you never saw so many long faces, including my own. We felt certain we were being ordered to our deaths.

At the last minute, for reasons unknown to us, the attack was called off, and I don't think I could begin to describe the relief we felt. I read later that there had been a breakdown in the truce talks, and that this attack was to be part of a major offensive all along the front. But new overtures were made in the talks, and the attack was called off.

Shortly after this we moved to Heartbreak Ridge. We had to cross a valley to get there, and the entire road through that valley, over two miles of it, was covered with camouflage netting. It was like a long dim tunnel, and it was very depressing to see, because it meant that we were going into positions where the enemy would be looking down our throats.

It turned out to be even worse than that. Our trenches in that sector were only about twenty meters in front of theirs. We were eyeball to eyeball. Just twenty meters of no man's land between us. We couldn't move at all in the daytime without getting shot at. Machine-gun fire would come in, grenades, small-arms fire, all from within spitting distance.

It was like World War I. We lived in a maze of bunkers and deep trenches. Some had been dug by previous occupants of the ridge. Some we dug ourselves. There were bodies strewn all over the place. Hundreds of bodies frozen in the snow. We could see the arms and legs sticking up. Nobody could get their dead out of there.

On Heartbreak it was just a matter of holding our positions. We'd send out a patrol once in a while, but only at night. It was suicide to move around in the daytime. Many times they'd attack us at night, so nobody slept after dark. You stayed wide awake. During the day we'd get shelled by artillery or mortars, or get sniped at, so you never got any real sleep.

Added to that, we were fighting North Koreans. There was a distinct difference between fighting them and fighting the Chinese. The Chinese were normal soldiers, in the sense that when they saw they couldn't do something they'd pull back. The North Koreans would come at you even when they couldn't do anything. Even when they knew it was hopeless and that they were going to be killed. They'd come right into your hole, try and shoot you or stab you or bite you if they didn't have a weapon. Just fanatical as hell. Maybe thirty or forty of them would come straight at us in a kind of banzai attack, where they'd all get killed, but it was just to distract us while more of them were trying to sneak around us somewhere else. And they were vicious people. They mutilated bodies. They shot prisoners. Just nasty, nasty people.

Heartbreak Ridge was bad news any way you looked at it.

But I finally made exec while I was up there. We had a new CO by that time, a big Polish guy from Pennsylvania who was making a real effort to be fair. A replacement came in, a lieutenant named Stevens who had been wounded in World War II on Okinawa and who'd been called up from the reserves. He was a nice guy, a real handsome guy. We all called him Steve. When he came to the company our exec was moved up to battalion, and I was made the executive officer while Steve took over my old platoon.

At this time the army required that we have one hot meal a day. I suppose it was for morale purposes. Conditions on Heartbreak were so miserable otherwise. You could choose either breakfast or supper—that is, you could eat your hot meal before the sun came up or after it went down. But to get to the mess tent you had to walk down the reverse slope of the hill, and the North Koreans were always lobbing mortar rounds over there. It was just random fire, but it was something you had to be careful about.

Steve and I got to be pretty close friends, and since we both preferred to eat our hot meal in the morning, each morning we'd walk down the hill together. And as we walked down we'd talk about various issues, or about the platoon, things that needed to be done, or the personalities of the men, who you could rely on and so forth.

On this one particular morning, I guess it was a week or two after Steve got there, I couldn't get my razor going. I used an electric razor plugged into an old radio battery, and the battery was acting up, so I sent Steve on ahead of me.

Finally I got myself shaved, and as I was walking down the hill a big blast blew apart the mess tent. A mortar round had landed right on it. The explosion killed a number of cooks, and it also blew Steve's legs off.

He'd been sitting at the mess table, where I'd have been sitting if that battery hadn't acted up, and the blast just kind of sheared him off below the hips.

I was one of the first to reach him. I helped get him out, and he was a mess. He survived the wound, but he didn't want to, because as we were taking him out he saw his legs still lying there under the table. He'd been a newspaper reporter from Vallejo, California, and I think he eventually went back to his work in Vallejo, but after they took him away I never had any contact with him again.

By this time, March of 1952, I had been in Korea longer than anybody in the division. You needed thirty-six points to rotate. You got four points for every month of line duty, so after nine months on line you had thirty-six points. I think I had something like fifty-two points by this time, but they kept telling me, "Well, we don't have a replacement for you."

That was nonsense, so one morning while I was back picking up the company payroll I stopped by the Inspector General's office and complained about being treated unfairly. I left a note asking that they look into my case and find out why I couldn't rotate home when I'd been there longer than anybody in the division.

The next time I went down there I got word from the IG to report to Yongdungpo to go home.

I didn't even go back to the company. I called my platoon sergeant and some of the other guys on the telephone, told them goodbye and left.

2. Private William Boldenweck, a Marine,
Remembers the Inchon Invasion (1950), 1997

There really wasn't much to do on the Navy's LST 611 on the morning of 15 September 1950, and not much more in the afternoon, at least for the Marines aboard, who stood along the rails—at least in the spaces where they could see—because there were huge steel floating piers lashed more than head high along the flanks of the ship, ready to be unslung and used as some sort of floating port.

The floaters were regarded with something less than affection as the 611 wallowed its way from Kobe, Japan, to the harbor of Inchon in Korea through the tail end of a massive typhoon. As the 12-foot seas struck the flat-bottomed LST midships, tilting her on her beam ends while the troops grabbed for handholds, the cold salt water swooshed its way up the gap between the piers and the hull, dumping geysers of icy water all over them. But Inchon harbor was calm; the weather was clear and sunny; and there wasn't anything happening except the roar of the 16-inch guns of the *USS Missouri,* pounding someone or something somewhere in the far distance, that and the sporadic small arms and mortar fire from Wolmi-do, a small fortified island at the end of a causeway from the Inchon beach.

George Company of the First Marines was taking the island, scrambling up boarding ladders cobbled together using scrap wood from ammo crates over a 15-foot sea wall and taking, we were to learn, some serious casualties.

But there was no viewing that battle, because of the portable steel piers and the distance. Maybe it was just as well. Some of us might have had second thoughts about the big adventure, and there'd be plenty of opportunity for that later.

Since Inchon Harbor has some of the world's most extreme tides, with a range of about 35 feet, George Company had landed in the morning at high tide, and the rest of us were scheduled to attack the beach—in Fox Company's case Blue Beach Two—at 1730, or 5:30 P.M. civilian time, so there was nothing much to do but sit around and listen, smoke, chat about nothing much, and take advantage of our Navy hosts' most generous gesture of denying themselves fresh water that we could all have showers, the last we'd get for weeks.

Finally, about 1600, the ship's public address system ordered us to form up in units and descend to the tank deck to board our amphibious tractors. As we single-filed down the ladders to the tank deck, sailors filled our canteen cups with hot, black coffee, while others handed us huge sugar cookies.

Cramming into the LVTs, we wriggled and struggled to try to get some sort of comfort, burdened as we were with our gear and weapons and the crew-served weapons, for this was Fox Company's section of the Second Battalion's Anti-Tank/Assault Platoon. Most of the group were carrying 3.5-inch rocket launchers or the packboards with 80 pounds of rockets lashed to them. The flamethrower, 72 pounds with two full tanks of napalm, was mine, and I eased out of it as soon as I could slide into a space.

William Boldenweck, an original memoir written in 1997 specifically for this book by this retired city editor of the San Francisco *Examiner,* who went ashore at Inchon in 1950 as an 18-year-old Marine. Reprinted by permission.

A pregnant silence grew across the tank deck, as the last armored and water-tight doors closed across the backs of the LVTs, then was broken by the PA system. "This is the captain speaking," said a deep voice. The captain said we'd been good passengers and that he hoped we'd had not too bad a crossing, closing with the traditional "Good Luck and Good Hunting!" Immediately, the deep-throated engines of the LVTs began cranking over, and the big steel tracks began clawing their way forward over the steel deck. The bows of the big tractors pointed higher and higher above the beach line as the track cleats pulled their way over the ribs of the bow ramp, until the center of gravity finally passed over the ramp's rim and the machines tilted over to splash into the water and growl their way into the rendezvous circle.

I'd shrugged my way out of the flamethrower's harness, and was trying to read a paperback I'd lugged along as an antidote to nervousness, until I looked up to see the bow gunner's legs swinging casually above me.

"Hey, can I come up?" I shouted up, and he shrugged and said, "Why not?" So I shinnied up alongside him and took a look around.

In a time when we're accustomed to seeing huge battle fleets and individual warships "up close and personal" on the TV screen, it might not seem so much, but the scene that confronted me in Inchon harbor puts the word "awesome" to a severe test.

The centerpiece was the battleship *Missouri*, firing a steady cadence of three 16-inch rounds from her turrets, flinging two-ton shells who knows how far over the horizon. Around her in the harbor were her supporting cruisers and destroyers, pummeling the hills around the port with an assortment of heavy shells.

To one side were the LSMRs (Landing Ship Medium, Rocket) kicking off row after row of five-inch rockets with a steady swishing roar as the tubes automatically reloaded and fired again, bathing the rocket ships' gun decks in a boiling cloud of black smoke and red flame.

Overhead, the gull-winged F-4 Corsair fighter planes were screaming down over the beach, pummeling everything with tanks of napalm, rockets, .50 calibre machine guns, and fragmentation bombs. The brilliant blue sky was dimmed by the clouds of battle smoke.

Quite a show, certainly the biggest and most exciting *I'll* ever see and, looking back, probably the last time *anyone* will ever see such a spectacle.

For a beginner, it was very reassuring. No one could live through such a bombardment, so obviously we'd just walk ashore with dry feet and it would be a couple of miles at least before there would be anybody in shape to shoot at us.

No doubt there were a lot of seasoned veterans of the Big War in those boats who knew damned well better, who had had the same innocent confidence heading into the beaches of well-fortified islands like Tarawa and Peleliu and had learned the hard way that a lot of people could live through a battering like that and fight well and effectively. In any case, the turret gunner said "OK" into his throat mike and punched me in the shoulder. "We gotta get below now," he shouted, and we slid down through the hatch and I shrugged into the flamethrower harness, as the sound of the engine picked up and we could feel movement as the tractors broke out of their circle and into a line to head for the sand.

Our tractor stopped abruptly, a little too quickly, and the driver shouted "You're gonna have to wade. We're stuck." (Uh-oh!)

Someone folded back the steel cover of the troop compartment, and we started climbing up and out into the sunshine.

The bombardment had stopped, and it was quiet. The harbor looked quite calm as I swung one leg over the side and tried to get a foothold. Lacking one, I kept sliding down until finally my arms were fully extended and I was hanging by my fingertips, but the 72-pound weight on my back kept pulling me down until there was bottom under my soles and I was in water over my shoulders.

It came to me that I couldn't have climbed back aboard to save my life, so there was nothing to do but start wading toward the beach with the thrower's gun grip held skyward in both hands. The water level kept dropping as I slogged landward but then began rising again.

The flamethrower straps had quick-release buckles at collarbone level, and as the water crept up over my chin I began thinking about sticking my thumbs up under them and dropping the damned thing, but those thoughts were driven away by the face of Gunny Laberere, the tough cajun who ran my company.

I wasn't sure that he'd shoot me or beat me into a pulp, though those seemed like real possibilities, but I supposed he'd order me to swim back out, and if I couldn't find it I should just keep on swimming and see if I could make it back to Japan because there was *no* way I was going to stay around on *his* beach without it.

Fortunately, the water level began dropping away from my clamped lips as I waded forward and eventually got down around my hips. Things were going fine by then, though I kept stealing glances at the hill beyond the beach and remembering training films of places like Iwo Jima and what could start coming at us from those hills. But finally we were ashore, without a shot fired at us. The gunny was sweating up a storm trying to organize us, and we were looking at each other with half-assed grins. The next day I learned that war can be kind of fun, sort of like cowboys and Indians. The day after that I learned that war is, in fact, hell.

3. General Douglas MacArthur Urges a Wider War, 1951

Dear Congressman Martin: I am most grateful for your note of the eighth forwarding me a copy of your address of February 12. The latter I have read with much interest, and find that with the passage of years you have certainly lost none of your old time punch.

My views and recommendations with respect to the situation created by Red China's entry into war against us in Korea have been submitted to Washington in most complete detail. Generally these views are well known and clearly understood, as they follow the conventional pattern of meeting force with maximum counter force as we have never failed to do in the past. Your view with respect to the utilization of the Chinese forces on Formosa is in conflict with neither logic nor this tradition.

From Douglas MacArthur to Rep. Joseph Martin. Reprinted in *Congressional Record,* 82nd Congress, 1st sess., April 5, 1951, Vol. 97, part 3 3389.

It seems strangely difficult for some to realize that here in Asia is where the Communist conspirators have elected to make their play for global conquest, and that we have joined the issue thus raised on the battlefield; that here we fight Europe's war with arms while the diplomats there still fight it with words; that if we lose the war to communism in Asia the fall of Europe is inevitable, win it and Europe most probably would avoid war and yet preserve freedom. As you point out, we must win. There is no substitute for victory.

With renewed thanks and expressions of most cordial regard, I am,

Faithfully yours,
Douglas MacArthur

4. President Harry Truman Fires MacArthur, 1951

With deep regret I have concluded that General of the Army Douglas MacArthur is unable to give his wholehearted support to the policies of the United States Government and of the United Nations in matters pertaining to his official duties. In view of the specific responsibilities imposed upon me by the Constitution of the United States and the added responsibility which has been entrusted to me by the United Nations, I have decided that I must make a change of command in the Far East. I have, therefore, relieved General MacArthur of his commands and have designated Lt. Gen. Matthew B. Ridgway as his successor.

Full and vigorous debate on matters of national policy is a vital element in the constitutional system of our free democracy. It is fundamental, however, that military commanders must be governed by the policies and directives issued to them in the manner provided by our laws and Constitution. In time of crisis, this consideration is particularly compelling.

General MacArthur's place in history as one of our greatest commanders is fully established. The Nation owes him a debt of gratitude for the distinguished and exceptional service which he has rendered his country in posts of great responsibility. For that reason I repeat my regret at the necessity for the action I feel compelled to take in his case. . . .

The course we have been following is the one best calculated to avoid an all-out war. It is the course consistent with our obligation to do all we can to maintain international peace and security. Our experience in Greece and Berlin shows that it is the most effective course of action we can follow.

First of all, it is clear that our efforts in Korea can blunt the will of the Chinese Communists to continue the struggle. The United Nations forces have put up a tremendous fight in Korea and have inflicted very heavy casualties on the enemy. Our forces are stronger now than they have been before. These are plain facts which may discourage the Chinese Communists from continuing their attack.

From Harry S. Truman. "Statement and Order by the President on Relieving General MacArthur of His Command," and "Radio Report to the American People on Korea and on U.S. Policy in the Far East," April 11, 1951. Reprinted in *Public Papers of the President of the United States: Harry S Truman . . . 1951* (Washington, D.C.: GPO, 1965), 222, 226.

Second, the free world as a whole is growing in military strength every day. In the United States, in Western Europe, and throughout the world, free men are alert to the Soviet threat and are building their defenses. This may discourage the Communist rulers from continuing the war in Korea—and from undertaking new acts of aggression elsewhere.

If the Communist authorities realize that they cannot defeat us in Korea, if they realize it would be foolhardy to widen the hostilities beyond Korea, then they may recognize the folly of continuing their aggression. A peaceful settlement may then be possible. The door is always open.

Then we may achieve a settlement in Korea which will not compromise the principles and purposes of the United Nations.

I have thought long and hard about this question of extending the war in Asia. I have discussed it many times with the ablest military advisers in the country. I believe with all my heart that the course we are following is the best course.

I believe that we must try to limit the war to Korea for these vital reasons: to make sure that the precious lives of our fighting men are not wasted; to see that the security of our country and the free world is not needlessly jeopardized; and to prevent a third world war.

5. General Omar Bradley, Chairman of the Joint Chiefs of Staff, Faces Congressional Cross-Examination on the Meaning of Limited War, 1951

Role of Asia in Strategic Planning

Senator Morse. General, would it be fair to say that in view of the military plans and war plans which the Joint Chiefs of Staff have had constantly under study and revision since the outbreak of the Korean War, it has been the opinion of the Joint Chiefs of Staff during that period of time, that if they were running the military plans of the Russians, they would like to draw the Allies into an all-out war in Asia?

General Bradley. Yes, sir. We are very definitely of that opinion that Russia, right now, is following a policy of trying to cause as much trouble in the world as possible, even to the point of conflicts and wars, and using as much as possible, her satellites' troops, and not her own.

Senator Morse. At the risk of repetition, but for the purpose of emphasis, I put the question this way, General:

Has it been the viewpoint of the Joint Chiefs of Staff, since the outbreak of the Korean War, that on the basis of the military potential we have been in a position to muster during that period of time, the security of the United States, on a global basis, dictated that we do what we could to avoid an all-out war, and keep the Korean War on a so-called limited basis?

From General Omar S. Bradley. Testimony Before the Senate Committee on Foreign Relations. *Military Situation in the Far East: Hearings to Conduct an Inquiry into the Military Situation in the Far East and the Facts Surrounding the Relief of General of the Army Douglas MacArthur from His Assignments in That Area.* 82nd Cong., 1st sess. 1951, part 2, 895–897, 954–955.

General Bradley. Yes. We feel that we are not in the best position to meet a global war. We feel that we are improving all the time our own position, and that of our allies, and we would like very much to avoid a war at this time, not only as to our own readiness, but the longer you can avoid a war the better chance you have of avoiding it altogether, in the end.

Senator Morse. During the period that the Korean War has been fought, has it been the position of the Joint Chiefs of Staff that keeping the war within the limitations that it has been fought in Korea would save us many more American lives and allied lives than would be the case if it had been extended into an all-out war in Asia?

General Bradley. Yes; and we also feel that by fighting this war in Korea, even on a limited basis, that we may be postponing other actions which may have been on the timetable, and we have possibly avoided the outbreak of war in other parts of the world.

And if we can continue to keep the attention focused on Korea without becoming too much involved in it, in other words if we can fight this limited action in Korea without its being spread, we may be going a long way toward avoiding world war III. . . .

Effect of Adopting MacArthur Recommendations

Senator Morse. Is it your opinion, General, and the opinion of the Joint Chiefs of Staff, that if prior to this time we had adopted General MacArthur's recommendations for a blockade, and for bombing the mainland of China, we would have greatly weakened America's military power as the result of the conflict that would have followed in Asia if Russia had decided to come into the war at that point?

General Bradley. Well, if I can answer your question in two parts: The extension at one time of bombing just across the Manchurian border when we only had a short distance to bomb it, might not have taken any more strength, but if by doing so it had brought Russia into the war, we would be in an infinitely worse position than we are today.

Now, no one knows whether or not Russia is going to come [in]. Some people think that if we bomb bases in Manchuria and China they will. Others think that they would not come in.

I do not think that they know—I do not think anyone knows, other than probably the 14 people in the Kremlin that form the Politburo.

However, our feeling is that as long as we are not suffering too much from the avoidance of going across and bombing it, that we shouldn't take the chance, whatever it is.

Now, it may be a big chance; it may be a little chance, no one knows; but we don't think the advantages of doing it now are great enough to outweigh the disadvantages of the possibility of bringing Russia into the war. . . .

Objectives of Our Mission in Korea

[Senator Cain.] General Bradley, will you please tell me what the United States and the United Nations set out to accomplish in Korea? I know that you and others have given definitions from time to time, but I just wish to burden you a

little bit by asking you to define our objectives in terms of the mission which was given to the Supreme Commander when the conflict began in June.

General Bradley. The mission given him at that time was to repel this aggression and drive the North Koreans back north of the thirty-eighth parallel. In substance that is what it was.

Senator Cain. General Marshall testified that our mission in Korea was to make Korea a free, independent, and democratic nation. General MacArthur testified as I recall that our mission in Korea was to make of Korea a free, united, and self-controlled nation.

General Bradley. That has always been our Government's political objective and it has never abandoned that as I understand it since 1945. In fact when arrangements were first made in 1945 that was set forth as an objective.

Russia prevented it by putting down a curtain along the thirty-eighth parallel. When we went in originally it was to repel the aggression and then as we went farther north and the United Nations again came out with a resolution to establish a unified Korea, united and free Korea; that was the mission then given to General MacArthur in late September.

Senator Cain. And yet to carry out that mission from a military point of view or that objective from a political point of view, it will, before we are through, if we do not change that mission, be required to defeat the enemy and to repel him, not from South Korea but we must repel the enemy from Korea, or otherwise, sir, how can we make Korea a free, independent, and democratic nation?

General Bradley. Well, I think we could have an intermediate military objective without abandoning the long range political objective which we agreed with the Russians on in 1945.

Senator Cain. . . . General Bradley, will you give us your opinion concerning whether or not our mission in Korea is a different one today from what that mission was in the early months of the Korean War?

General Bradley. I doubt if there is any change. I think our long-range political objective is still that we would like to see a free and united Korea.

Senator Cain. But at the present time————

General Bradley. As far as the military, immediate military objective, is concerned, I think we would consider it a victory with something less than that.

6. General Matthew Ridgway, MacArthur's Successor, Keeps the War Limited, 1951

Much in my mind as I took over Supreme Command of the UN forces was the proper relationship between myself and General Van Fleet, and the Corps Commanders in the field. I had no desire to try to hold all the reins in my own hand, as MacArthur had done prior to my assuming command of the Eighth Army. Nor had I ever thought it proper for a distant commander to try to keep tactical control when he had able and trusted commanders on the spot. I was determined, instead, to follow what I had seen habitually practiced in combat in Europe. That is, I

From *The Korean War* by Matthew B. Ridgway. Copyright © 1967 by Matthew B. Ridgway. Used by permission of Doubleday, a division of Bantam Doubleday Dell Publishing Group, Inc.

would accord the Army Commander, General Van Fleet, the latitude his reputation and my high respect for his ability merited, while still retaining the right of approval or disapproval of his principal tactical plans. And in appraising these plans I intended on each occasion to consult personally and separately not only with the Army Commander himself, but with the Corps and Division Commanders of the Eighth Army, all of whom I knew intimately. I wanted in every instance to get for myself the feel of the situation as these officers responsible for execution of the plans might sense it. With this firsthand knowledge of their views added to all other relevant information, I would be in a position to make sound decisions—for which I as Theater Commander would accept full and sole responsibility.

In reaching my decisions I wanted to keep always in mind the clear policy decisions communicated to me by President Truman and the Joint Chiefs of Staff, the most immediate of which was to avoid any action that might result in an extension of hostilities and thus lead to a worldwide conflagration. General Van Fleet; Vice-Admiral Joy, Commander Naval Forces, Far East; and General Stratemeyer, Commander Far East Air Forces, were all apprised of this basic guideline and each commander had expressed his full understanding and agreement.

Pending receipt of a summarization of up-to-date missions and policies from Washington, and in keeping with the broad policy directive just mentioned, I undertook to place reasonable restrictions on the advances of the Eighth and ROK Armies. Specifically I charged General Van Fleet to conduct no operations in force beyond the Wyoming Line without prior approval from GHQ. And I wished to be informed ahead of time of whatever advances beyond the Utah Line the Eighth Army Commander felt were warranted.

In all this I was studiously trying to avoid those practices on the part of my predecessor that I regarded as faulty. In any event, one of my cardinal rules of battle leadership—or leadership in any field—is to be yourself, to strive to apply the basic principles of the art of war, and to seek to accomplish your assigned missions by your own methods and in your own way. General MacArthur's ways were not mine. MacArthur, besides being a dominating personality, had military experience vastly greater than that of any officer under his command. He had overridden strongly voiced and almost unanimous opposition from subordinate commanders as well as from principal staff officers and had achieved a brilliant success. It was only natural that he would have far more confidence in his own judgment than in that of any of his commanders. But beyond that he actually lacked confidence in one of his two ground commanders during the first six months of the Korean War. Consequently he had undoubtedly felt justified in holding a tight rein on his field commanders and in making all major tactical decisions himself, leaving only details of execution to the discretion of his field subordinates.

By contrast, I had full confidence in General Van Fleet, a courageous and competent field commander. Moreover, I had always felt that the views of subordinate field commanders were entitled to the most thoughtful consideration. Even so, I had to walk that tightrope familiar to all top commanders in any profession, civilian as well as military: To maintain the proper balance between according sufficient latitude to the subordinate commander in carrying out broadly stated directives, and in exercising adequate supervision, as befitted the man who would bear the ultimate responsibility for the success or failure of the entire effort. I sought during all my time in Tokyo to maintain that balance.

There were two top-priority tasks, practically of equal importance, as I now saw them. One was to grasp the dimensions of the primary mission assigned me by my superiors in Washington, namely, the defense of Japan. This meant that I must immediately review existing plans and satisfy myself of their adequacy to meet the possible though unlikely contingency of a Soviet attack. The other was to take all proper feasible actions within my authority for carrying out the policy firmly and clearly stated by President Truman of preventing enlargement of the conflict into a general war.

In connection with the top-priority tasks, the first action I considered necessary was to request a summarized clarification of the many directives issued by the JCS during the preceding months or deriving from policies enunciated by the President and the Secretary of Defense. In addition to the mission of defending Japan in case of attack, a mission assigned unilaterally by my government, I had other missions as the United Nations Commander in Korea. These were to maintain the integrity of UN forces; to continue to fight in Korea as long as, in my judgment, such action offered a reasonable chance of success; to maintain a blockade of the entire Korean coast; and to stabilize the situation in Korea or evacuate to Japan if forced out of Korea. There were others, still on the books, which ceased to have any meaning since the forced retrograde movement of the UN ground forces in late 1950.

At the same time it was highly important that I make my wishes unmistakably clear to General Van Fleet with respect to the tactical latitude within which he was to operate. These two tasks, in turn, called for action along parallel lines.

The first was to place reasonable restrictions on Eighth and ROK Armies' advance, pending the drafting of carefully phrased letters of instruction which would go not only to General Van Fleet but also to Admiral Joy and General Stratemeyer. These letters would define objectives and policies in broad but clear outline. I quickly initiated this action by confirming oral instructions I had issued on the day of Van Fleet's arrival and adding this prescription: "I desire that there be no operations conducted in force beyond the WYOMING LINE (Junction of IMJIN and HAN Rivers—CHORWON—HWACHON RESERVOIR—TAEPO-RI) without prior approval of this headquarters. To the extent you feel the situation warrants, please inform me prior to advance beyond the UTAH LINE [a line considerably short of WYOMING]."

The second of the two tasks, drafting letters of instructions, I put in train at once, even though these letters might not be put in final form until a summary of up-to-date missions and policies had been received from Washington. Meanwhile, however, I freely consulted with the three commanders, and by the time the letters were issued, on April 25, 1951, each commander had stated his full agreement with the contents.

The letters of instruction were accompanied by a memorandum, the purpose of which, I said, was to present certain concepts intimately related to the letters and constituting, in themselves, instructions of basic and equal importance. Extracts from the memorandum of transmittal and the letter of instructions to General Van Fleet follow. . . .

Extract From the Memorandum

"The grave and ever-present danger that the conduct of our current operations may result in an extension of hostilities, and so lead into a world-wide conflagration, places a heavy responsibility upon all elements of this Command, but particularly upon those capable of offensive action.

"In accomplishing our assigned missions, this responsibility is ever-present. It is a responsibility not only to superior authority in the direct command chain, but inescapably to the American people. It can be discharged only if every commander is fully alive to the possible consequences of his acts; if every commander has imbued his command with a like sense of responsibility for its acts; has set up, and by frequent tests has satisfied himself of the effectiveness of his machinery for insuring his control of the offensive actions of his command and of its reactions to enemy action; and, in the final analysis, is himself determined that no act of his command shall bring about an extension of the present conflict, except when such act is taken in full accordance with the spirit of the accompanying Letter of Instructions.

"In the day to day, in fact hour to hour, performance of his duties, I therefore desire that every responsible commander, regardless of rank, bear constantly in mind that the discharge of his responsibilities in this respect is a sacred duty."

While the foregoing had less application to the ground forces than to the naval and air components of my command, where the action of a single Navy ship or Air Force plane could bring on the most serious consequences, they nevertheless served to focus attention on this vital point, as I explained orally to General Van Fleet during my next visit to his headquarters.

Extract From the Letter of Instructions to the Commanding General, Eighth Army

1. a. Until our Intelligence justifies different concepts, you will base your operations on the assumptions:

(1) That forces opposed to you are fixed in their determination either to drive you from the Peninsula, or to destroy you there, and

(2) That the U.S.S.R. may at any time elect to exercise present capabilities by the direct military intervention of its armed forces, ground, sea, and air, against United Nations forces in this Theater, and that such intervention, if made, will be coordinated with the exercise of their offensive capabilities by Chinese Communist and North Korean Peoples Army military forces, all so timed as to take maximum advantage of weather and of its effect on terrain.

b. You will further base your operations on the assumptions:

(1) That your own forces will be brought to and maintained at approximately Tables of Organization and Equipment strength, but that you will receive no major reinforcements in combat organizations or service support units.

(2) That the duration of your operations cannot now be predicted.

(3) That you may, at any time, be directed by competent authority to initiate a withdrawal to a defensive position and there be directed to defend indefinitely.

(4) That you may at any time be directed by competent authority to initiate a retirement designed to culminate in an early evacuation of the Korean Peninsula.

2. a. Your mission is to repel aggression against so much of the territory (and the people therein) of the Republic of Korea, as you now occupy and, in collaboration with the Government of the Republic of Korea, to establish and maintain order in that territory. In carrying out this mission you are authorized to conduct military operations, including amphibious and airborne landings, as well as ground operations in Korea north of the 38th parallel, subject to the limitations imposed in b(1) below, and subject to the further limitation, that under no circumstances will any

of your forces of whatever strength cross the Manchurian or U.S.S.R. borders of Korea, or will any of your non-Korean forces even operate in North Korean territory contiguous to those borders.

b. In the execution of this mission you will be guided by the following prescriptions:

(1) Advance of major elements of your forces beyond the general line: Junction of IMJIN and HAN Rivers—CHORWON—HWACHON RESERVOIR—TAEPO-RI, will be on my orders only. [This was the WYOMING LINE.]

(2) You will direct the efforts of your forces toward inflicting maximum personnel casualties and matériel losses on hostile forces in Korea, consistent with the maintenance intact of all your major units and the safety of your troops. The continued piecemeal destruction of the offensive potential of the Chinese Communist and North Korean armies contributes materially to this objective, while concurrently destroying China's military prestige.

(3) You will maintain the offensive spirit of your Army and retain the initiative, through maximum maneuver of firepower, within the limitations imposed by logistics and terrain, and without undue sacrifice of men or equipment.

(4) You will exploit the enemy's every weakness and take advantage of every opportunity to show the world the true measure of the combat effectiveness of the forces opposing you.

(5) * * *

(6) Acquisition of terrain in itself is of little or no value.

(7) You will support the Commander, Naval Forces Far East, and the Commanding General, Far East Air Forces, in the discharge of their assigned missions.

3. a. Copies of these instructions, which provide the basis for your planning, should be furnished only to United States officers under your command who "need to know." However, the restrictive provisions of these instructions, designed to prevent expansion of the Korean conflict, will be disseminated to the extent necessary to guarantee understanding and compliance by all members of your command.

b. * * *

c. You are invited to discuss these instructions with me at any time for the purpose either of clarifying any feature of them, or of proposing changes therein.

M. B. Ridgway
Lieutenant General, U. S. Army

▲ E S S A Y S

Historians continue to differ over the MacArthur-Truman controversy. In the first essay, written in 1993, D. Clayton James of the Virginia Military Institute, a sympathetic biographer of MacArthur, summarizes his interpretation that the conflict between the two men occurred in part because of unfortunate miscommunication and resulted in the president's mistreatment of MacArthur. In the second essay, Roy Flint, a retired brigadier general, historian of the Korean War, and former head of the history department at West Point, agrees with Truman and Bradley that MacArthur suffered from the narrow vision of a theater commander and ignored the implications of his recommendations in regard to the nation's larger global needs and strategies.

In Defense of MacArthur:
Miscommunication and Mistreatment

D. CLAYTON JAMES

The dismissal of General MacArthur in April 1951 is a watershed in the history of American strategic direction in the Korean conflict. For the ensuing two years and three months of hostilities and truce negotiations no major challenge would be offered to the Truman administration's manner of limiting the war except by a few Allied leaders who urged more compromises with the communists at Panmunjom than the Americans wished to make for the sake of a quicker end to the fighting. With the removal of MacArthur, moreover, the post-1945 trend of increasing input by the State Department in military policy was accelerated. By the bellicose nature of his criticism of the Truman administration's direction of the war, MacArthur had placed himself in the position of championing a military solution in Korea in the American tradition of preferring strategies of annihilation, instead of attrition. He left the scene as an uncompromising warrior, though, in actuality, his differences with Truman were not as simplistic as they appeared. During World War II, as in the Korean conflict, for instance, he had argued for a balanced global strategy that accorded high priorities to not only Europe but also Asia and the Pacific. In view of the sites where American boys have died in combat since 1945, perhaps that and other arguments of the fiery old general need not have been dismissed so lightly.

Contrary to popular accounts, the strategic aspect of the Truman-MacArthur controversy was not based on the President's advocacy of limited war and the general's alleged crusading for a global war against communism. MacArthur wanted to carry the war to Communist China in air and sea operations of restricted kinds, but he never proposed expanding the ground combat into Manchuria or North China. Both Washington and Tokyo authorities were acutely aware that the Korean struggle could have escalated into World War III if the Soviet Union had gone to war, but at no time did MacArthur wish to provoke the USSR into entering the Korean War. He predicted repeatedly that none of his actions would lead to Soviet belligerency, which, he maintained steadfastly, would be determined by Moscow's own strategic interests and its own timetable.

Yet there were significant strategic differences between Truman and MacArthur. The "first war," against North Korea, did not produce any major collisions between the general and Washington except on Formosa policy, which did not reach its zenith until the Communist Chinese were engaged in Korea. The strategic plans of MacArthur for a defensive line at the Naktong, for an amphibious stroke through Inchon and Seoul, and for a drive north of the 38th parallel all had the blessings of the President and the Joint Chiefs before they reached their operational stages. Even the Far East commander's plans for separate advances by the Eighth Army and the X Corps into North Korea and for an amphibious landing at Wonsan, though they raised eyebrows in Washington, did not draw remonstrances from his superiors, who viewed such decisions as within the purview of the theater chief. Sharp differences between MacArthur and Washington leaders only emerged after the euphoric days of October 1950 when it seemed the North Korean Army was beaten and the conflict was entering its mopping-up phase. Perhaps because of the widespread optimism that prevailed most of that month, neither Tokyo nor Washington officials were aware of a strategic chasm developing between them.

On September 27 the Joint Chiefs, with unmistakably clear wording, directed MacArthur, whose troops were to enter North Korea within four days, to employ only ROK forces in the provinces bordering Siberia and Manchuria. Two days after returning from the Wake Island conference with Truman, the general proclaimed on October 17 a line from Sonchon to Songjin north of which non-ROK units would not be used; the new line was well above a more defensible belt across the narrow waist of North Korea, which was still deep in North Korea. The latter line was preferred by the JCS, but the theater commander was not challenged, though Collins later called it "the first, but not the last, stretching of MacArthur's orders beyond JCS instructions." Then came a bombshell for the Joint Chiefs one week hence when MacArthur abolished the Sonchon-Songjin restraining line and ordered his ground commanders "to drive forward with all speed and full utilization of their forces" in order "to secure all of North Korea." The JCS promptly informed him that he had violated the directive excluding non-ROK units from the border provinces; he was told to explain his action, which was "a matter of some concern" to them. He brazenly responded, "There is no conflict that I can see with the directive . . . [which] stated: 'These instructions . . . may require modification in accordance with developments.' " He argued that ROK units involved in the drive were not of adequate strength or stability to secure the region, and he reminded them that Secretary of Defense Marshall had told him on September 30 "to feel unhampered tactically and strategically" in advancing through North Korea.

"The Joint Chiefs of Staff," attests the JCS chronicle, "apparently accepted his defense of his latest action; at any rate, they did not countermand his order." Since Red China's impending intervention was precipitated in part by the American spearheads approaching its border, the JCS might well have considered more carefully the ramifications of MacArthur's bold advance toward the Yalu River. At the Senate hearings on the Far East chief's dismissal later, Collins testified that this was the first of a number of violations of directives by him during the Korean conflict and that it showed that MacArthur was "not in consonance with the basic policies" of the administration. "In any event," Collins remarked subsequently, "it was too late for the JCS to stop the movement of American forces north of the restraining line."

Perhaps it might not have been too late to avert war with Communist China if the Joint Chiefs had focused less on MacArthur's impudence toward them and more on the strategic consequence at stake in the Far East commander's move, namely, the escalation of the war by Communist China rather than by the USSR. While MacArthur had largely discounted the possibility of the Soviet Union's entry into the war, he had not seemed greatly concerned about Communist China's possible belligerency. As he had cockily assured the President at Wake, his air power would decimate the Chinese Communist Forces if they tried to advance south of the Yalu. The aggressive move up to the border with American troops in the lead was imprudent adventurism on MacArthur's part, but, on the other hand, the Joint Chiefs' timidity toward him and their priority on his effrontery to them at such a critical strategic juncture left them fully as liable as he was for the decisive provocation of Peking.

Communist Chinese units in unknown strength struck the Eighth Army and X Corps in savage but brief attacks, October 25–November 7, and then disappeared into the mountains of North Korea. When the JCS told MacArthur that the CCF intervention, though limited, might lead to a new directive altering his current mission to liberate all of North Korea, he replied heatedly, "It would be fatal to weaken the fundamental and basic policy of the United Nations to destroy all resisting armed forces in Korea and bring that country into a united and free nation." He said that his final push to the Yalu would begin soon and that its curtailment "would completely destroy the morale of my forces"; indeed, South Korean resentment would be so strong that the ROK Army "would collapse or might even turn against us." The JCS and the National Security Council decided not to change his directive. MacArthur's tactics of intimidation and hyperbole could be quite effective at times, particularly when his superiors were unsure of their position. Acheson observed in hindsight, "Here, I believe, the Government missed its last chance to halt the march to disaster in Korea. All the President's advisers in this matter, civilian and military, knew that something was badly wrong, though what it was, how to find out, and what to do about it they muffed."

On November 18, MacArthur notified the JCS that six days hence the United Nations Command would begin an offensive toward the Yalu, which he hoped would bring the war to a swift end. On November 21, high-ranking officials of the Defense and State departments met at the Pentagon to consider changing MacArthur's directive and halting the offensive, especially in view of mounting concern among UN members over Peking's repeated threats of intervention and growing interest in a British plan for a demilitarized zone along the Yalu in North Korea. . . .

On the night of November 25, the United Nations offensive came to an abrupt end when 180,000 CCF troops attacked the Eighth Army on the west side of the peninsula and 120,000 others hit the X Corps on the east side. MacArthur frantically notified the JCS: "We face an entirely new war. . . . Our present strength is not sufficient to meet this undeclared war. . . . The resulting situation presents an entirely new picture which broadens the potentialities to world-embracing considerations beyond the sphere of decisions by the Theater Commander." He declared that he was ordering his forces to "pass from the offensive to the defensive," and he urgently requested new policy guidance from Washington. The JCS approved his shift to the defensive but recommended that the UN forces set up a continuous line of defense across the waist of North Korea, the narrowest width of the entire peninsula. He countered, however, that such a cordon defense could be penetrated easily and got approval instead for the Eighth Army and X Corps to withdraw to beachheads around Pusan and Hungnam, respectively. There, he stated ominously, his troops could try to make defensive stands and, if unable, could be evacuated by sea to Japan.

So far in this fast-developing drama MacArthur and his superiors agreed that their intelligence systems had not provided sufficient warning of the impending CCF assaults, while they differed on whether the Yalu offensive should have been led by ROK, instead of American, troops and whether, once the UNC drive had been thwarted, their forces should stand and fight along the waist of North Korea or should retreat to the port beachheads. The latter alternatives were soon beyond choosing by Tokyo or Washington authorities. With the notable exception of the 1st Marine Division's masterful fighting withdrawal from the Chosin Reservoir, most elements of the Eighth Army and X Corps began rapid movements southward that some correspondents labeled "bugouts," with many units breaking contact with the enemy and abandoning large quantities of weapons and supplies. This disastrous setback was caused primarily by swift Chinese infiltration and envelopment more than by panic and confusion among the UNC soldiers. Once the necessity to pull out of North Korea became quickly evident, neither MacArthur nor his Washington superiors could consider long-range strategic plans until the issue of stopping the Chinese or evacuating the peninsula was settled.

With the British and other Allied governments urging restraint in responding to the Chinese intervention, the Truman administration began to back away rapidly from its aim of liberating North Korea. In the absence of a new directive from Washington, however, MacArthur continued to believe that his ultimate strategic objective was to conquer North Korea for the purpose of reunifying the peninsula under a free and democratic government, presumably the not-quite-liberal regime of President Syngman Rhee of South Korea. Seoul would be recaptured by communist troops on January 4, 1951; another ten days would pass before the Eighth Army, now under the command of Lieutenant General Matthew Ridgway, would stop the Chinese advance considerably south of the 38th parallel. MacArthur, not realizing the wondrous turnaround Ridgway was about to accomplish, was in desperate search for ways to regain the initiative in the ground war. He hit upon five, each of which accelerated his collision course with Washington over strategy: expanding air operations, employing naval surface forces directly against Red China, taking advantage of the Nationalist Chinese divisions on Formosa, getting four divisions in the United States that were earmarked for NATO shipped to the Far East Command instead, and raising the specter of abandoning the Korean peninsula if he did not get approval of some or all the above ways to bring relief to the battered UN ground forces in Korea. . . .

On December 6, an irate President issued two directives: the first decreed that all American officials abroad must hence clear public statements on foreign or military policy through the State or Defense departments, respectively; the second ordered such persons "to exercise extreme caution in public statements, to clear all but routine statements with their departments, and to refrain from direct communication on military or foreign policy with newspapers, magazines, or other publicity media in the United States." MacArthur's continued violations of these directives, especially in March and April 1951, exhausted Truman's tolerance of the defiant old warrior. To his last days MacArthur would argue that Chiang's forces ought to have been used, mainly to preserve the lives of American boys. Truman and his senior advisers, in turn, continued to insist that involvement of the Nationalist

Chinese would have resulted in diplomatic and logistical nightmares. The successes of the rejuvenated Eighth Army under Ridgway and then Van Fleet from January to June 1951 did not decide the rightness of either side on this issue, but they surely made MacArthur's argument academic.

The final manpower source MacArthur hoped to tap was the contingent of four American divisions said to be going soon to Europe. In correspondence and public statements during the Great Debate in Congress, MacArthur gave his support to the Wherry-Taft faction that opposed the administration's plan to send the units to NATO. While MacArthur found it impossible to comprehend the Pentagon's word to him that he could expect no sizable reinforcements in Korea, Secretary of Defense Marshall announced in mid-February that Eisenhower would establish NATO's supreme headquarters near Paris in April and that four U.S. Army divisions would be transferred to West Europe during the coming months. It seems more than coincidental that the Senate's approval of these moves took place on April 4, exactly one week prior to MacArthur's dismissal. With its firm positions on the Great Debate and on MacArthur, the Truman administration made unmistakably clear its limited commitment to the war in Korea.

While the Great Debate was heating up on Capitol Hill, the beginning of MacArthur's end occurred when Collins, his Army superior and the executive agent for the JCS in Far East matters, visited Tokyo and the Korean front on January 15–17, accompanied by Vandenberg, the Air Force chief. Their trip had been precipitated by a false dilemma MacArthur had posed to his superiors the previous week: As Truman saw it, the Tokyo commander declared the only alternatives were to "be driven off the peninsula, or at the very least suffer terrible losses." Collins reported that during their meeting at MacArthur's GHQ in Tokyo, MacArthur again appealed for the four divisions. Upon visiting Ridgway and his troops in Korea, however, Collins found a renovated force preparing to go on the offensive. He was able to return to Washington with the good news, backed by Vandenberg's findings also, that MacArthur was not only uninformed about the situation at the front but also deceitful in posing the false dilemma of evacuation or annihilation if they did not approve his proposals and troop requests. Ridgway's counsel, rather than MacArthur's, was thereafter increasingly sought by the Joint Chiefs and the President.

MacArthur had been found wanting in both strategy and stratagem. Far more crucial, the U.S. government had reaffirmed its foremost global priority to be the security of its Atlantic coalition. Similar to his plight during the Second World War, MacArthur again was arguing in futility for greater American strategic concern about Asia and the Pacific against a predominantly Europe-first leadership in Washington. Having spent over twenty-five years of his career in the Far East, MacArthur may have been biased in speaking out for a higher priority on American interests in that region. There is little question, however, that communist expansionism was mounting in East and Southeast Asia and that American leaders knew little about the susceptibilities of the peoples of those areas. To MacArthur, his struggle to get Washington's attention focused on the Pacific and Asia must have seemed as frustrating as the efforts by him and Fleet Admiral Ernest King to get more resources allocated to the war against Japan.

Despite the warmongering allegations leveled against him, MacArthur never proposed resorting to nuclear weapons while he was Far East chief. In December 1952, he did suggest in a private talk with Eisenhower and Dulles, the President-elect and the next secretary of state, that a line of radioactive waste materials be air-dropped along the northern border of North Korea, to be followed by conventional amphibious assaults on both coasts as well as atomic bombing of military targets in North Korea to destroy the sealed-off enemy forces. He saw this as "the great bargaining lever to induce the Soviet [Union] to agree upon honorable conditions toward international accord." It must be remembered, however, that he had been out of command for twenty months, and, besides, Eisenhower and Dulles scorned his counsel and never sought it again.

In truth, Presidents Truman and Eisenhower, not MacArthur, both considered the use or threat of nuclear force in the Korean War. On November 30, 1950, Truman remarked at a press conference that use of the atomic bomb was being given "active consideration," but Allied leaders, with British Prime Minister Clement R. Attlee in the forefront, exhibited such high states of anxiety over his comment that the President never openly discussed that option again. In January 1952, however, he confided in his diary that he was considering an ultimatum to Moscow to launch atomic raids against Soviet cities if the USSR did not compel the North Koreans and Red Chinese to permit progress in the Korean truce negotiations. "This means all out war," he wrote angrily but wisely reconsidered the next day. In the spring of 1953, President Eisenhower tried to intimidate the Chinese and North Koreans into signing an armistice on UN terms by threatening to use nuclear weapons, which by then included hydrogen bombs. MacArthur had nothing to do with these nuclear threats. Nevertheless, the canard of MacArthur as a warmonger who was eager to employ nuclear weapons in the Korean conflict has persisted in popular and scholarly writings over the years.

A Threat to Civil-Military Relations?

MacArthur's record of arrogant and near-insubordinate conduct during the previous decade on the world stage was well known to the leaders in Washington in 1950–1951. During World War II, President Roosevelt and General Marshall, the Army chief of staff, had been greatly annoyed when he attempted to get Prime Ministers Churchill and Curtin to press for more American resources to be allocated to the Southwest Pacific theater in 1942. MacArthur appeared to encourage anti-Roosevelt groups in American politics who tried in vain to stir up a draft of him for the Republican presidential nomination in 1944. As for defiance of his military superiors, MacArthur launched a number of amphibious operations prior to obtaining authorization from the Joint Chiefs. Admiral Morison observes that "the J.C.S simply permitted MacArthur to do as he pleased, up to a point" in the war against Japan.

On several occasions during the early phase of the occupation of Japan, MacArthur defied Truman's instructions for him to come to Washington for consultations, the general pleading his inability to leave "the extraordinarily dangerous and inherently inflammable situation" in Japan. Truman was so irked that he quoted two of the general's declinations in his memoirs written nearly a decade afterward. In 1948, MacArthur again appeared willing to run against his commander in chief, but his right-wing supporters were unable to secure the Republican nomination for him. His dissatisfaction with Washington directives during the later phases of the occupation almost led to his replacement by a civilian high commissioner. His growing alienation from administration policies during the first eight months of the Korean fighting gave rise to speculation that he might head an anti-Truman ticket in the 1952 presidential race.

The administration officials who testified at the Senate hearings on MacArthur's relief clearly indicated that they viewed his attitude and conduct as insubordinate and a threat to the principle of civilian supremacy over the military. Secretary of Defense Marshall, probably the most admired of the witnesses representing the administration, was adamant about MacArthur's unparalleled effrontery toward his superiors:

> It is completely understandable that, in fact, at times commendable that a theater commander should become so wholly wrapped up in his own aims and responsibilities that some of the directives received by him from higher authorities are not those that he would have written for himself. There is nothing new about this sort of thing in our military history. What is new, and what had brought about the necessity for General MacArthur's removal, is the wholly unprecedented situation of a local theater commander publicly expressing his displeasure at and his disagreement with the foreign and military policies of the United States.
>
> It became apparent that General MacArthur had grown so far out of sympathy with the established policies of the United States that there was grave doubt as to whether he could any longer be permitted to exercise the authority in making decisions that normal command functions would assign to a theater commander. In this situation, there was no other recourse but to relieve him.

The evidence accumulated in the Senate investigation of May and June 1951 demonstrates that virtually all of his transgressions fell under the category of disobedience of the President's "muzzling directives" of December 6, 1950. The general's responses, in turn, had revealed his deep opposition to administration policies. The press had widely publicized his blasts; indeed, many of his missives had gone to national news magazines and major newspapers by way of interviews with and correspondence to their publishers and senior editors or bureau chiefs. His false dilemma about evacuation or annihilation, which was rankling enough to his superiors since he seemed to pass responsibility to them, was a frequent theme in his flagrantly defiant public statements. McCarthyism had already left the national press in a feeding frenzy, so it was natural for reporters eager to exploit the popular hostility against Truman and Acheson to give lavish attention to the anti-administration barbs of one of the nation's greatest heroic figures of World War II.

Most heinous to Commander in Chief Truman were the general's ultimatum to the head of the Chinese Communist Forces on March 24 and his denunciation of administration policy read in the U.S. House of Representatives on April 5. The general had been told that Truman would soon announce a new diplomatic initiative to get a Korean truce before Ridgway's army advanced across the 38th parallel again. MacArthur arrogantly and deliberately wrecked this diplomatic overture by issuing his own public statement directed to the CCF leader, which scathingly criticized Red China's "complete inability to accomplish by force of arms the conquest of Korea," threatened "an expansion of our military operations to its coastal areas and interior bases [that] would doom Red China to the risk of imminent military collapse," and offered "at any time to confer in the field with the commander-in-chief of the enemy forces in the earnest effort to find any military means whereby realization of the political objectives of the United Nations in Korea . . . might be accomplished without further bloodshed."

In sixteen or more instances in the previous four months the volatile Far East chief had made statements sharply chastising the administration for its errors or absence of policy in the Far East. MacArthur was bent now upon some dramatic gesture to salvage his waning stature. By late March, the UN commander became so paranoid that he believed that he had ruined a plot created by some in the United Nations, the State Department, and high places in Washington to change the status of Formosa and the Nationalists' seat in the UN.

Upon reading MacArthur's shocking statement of the 24th, the President firmly but secretly decided that day to dismiss him; only the procedure and the date had to be settled. Truman heatedly remarked to an assistant that the general's act was "not just a public disagreement over policy, but deliberate, premeditated sabotage of US and UN policy." Acheson described it as "defiance of the Chiefs of Staff, sabotage of an operation of which he had been informed, and insubordination of the grossest sort to his Commander in Chief." Astoundingly, however, the President, through the JCS, sent him a brief and mildly worded message on March 25 reminding him of the directives of December 6 and telling him to contact the Joint Chiefs for instructions if the Chinese commander asked for a truce.

The message from Washington on March 20 alerting him to the impending peace move also set off MacArthur's second climactic act of self-destruction in his endeavor to redirect American foreign and military policies to a greater focus on Asia's significance to the self-interests of the United States. That same day the general wrote Representative Joseph W. Martin, Jr., the House minority leader and a strong Asia-first and Nationalist China crusader. Martin had asked for comments on a speech by the congressman hitting Truman's weak support of Formosa, his limited-war strategy in Korea, and his plans to strengthen NATO. In his letter, MacArthur endorsed his friend Martin's views with enthusiasm but offered nothing new, even admitting that his positions "have been submitted to Washington in most complete detail" and generally "are well known." What made the general's comments different this time were their coincidence with the sensitive diplomatic maneuvering, Martin's dramatic reading of the letter on the floor of the House, and the front-page headlines MacArthur's words got. . . .

At the Senate hearings, MacArthur claimed the letter to Martin was "merely a routine communication." On the other hand, Truman penned in his diary on April 6: "MacArthur shoots another political bomb through Joe Martin. . . . This looks like the last straw. Rank insubordination. . . . I call in Gen. Marshall, Dean Acheson, Mr. Harriman and Gen. Bradley before Cabinet [meeting] to discuss situation." Acheson exclaimed that the Martin letter was "an open declaration of war on the Administration's policy." When Truman conferred with the above "Big Four," as he called them, he did not reveal that his mind had been made up for some time;

instead, he encouraged a candid discussion of options and expressed his desire for a unanimous recommendation from them as well as the three service chiefs, Collins, Sherman, and Vandenberg.

Over the weekend Truman talked to key members of the Cabinet to solicit their opinions, while top State and Defense officials met in various groupings to discuss the issue. At the meeting of the President and the Big Four on Monday, April 9, the relief of General MacArthur was found to be the unanimous verdict of the President, the Big Four, and the service chiefs. . . .

MacArthur was the first to testify at the Senate hearings, and when he expounded on the harmonious relationship and identity of strategic views between him and his military superiors, he seems to have believed this sincerely, if naively. One by one, Marshall, Bradley, Collins, Sherman, and Vandenberg would later tell the senators that they were not in accord with MacArthur on matters of the direction of the war, relations with civilian officials, the value of the European allies, and the priority of the war in the global picture, among other differences. Not aware of how united and devastating against him his uniformed superiors would be, MacArthur set about describing a dichotomy in the leadership of the war from Washington, with Truman, Acheson, Harriman, and other ranking civilians of the administration, especially the State Department, which tended to have unprecedented input in military affairs by 1950–1951, being responsible for the policy vacuum, indecisiveness, and protracted, costly stalemate. On the other hand, he and the Pentagon leaders, along with most of the other senior American officers of the various services, wanted to fight in less limited fashion and gain a decisive triumph in order to deter future communist aggression.

MacArthur, thinking he spoke for his military colleagues, told the senators that Truman and his "politicians" favored "the concept of a continued and indefinite campaign in Korea . . . that introduces into the military sphere a political control such as I have never known in my life or have ever studied." He argued that "when politics fails, and the military takes over, you must trust the military." Later he added: "There should be no non-professional interference in the handling of troops in a campaign. You have professionals to do that job and they should be permitted to do it." As for his recommendations for coping with the entry of the Red Chinese onto the battlefield, he maintained that "most" of them, "in fact, practically all, as far as I know—were in complete accord with the military recommendations of the Joint Chiefs of Staff, and all other commanders." Referring to a JCS list of sixteen courses of action that were under consideration on January 12, which included three of the four he had recommended on December 30, he claimed with some hyperbole, "The position of the Joint Chiefs of Staff and my own, so far as I know, were practically identical." He pictured his ties with the JCS as idealistic, indeed, unrealistic: "The relationships between the Joint Chiefs of Staff and myself have been admirable. All members are personal friends of mine. I hold them individually and collectively in the greatest esteem." It was a desperate endeavor to demonstrate that the basic friction lay between the civilian and the military leadership, not between him and the Pentagon, but it became a pathetic revelation of how out of touch he was with the Joint Chiefs. For want of conclusive proof as to his motivation, however, leeway must be allowed for MacArthur's wiliness, which had not altogether abandoned him: He may have been trying to exploit tensions between the State and Defense departments, with few uniformed leaders holding Acheson and his lieutenants in high regard.

Fortunately for MacArthur, Marshall and the Joint Chiefs, who had chafed over Acheson's obvious eagerness to see the proud MacArthur fall, felt an affinity with this senior professional in their field who had long commanded with distinction. They could not bring themselves to court-martial him. Further, Truman's terrible ratings in the polls—worse than Nixon's at the ebb of Watergate—and the firestorm that McCarthyism had produced for him and Acheson weakened him so politically that a court-martial of MacArthur would have been foolhardy in the extreme. During the first five days after MacArthur's relief, a White House staff count showed that Truman received almost thirteen thousand letters and telegrams on the issue, of which 67 percent opposed the President's action. By the end of the Senate hearings on the general's relief, much of the public, Congress, and the press had lost interest in the inquiry, though polls indicated that a majority of those who cared enough to give an opinion now were against MacArthur. The notion that he might have touched off World War III was on its way to becoming one of the more unfortunate myths about the general.

Insubordination, or defiance of authority, was the charge most frequently leveled against MacArthur at the time and later by high-ranking officials of the Truman administration, including those in uniform. Of course, there was no doubt of his insubordination in the minds of the two chief architects of his dismissal, Truman and Acheson. On numerous occasions during his days of testimony before the Senate committees, it will be recalled, MacArthur himself said that the nation's commander in chief was empowered to appoint and dismiss his uniformed leaders for whatever reason, which surely included rank insubordination. There was no serious question about Truman's authority to relieve MacArthur, but the President and the Joint Chiefs found such great difficulty in dismissing him because there was no genuine threat to the principle of civilian supremacy over the military in this case. MacArthur was not an "American Caesar" and held very conservative views of the Constitution, the necessity of civilian control, and the traditions and history of the American military. When the President finally decided to gird his loins and dismiss MacArthur, the action was swift and Ridgway replaced him smoothly and effectively in short order. All the President had to do was issue the order to bring about the change in command, and it was clear that his power as commander in chief was secure and unchallenged. The President and his Far East commander had differed over strategic priorities and the direction of the war, but their collision had not posed a serious menace to civilian dominance over the military in America.

Breakdowns in Command and Communication

A significant and often overlooked reason for the termination of MacArthur's command was a breakdown in communications between him and his superiors. During the Second World War, MacArthur and the Joint Chiefs of Staff sometimes differed in ways that indicated misperceptions more than strategic differences, but the two sides and their key lieutenants had personal ties between them that were lacking between the Tokyo and Washington leaders of 1950–1951. During the Korean War, the camps of Truman and MacArthur strongly influenced each man's perception of the other. This is not to say that on their own Truman and MacArthur would have become cordial friends. But their lieutenants undoubtedly were important in molding their judgments. Their only direct contact had been a few hours at Wake Island on October 15, 1950, of which a very small portion had been spent alone. Despite the fact that they had never met before and were never to talk again, they would go to their graves implacable enemies.

If the Truman-MacArthur personal relationship was limited to one brief encounter, the personal links between the Far East leader and the seven men who were the President's principal advisers on the Korean War—the Big Four and the service chiefs—were almost nil. Acheson never met him. Marshall visited him once during World War II while going to Eisenhower's headquarters numerous times. Bradley and Harriman had no personal ties with MacArthur at all prior to June of 1950, although each traveled to Tokyo to confer with him after the Korean hostilities commenced. None of the Big Four was an admirer of MacArthur's flamboyant leadership style, yet Marshall, who had been his military superior in World War II, had treated him with commendable fairness despite the Southwest Pacific commander's sometimes difficult ways. All of the Big Four were strongly committed to the security of West Europe, and all had considerable experience and friends there.

None of the service chiefs had any personal contacts with MacArthur of any importance prior to the outbreak of war in Korea, whereupon they made a number of trips to Tokyo to meet with him and his senior commanders and staff leaders. Collins was on the faculty of the United States Military Academy during MacArthur's last year as superintendent (1921–1922), and Vandenberg was a cadet for the three years (1919–1922) of his tenure. Neither of them, however, really got to know the aloof superintendent, though both knew much about him, especially his hero image from the battlefields of France and his efforts to bring reforms to the school despite faculty and alumni resistance. Collins and Vandenberg achieved their senior commands in the Second World War in the European theater; the former had seen combat first in the Solomons, which was not in MacArthur's theater. When he was on Admiral Chester W. Nimitz's staff during the war in the Pacific, Sherman conferred with MacArthur at three or more intertheater planning sessions. Sherman, who had the most significant pre-1950 personal contact with MacArthur, was his strongest supporter of the seven men on a number of his ideas and plans, notably the Inchon assault. On the other hand, Marshall, the oldest of the seven (like MacArthur, born in 1880), and the officer with seniority in the service, was the last of the group to be persuaded that MacArthur should be relieved of his commands.

Of these key advisers to the President, Acheson stands out for his vituperativeness toward the Tokyo commander. In a bitter exchange of press statements in the autumn of 1945 contradicting each other over estimated troop strength needed in occupied Japan, Acheson and MacArthur seemed to exhibit a deep and natural incompatibility. Acheson blamed MacArthur in part for trouble in getting his approval as under secretary of state passed by the Senate that fall. When he was secretary of state later, he visited Europe often but never Japan, and in 1949 he was behind the move to oust the general as head of the Allied occupation. Certainly as proud and arrogant as MacArthur, Acheson could be invidious. Writing nearly two decades after the dismissal, Acheson still harbored deep wrath: "As one looks back in calmness, it seems impossible to overestimate the damage that General Mac-Arthur's willful insubordination and incredibly bad judgment did to the United States in the world and to the Truman Administration in the United States." Acheson was the abiding voice in Truman's ear from 1945 onward urging him to dump "the Big General," and it was he who primarily continued to stoke the long-cold coals even after most of his cohorts had let the fire die as far as public statements were concerned.

The sorry spectacle of MacArthur testifying at the Senate hearings about his harmonious relations with the Joint Chiefs not only exposed his ignorance of the situation but also pointed up how poorly the JCS had communicated their doubts and anxieties, as well as their anger, to the theater commander. It was an invitation to trouble to place him in the UN command in the first place because of both his prior record of defying authority and his long career of distinction and seniority in comparison to theirs. It should have been understood from the beginning of the Korean War that his past achievements gave him no claim to special privileges in obeying orders and directives, especially in such an unprecedented limited conflict that could quickly become a third world war. Time after time, especially after the Red Chinese intervention, the Joint Chiefs retreated from the policy guidance and new directives they should have given MacArthur and should have demanded his obedience. Instead, his intimidation of the Joint Chiefs led them to appease him.

On the other hand, MacArthur discovered that he could not awe or intimidate Truman. Indeed, at the end, the President dismissed him so abruptly and crudely that the general heard of it first from a commercial radio broadcast. Speaking as a professional, MacArthur later said, "No office boy, no charwoman, no servant of any sort would have been dismissed with such callous disregard for the ordinary decencies." For MacArthur, his erroneous image of Truman as a fox terrier yapping at his heels instead of a tough, decisive commander in chief was a costly failure in communication.

If the Joint Chiefs had been more responsible in keeping MacArthur on a short leash, perhaps the collision course between the President and the general might have been averted. The absurd spectacle of the Senate investigation into the general's relief, which bestowed upon Pyongyang, Peking, and Moscow an abundance of data on American strategy in the midst of war, surely could have been avoided. While MacArthur's career was terminated by the confrontation, Truman's also was cut short, the controversy mightily affecting his chances for reelection. Truman won over MacArthur, but it was a Pyrrhic victory politically.

MacArthur's relief was, in part, a legacy of World War II and the strategic priorities of that conflict. Roosevelt and his Joint Chiefs of Staff had early agreed to the British priority on the defeat of Germany because the Atlantic community of nations was vital to American national security and the threat by Japan was more distant. In the midst of another Asian war, MacArthur was sacrificed by a different President and his Defense and State advisers, who did not consider American strategic interests as menaced in East Asia as in Europe. It remains to be seen whether a century hence the Far East will loom as important to American self-interests as MacArthur predicted.

In Defense of Truman: MacArthur Had Limited Vision as a Theater Commander

ROY K. FLINT

The primary constitutional issue to emerge from the Korean War was the extension of presidential authority in wartime into the technical realm of the professional soldiers, who as recently as World War II had exercised not only the detailed but also the broader direction of the nation's wars once the fighting began. But in the late 1950s, when the United States assumed leadership of the anti-Soviet coalition in the UN and the North Atlantic Treaty Organization (NATO), the President had to take a more active role as Commander-in-Chief, even as he fulfilled his traditional foreign policy role. The Truman-MacArthur controversy was but an extension of this trend, as the President responded in the atomic era to a broader understanding of war, one which blurred any distinction that may have existed between foreign policy and armed conflict. President Truman's relief of General MacArthur confirmed civilian control over the military services and revealed the General as an heroic figure, single-mindedly committed to victory on the battlefield, but seemingly without any real appreciation of the larger political implications of the war that he was fighting. . . .

MacArthur had been defeated before. He had built a noble cause and a great reputation out of defeat in the Philippines early in World War II. He had used that defeat to create an image of heroic leadership for himself around which he mustered an American-Australian-New Zealand offensive force. Then, too, he had been forced to accept a priority on men and materiel lower than that given to the European theater. Nevertheless, he had designed a brilliant scheme of offensive operations through the islands of the South Pacific and was able to return to the Philippines and ultimately to vanquish totally his earlier conquerors. In Korea, events had transpired in remarkably similar fashion. Once again he faced early defeat while his nation hastily patched together reinforcements. Once again he had to accept a lower priority. At Inchon he had reversed the flow of the war in a singularly brilliant victory that rivaled those of Napoleon in its conception. But there the parallel ended, for in World War II there had been no China able to come to the aid of the Japanese, no Soviet Union poised ominously nearby. In the anguish of his personal defeat, MacArthur could not see that difference so clearly.

To MacArthur there was "no substitute for victory," particularly now, in the twilight of his long and successful life. The war in Korea was there to be won, not lost or, perhaps even worse, left deadlocked and inconclusive. If communists chose to fight it out in Asia, then that is where the priority of American efforts should be—not in Europe, but in Asia. And all of the nation's combat power should be marshaled there to ensure a victorious outcome. This was the bedrock of his personal belief and his professional judgment. He had consistently argued to this

From Roy K. Flint, "The Truman-MacArthur Conflict: Dilemmas of Civil-Military Relationships in the Nuclear Age," *The United States Military under the Constitution of the United States, 1789–1989,* ed. Richard H. Kohn (New York University Press, 1991). Reprinted by permission of the publisher.

conclusion, and the directives that he had received from the Joint Chiefs seemed to indicate their general agreement, at least with the goal of winning in Korea. But that was about to change: the Joint Chiefs were now obligated to a course of action that would accept MacArthur's reverse, a policy that sought only to retain a foothold—a tie—in Korea. MacArthur saw this as a dangerous policy in the world-wide struggle with communism. To be defeated in battle was, MacArthur knew, the lot of a soldier—unwanted, but not unexpected. To be defeated and then denied the opportunity to strike back to set things right was bad politics, professionally wrong, and personally humiliating. At this stage in MacArthur's life, public policy had merged with his personal image of himself in history. Which was more impor-tant to him is to this day impossible to judge with certainty. But after a singularly successful career that earned for him the highest accolades a soldier could receive, he was about to be forced to finish his career with a defeat of historic proportions. Thus he determined to head off personal disaster in any way possible.

MacArthur had always relied upon his reputation and strong personality to achieve his ends. Still the national hero, his hauteur was accepted as a natural trait of a great old soldier. In fact, it could be argued that without his arrogance, he would never have possessed the confidence to withhold the forces from the Pusan defense he then used so boldly to surprise the North Koreans at Inchon. But on a more mundane level, the trait caused nothing but trouble. Even before the interven-tion of the Chinese, the General and the President had disagreed over American policy regarding Taiwan. Early in the war, MacArthur had made an ill-advised visit to Chiang Kai-shek to discuss their mutual interests in East Asia. A public state-ment issued by Chiang cast MacArthur more in the light of an independent sover-eign than an American general. Truman was irritated, but inclined to overlook the indiscretion. Later, in a letter to the Veterans of Foreign Wars, MacArthur stressed the strategic importance of Taiwan and called for continued American control over the island. Just as the United States might profitably use Taiwan as a base against China, so too would it be a formidable threat to the United States in the Pacific if controlled by the Chinese. Now the soldier had gone too far. . . .

MacArthur's first reaction to defeat at the hands of the Chinese was defensive. As the criticism of American policy and his leadership mounted in foreign capitals, in the press, and even in his own government, MacArthur spoke sharply in his own defense. Early in December, he complained to the press that the restrictions placed on him were "without precedent in military history." Truman, his anger aroused, framed an executive order to all cabinet members and special staff on 5 December that admonished them to reduce the number of public speeches dealing with for-eign and military policy issues. While the order affected all administration officials and military officers, it was aimed specifically at MacArthur and intended to stop his free use of the press as a means of transmitting his private views. . . .

MacArthur's message to the enemy commander and his letter to Congressman Martin were the immediate causes of relief. But the Commander-in-Chief's disaf-fection with the General was rooted in the nature of the war. What had been miss-ing all along was close coordination between battlefield goals and worldwide coalition goals. Having assumed the leadership in both areas, the President and his advisors had allowed the battlefield objective, which after the Inchon victory became defeat of the North Korean Army and occupation of North Korea, to coexist with the broader coalition goal of avoiding a wider war, a goal that proved after Chinese interventions to be incompatible with the occupation of North Korea. Either MacArthur should have been given the resources to take North Korea regardless of the risks, or he should have been stopped short of the Manchurian border in order to avoid provoking a wider war. After directing MacArthur to cross into North Korea without the resources to defeat both the North Koreans and the Chinese, the administration found itself faced with the worst possible outcome: a divided Korea and a war with China. Clearly, the Truman administration was ready neither psychologically nor in organization to fight such a war. Not surprisingly, the President and the General clashed over this fundamental issue.

MacArthur's relief shocked the American people. Many saw the President's act as that of a small-minded man. MacArthur represented to them respected traditions and widely held attitudes about war and the meaning of victory. His disagreement with Truman's policy of seeking a settlement short of enemy capitulation was probably shared by a majority of Americans. Although short-lived, the clamor on the General's behalf amounted to a sizable political uprising, enjoyed greatly by the President's political opposition. Pressing their advantage, the Republicans in Congress forced a senatorial investigation of the facts behind the incident. During May and June, lengthy hearings, which for the most part were open to public scrutiny, enabled MacArthur's advocates to vie with administration spokesmen in a political struggle over the history and future of American foreign policy—the real issue, as all knew. With the airing of contending arguments, and after the emotionalism surrounding the General's return to the United States died down, a consensus emerged among Americans that generally supported Truman's actions. Thus, in the end, the President won widespread support for his views that America's real interests lay with her European and NATO allies and that the fighting in Korea should be contained and ended as quickly as possible to avoid widening the conflict into a third world war. Nevertheless, during the last two years of the war, frustrated critics decried the difficult negotiations and condemned the wasteful and seemingly meaningless war of attrition fought along the line of contact in Korea. Eventually, though the President controlled his enemies in Congress with the Democratic majority, disenchantment with protracted war became the major political issue in the Presidential election of 1952 and perhaps played the crucial role in the electoral victory of Dwight D. Eisenhower.

Less conspicuous, but perhaps more important both to the military profession and to the system of government under the Constitution, was the impact on the American practice of command and the civil-military relationships under which command of American forces functioned. The sacking of Douglas MacArthur reaffirmed the traditional civilian supremacy over the military. Even though partisan Republican support for MacArthur grew hysterical at times, few seriously doubted that the facts warranted relief of a general who challenged a fundamental principle of American constitutional government. It is possible to argue, at least in theory, that MacArthur's loyalty was to the Constitution rather than to the political administration that was temporarily running the government. MacArthur considered it his duty to speak out on issues that he thought were vital to the security of his country. If he was stifled, who then would warn the country of danger? Nevertheless,

MacArthur's oath of office demanded that he obey the legal orders of his superiors. This he failed to do when he defied the Executive Order of 5 December requiring the clearance of public statements by senior government officials.

President Truman extended executive control to the battlefield when he relieved MacArthur. If they adhered to the traditional practice of high command, the President and the Joint Chiefs would have had to give in to their battlefield commander's arguments and demands for freedom of action. In this contest, MacArthur held the upper hand; and the administration, trying to reach wise decisions from the other side of the world, subordinated long-term political policy to tactical expediency. In retrospect, the Chinese attacks in late October-early November, followed by a two-week lull, might have served as a warning to advance no further. Had the President and the Joint Chiefs interpreted the lull as a signal, they might have ordered MacArthur to withdraw to more advantageous positions. While there is no assurance that the Chinese would have withheld further attacks, a withdrawal would certainly have changed the situation; MacArthur would almost certainly have been indignant, but the tactical disaster might have been averted.

For failing seriously to consider consolidation short of the border, the President and his senior military leaders must take responsibility. The Department of Defense and the Joint Chiefs of Staff, relatively new organizations trying to keep local the first open war in the atomic age, were prudently cautious at the outset of the war. Overburdened by their worldwide responsibilities, however, they quickly abandoned their wary approach. The Joint Chiefs, conservative in their response to the Inchon plan and then overbold in their assessment of the risks to be incurred by crossing the thirty-eighth parallel, failed to see their inconsistency and permitted their error to be built into the President's decision to cross. Moreover, after the spectacular success at Inchon, they were only too willing to give the victorious MacArthur wide latitude in winding up the whole Korean affair while they concentrated their attention on the rearmament of the United States and the reinforcement of NATO. As a consequence, the Joint Chiefs saw the drive into North Korea through the eyes of MacArthur. Too late, they realized that the military situation was not as he had portrayed it.

Yet what were they to do? The Joint Chiefs, as well as the President and his top civilian advisors, were grappling with an entirely new experience. Never before had the direction of battle contained such far-reaching implications as it did in Korea in the atomic age. In World War II, devolution of authority and responsibility to unified military commanders was found to be the only effective way to direct the efforts of air, sea, and ground forces. Under these conditions, MacArthur and the other theater commanders succeeded magnificently. The Joint Chiefs themselves had been a part of that system and fully endorsed it. But once the Soviet Union gained possession of atomic weapons and the means to deliver them against United States territory, there was an urgent need to coordinate closely the policies of the President, the strategies of the Joint Chiefs, and the operations of the theater commander so as to prevent a local war from escalating into a global conflict. Instinctively the President and his advisors understood this, but they had not thought through a new division of responsibility between Washington and a theater commander, nor an alternative system of control. A conflicting instinct was not to risk the consequences of tampering with tradition. As Truman said: "You pick your man, you've got to back him up." In the end, it took MacArthur's challenge to the authority of the President to force a change in the American concept and system of military command at the theater level, that point at which strategy and operations meet in the person of the theater commander. After the defeat in North Korea, the administration finally subordinated the freedom of action traditionally accorded the local commander to the demands of global strategy in the age of atomic weapons. Eventually, this priority forced the dismissal of Douglas MacArthur and the conflict in civil-military relationships known since as the Truman-MacArthur controversy.

♠ F U R T H E R   R E A D I N G

Bevin Alexander, *Korea: The First War We Lost* (1986).

Joseph H. Alexander and Merrill L. Bartlett, *Sea Soldiers in the Cold War: Amphibious Warfare, 1945–1991* (1995).

Roy E. Appleman, *Disaster in Korea: The Chinese Confront MacArthur* (1989).

———, *South to the Naktong, North to the Yalu: June-November 1950* (1961).

Jeffrey G. Barlow, *The Revolt of the Admirals: The Fight for Naval Aviation, 1945–1950* (1994).

Albert D. Biderman, *March to Calumny: The Story of American POW's in the Korean War* (1963).

Clay Blair, *The Forgotten War: America In Korea, 1950–1953* (1987).

William T. Bowers, William M. Hammond, and George L. MacGarrigle, *Black Soldier, White Army: The 24th Infantry Regiment in Korea* (1996).

Malcolm W. Cagle and Frank A. Manson, *The Sea War in Korea* (1957).

Jian Chen, *China's Road to the Korean War: The Making of the Sino-American Confrontation* (1994).

J. Lawton Collins, *War in Peacetime* (1969).

Bruce Cumings, *The Origins of the Korean War*, 2 vols. (1981, 1990).

Richard M. Dalfiume, *Desegregation of the U.S. Armed Forces: Fighting on Two Fronts, 1939–1953* (1969).

T. R. Fehrenbach, *This Kind of War: A Study in Unpreparedness* (1963).

Sergei N. Goncharov, John W. Lewis, and Xue Lutai, *Uncertain Partners: Stalin, Mao, and the Korean War* (1993).

Joseph C. Goulden, *Korea: The Untold Story of the War* (1982).

Jon Halliday and Bruce Cumings, *Korea: The Unknown War* (1988).

Max Hastings, *The Korean War* (1987).

Richard F. Haynes, *The Awesome Power: Harry S. Truman as Commander in Chief* (1973).

Robert D. Heinl, Jr., *Victory at High Tide: The Inchon-Seoul Campaign* (1968).

Frances H. Heller, ed., *The Korean War: A 25-Year Perspective* (1977).

Trumbull Higgins, *Korea and the Fall of MacArthur: A Precis in Limited War* (1960).

D. Clayton James, *Refighting the Last War: Command and Crisis in Korea, 1950–1953* (1993).

———, *The Years of MacArthur, Triumph and Disaster, 1945–1964* (1985).

Burton I. Kaufman, *The Korean War: Challenges in Crisis, Credibility, and Command* (1986).

Douglas MacArthur, *Reminiscences* (1964).

S. L. A. Marshall, *Pork Chop Hill: The American Fighting Man in Action, Korea, Spring 1953* (1956).

Donald R. McCoy, *The Presidency of Harry S. Truman* (1984).

Geoffrey Perret, *Old Soldiers Never Die: The Life of Douglas MacArthur* (1996).

Forrest C. Pogue, *George C. Marshall, Statesman, 1949–1959* (1987).

David Rees, *Korea: The Limited War* (1964).

Matthew B. Ridgway, *The Korean War* (1967).

David Alan Rosenberg, "The Origins of Overkill: Nuclear Weapons and American Strategy, 1945–1960," *International Security* 7 (Spring 1983): 3–71.

Charles R. Shrader, *Communist Logistics in the Korean War* (1995).

John W. Spanier, *The Truman-MacArthur Controversy and the Korean War* (1959).

Shelby L. Stanton, *America's Tenth Legion: X Corps in Korea, 1950* (1989).

William J. Stueck, Jr., *The Korean War: An International History* (1995).

John Toland, *In Mortal Combat: Korea, 1950–1953* (1991).

Rudy Tomedi, *No Bugles, No Drums: An Oral History of the Korean War* (1993).

Harry S. Truman, *Memoirs* 2 vols. (1955–1956).

Shu Guang Zhang, *Mao's Military Romanticism: China and the Korean War, 1950–1953* (1995).

C H A P T E R
14

The Vietnam War: Political-Military Decisions and Combat Experiences

Why did the United States lose in Vietnam? Could a different strategy have won? Should the United States government have committed the American armed forces to fight there? What was the nature of the American military experience in Vietnam? Historians continue to debate these and other questions about the massive American military effort in Southeast Asia in the 1960s and early 1970s. The nature of the military experience certainly varied depending on many factors such as branch of the armed forces, type of military service, and the time and place of the tour of duty. As in other aspects of American life, the Vietnam experience of American service people could also be influenced by factors of race, class, ethnicity, and gender as well as by the personality and circumstances of particular individuals, although common exposure to danger and the need for mutual protection can submerge differences among members of combat units. Historians continue to debate the extent to which military unit cohesion broke down in Vietnam and the reasons for that development. When and why did significant numbers of American service people turn against the war? Were they against the war itself or against the way it was being fought?

Although the majority of historians consider the war to have been unwinnable for the United States, some military analysts have suggested that different strategies might have produced more effective results, possibly even the prevention of a North Vietnamese victory in South Vietnam. Their prescriptions vary. Some suggest the military emphasis should have been shifted away from conventional unit warfare to psychological and counterguerrilla pacification efforts to protect and win the allegiance of the rural South Vietnamese population. Some believe that conventional warfare should have been increased, including wider bombing of North Vietnam. There are those who argue for greater effort in cutting off the North Vietnamese supply routes to South Vietnam through neighboring Laos and Cambodia and the establishment of a more effective barrier between North and South Vietnam. It was, of course, President Lyndon B. Johnson who made the decision to commit U.S.

combat units to Vietnam beginning in 1965. Johnson's priorities as president be-
tween 1963 and 1969 were his domestic reform program and his re-election, and
to those ends he sought to forestall either the collapse of Washington's South
Vietnamese ally or a full-scale American mobilization for a war that might prove
unwinnable and simultaneously destructive of Johnson's domestic achievements.
Weaving between the conflicting pressures from "hawks" and "doves" in Congress,
his party, and the public, Johnson carefully sought to control the U.S. military, es-
calating the American part in the war according to his own decisions about what
was necessary and what was politically acceptable in the United States.

An important part of the debate over the American military role in Vietnam
concerns not simply Johnson's decisions, which have been debated for many years,
but more recently, the role of senior military officers. What was the view of the
Joint Chiefs of Staff and other experienced commanders about the war in Vietnam?
Did they think from the beginning that it was unwinnable? Or did they think that
President Johnson, because of his policy of gradual and incremental escalation,
was preventing the American military from winning the war? What kind of advice
was the senior brass giving the president? If they disagreed with his policy, why did
they not resign and speak out publicly? What is the responsibility of a military offi-
cer if after studied professional judgment, he or she disagrees with the commander
in chief, particularly on a matter that can lead to deaths of many Americans and
others? As with the controversy between General MacArthur and President
Truman in the Korean War, the question of the responsibilities of the Joint Chiefs
of Staff during the Vietnam War raises highly significant questions about civil-
military relations and limited war, and the problems they pose for the military
profession and for American democracy.

♠ D O C U M E N T S

On March 4, 1964, President Lyndon B. Johnson met with the Joint Chiefs of Staff
(JCS) after directing Secretary of Defense Robert McNamara and JCS chairman General Maxwell Taylor to go on a fact-finding mission to Saigon, South Vietnam, March
8 to 12, 1964. The first document, Taylor's notes of the March 4th meeting, illustrates
some of the differences between the JCS and the president over the American military
role in the war before the November 1964 U.S. presidential election. Returning from
Vietnam, where the new Saigon government of General Nguyen Khanh was unstable
and the Communist Viet Cong was gaining in the countryside, McNamara gave the
president the report he wanted. As shown in the second document, which lists the recommendations at the end of the Secretary of Defense's report, McNamara suggested
increased U.S. advisory and assistance efforts rather than the initiation of any overt
U.S. military involvement (at least before the American presidential election in November). The service chiefs objected at their meeting with General Taylor on March
14, 1964, when Taylor showed them McNamara's March 13th draft of his report. The
third document, a transcription by the editors of this volume of handwritten notes of
the March 14th JCS meeting taken by Lieutenant General Harold K. Johnson, then
deputy Army Chief of Staff and deputy Chief of Staff for operations on the JCS, indicates that all of the service chiefs contended that McNamara's proposal did not go far
enough. Indeed, Army Chief of Staff Earle G. Wheeler at first refused to go along,
saying "[I] Will not be party to proposals that this action can be done with mirrors,"

but his non-concurrence was later withdrawn. McNamara did not change his recommendations; they remained the same in the March 16th report (Document Number Two) that he submitted to President Lyndon Johnson on March 16. Nor did he forward to the president a toned-down summary of the chiefs' views prepared by General Taylor. The president met with the National Security Council (NSC) (among whose members were the Vice President, Secretaries of Defense, State, and Treasury, as well as the Director of the Central Intelligence Agency, and the Chairman of the Joint Chiefs of Staff) and other invited participants to discuss the Defense Secretary's report on March 17, 1964. As indicated in the fourth document, the summary record of that meeting written by the executive secretary of the NSC, Bromley Smith, General Taylor told the president and the NSC that the service chiefs "support the McNamara report." Taylor added that "the Chiefs believed the proposed program was acceptable, but it may not be sufficient to save the situation in Vietnam." The president approved the McNamara recommendations (which he had inspired), stating that the "proposals did not foreclose action later if the situation did not improve as we expected." For the public, the White House then issued a press release. That press release of March 17, 1964, the fifth document, downplayed any U.S. military role and put forward an optimistic view of the ability of the South Vietnamese Government of General Khanh itself to drive back the communist-led insurgents. After President Johnson's reelection in November, he began the U.S. military build-up in South Vietnam. By April 1965, there were 90,000 American troops there, and that month, the president authorized U.S. ground force units to take the offensive.

President Johnson's incremental escalation continued from 1965 through 1968. In early 1968, in the wake of the defeat of a major Communist offensive during the February "Tet" holidays and General Westmoreland's February 27th request for 206,000 additional troops (to raise the U.S. forces in Vietnam to 731,000), former army Colonel John Paul Vann, who had left the army in disgust over the brutality and ineffectiveness of the U.S. strategy in Vietnam only to return in 1965 as a civilian worker in the Civil Operations and Revolutionary Development Support (CORDS) pacification program, wrote, in the sixth document, a "personal and confidential" letter from Saigon to a friend at the State Department in Washington, assessing the situation in Vietnam in the aftermath of the Tet offensive. The individual American military experience in Vietnam varied enormously as the following documents illustrate. In the seventh document, Lieutenant Commander Theodore R. ("T. R.") Swartz, pilot of a Navy A4C Skyhawk aboard the carrier, *U.S.S. Bon Homme Richard,* recalls the excitement of the Navy's air strikes in operation ROLLING THUNDER, the bombing campaign over North Vietnam, and aerial combat with MIG fighters and surface-to-air missiles (SAMs) in 1967. In the eighth document, Army Specialist 4 Richard J. Ford III, an African-American soldier, has bitter memories of the war and racism from his tour of duty, June 1967 to July 1968, with a long-range reconnaissance patrol (LURP) in the 25th Infantry Division. In the ninth document, the 1976 published memoir of General William C. Westmoreland, the U.S. military commander in Vietnam maintains that American forces came close to prevailing militarily, but lost the war because of the absence of support from the public and the lack of political will on the part of the Johnson Administration and the failure to recognize the Tet Offensive as a "victory." In the tenth document, Ron Kovic, whose memoir, *Born on the Fourth of July* became a bestselling book and motion picture, tells a conference in 1985 about his transition from a John Wayne idolizing, decorated combat Marine to a vigorous antiwar dissenter and about the haunted reactions of this gravely wounded veteran to memories of the Vietnam War—a war that tore him and the nation apart.

1. The Joint Chiefs of Staff Differ with the President over Restraints on the U.S. Role in the Vietnam War, 1964

Memorandum by Gen. Maxwell Taylor, Chairman, JCS, of a Conversation Between the JCS and the President, Washington, March 4, 1964

4. He [the President] then opened the subject of our coming trip to Saigon and asked what course I was inclined to recommend at this moment. I told him that, in general, I felt our program should consist of two main parts; one, an intensive continuation of the counterinsurgency campaign within South Vietnam and, second, a progressive program of selective air and naval attacks against North Vietnam using means beyond those employed in the past. The other Chiefs expressed themselves generally in accord. They also were of the opinion that it was unlikely that the Chicoms [Chinese Communists] would intervene in strength. However, once embarked on the program the US must carry it to success, cost what may.

5. The President accepted the need for punishing Hanoi without debate, but pointed to some other practical difficulties, particularly the political ones with which he was faced. It is quite apparent that he does not want to lose South Vietnam before next November nor does he want to get the country into war.

6. The President is impressed with the danger of another coup. He feels we must make General [Nguyen] Khanh [current South Vietnam leader] "our boy" and proclaim the fact to all and sundry. He wants to see Khanh in the newspapers with McNamara and Taylor holding up his arms.

2. Secretary of Defense Robert McNamara Recommends a Limited Graduated U.S. Response in Vietnam, 1964

[16 March 1964; first draft 13 March 1964]

I recommend that you instruct the appropriate agencies of the U.S. Government:

1. To make it clear that we are prepared to furnish assistance and support to South Vietnam for as long as it takes to bring the insurgency under control.

2. To make it clear that we fully support the Khanh government and are opposed to any further coups.

3. To support a Program for National Mobilization (including a national service law) to put South Vietnam on a war footing.

4. To assist the Vietnamese to increase the armed forces (regular plus paramilitary) by at least 50,000 men.

5. To assist the Vietnamese to create a greatly enlarged Civil Administrative Corps for work at province, district and hamlet levels.

6. To assist the Vietnamese to improve and reorganize the paramilitary forces and to increase their compensation.

"Memorandum of a Conversation Between the Joint Chiefs of Staff and President Lyndon B. Johnson, Washington, March 4, 1964, *Foreign Relations of the United States, 1964–1968, Volume I: Vietnam 1964* (Washington, D.C.: GPO, 1994) p. 129.

Memorandum from Secretary of Defense Robert S. McNamara to President Lyndon B. Johnson. *Foreign Relations of the United States, 1964–1968, Volume I: Vietnam 1964* (Washington, D.C.: GPO, 1992), 166–167.

7. To assist the Vietnamese to create an offensive guerrilla force.

8. To provide the Vietnamese Air Force 25 A-1H aircraft in exchange for the present T-28s.

9. To provide the Vietnamese Army additional M-113 armored personnel carriers (withdrawing the M-114s there), additional river boats, and approximately $5–10 million of other additional material.

10. To announce publicly the Fertilizer Program and to expand it with a view within two years to trebling the amount of fertilizer made available.

11. To authorize continued high-level U.S. overflights of South Vietnam's borders and to authorize "hot pursuit" and South Vietnamese ground operations over the Laotian line for the purpose of border control. More ambitious operations into Laos involving units beyond battalion size should be authorized only with the approval of Souvanna Phouma. Operations across the Cambodian border should depend on the state of relations with Cambodia.

12. To prepare immediately to be in a position on 72 hours' notice to initiate the full range of Laotian and Cambodian "Border Control" actions (beyond those authorized in paragraph 11 above) and the "Retaliatory Actions" against North Vietnam, and to be in a position on 30 days' notice to initiate the program of "Graduated Overt Military Pressure" against North Vietnam.

3. Joint Chiefs of Staff Complain that McNamara's Proposals Will Not Win the War, 1964

[The Joint Chiefs of Staff in March 1964:
Gen. Maxwell Taylor, Chairman, Joint Chiefs of Staff (CJCS)
Gen. Earle G. Wheeler, Chief of Staff, US Army (C/S Army)
Adm. David McDonald, Chief of Naval Operations (CNO)
Gen. Curtis LeMay, Chief of Staff, US Air Force (C/S USAF)
Gen. Wallace M. Greene, Jr., Commandant US Marine Corps (CMC)]

[Special JCS Meeting 14 March 1964]

. . . .

CSA [Chief of Staff Army Wheeler] talked first. . . .

Program not adequate in itself to win the war.

CNO [Chief of Naval Operations McDonald] talked:

    a. Overall assessment seems to be OK

    b. Actions do not go far enough. [It is] Not strong enough paper.
       U.S. must take stronger action. Doubt that SVN [South Vietnam] can win fight alone.

    c. Has President gotten Chiefs' views on value of SE Asia [?]

    d. . . . Highlight importance of SEA [Southeast Asia]

    e. Take stronger stand on borders of both LAOS and CAMBODIA

Document (transcribed by the editors from General Johnson's handwritten notes); US Army Chief of Staff, General Harold K. Johnson, Notes on JCS Meeting, 14 March 1964–11:00 A.M., Box 126, Notes on Meetings of the JCS Jan-Apr 1964, General Harold K. Johnson Papers, U.S. Army Military History Institute, Carlisle, Pa.

f. [Allow] Hot pursuit [into] both L & C [Laos and Cambodia]—NOW

g. [Allow] Faster retaliatory action against [communist] offenses—3 hrs [hours] instead of 3 days.

CJCS [Chairman of the Joint Chiefs of Staff Taylor] rebuttal—Need time to determine what you retaliate against.

CNO [McDonald] thinks [it is] too long [a] period—period. Also 30 day [delay on] reaction time is much too long.

h. Pull U.S. dependents out. Could it be done at time SVN [South Vietnam] announces war footing[?]

CJCS [Taylor]—[You want to] Make Saigon look like a war capital?

[CNO McDonald]—Yes

[CS]AF [LeMay] agrees.

CSA [Wheeler] disagrees—[he] wants it to be in conjunction with a significant war related action. ([unclear] step-up). . . .

CNO [McDonald] really argues the case hard—active war area—should create a better US image and set an example for [the] Vietnamese.

[Recommendations regarding the memorandum:]

i. 1. Strengthen paper [by recommending options of]
2. Hot pursuit into CAMBODIA now.
3. Strengthen [U.S. and SVN's] control of MEKONG [delta area].
4. [Allow] High & low level reconnaissance—[of communist sanctuaries and lines of communications & supply in Laos and Cambodia] using US planes.
5. Reduce 72 hrs reaction to 24 [hours].
   Reduce 30 day mining capability to 72 hours.

MARINE CORPS CMDT. [Commandant, General Greene:]

Concur w[with] 10 of 12 recommendations.

Do not like [number] 7.—Should be reworded to use term other than guerrilla.

Do not like [number] 10—Have no comment on fertilizer.

12 recommendations offer little more than continuation of current program—hopefully a little better.

j. Separate service positions have not been examined by JCS.

Need an estimate of the situation.

Some discussion—argument heat[ed] as to just where we stand.

CMC [Commandant of Marine Corps] tabled an estimate.

Earlier paper had 23 points, only 4 of which are considered in this paper.

LOOK up the old paper and check on just what it says.

CMC [Commandant of Marine Corps] believes strongly that his 23 actions are imperative [including especially the introduction of Marines into enclaves in South Vietnam]

CSAF [Chief of Staff of Air Force LeMay]:—

a. Paper does not go far enough.

b. Ascending force must be included in paper. [The] Recommendations [in the paper] will not win the war.

c. [Stable] Political base [in South Vietnam] will not be created until more overt actions are taken.

CJCS [Chairman JCS Taylor]—Probably no common understanding of political base—Need US governmental announcement of support.

CSAF [Chief of Staff Air Force LeMay]—Must do it now.

US people will be behind aggressive action.

Vietnamese will support; in fact are eager for such support.

CJCS [Chairman JSC Taylor]: [I] Have [a] sense of the [position of the] Chiefs.

go [into] Cambodia

[Secretary of Defense McNamara's Proposals] Will not win [the war].

CSA [Wheeler]—Close to Army position. [I] Will not be party to proposals that this action can be done with mirrors.

CNO [McDonald]—Wants [control of] MEKONG [delta] included.

Chairman sup[poses?] it is.

Wants! Mar[ch] Chiefs' position reaffirmed.

To CSA [Chief of Staff of the Army]: This is not a continental war. [It is] Tailor made for kind of forces we have (Air and naval can interdict) South of Hanoi—VC [Viet Cong] effort is canalized.

Meet again.

Army non-concurrence with/drawn on 2343/344 [reference unclear]

4. National Security Council Endorses the Johnson-McNamara Plan for Limited U.S. Response, 1964

[NCS Meeting, 17 March 1964]

Secretary Rusk presented the recommendations on pages 17 and 18 of Secretary McNamara's report on Vietnam 16 March. He said that no one could guarantee that the proposed program would ensure success, but that if the situation in South Vietnam continued to deteriorate, the proposed recommendations provided for readying forces which could be used if it were decided later to take the war to North Vietnam.

Secretary McNamara said he had no additional comments to make but asked General Taylor to present the military actions discussed in the report. General Taylor began by commenting that high-level overflights of North Vietnam are now possible, but if we required low-level reconnaissance, we will have to use U.S. planes overtly. General Taylor then covered the sections of the report, including border control actions, retaliatory actions, and the graduated overt military pressure program. He said that the kinds of military actions he described would produce strong reactions in Cambodia and in North Vietnam including, as a final act, asking the Chinese Communists to come to their support. Risk of escalation would be greatest if we undertook the overt military pressure program, and before doing so, we would want to improve the readiness of U.S. naval forces in the Pacific.

General Taylor said the Chiefs support the McNamara report. They favor readying forces now which would be required if it were decided later to take

Summary Record of the 524th Meeting of the National Security Council, Washington, March 17, 1964, *Foreign Relations of the United States, 1964–1968, Volume I: Vietnam, 1964* (Washington, D.C.: GPO, 70–172.)

further military action than that recommended in the report. The Chiefs also want to examine the possibility of reducing from 72 to 24 hours the prior notice required to undertake actions against North Vietnam.

Secretary McNamara said that each Department and Agency concurs with the recommendations which fall in its area of responsibility. Ambassador Lodge agrees with all the recommendations except for his views on the need for overt reconnaissance of Cambodia. Mr. McGeorge Bundy pointed out that Ambassador Lodge's recommendation on Cambodian reconnaissance has been overtaken by events. No decision on this matter can be taken until we have further information about the conversations which are taking place between Khanh and the Cambodians.

The President said it was his understanding that Ambassador [to South Vietnam Henry Cabot] Lodge approved all the recommendations in the report except the one which has been overtaken by events and which he can be told lies in the area of unfinished business. The President then asked Secretary McNamara to summarize all twelve of his recommendations.

Secretary McNamara said as to cost, the program proposed would involve an expenditure of between $50 million and $60 million by the South Vietnamese, but that the actual cost to us would be approximately $30 million. Some of the cost will be covered by PL 480 funds and the remainder will come from reallocation of funds to meet the new plans. No supplemental budget request will be necessary.

Secretary McNamara covered very briefly all twelve recommendations. He agreed that the Joint Chiefs of Staff should study the proposal to reduce the 72-hour notice proposal contained in Recommendation 12. He agreed that this time should be reduced if it is possible to do so without resulting in the maldeployment of our forces in the Pacific.

The President asked Secretary McNamara if his program would reverse the current trend in South Vietnam. Secretary McNamara replied that if we carry out energetically the proposals he has made, Khanh can stem the tide in South Vietnam, and within four to six months, improve the situation there.

The President summarized the alternatives to the recommended course of action, i.e., putting in more U.S. forces, pulling out of the area, or neutralizing the area. He said the course we are following is the only realistic alternative. It will have the maximum effectiveness with the minimum loss.

General Taylor said the Chiefs believed the proposed program was acceptable, but it may not be sufficient to save the situation in Vietnam. He commented that the Chiefs' interest in military action against North Vietnam was based on their belief that action against North Vietnam might be necessary to make effective the program recommended by Secretary McNamara.

Secretary McNamara commented that Khanh had told him that he opposed taking the war to North Vietnam now because he felt that the South Vietnamese need a more secure base in the South before undertaking expanded military action.

The President said the McNamara proposals did not foreclose action later if the situation did not improve as we expected. He asked whether anyone present had any objections. Hearing none, he said the recommendations were approved.

The President, accompanied by Secretaries Rusk and McNamara, USIA Director [Carl T.] Rowan, and Mr. McGeorge Bundy, went to his office where a draft press statement was revised and later issued. . . .

5. White House Issues Optimistic Statement on South Vietnam, 1964

[Press release, 17 March 1964]

Secretary McNamara and General Taylor, following their initial oral report of Friday, today reported fully to President Johnson and the members of the National Security Council. The report covered the situation in South Viet-Nam, the measures being taken by General Khanh and his government, and the need for United States assistance to supplement and support these measures. There was also discussion of the continuing support and direction of the Viet Cong insurgency from North Viet-nam.

At the close of the meeting the President accepted the report and its principal recommendations, which had the support of the National Security Council and Ambassador Lodge.

Comparing the situation to last October, when Secretary McNamara and General Taylor last reported fully on it, there have unquestionably been setbacks. The Viet Cong have taken maximum advantage of two changes of government, and of more long-standing difficulties, including a serious weakness and over-extension which had developed in the basically sound hamlet program. The supply of arms and cadres from the north has continued; careful and sophisticated control of Viet Cong operations has been apparent; and evidence that such control is centered in Hanoi is clear and unmistakable.

To meet the situation, General Khanh and his government are acting vigorously and effectively. They have produced a sound central plan for the prosecution of the war, recognizing to a far greater degree than before the crucial role of economic and social, as well as military, action to ensure that areas cleared of the Viet Cong survive and prosper in freedom.

To carry out this plan, General Khanh requires the full enlistment of the people of South Viet-Nam, partly to augment the strength of his anti-guerrilla forces, but particularly to provide the administrators, health workers, teachers, and others who must follow up in cleared areas. To meet this need, and to provide a more equitable and common basis of service, General Khanh has informed us that he proposes in the near future to put into effect a National Mobilization Plan that will provide conditions and terms of service in appropriate jobs for all able-bodied South Vietnamese between certain ages.

In addition, steps are required to bring up to required levels the pay and status of the paramilitary forces and to create a highly trained guerrilla force that can beat the Viet Cong on its own ground. Finally, limited but significant additional equipment is proposed for the air forces, the river navy, and the mobile forces.

"White House Statement on the Situation in South Viet-nam," March 17, 1964 in *Public Papers of the Presidents of the United States. Lyndon B. Johnson: Containing the Public Messages, Speeches, and Statements of the President. 1963–1964.* (Washington, D.C.: GPO, 1965).

In short, where the South Vietnamese Government now has the power to clear any part of its territory, General Khanh's new program is designed to clear and to hold, step by step and province by province.

This program will involve substantial increases in cost to the South Vietnamese economy, which in turn depends heavily on United States economic aid. Additional, though less substantial, military assistance funds are also needed, and increased United States training activity both on the civil and military side. The policy should continue of withdrawing United States personnel where their roles can be assumed by South Vietnamese and of sending additional men if they are needed. It will remain the policy of the United States to furnish assistance and support to South Viet-Nam for as long as it is required to bring Communist aggression and terrorism under control.

Secretary McNamara and General Taylor reported their overall conclusion that with continued vigorous leadership from General Khanh and his government, and the carrying out of these steps, the situation can be significantly improved in the coming months.

6. Colonel John Paul Vann, a Field Officer, Denounces Inflated "Body Counts," 1968

[7 March 1968]

I finally secured a copy of your memo for the record of my visit and conversation with you in Washington. Despite the limited number of addressees, it apparently received rather wide distribution in Saigon. I found no inadequacies in your interpretation of what I said or meant and I think the events of the past five weeks tend to support the observations I made then.

I had an interesting visit with Phil Habib when he came over with General Wheeler, and subsequent to that, I had a three hour private luncheon with Ambassador Bunker. Both gentlemen received a considerably different evaluation of the events of the last five weeks than they had received through MACV channels. Both seemed to accept the fact that the MACV reporting system had a built-in upgrading factor which makes military assessments far more optimistic than is justified.

I participated (as a spectator) this past Monday (4 March) in an update briefing of General Westmoreland. I could not help but feel sorry for General Westmoreland since the purpose of his visit to our command was to kick ass and energize offensive operations, and all the wind was taken out of his sails by briefings (both US and Vietnamese) which indicated to him:

    a. The reported enemy KIA within III CTZ since 29 January of 16,000 was "absolutely valid," and "did not contain a large number of recently recruited youths or ammunition bearers."

    b. Further, the General was smothered with statistics as to the number of offensive operations that had been conducted during the month of February and the fact that we were consistently "killing 300 VC a day."

John Paul Vann to LeRoy Wehrle, 7 March 1968, John Paul Vann Papers, U.S. Army Military History Institute. Carlisle, Pa.

c. Not a single word of the briefing given to the General dwelt upon the many problems of GVN inactivity and the clutched-up defensive attitude of most province and district chiefs and their troops that exists within this CTZ.

d. Not one mention was made of the fact that the VC guerrillas were being given more freedom to intimidate the rural population than ever before in the past two and one half years.

The regrettable thing about all this is that General Westmoreland apparently came out (almost for the first time) specifically to challenge some of our claims and to do a little ass-kicking. Even with the counterattack received, the General did make a rather excellent speech emphasizing the need to go on the offensive and to take advantage of the obviously weakened and exposed condition of the VC. As I said at the start, I feel sorry for him because even his best subordinates (and I consider General Weyand his best) continually screen him from the realities of the situation in Vietnam. As an honorable man, he has no choice but to accept what they say and to report it all to his superiors.

I am also enclosing a message I sent to my troops on or about the 20th of February emphasizing the need to take advantage of the enemy's exposed position. You may find it of interest. I will admit to you that I attempted to be (as an incentive to the troops) more positive in my message than the situation actually warranted. Nevertheless, to quote an old Roosevelt saying, "The only thing we have to fear is fear itself." God knows the Vietnamese could not be more (at province and district level) in a defensive posture than they have continued to be since the first day of Tet. To sum it up, I consider that the enemy has less capability and is more vulnerable today than at any time before and that he has never been permitted freer access to the population than he has today. Obviously, we must correct this and do it fast.

I find it quote insulting (to Ambassador Bunker) that such criticism as was leveled by the press was leveled only at General Westmoreland. Quite obviously, the failures here in Vietnam have been more than failures in the military and failures in intelligence. I find it distressing that there does not seem to be any concerted effort being made in the intelligence community to assess the reasons for the massive intelligence failure that occurred. It is almost inconceivable that our penetrations and intelligence operations are so inept as to have permitted this to happen. I say this in recognition that we may have had "strategic" intelligence on the movement of the enemy forces toward the population centers, but we had a complete void of "tactical" intelligence that specified the targets, the methods of infiltration, the time and dates and locations.

I find it strange that no significant responsible official on either the Vietnamese or the US side is being relieved as a result of the VC Tet offensive. (The change of command in II and IV Corps had nothing to do with this subject.)

Well, enough for now. Will appreciate hearing from you when you have a chance.

Sincerely,

John P. Vann
Dep/CORDS

7. Lieutenant Commander Theodore R. ("T. R.") Swartz Thrills to Aerial Combat and Air Strikes (1967), 1989

In VA-76 we had some real warriors, guys like John Waples, Les Jackson, and Paul Hollingsworth. We lost the CO—Guy Fuller—to a SAM and the XO, Ken Cameron, went down early. . . .

It was kind of fun over the beach, like pro football where you take the ball, get on the field, kick everybody's ass, and come home. We weren't concerned with what the hell the war was all about; we were more concerned with getting it done right, getting everybody back, and doing some good damage to the enemy. The shots, of course, were still called by somebody way higher than us, but we were able to go up North of the 20th Parallel, into the Haiphong and Hanoi area, and targeting was fairly well open.

You don't forget how to be a fighter pilot, and I didn't let anyone in the squadron forget there was a real possibility one day they might have a MiG on their ass, and they ought to have an attitude developed in a training frame-of-mind that takes them to the point to not only get the son-of-a-bitch off their ass, but blow his brains out or at least scare him. A MiG pilot had no idea the A-4 didn't carry weapons that could hurt him, and he probably felt as apprehensive as we were. I think if you go up and meet somebody in the air and just act aggressive and point the airplane at him, and push him out in front of you, and shoot at him regardless of what the hell it is, he's going to think twice about who in the hell you are. I believe that is what I was pushing for in the attack community, because while we had gone through defensive tactic drills and offensive business, it wasn't getting sponsored a whole hell of a lot. . . .

A[n] interesting strike occurred in the early morning on July 21 when VF-24 and -211 bagged four MiGs. Mike Cater from VA-212 had the lead and I was Iron Hand, and Iron Hand was a good mission. Jack Monger was a good CAG, and he let a lot of us junior guys lead, and by junior I mean middle of the road lieutenant commanders. It gave us a lot of experience and a lot of confidence. As a strike lead, you got to look around and were pretty busy. As Iron Hand, you got to look around and duel the big red SAM.

At the time, we had the Shrike, and the little scope in the airplane that gave you targeting of the SAM. We didn't have many Shrikes; in fact, some of the missions were flown carrying the Shrike with orders not to shoot the damn thing, just go up and listen. For a while, we carried Zuni rockets, smoking them off to see if the jerks on the ground would shut down their radar, and I have no idea whether that worked or not.

The little A-4 was about as good an airplane as you could get to go out and duel with the SAM. It was maneuverable, and as long as you kept your heart going, your eyes out of the cockpit and saw all the SAMs, you'd stay alive. As Iron Hand, our job was to attract the SAMs, so we just went out and chummed, got the SAMs

Account of U.S. Navy's "Alpha" full carrier air strikes in the operation "Rolling Thunder": bombing campaign of North Vietnam in spring and summer 1967, printed in J. L. Levinson, *Alpha Strike Vietnam: The Navy's Air War, 1964–1973* (Novato, CA: Presidio Press, 1989). Reprinted with permission from *Alpha Strike Vietnam* © 1989 Jeffrey L. Levenson.

in the air, called them in the air, and protected the strike group. I flew a lot of Iron Hand and had only two or three close encounters, usually because I became triangulated. One site would shoot at me, and I'd turn into it; then another would shoot from behind, and you'd turn around to look at that one; then there'd be a third lift-off. The guys on the ground knew what Iron Hands were doing, and if the system worked right, they could get you. One particular day, I was worked down to about five hundred feet trying to get away from them. Fortunately it was a pretty non-defended area for guns, or else they would have eaten me up. The guys on the ground were good; they'd try and fake you out by bringing up the missile command guidance linkup, which really scared the hell out of you. The warning lights came on, and you'd think they're steering a missile when they weren't.

That morning I was Pouncer One, and because of our limited Iron Hand resources, Timmy Hubbard, an F-8 Crusader pilot, flew cover for me. I was up in front of the strike group about two or three miles, with my head in the scope and listening to the noise, the radar frequencies, and telling the guys information like there's a SAM site over in the valley to the right. Timmy Hubbard is on my right wing, and a pack of these bombers are behind us. Incredibly, a flight of eight MiG-17s crept between Timmy Hubbard and myself, and the strike group. They're all in a God damn column, like they're out for a Sunday parade. Waples saw them first, and Mike Cater looks up and says, "Jesus, they're dropping bombs." Well, in fact, they dropped fuel tanks. Waples said to me, "T. R., check your six, you've got a couple of MiGs back there." I looked around and said, "Two, shit, there's eight of them," and I call out something like "Get 'em Crusaders!" Red Issacks was in the strike; Phil Dempewolf; and Bob Kirkwood was the other MiG killer—all from VF-24 flying the F-8. In the melee that followed, four MiGs fell out of the sky, one of them Hubbard's.

[His plane] loaded as the morning flak suppressor, Timmy carried Zunis and poked a couple of those at the MiG, then put every bullet he had into that damn airplane, and the thing didn't fall out of the air. Timmy hollered "I'm ammo minus, and I'm running out of fuel. I've got to go." I said, "Okay, Pouncer Two," and I figured, Shit, here's number two. I've got a cripple and another God damn MiG. Well, Hubbard drives up beside this guy, and I'm one thousand feet from him, and about the time he gets beside the MiG, the guy gets out of the airplane, and the airplane blows up. So it was a confirmed kill for Timmy.

In all the confusion—and I'm taking pictures, doing a little Iron Hand, flying the stick, and listening to the bombers roll in—I end up kind of tailing the strike group. The Crusaders are milling around; they've managed to get four MiGs, and there's still four left. Red Issacks, he has two 17s behind him and they're both shooting at him, and his God damn left wing is on fire. He's burning bad and he said, "This is Page Boy Two. I'm hit, I'm burning. I've got two MiGs behind me." I said, "Okay, Red, turn right," because we were pretty close to the border, and I don't want him to go into China. I said, "Turn right, and I'll take care of the MiGs behind you." I came smoking across the circle we're flying with a Shrike on one wing and Zunis on the other, and arm up the Zunis. I poke two Zunis at these two airplanes at about one thousand feet, God damn near head on. [The Zunis] whizzed right through them, just scared the shit out of them, and they got off Red's ass. Red's wingman was some kid on his first God damn strike or something—lost the whole thing, never saw anything, and finally made it back to the ship.

One other incident took place that day between Bobby Kirkwood and Phil Dempewolf. I'm on top of these two when Kirkwood shoots a Sidewinder and gets a MiG. Dempewolf also shoots a Sidewinder, and it heads straight for Kirkwood's tailpipe. I'm looking down on this incredulously, and I'm saying to myself, Self, I know what I'm going to tell Kirkwood as soon as he's hit. I'm going to say, Hey Bobby, you've just been hit with a Sidewinder, that's your problem, better get ready to jump out of that thing. Just as the God damn Sidewinder approaches his tailpipe, Kirkwood launches another one, and the Sidewinder headed for him goes after the one he launched, lops off the starboard horizontal stabilizer of his airplane, and puts roller markers on the underside of the wing.

One of the missiles hit the MiG, and the other flies through the debris. Kirkwood keeps on going. Meanwhile, I've got my hands full and decide not to say shit about the whole thing because Kirkwood is still flying the airplane, and he doesn't have utility or hydraulic failure.

We got back, had this big debrief, and I said, "Okay, now I'm going to tell my story." They said, "Impossible," and I said, "Go out and look at the airplane." We went up on deck and the [plane's] starboard horizontal stabilizer was sliced off, and there's a big God damn line down the underside of the wing made by the stainless steel guidance and balance fins of the Sidewinder. Kirkwood about shit, and Dempewolf tried to claim a half kill. He's lucky he didn't get his ass kicked, but it was funnier than hell.

I don't know why I happened to get so lucky. I won one, had a draw on July 21, and saw some for the third time over the Hanoi lake. I guess it was being at the right place at the right time—there was a helluva lot of fighter pilots that never saw a MiG—and it was pretty active in 1967.

8. Specialist 4 Richard J. Ford III, a Black Soldier, Recounts the War and Racism (1967–1968), 1984

It was in June 1967. My MOS was mortarman, but they made me a rifleman first and sent me to Company C, 3rd Brigade, 25th Infantry Division. We was operating in Chu Lai, but we was a floatin' battalion.

It was really weird how the old guys would ask you what you want to carry. It wasn't a thing where you get assigned an M-14, M-16. If you want to carry an M-16, they say how many rounds of ammo do you want to carry? If you want to carry 2,000, we got it for you. How many grenades do you want? It was really something. We were so in the spirit that we hurt ourself. Guys would want to look like John Wayne. The dudes would just get in the country and say, "I want a .45. I want eight grenades. I want a bandolier. I want a thousand rounds ammo. I want ten clips. I want the works, right?" We never knew what the weight of this ammo is gon' be.

A lot of times guys be walkin' them hills, choppin' through them mountains, and the grenades start gettin' heavy. And you start throwin' your grenades under

From Wallace Terry. *Bloods: An Oral History of the Vietnam War by Black Veterans* (New York: Random House, 1984), 37–42.

bushes and takin' your bandoliers off. It wasn't ever questioned. We got back in the rear, and it wasn't questioned if you felt like goin' to get the same thing again next time.

Once I threw away about 200 rounds of ammo. They designated me to carry ammo for the M-60 machine gun. We was going through a stream above Chu Lai. I'm carrying my C rations, my air mattress, poncho, five quarts of water, everything that you own. The ammo was just too heavy. I threw away the ammo going through the river. I said it got lost. The terrain was so terrible, so thick, nobody could question that you lost it.

I come from a very religious family. So I'm carrying my sister's Bible, too. All my letters that I saved. And a little bottle of olive oil that my pastor gave me. Blessed olive oil. But I found it was a lot of guys in basic with me that were atheist. When we got to Vietnam there were no atheist. There was not one atheist in my unit. When we got hit, everybody hollered, "Oh, God, please help, please." And everybody want to wear a cross. Put a cross on their helmet. Something to psych you up.

Black guys would wear sunglasses, too. We would put on sunglasses walking in the jungle. Think about it, now. It was ridiculous. But we want to show how bad we are. How we're not scared. We be saying, "The Communists haven't made a bullet that can kill me." We had this attitude that I don't give a damn. That made us more aggressive, more ruthless, more careless. And a little more luckier than the person that was scared.

I guess that's why I volunteered for the LURPs and they brought me into Nha Trang. And it was six other black fellas to go to this school at the 5th Special Forces. And we would always be together in the field. Sometimes it would be Captain Park, this Korean, with us. Most of the time it was us, five or six black dudes making our own war, doing our thing alone.

There was Larry Hill from New York. Garland from Baltimore. Holmes from Georgia. Louis Ford from New Orleans. Moon from Detroit, too. They called him Sir Drawers, 'cause he wouldn't wear underwear. Said it gave him a rash. And this guy from Baton Rouge named Albert Davis. He was only 5 feet 9. Only 120 pounds. He was a terrific soldier. A lot of guts, a lot of heart. He was Sir Davis. I was Sir Ford. Like Knights of the Round Table. We be immortal. No one can kill us.

I didn't believe Nha Trang was still part of Vietnam, because they had barracks, hot water, had mess halls with three hot meals and air conditioning. Nha Trang was like a beach, a resort. They was ridin' around on paved streets. They be playing football and basketball. Nobody walked around with weapons. They were white. And that's what really freaked me out. All these white guys in the rear.

They told us we had to take our weapons to the armory and lock 'em up. We said naw. So they decided to let us keep our weapons till we went to this show.

It was a big club. Looked like 80 or 90 guys. Almost everybody is white. They had girls dancing and groups singin'. They reacted like we was some kind of animals, like we these guys from the boonies. They a little off. I don't know if I was paranoid or what. But they stare at you when you first come in. All of us got drunk and carryin' on. I didn't get drunk, 'cause I didn't drink. And we started firin' the weapons at the ceiling. Telling everybody to get out. "Y'all not in the war." We was frustrated because all these whites were in the back having a big show. And they were clerks. Next thing I know, about a hundred MPs all around the club. Well, they took our weapons. That was all.

The next day Davis got in trouble 'cause he wouldn't salute this little second lieutenant. See, we weren't allowed to salute anybody in the field. Officers didn't want you to. A sniper might blow his head off. The captain wanted to be average. He say, "I'm just like you, brother." When we got in the rear, it was hard for us to adjust to salutin' automatically.

When we got to be LURPs, we operated from Hill 54. Then they'd bring us in for like three days. They'd give you steak, all the beer you could drink. They know it's your last time. Some of us not coming back. We'd eat half the steaks, throw 'em away, have a ball. Go into town, and tear the town up.

Davis couldn't make no rank 'cause he got court-martialed for somethin' we do in town. We stole a jeep. Went to town. Tuy Hoa was off limits. Davis turned the jeep over comin' around one of them curves. But Davis was a born leader. He went back to the unit and got some more fools to get another jeep to push this jeep up. But he got court-martialed for stealin' the jeep. And for having United States currency.

Davis would take American money into town. Somebody send him $50, he get 3 to 1. Black market. First chance we go to town, he go get some cash. 'Cause he stayed high all the time. Smokin' marijuana, hashish. At mama san's house.

And some guys used to play this game. They would smoke this opium. They'd put a plastic bag over their head. Smoke all this smoke. See how long you could hold it. Lot of guys would pass out.

In the field most of the guys stayed high. Lot of them couldn't face it. In a sense, if you was high, it seemed like a game you was in. You didn't take it serious. It stopped a lot of nervous breakdown.

See, the thing about the field that was so bad was this. If I'm working on the job with you stateside and you're my friend, if you get killed, there's a compassion. My boss say, "Well, you better take a couple of days off. Get yourself together." But in the field, we can be the best of friends and you get blown away. They put a poncho around you and send you back. They tell 'em to keep moving.

We had a medic that give us a shot of morphine anytime you want one. I'm not talkin' about for wounded. I'm talkin' about when you want to just get high. So you can face it.

In the rear sometimes we get a grenade, dump the gunpowder out, break the firing pin. Then you'll go inside one of them little bourgeois clubs. Or go in the barracks where the supply guys are, sitting around playing bid whist and doing nothing. We act real crazy. Yell out, "Kill all y'all motherfuckers." Pull the pin and throw the grenade. And everybody would haul ass and get out. It would make a little pop sound. And we would laugh. You didn't see anybody jumpin' on them grenades.

One time in the field, though, I saw a white boy jump on a grenade. But I believe he was pushed. It ain't kill him. He lost both his legs.

The racial incidents didn't happen in the field. Just when we went to the back. It wasn't so much that they were against us. It was just that we felt that we were being taken advantage of, 'cause it seemed like more blacks in the field than in the rear.

In the rear we saw a bunch of rebel flags. They didn't mean nothing by the rebel flag. It was just saying we for the South. It didn't mean that they hated blacks. But after you in the field, you took the flags very personally.

One time we saw these flags in Nha Trang on the MP barracks. They was playing hillbilly music. Had their shoes off dancing. Had nice, pretty bunks. Mosquito nets over top the bunks. And had the nerve to have this camouflaged covers. Air conditioning. Cement floors. We just came out the jungles. We dirty, we smelly, hadn't shaved. We just went off. Said, "Y'all the real enemy. We stayin' here." We turned the bunks over, started tearing up the stereo. They just ran out. Next morning, they shipped us back up.

In the field, we had the utmost respect for each other, because when a fire fight is going on and everybody is facing north, you don't want to see nobody looking around south. If you was a member of the Ku Klux Klan, you didn't tell nobody.

Take them guys from West Virginia, Kentucky. First time they ever seen blacks was when they went in the service. One of them told me that the only thing he hate about the service was he had to leave his sheep. He said he used to never wear boots or shoes. He tell us how he cut a stump, put the sheep across the stump, and he would rape the sheep. Those guys were dumb, strong, but with no problems about us blacks. Matter of fact, the whites catered to the blacks in the infantry in the field.

Captain one time asked Davis what kind of car he gonna have when he get back in the States. Davis told him, "I'm not gonna get a car, sir. I'm gonna get me a Exxon station and give gas away to the brothers. Let them finish burnin' down what they leave." It wasn't funny if he said it in the stateside. But all of 'em bust out laughing.

We used to bathe in the stream. Shave and everything. Captain was telling Davis he had some Ivory soap. Davis said, "I don't take baths. Water rusts iron and put knots on the alligator's back." Creole talk. Everybody laugh. They know he don't bathe, but he was a terrific soldier. Small fella. He had one of the Napoleon complexes. Always had to prove something. He wasn't scared. He had more heart than anybody. They respected him, and they knew if you need fire cover or need help, he right there.

Right after Tet, the mail chopper got shot down. We moved to Tam Ky. We didn't have any mail in about three weeks. Then this lady by the name of Hanoi Helen come on the radio. She had a letter belong to Sir Drawers. From the chopper that was shot down. She read the letter from his wife about how she miss him. But that didn't unsettle the brothers as much as when she got on the air after Martin Luther King died, and they was rioting back home. She was saying, "Soul brothers, go home. Whitey raping your mothers and your daughters, burning down your homes. What you over here for? This is not your war. The war is a trick of the Capitalist empire to get rid of the blacks." I really thought—I really started believing it, because it was too many blacks than there should be in infantry.

And take the Montagnards, the brothers considered them brothers because they were dark. They had some of the prettiest ladies, pretty complexion, long hair, and they didn't wear no tops. Breasts would be exposed. And the Montagnard be walking with his water buffalo, his family, his crossbow. You waved at them, kept on walking. The people in Saigon didn't have anything to do with Montagnards. It was almost like white people in the States didn't have anything to do with blacks in the ghetto. So we would compare them with us.

I remember when we was stealing bananas in Pleiku and here come a bunch of Montagnards. Some white guys were talking about them: "Now I'd like to bang one of them." I remember Davis said, "Yeah. But you get that thought out your mind, 'cause I'll blow your brains out just for thinking it."

9. General William C. Westmoreland, Commander, U.S. Military Assistance Command Vietnam (MACV), Argues that the U.S. Could Have Won, 1976

As American commander in Vietnam, I underwent many frustrations, endured much interference, lived with countless irritations, swallowed many disappointments, bore considerable criticism. I saw any number of my proposals, which I was convinced were legitimate and would speed the conclusion of the American assignment, disapproved—such matters as troop strength, for example, minimum versus optimum force, drives into Laos and Cambodia, and so on. I took issue with the strategy of graduated response in the bombing of North Vietnam, with bomb halts, with holiday ceasefires. Yet I realized that air operations against North Vietnam were outside my jurisdiction, however much I might have thought they should have been part of it; and I saw the bombing policy not as leading to failure but only as delaying success.

Once the penchant of niggling officials in Washington for quibbling over B-52 bomb targets had passed, President Johnson and Secretary McNamara afforded me marked independence in how I ran the war within the borders of South Vietnam, and no commander could ever hope for greater support than I received from Admiral Sharp at CINCPAC and from General Wheeler and the other members of the Joint Chiefs. Yet a commander must recognize that political considerations will never allow total independence. Politicians are too imbued with French Premier Georges Clemenceau's dictum, however erroneously quoted, that "war is too important to be left to the generals." A commander must learn to live with frustration, interference, irritation, disappointment, and criticism, as long as he can be sure they do not contribute to failure. I suffered my problems in Vietnam because I believed that success eventually would be ours despite them, that they were not to be, as Napoleon put it, instruments of my army's downfall.

Only once did the possibility of resigning enter my mind, and that was not because of a question of success or failure. That happened early in 1968 when I saw the Joint Chiefs for a time leaning toward a parochial decision favoring one of the armed services in a matter that I saw as the field commander's prerogative and one that, if taken, would have been detrimental to my command.

Despite the long years of support and vast expenditure of lives and funds, the United States in the end abandoned South Vietnam. There is no other true way to

Gen. William C. Westmoreland. *A Soldier Reports* (NY: Doubleday, 1976), excerpts from pages 261–262, 408–412.

put it. We not only failed to react to the gross violations by the North Vietnamese of a solemn international agreement; we also failed to match the material support that the big Communist powers provided the North Vietnamese. We failed even to replace all expended South Vietnamese arms and equipment, as we were entitled to do by terms of the cease-fire agreement; and it was clear, as South Vietnam began to collapse, that the United States Congress was about to eliminate all assistance.

Presumably reflecting the attitude of a majority of the American people, the Congress was tired of the Vietnam struggle. . . .

The American people were tired of a war that had gone on for more than seventeen years, one in which their sons had been directly involved in a combat role for over seven years, one in which the vital security of the United States was not and possibly could not be clearly demonstrated and understood. Yet it need not have been that way.

Between 1963 and 1965, for example, when political chaos gripped South Vietnam and the lack of cohesiveness in the nation's heterogeneous society became clearly evident, the United States could have severed its commitment with justification and honor, though not without strong political reaction at home. Had not President Kennedy pledged the nation to bear any burden, meet any hardship, support any friend, and oppose any foe to assure the survival and the success of liberty? Indeed, Vietnam may have served a purpose for John F. Kennedy. Following his disastrous meeting with Khrushchev in Vienna in 1961, Kennedy allegedly told James Reston of the New York *Times:* "Now we have a problem in making our power credible, and Vietnam looks like the place."

Even after introduction of American combat troops into South Vietnam in 1965, the war still might have been ended within a few years, except for the ill-considered policy of graduated response against North Vietnam. Bomb a little bit, stop it a while to give the enemy a chance to cry uncle, then bomb a little bit more but never enough to really hurt. That was no way to win.

Yet even with the handicap of graduated response, the war still could have been brought to a favorable end following defeat of the enemy's Tet offensive in 1968. The United States had in South Vietnam at that time the finest military force— though not the largest—ever assembled. Had President Johnson changed our strategy and taken advantage of the enemy's weakness to enable me to carry out the operations we had planned over the preceding two years in Laos and Cambodia and north of the DMZ, along with intensified bombing and the mining of Haiphong Harbor, the North Vietnamese doubtlessly would have broken. But that was not to be. Press and television had created an aura not of victory but of defeat, which, coupled with the vocal antiwar elements, profoundly influenced timid officials in Washington. It was like two boxers in a ring, one having the other on the ropes, close to a knock-out, when the apparent winner's second inexplicably throws in the towel.

Aside from making the grave error of graduated response, failing to exploit the enemy's defeat in the Tet offensive, and abandoning South Vietnam in the end, the United States made other serious strategic mistakes in Vietnam and Southeast Asia: waiting so long to make incursions into Laos and Cambodia and even when eventually doing so, reducing their effectiveness by restrictions; failing to demonstrate to the North Vietnamese that they were vulnerable just north of the DMZ;

delaying so long in setting up a viable pacification organization in South Vietnam; going so slowly in re-equipping the ARVN, particularly with M-16s; failing to provide an international force along the DMZ; stopping the bombing of the enemy and thus facilitating the North Vietnamese build-up for the conventional invasion of 1972; failing to assure a strong ARVN chain of command in the northern provinces in anticipation of the 1972 offensive; not a strategic error in the usual sense but nonetheless of strategic impact, the policy of blanket educational draft deferments that created a working man's war and contributed to dissent at home.

Many of the errors could be traced to strong control of the conduct of the war from Washington, a policy born jointly of the failure of the Bay of Pigs invasion of Cuba in 1961, which demonstrated the perils of decentralization, and of the successful outcome of the Cuban missile crisis in 1962, which seemed to indicate that command from the White House was the only way to handle crisis and war in the nuclear age. Yet never was there created a central organization in Washington capable of exercising the necessary control; in the final analysis only the President could make a decision and then only after having listened to a host of sometimes conflicting voices.

Creating a unified command for all of Southeast Asia would have gone a long way toward mitigating the unprecedented centralization of authority in Washington and the preoccupation with minutiae at the Washington level. A unified commander provided with broad policy guidance and a political adviser would have obviated the bureaucratic wrangles that raged in Washington and resulted in military decisions strongly influenced by civilian officials who, however well-intentioned, lacked military expertise either from experience or study. Instead of five "commanders"—CINCPAC, COMUSMACV, and the American ambassadors to Thailand, Laos, and South Vietnam—there would have been one man directly answerable to the President on everything. Although that kind of organization might have created ripples within the service-conscious Joint Chiefs of Staff, the Joint Chiefs traditionally fall in line when the Commander in Chief speaks. Such an arrangement would have eliminated the problem of co-ordination between the air and ground wars that was inevitable with CINCPAC managing one, MACV the other.

Influencing many of the major decisions was an almost paranoid fear of nuclear confrontation with the Soviet Union and a corresponding anxiety over active participation by Chinese Communist troops. On those matters the President's advisers took undue council of their fears, for much of the time the Chinese Communists were heavily involved in their own internal problems—including the machinations of the "Red Guards"—and later the two Communist countries were preoccupied with friction along their common border, where the Soviet Union massed a threatening number of troops. Nor could the policy makers in the Departments of State and Defense conceive of the toughness and pertinacity of the North Vietnamese Communists. Surely they would back down in the face of threat or token commitment of forces by the world's greatest power; had not even the Russians backed down over Berlin and Cuba?

President Johnson's policy of guns *and* butter—pursuit of the "Great Society"—also exerted a strong influence. It further limited the President's strategic options, and it virtually foreordained the kind of long war that democracies are ill-prepared to sustain. When the President and his Administration failed to level with the American people about the extent and nature of the sacrifice that had to be made, they contributed to a credibility gap that grew into an unbridgeable chasm. A low-key approach means that some make sacrifices while most do not, and even those who make no sacrifice dislike it because their consciences trouble them. If a war is deemed worthy of the dedication and sacrifice of the military services, it is also worthy of the commitment of the entire population.

So too President Johnson erred in relying on the Gulf of Tonkin resolution as his authority from the Congress to do what he deemed necessary in Southeast Asia. When dissent developed in 1966 and 1967, he would have been well advised to have gone back to the Congress for reaffirmation of the commitment to South Vietnam, a vote either of confidence or rejection after the manner of the parliamentary system practiced in Great Britain and elsewhere. Given the American system of congressional elections every two years, a long undeclared war was bound to become a political issue. President Johnson with his normally keen appreciation for politics should have anticipated that and should have forced the Congress to face its constitutional responsibility for waging war.

By failing to level with the people and failing to impel the Congress to commit itself, the President allowed public opinion to become a leaden liability. Unlike Kennedy, Johnson did not have the background or style to carry public opinion with him, and he became a prisoner of it. If he declined to negotiate, when he well knew that the Communists entertained no idea of genuine negotiations except on their own terms, he appeared to many Americans to want the war to continue, however absurd that assumption might be. In the face of strident cries from the press, carping by legislators, and wild displays by demonstrators, he stopped the bombing when he knew that that would do nothing to stop the war but probably would prolong it. A most sensitive and conscientious statesman, President Johnson no doubt did his best; it was perhaps a situation beyond the mastery of any man. . . .

10. Sergeant Ron Kovic, Marine Veteran, Agonizes over the Meaning of the War and Recalls His Transition from Warrior to Dissenter, 1985

Ron Kovic: I'd like to first respond to something that wounded me very deeply last night. I patiently sat in the back of the room as James Webb began his keynote address. I began to realize that something very dangerous was happening . . . there was an attempt to undo everything that I and others had done. This man, in a very insensitive and callous fashion, was trying to negate my suffering, and the suffering of thousands and thousands of Americans and Vietnamese.

I was very upset. I felt physically wounded. I felt my wound come back to me. I was shot on January 20, 1968, through the right foot and the right shoulder. The bullet that hit my shoulder went through my lung and it severed my spinal cord, paralyzing me for life. It's taken me almost eighteen years to come to terms with

Ron Kovic, Marine veteran and author of *Born on the Fourth of July*, statements at a 1985 conference on the Vietnam War at the Asia Society in New York City, reprinted in *"Reading the Wind": The Literature of the Vietnam War*, An Interpretive Critique by Timothy J. Lomperis. (Durham, N.C.: Duke University Press, 1987; published for the Asia Society), pp. 26–27, 30–31. Reprinted with permission of The Asia Society.

my paralysis. I'm paralyzed from my mid-chest down—I can't feel or move any-thing from my chest down. I will never be able to walk again, or to make love. But I'm not complaining to you. I'm telling you that I'm strong and that I have my life together now. I feel a wholeness that I never believed in 1968 I would ever be able to feel.

That one speech last night drove deep into that wholeness, wounded me again, and allowed me to feel the weight of my injuries. I'm very proud of everybody here in the room—I'm very proud of all of you—and this talk last night: it tried to demean the precious and courageous and beautiful and sensitive and compassion-ate and compelling work that has been achieved by the authors in this room. I was very saddened and wounded. I looked to the person next to me and I said, "I'm feeling hurt again. I'm feeling wounded again." Then I turned to the person once more and I said, "No. You know what? I'm feeling America's wound. And I'm feeling how deep and grievous it is."

I wasn't angry at Jim. I was sad because this wound has not healed. It may never heal. . . .

Lightning Bolt II   The Rage

Ron Kovic: When I saw the wall [the Vietnam memorial] for the first time, I said, "My God, 58 thousand American boys killed because of the United States Govern-ment's foreign policy." Fifty-eight thousand killed because they lied to us, because they used us, because they fed us with all this crap about John Wayne and being a hero and the romance of war and everything we watched on television. They set up my generation, they set us up for that war. They made us believe that war was go-ing to be something glorious and something beautiful, just like they set up the vet-erans of World War I. The bands were playing. Everybody told us to go.

We had been the children of the Second World War. The Children, and we had gone without question. Many of us believed, and I have in the beginning of my book John F. Kennedy's January 20th, 1961, inaugural address, "Ask not what your country can do for you, but what you can do for your country." Millions of us were deeply touched by what John F. Kennedy said on that January day in 1961. I sat in my living room at 227 Toronto Avenue in Massapequa and tears streamed down my face because I felt that I had a purpose in my life. I felt that I had an obligation to serve my country. And I was used, and that's one of the great tor-ments of that war. All of this youth and beauty and life and all of this intelligence, and we were innocent. We really became intelligent when we realized that we had been used, and that our generation had been crushed by their madness and their lies and their ignorance.

When I see that wall, I see beautiful young men, I see sensitive men, I see high school graduates. I see myself on that goddamn wall and my whole generation plastered up there. I think about the twelve friends I have on that wall and how they'll never be able to say the things that I am saying right now. Did you ever think for a moment, did you ever think for one moment in your life, what would they say? What would the dead on that wall say? If they could speak, what would they say? "Gee whiz, I really love it here. It's really great being dead. It's really great being in the ground at 21 and not being able to breathe or to make love or to have a life." What if the dead could speak, because who speaks for the dead in this country? The government speaks for the dead. . . .

Let me lastly say that the wall stirs up deep emotions for all of us, and everyone will have their own interpretation of that wall. I was with Jan Scruggs [one of the directors of the Vietnam Memorial project] the other night. We did a television show together and I thanked him. I thanked him and I thank you [John Wheeler, the questioner of Kovic and another director of the project] for putting that wall up. I thank you for reminding all of us of our generation. I have only one criticism: that the words, "never again, never again," were not put above the names on that wall so that we do not kill another generation and we do not repeat the madness and insanity and the callous disregard for youth. Are we going to learn, are we going to grow, are we going to repeat it again? What kind of country is this, if we would ever let it happen again?

◣ *E S S A Y S*

Robert Buzzanco of the University of Houston and author of a 1996 book, *Masters of War: Military Dissent and Politics in the Vietnam Era,* in an essay written especially for this volume, criticizes the top civilian leadership, including Presidents Kennedy and Johnson, for ignoring military warnings against U.S. combat commitment in Vietnam. In the second essay, also written specifically for this volume, Major H. R. McMaster, commander of an Army tank unit in the Persian Gulf War, a Ph.D. in History from the University of North Carolina, and author of a 1997 book, *Dereliction of Duty: Johnson, McNamara, the Joint Chiefs of Staff, and the Lies that Led to Vietnam,* places particular blame not simply on the civilian leadership, primarily President Johnson and Secretary of Defense McNamara, but also on the Joint Chiefs of Staff, whom he accuses of abdicating their responsibility and failing to confront the president on a policy they considered fatally flawed.

Senior Military Officers Warned Against Vietnam

ROBERT BUZZANCO

American intervention in Vietnam was a profound tragedy, driven by a generation of American leaders who ignored their own judgments about events and conditions in Indochina. Despite recognizing the political, strategic, and moral barriers to success—both indigenous and international—civilian and military leaders assumed and expanded commitments to Vietnam, which only led to ultimate disaster. Rather than admit the shortcomings of U.S. policies, national leaders—compelled by larger forces such as containment, liberal political economy, domestic politics, and credibility—moved inexorably deeper into the abyss. As a result, the United States suffered a military defeat in Vietnam, with 58,000 Americans and millions of Vietnamese dead and a small nation devastated, which many ranking officials anticipated long before the war ended.

Written in 1997 specifically for this volume by Robert Buzzanco, author of *Masters of War: Military Dissent and Politics in the Vietnam Era* (NY: Cambridge Univ. Press, 1996). Reprinted with the permission of the author.

Vietnam qualifies as a military tragedy because so many influential national leaders realized for so long that they had little ability to succeed there, but continued along the path toward deeper involvement nonetheless. Individual opinions and the character of American officials meant little as systemic concerns about economic hegemony, prestige, power, and civil-military relations conditioned American decisions. Throughout the Vietnam era, many of the most influential U.S. military leaders recognized the peril of military involvement in Indochina and were mostly pessimistic about their chances for victory there; yet they accepted progressive responsibility for the war. For its part, the civilian establishment was unmoved by military objections about Vietnam and went to war there anyway. Under such circumstances, failure was always a strong possibility, if not a likelihood.

Throughout the war, ranking U.S. military representatives understood that political and military conditions in Vietnam were not favorable, and they were unlikely to measurably improve. As such, American officers recognized that the war was to be lost or won because of conditions in Vietnam, not, as many would later claim, because of weak politicians, the antiwar movement, or the media at home. Specifically, they saw that the enemy—whether it be the Viet Minh, National Liberation Front, Viet Cong, or People's Army of Vietnam—was militarily potent and politically popular and it represented the nationalist hopes of the people, while the ally—the Republic of Vietnam [RVN] and its Army in the south—had frequent and fundamental crises of legitimacy and stability; in terms of global strategy, service officials never considered Vietnam to be more than an area of peripheral interest; and militarily the brass was aware of the dangers of guerrilla warfare in the jungles of Indochina and never could agree on the way the war should be fought. Time and again, the military's reports and analyses of conditions in Vietnam offered bleak and pessimistic litanies about the problems facing American forces there. In the end, however, the military's objections remained subordinate to larger goals, and the war grew and dragged on.

U.S. military opposition to involvement in Vietnam was already evident at the end of World War II. American military and intelligence officials had worked alongside nationalist leader Ho Chi Minh during the war and had drawn favorable impressions of him. In 1949, the Joint Chiefs of Staff [JCS] noted the "widening political consciousness and the rise of militant nationalism among the subject people" of Vietnam and thus wisely argued that American involvement would be "an anti-historical act likely in the long run to create more problems than it solves and cause more damage than benefit." Throughout the early 1950s, and especially amid the 1954 Dien Bien Phu crisis, American officers, particularly Army Chief of Staff General Matthew Ridgway, firmly opposed any military commitment to Vietnam. They understood that the Nationalist-Communist forces of Ho and the Viet Minh who were fighting the French had broad popular appeal and would likely be viewed as the liberators of the Vietnamese people—Army officials estimated that 80 percent of the population supported Ho, but that 80 percent of his supporters were not Communists. Many further recognized that American units were "too ponderous" to fight in a guerrilla environment, that the country of Vietnam had virtually no logistics or communications capacity, and that the Viet Minh possessed the politico-military initiative throughout the country.

Such military sentiment was still pervasive in the following decade. Officers remained well aware of the problems confronting any U.S. military role in Vietnam and continued to offer candid and often bleak appraisals of American chances for success. During the Kennedy years, armed forces leaders showed no real desire for war in Vietnam in spite of the hawkish young president's escalation there. While JFK was increasing the number of U.S. "Advisors" from 800 to 16,000, beginning a war of attrition, deploying helicopters, and allowing the military to use napalm and defoliants in Vietnam, the military was hoping to avoid an armed engagement in Indochina. As Army Chief of Staff General George Decker explained, "there was no good place to fight" in Southeast Asia. Admiral Harry D. Felt, the military's Pacific Commander, likewise "strongly opposed" any troop deployments to Vietnam because the Vietnamese would likely do even less as U.S. soldiers took responsibility for fighting the VC. Felt's goal was thus to "help the Vietnamese get organized, get trained, [be] given the military equipment to fight their own war, but to keep U.S. troops out of that country." The presence of Americans in Vietnam, the Admiral added, would cause a "big fuss" throughout Asia "about the reintroduction of the forces of white colonialism."

The military's reluctance to fight in Vietnam stemmed from its awareness of conditions there. As General Lionel McGarr, the chief of the U.S. advisory group in Vietnam, reported, the NLF in 1961 already controlled 60 percent of South Vietnam and was gaining more, which was a "fatal" trend in his estimation. Worse, southern officials had made "little or no progress in developing an overall plan" for the war. Marine Commandant General David Shoup, later an outspoken antiwar activist, also opposed U.S. involvement "with no qualms whatever" because of the social chaos and military deficiencies of the ally in the south. General Wallace Greene, Shoup's successor as Commandant, agreed and told Marine officers that "frankly, . . . we do not want to get any more involved in Vietnam." Such resistance, Shoup maintained, was shared by "every responsible military man to my knowledge." Yet, into late 1963, there were no signs of American retreat in Indochina.

As Lyndon Johnson assumed the presidency in November 1963, he made clear his commitment to staying JFK's course, which meant "seeing things through in Vietnam." Fear of being blamed at home for "losing" Vietnam, as Truman had "lost" China, and his own commitment to economic hegemony and containment led the president to see Vietnam as a test case of American resolve. Accordingly, in just eighteen months, LBJ would quintuple the number of American military personnel there, authorize offensive operations, begin a massive air campaign, and introduce combat forces into the RVN in the south. What had been a limited advisory effort at the outset of the decade had become an "Americanized" war by 1965. And, once again, the military was not a driving force toward intervention.

The reluctance of the brass to wage war in Vietnam, if anything, grew even more clear in the first phase of LBJ's presidency. As Johnson took increasingly aggressive measures in Vietnam, he did so, as his predecessor had, with a clear awareness of the peril and problems facing him there. Military leaders continued to forward candid appraisals of conditions in Vietnam and repeatedly challenged the president and his secretary of defense, Robert McNamara, on their handling of the war. Throughout 1964 and early 1965, General Maxwell Taylor, past army chief and JCS chair and then ambassador to Saigon, sent a cascade of bleak and critical reports back to Washington about the situation in Vietnam. To Taylor, an increased U.S. military effort would lead to significant casualties, allow the South Vietnamese to relax as Americans took over the war, and lead to increasing resentment among the native peoples at the introduction of Caucasian forces into Indochina. As more American forces entered Vietnam, the General warned, RVN leaders would certainly "seek to unload other ground force tasks upon us," and lead to friction between American and Vietnamese officials over command arrangements.

Taylor saw the cultural barriers endemic to such military moves as well. The American "white-faced soldier" was not a "suitable guerrilla fighter for Asian forests and jungles," he realized. The French had discovered such shortcomings in their war against Ho in the early 1950s, and Taylor was full of "doubt that U.S. forces could do much better." Indeed, the general was so pessimistic that in 1965 he was urging "hard soul searching" on Vietnam and called for a reappraisal of U.S. options there, "which might entail ultimate withdrawal." Even the U.S. military commander in Vietnam, General William Westmoreland, essentially agreed with Taylor, pointing out that "a purely military solution is not possible" to the crisis in Vietnam. As late as January 1965, just ten weeks before the ground force deployments to Da Nang, Westmoreland remained opposed to such a move. Conceding that the American advisory effort had failed, the Commander saw "even less reason to think that U.S. *combat* forces would have the desired effect." The involvement of American soldiers in the Vietnam war, Westmoreland presciently concluded, "would at best buy time and would lead to ever increasing commitments until, like the French, we would be occupying an essentially hostile foreign country."

Such military views notwithstanding, LBJ took clear and decisive steps toward war in early 1965, first authorizing Operation Rolling Thunder, the most intense sustained air campaign in history, and, in March, sending Marine units ashore at Da Nang. The armed services accepted those decisions, but their anxiety about and criticism of intervention continued. Perhaps most importantly, the years between 1965 and 1968 were marked by one of the more divisive interservice conflicts over strategy in modern U.S. warfare. Westmoreland, per LBJ's dictum to "nail the coonskin to the wall" as soon as possible and thus keep Vietnam from eclipsing domestic issues, hoped to win via a strategy of attrition in which he would employ America's massive technological power in a torrent of firepower and air strikes against a group of scrappy Third World revolutionaries. Such an approach, as many officers charged, was fraught with peril. Marine leaders such as Commandant Wallace Greene and Pacific Commander Victor Krulak excoriated the Westmoreland strategy.

American firepower, they explained, was being used against the villagers of southern Vietnam, the very people the U.S. was there to "save." Attrition, to Krulak, was "wasteful of American lives" and it promised only "a protracted, strength-sapping battle with small likelihood of a successful outcome." The enemy, he explained, had a huge advantage in manpower, so U.S. forces could never erode Vietnamese forces to the point where victory would be likely. Commandant

Greene agreed and compared Westmoreland's strategy of attrition to "a grindstone that's being turned by the Communist side, and we're backing into it and having our skin taken off of our entire body without accomplishing a damn thing because they've got enough to keep the old stone going." The enemy's casualty rate "may be fifty times what ours is" but, Greene cautioned, the Communists will "be able to win through their capability to wage a war of attrition." Greene and Krulak thus urged a strategy of pacification, providing security and development to the villagers in the south while turning over responsibility for engaging the enemy to the RVN's forces.

So too did significant segments of the Army. In 1966, at the behest of Army Chief General Harold K. Johnson, junior officers prepared the so-called PROVN report, the "Program for the Pacification and Long-Term Development of South Vietnam." To gain "victory," the PROVN authors insisted, it was imperative to gain the support of the Vietnamese people at the local levels. The grassroots was where "the war must be fought . . . [and] won" and that could not be done through the massive use of firepower. The PROVN study, like the Marines' critique, was essentially ignored and attrition continued. Army officers also criticized the air war, which they believed had been seriously overhyped. Westmoreland himself doubted that U.S. air power could force the enemy to relent, and feared that excessive force could provoke a reaction by North Vietnam "that might overwhelm the existing unstable government" in the south in 1965. Admiral U.S. Grant Sharp, the Pacific Commander and a strident advocate of air power, had to concede that "the influx of men and materials" from north to south Vietnam had continued "despite considerable air effort expended to hinder infiltration." And Harold K. Johnson later contended that "if anything came out of Vietnam it was that airpower couldn't do the job."

Clearly, then, American military leaders recognized the perils of intervention and barriers to success in Vietnam, and had made known their objections. Yet, in the end, they supported and escalated a war that they understood was likely to end in failure. In large measure, this seemingly paradoxical or incoherent behavior stemmed from the nature of civil-military relations in the 1960s. From the "New Look" in the 1950s to the "Whiz Kids" in the early McNamara years, armed forces leaders had been engaging in political conflict with the civilian establishment over budgets and policy influence. In the Vietnam era, then, the brass, fearing the worst, accepted commitments in Indochina but always wanted to make sure that the civilian leadership would be held responsible when things turned sour. As early as 1961 General McGarr, seeing a "slimmer and slimmer" chance to "pull this one out of the fire," feared that the military would be blamed for the likely disaster in Vietnam. "As I am jealous of the professional good name of our Army," the General candidly admitted, "I do not wish it to be placed in the position of fighting a losing battle and being charged with the loss." Civilian officials were likewise concerned about the politics of failure. Jack Valenti, LBJ's trusted aide, urged the president to "sign on" the JCS before making a military commitment to Vietnam. Fearing a repeat of the MacArthur-Truman controversy, Valenti wanted to avoid recriminations between the brass and White House over Vietnam, and the JCS's support would be vital so that "our flank will have been covered in the event of some kind of flap or investigation later." In turn, Admiral Sharp warned Westmoreland of the "grave political implications" involved in committing U.S. troops in a losing engagement.

Such civil-military distrust and scheming continued to hamper American efforts as the war grew. By early 1967, JCS Chair Earle Wheeler was ordering Westmoreland to suppress statistics about enemy military success because, if made public, "they would, literally, blow the lid off of Washington." Admiral Sharp similarly instructed the Commander in Saigon to continue requesting more forces from the White House "even though you are not going to get them." In that way, LBJ, not the brass, would then be accountable for the U.S. failure. This point was not lost on the military, as American officers time and again lamented that the armed forces would "take the fall" for the Vietnam disaster. Civilian leaders were hoping to avoid responsibility as well. In February 1968, amid the Tet Crisis, LBJ worried aloud that Westmoreland and Wheeler would "ask for something, not get it [and then I would] have all the blame placed on me."

Now, thirty years later, there is plenty of blame to go around. U.S. officers early on understood the dangers of involvement in Vietnam and made their views known to their civilian superiors, and once committed to war in Indochina military leaders were deeply divided over how to fight the war there. For their part, civilian officials overlooked the military's objections because Vietnam had become a test case of American credibility, containment, and economic hegemony. Rather than confront the objective conditions in Vietnam—a militarily and politically superior enemy and a weak ally—American politicians and generals played politics to avoid blame for the coming failure. So while enemy forces were gaining a military victory in Vietnam, U.S. officials were looking for political vindication at home.

Senior Military Officers Were Derelict in Going Along

H. R. MCMASTER

As early as May of 1964, President Lyndon Johnson seemed to realize that an American war in Vietnam would be a costly failure. In a taped telephone conversation, he confided to his national security advisor, McGeorge Bundy, ". . . looks like to me that we're getting into another Korea. It just worries the hell out of me. I don't see what we can ever hope to get out of this." Vietnam was, Johnson observed, "the biggest damn mess that I ever saw . . . It's damn easy to get into a war, but . . . it's going to be harder to ever extricate yourself if you get in." Despite the president's premonition of disaster, a complicated chain of events and a complex web of decisions slowly transformed the conflict in Vietnam into an American war. Most historical investigations of how America entered the war have ignored the crucial developments of 1964 that shaped the president's approach to the war and created the conditions for a gradual intervention: the decisions that Americanized the war did not take place during the period February through July 1965 alone. Broad studies of post–World War II American involvement in Vietnam overempha-

---

"Web of Deceit: Civil-Military Relations and the Americanization of the Vietnam War" written in 1997 specifically for this volume by H. R. McMaster, Ph.D., author of *Dereliction of Duty: Johnson, McNamara, the Joint Chiefs of Staff, and the Lies that Led to Vietnam* (New York: HarperCollins, 1997).

size the continuities of American foreign policy, particularly the priority of containing communism. Containment was an important factor in Vietnam policy, but it did not make either entrance into the war or the manner in which the war was conducted inevitable. Indeed, not only was America's war in Vietnam not inevitable, it was only made possible by lies and deceptions aimed at the American public, Congress, and even members of LBJ's own administration. Although impersonal forces, such as the ideological imperative of containing communism, the bureaucratic structure, and institutional priorities influenced Lyndon Johnson's Vietnam decisions, those decisions depended primarily upon the character of the president, his motivations, and his relationships with his principal advisors. The president's fixation on short-term domestic political goals, combined with a civil-military relationship based in distrust and deceit, rendered the administration incapable of dealing adequately with the complexities of the situation in Vietnam.

No one clear decision led to direct American military intervention. There were several "turning points," however, in the American escalation between November 1963 and July 1965. The first was the near simultaneous assassinations of Ngo Dinh Diem and John F. Kennedy. After November 1963, America confronted what in many ways was a new war in South Vietnam. Having grown distressed over the South Vietnamese Government's brutal repression of Buddhist unrest, the Kennedy administration fomented a coup against long-time ally Ngo Dinh Diem that resulted in Diem's and his brother Nhu's deaths. With Diem gone, as President John F. Kennedy observed two weeks before his own death, the United States had "a responsibility to help this new government to be effective in every way we can." As America's responsibilities in South Vietnam widened, the Viet Cong sought to take advantage of the instability associated with the sudden change of government. The dynamic situation in the South after the Diem coup added impetus to deliberations in Washington. The new American president, Lyndon Johnson, and his advisors concluded that the situation in South Vietnam demanded action beyond military advice and support.

The next turning point occurred in the spring of 1964 when the Johnson Administration adopted "graduated pressure" as its strategic concept for the Vietnam War. Graduated pressure, which envisioned starting the application of force at a very low level and gradually increasing the use of force in scope and intensity, became the blueprint for deepening the American military commitment to maintaining South Vietnam's independence. Graduated pressure aimed to affect the enemy's calculation of interests through carefully selected and controlled actions designed to send the right "signal" to the enemy. In August 1964, the initial elements of graduated pressure, covert operations against North Vietnam, were already under way when the United States crossed the threshold of direct American military action against the North. After an August 2, 1964, North Vietnamese gunboat attack on U.S. destroyers in the Gulf of Tonkin, Lyndon Johnson seized on an ambiguous report of a second attack on August 4 to mount a political "coup" against his opponent in the November presidential election, Barry Goldwater. The Gulf of Tonkin resolution, which resulted from LBJ's guileful handling of the supposed second attack, gave the president *carte blanche* for escalating the war.

From September 1964 to February 1965, Lyndon Johnson advanced his domestic political agenda while his secretary of defense, Robert S. McNamara, refined and built consensus behind the strategic concept of graduated pressure. After previously refusing to respond militarily to Viet Cong attacks on U.S. soldiers and facilities, the president again raised U.S. intervention to a higher level in February and March 1965. After an attack on the U.S. air base at Pleiku, Johnson decided on February 9 to begin a systematic program of limited air strikes against targets in North Vietnam. On February 26, Johnson decided to commit U.S. ground forces to the South. Lastly, on March 15, 1965, he quietly gave U.S. ground forces the mission of "killing Viet Cong." All of those decisions, none in itself tantamount to a clear decision for war, nevertheless transformed America's commitment in Vietnam.

Viewed together, those decisions might create the impression of a deliberate determination on the part of the Johnson Administration to go to war. On the contrary, LBJ did not want to go to war in Vietnam and was not planning to do so. The president, rather, sought to avoid or to postpone indefinitely an explicit choice between war and disengagement from South Vietnam.

Johnson was a profoundly insecure man who feared dissent and was obsessed with preventing potentially damaging leaks to the press. In 1964, LBJ was preoccupied with winning the presidency in his own right. He saw Vietnam principally as a danger to that goal. After the election, he feared that a congressional or public debate over Vietnam policy would jeopardize the passage of his Great Society legislation through Congress. The Great Society was to be Lyndon Johnson's domestic political legacy and he could not tolerate the risk of its failure. McNamara would help the president first protect his electoral chances and then pass the Great Society by offering a strategy for Vietnam that appeared cheap and could be conducted with minimal public and congressional attention. McNamara's strategy of graduated pressure permitted Johnson to pursue his objective of not losing the war in Vietnam while postponing the "day of reckoning" and preserving an illusion of continuity with the policies of previous administrations.

LBJ's desire for consensus, rather than for wide-ranging debate on policy issues, shaped his relationship with the Joint Chiefs of Staff (JCS) and other advisors and determined who exerted influence over Vietnam policy. When the situation in Vietnam seemed to demand military action, Johnson did not turn to the JCS to explore the long-term costs and consequences of expanding the American military effort. He turned instead to his civilian advisors to determine how to postpone a decision. LBJ used McNamara to shield him from calls for more resolute action in Vietnam. The defense secretary's trips to Saigon created the impression that military recommendations were under serious study. The formation of *ad hoc* interdepartmental study groups had a similar effect. Additionally, McNamara used JCS Chairman Maxwell Taylor to prevent the chiefs' recommendations from even being considered. Taylor, who believed that the JCS chairman should be a "true believer in the foreign policy and military strategy of the administration which he serves," shielded LBJ from the views of his less politically sensitive colleagues while telling the chiefs that their recommendations had been given full consideration. To keep the chiefs from expressing dissenting views, Taylor helped to craft a civil-military relationship in which the president obscured the finality of decisions and made false promises that the JCS conception of the war might one day be realized. Meanwhile, with the JCS relegated to a position of little influence, the

Johnson administration's civilian planners developed a flawed strategy for fighting what seemed to them a war without precedent.

McNamara was confident in his ability to satisfy the president's desire to postpone a decision between war and disengagement in Vietnam. McNamara believed fervently that nuclear weapons and the Cold War international political environment had made traditional military experience and thinking not only irrelevant, but often dangerous for contemporary policy. Accordingly, McNamara, along with systems analysts and other civilian members of his own department and the department of state developed plans for Vietnam independent of military advice. Bolstered by what he regarded as a personal triumph during the Cuban missile crisis, McNamara drew heavily on that experience and applied it to Vietnam. One of the principal assumptions of graduated pressure, that carefully controlled and severely limited military actions were reversible, and therefore could be carried out at minimal risk and cost, allowed McNamara and Johnson to avoid confronting many of the possible consequences of those actions. Graduated pressure created the illusion that attacks on North Vietnam were means of communication and alternatives to acts of war, not acts of war themselves. Because the favored means of communication (bombing fixed installations and economic targets) were not appropriate for the mobile forces of the Viet Cong, McNamara and his colleagues pointed to the infiltration of men and supplies into South Vietnam as proof that the source and center of the enemy's power lay north of the 17th parallel, and specifically in Hanoi. They derived their definition of the enemy's source of strength from the strategy of graduated pressure rather than from a critical examination of the reality in South Vietnam.

Graduated pressure was fundamentally flawed in other ways. The strategy ignored the uncertainty of war and the unpredictable psychology of an activity that involves killing, death, and destruction. To the North Vietnamese, military action, involving as it did attacks on their forces and bombing of their territory, was not simply a means of communication. The human sacrifices of war evoke strong emotions that create a dynamic that defies systems analysis quantification. Once America crossed the threshold of war against North Vietnam with covert raids and the Gulf of Tonkin "reprisals," the future course of events depended not only on decisions made in Washington, but also on enemy responses and actions that were unpredictable. McNamara, however, viewed the war as another business management problem that, he assumed, would ultimately succumb to his reasoned judgment and others' rational calculations. He and his assistants thought that they could predict with great precision what amount of force applied in Vietnam would achieve the results they desired, and they believed that they could control that force with great precision from halfway around the world. There were, however, compelling contemporaneous arguments that graduated pressure would not affect Hanoi's will sufficiently to convince the North to desist from its support of the South, and that such a strategy would probably lead to an escalation of the war. Others, including Army Chief of Staff Harold K. Johnson, doubted that even the total destruction of North Vietnam would end the insurgency in the South. Nevertheless, Robert McNamara refused to consider the consequences of his recommendations and forged ahead oblivious to the nature of the conflict in South Vietnam and the human and psychological complexities of war.

Despite their recognition that graduated pressure was fundamentally flawed, the JCS were unable to articulate effectively either their objections or alternatives. Inter service rivalry was a significant impediment. Although differing perspectives were understandable given the chiefs' long experience in their own services and their need to protect the interests of their services, the JCS were obligated by law to render their best advice. Their failure to do so and their willingness to present single-service remedies to a complex military problem prevented them from thinking effectively about strategy. The chiefs, in large measure, abdicated their statutory responsibility as "principal military advisers."

When it became clear to the chiefs that they were to have little influence on the policymaking process, they refused to confront the president with their objections to McNamara's approach to the war. Instead, they attempted to work within that strategy in order to remove over time the limitations to further action. Unable to develop an alternative to graduated pressure, the chiefs became fixated on means and pressed for an escalation of the war by degrees. They hoped that graduated pressure would evolve over time into a fundamentally different strategy, more in keeping with their general belief in the necessity of greater force and its more resolute application. In so doing, they gave tacit approval to graduated pressure during the critical period in which the president escalated the war. They failed to make a recommendation for the total force that they believed would ultimately be required in Vietnam and accepted a strategy that they knew would lead to a large but inadequate commitment of troops, for an extended period of time with little hope for success.

Johnson and McNamara were far from disappointed with the Joint Chiefs' failings. Johnson, because his priorities were domestic, had little use for military advice that recommended actions inconsistent with those priorities. McNamara had resolved to use JCS weaknesses against them. He reported to LBJ in March 1964 that a "divide and conquer" approach to the JCS was "coming along pretty well." For military advice, McNamara relied primarily on the Defense Department's "whiz kids," a group of young analysts and attorneys whom McNamara and Kennedy had drawn into government service. The whiz kids considered military experience a liability because military officers took too narrow a view and based their advice on antiquated notions of war. McNamara's top analyst, Alain Enthoven, likened leaving military decision-making to the professional military to allowing welfare workers to develop national welfare programs. Enthoven, convinced that "there was little in the typical officer's early career that qualifies him to be a better strategic planner than . . . a graduate of the Harvard Business School," used statistics to analyze defense programs and issues and then gave the secretary of defense and the president information needed to make decisions. The whiz kids saw no limits to the applicability of their methods. They sought to achieve maximum political payoff in Vietnam at minimal military cost and assumed that Ho Chin Minh, when faced with the threat of American military "muscle," would behave reasonably and end Hanoi's support for the Vietnamese Communist insurgency in South Vietnam.

Rather than advice, McNamara and Johnson extracted from the JCS acquiescence and silent support for decisions already made. Even as they relegated the chiefs to a peripheral position in the policymaking process, McNamara and Johnson were careful to preserve a facade of consultation to prevent the JCS from opposing the administration's policies either openly or behind the scenes. As American involvement in the war escalated, Johnson's vulnerability to disaffected senior military officers increased because he was purposely deceiving the Congress and the public about the nature of the American military effort in Vietnam. To keep the chiefs on the team, the president and the secretary of defense deliberately obscured the nature of decisions made and left undefined the limits that they envisioned on the use of force. In April 1965, LBJ promised the JCS to invest whatever money, materiel, or effort necessary "to win the game" in South Vietnam and "start killing more Viet Cong." Johnson played for the chiefs' sympathy, citing opposition to his policy and referring to himself as the "coach" and the JCS as "his team."

The ultimate test of the chiefs' loyalty came in July 1965. The administration's lies to the American public had grown in magnitude as the American military effort in Vietnam escalated. The president had misrepresented the mission of U.S. ground forces in Vietnam, distorted the views of the chiefs to lend credibility to his decision against mobilization, grossly understated the numbers of troops General Westmoreland had requested, and lied to the Congress about the monetary cost of actions already approved and of those awaiting final decision. The chiefs did not disappoint the president. In the days before the president made his duplicitous July 28, 1965, public statement concerning Westmoreland's request for additional ground combat units, the chiefs withheld from congressmen their estimates of the amount of force that would be needed in Vietnam thereby lending silent support to the president's deceptions.

Several factors kept the chiefs from challenging the president's subterfuges. The professional code of the military officer prohibits him or her from engaging in political activity. Actions that could have undermined the administration's credibility and derail its Vietnam policy could not have been undertaken lightly. The chiefs felt loyalty to their commander-in-chief. In particular, Army General Earle Wheeler, who succeeded Maxwell Taylor as JCS Chairman in July 1964, believed that the war in Vietnam could "be lost in Washington if Congress loses faith." Additionally, the Truman-MacArthur controversy during the Korean War had warned the chiefs about the dangers of overstepping the bounds of civilian control. Loyalty to their services also weighed against opposing the president and the secretary of defense. Army Chief of Staff Harold K. Johnson, for example, did not resign because he thought he had to remain in office to protect the Army's interests as best he could. Chief of Naval Operations David McDonald and Marine Corps Commandant Wallace Green compromised their views on Vietnam in exchange for concessions to their respective services. None of the chiefs had sworn an oath to his service, however. They had all sworn, rather, to "support and defend the Constitution of the United States." General Greene recalled that congressional requests for his assessment put him in a difficult situation, and indeed they had. The president was lying, and he expected the chiefs to lie as well or, at least, to withhold the whole truth. Although the president should not have placed the chiefs in that position, the flag officers should not have tolerated it when he had.

Because the Constitution locates civilian control of the military in Congress as well as in the executive branch, the chiefs could not have been justified in deceiving the peoples' representatives about Vietnam. As cadets are taught at West Point, the JCS relationship with Congress is challenging and demands that military officers possess a strong character and keen intellect. While the chiefs must present Congress with their best advice based on their professional experience and education, they must be careful not to overstep the bounds of civil control or undermine their credibility by crossing the line between advice and advocacy of service interests.

The way in which the United States went to war in the period between November 1963 and July 1965, not surprisingly, had a profound influence on the conduct of the war and on its outcome. Because Vietnam policy decisions were made based on domestic political expediency and because the president was intent on forging a consensus position behind what he believed was a middle policy, the administration deliberately avoided clarifying its policy objectives and postponed discussing the level of force that the president was willing to commit to the effort. Indeed, because the president was seeking a political consensus built on lies and obfuscation, members of the administration believed that ambiguity in the objectives for fighting in Vietnam was a strength rather than a weakness. Civilian planners in the Defense and State Departments believed that it would be possible to preserve American credibility after a show of force against the Communists in which American forces were "bloodied." That conclusion, combined with the belief that the use of force was merely another form of diplomatic communication, directed the military effort in the South at achieving stalemate rather than victory. After the U.S. became committed to war, however, and more American soldiers, airmen, and Marines had died in the conflict, it would become impossible simply to disengage and declare America's credibility intact, a fact which should have been foreseen. The chiefs sensed the ambiguity in LBJ's policy, but did not directly challenge the views of civilian planners in that connection. As a result, when the United States went to war, the JCS pursued objectives different from those of the president and the secretary of defense. When the chiefs requested permission to apply force consistent with their conception of U.S. objectives, the president and McNamara, based on their goals and domestic political constraints, rejected JCS requests, or granted them only in part. The JCS and McNamara became fixated on means rather than on ends, and on tactics rather than on a strategy designed to connect military actions to achievable policy goals.

Because forthright communication between top civilian and military officials in the Johnson Administration was never developed, there was no reconciliation of McNamara's intention to limit the American military effort sharply and the chiefs' assessment that the United States could not possibly win under such conditions. If they had attempted to reconcile those positions, they could not have helped but recognize the futility of the American war effort.

The JCS became accomplices in the President's deception and focused on a tactical task, killing the enemy. General William Westmoreland's "strategy" of attrition in South Vietnam was, in essence, the absence of a strategy. The result was military activity (bombing North Vietnam and killing the enemy in South Vietnam) that did not aim to achieve a clearly defined objective. As American casualties mounted and the futility of the war became apparent, the American public lost faith in the effort. The chiefs did not request the number of troops necessary to impose a military solution in South Vietnam until after the Tet offensive in 1968. By that time, however, the president was besieged by opposition to the war and was unable even to consider the request.

Johnson thought that he would be able to control the United States' involvement in Vietnam. That belief, based in the strategy of graduated pressure and the confident assurances of Robert McNamara, proved, in dramatic fashion, to be false. If LBJ was surprised by the consequences of his decisions during the period November 1963 to July 1965, he should not have been so. He had disregarded the advice he did not want to hear in favor of a policy based on the pursuit of his own political fortunes and his beloved domestic programs.

The war in Vietnam was not lost in the field, nor was it lost on the front pages of the *New York Times* or on the college campuses. It was lost in Washington, D.C. even before Americans assumed responsibility for the fighting in 1965 and before they realized the country was at war. The disaster in Vietnam was a uniquely human failure, the responsibility for which was shared by Lyndon Johnson and his principal military and civilian advisors. During the critical period in which Vietnam became an American war, a deceitful and manipulative civil-military relationship allowed the president to neglect the consequences of his decisions and deny the American Congress and public a say in the most momentous issue a nation must face.

⚔ F U R T H E R   R E A D I N G

Christian G. Appy, *Working-Class War: American Combat Soldiers and Vietnam* (1993).

Larry Berman, *Lyndon Johnson's War: The Road to Stalemate in Vietnam* (1989).

Michael R. Beschloss, ed., *Taking Charge: The Johnson White House Tapes, 1963–1964* (1997).

Walter J. Boyne, *Beyond the Wild Blue: A History of the United States Air Force, 1947–1997* (1997).

Robert Buzzanco, *Masters of War: Military Dissent and Politics in the Vietnam Era* (1996).

Larry E. Cable, *Conflict of Myths: The Development of American Counterinsurgency Doctrine and the Vietnam War* (1986).

Jeffrey J. Clarke, *U.S. Army in Vietnam; Advice and Support: The Final Years, 1965–1973* (1988).

Mark Clodfelter, *The Limits of Air Power: The American Bombing of North Vietnam* (1989).

William Colby and James McCargar, *Lost Victory: A Firsthand Account of America's Sixteen-Year Involvement in Vietnam* (1989).

Graham A. Cosmas and Terrence P. Murray, *U.S. Marines in Vietnam, 1970–1971* (1986).

Victor Croziat, *The Brown Water Navy: The River and Coastal War in Indochina and Vietnam, 1948–1972* (1984).

Phillip B. Davidson, *Vietnam at War, The History: 1946–1975* (1988).

Charles DeBenedetti and Charles Chatfield, *An American Ordeal: The Antiwar Movement of the Vietnam Era* (1990).

Bernard Edelman, ed., *Dear America: Letters Home from Vietnam* (1985).

H. Bruce Franklin, *M.I.A., or, Mythmaking in America* (1992).

Lloyd C. Gardner, *Pay Any Price: Lyndon Johnson and the Wars for Vietnam* (1995).

Leslie H. Gelb and Richard K. Betts, *The Irony of Vietnam: The System Worked* (1979).

William M. Hammond, *U.S. Army in Vietnam: Public Affairs: The Military and the Media, 1962–1968* (1988).

George Herring, *America's Longest War: The United States and Vietnam, 1950–1975*, 3d ed. (1996).

Craig Howes, *Voices of the Vietnam POWs: Witnesses to Their Fight* (1993).

Lyndon Baines Johnson, *The Vantage Point: Perspectives of the Presidency, 1963–1969* (1971).

Jeffrey P. Kimball, ed., *To Reason Why: The Debate About the Causes of U.S. Involvement in the Vietnam War* (1990).

Douglas Kinnard, *The Certain Trumpet: Maxwell Taylor and the American Experience in Vietnam* (1991).

Andrew F. Krepinevich, Jr., *The Army and Vietnam* (1986).

Jeffrey L. Levinson, *Alpha Strike Vietnam: The Navy's Air War, 1964–1973* (1989).

Guenter Lewy, *America in Vietnam* (1978).

H. R. McMaster, *Dereliction of Duty: Lyndon Johnson, Robert McNamara, the Joint Chiefs of Staff, and the Lies That Led to Vietnam* (1997).

Robert S. McNamara, *In Retrospect: The Tragedy and Lessons of Vietnam* (1995).

Harold G. Moore and Joseph L. Galloway, *We Were Soldiers Once . . . And Young* (1992).

Richard R. Moser, *The New Winter Soldiers: GI and Veteran Dissent During the Vietnam Era* (1996).

Charles C. Moskos, *The American Enlisted Man: The Rank and File in Today's Military* (1970).

John E. Mueller, *War, Presidents, and Public Opinion* (1973).

Bernard C. Nalty, *Air Power and the Fight for Khe Sanh* (1973).

Elizabeth M. Norman, *Women at War: The Story of Fifty Military Nurses Who Served in Vietnam* (1990).

Bruce Palmer, Jr., *The 25-Year War: America's Military Role in Vietnam* (1984).

R. L. Schreadley, *From the Rivers to the Sea: The U.S. Navy in Vietnam* (1992).

D. Michael Shafer, ed., *The Legacy: The Vietnam War in the American Imagination* (1990).

Ulysses S. Grant Sharp, *Strategy for Defeat: Vietnam in Retrospect* (1978).

Neil Sheehan, *A Bright Shining Lie: John Paul Vann and America in Vietnam* (1988).

Dennis E. Showalter and John G. Albert, eds., *An American Dilemma: Vietnam, 1964–1973* (1993).

Melvin Small, *Johnson, Nixon, and the Doves* (1988).

Lewis Sorley, *Honorable Warrior: General Harold K. Johnson and the Ethics of Command* (1998).

Ronald H. Spector, *The U.S. Army in Vietnam: Advice and Support: The Early Years* (1983).

Shelby L. Stanton, *Green Berets at War: U.S. Army Special Forces in Southeast Asia, 1956–1975* (1985).

Harry G. Summers, Jr., *On Strategy: A Critical Analysis of the Vietnam War* (1982).

Maxwell D. Taylor, *Swords and Plowshares* (1972).

Truong Nhu Tang, *A Vietcong Memoir* (1985).

Wallace Terry, ed., *Bloods: An Oral History of the Vietnam War by Black Veterans* (1984).

E. H. Tilford, Jr., *Setup: What the Air Force Did to Vietnam and Why* (1991).

Frank Uhlig, Jr., ed., *Vietnam: The Naval Story* (1986).

Brian VanDeMark, *Into the Quagmire: Lyndon Johnson and the Escalation of the Vietnam War* (1991).

Keith Walker, ed., *A Piece of My Heart: The Stories of 26 American Women Who Served in Vietnam* (1985).

James E. Westheider, *Fighting on Two Fronts: African Americans and the Vietnam War* (1997).

William C. Westmoreland, *A Soldier Reports* (1976).

James J. Wirtz, *The Tet Offensive: Intelligence Failure in War* (1991).

C H A P T E R
15

The Persian Gulf War
and Peacekeeping
in the Post–Cold War World

Since the mid-1970s, the U.S. armed forces have undergone a number of significant changes. At the end of the Vietnam War, the selected draft was ended, and the resulting All-Volunteer Force included increased percentages of minorities and women (the latter contributing to a major debate over whether women should be included in combat units). Reservists became an integral part of the new Total Force structure. With the breakup of the Soviet empire beginning in 1989, the collapse of the Communist regimes in Russia and Eastern Europe, and the end of the Cold War, the United States faced a new international environment. In the strategic planning for a post–Cold War world, the U.S. armed forces were to be prepared to fight regional wars if necessary, potentially containing rogue states on the Korean peninsula and around the Persian Gulf. The U.S. military also began to prepare for a number of new missions, including countering terrorism and drug-trafficking; protecting borders; and, most prominently, engaging in UN-directed humanitarian peacekeeping missions in countries torn by ethnic, political, and other civil strife.

The largest military operation of the post–Cold War period was the Persian Gulf War of 1990–1991. In the wake of Iraqi dictator Saddam Hussein's conquest of neighboring oil-rich Kuwait in August 1990, President George Bush put together a UN-sponsored military coalition from 24 Arab and other nations. Operation DESERT SHIELD blocked Iraqi forces from pushing beyond Kuwait. Then, between January 15 and February 27, 1991, in Operation DESERT STORM, the Allied forces liberated Kuwait. The air campaign lasted just over a month; the ground offensive achieved its objectives in less than a week. Under the command of U.S. Army General H. Norman Schwarzkopf, the Allied forces completely routed the Iraqi army, capturing some 86,000 enemy soldiers, and driving Saddam's Republican Guards and other units back into Iraq. It was a massive application of force, producing a dramatic military victory. The 254,000 Allied forces suffered only 92 combat deaths and some 300 wounded in liberating Kuwait. After the cease-fire, President Bush declared that the "Vietnam Syndrome" was over.

Subsequently, the major military debates about the Persian Gulf War have involved the war aims, means, and results. Military analysts and the armed forces themselves have debated the services' relative contributions to victory and what the Persian Gulf War portended for the future of warfare and for each branch of the service. Did airpower win the war? Or can war only be won on the ground? The debate over the war aims and results began as soon as the proclamation of the ceasefire, for the Allied ground offensive stopped at the border of Iraq, thus leaving Saddam Hussein in power in Baghdad and able with his remaining forces to crush subsequent internal uprisings against his regime. Some argued that Saddam's aggressive regime, with its ability to build and store chemical and nuclear weapons of mass destruction, should be toppled by a continuation of the war. Others warned of high Allied casualties and the withdrawal of Arab support if the United States had sought to lead the invading forces into the urban areas of Iraq.

In regard to UN peacemaking and peacekeeping operations in the post-Cold War world, the U.S. military in the 1990s was prominently involved in operations in Somalia, Haiti, and most extensively in Bosnia. After five years of bloody civil war in Bosnia among ethnic Serbs, ethnic Croats, and Bosnian Muslims, the combination of a massive NATO air campaign and a Croat-Muslim ground offensive in 1995 brought three contending Balkan presidents to Wright-Patterson Air Force Base in Dayton, Ohio; there they signed the accords that ended the civil war and provided for a Bosnian Republic of two "entities," divided 49 percent for the Bosnian Serbs and 51 percent for a federation of Muslims and Croats. To enforce the agreement, NATO and other nations agreed after the formal signing of the peace accord in December 1995 to send to Bosnia 60,000 peacekeeping troops, 20,000 of them U.S. soldiers (Britain and France were the other main contributors). Americans were divided over the deployment of U.S. troops in the strife-torn Balkans. Their position was based mainly on whether or not they thought there were American national interests or overriding humanitarian needs there. Military analysts and others debated the roles and missions of the military in such peacekeeping operations. Were the military acting as soldiers? As police? As humanitarian relief workers? What was the acceptable use of force in such complex civil-military functions?

Although President Bill Clinton initially declared that the American peacekeepers would be withdrawn within one year, continuing political conflicts in the region kept the peacekeepers in Bosnia for several years, although in reduced numbers. With ethnic civil strife rampant in many parts of the world, and with the American public displaying differing views, from the public rejection of that role in Somalia to reluctant acceptance in Bosnia, the future of the peacekeeping role of the United States armed forces remained an open question.

♠ D O C U M E N T S

In the first document, a debate in *Army Magazine* in March 1980, over whether women should be included in combat units, Major Richard A. Gabriel, a reserve army officer and a professor of political science at St. Anselm's College in Manchester, New Hampshire, argues that the presence of women could impede the ability of troops to maintain cohesive bonding under fire; Major Doris H. Kessler, a member of the Army's Adjutant General's Corps, and at the time a member of the CINC-PAC staff,

Hawaii, countered that in the modern military, women possess the qualities to defend the nation and must be entrusted with its firepower. In the second document, Air Force Captain Jack Thompson, an F-16 pilot in the Persian Gulf War, recalls being part of an air strike against a nuclear research facility south of Baghdad in the opening days of the war, January 1991. In the third document, Army Captain H. R. McMaster, commander of Eagle Troop, 2nd Squadron, 2nd Armored Cavalry Regiment, recounts the engagement of his troop of Abrams tanks and Bradley Fighting Vehicles on the second day of the ground offensive, February 26, 1991, as the outnumbered Americans surprised and stormed through an Iraqi position, destroying 30 enemy tanks, 20 personnel carriers, and several dozen trucks, and capturing several hundred enemy prisoners. General H. Norman Schwarzkopf was praised for his victory, but criticized by some for stopping at the Iraqi border after liberating Kuwait; in the fourth document, the conclusion to his 1992 memoir, he addresses some of the major criticism of his goals and methods. The air war against Iraq proved so spectacular, particularly as projected by the media, that some commentators believed it presaged a "revolution in warfare." Others, particularly in the Army, Navy, and Marines, contested such a view. Consequently, the Secretary of the Air Force commissioned an independent study, the Gulf War Air Power Survey, which, like the U.S. Strategic Bombing Survey following World War II, sought to assess the strategic effectiveness of airpower. The fifth document, an excerpt from a 1995 reprinting of the Survey's 1993 Summary Report, pinpoints the major accomplishments of the air forces of the Allied Coalition.

With the end of the Cold War, a major new role of the U.S. Army is a peacekeeping mission. In the sixth document, a speech on December 7, 1995, to the Center for Strategic Studies in Washington, D.C., Secretary of Defense William Perry justifies President Bill Clinton's decision to send U.S. military units as peacekeepers to Bosnia, the largest American peacekeeping mission in the twentieth century.

1. Major Doris Kessler and Major Richard Gabriel, Both U.S. Army, Debate Women in Combat, 1980

Major Doris H. Kessler

America has viewed its women as everlasting children and has protected them as it protects a child. In its solicitude, America has tried to protect women from challenges, experiences and opportunities that would lead to women hurting themselves, being taken advantage of, but most of all, developing male-like characteristics such as self-reliance and physical and psychological toughness.

Although all children develop these characteristics as they grow into adulthood, women have been taught not to exhibit them, and society has ignored the fact that women possess them by continuing to safeguard its adult females. It is no accident that one still sees concessionaires' signs advertising a special "ladies night" or free admission for "women and children."

Lately however, society's protection of women has lessened. National need has been the primary reason for reevaluating attitudes about what women should

"Women in Combat? Two Views," Maj. Doris Kessler and Maj. Richard A. Gabriel, *Army* Magazine, Vol. 30, no. 3 (March 1980), pp. 44–45, 47–50, 52. From *Army* Magazine, March 1980, Copyright 1980 by the Association of the U.S. Army and reproduced by permission.

be allowed to do, particularly in the armed forces. The need exists because enough men can no longer be drafted into jobs necessary to sustain the Army. National need has also governed national attitudes formulated in the past.

For example, during World War II the country had to depend upon segments of its population it had previously considered less than full-fledged adults. Black men were drafted into the services and given the attribute of "brave men," although before that time, black men had been called "boys."

Women were called from the home and put into defense plants to work in jobs previously considered too hard for them. When the crisis was over, both groups were asked to step back into their former, less responsible roles. One group did not, but women did because they felt it was incumbent upon them to return to the homes that the fighting men had defended.

But young women today feel no similar obligation to the nation's men. Their childhood impressions of men include the antiwar demonstrations of the 1960s; furthermore, the war in Vietnam did not impose the same global threat on home and family as did World War II.

The idea that a man will fight to protect the home and woman who tends it is alien to them. Young women see themselves as those best fit to defend what is important to them, whether it be the home, the right to train for and maintain a nontraditional job, or to take a more active part than previously sought in the military defense of the country.

The nation's leaders and those who direct military affairs have sanctioned the attitudes of today's young women, but the extent of their approval has not yet been clearly defined. They have opened more and more military occupational specialties (MOSs) to women largely because men can no longer be drafted into the military service.

Whether or not the decision-makers will open the combat arms to women and let them serve in the infantry, armor and artillery remains an unanswered question. The need to fill these ranks in the volunteer Army, however, has driven our national leaders to a decision point on the matter.

Faced with the results of the low birth rate that started in the late 1950s, our leaders have found there are not enough acceptable males between the ages of 18 and 35 to fill the combat arms on a volunteer basis, while the requirement to maintain a standing Army continues. In order to solve this problem, our national leaders must look at alternatives and decide whether to maintain the volunteer Army and make it more workable by expanding the pool of available adults, or whether to institute a draft.

Expanding the pool of available adults is necessary if the volunteer Army is to be maintained, and that expanded pool will have to include women with the combat restriction lifted if it is to be effective.

Many methods—including a multimillion dollar advertising campaign—have been tried to prop up the volunteer concept. These methods include offering bonuses to males who volunteer for the combat arms, lowering standards, and raising the ceiling on the number of women allowed in the Army, with the assumption that men would be released to fight. Yet the shortfall continues.

I was a recruiting officer in New York City at the time that some of the planning for and the beginning stages of the volunteer Army were implemented. My duty assignment brought me into contact with the Manhattan office of the agency that handled the multimillion dollar Army advertising campaign. I was well briefed by them and read their working papers dealing with demographics, public opinion and population trends.

The fact remains that there are not enough qualified males to volunteer for the combat arms. To overcome this problem, the nation must look to *all* its adults between the ages of 18 and 35 as potential volunteers. This new perspective will require that the nation rethink its long-standing image of women and acknowledge their adulthood, with full awareness that adulthood predicates psychological soundness under stress, physical stamina in hardship, and the quality of self-reliance that precludes protection from others or self.

Stated more explicitly, the nation must recognize that its women possess the qualities to defend the country and learn to trust them with its firepower.

Whether our national leaders or our citizens at large are willing to trust women with national defense, and under what conditions, is a matter of conjecture. However, when concerns about national security arise and manpower requirements are discussed, the idea of a draft traditionally comes to the fore because our national experience has taught us that a draft is the most direct route to solving manpower problems.

Our national experience has also taught us the concept of an all-male draft. But the country cannot assume that an all-male draft would be implemented. In fact, it is unlikely that such a draft could be carried out today.

Too many anti-discrimination laws have been passed and too many sex equity precedents have been set since the country last relied upon an all-male draft.

It would be stopped in the courts with a decision for either males petitioning against an all-male draft because of the discrimination or females appealing it with a class suit.

The momentum of equality in modern times and laws that sanction it preclude an all-male draft, but conscription must remain an option open to the country to be used in time of an emergency. Today, it is necessary to extend our traditional concept of draft, all-male, to one of a male-female draft.

This is possibly the only kind that could be carried out, and its implementation would depend upon the manpower demands the world situation placed upon the military.

If, however, the combat restriction against women is not lifted in a volunteer Army environment and full mobilization required a male-female draft, women would continue to be assigned to traditionally female MOSs, even if massive expansion of the combat arms required more manpower than provided by existing qualified males.

It is unlikely that our national leaders would be impractical enough to try assigning women, by force of law, to the same MOSs they had denied them on a voluntary basis. Full mobilization and implementing a draft is a "what if" situation. But since the future is unpredictable, it seems unwise for the nation's leaders to impose limitations on themselves when they cannot see the future. It would be wiser for them to open all MOSs now and allow women to compete and qualify for them as do the males.

It would set a pattern of responsibility and a precedent that could be used as an insurance policy in the future. Also, allowing women into excluded MOSs would build bridges: men and women would associate with one another, train with one another and start functioning as a team—another asset accrued for the future, especially since the excluded MOSs are the most critical in the armed forces.

There will be problems and growing pains as happens when women are new in any field. Traditional relationships are upset and old responses are no longer appropriate. But it is better to work these problems through in today's noncritical environment than to try to deal with them in a crisis. . . .

. . . I developed a real and deep perspective on policies concerning women and their rationale, plus insight into attitudes and knowledge of troop capabilities as an instructor at the WAC Training Center, Ft. McClellan, Ala., as a recruiting officer in New York City, as a commanding officer at Ft. Jackson, S.C., and later battalion XO at the same post, and, most recently, as a management information systems officer (MISO) working on WITA (Women in the Army), a DA study on the utilization of women in the Army. . . .

Over the years, I observed the axis of young women's attitudes moving toward more assurance and self-confidence and their actions toward more meaningful accomplishment. On the other hand, when I was the MISO for the WITA project, where I collected, classified and programmed the statistical data from over 30,000 survey questionnaires, I was struck by the fact that the attitudes of men surveyed, particularly attitudes about women, had *not* changed. Their attitudes were the same as the male high school students of 20 years ago.

But other old customs have been overridden with modern attitudes. The only questions are: when will present attitudes about women change, and when will society allow women to follow other segments of the population, formerly restricted by the military, into a position of unabridged professionalism? . . .

And this situation, should it be allowed to continue, cannot help but diminish the total Army.

Major Richard A. Gabriel

The primary function of an armed force, especially its ground components, is to conduct combat operations as effectively as possible. An army is a very specific social institution, one dedicated to the application of systematic violence.

It is clear that military forces have also performed secondary roles for their societies. Thus, in less-developed countries the army is often used to siphon those elements in the society which tend to be disruptive of governmental control. In other, more industrialized states, military organizations are used as vehicles of social welfare and educational opportunity. . . .

The point that must be stressed, however, is that an army is primarily an instrument of warfare. Whatever secondary functions it performs or has forced upon it by its host society, such as accelerating social mobility or even being an employer of last resort, must be assessed in the context of how these additional roles affect the ability of the army to fight.

Secondary functions grafted upon a military force must never be undertaken in such a manner as to erode its ability to conduct effective combat operations. When this happens social priorities become deranged.

In assessing the role that women should play in the military it seems clear that whatever one they play and whatever limits are placed upon this role can only be justified in terms of the effects that either may have on the Army's combat abilities. A military force that performs alternative social functions at the expense of its ability to wage war ceases to be an effective instrument of policy. It becomes an inadequate instrument of social violence in the international system.

Thus, the role of women in military service can only legitimately be addressed in terms of the impact that the total integration of women will have on the capabilities of the army to effectively undertake concerted social violence.

The idea of totally integrating women into the military force at all levels and in all functions, especially combat and leadership functions in ground units, is a relatively new idea in the United States. It has come about as the result of two fundamental social phenomena which have emerged during the last decade: the failure of the all-volunteer force to recruit sufficient manpower during the last few years, and the ideological thrust of the women's rights movement.

The failure of the volunteer Army to recruit sufficient manpower has forced those committed to the volunteer concept to fill their quotas and maintain personnel strength by encouraging the enlistment of women. . . .

As long as conscription is ruled out as a way of obtaining sufficient manpower, female entrance into military service will continue and with it the pressure for an expansion in the roles female soldiers are allowed to play.

The second factor contributing to increased female participation in the armed forces is the ideological thrust of the women's rights movement, the fundamental premise of which is the probably correct notion that women are as technically competent and as skill-proficient as men in all or nearly all areas of occupational competence.

Thus, it is but a short jump to the proposition that the utilization of women's skills in the military can be just as effective as men's.

Taken with the larger thrust of American society towards securing equal rights for all minorities, this argument has become an effective lever for prying open the gates of military service and expanded social roles for women.

The result of the convergence of both these forces within the last decade has produced a dramatic increase in the number and jobs of women in the American armed forces in peacetime, especially the ground forces. No longer is it rare to find women as pilots, missilemen, squad leaders, or in other roles traditionally reserved to men. The increased role of women in the military is the logical consequence of the impact of larger social, economic, and political forces rampant in society.

There is a problem, however: both the premises upon which the expanded role of women in the military service has been justified are of questionable validity. Indeed, to implement women as rapidly as we have may actually be disastrous for the fighting ability of U.S. military forces. For example, the decision to use women to fill the manpower shortage created by the failure of the volunteer force is based upon an analogy with the civilian business sector.

By 1965, large numbers of women were entering the civilian labor force with great success. The success of women in the civilian labor force coupled with the pressures upon military planners to meet manpower quotas for the volunteer force led military planners to conclude that the same strategy of recruiting women could succeed equally well in the military.

The argument was further buttressed by the military's own metamorphosis, begun in the 1960s by Secretary of Defense Robert S. McNamara, characterized by a movement away from a traditional institution based upon warrior-leader roles and male bonding toward a more managerial, entrepreneurial institution based in economic incentives.

This change coupled with the business analogy that women were doing well in traditional male roles in the civilian sector led military planners to conclude that the recruitment of women to fulfill manpower requirements could work just as effectively in the military.

The problem with this reasoning, although it seems superficially sound, is that the military, especially its ground component, is not the equivalent of a civilian business in any meaningful sense. It most certainly is not equivalent in terms of those factors required to develop and sustain unit cohesion and battle effectiveness.

Indeed, equating the military with civilian business led to many of the organizational problems encountered during the Vietnam war and it is largely responsible for many of the failures of the all-volunteer force.

The requirements of combat effectiveness and cohesion are rooted fundamentally in sociopsychological forces which bind men together more than in the acquisition of technical skills. Military planners, ignoring the argument that a military unit is more than the equivalent of individuals exercising technical skills, lurched ahead and increased the number of women in military service.

The Department of Defense (DoD) convinced itself of its own argument that military units are analogous to, if not identical with, civilian economic institutions and that the same factors responsible for success in the civilian sector would produce effective military units. The fact that the argument is demonstrably false has made no difference.

The argument rooted in the ideology of the women's rights movement is also subject to serious question. The ideological thrust of that movement has as its base the equation of levels of technical competence for the sexes. The argument suggests, no doubt correctly, that the technical skill levels of men and women are identical; the justification for an expanded role for women in the military is based on the false assumption that technical skills are the major contributing factor to the combat effectiveness of military units. The fallacy resides here.

The fact is that combat effectiveness is only partially, and probably only a small part, the result of well-applied technical skills. Most skills in the military, especially combat skills, are learnable by virtually anyone within six to eight weeks. But military unit effectiveness and cohesion are far more the result of sociopsychological bonding—anthropologically, male bonding—among soldiers within combat groups.

Without this crucial bonding, units disintegrate under stress no matter how technically proficient or well-equipped they are. The key variable to the effectiveness of a military unit is not the technical abilities of its troops, although a certain level of technical competence is required, but the ability of troops to maintain cohesive bonding groups under fire. With regard to the role of women, if examined in terms of technical competence, the question is misplaced.

The important question is the effect of the presence of females upon the psychological bonds of the battle group. Military planners have failed to ask this question because their belief in the analogous nature of civilian and military groups has blinded them to its importance. . . .

The key question remains: what is the effect of total integration of females likely to be on the combat performance of military units? The truth is that we have no definitive answer. Little in the way of systematic research has been addressed to the question. What data is available, such as a few studies of female participation in guerrilla bands, is inapplicable to a large, modern, standing army. In an empirical sense, the question remains moot.

What is devastatingly certain, however, is that we have tinkered with the very foundations of our military forces without any sound sociological or psychological research from which to predict the results of our organizational restructuring. Driven by ideology and the equation of military tasks with civilian business, we have proceeded to integrate females in our military forces with scant regard for the possible consequences. . . .

An aspect bearing directly upon the ability of military groups to integrate females is that it is likely to require among the male members their complete redefinition of themselves as "men." Generally, the definition of "manhood" does not accept females as equals, but as charges to be protected.

This psychological orientation, however contrary it may run to ideals of sexual equality, is most strongly apparent among males from low socioeconomic levels, precisely the segment of the population which provides the greatest number of soldiers in the enlisted ranks, especially under the volunteer concept.

If females are integrated, especially in combat roles, it may necessitate that low socioeconomic-status males redefine in their minds what constitutes manhood, since historically combat and military service have been the most "male" of pursuits. It is, however, unlikely that these soldiers can or will redefine their role as men. To do so would challenge their entire personalities. . . .

There is a clear need for further research on the question. What is beyond belief is that DoD has moved so quickly to implement female integration without first examining its probable impact upon combat performance. At the very minimum, there is a need to undertake a major study which has as its central concern the impact of female integration on the ability of military units to fight.

Until such a study is undertaken and recommendations made, two options might be considered:

• First would be the creation of a special, totally integrated small-unit force, perhaps of battalion size, complete with a sexually integrated leadership corps at all levels. This unit would be earmarked for immediate use in combat should the need arise. Once it is exposed to actual field conditions it would be possible for

DoD officials to examine its performance and assess the levels of cohesion and effectiveness relative to that of nonintegrated units. Until this force can be studied under combat stress, it is suggested that any further integration of females in combat roles be halted.

• If this is too extreme a solution, then perhaps women's combat-related roles should be limited to those areas in which technical capacities are more important to combat effectiveness than cohesion and psychological bonding. Perhaps women could serve as aircraft pilots, helicopter gunners and maybe even tankers.

If it turns out that female integration *does* work, that it has no adverse effects on combat performance, then women should be fully integrated into the military force and perhaps, even subject to conscription.

In the meantime, however, we ought not to forget that the task of a military force is to conduct war. Any change in its structure or values cannot be permitted if it affects its fighting ability. If integration does affect performance, it must be resisted; if not, then permit it by all means.

2. Captain Jack Thompson, a Fighter-Bomber Pilot, Recalls a Raid on a Nuclear Facility near Baghdad, 1991

This is the story of my most unforgettable mission as an F-16 pilot during Desert Storm. On 19 January 1991, our objective was to destroy a nuclear research facility south of Baghdad. The strike package consisted of 36 F-16s, each carrying two Mk-84 2,000-pound bombs. At that time I was part of the 69th Tactical Fighter Squadron from Moody AFB. We had deployed two weeks earlier and were assigned to a provisional wing already established by Hill AFB. We were equipped with low-altitude navigation and targeting infrared for night (LANTIRN) systems, which allowed us to fight at night. That is how we were primarily used. I flew the first night of the war on 17 January 1991. I didn't fly the next day, so I took advantage of a chance to sleep.

My second combat sortie was my first daytime sortie. The afternoon time over target (TOT) denied us the added security of night flying. I will describe this mission from takeoff through air refueling, ingress, and egress, to return to base (RTB).

Takeoff and air refueling procedures made it difficult to fly the prebriefed formation. Anytime we carry live ordnance, we are restricted by TACR 55-116 to a minimum of 20-second spacing between aircraft. This translates to over 11 minutes (approximately 60–80 miles) between the first and last aircraft of the strike package. Luckily, we were far enough from the forward edge of the battle area (FEBA) for everyone to catch up and build the fighting formation.

If we had been closer to the FEBA, we would not have had time to regroup, especially if we were late taking off and didn't have time to orbit. I was back in the

From Captain Jack Thompson. "A View from the Cockpit," in Captain Michael P. Vriesenga. *From the Line in the Sand: Accounts of USAF Company Grade Officers in Support of Desert Shield/Desert Storm* (Maxwell AFB, AL: Air University P., 1994), 229–233.

pack, number 31 of 36 aircraft. Eventually I rejoined my flight, and we headed for the tankers. Refueling also made staying in formation difficult. Although we were one big package, we were broken down into flights of four. Each flight had a specific TOT and a certain point in the target area where we were expected to bomb. Since I was number three of my four-ship formation, I was responsible for backing up my flight lead in his responsibilities of navigation and timing, radar search, and returning the flight home safely.

There were five tankers in formation as we rejoined to receive our fuel. Eight F-16s rejoined on each tanker except the last one, which only had four fighters. The tankers were responsible for dropping us off at the Kuwaiti border on time. We would then dash to Baghdad. Timing was crucial on this mission to avoid conflicts between our strike package and others. We all refueled several times, because we wanted as much fuel as possible for the trip "downtown." I knew that fuel was crucial on this mission; every ounce would count. We were in and out of the clouds during refueling, making a demanding task even more complicated.

Finally, our flight finished refueling and we climbed 1,000 to 2,000 feet above the tankers to be in clear weather. We could no longer see the rest of the strike package or the tankers, relying on timing to make our jump on the planned route. We were a few minutes early, so we orbited so as to start the route on time. The altitude, and the combination of heavy fuel loads and bombs, made the airplanes sluggish and unresponsive. My flight lead and his wingman flew out in front of my element by about six miles. I kept asking lead to slow down so I could return to formation, but he didn't respond. I didn't feel comfortable flying over enemy territory out of the briefed formation, so I selected minimum afterburner to close the gap. Unfortunately, I was burning fuel I couldn't afford to use. I returned to position over Kuwait, but with 1,000 pounds less fuel than I had planned for at this point on the route. I wasn't about to turn back. I started thinking of ways I could return home from the target with enough fuel to meet the tankers waiting for us on the egress. We headed for Baghdad with our fangs out.

Our ingress to the target was uneventful except for a 40-mile radius around Baghdad. AWACS hadn't called out any air threats. With F-15s escorting our strike package, the Iraqi Air Force probably thought it was best that they didn't come out to play. F-4G Wild Weasels joined our package, ready to slam any surface-to-air missile (SAM) radars that attempted to shoot us down. My four-ship was now about 20 miles behind the mission commander's four-ship and there were six other flights in between. When we were approximately 40 miles south of Baghdad, I saw SAMs searching for the front of the strike package.

SAM launches and break calls filled the radios as the first F-16s bore down on the target. My radar warning receiver (RWR), which is only a rich man's radar detector, beeped and squeaked in my ears that the Iraqi SAM operators were looking at me. Suddenly, I saw a flash off my right wing, then a steady contrail arching upward. At the same time, I heard the call "Magnum" over the radio. Magnum is the Wild Weasel term for launching an antiradiation missile. I smiled to myself, thinking there was one less SAM to worry about. SAMs continued to fill the sky as we approached the target, and the fog of war hit me right between the eyes.

Fifteen miles from the target, I passed two F-16s going the wrong way, completely confusing me and dumping what little situational awareness I thought I had. My immediate reaction was that my flight lead and his wingman had just dropped their bombs and were egressing the target area, almost colliding with me in the process. I immediately queried lead and asked him where he was going since I still showed the target 15 miles in front of me. He quickly responded that he was 13 miles from the target on his bomb run. I said a quick mental prayer thanking the Lord for not letting me screw up. I later learned that the two F-16s that almost hit me had jettisoned their bombs in threat-reacting, and were "getting out of Dodge."

During my bomb run, I was continually dodging SAMs. I committed a fighter's cardinal sin: I lost sight of lead. Under the circumstances there wasn't much I could do. When you are threat-reacting to a SAM, trying to stay alive, you do what needs to be done and worry about the consequences later. Fortunately, my wingman still had me in sight. He was giving me some mutual support as we rolled in on the target. Lead screamed over the radio that the target was obscured by smoke, making it impossible to see. We were dropping dumb bombs, so we didn't have the luxury of laser-guided accuracy. I dropped my bombs where the fire control computer, which was constantly being updated by global positioning system (GPS) satellites, thought the target was. Although not as accurate as laser-guided munitions, that's about as accurate as you can get with dumb bombs, especially on long sorties. I felt the jet "thump" as the bombs released, and I selected full afterburner to get away from the hornet's nest as fast as possible. The RWR continued to howl in my ears, and I could see antiaircraft artillery smoke below me. My fuel was still lower than planned, but not as bad as I had expected. I decided not to jettison my empty fuel tanks yet. I turned for home as fast as the jet would go.

Once I was out of the target area and my RWR quieted, I tried to sort some things out for the RTB. My wingman had lost sight of me while pulling off target, and I was trying to find out where he was. Somehow, he had ended up about 12 miles in front of me. I hooked up with a couple of other F-16s and would worry about my wingman later. He had also found some buddies to race home with. Contrails filled the skies over Iraq as our strike package streaked southward. It reminded me of the movie, *Memphis Belle.* Although I was still over Iraq, about 100 miles north of Saudi, I started to relax. A distressed radio call brought me back to reality. An F-16 had been hit by a SAM and was going down. The pilot was doing his best to keep her flying, keeping his cool on the radio. He pointed south trying to cross the border before his engine let go. He didn't make it. The jet finally quit flying, and he said he was ejecting. Someone said over the strike frequency, like a voice from God, "GOOD LUCK." Later I learned he became one of our first POWs. He was part of a strike package just behind ours, and it hit home like a freight train. At the Saudi border, our four-ship finally re-formed, only to find out that one tanker was to service all 36 jets. I knew a lot of pilots would be scrambling to get there first, and I didn't have time to waste. I told lead I was diverting to the closest Saudi divert field. He said he was headed there too. After landing and shutting down, lead's engine dumped all its oil on the ramp. Maintenance troops told him he probably had less than 5 minutes of flying time left before all the oil was gone, making engine seizure imminent. That was the most serious maintenance problem we had during the war; the jets held up far beyond what we expected.

That completed the most memorable and hair-raising mission I flew in the war. I flew 41 more combat sorties, including going back to Baghdad a week later. None were as threatening as that one. I think psychologists call it a "significant emotional event." It certainly is one I'll never forget, from the takeoff and air refueling, to the harried ingress and high stakes video game of SAM-dodging and threat-reacting. The egress and RTB were forever etched into my mind as I listened to that F-16 pilot trying to nurse his sick airplane home before ejecting. And even though he has returned home safely, I'll never forget the feeling of helplessness as I listened to a brother going down, knowing there wasn't a thing I could do about it.

3. Captain H. R. McMaster Recounts a Tank Battle in the Desert (1991), 1994

[26 February 1991]

At 1525 hours, the troop once again received orders to attack. I relayed the order enthusiastically. Although we knew the general locations of large enemy units, we had not received detailed intelligence about the enemy we were about to encounter. I had a feeling, however, that this time we would meet the enemy. LT Tim Gauthier, one of my platoon leaders and known for his deadpan sense of humor, asked on the radio, "What kind of contact can we expect?" I replied, "Enemy contact." He said, "Roger, that's the best kind," and the troop rolled forward through the blowing sand.

The sun fought its way through the clouds, but the sandstorm continued to preclude long-range observation. As the troop crested a slight rise, air burst artillery fell on LT Petschek's lead scout platoon and the mortar section. The troop did not break strike. Soldiers closed their hatches and swung to the south around the impact area. I remember feeling proud of how the troop reacted. Falling artillery is something difficult to replicate in training, but the troopers reacted exactly as we had practiced.

At 1556 hours SSG McReynolds of 3rd Platoon reported four enemy soldiers surrendering in a bunker complex just north of the troop's southern boundary. Without hesitation, McReynolds and his two scout observers dismounted, searched the enemy prisoners, loaded them on the front of the Bradley, and sped toward the first sergeant's track. As McReynolds was departing, SGT Harris' Bradley came under heavy machine gun fire from a village east of the bunker complex.

I decided to hit the enemy position hard and bypass it to the north. We could see gun barrels protruding from windows in the gray cinderblock buildings. Several enemy vehicles with machine guns mounted were parked in the narrow streets. Scouts from 1st and 3rd Platoons fired 25-millimeter chain gun high explosive ammunition into the buildings and across the wall of dirt that the enemy had constructed around the village. I brought all nine tanks on line and gave them a fire command which resulted in the near-simultaneous firing of nine 120 millimeter

Capt. H. R. McMaster, "Eagle Troop," in *Personal Perspectives on the Gulf War* (Arlington, VA: Association of United States Army, The Institute of Land Warfare, n.d., © 1994) pp. 33–38. McMaster's account of the tank battle between his unit "Eagle Troop" and Iraqi tanks in 1991. Reprinted by permission of the author.

HEAT (high explosive antitank) rounds into the buildings. Rounds impacted into each of the buildings, blew gaping holes in them, and collapsed several roofs. Subsequently, fires started and the blowing smoke obscured the troop from the enemy. We would take no more fire from the village.

The troop resumed movement eastward. First platoon was moving tentatively and, unknown to me, had just sighted an enemy armored vehicle to the east. I decided to switch the formation to tanks in the lead and instructed the tank platoons to "follow my move." SGT Moody detected two enemy tanks and began firing on them with TOW missiles. Magee yelled, "Tank, we hit a tank!" on the platoon radio net. I had taken the point and the tanks were passing through the scouts in a nine-tank wedge. LT Mike Hamilton's 2nd Platoon was coming up on my left and LT Jeffrey DeStefano's 4th Platoon was on my right.

It was 1618 hours. The sandstorm had not let up. I was issuing final instructions to the troop when my tank crested another, almost imperceptible rise. As we came over the top, SSG Koch yelled, "Tanks direct front!" In an instant, I counted eight tanks in dug-in fighting positions. Large mounds of loose dirt were pushed up in front of the vehicles and they were easily discernible to the naked eye. They had cleverly established their position as a reverse slope defense to they could surprise us as we came over the rise. We, however, had surprised them. We had destroyed their scouts earlier in the day and, because of the sandstorm, they had neither seen nor heard us.

They were close! Koch hit the button on the laser range finder and the display under the gun sight showed 1,420 meters. I yelled, "Fire, fire Sabot." A HEAT round was loaded but Taylor would load a high velocity kinetic energy round next: a tank defeating depleted uranium dart which travels at about one mile per second. As Koch depressed the trigger, the gun breach recoiled and the HEAT round flew toward the enemy tank. We were still moving forward but the tank's stabilization system kept the gun right on target. The enemy tank exploded in a huge fireball as Koch swung onto another tank. This tank was much closer and was positioned forward of the main defense. It was swinging its turret toward our tank. Taylor actuated the ammunition door. As the door slid open, he grabbed a Sabot round, slammed it in the breach, and screamed, "Up!" Only three seconds had elapsed since we destroyed the first tank. I was talking on the radio as Koch let the round go. The enemy tank's turret separated from its hull in a hail of sparks. The tank hull burst into flames as the penetrator ignited the fuel and ammunition compartments.

PFC Hedenskog slowed the tank down to about 20 kilometers per hour. He spotted an enemy minefield and was weaving between the mines while trying to keep the tank's thick frontal armor toward the most dangerous enemy tank. Hedenskog knew he was setting the course for the troop. He guided the tank to the right so both tank platoons would hit the enemy position. Two T-72s fired on us but their rounds fell short on either side of the tank. Taylor threw in another SABOT round. As Koch destroyed another T-72, our two tank platoons crested the ridge. The seconds of solo fighting had seemed an eternity. All of the troop's tanks were now in the fight. Eight more T-72s erupted into flames as the tanks fired their first rounds. Two more enemy tank rounds fell short of LT DeStefano's and SSG Henry Webster's tanks. Our tanks, however, were not missing and were closing rapidly on the enemy's front line of defense. Enemy antipersonnel mines popped harmlessly under the tracks of the advancing tanks. An antitank mine exploded loudly under MAJ MacGregor's tank but inflicted only minor damage. The enemy was now in a panic. The few seconds of surprise was all we had needed. Enemy tanks and BMPs (Soviet-made armored personnel carriers) erupted in innumerable fire balls. The troop was cutting a five-kilometer-wide swath of destruction through the enemy's defense.

Radio traffic was relatively calm during the battle. I directed the tanks to keep information and assault through the enemy position. Third Platoon's Bradleys were arrayed in depth behind fourth platoon's tanks and protected the troop's right flank. They continued to fire into the village and beyond it to the south. Their job was particularly critical because 3rd Squadron, unaware of our contact with the enemy, had halted Iron Troop and the flank was open.

First platoon moved behind the tanks to "scratch their backs" with machine gun fire and clear pockets of enemy dismounted resistance. The enemy had prepared deep bunkers and waist-deep trenches just forward of the tank and BMP positions. The scouts were firing 25 millimeter high explosive and armor piercing ammunition into enemy personnel carriers and these bunkers.

We continued to attack east in this configuration. The enemy had made the town an infantry strongpoint and anticipated that we would bypass it to the north or south. An enemy defense consisting of thirty tanks, fourteen BMPs, and several hundred infantry had awaited us on the east side of the village along the 70 easting. We had done what the enemy anticipated. The surprise we gained and the speed and ferocity of our attack, however, was compensating for the enemy's greater numbers and the inherent advantages of their defense.

It was 1622 hours. Our tanks were now even with the enemy's first line of defense. All of their tanks that were directly forward of the troop were in flames. The enemy's defenses, however, extended farther to the south and DeStefano's tanks and Gauthier's Bradleys were heavily engaged on our right flank. At one point, 3rd Platoon took effective fire from a bunker which housed an enemy 23 millimeter anti-aircraft gun. The platoon launched two TOW missiles simultaneously. The first collapsed the bunker and the second destroyed the AA gun. In a particularly tense moment LT Gauthier's gunner, SGT Hovermale, swung his Bradley turret onto a T-72 tank just as it fired on him. The enemy tank missed and its explosive round threw dirt into the air. Hovermale returned fire with a TOW missile and destroyed the enemy tank as it was attempting to reload. SGT Digbie's Bradley was also engaging enemy vehicles along the troop's southern flank. His gunner, SGT Cooper, expended both TOW missiles in the launcher and Digbie excitedly yelled over the intercom to PFC Bertubin and SP4 Frazier to reload. The two soldiers in the back of the Bradley couldn't get the hatch open to gain access to the launcher. Bertubin, a college graduate and intercollegiate wrestler from Fort Walton Beach, Florida, frantically kicked at the hatch release and broke it. Frazier tossed off his crewman's helmet and jumped out of the Bradley despite heavy small arms fire. Bertubin handed Frazier two missiles, then climbed on top of the Bradley to slam them into the launcher. Bertubin startled SGT Digbie when he tapped him on the shoulder to tell him that the TOWs were loaded.

As our tanks drove around the destroyed enemy vehicles, secondary explosions threw flames and hunks of metal over our heads. Perhaps to avenge the fate of their comrades in the armored vehicles, enemy infantry fired their assault rifles and machine guns at us. The bullets, of course, had no effect on our tanks and Bradleys. We cut the infantry down with machine gun fire. Some of the enemy tried to lay low in their bunkers or play dead then jump up behind the tanks with their rifles and rocket propelled grenades (RPGs). They fell prey to the Bradleys' 25 millimeter and coaxial machine guns. LT Hamilton decided to leave unmolested an enemy squad of infantry who were not firing on him. He called back to LT Petschek to keep his eyes on them. After Hamilton's tank passed, the enemy raked it with machine gun fire while others prepared to fire a rocket propelled grenade. Petschek's and Patterson's Bradleys dropped them with their machine guns and cannons.

The troop's fire support officer called in artillery forward of the troop's advance. He kept his vulnerable FIST-V right behind the tanks so he could be in position to adjust the artillery. We were closing on the enemy fast and, moments later, I had to tell him to cancel the mission. I didn't want to risk running into our own fires.

LT Gifford called me from the command post to remind me that the 70 easting was the limit of advance. We were already beyond it. I told him, "I can't stop. We're still in contact. Tell them I'm sorry." Gifford explained the situation to the squadron headquarters on the radio. MAJ MacGregor was forward with our tanks and fully understood the situation. If we had stopped, we would have forfeited the shock effect we had inflicted on the enemy. Had we halted, we would have given the enemy farther to the east an opportunity to organize an effort against us while we presented them with stationary targets. We had the advantage and had to finish the battle rapidly. We would press the attack until all of the enemy were destroyed or until they surrendered.

As we drove through the smoke, we detected more tanks and armored vehicles behind the most forward enemy positions. The enemy had positioned some tanks and BMPs in depth and a reserve of seventeen T-72s were parked in a coil two kilometers further to the east. Our assault through the enemy's front line of defense had taken us to our southern limit so I began to steer the troop northeast toward the enemy reserve position. We were using a Global Positioning System on top of the tank to keep us properly oriented. The left side of the troop was hitting the enemy's reserve while Gauthier's 3rd and DeStefano's 4th Platoons were still heavily engaged to the south. The reserve tanks were positioned on a subtle ridge. My tank and 2nd Platoon were firing uphill and, as we gained elevation, more of the enemy came into view. We drove our tanks into the center of the position and destroyed many of the enemy vehicles from the rear.

At 1640 hours I finally found a place where I could halt the troop. It was just short of the 74 easting centered slightly south of where the enemy reserve position had been. Second Platoon halted just east of the burning T-72s that never had the opportunity to deploy out of their assembly area. Dominant terrain is difficult to discern in a relatively featureless desert but this was it. The small ridge allowed observation out to several kilometers in all directions. It was apparently the end of the enemy's defense.

As we halted, I anxiously called each platoon to ensure that all had made it through. I could not see most of the troop because of blowing sand. I was greatly relieved and thanked God when the platoon leaders and the first sergeant reported that they had taken no casualties. The troop had assaulted through four kilometers of heavily defended ground, and in 23 minutes had reduced the enemy position to a spectacular array of burning vehicles. . . .

I jumped on top of my tank to give the crew room to cross-load ammunition while I monitored the radio. I surveyed the fires which surrounded the troop. It seemed as if the action had lasted only seconds. I had felt no significant emotion during the battle. I think I had simply been too busy. I realized that I had not eaten all day. I tore into an MRE (meal, ready to eat) package and devoured a dinner of cold potatoes and ham. I gulped down some water and the quick infusion seemed to slow the flow of adrenaline. . . .

As the sun rose the next morning, the true extent of the damage inflicted on the enemy became apparent. Countless enemy tanks, personnel carriers, trucks, and bunkers were still smoking or in flames. Our Bradleys and tanks destroyed over 30 enemy tanks, approximately 20 personnel carriers and other armored vehicles, and about 30 trucks. The artillery strike had destroyed another 35 enemy trucks, large stocks of fuel, ammunition, and other supplies, and several armored vehicles. Enemy dead littered the battlefield. The day involved taking more prisoners and collecting and treating more enemy wounded.

I suddenly became aware of how filthy I was. I had not bathed in six days. The charcoal lining of the still damp chemical suit had coated my skin. I stood naked on the back deck of my tank and took a crude and largely ineffective bath with a wash cloth. The prisoners, from a culture which imbues them with physical modesty, were visibly shocked at my behavior.

We surprised the enemy on the 26th of February. That surprise and the bold action and teamwork of the troop's soldiers contributed the rout that is now known as the Battle of 73 Easting. In general, the Iraqis were unprepared for the United States Army. Our Army was better trained and equipped. The most decisive factor, however, was the American soldier. Our soldiers were aggressive in battle yet demonstrated great discipline and compassion for their enemy. They were exceptionally well-led by their noncommissioned officers and platoon leaders. Because of strong leadership and confidence gained through tough, realistic training, the soldiers approached their first combat action without any hesitation or sense of foreboding. I am grateful that I had the opportunity to serve with them in this action.

4. General H. Norman Schwarzkopf Defends Strategy and War Aims, 1992

Since my retirement from the Army a year ago, I have traveled extensively throughout the United States and Europe. Everywhere I go I am asked the same questions regarding the conduct and the outcome of the Gulf War. As the postwar euphoria receded, the analyses began. Some people started questioning, and some criticizing, both what we accomplished in the gulf and how the war was fought. Here are my answers to the five questions I am most often asked.

The first question, of course, is, *Why didn't we go all the way to Baghdad and "finish the job"?*

It should be clearly understood that the option of going all the way to Baghdad was never considered. Despite all of the so-called experts who, with twenty-twenty hindsight, are now criticizing that "decision," at the time the war ended there was not a single head of state, diplomat, Middle East expert, or military leader who, as far as I am aware, advocated continuing the war and seizing Baghdad. The United Nations resolutions that provided the legal basis for our military operations in the gulf were clear in their intent: kick the Iraqi military force out of Kuwait. We had authority to take whatever actions were necessary to accomplish that mission, including attacks into Iraq; but we had no authority to invade Iraq for the purpose of capturing the entire country or its capital.

If we look back to the Vietnam War we should recognize that one of the reasons we lost world support for our actions was that we had no internationally recognized legitimacy for our intervention in Vietnam. In the gulf the case was exactly the opposite; we had no less than nine United Nations resolutions authorizing our actions, and we had the support of virtually the entire world. But that support was for us to kick Iraq out of Kuwait, not to capture Baghdad.

If we look at the battle maps of the ground war, we can see that no Arab forces ever entered Iraq. Only British, French, and American troops fought on Iraqi territory. In this book I have discussed in some detail the sensitivity of our allies concerning one Arab nation's attacking another. I am convinced that had a decision been made to invade all of Iraq and capture Baghdad, the coalition that we worked so hard to preserve would have fractured. I am equally convinced that the only forces that would have participated in those military actions would have been British and American. Even the French would have withdrawn from the coalition.

Had the United States and the United Kingdom gone on alone to capture Baghdad, under the provisions of the Geneva and Hague conventions we would have been considered occupying powers and therefore would have been responsible for *all* the costs of maintaining or restoring government, education, and other services for the people of Iraq. From the brief time we did spend occupying Iraqi territory after the war, I am certain that had we taken all of Iraq, we would have been like the dinosaur in the tar pit—we would still be there, and we, not the United Nations, would be bearing the costs of that occupation. This is a burden I am sure the beleaguered American taxpayer would not have been happy to take on.

Finally, we should not forget how Saddam tried to characterize the entire war. He was quick to proclaim that this was *not* a war against Iraq's aggression in Kuwait, but rather the western colonialist nations embarking as lackeys of the Israelis on the destruction of the only Arab nation willing to destroy the state of Israel. Had the United States and the United Kingdom alone attacked Iraq and occupied Baghdad, every citizen of the Arab world today would be convinced that what Saddam said was true. Instead, they know that the armed forces of western *and* Arab nations fought side by side against Iraq's aggression and that when Kuwait was liberated the western nations withdrew their military forces and went home. For once we were strategically smart enough to win the war *and* the peace.

The next question I inevitably get is a follow-up one: *Since Saddam is still alive and in control in Iraq, wasn't the whole war fought for nothing?*

I will confess that emotionally I, like so many others, would have liked to see Saddam Hussein brought to some form of justice. He may still be. But to best address the question, we must consider what would have happened if Saddam had been allowed to succeed with his aggression—if the Gulf War hadn't been fought.

First, he would now control all the oil from Kuwait and perhaps from the entire Arabian Peninsula. Let's not forget that prior to the war, Saddam's threats were against *both* Kuwait and the United Arab Emirates. The only way to get to the United Arab Emirates from Kuwait is through Saudi Arabian oil-producing territory. But even if we assume that he would have limited his aggression to Kuwait, he would have sent a powerful signal to the rest of the gulf nations which they could not have ignored. They would have been intimidated in every future decision. Saddam would have achieved his stated aim of dramatically raising the price of oil on the world market, with the resultant stress on an already shaky world economy. Worse yet, if he followed the patterns of the past, his greatly increased oil revenues would have gone to the strengthening of his already strong (relative to other Middle Eastern nations) military forces and the expansion of his developing nuclear and biological and existing chemical arsenals. It is not hard to imagine what this could have meant to the future of Israel and the cause of world peace.

Instead, a defanged Saddam has been forced to retreat behind his own borders. His nuclear, biological, and chemical military capabilities have been destroyed and will stay that way if we can figure out how to prevent him from getting them in the future the same way he got them in the past—from unscrupulous firms, both western and eastern, more interested in the corporate bottom line than in world peace. Saddam's military forces suffered a crushing defeat and are no longer a threat to any other nation. Perhaps of greatest importance, because he did the unthinkable, attacked a brother Arab and subsequently lost face in a humiliating military rout, Saddam's irrational, militant voice is no longer relevant in Arab politics. Largely as a result of this and the coalition's gulf victory, the Middle East peace process is moving forward; Palestinians, other Arabs, and Israelis are sitting down at the negotiating table, and our hostages have been freed. Do I think it was worth it? You bet I do.

Finally, despite what we may see in *Rambo* films, catching and bringing to justice someone like Saddam is not a simple task. In Panama, a small country where we had thousands of American eyes in place even before military operations began, we still couldn't find a guy named Noriega for quite some time. I'm not sure that even with a full-scale invasion we would have ever found Saddam in the large armed camp that is Iraq.

What about all of the incidents of friendly fire we have heard about since the end of the war?

I detest the term "friendly fire." Once a bullet leaves a muzzle or a rocket leaves an airplane, it is not friendly to anyone. Unfortunately, fratricide has been around since the beginning of war. The very chaotic nature of the battlefield, where quick decisions make the difference between life and death, has resulted in numerous incidents of troops being killed by their own fires in every war that this nation has ever fought. Even at the National Training Center, where "kills" are simulated by lasers and computers, many incidents of fratricide are observed. This does not make them acceptable. Not even one such avoidable death should ever be considered acceptable. And in a war where so few lives were lost on our side, the tragedy is magnified when a family loses a son or daughter in such a way.

In the Gulf War our problem was that our technological ability to engage targets exceeded our ability to identify targets clearly. For years we had been working on the ability to attack enemy targets at great ranges since, in order to succeed against massed Soviet tank forces, we would need to destroy as many of them as possible before they could engage our forces. We found that the desert environment enhanced this ability to acquire and engage targets at great distances.

Early on, we became aware of the danger posed to our own forces by this enhanced capability and challenged the development community to come up with some way to discriminate definitely between friend and foe. Unfortunately, no technological solution was found that wouldn't have increased the danger to our forces of being destroyed by the enemy. Simply stated, anything that would have made our forces more recognizable to us would also have made them more recognizable to the enemy. We then had to rely on other procedures for identification, which we emphasized and reemphasized at every level. The most common of these of course was to look at "position on the battlefield." If you know that no friendly forces are in front of you, then anything you see must be the enemy.

Regrettably, in the confusion of battle innocent mistakes were made and lives were lost. We must find a better and safer way to do our jobs. In every after-action report submitted by my former headquarters and those of my component commanders, this problem has been highlighted as one that demands immediate attention and action. All the services are dedicated to finding a technological solution to this long-standing dilemma.

Another question I am often asked is, *How did our high-tech equipment really work?*

My answer is always the same: "Beyond our wildest expectations." In the early days of our deployment we did run into unanticipated problems as a result of the harsh desert environment. We found that the fine, dustlike sand of Saudi Arabia caused the air filters to clog on some of our armored vehicles. This problem was quickly solved when American technology came up with new filters. We found that sand eroded our helicopter blades, so the experts came up with tape for the blades that reduced the erosion. Just like other extreme environments, such as the Arctic and the jungle, the desert environment posed special challenges that we had to adjust to, but good old American ingenuity always came through. We learned to adapt, and our equipment continued to operate despite all the predictions to the contrary. After four days of battle, our maintenance levels were higher than those found in most units during peacetime.

Certain systems have been singled out for criticism by individuals serving their own purposes. One of these is the Patriot missile. The critics have only succeeded in illuminating their lack of knowledge about what the Patriot was designed to do. The Patriot was designed to defend a *point* target—such as an airfield, supply depot, or headquarters—against incoming enemy aircraft or missiles. I don't know of a single case where the Patriot wasn't one-hundred-percent successful in defending the facility it was deployed to protect. The fact that it also often performed splendidly as an *area* defense weapon was pure gravy and provided a degree of protection for whole cities that we had never expected to have. Similar criticism has been leveled at Air Force precision munitions, stating that they didn't always hit their target the first time; sometimes it took two or even three to destroy a target. Maybe so, but were any of those critics in Vietnam? I would have given my left arm if our Air Force could have had half the capability in Vietnam that it demonstrated in the gulf. Sure our high-tech munitions didn't work perfectly one hundred percent of the time, but that is not unusual considering their complexities and the fact that many were developed at an accelerated pace because of the war. But they were so vastly superior to anything we had before, and to anything our enemies have now, that the American people can feel very proud of the *American* technology that produced them.

Finally, I am often asked to comment on *the nature of future conflicts and the size of our armed forces.*

I feel that retired general officers should never miss an opportunity to remain silent concerning matters for which they are no longer responsible. Having said that, I believe a few general (no pun intended) comments are in order. I am quite confident that in the foreseeable future armed conflict will not take the form of huge land armies facing each other across extended battle lines, as they did in World War I and World War II or, for that matter, as they would have if NATO had faced the Warsaw Pact on the field of battle. Conflict in the future will be similar to that which we have seen in the recent past. Both of the military operations in which we were involved in the Middle East were a result of regional conflicts that grew to proportions that began to impact the rest of the world. The "tanker war" was a result of the Iran-Iraq war, and, of course, the Gulf War came about as a result of a dispute between Iraq and other oil-producing nations. As I have stated earlier, when I took command of Central Command there were thirteen such conflicts occurring in my area of responsibility alone. Since that time many have abated, but others far more troublesome have emerged to take their place. One need only look at the tragic events taking place in what we used to call Yugoslavia or the ethnic, religious, and nationalistic clashes in the former Soviet Union to realize that such dangerous regional conflicts will be with us for years to come. Any one of them could lead us to war.

What then does this tell us about the future size of our armed forces? First, it does tell us that reductions are possible. But it does not tell us that reductions by arbitrary amounts set *solely* on the basis of political or fiscal considerations are the answer. It frightens me when I hear someone propose a hundred-billion-dollar cut in our armed forces without any rationale other than that the money can be used elsewhere. The purpose of our armed forces is to protect our national interests and defend our country. Before we allow deep cuts in our forces we should be sure that we have made a thorough analysis of what our national interests will be for the next twenty years and where and how we might be required to commit our forces. Only then can we honestly assess what size our armed forces should be. Then the cuts can be made. I am told that just such an analysis is currently under way in the Department of Defense.

Finally, we must ensure that our forces remain flexible enough to handle unforeseen contingencies. The future is not always easy to predict and our record regarding where we will fight future wars is not the best. If someone had asked me on the day I graduated from West Point, in June 1956, where I would fight for my country during my years of service, I'm not sure what I would have said. But I'm damn sure I would *not* have said, "Vietnam, Grenada, and Iraq."

The day I left Riyadh to return to the United States, General Khalid made a statement in a speech that every American should think about. He said, "If the world is only going to have one superpower, thank God it is the United States of America." When I think about the nations in the past fifty years that could have emerged as the world's only superpower—Tojo's Japan, Hitler's Germany, Stalin's Russia, Mao's China—and the darkness that would have descended on this world if they had, I appreciate the wisdom of Khalid's words. Because we have emerged as the only remaining superpower, we have an awesome responsibility both to ourselves as a nation and to the rest of the world. I don't know what that responsibility will mean to the future of our great country, but I shall always remain confident of the American people's ability to rise to *any* challenge.

5. U.S. Government Report Assesses the Effectiveness of Air Power During the Gulf War (1993), 1995

Control of the Air

To wage the air campaign, the Coalition had to control the air space over Iraq. When war came, Coalition air forces soon bottled up the Iraqi air force on its airfields and largely prevented effective employment of Iraq's integrated air defense system and radar-guided surface-to-air missiles (SAMs). Save for low-altitude antiaircraft artillery (AAA) and infrared SAMs in highly defended areas like Baghdad and the portions of the Kuwaiti theater occupied by Republican Guard divisions, the Coalition air forces quickly gained relatively unimpeded freedom of action. Air superiority (that is, the ability of one side's aircraft to operate in selected airspace at a given time without prohibitive interference from the other side) was achieved by the end of 17 January 1991; by 27 January, General Schwarzkopf could declare air supremacy, meaning that the Iraqi air force no longer existed as a combat-effective force.

To a considerable extent, the Iraqis conceded control of the air to the Coalition even before the war began. The Iraqi air force on 17 January apparently intended to ride out the initial Coalition bombing raids inside supposedly bombproof shelters while attempting some defensive counter-air action under close control from Iraq's integrated air defense system. The Iraqis may have hoped to disrupt the Coalition air campaign somewhat, inflicting occasional losses on Coalition air forces by at-

From Thomas A. Keaney and Eliot A. Cohen. *Revolution in Warfare?: Air Power in the Persian Gulf* (Annapolis, MD: Naval Institute P., 1995), 48–51, 78–79, 93–95, 101–104; a reprint of *Gulf War Air Power Survey Summary Report* (Washington, D.C.: GPO, 1993).

tacking stragglers and egressing strike aircraft low on fuel. This limited use of its air force mirrored Iraq's policy in the Iran-Iraq War, when neither side attempted to establish real air superiority. The Iraqi leadership believed that the army, not the air force, determined victory in modern war and that an air force had value primarily as a "force-in-being"—a protected deterrent against regional rivals.

In the weeks preceding Desert Storm, Saddam Hussein confidently predicted that after the initial air strikes, the Iraqi army would still be "safe and sound and ready for battle" when Coalition ground forces appeared. As in the Iran-Iraq War, ground-based air defenses, rather than Iraqi fighters, would be relied upon to blunt any Coalition air strikes that might occur. In such circumstances, Coalition air-control operations were less a contest between opposing air forces than a concerted effort by the Coalition to minimize its losses while destroying the Iraqi air force on the ground, thereby denying Iraqi's [*sic*] goal of holding its air force in reserve either for a last stand or for post-war use.

Freedom of Action

The opening hours of the war saw Coalition air forces bomb key command and control elements of Iraq's strategic air defense system such as sector and intercept operations centers. Coalition fighters mounted offensive fighter sweeps over the main Iraqi fighter bases with the intent of shooting down any Iraqi fighters that became airborne. British Tornados attacked takeoff surfaces at key airfields with JP-233 (an airfield-attack system containing specialized cratering and mining submunition) in order to limit the numbers of launched Iraqi fighters to quantities the Coalition fighters could readily handle. And sophisticated attacks involving drones and HARMs (high-speed antiradiation missiles) were launched against Baghdad and other areas where Iraq's radar-guided SAMs were concentrated. These efforts were designed to bottle up the Iraqi air force on the ground and eliminate the threat of radar-guided SAMs at medium and higher altitudes, thereby permitting Coalition aircraft to operate there with little risk of significant attrition.

The air-to-air portion of this effort, which averaged some 340 sorties daily over the course of Desert Storm, quickly persuaded the Iraqi air force to stand down. By the ninth day of the war (25 January), Coalition fighters had downed sixteen Iraqi MiG-29s, MiG-25s, and F-1s, and Iraqi flight activity had largely ceased. By the end of Desert Storm, Coalition air forces had shot down thirty-three Iraqi fixed-wing aircraft (five MiG-29s, eight Mirage F-1s, two MiG-25s, eight MiG-23s, two Su-25s, four MiG-21s, three Su-7/17s, and one IL-76) and five helicopters while suffering, at most, one air-to-air loss on the opening night of the war.

Although the thirty-three-to-one box score provides some insight into the degree to which Coalition forces dominated in air-to-air combat, it is by no means the entire story. More than 40 percent of the Coalition's kills from 17 January through 28 February involved beyond-visual-range (BVR) shots. The Gulf War was the first conflict in history in which a large percentage of the air-to-air engagements that produced confirmed kills involved BVR shots: namely, the sixteen out of thirty-three victories against fixed-wing Iraqi aircraft credited to Coalition fighters during Desert Storm. These BVR shots were possible because Coalition fighters, operating in conjunction with platforms such as the E-3 AWACS (Airborne

Warning and Control System) could shoot BVR with little risk of accidentally hitting friendly aircraft. . . .

The Strategic "Core" in Retrospect

Regardless of the private hopes airmen may have had during the Gulf War that air power might achieve the Coalition's military objectives without a ground campaign, the modest fraction of the air-to-surface attacks focused against the strategic core concentrated primarily on the more pragmatic objectives laid out in this and the previous chapter. Planners wished to exert pressure from the outset directly against the heart of Iraqi power, an idea consistent with other strategic bombing campaigns. Strategic air attacks were, in some cases, less effective than air planners had hoped for or believed, as in the case of the Iraqi nuclear weapons program. By mid-1992, for example, U.N. Security Council inspection teams had identified and destroyed more of Iraq's nuclear missile programs than had the air campaign. In other cases, such as that of Iraq's electrical power system, the Coalition met its immediate military objectives. In yet other cases, such as the L&CCC [Leadership (L) & Telecomms/C3] target categories, effectiveness cannot be precisely estimated. . . .

The data support several conclusions. First, CENTCOM's initial counts of equipment destroyed were inflated, but so too was the target base, and the errors offset one another. In other words, CENTCOM's *percentages* of equipment destroyed by the beginning of the ground war were in line with later observations, though the *numbers* of pieces destroyed were inflated. Second, equipment attrition did not occur evenly throughout the theater but varied from high attrition to lower attrition by division, moving south to north and from west to east in the theater. Highest attrition took place in the western frontline divisions; lowest in the divisions in the northeast corner of the theater.

A related issue to Iraqi attrition of equipment is the Iraqis' loss of personnel during the air war. CENTCOM produced no estimates of Iraqi personnel losses during or after the war, nor did the 1991 Department of Defense *Conduct of the Persian Gulf War.* Iraq itself has given estimates on [the] number of Iraqi noncombatants killed but has not addressed its military losses. Prisoner reports that addressed the number of soldiers in each unit that were killed, wounded, or had deserted during the air war enable some estimates of the size of the Iraqi army in the theater at the beginning of the ground war. Starting from a figure of 336,000, the estimated personnel manning the Iraqi army at the beginning of the air war . . . the Iraqi army saw desertions of 25–30 percent. In addition, that army suffered a smaller number of casualties to the air attacks—probably less than 10 percent of the force. As a result, the remaining strength of the Iraqi army by 24 February numbered approximately 200,000 to 222,000.

The air interdiction, the damage to the communications and supply systems, along with the equipment attrition during the air war, clearly affected the Iraqi soldiers beyond the inflicting of casualties during that period. The Iraqi soldier, by and large, lost his determination to fight. The Iraqis did not defect or surrender in droves during the air and ground war because their armor and artillery were being destroyed (in fact, statements by Iraqi prisoners of war indicate they appreciated the discrimination of the air forces in aiming at the equipment and not them) but because many were short of food and water. The true effects of these attacks, in other words, came not from specific targets destroyed but from the combination of targets attacked and the intensity with which those attacks took place.

The pervasive impression left by the interrogation reports of prisoners was the sense of futility felt by the Iraqis after weeks of extensive bombing. When the bombing started, their ground transportation began to crumble. Many, particularly the frontline forces, ran short of water, food, fuel, and all spare parts. Some units had their supply stocks destroyed. Training in the units ceased. Soldiers moved apart from their equipment because they well understood what the targets were. Many captured Iraqis stated that they thought the air campaign would last several days to a week at most. When it did not end, the sense of futility and inevitability of the outcome became more apparent. Some frontline soldiers decided not to fight, others deserted, and still others remained in place; but the effect on the capability of the Iraqi units was the same. The deserters from the frontline divisions told their interrogators that most of those remaining in their units would surrender at the first opportunity without any resistance. That is exactly what happened.

The ground offensive ended quickly, but units qualified to fight and willing to resist may well have remained. Few of those units were in the front lines, however. When the soldiers and officers in these frontline units decided not to resist, any opportunity for an organized defense in the theater collapsed. The Iraqi strategy called for the operational and strategic reserves to move to resist the points of the Coalition ground attack, but these reserve forces were fooled not only by the direction of the attack but also by how fast it was upon them. The utter collapse of the Iraqi front lines made any planned movements by the reserves irrelevant. The reserve forces were themselves under attack before they had a chance to maneuver or present an organized defense.

Air Power with Engaged Ground Forces

The effectiveness of air power in supporting engaged ground forces during Desert Storm is particularly challenging to assess because the support took place only during the one-hundred-hour ground war and briefly during the Iraqi incursion into the Saudi town of Al Khafji. The brief time involved and the conditions under which the engagements took place—against thoroughly demoralized Iraqi troops, many in full flight or surrendering even before being engaged—make any generalizations based on these circumstances questionable. Moreover, the speed of the ground action added to the complexity of making a precise accounting of specific actions that took place. After the war, no theater-wide survey was undertaken, although various organizations attempted reconstructions of some of the battlefield engagements.

Even the limited data make clear, nevertheless, that Iraqi forces were significantly more vulnerable on the move, day or night, than they were dug in and surrounded by air defenses. The JSTARS aircraft, a test aircraft brought to the theater just before the air war, proved enormously capable of identifying the path of attacking or retreating columns of Iraqi equipment and provided both battlefield intelligence and targeting information. Moreover, vehicles out of revetments and on the move were vulnerable to more weapons, such as aircraft cannon fire and air-delivered mines. It is not surprising, then, that the success of attacks on moving columns of armor was substantially greater than those attacks on similar forces protected by berms, camouflage, and other defensive and deceptive measures.

From 29 through 31 January—the time of the Al Khafji battle—Iraqi ground movements were a subject of much conjecture. While Iraqi forces were detected moving south in eastern Kuwait, CENTCOM suspected that the move was a feint for a larger maneuver farther to the west, at the tri-border area, by perhaps the Republican Guard divisions. This suspicion was helped along by pilot reports indicating that the Tawakalna Division had moved from its previous position (and was unlocated) and that the Madinah Division was observed moving south. In this situation, the JSTARS capabilities took on tremendous value, to both evaluate the amount and nature of movement throughout the theater and track the specific movements of Iraqi forces in southeast Kuwait.

All indications are that the air attacks on the Iraqi army during the Al Khafji incursion had a devastating effect. Iraqi equipment attrition as recorded by CENTCOM increased fourfold for the period 29 January to 3 February over what it had been for the entire air campaign up to that point. Even allowing for overcounting of the losses, the impact on the Iraqis was tremendous. While a number of prisoner-of-war reports mention the effects, the most telling one was the comment by a veteran of the Iran-Iraq War, who remarked that his brigade underwent more damage in thirty minutes than it had in eight years in the previous war. . . .

Air power had two important effects on the Iraqi army during the four days of the ground war: one imposed during those four final days, the other imposed during the preceding weeks of the campaign. Air strikes during the air war had made the Iraqi forces in some cases unwilling and in other cases unable to maneuver or mount an effective defense. Lack of communications, equipment attrition, and destruction of the theater distribution system had combined to bring about these conditions. The rout of maneuvering Iraqi forces during the engagement at Al Khafji gave those forces a preview of what was in store. During the ground war, concentrated attacks on the Iraqi heavy divisions prevented them from playing any role other than self-defense, and several of these divisions did not even do that. In some instances involving frontline Iraqi divisions, air power had merely to show up to prompt the forces to surrender.

Estimates of air power's worth during the ground war must look beyond the last four days themselves. The most important contribution of air power in the Kuwaiti theater during the ground war, and a prime reason why the ground campaign was so short and so overwhelming, was the success of air interdiction in preventing the heavy divisions from moving or fighting effectively. In other words, the interdiction sorties after 23 February were just a continuation of the campaign that began on 17 January.

Nor were the interdiction sorties dissimilar from the close air support sorties flown: interdiction and close air support sorties often occurred just a few miles apart. What the events on the ground made clear is that airpower essentially paralyzed or demoralized the Iraqi heavy divisions on which the Iraqi strategy depended. The remnants of some divisions were destroyed in place or surrendered with little resistance; others fled the theater without much of their equipment, while those farther to the rear were able to make a more orderly departure. Those left with a will to fight were able to do little more than face the attack and return fire, with no hope of maneuvering or being reinforced or achieving even tactical success. The engagements of the Marines with elements of the Iraqi 3d Armored Division at Kuwait International Airport on 26 February and of VII Corps with elements of the Tawakalna, 12th, and Madinah Divisions on 26 and 27 February were just such desperate actions.

Ironically, the loss of equipment, a key index of bomb damage assessment used during the war, was not decisive in any direct way. The Iraqi army did not run out of tanks, armored personnel carriers, or artillery; in fact, much of the equipment remaining intact at the start of the ground offensive was abandoned, or was at least unoccupied, when the Coalition ground forces reached it. Reports of AH-64 strikes describing the attacks on armor columns noted that when firing began on the first tank, the crews of the other tanks began abandoning their vehicles. The total number and operability of the tanks had less meaning under those conditions.

Air power had destroyed not only large amounts of equipment, it had also destroyed the confidence of the Iraqi soldiers that the equipment would do them any good. On the contrary, the equipment was seen as a magnet for air strikes. Whether the Iraqi troops could have held on and for how long, even without a ground attack, are matters for speculation. The demonstrable fact is that the Iraqis simply could not react once the ground attack took place and Coalition forces swept through the theater. One can only guess at possible differences in Iraqi resistance if the Coalition ground forces had had less air support or had there been a shorter air campaign. Certainly, though, air power made that resistance disorganized and totally ineffective.

6. Secretary of Defense William Perry Justifies Sending U.S. Peacekeepers to Bosnia, 1995

From the beginning, many have said that we, the United States, have no business getting involved in the civil war in Bosnia, a faraway land, indeed a land that has people names and place names we can't even pronounce. That view, I believe, was summarized well, I believe, four years ago by then-Secretary of State [James] Baker, who captured it in a particularly homey way. He said, "We don't have a dog in that fight."

Contrast that with the view of others, who, from the beginning, believed that we, the United States, should have entered that war years ago to defend the Bosnian government from a war of aggression by the Serbs. They evoked images of the Spanish Civil War, and they said, "Send not to ask for whom the bell tolls; it tolls for thee."

Secretary of Defense William Perry, "Bosnia: Creating an Environment of Hope," Remarks delivered at the Center for Strategic and International Studies, December 7, 1995 reprinted in *Defense Issues*, vol. 1, no. 2. *Defense Issues* is available on the Internet via the World Wide Web at http://www.defenselink.mil/pubs/di_index.html.

The public debate today is confused by a misperception that the administration has moved from this first view, namely, that Bosnia has nothing to do with us—to the second view, that we should intervene. That is not correct. And if I do nothing else today, I would like to clarify that misperception.

The administration view consistently for the last 2½ years has acted on a belief different from either of those views; namely, that we would not enter the war to impose a peace. We took that view because we believed that to do that would require several hundred thousand American troops and would entail thousands of American casualties. But that did not mean that Bosnia had nothing to do with the United States. Instead, we said we would take strong steps to minimize civilian casualties, all the while working to achieve a peace settlement.

That first step has had relatively good success. Civilian casualties dropped from . . . over 100,000 in 1992, to 12,000 in [19]93, to just over 2,000 last year [1994]. Nobody is celebrating 2,000 casualties, but the effort, the very substantial effort by the United States and the NATO nations to reduce the civilian casualties, was in fact successful.

Now finally, the determined effort to negotiate a peace agreement has been successful. For the first time in four years, there is a real prospect of stopping the killings and the atrocities. But all of the parties in Dayton [Ohio] who accepted this agreement accepted it only on the conditions that the peace would be implemented by a NATO-led military force and that the United States would . . . participate in that force, indeed provide the leadership for it.

Without U.S. participation in the peace implementation force, the parties would withdraw from the peace agreement and we would see a resumption of the killings and the atrocities. Therefore, we will participate.

I understand all too well the risks to our soldiers who will be in the implementation force, and I have discussed them fully and frankly with those soldiers who are going to go. Two weeks ago, I met with 700 soldiers from the 1st Armored Division. This is going to be the backbone of U.S. ground forces that deploy to Bosnia. I talked with the division commanding general, all of the brigade commanders, all of the battalion commanders, all of the company commanders, platoon commanders, the first sergeants, the sergeant majors. In short, I talked to the entire leadership of this division. They had five basic questions that they wanted me to answer: Why are we going into Bosnia? What will our mission be? Who's going in with us? When will we go in? And when will we come out?

To the best of my ability, I answered those questions fully and frankly for them, and today I want to share with you the answers which I gave our soldiers.

Why are we going in? The simplest way of expressing that is that there's only one real alternative to going in, and that is a restart of the war. I have testified at five different congressional hearings, I've met with congressmen, [and] public interest groups dozens of times in the last few months. I hear all of these proposals of why don't we do this, that or the other thing. That is evading the issue. We have two alternatives in front of us: We can participate in the peace implementation force with the risks involved with that, or we can walk away from it. And if we walk away from it, make no mistake, there will be a restart of the war.

Not only will that lead to a resumption of the killings, but there's a very real risk of this war spreading. I have testified to that many times, and many in Congress have expressed skepticism on that point. I wish they could have shared the concern and the apprehensions that I've had many times in the last few years about the real danger of a war erupting between Serbia and Croatia, for example. Just two months ago, I would have given you an even chance that that war was going to explode and dwarf the war in Bosnia by comparison. And a war between Serbia and Croatia would clearly threaten Slovenia and Hungary.

From the beginning, there has been a palpable danger that the war would spread to the south, to Macedonia and Kosovo, Albania. That would threaten Greece and Turkey, two of our NATO allies.

So there are risks to U.S. participation in this peace force. I've talked about them candidly and fully with our soldiers and with the Congress. But if the war restarts, the dangers, the problems, the risks are even greater. If this war erupted and included conflicts in Greece and Turkey, and we felt obliged to intervene at that stage, we're not only intervening in a much wider war, but we're intervening in a war, instead of going in to enforce a peace—a much greater risk.

I talked to the soldiers about what our mission was, what we're going to do when we get there. I started off by telling them what it was not. We are not going into Bosnia to fight a war. For 2½ years, this administration has said we're not going to fight a war in Bosnia, we're not going to enter the war. But we've also said if we can get a peace agreement, we will assist in the implementation.

Now, we have a simple dichotomy: We are not committing U.S. ground troops unless we get a peace agreement. That's what we have said for 2½ years. It's now also true that we will not have a peace agreement unless we commit U.S. troops.

So the mission is to implement a peace. The tasks are limited and they're clear. Our soldiers understand them. They are not involving nation building. There will be a very important set of civil functions going along in parallel to IFOR [the peace implementation force], but U.S. troops and the NATO troops do not have the responsibility and will not be executing these functions of rebuilding the infrastructure—of rebuilding the economy, of overseeing elections, resettling refugees. All of these are very important civil functions. Success in Bosnia ultimately depends on the success of those civil functions. The task of the NATO force will be to create a secure environment so that other organizations and other institutions can conduct those important civil functions.

This will be an operation with risks, and there will be casualties, but we will do—we are doing everything that is possible to minimize those risks, first of all, and most important, by only going in with a peace agreement already signed, with the parties already agreeing not only to have peace but to assist in the implementation of the peace.

Even with that agreement, we believe that there will be individuals and gangs who will not accept the judgment of their leaders and may, therefore, try to resist. We do not expect to meet an army—we do not expect to meet organized opposition—but we do expect to run into gangs who may try to harass this force. Therefore, we're going in with a large and a very well-armed force.

In our debate and in our discussion about the size of the force to go in, both at NATO and the United States, we considered sending a much smaller force in, maybe half the size of what is being proposed, with the thought that if we run into trouble, we will send in reinforcements. We concluded that was the wrong philosophy, that we should send in a large force and, if we don't run into trouble, then we can start drawing them down. If we err in the size of this force, we have erred on the size of it being too large.

This force is also very well-trained. Every battalion in the 1st Armored Division in the last two months has undergone extensive training, including more than a week at the Grafenwoehr [Germany] Training Range, where they are undergoing checks in training and exercises in the basic combat skills. Then they spent another week at our Hohenfels training range in Germany. There we have created a mini-Bosnia, and we put them through simulated exercises of the kind of situations and scenarios which we expect they could run into in Bosnia. At that training range we have a simulated Serbian army, Bosnian Serb army, a simulated Federation army. We have villagers, mayors, paramilitary groups, CNN. We have everything that resembles the kind of issue that they're going to run into when they get into Bosnia. We had the cold, miserable weather; that came for free. And we had potholes in the road, and that came for free. . . .

The specific tasks that they will have are spelled out in the military annex to the Dayton agreement. . . . [L]et me just mention a few, two in particular that are important.

One of them is to enforce—mark and enforce—a zone of separation. The Bosnian Serb army will still exist, Bosnian Federation army still exists, and those will be separated. There will be two kilometers on either side of a zone of separation in which all soldiers and all weapons will have to be removed. This minimizes the chance of border conflicts. We will then monitor that and patrol that zone to be sure that that zone of separation is maintained.

The Dayton agreement also requires that all heavy weapons and all troops be returned to cantonment and barracks within 120 days. We will monitor and oversee that to be sure that that is complied with.

More generally, what we will be doing is enforcing the cessation of hostilities and providing a secure environment so that the people in Bosnia can start getting their lives back together again and that these organizations which are conducting the functions I described to you, the rebuilding functions, will have a secure environment in which they can perform their tasks. We do not expect those tasks, those civil tasks, to be finished during the time of the IFOR presence in Bosnia, but we expect them all to be well started.

I told our soldiers that we would not be going alone into Bosnia. Indeed, all of the NATO nations that have armed forces—that is, all NATO nations except Iceland—will be participating. The British are going in with 13,000 troops; the French with about 8,000; Germans, about 4,000; Italians and Spaniards, 2,000 each; all other NATO nations, about 1,000 each. Proportional to the size of their armies, proportional to their countries, these contributions are equal to, or somewhat greater than, those of the U.S. So this is not—nobody in NATO is taking a "Let-George-do-it" attitude. Everybody is pitching in to do this job. . . .

And finally, with the American division, we are going to have a Russian brigade consisting of perhaps 2,000 to 3,000 soldiers.

I attended a NATO meeting in Williamsburg, Va., two months ago in October, and we discussed the imminence of this NATO operation and the potential role of the Russians. I had a meeting scheduled with the minister of defense of Russia,

[Gen. Pavel] Grachev, the day after the meeting in Williamsburg, and so I sought guidance from my fellow NATO defense ministers. I got unanimous guidance on two important points.

The first, they all agreed it was very important to have Russian participation, not just for Bosnia, but for, really, the future security of Europe. When we tackled this first big security problem which Europe has faced since the Cold War, we wanted to tackle it with Russia, working cooperatively with them, not in a confrontation mode with Russia. That will affect the security of Europe for years to come. . . .

The last question which our soldiers were very concerned about was: When are we coming out? There's been a wonderful debate in this town [Washington] on when we are coming out.

The answer is really very simple. We're coming out in about a year. I say "about"; I mean within weeks of a year. It's not 365 days. Pulling 20,000 troops out is not done to that degree of precision, but they're coming out in about a year. So all of the discussion on exit strategy is sort of moving off in the wrong direction.

The NATO commitment, the U.S. agreement and the Dayton agreement, by the way, calls for the forces to be there about a year. We will be very close to that time. . . .

▲ E S S A Y S

In the first essay, Richard P. Hallion, U.S. Air Force historian, in a 1992 book, *Storm over Iraq: Air Power and the Gulf War,* credits air power, specifically the Air Force's land-based planes, not the Navy's carrier-based fighter-bombers, with winning the war against Iraq with their precision bombing. In contrast, in the second essay, Eliot A. Cohen, a reserve army officer and professor of strategic studies at the School of Advanced International Studies at the Johns Hopkins University and from 1991 to 1993 the Director of the Gulf War Air Power Survey, an independent study commissioned by the Secretary of the Air Force, concludes, in a 1994 article in the prestigious journal, *Foreign Affairs,* that surgical air power alone cannot win wars.

Land-Based Air Power Brought Victory in the Gulf War

RICHARD P. HALLION

The success of air power in the Gulf war was neither universally predicted nor assumed in the weeks and months before Desert Storm broke. Indeed, while many analysts expected air power to influence the outcome of the war, few expected it to be the war's decisive force. In part this stemmed from air power's mixed record in previous conflicts. While military historians could argue that air had already been the single most important form of military power since 1939 and the outbreak of the Second World War, its application in wars since that time had often been

---

Richard P. Hallion. *Storm Over Iraq: Air Power and the Gulf War* (Washington, D.C.: Smithsonian Institution Press, 1992). Reprinted by permission of Smithsonian Institution Press.

haphazard, not sustained, disappointing, or obscured by equally complex and involved land and sea operations. Only one previous war came close to being a decisive victory for air power alone: the June 1967 Arab-Israeli war—but this was the last "pre-missile era" air war, and, as such, one whose lessons had to be qualified in light of the experience in Vietnam and later conflicts. Few commentators discussed the June 1967 war or its successors when predicting potential outcomes of a Gulf conflict as the crisis escalated over the fall and winter of 1990–91. Even more surprising, few air power historians ventured to make any sort of predictions about what might happen in the Gulf. With the vast preponderance of media consultants being specialists either in land or sea warfare, it is not surprising that they consistently ignored or (at best) underestimated air power and its potentialities. Only rarely did someone speak favorably of air power, and in those few cases, moderators usually carefully sandwiched such remarks between ones much more critical or "realistic." . . .

The Strategic Air Campaign: Decisive Accomplishment

Overall, the coalition air campaign accumulated a total of 109,876 sorties over the 43-day war, an average of 2,555 sorties per day. Of these, over 27,000 targeted Scuds, airfields, air defenses, electrical power, biological and chemical weapons, headquarters, intelligence assets, communications, the Iraqi army, and oil refining. Aerial tanking was crucial to producing these sortie figures. During Desert Storm, Air Force tankers exceeded even their Desert Shield support record, flying 15,434 sorties—nearly 60,000 flying hours—refueling 45,955 aircraft (20 percent of which were Navy or Marine airplanes), and off-loading 110.2 million gallons of aviation fuel. American airmen dropped 84,200 tons of munitions in the course of approximately 44,145 combat sorties, 67 percent of which were flown by the Air Force, 19 percent by the Marine Corps, and 14 percent by the Navy. Of the 84,200 tons, the Air Force dropped 72 percent, roughly 60,624 tons of both "smart" and "dumb" weapons. The Navy and Marine Corps shared the remaining 28 percent. The Air Force dropped 70 percent (53,964 tons) of the dumb bomb tonnage (76,800 tons total) expended in the war, the Marine Corps and the Navy roughly splitting the remaining 30 percent.

Approximately 9 percent—7,400 tons—of the total tonnage expended by American forces was precision munitions. The Air Force dropped 90 percent (6,660 tons), the Marine Corps and the Navy accounting for the remaining 10 percent (740 tons), although a significant proportion of this—about a third—consisted of ship- and sub-launched TLAM cruise missiles. Roughly 30 percent of all Air Force precision tonnage was dropped by F-117s. . . . Altogether, the precision munitions—particularly the laser-guided Paveway bombs—offered very high leverage, accomplishing approximately 75 percent of the damage inflicted upon Iraqi strategic and operational-level targets. Accuracy of smart bombs was such that successful strikes were the norm, not the exception. "To find yourself being blasé about zero CEP [circles inscribing bombing errors about aim points] accuracy is really astounding, but that's the way it was," one F-117 mission planner recollected.

Although prewar campaign planning set generally sequential phases to the air war, giving the impression that the campaign would turn from "strategic" to "tactical" targets, and eventually (after G-day) to direct support of ground forces via close air support and battlefield air interdiction strikes, in fact the actual campaign as executed had considerable overlap; right to the end of the war, all phases of the air plan were still being flown simultaneously, though at varying levels of effort. The even greater force buildup that accompanied the second phase of the Desert Shield deployment also changed the strategic air campaign. Planners had initially anticipated that the "Phase I" strategic air campaign would sharply drop off by day 7 of the air campaign, from about 700 sorties per day to less than 100 per day. In fact, the added air assets enabled the coalition air forces to fly approximately 1,200 strategic sorties per day at the outset—almost twice as many as the planners initially had anticipated prior to war—and sorties never dropped to less than 200 per day over the first 35 days. Air defense suppression, the "Phase II" of the plan, likewise proved more extensive than in prewar plans. "Phase III" attacks against the Iraqi field army, instead of beginning about day 5 and building to about 1,200 sorties per day, started on day 1. After G-day, attacks against Iraqi forces reached nearly 1,700 sorties per day during the four-day ground operation at the end of the war. . . .

One can get some perspective on the scope of the Gulf air war by comparing it to some predecessors. **Table 6.3** presents U.S. Air Service, U.S. Army Air Forces, and U.S. Air Force bomb tonnage statistics extracted from various wars, compared with Air Force tonnage dropped in the Gulf war. Viewed in this fashion, the Gulf war was not, as some of its critics alleged, an exercise in massive and unrestrained bombing unparalleled in previous air war history; neither the sortie rates nor the bomb tonnage statistics made it so. The Air Force's tonnage expenditure in the Gulf war was only 11 percent of that expended against Japan (537,000 tons), less than 4 percent of that expended against Nazi Germany (1,613,000 tons), and less than 1 percent of the tonnage that the Air Force dropped in Southeast Asia. In measures of tonnage dropped per month, the Gulf air war ranked significantly below Vietnam, and very much below the Second World War. Yet it was more decisive overall in what it achieved than any of these previous wars.

What made it decisive was what the strategic air campaign managed to accomplish. One can comprehend what strategic air power achieved in the Gulf war by looking at five separate categories of effort: attacks on command and control, power generation, refined fuel and lubricants production, the transportation infrastructure, and the Iraqi air force.

First, the strategic air campaign struck forty-five key targets in the Baghdad area with F-117A–dropped precision-guided bombs or cruise missiles, which left the Hussein regime confused, and ignorant of what was happening above them. Yet the strategic air campaign did this without "carpet-bombing" Baghdad or inflicting massive civilian casualties as, say, the bomber raids on Berlin that forced Hitler underground had caused during the Second World War. Indeed, as was reported by one physician who visited Iraq after the war, the strategic air campaign hit with "neurosurgical precision." The war revealed an interesting synergy between airlift and strike operations. Because of the leverage precision weapons offer, and the

Table 6.3   USAS/USAAF/USAF Bomb Tonnage Statistics for Five Conflicts

War	Tonnage	Length	Tonnage/Month
World War I	137.5	8.0 months	17.19
World War II	2,150,000.0	45.0 months	47,777.78
Korea	454,000.0	37.0 months	12,270.27
Vietnam/SE Asia	6,162,000.0	140.0 months	44,014.29
Gulf War	60,624.0	1.5 months	40,416.00

ease with which they are moved (the total precision munitions tonnage used in the war would have required only 450 C-141 airlift sorties to deliver) the airlifter in effect becomes the "first stage" of a "two-stage bomber." It carries the munitions around the globe and deposits them on an airfield. Then the munitions, in football terms, are "lateraled" to a strike airplane that carries the bomb over the "goal line." (The most telling example of this came late in the war, when two 4,700-pound GBU-28s arrived in the Gulf via a C-141, and, less than five hours later, were loaded on F-111Fs to go after a specially hardened command bunker; their bomb casings were still warm from the molten bomb mix poured in them back at Eglin AFB just hours before.)

Second, the strategic air campaign shut down the Baghdad electrical power grid by attacking twenty-seven selected generation plants and transmission facilities across the country. The power strikes, which included cruise-missile attacks and a little over 200 manned aircraft sorties, were particularly significant, for to modern military forces—and Iraq's were very modern indeed—electrical power is a vital necessity. It cannot be stockpiled and thus, by targeting power generation, one shuts down so many other military facilities that large-scale bombing is unnecessary—one has achieved *passive,* as opposed to *active,* destruction. Again, the unprecedented accuracy of modern munitions meant that the coalition achieved maximum military effect with minimal force, minimal sorties, and minimal—in fact, no—friendly casualties. One airplane dropping two precision-guided bombs sufficed to destroy a single power-generating station's transformer yards. During World War II, in contrast, the Eighth Air Force found it took two full combat wings, a force of 108 B-17 bombers (flying in six combat "boxes" of eighteen aircraft each), dropping a total of 648 bombs (six 1,100-pound bombs per airplane) to guarantee a 96-percent chance of getting just two hits (the minimum necessary to disable a single power-generating plant for several months) on a single power-generating plant measuring 400 by 500 feet. Thus, by the time of the Gulf war, a single strike airplane carrying two "smart" bombs could function as effectively as 108 World War II B-17 bombers carrying 648 bombs and crewed by 1,080 airmen. Further, for the number of bomber sorties in World War II required to disable just two power stations, the coalition disabled the transformer capacity of every targeted power generation facility in Iraq.

Third, the strategic air campaign targeted fuel and lubricants—the lifeblood of any military machine. Iraq was a major petroleum and electrical power exporter, with one of the most modern petroleum extraction, cracking, and distillation industries in the world. Before the war, it already possessed fifty times more reserve oil, per person, than the United States; after seizing Kuwait's oil assets, Saddam Hussein's government controlled more than 10 percent of the world's oil production capacity and 20 percent of the world's known oil reserves. The oil campaign was as decisive as it had been in World War II, but in a shorter time, with greater effectiveness, and with incomparably fewer losses. Further, it only targeted Iraq's militarily significant refined product production, and not its crude oil production facilities; there was no desire to impose greater hardship on Iraq than necessary. In the Second World War, American bombers dropped 185,841 tons of bombs during 50,000 sorties against 69 Nazi refineries (an average of nearly 2,700 tons of bombs and 725 sorties per refinery), cutting refined petroleum production by 60 percent. Of this total bomb tonnage, only 15 percent—approximately 27,876 tons, an average of only 404 tons per refinery—actually hit within the target area. In contrast, in the Gulf war, strike aircraft flying slightly over 500 sorties precisely dropped 1,200 tons of bombs on 28 Iraqi oil facilities (an average of only 43 tons and 18 sorties per facility), effectively ending refined petroleum production.

Thus, for less than half the tonnage dropped on a single German refinery during the Second World War, Allied strike aircraft destroyed all of the Iraqi facilities targeted for attack, a clear indication of the greater precision and destructiveness of modern air attack. (It should be noted that the Iraqi refineries were at least as large as and more sophisticated than German ones had been.) Therefore, for only 2.5 percent of the sorties as would have been required in World War II, and for only 1.5 percent of the bombs that would have been necessary in that earlier conflict, the Gulf attackers shut down Iraq's refined petroleum production. Within three days of the commencement of the oil campaign, Iraqi refined oil production was only 50 percent of its prewar level; within five days, it was at 10 percent, and five days later it was at zero.

Fourth, the strategic air campaign achieved clearcut interdiction of Iraqi transport into the Kuwaiti theater of operations. This was the first clearcut case of air interdiction in military aviation history. At the start of the war, there were fifty-four key railroad and highway bridges vital to the supply of Iraqi forces in Kuwait, most on roads running southeast from Baghdad into Basra and Kuwait. At the end of the war, forty-one of the fifty-four were dropped (others had not been targeted for various reasons), and thirty-two pontoon bridges hastily built to offset the Allied air attacks had been destroyed as well. It had taken only 450 bomb-dropping sorties to accomplish this. As a result, the flow of supplies and some key communications between Iraq and Kuwait were totally disrupted. By the third week of the war, transport south from Baghdad was so badly damaged that the amount of supplies getting to Basra—the major trans-shipment point for the Iraqi army in Iraq—was far below the amount necessary to maintain any sort of meaningful combat effectiveness. Historically, bridges have been profoundly difficult targets that have quickly become flak traps for attacking aircraft. The precision-guided bomb, either a laser-guided or electro-optical-guided weapon, dramatically revised that relationship. Now, strike aircraft such as the F-15E, Tornado, Jaguar, and F-117 could achieve virtual "one bomb, one hit" results.

Fifth, the strategic air campaign destroyed the Iraqi air force, preventing it from coming to the aid of the Hussein regime and its fielded forces in Iraq. As mentioned previously, the Iraqi air force played little role in the war, for two reasons. First, Saddam Hussein evidently believed that the coalition could not sustain its air effort beyond four or five days, and then the Iraqis could come out of their shelters and fight. Second, it was the smartest thing they could do, for when they did venture out, they ran into a veritable buzz-saw of eager Eagle, Tomcat, and Hornet pilots ready to do battle. During the immediate prewar period, the first two weeks of January, the Iraqi air force had averaged approximately fifty-five "shooter" sorties per day, and another forty or so sorties by support aircraft. On the first night of the war, the IQAF flew about twenty-five "shooter" sorties and ninety or so support ones. For the first week, Iraqi fighter sorties averaged about thirty per day, but they quickly found that Allied fighters—and pilots—were better. For example, on January 17, two Navy F/A-18s approaching H-3 airfield in western Iraq with four 2,000-pound bombs apiece received a warning of two MiG-21s coming head-on. With hardly a pause, the Hornet drivers switched from air-to-ground radar viewing to air-to-air mode, locked up the MiGs, and shot both down with an AIM-9 and AIM-7 apiece. They then switched back to air-to-ground radar mode, pressed on, and accurately bombed their target from an altitude of 18,850 feet, something that would have been unthinkable in any previous air war. Altogether, sixteen Iraqi fighters fell before F-15s and F-18s—fourteen to Eagles and two to Hornets—during that first week. Very quickly, the Iraqis decided not to fight, and it showed. For example, frustrated Navy Tomcat crews watched their radars as MiGs consistently fell back 40 to 50 miles beyond oncoming coalition strike packages, and the commander of the Air Force's 1st Tactical Fighter Wing, Col. John McBroom, remarked, "If somebody were going after my homeland, I'd [fight] a little harder."

Coalition air leaders were initially uncertain of their success in so effectively shutting down Saddam Hussein's air force; accordingly, they feared a possible "Air Tet" that Iraq might spring for maximum destructive and propaganda effect. Historically, there was a disturbing precedent: the New Year's 1945 attack by the battered remnants of the Luftwaffe against Allied air bases in Western Europe, which came as a great shock and destroyed a number of Allied aircraft, demonstrating that no air force is down and out until it is planted in the ground. Thus, on January 23, day 7 of the war, the coalition began an active program of "shelter busting." If the IQAF would not fight, it would be bombed in place. The airfield strikes were more complex than might have been imagined, and not just because of air defenses. Iraq's many fields were large, with redundant hangar and taxiway facilities. Tallil airfield, for example, covered 9,000 acres, twice the size of London's Heathrow Airport, and only slightly smaller than Washington's expansive Dulles Airport. Allied strike aircraft carrying hardened laser-guided bombs began striking Iraqi shelters, which had been patterned on Warsaw Pact models designed to withstand the rigors of nuclear attack. The impact was immediate. On day 9, January 25, the IQAF appeared to "stand down," to take stock of what was happening to it. Then, the next day, it "flushed" to Iran. Why the IQAF fled to Iran is not precisely known; was it a prearranged deal? Was it an act of defiance to Saddam—a recognition that the war was lost and an effort to try to salvage a useful force out of the disaster that had hit Iraq? The answer may never be fully known. In any case, Iraqi fighters and support aircraft fled for the border (leading to a popular joke that Iraqi fighters had a bumper sticker reading, "If you can read this, you're on your way to Iran"). More than 120 left, trying desperately to evade the probing eye of AWACS and the F-15's powerful air-to-air radar. Some ran out of fuel and crashed over Iranian territory. Others fell before Air Force F-15 barrier patrols (the last on February 7), raising total coalition fighter-vs.-fighter victories by the end of the war to 35, with no friendly losses. Meanwhile, back in Iraq, over 200 aircraft were destroyed on Iraqi airfields, and hardened 2,000-pound bombs devastated Iraq's supposedly impregnable shelters and the aircraft within many of them. Eventually day and night air strikes destroyed or seriously damaged 375 shelters out of a total of 594. One night, F-117s launched a particularly effective series of attacks and were rewarded by seeing fireballs blasting out of shelter doors after they had been penetrated by hardened bombs. In sum, then, the Iraqi air force died ignominiously.

All success in war is, unfortunately, accompanied by loss, and each loss is tragic and profound; sadly, the Gulf war was no exception. But what was different about this war was the remarkably low loss rate of Air Force and coalition aircraft. Optimists predicted losing one-half of 1 percent of all sorties (150 aircraft over a 30,000 sortie campaign, a .005 loss rate) with roughly a quarter of all shot-down air crews killed, a quarter captured, and half rescued or able to return to friendly territory. Thoughtful pessimists estimated losses at 2 percent (which the Israelis had suffered in their spectacularly successful campaign of 1967). The Air Force Studies and Analysis Agency estimated 4 percent. Dire pessimists—and there were some—forecast losses as high as 10 percent, equivalent to the casualties experienced by RAF Bomber Command and the Eighth Air Force during the worst days of 1943. In October, while briefing President Bush, Brigadier General Glosson had estimated the coalition would lose no more than eighty (more likely around fifty) aircraft; in fact, it lost forty-two. Two days before the war, Lieutenant General Horner had remarked to Glosson that he anticipated losses of thirty-nine Air Force airplanes (and possibly one hundred overall to the coalition). Given the number of combat sorties that CENTAF flew, this would have generated a loss rate per combat sortie of .00132 (slightly more than one-tenth of one percent) for the Air Force. In actuality, the Air Force lost fourteen aircraft in the war, giving an overall Air Force loss rate in Desert Storm of .00047—one-twentieth of 1 percent—per CENTAF combat sortie, which was unprecedented in military aviation history. . . .

Toward the Future

Writing in 1945, the noted British military analyst Maj. Gen. J. F. C. Fuller stated that "the barbarism of any period pales before the barbarism of today . . . From the javelin and the arrow to the Superfortress and the rocket-bomb, the very power to destroy, first slowly and then at terrific speed, has intoxicated man." As a means of illustrating his dismal point, he compared the destruction of Madgeburg during the Thirty Years War, and the subsequent massacre of its 30,000 inhabitants, with the destruction of Hamburg in 1943 by RAF Bomber Command. In the years after the Second World War, it was the images of bombed cities that haunted air power—the postwar photographs of Berlin and Tokyo rubble, the blasted ruin of Hiroshima and Nagasaki. It had taken the massive application of destructive force with unprecedented ferocity to eliminate the military strength of Nazi Germany and Imperial Japan, at a cost of hundreds of thousands of civilian lives. It was the anticipation of even greater levels of destruction by atomic and nuclear bombing that compelled the disarmament movement from the 1950s through the 1980s. But the reality was vastly different. At the end of the Gulf war, the ability of Iraq to threaten its neighbors was no less incapacitated than that of Japan and Germany in 1945, but Baghdad was intact. Its civilian population was virtually untouched directly by the war. Humane values had, in fact, prevailed.

Surgical Air Power Alone Cannot Win Wars

ELIOT A. COHEN

War and Organization

The successes of the air campaign in the gulf rested almost as much on organizational innovations as on technology. To speak of a revolution in warfare as a purely technological affair is to miss half the significance of the war. In the Gulf War, for example, Lieutenant General Charles Horner, the commander of CENTAF (the Air Force component of Central Command), also controlled in some measure the airplanes of all the services, as well as helicopters flying above 500 feet and Navy Tomahawk cruise missiles. In this respect he embodied a doctrine dear to airmen for half a century: "Control of available air power must be centralized and command must be exercised through the Air Force commander if this inherent flexibility and ability to deliver a decisive blow are to be fully exploited." "Centralized planning, decentralized execution" remains a catchphrase of Air Force doctrine, much as "don't divide the fleet" preoccupied American naval strategists in earlier times.

In practice, though, Horner's authority had its limits. The Navy controlled maritime air operations, the Marines determined the assignments of their short take-off and landing aircraft plus at least half of their fighter-bombers, while the allies exercised discretion regarding which targets they would attack. Special operations forces—which in effect constitute a fifth armed service—continued to struggle for control of their own air operations.

Horner, directing 1,800 combat aircraft, had a staggering fleet at his command. Nonetheless, even his gently wielded centralized control elicited suspicion and hostility from officers in other services who feared an Air Force attempt to dominate all aerial warfare. Grudgingly conceding the necessity of a single command center, they argued that in theory it could dilute the synergy of, for example, Marine air and ground forces, and that in practice it proved cumbersome and slow.

Eliot A. Cohen, "The Mystique of U.S. Air Power," *Foreign Affairs* 73, 1 (January/February 1994): 116–124. Reprinted by permission of *Foreign Affairs*. Copyright 1994 by the Council on Foreign Relations, Inc.

The centralized control of air power made for a much more coherent campaign than would otherwise have occurred. But, as officers from the other three services bitterly observed, the centralized control rested overwhelmingly in the hands of Air Force officers. Although the core planning staff, the so-called "Black Hole," included representatives from the Navy, Army and Marine Corps, as well as the British and Saudi air forces, its membership came predominantly from the Air Force. In theory a joint targeting board should have selected targets; in practice it did very little. Furthermore, much of the inspiration for the Black Hole's targeting decisions came from an Air Force staff in the Pentagon, an organization known as "Checkmate" led by Colonel John Warden, a fervent believer in air power.

Thus, an Air Force staff (nominally under Joint Staff auspices) dominated the flow of targeting information and proposals to the theater. . . .

The abundance of reliable and secure voice, data and facsimile communications to (and within) the theater transformed command and control. Communications technology subverted hierarchies and rendered abundant exchanges between the theater and the United States both inevitable and desirable. During the Persian Gulf War staffs in Colorado relayed warnings of Scud launches to Riyadh and Tel Aviv, and the now-defunct Tactical Air Command near Norfolk, Virginia, managed CENTAF logistical accounts. Watching CNN and using other sources of instantaneous news, the chairman of the Joint Chiefs of Staff (and, to only a slightly smaller degree, his civilian superiors) monitored the day-to-day activities of U.S. Central Command's (CENTCOM) forces. The new technologies threaten age-old principles such as unity of command and delegation of authority. Those pieces of military folk wisdom have so much authority that they will persist in peacetime even if they must disappear in war. A new concept of high command, one that acknowledges that technology inevitably diffuses authority, will have to take root.

Information gathering and processing technology can help but not solve the problem of bomb damage assessment. In many cases, commanders sent out sorties uncertain about the degree of damage a target had already received. Part of the problem stemmed from excessive reliance on intelligence derived from satellites rather than locally controlled reconnaissance aircraft. The theater intelligence staff was small in number and had little experience in tasking the array of satellites at its disposal. There remained, moreover, the sheer difficulty of knowing what damage has been done. From an overhead photograph, for example, it may prove difficult to figure out whether a small black hole on top of a hardened aircraft shelter indicates a hit by a dud bomb, an explosion in the thick, rubble-filled space between the shelter's inner and outer walls, an explosion within the shelter or an artful paint job by Iraqi camouflage experts. And unless reconnaissance units can keep targets under near-constant surveillance from many angles and with different kinds of sensors, intelligence analysts may not know which projectile did what kind of damage. Finally, functional damage may differ sharply from physical damage. Air Force planners desired the first, hoping, for example, that a few hits on a command post would discourage the Iraqis from using it, even if according to normal measures of damage (which depend mainly on engineering criteria) the facility had not received a mortal blow. Not surprisingly, they became increasingly frustrated with intelligence reports that paid more attention to physical than functional damage.

The problem of bomb-damage assessment means that the fog of war will persist, although intelligence services will work to develop ever more sophisticated means of interpreting imagery and cross-checking damage through different sources of information. . . . In future conflicts, where commanders might have less time or much smaller forces, an inability to track damage to an enemy could prove crippling. Even in retrospect it has proven extremely difficult to decipher the air war's effects. . . .

The War and American Influence

Reliance on air power has set the American way of war apart from all others for well over half a century. Other countries might field doughty infantry, canny submariners or scientific artillerists comparable in skill and numbers to America's. Only the United States, however, has engaged in a single-minded and successful quest for air superiority in every conflict it has fought since World War I. Air warfare remains distinctively American—high-tech, cheap in lives and (at least in theory) quick. To America's enemies—past, current and potential—it is the distinctively American form of military intimidation.

Air warfare plays to the machine-mindedness of American civilization. Aircraft can direct massive and accurate destructive force at key points without having to maneuver cumbersome organizations on land or sea. Air power can indeed overawe opponents, who know quite well that they cannot hope to match or directly counter American strength. On the other hand, these enemies will find indirect responses. The Saddam Husseins of the world have surely learned that they need not take American children hostage to deter bombardment; they can take their own citizens' young with no less effect. When F-117s struck the so-called al-Firdos bunker—a perfectly appropriate military target—on February 13, they apparently killed the wives and children of Iraqi leaders using the facility as a shelter. For the next four days all air operations against Baghdad ceased, and when they resumed, politically motivated controls reduced the number of targets to the barest handful. Mobility, when abetted by camouflage and tight communications security, can also shield a potential opponent from harm. Publicly available evidence does not suggest that air attacks destroyed any Scud missile launchers, for example.

The soldier or marine will surely say to the air power enthusiast that nothing can substitute for the man with the bayonet. True, but some politically desired effects (elimination of electrical power in Baghdad, for example) required no use of ground forces. And in some cases the United States has proved unwilling to use ground forces to achieve its objective (for example, the overthrow of Saddam). Air power may not decide all conflicts or achieve all of a country's political objectives, but neither can land power.

All forms of military power seem likely to benefit from the imminent arrival of "nonlethal" or "disabling" technologies, which offer the prospect of war without casualties. But here, perhaps, lies the most dangerous legacy of the Persian Gulf War: the fantasy of near-bloodless uses of force. Set aside, for the moment, the question of so-called nonlethal weapons. No military technology (indeed, no technology at all) works all the time. Inevitably, even the best-aimed laser-guided bomb will lose its fix on a target because of a passing cloud or a steering mechanism failure, and hurtle into an orphanage or hospital. As one wise engineer puts it, "[T]he truly fail-proof design is chimerical."

In many cases, so-called nonlethal weapons will prove just the reverse. The occupants of a helicopter crashing to earth after its flight controls have fallen prey to a high-power microwave weapon would take little solace from the knowledge that a nonlethal weapon had sealed their doom. Some of these weapons (blinding lasers for example) may not kill, but have exceedingly nasty consequences for their victims. And in the end a disabling weapon works only if it leaves an opponent vulnerable to full-scale, deadly force.

War is Cruelty

The simple and brutal fact remains that force works by destroying and killing. In the Gulf War the commanding generals ostentatiously, indeed obsessively, abjured Vietnam-style body counts, but that did not diminish the importance of terrifying enemy soldiers through the fear of violent death from tons of ordnance raining down on them. And fear of violent death only comes from the imminent possibility of the real thing. True, in the Gulf War relatively small numbers of Iraqis (perhaps 2,300 civilians and up to 10,000 soldiers) died before the ground war, although others suffered indirectly from the combined effects of air attack and the coalition embargo. That so few died reflects, among other things, the potential of the new technologies and the scrupulous regard for civilian life shown by coalition planners. But the essential ingredient of fear remained constant.

Sometimes fear does not suffice. The objectives of conflicts such as the war with Iraq will frequently mandate killing. The destruction of some 50 percent of the Republican Guard's armor (in roughly equal proportions by air and ground action) made little difference outside the Kuwait theater. The Republican Guard remained at war's end an organized force and, after drawing on ample stocks of weapons in Iraq proper, put down the Kurdish and Shi'ite uprisings. To stop that and to undermine Saddam's regime (which the Bush administration certainly wished to do) would have required killing or wounding the men who constituted the bulwark of the regime. This uncomfortable fact, long known to the Israelis, who have had few scruples about killing German rocket scientists in the past or rogue super-gun designers in more recent years, sits poorly with Americans. When General Michael Dugan, Chief of Staff of the United States Air Force, hinted to journalists in September 1990 that the most effective use of air power might consist of attacks on Saddam Hussein, his intimate associates and key members of the Iraqi general staff and Ba'ath Party, he only pointed to the truth, impolitic as his outraged superiors found it.

It appears likely that civilian populations or large portions of them will continue to be the objects of terror. General William Tecumseh Sherman described the grim purpose of his 1864 march through Georgia and South Carolina thus: "My aim then was, to whip the rebels, to humble their pride, to follow them to their inmost recesses, and make them fear and dread us. 'Fear of the Lord is the beginning of wisdom.'" Sherman's troops did not massacre the inhabitants of the South: they merely ruined their private and public possessions, attacking (as a contemporary strategic analyst might antiseptically observe) the region's "economic infrastructure." In many cases today, war means bringing power, particularly air power, to bear against civil society. Those who hope for too much from air power desire to return to a mode of warfare reminiscent of the mid-eighteenth century in western Europe—war waged by mercenary armies isolated from society; war with (by modern standards, at any rate) remarkable efforts to insulate civilians from its effects. Sherman, reflecting the character of armed struggle in his century as well as ours, believed that in modern conditions civil society must inevitably become a target.

As leaders attempt to use their civilians as hostages against American air power this will become ever more true, whether we like it or not. Moreover, throughout the nineteenth and twentieth centuries military power has become increasingly intertwined with civil society. The electric generators that keep a defense ministry's computers running and its radars sweeping the skies also provide energy for hospitals and water purification plants. The bridges indispensable to the movement of military forces support the traffic in food, medicine and all other elements of modern life for large civilian populations. Sherman faced a similar situation when he besieged Atlanta. "You cannot qualify war in harsher terms than I will," he told the hapless leading citizens of that city. "War is cruelty, and you cannot refine it."

The Use of Air Power

American air power dominated the Persian Gulf War as no other conflict since World War II. Special circumstances helped account for this achievement, but in the end airmen were probably correct in their belief that this war marked a departure. No other nation on earth has comparable power, nor will any country accumulate anything like it, or even the means to neutralize it, for at least a decade and probably much longer. American air power has a mystique that it is in the American interest to retain. When presidents use it, they should either hurl it with devastating lethality against a few targets (say, a full-scale meeting of an enemy war cabinet or senior-level military staff) or extensively enough to cause sharp and lasting pain to a military and a society. But both uses of force pose problems. The first type represents, in effect, the use of air power for assassination, a procedure not without precedent (American pilots stalked and slew Japan's Admiral Isoroku Yamamoto in 1943). But it sets troubling precedents and invites primitive but nonetheless effective forms of revenge. The second involves the use of air power in ways bound to offend many, no matter what pains commanders take to avoid the direct loss of human life. To strike hard, if indirectly, at societies by smashing communication or power networks will invite the kind of wrenching television attention that modern journalists excel at providing.

Still, to use air power in penny packets is to disregard the importance of a menacing and even mysterious military reputation. "The reputation of power is power," Hobbes wrote, and that applies to military power as well as to other kinds. The sprinkling of air strikes over an enemy will harden him without hurting him and deprive the United States of an intangible strategic asset. American leaders at the end of this century indeed have been vouchsafed with a military instrument of a potency rarely known in the history of war. But glib talk of revolutionary change obscures the organizational impediments to truly radical change in the conduct of war and, worse, its inherent messiness and brutality. In the end, students of air power will serve the country well by putting the Persian Gulf War in a larger context, one in which the gloomy wisdom of Sherman tempers the brisk enthusiasm of those who see air power as a shining sword, effortlessly wielded, that can create and preserve a just and peaceful world order.

♠ F U R T H E R   R E A D I N G

Deborah Amos, *Lines in the Sand: Desert Storm and the Remaking of the Arab World* (1992).

Les Aspin and William Dickinson, *Defense for a New Era: Lessons of the Persian Gulf War* (1992).

Rick Atkinson, *Crusade: The Untold Story of the Persian Gulf War* (1993).

A. J. Bacevich, James D. Hallums, Richard H. White, and Thomas F. Young, *American Military Policy in Small Wars: The Case of El Salvador* (1988).

Arthur H. Blair, *At War in the Gulf: A Chronology* (1992).

Daniel P. Bolger, *Americans at War, 1975–1986: An Era of Violent Peace* (1988).

Eliot A. Cohen, "The Mystique of U.S. Air Power," *Foreign Affairs* 73 (January/February 1994): 109–124.

Lawrence Freedman and Efraim Karsh, *The Gulf Conflict, 1990–1991: Diplomacy and War in the New World Order* (1993).

Norman Friedman, *Desert Victory: The War for Kuwait* (1991).

Michael R. Gordon and Bernard E. Trainor, *The General's War: The Inside Story of the Conflict in the Gulf* (1995).

Stephen R. Graubard, *Mr. Bush's War: Adventures in the Politics of Illusion* (1992).

David Locke Hall, *The Reagan Wars: A Constitutional Perspective on War Powers and the Presidency* (1991).

Richard P. Hallion, *Storm Over Iraq: Air Power and the Gulf War* (1992).

Dilip Hiro, *Desert Shield to Desert Storm: The Second Gulf War* (1992).

Michael H. Hoffman, "War, Peace, and Interventional Armed Conflict: Solving the Peace Enforcer's Paradox," *Parameters* 25 (Winter 1995–1996): 41–52.

Jeanne Holm, *Women in the Military: An Unfinished Revolution* (1992).

Robert H. Jackson, "Armed Humanitarianism," *International Journal* 48 (Autumn 1993): 579–606.

James Turner Johnson and George Weigel, *Just War and the Gulf War* (1991).

Thomas A. Keaney and Eliot A. Cohen, *Revolution in Warfare?: Air Power in the Persian Gulf* (1995).

Doris H. Kessler and Richard A. Gabriel, "Women in Combat? Two Views," *Army* 30 (March 1980): 44–45, 47–50, 52.

Ariel E. Levite, Bruce W. Jentleson, and Larry Berman, *Foreign Military Intervention: The Dynamics of Protracted Conflict* (1992).

Molly Moore, *A Woman at War: Storming Kuwait with the U.S. Marines* (1993).

Charles C. Moskos and John Sibley Butler, *All That We Can Be: Black Leadership and Racial Integration the Army Way* (1996).

Jeffrey Record, *Hollow Victory: A Contrary View of the Gulf War* (1993).

H. Norman Schwarzkopf, *General H. Norman Schwarzkopf, The Autobiography, It Doesn't Take a Hero* (1992).

Jean Edward Smith, *George Bush's War* (1992).

Judith Hicks Stiehm, ed., *It's Our Military Too! Women and the U.S. Military* (1996).

Richard M. Swain, *"Lucky War": Third Army in Desert Storm* (1994).

U.S. General Accounting Office, *Operation Desert Storm: Evaluation of the Air War* (1996).

Michael P. Vriesenga, ed., *From the Line in the Sand: Accounts of USAF Company Grade Officers in Support of Desert Shield/Desert Storm* (1994).

Daniel Wirls, *Buildup: The Politics of Defense in the Reagan Era* (1992).

Bob Woodward, *The Commanders* (1991).

Susan L. Woodward, *Balkan Tragedy: Chaos and Dissolution After the Cold War* (1995).